D0146654

Your FREE research companion!

Research Writer for
Criminal Justice CD-ROM

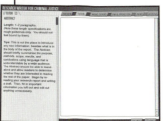

Included FREE with every new copy of this text, the **Research Writer for Criminal Justice CD-ROM** puts successful research papers within your grasp!

The **Research Writer for Criminal Justice CD-ROM** takes the mystery out of the writing process, allowing you to put your research into perspective.

The CD-ROM serves as your step-by-step guide, offering helpful tips and hints along the way. You can even check your progress by e-mailing your report to your instructor at any stage along the writing process. When you're done, the program can format your paper as a Microsoft® Word document according to standard research report guidelines.

And be sure to visit the Maxfield/Babbie Book Companion Web Site

http://cj.wadsworth.com/ maxfield_babbie/research_ methods4e

An abundance of outstanding resources is now available to you when *you* need them! In addition to study aids such as *Chapter Outlines* and *Flash Cards*, this **new** book-specific Web site also includes four electronic appendices, criminal justice data for SPSS® analysis, a compelling research project, and quantitative and qualitative data analysis software primers.

Put the power of multimedia to work for *you*—explore the *Research Writer for Criminal Justice CD-ROM* today!

Research Methods
for CRIMINAL JUSTICE
and CRIMINOLOGY

FOURTH EDITION

Michael G. Maxfield

Rutgers University

Earl Babbie

Chapman University

THOMSON

WADSWORTH

Australia · Canada · Mexico · Singapore · Spain · United Kingdom · United States

Dedication

Mary Maxfield Fauth   Molly Maxfield   Sheila Babbie

Senior Acquisitions Editor, Criminal Justice: Jay Whitney
Development Editor: Julie Sakaue
Editorial Assistant: Elise Smith
Technology Project Manager: Susan DeVanna
Marketing Manager: Dory Schaeffer
Marketing Assistant: Andrew Keay
Advertising Project Manager: Stacey Purviance
Project Manager, Editorial Production: Jennie Redwitz
Art Director: Vernon Boes/Carolyn Deacy
Print/Media Buyer: Karen Hunt

Permissions Editor: Joohee Lee
Production Service: Melanie Field,
    Strawberry Field Publishing
Text Designer: Brad Greene
Copy Editor: Tom Briggs
Illustrator: G&S Typesetters, Inc.
Cover Designer: Yvo
Cover Image: Charles Nes/Getty Images
Compositor: G&S Typesetters, Inc.
Text and Cover Printer: Phoenix Color Corp

COPYRIGHT © 2005 Wadsworth, a division of Thomson Learning, Inc. Thomson Learning™ is a trademark used herein under license.

ALL RIGHTS RESERVED. No part of this work covered by the copyright hereon may be reproduced or used in any form or by any means—graphic, electronic, or mechanical, including but not limited to photocopying, recording, taping, Web distribution, information networks, or information storage and retrieval systems—without the written permission of the publisher.

Printed in the United States of America
2 3 4 5 6 7 08 07 06 05 04

For more information about our products, contact us at:
Thomson Learning Academic Resource Center
1-800-423-0563

For permission to use material from this text or product, submit a request online at **http://www.thomsonrights.com**. Any additional questions about permissions can be submitted by email to **thomsonrights@thomson.com**.

ExamView® and ExamView Pro® are registered trademarks of FSCreations, Inc. Windows is a registered trademark of the Microsoft Corporation used herein under license. Macintosh and Power Macintosh are registered trademarks of Apple Computer, Inc. Used herein under license.

Library of Congress Control Number: 2003114705

Student Edition: ISBN 0-534-61560-0
Instructor's Edition: ISBN 0-534-61566-X

Wadsworth Thomson Learning
10 Davis Drive
Belmont, CA 94002-3098
USA

Asia
Thomson Learning
5 Shenton Way #01-01
UIC Building
Singapore 068808

Australia/New Zealand
Thomson Learning
102 Dodds Street
Southbank, Victoria 3006
Australia

Canada
Nelson
1120 Birchmount Road
Toronto, Ontario M1K 5G4
Canada

Europe/Middle East/Africa
Thomson Learning
High Holborn House
50/51 Bedford Row
London WC1R 4LR
United Kingdom

Image Credits:
pp. 1, 2, 29, 51: © Royalty-Free/Corbis
pp. 77, 78, 114, 142, 174: © PictureArts/Corbis
pp. 207, 208, 245, 281, 318: © PictureArts/Corbis
pp. 353, 354, 392: © Royalty-Free/Corbis

Contents

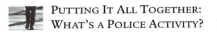

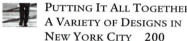
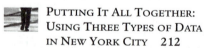

Preface

One of my[*] most oddly rewarding teaching experiences took place not in the classroom but on the streets of downtown Indianapolis. On my way to a meeting with staff from the Indiana Department of Correction, I recognized a student from the previous semester's research methods class. Ryan was seated on a shaded bench, clipboard in hand, watching pedestrians make their way down the sidewalk. After we had exchanged greetings, I learned that Ryan had landed a summer internship with the city's planning department and was currently at work conducting a study of pedestrian traffic.

"Ha!" I exclaimed, recalling student complaints about how research methods are not relevant (what I have since referred to as "Ryan's lament"). "And you whined about how you were never going to use the stuff we talked about in class."

Ryan responded that the systematic study of pedestrians was interesting, and he admitted that some course topics did, in fact, relate to his work as an intern. He also said something about not really knowing what actual research involved until he began his current project. Ryan remained attentive to people passing by while we chatted for a few minutes. I was pleased to see that he was a careful observer, applying some of the skills he had learned in my course only a few weeks after the semester's end.

Later, thinking more about the encounter, I recognized the need to change my approach to teaching the course. Ryan clearly enjoyed his experience in doing research, but he had not recognized how much fun research could be until after he left the classroom. As a result, I restructured the course to involve students more actively in the research process. I resolved to be more diligent in linking fundamental concepts of research methods to a broad spectrum of examples, and I became determined to show students how they, like Ryan, could apply systematic inquiry and observation techniques to a wide variety of situations in criminal justice and other policy areas.

Collaborating with Earl Babbie to produce this textbook, I joined a colleague whose writing embodied my efforts to engage students in the learning process. Earl's classic text, *The Practice of Social Research,* has always been an enviable model of clarity—generating student interest while still presenting a rigorous treatment of social science research methods.

As has always been the case with *Practice,* our text illustrates principles of doing research with examples specifically selected to appeal to students. We have sought to convey something of the excitement of doing research that Ryan discovered as he observed pedestrians in downtown Indianapolis.

A Familiar, Comfortable Approach

This text has several distinctive features. Anyone who has taught with or learned from *The Practice of Social Research* will recognize much in our collaborative effort. This enables instructors of criminal justice research methods to organize their course around a familiar approach, capitalizing on the strengths and popularity of Earl Babbie's superb text. At the same time, we have designed our book to address the particular needs of research methods for criminal justice and criminology.

Features of the New Edition

All editions of our text *Research Methods for Criminal Justice and Criminology* have retained much of the raw material from *Practice,* albeit revised and otherwise adapted for students in criminol-

---

Note: In this Preface, the first-person singular refers to Michael Maxfield, while the first-person plural refers to Maxfield and Earl Babbie.

ogy and criminal justice. In preparing the Fourth Edition, we stayed with what has proved to be a popular formula. But we have also responded to suggestions from several people—reviewers, colleagues, and instructors—who used earlier editions.

Two important structural changes are most apparent: two chapters have been merged, and our discussion of research ethics has been moved forward. We did not undertake these changes lightly, recognizing that they may require instructors to reorganize their courses somewhat. But reviewers and others offered compelling reasons for combining chapters and moving some material around. Here's an overview of what's new in this edition.

Ethics and Criminal Justice Research

Reviewers and users from the First Edition onward have offered suggestions about the location of the chapter on research ethics. Most suggested that the chapter appear earlier, and some instructors have even urged that it be the first chapter in the text. We were reluctant to make that change in earlier revisions because we felt students would gain a better appreciation of ethics after learning more about research techniques. On the other hand, from our own teaching experiences we can recall (pleasantly) that students asked spontaneous questions about ethics while we were covering research methods. In fact, I have been covering ethics in the first weeks of my own research methods course, predating the text reorganization by at least a couple of years.

The ethics chapter is revised in other ways. Reviewers have commented on the special ethical problems encountered in field research. A new box on ethics in extreme field research illustrates this through the actual experiences of a graduate student doing research on drug use in New York City dance clubs. Other revisions reflect the evolving role of institutional review boards at research universities. No one disputes the need to protect human subjects from possible harm, but many researchers are frustrated by what they see as unduly burdensome regulations.

Reviewers also called for an update on ethics codes issued by professional associations. We cite and briefly comment on the code recently issued by the Academy of Criminal Justice Sciences. Updating ethics and the American Society of Criminology (ASC) was easier in one respect: ASC officials have not yet presented a code of ethics for consideration by members.

Causation and Validity

Some users of earlier editions commented favorably on devoting a chapter to causation and validity, but many others had difficulty with these topics. Seemingly equal numbers of people felt the chapter was too long or too short. There does appear to be consensus on the view that causation and validity are among the most difficult topics for undergraduates. Accordingly, we moved our discussion of cause and validity from the old Chapter 3 into Chapter 4 on general issues in research design. Earl Babbie introduced a similar restructuring in the Tenth Edition of *Practice*.

Chapter 4 now includes quite a lot of material. However, preliminary reviews of this new chapter, even from one self-confessed causation enthusiast, have been positive. We are pleased that the chapter reads smoothly and retains the most important features of the topic from previous editions.

Qualitative and Quantitative

Reflecting on our own graduate training more than a few years past, memories of the quantitative/qualitative debate remain fresh. Some reviewers have objected to what they perceive as a quantitative bias in the text, pointing to the lack of a chapter titled something like "Qualitative Field Research." A quick review of the contents in this and previous editions will fail to locate a chapter titled something like

"Quantitative Designs." To be even more precise, an index search of all text files for this edition finds the word "qualitative" appearing in 34 paragraphs, headings, and citations while the word "quantitative" appears in 32. Lest we be charged with conducting a quantitative analysis to illustrate a qualitative point, we cheerfully plead "guilty"!

Chapter 1 addresses the traditional qualitative/quantitative distinction directly, concluding with a position carried over into all other chapters: (1) each approach has advantages; (2) researchers are best advised to draw on elements of each approach as appropriate; and (3) the best advice is to do the best you can. In Chapter 4, we describe threats to validity as illustrations of how research findings might be wrong, an approach that applies to all methods. Chapters on measurement (5 and 6) and making observations (9, 10, 11) examine a range of approaches. Design is also discussed in several chapters, though most thoroughly in Chapters 7 and 12.

Trying to even more explicitly bridge the historical divide, we have expanded our discussion of scientific realism. By focusing on mechanisms in context, this approach really does offer the best of both worlds. We amplify this in Chapters 7 and 12 by introducing Charles Ragin's distinction between case-oriented and variable-oriented research. The former examines a small number of variables over a large number of cases, while the latter examines a variety of variables for a small number of cases. We also draw (in Chapter 7) on Robert Yin's work to emphasize that the phrase "case study" is often misunderstood and used inappropriately. In a similar vein, though Donald Campbell's name is often associated with advocacy of experimental designs, he emphasized the importance of both qualitative and quantitative designs for evaluation (Campbell, 1979).

The result is an approach that truly does draw on the strengths of each. We don't claim to be revolutionary in this regard. However, instructors who recognize that a variety of techniques are used in criminal justice and criminology research will feel even more comfortable with this edition of the text.

Policy Analysis

This edition continues to add different examples of applied research. In some respects, a few criminal justice agencies almost seem to have jumped ahead of researchers in their use of crime mapping and similar analytic tools. We briefly describe new applications in Chapter 12. The Internet is the best resource for illustrations of crime mapping, as more law enforcement and even regional planning agencies grant public access to maps. We refer students to these in several chapters.

Survey Technology

The Internet continues to develop as a viable conduit for survey research. Chapter 9 discusses how sampling, item presentation, and analysis capabilities continue to expand. The chapter also cautions that Web-based surveys have their own problems, not the least of which is a higher-tech version of junk mail and telemarketing.

Internet Resources

At the end of each chapter, we advise students to take advantage of the great new Web site Wadsworth has put together for this edition of the text. There students will find many useful learning resources to help them review the material we present in the book. We have also provided Internet exercises and InfoTrac College Edition exercises to encourage students to link chapter concepts with real-world applications found on relevant Web sites and in journal articles. To guide students in doing the exercises, we have provided directions or questions that help students to gain a deeper understanding and appreciation of what they've just learned in the chapter. We have been careful to include only stable Web sites to ensure that they will still be active when students visit them over the cycle of this edition, and with InfoTrac® College Edition—a robust online library—students will be able to access a wealth of relevant news and journal articles when doing the exercises or research on their own.

The Research Writer for Criminal Justice CD-ROM

We are excited about the addition of a new CD-ROM to the text, the Research Writer for Criminal Justice. The CD-ROM was added to complement Appendix C, The Research Report, and is automatically bundled free with every new copy of the text. The Research Writer for Criminal Justice helps students tackle the task of writing research reports by taking some of the mystery out of the endeavor; it provides them with a template that they can use as they write their research projects. The template guides students through the process of writing a research report, from the beginning idea to the documentation of the last source. Moreover, students can access helpful hints and tips as they write with just a click of a button. They can also email their work at any stage of the process to their instructor, and they can even export their work to Microsoft Word where the document will be formatted in a style consistent with standard research projects. We hope students find this CD-ROM exciting and helpful.

Notable Features Retained and Updated

Putting It All Together: Crime in New York City

The previous edition introduced "Putting It All Together," a running example of research on the question of whether changes in policing were responsible for reducing crime in New York City. The running example has been retained and updated to reflect the role of researchers from the Rutgers University School of Criminal Justice in studying links between policing and crime. William Sousa's (2003) dissertation is now complete, but it has not settled the issue to everyone's satisfaction. Nevertheless, serious

crime continues to be reduced in New York City as of this writing, whereas the declines of the 1990s have reversed in many other large cities.

We continued the example in the Fourth Edition because it vividly illustrates different elements of social science research, from research purposes through measurement, design, data collection, and simple analysis as they emerge in each chapter. Information presented reflects the experiences of Sousa and other researchers from Rutgers. Each chapter's installment (two each in Chapters 4 and 8) bridges general principles of research methods with the nuts-and-bolts issues that emerged during the course of this project.

Measurement

Many people believe that measurement presents the greatest challenge in doing social science research. We feel this is especially true for criminal justice. In response to suggestions, the two chapters on measurement (Chapters 5 and 6) include additional examples and more in-depth discussion to illustrate the importance of conceptualization and measurement. As in earlier editions, throughout the text we remind students to be careful but creative when it comes to measurement.

Agency Records as Data Sources

Reviewers and colleagues reacted favorably to our discussion of agency records in earlier editions. This chapter remains a unique feature of our text, and we have added material to reflect the growing sophistication of data management systems in justice agencies.

This edition includes a new extended example by one of my students at Rutgers. In Chapter 11, Marie Mele describes how she worked with staff from a large police department in the Northeast to build an enhanced data system for tracking domestic violence cases. The new system produced data for her research and improved operations in a domestic violence investigative unit. Though it's presented in the chapter on using agency records, this example also illustrates key principles of measurement, data collection, and applied research.

Design Building Blocks

Research methods seems to be one of those courses in which students feel driven to memorize the book, lectures, practice questions, last semester's notes purchased from a friend, or whatever. The strange vocabulary of the subject probably encourages this tendency, which seems to be especially troublesome when teaching research design. All those Xs and Os must be faithfully recorded, memorized, and associated with the right label.

Although the XO diagrams in Chapter 7 will be familiar to many instructors, we encourage students to become engaged in learning research methods by describing how common research designs represent creative uses of design building blocks. In Chapter 7 and elsewhere, we describe how the fundamentals of subject selection, making observations, and administering or withholding a treatment represent basic building blocks of design. Then we offer examples to illustrate different ways to combine those building blocks. Rather than trying to shoehorn a research problem into some pattern of Xs and Os that appears in their books, we urge students to learn what these building blocks represent and what different building blocks can be expected to accomplish.

Survey Research and Sampling

One of the strengths of *The Practice of Social Research* has always been a comprehensive but eminently readable treatment of sampling and survey methods. Our criminal justice text (in Chapters 8 and 9) retains Earl's general approach, but it also points to some of the more specialized criminal justice applications. These range from victim and self-report surveys to specialized interviews with nonprobability samples. Again, our approach focuses on arming students with the principles of survey methods so that they can adapt these general tools to a variety of uses. A new box in this chapter directs students to Web sites that present examples of survey questionnaires. The chapter also includes more material on special-purpose crime surveys, such as those seeking to measure family violence.

Applied Research and Policy Experiments

This edition retains a chapter devoted to applied criminal justice research; Chapter 12 examines program evaluation and policy analysis. In addition, we link policy and management applications to virtually every stage of the research process, from theory in Chapter 2 through data interpretation in Chapter 13. We feel this approach is crucial for two complementary reasons. First, students whose interests center on criminal justice policy must understand that applied research is as dependent on theory and reasoned expectations as is basic research. Second, basic research in criminology or criminal justice is usually conducted in some applied context, so the researcher interested in some causal proposition about, say, drug use and violence must recognize that these are not simply abstract constructs. Most measures of drug use and violence will be operationalized with legal or policy definitions of those constructs in mind.

Randomized field experiments have become the designs of choice for many applied studies. Our chapters on experimental and quasi-experimental designs (Chapter 7) and applied research describe the advantages of randomized designs. However, we also caution students that all designs have weaknesses and no design is well suited for all research purposes. Unfortunately, the weaknesses of randomized experiments are sometimes overlooked by their champions and by many textbooks. Our treatment of this topic, encouraging students to think carefully and creatively, is more balanced and will enable students to better recognize appropriate and inappropriate uses of experiments. Expanded material on scientific realism reinforces this perspective.

Statistics

Chapter 13 guides students through fundamental principles of descriptive and inferential statistics. Our coverage here is conceptual and brief, reflecting our view that criminal justice research design, measurement, and data collection require the concerted attention of students for a full semester. We also believe that understanding these issues is a necessary foundation for doing meaningful statistical analysis. Future producers and consumers of criminal justice research must understand how concepts become observations and how observations become data before they learn the details of data analysis.

At the same time, our approach to statistics is both thorough and conceptually sound. As a result, instructors who wish to cover data analysis in more detail (perhaps in a second semester course) will find Chapter 13 an excellent point of departure.

Appendices

Now that we have a companion Web site to accompany this text, we've moved the appendices from the CD-ROM to the Web site for greater access anywhere, anytime. Each appendix has been updated to reflect new Web-based resources.

Appendix A includes examples and general information about evolving library and information technology. Depending on the availability of tools and resources on your campus, we suggest that you supplement Appendix A with guides or manuals that document campus facilities and routines.

Appendix B describes the National Criminal Justice Reference Service (NCJRS), a specialized library and information tool for criminal justice research and policy development. The NCJRS was rather late in developing a useful Web site, but now provides ready access to publications issued by Justice Department agencies. Because more agencies are issuing reports in electronic format, virtually all students have access to documents previously available only in a small number of specialized collections. Appendix B leads students to several sources.

Appendix C presents guidelines on writing research reports. If your course will require a proposal or research report, we recommend that students review this appendix early in the term. See also Chapter 4 for further information on proposals. You may wish either to supplement or to modify our suggestions to reflect your own preferences. To complement this appendix, Wadsworth has replaced the CD-ROM that accompanied the Third Edition with the Research Writer for Criminal Justice CD-ROM.

Appendix D describes major sources of secondary data, most notably the National Archive of Criminal Justice Data (NACJD) and the Interuniversity Consortium for Political and Social Research (ICPSR). If adequate computing resources are available, students can retrieve information about NACJD and ICPSR holdings over the Internet. If not, online data analysis of selected collections is available at the NACJD.

Supplements

A number of resources are available to facilitate instruction and student comprehension and are available to qualified adopters. Please consult your local sales representative for details. The supplement package includes the following:

- For each chapter, the *Instructor's Manual* offers instructors lecture suggestions, learning objectives, chapter summaries and outlines, key terms, class discussion exercises, and a test bank with numerous multiple choice, true-false, fill-in-the-blank, and essay questions.
- ExamView® Computerized Testing, an easy-to-use assessment and tutorial system, enables instructors to create, deliver, and customize tests and study guides (both print and online) in minutes. Tests appear on screen exactly as they will print or display online. Using ExamView's complete

word-processing capabilities, you can also enter an unlimited number of new questions or edit questions included with ExamView.

- Designed to aid students in learning chapter concepts, the *Study Guide* offers students chapter-specific learning objectives, chapter summaries and outlines, key terms, and self-tests that include numerous multiple choice and true-false questions and exercises.

- The Research Writer for Criminal Justice CD-ROM serves as a step-by-step guide to writing research papers, offering helpful tips and hints along the way. Students can even check their progress by e-mailing their report to their instructor at any stage in the writing process. When they're done, the program can format their paper as a Microsoft® Word document according to standard research report guidelines.

- With this Fourth Edition, Wadsworth has added a companion Web site to the suite of supplements designed to aid students in mastering research methods. At *http://cj.wadsworth.com/maxfield_babbie/research_methods4e*, students can access useful learning resources for each chapter of the book. Resources include Tutorial Quizzes, flash cards, chapter outlines and summaries, and many other study aids. Students will also find special features such as four electronic appendices and quantitative and qualitative data analysis primers. The following four appendices are now available on the companion Web site:

  Appendix A: Using the Library: Traditional and Computer-Based Information Sources
  Appendix B: National Criminal Justice Reference Service
  Appendix C: The Research Report
  Appendix D: Sources of Secondary Data

- Four months of free access to InfoTrac® College Edition is automatically bundled with every new copy of this text. This world-class online library offers the full text of articles from almost 5000 scholarly and popular publications — updated daily and going back as much as 22 years. Through InfoTrac College Edition, users now also have instant access to *InfoWrite,* a handy resource that covers paper writing, critical thinking, and more.

Acknowledgments

Several reviewers made perceptive and useful comments on various drafts of the book. We are especially grateful to them for their insights and suggestions: James Ballard, Grand Valley State University; David Jenks, California State University, Los Angeles; Mark Lanier, University of Central Florida; Joan McDermott, Southern Illinois University at Carbondale; J. Mitchell Miller, University of South Carolina; Nathan Moran, Midwestern State University; Theodore Skotnicki, Niagara County Community College; William Tafoya, University of New Haven; and Robert Wadman, Weber State University.

Other colleagues offered suggestions, comments, and advice: Patricia Brantingham, Simon Fraser University; Judith Collins, Michigan State University; Robyn Dawes, Carnegie Mellon University; Brian Forst, American University; Michael Maltz, University of Illinois at Chicago; Mangai Natarajan and her Fall 2003 class in research methods, John Jay College of Criminal Justice; and Cathy Spatz Widom, The New Jersey Medical School.

Students at the Rutgers University School of Criminal Justice offered advice, feedback, and contributions for this and earlier editions. I thank Carsten Andresen, Dr. Gisela Bichler-Robertson (now at California State University, San Bernardino), Dr. Sharon Chamard (now at University of Alaska), Dr. Jarret Lovell (now at California State University, Fullerton), Dr. Marie Mele (now at LaSalle University), Dina Perrone, and Christopher Sullivan. Dr. William Sousa merits special thanks for generously sharing information about his own research.

Finally, Earl and I are very grateful for the patient, professional assistance from people at Wadsworth: Jay Whitney, Julie Sakaue, Susan DeVanna, Dory Schaeffer, Stacey Purviance, Jennie Redwitz, and Joohee Lee.

Part One

An Introduction to Criminal Justice Inquiry

What comes to mind when you encounter the word *science?* What do you think of when we describe criminal justice as a social science? For some people, science is mathematics; for others, it is white coats and laboratories. Some confuse it with technology or equate it with difficult high school or college courses.

Science is, of course, none of these things per se, but it is difficult to specify exactly what science is. Scientists, in fact, disagree on the proper definition. Some object to the whole idea of social science; others question more specifically whether criminal justice can be a social science.

For the purposes of this book, we view science as a method of inquiry—a way of learning and knowing things about the world around us. Like other ways of learning and knowing about the world, science has some special characteristics. We'll examine these traits in this opening set of chapters. We'll also see how the scientific method of inquiry can be applied to the study of crime and criminal justice.

Part One of the book lays the groundwork for the rest of the book by examining the fundamental characteristics and issues that make science different from other ways of knowing things. Chapter 1 begins with a look at native human inquiry, the sort of thing all of us have been doing all our lives. Because people sometimes go astray in trying to understand the world around them, we'll consider the primary characteristics of scientific inquiry that guard against those errors.

Chapter 2 deals specifically with the social scientific approach to criminal justice inquiry and the links between theory and research. The lessons of Chapter 1 are applied in the study of crime and criminal justice. Although special considerations arise in studying people and organizations, the basic logic of all science is the same.

Ethics is one of these special considerations we face in studying people. In Chapter 3, we'll see that most ethical questions are rooted in two fundamental principles: (1) Research subjects should not be harmed, and (2) their participation must be voluntary.

The overall purpose of Part One, therefore, is to construct a backdrop against which to view more specific aspects of research design and execution. By the time you complete the chapters in Part One, you'll be ready to look at some of the more concrete aspects of criminal justice research.

Chapter 1

Crime, Criminal Justice, and Scientific Inquiry

People learn about their world in a variety of ways, and they often make mistakes along the way. Science is different from other ways of learning and knowing. We'll consider the foundations of social science, different purposes of research, and different general approaches to social science.

(continued)

Introduction

*Criminal justice professionals are both consumers
and producers of research.*

Spending a semester studying criminal justice
research methodology may not be high on your
list of "Fun Things to Do." Perhaps you are or
plan to be a criminal justice professional and
are thinking, "Why do I have to study research
methods? When I graduate, I'll be working in
probation (or law enforcement, or corrections,
or court services), not conducting research! I
would benefit more from learning about probation counseling (or police management, or corrections policy, or court administration)." Fair
enough. But as a criminal justice professional,
you will need to be a *consumer* of research. One
objective of this book is to help you become an
informed consumer of research.

For example, in the section "Two Realities,"
we will see how findings from the Kansas City
Preventive Patrol Experiment appeared to contradict a traditional tenet of law enforcement—
that a visible patrol force prevents crime. Acting
as a consumer of research findings, a police offi-

cer, supervisor, or executive should be able to understand how the research was conducted and
how the study's findings might apply in his or
her department. Because police practices vary
from city to city, a police executive would benefit from being aware of research methods and
knowing how to interpret findings.

Most criminal justice professionals, especially those in supervisory roles, routinely review
various performance reports and statistical tabulations. In the past 30 years or so, thousands of
criminal justice research and evaluation studies
have been conducted. The National Criminal
Justice Reference Service (NCJRS) was established to archive and distribute research reports
to criminal justice professionals and researchers
around the world. Many such reports are prepared specifically to keep the criminal justice
community informed about new research developments. In addition, the Internet has become
an invaluable source of information about criminal justice research and policy; NCJRS documents now are available on the Web at http://
www.ncjrs.org. An understanding of research
methods can help decision makers critically

HOME DETENTION

Home detention with electronic monitoring (ELMO) was widely adopted as an alternative punishment in the United States in the 1980s. The technology for this new sanction was made possible by advances in telecommunications and computer systems. Prompted by growing prison and jail populations, not to mention sales pitches by equipment manufacturers, criminal justice officials embraced ELMO. Questions about the effectiveness of these programs quickly emerged, however, and led to research to determine whether the technology worked. Comprehensive evaluations were conducted in Marion County (Indianapolis), Indiana. Selected findings from these studies illustrate the importance of understanding research methods in general and the meaning of various ways to measure program success in particular.

ELMO programs directed at three groups of people were studied: (1) convicted adult offenders, (2) adults charged with a crime and awaiting trial, and (3) juveniles convicted of burglary or theft. People in each of the three groups were assigned to home detention for a specified time. They could complete the program in one of three ways: (1) successful release after serving their term, (2) removal due to rule violations, such as being arrested again or violating program rules, or (3) running away, or "absconding."

The agencies that administered each program were required to submit regular reports to county officials on how many individuals in each category completed their home detention terms. The accompanying table summarizes the program completion types during the evaluation study:

	Convicted Adults	Pretrial Adults	Juveniles
Success	81%	73%	99%
Rule violation	14	13	1
Abscond	5	14	0

evaluate such reports and recognize when methods are properly and improperly applied. The box titled "Home Detention" describes an example of how knowledge of research methods can help policy makers avoid mistakes.

Another objective of this book is to help you *produce* research. In other courses you take or in your job, you may become a producer of research. For example, probation officers sometimes test new approaches to supervising or counseling clients, and police officers try new methods of working with the community and with witnesses and suspects. Many cities and states have a compelling need to assess how changes in sentencing policy might affect jail and prison populations. Determining whether such changes are effective is an example of applied research. A problem-solving approach, rooted in systematic research, is being used in more and more police departments, and in many other criminal justice agencies as well. Therefore, criminal justice professionals need to know not only how to interpret research accurately but also how to produce accurate research.

What Is This Book About?

This book focuses on how we know what we know.

This book focuses on how we learn and know things, not on what we know. Although you will come away from the book knowing some things you don't know right now, our primary purpose is to help you look at *how* you know things, not *what* you know.

Two Realities

Ultimately, we live in a world of two realities. Part of what we know could be called our "experiential reality"—the things we know from direct experience. For example, if you dive into a glacial stream flowing down through the Canadian Rockies, you don't need anyone to tell you that the water is cold; you notice that all by

These figures, reported by agencies to county officials, indicate that the juvenile program was a big success; virtually all juveniles were successfully released.

Now consider some additional information on each program collected by the evaluation team. Data were gathered on new arrests of program participants and on the number of successful computerized telephone calls to participants' homes:

	Convicted Adults	Pretrial Adults	Juveniles
New arrest	5%	1%	11%
Successful calls	53	52	17

As the table shows, many more juveniles were arrested, and juveniles successfully answered a much lower percentage of telephone calls to their homes. What happened?

The simple answer is that the staff responsible for administering the juvenile program were not keeping track of offenders. The ELMO equipment was not maintained properly, and police were not visiting the homes of juveniles as planned. Because staff were not keeping track of program participants, they were not aware that many juveniles were violating the conditions of home detention. And because they did not to detect violations, they naturally reported that the vast majority of young burglars and thieves completed their home detention successfully.

A county official who relied on only agency reports of program success would have made a big mistake in judging the juvenile program to be 99 percent successful. In contrast, an informed consumer of such reports would have been skeptical of a 99 percent success rate and searched for more information.

Source: Adapted from Maxfield and Baumer (1991) and Baumer, Maxfield, and Mendelsohn (1993).

---

yourself. And the first time you step on a thorn, you know it hurts even before anyone tells you. The other part of what we know could be called our "agreement reality"—the things we consider real because we've been told they're real, and everyone else seems to agree they are real. A big part of growing up in any society, in fact, is learning to accept what everybody around us "knows" to be true. If we don't know those same things, we can't really be a part of the group. If you were to seriously question a geography professor as to whether the sun really sets in the west, you'd quickly find yourself set apart from other people. The first reality is a product of our own experience; the second is a product of what people have told us.

To illustrate the difference between agreement and experiential realities, consider preventive police patrol. The term *preventive* implies that when police patrol their assigned beats they prevent crime. Police do not prevent all crime, of course, but it is a commonsense belief

that a visible, mobile police force will prevent some crimes. In fact, the value of patrol in preventing crime was a fundamental tenet of police operations for many years. O. W. Wilson, a legendary police chief in Chicago and the author of an influential book on police administration, wrote that patrol was indispensable in preventing crime by eliminating incentives and opportunities for misconduct (Wilson and McLaren, 1963:320). A 1967 report on policing by President Lyndon Johnson's Commission on Law Enforcement and Administration of Justice (1967:1) stated that "the heart of the police effort against crime is patrol. . . . The object of patrol is to disperse policemen in a way that will eliminate or reduce the opportunity for misconduct and to increase the probability that a criminal will be apprehended while he is committing a crime or immediately thereafter."

Seven years later, the Police Foundation, a private research organization, published results from an experimental study that presented a dramatic challenge to conventional wisdom. Known as the "Kansas City Preventive Patrol Experiment," this study compared police beats with three levels of preventive patrol: (1) control beats, with one car per beat, (2) proactive beats, with two or three cars per beat, and (3) reactive beats, with no routine preventive patrol. After almost one year, researchers examined data from the three types of beats and found no differences in crime rates, citizen satisfaction with police, fear of crime, or other measures of police performance (Kelling, Pate, Dieckman, and Brown, 1974).

Researchers and law enforcement professionals alike were surprised by these findings. For the record, the Kansas City researchers never claimed to have proved that preventive patrol had no impact on crime. Instead, they argued that police should work more closely with community members and that routine patrol might be more effective if combined with other strategies that used police resources in a more thoughtful way.

Additional studies conducted in the 1970s cast doubt on other fundamental assumptions about police practices. For example, a quick response to crime reports made no difference in arrests, according to a research study in Kansas City (Van Kirk, 1977). And criminal investigation by police detectives rarely resulted in an arrest (Greenwood, 1975).

We mention these examples not to attack routine law enforcement practices. Rather, we want to show that systematic research on policing has illustrated how traditional beliefs—agreement reality—can be misleading. Simply increasing the number of police officers on patrol does not reduce crime because police patrol often lacks direction. Faster response time to calls for police assistance does not increase arrests because there is often a long delay between the time when a crime occurs and when it is reported to police. Clever detective work seldom solves crimes because investigators get most of their information from reports prepared by patrol officers, who in turn get their information from victims and witnesses.

Traditional beliefs about patrol effectiveness, response time, and detective work are examples of agreement reality. In contrast, the research projects that produced alternative views about each law enforcement practice represent experiential reality. These studies are examples of **empirical**[*] research, the production of knowledge based on experience or observation. In each case, researchers conducted studies of police practices and based their conclusions on observations and experience. Empirical research is a way of learning about crime and criminal justice, and explaining how to conduct empirical research is the purpose of this book.

In focusing on empirical research, we do not intend to downplay the importance of other ways of knowing things. Law students, for example, are trained in how to interpret statutes and judicial opinions. Historians take courses on methods of historical interpretation, mathematics majors learn numerical analysis, and students of philosophy study logic. If you are a criminal justice major, many of the other courses you take—say, a course on theories of crime and deviance—will add to your agreement reality.

The Role of Science

Science offers an approach to both agreement reality and experiential reality. Scientists have certain criteria that must be met before they will agree on the reality of something they haven't personally experienced. In general, an assertion must have both *logical* and *empirical* support: It must make sense, and it must agree with actual observations. For example, why do earthbound scientists accept the assertion that it's cold on the dark side of the moon? First, it makes sense because the surface heat of the moon comes from the sun's rays. Second, scientific measurements made on the moon's dark side confirm the assertion. Therefore, scientists accept the reality of things they don't personally experience—

---

[*] Words set in **boldface** are defined in the Glossary at the end of the book.

they accept an agreement reality—but they have special standards for doing so.

More to the point of this book, however, science offers a special approach to the discovery of reality through personal experience. Epistemology is the science of knowing; methodology (a subfield of epistemology) might be called "the science of finding out." This book focuses on criminal justice methodology—how social science methods can be used to better understand crime and criminal justice policy. To understand scientific inquiry, let's first look at the kinds of inquiry we all do each day.

Personal Human Inquiry

Everyday human inquiry draws on personal experience and secondhand authority.

Most of us would like to be able to predict our future circumstances. We seem quite willing, moreover, to undertake this task using causal and probabilistic reasoning. First, we generally recognize that future circumstances are somehow caused or conditioned by present ones. For example, we learn that getting an education will affect how much money we earn later in life and that running stoplights may result in an unhappy encounter with an alert traffic officer. As students, we learn that studying hard will result in better examination grades.

Second, we recognize that such patterns of cause and effect are probabilistic in nature: The effects occur more often when the causes occur than when the causes are absent—but not always. Thus, as students, we learn that studying hard produces good grades in most instances, but not every time. We recognize the danger of ignoring stoplights without believing that every such violation will produce a traffic ticket.

The concepts of causality and probability play a prominent role in this book. Science makes causality and probability more explicit and provides techniques for dealing with them more rigorously than does casual human inquiry.

As we look at our own personal inquiry, it is important to distinguish between prediction and understanding. Often, we can predict without understanding, such as predicting rain when our knees ache. And often, even if we don't understand why, we are willing to act on the basis of what appears to be predictive ability. Thus, racetrack buff who finds that the third-ranked horse in the third race of the day always wins will probably keep betting without knowing, or caring, why it works out that way.

Attempts to predict often occur in a context of knowledge and understanding. If we can understand why things are related to one another, why certain regular patterns occur, we can predict better than if we simply observe and remember those patterns. For example, college dormitories are often targets of burglary during semester breaks. If you understand something about the opportunity structure of burglary (it's more likely when a suitably motivated offender knows that a dwelling will be unoccupied), you will be able to predict that hanging a sign on your room that says, "Off to Jamaica! See you in two weeks!" invites trouble. Thus, human inquiry attempts to answer both *what* and *why* questions, and we pursue these goals by observing phenomena and figuring them out.

However, our attempts to learn about the world are only partly linked to personal inquiry and direct experience. Another, much larger, part comes from the agreed-on knowledge that others give us. This agreement reality both assists and hinders our attempts to find out things for ourselves. Two important sources of secondhand knowledge—tradition and authority—deserve brief consideration here.

Tradition

Each of us is born into and inherits a culture made up, in part, of firmly accepted knowledge about the workings of the world. We may learn from others that planting corn in the spring will result in the greatest assistance from the gods, that the circumference of a circle is approximately $3\frac{1}{7}$ times its diameter, or that driving on the left side of the road (in the United States) is dangerous. We may test a few of these "truths" on our own, but we simply accept the

ARREST AND DOMESTIC VIOLENCE

In 1983, preliminary results were released from a study on the deterrent effects of arrest in cases of domestic violence. The study reported that male abusers who were arrested were less likely to commit future assaults than offenders who were not arrested. Conducted by researchers from the Police Foundation, the study used rigorous experimental methods adapted from the natural sciences. Criminal justice scholars generally agreed that the research was well designed and executed. Public officials were quick to embrace the study's findings that arresting domestic violence offenders deterred them from future violence.

Here, at last, was empirical evidence to support an effective policy in combating domestic assaults. Results of the Minneapolis Domestic Violence Experiment were widely disseminated, in

part due to aggressive efforts by the researchers to publicize their findings (Sherman and Cohn, 1989). The attorney general of the United States recommended that police departments make arrests in all cases of misdemeanor domestic violence. Within 5 years, more than 80 percent of law enforcement agencies in U.S. cities adopted arrest as the preferred way of responding to domestic assaults (Sherman, 1992:2).

Several things contributed to the rapid adoption of arrest policies to deter domestic violence. First, the experimental study was conducted carefully by highly respected researchers. Second, results were widely publicized in newspapers, in professional journals, and on television programs. Third, officials could understand the study, and most believed that its findings made sense. Finally, mandating arrest in less serious cases of domestic violence was a straightforward and politically attractive approach to a growing problem.

---

great majority of them. These are the things that "everybody knows."

Tradition, in this sense, has some clear advantages for human inquiry. By accepting what everybody knows, we are spared the overwhelming task of starting from scratch in our search for regularities and understanding. Knowledge is cumulative, and an inherited body of information and understanding is the jumping-off point for the development of more knowledge.

Authority

Despite the power of tradition, new knowledge appears every day. In addition to our own personal inquiries, throughout life we learn about the new discoveries and understandings of others. Our acceptance of this new knowledge often depends on the status of the discoverer. For example, you are more likely to believe a judge who declares that your next traffic violation will result in a suspension of your driver's license than to believe your parents when they say the same thing.

Like tradition, authority can both help and

hinder human inquiry. We do well to trust the judgment of individuals who have special training, expertise, and credentials in a matter, especially in the face of contradictory arguments on a given question. At the same time, inquiry can be greatly hindered by the legitimate authorities who err within their own special province. Biologists, after all, do make mistakes in the field of biology, and biological knowledge changes over time. Most of us assume that over-the-counter medications are safe when taken as directed, trusting the authority of drug manufacturers and government agencies. However, in the late 19th century, our trust might have led us to buy a bottle of Bayer Heroin, then available as an over-the-counter pain relief medication (Inciardi, 1986). The box titled "Arrest and Domestic Violence" illustrates the difficult problems that can result when criminal justice policy makers accept too quickly the results from criminal justice research.

Inquiry is also hindered when we depend on the authority of experts speaking outside their realm of expertise. For example, con-

Sherman and Berk (1984), however, urged caution in uncritically embracing the results of their study. Others urged that similar research be conducted in other cities to check on the Minneapolis findings (Lempert, 1984). Recognizing this, the U.S. National Institute of Justice sponsored more experiments—known as replications—in six other cities. Not everyone was happy about the new studies. For example, a feminist group in Milwaukee opposed the replication in that city because it believed that the effectiveness of arrest had already been proved (Sherman and Cohn, 1989:138).

Results from the replication studies brought into question the effectiveness of arrest policies. In three cities, no deterrent effect was found in police records of domestic violence. In other cities, there was no evidence of deterrence for longer periods (6–12 months), and in three cities, researchers found that violence actually escalated when offenders were arrested (Sherman, 1992: 30). For example, Sherman and associates (1992: 167) report that in Milwaukee "the initial deterrent effects observed for up to thirty days quickly disappear. By one year later [arrests] produce an escalation effect." Arrest works in some cases but not in others. As in many other cases, in responding to domestic assaults, it's important to carefully consider the characteristics of offenders and the nature of the relationship between offender and victim.

After police departments throughout the country embraced arrest policies following the Minneapolis study, researchers were faced with the difficult task of explaining why initial results must be qualified. Arrest seemed to make sense; officials and the general public believed what they read in the papers and saw on television. Changing their minds by reporting complex findings was more difficult.

sider the political or religious leader, lacking any biochemical expertise, who declares marijuana to be a dangerous drug. The advertising industry plays heavily on this misuse of authority by having popular athletes discuss the nutritional value of breakfast cereals and having movie stars evaluate the performance of automobiles.

Both tradition and authority, then, are double-edged swords in the search for knowledge about the world. Simply put, they provide us with a starting point for our own inquiry, but they may lead us to start at the wrong point or push us in the wrong direction.

Errors in Personal Human Inquiry

Everyday personal human inquiry reveals a number of potential biases.

Aside from the potential dangers of relying on tradition and authority, we often stumble when we set out to learn for ourselves. Let's con-

sider some of the common errors we make in our own casual inquiries and then look at the ways science provides safeguards against those errors.

Inaccurate Observation

The keystone of inquiry is observation. We can never understand the way things are without first having something to understand. We have to know *what* before we can explain *why*. On the whole, however, people are rather sloppy, and even unconscious, observers of the flow of events in life. We fail to observe things right in front of us and mistakenly observe things that aren't so. Do you recall, for example, what your instructor was wearing on the first day of this class? If you had to guess now, what are the chances you would be right?

In contrast to casual human inquiry, scientific observation is a conscious activity. Simply making observations in a more deliberate way helps to reduce error. If you had gone to the first class meeting with a conscious plan to observe and record what your instructor was wearing, you'd have been more accurate.

In many cases, using both simple and complex measurement devices helps to guard against inaccurate observations. Suppose, for example, that you had taken color photographs of your instructor on the first day. The photos would have added a degree of precision well beyond that provided by unassisted human senses.

Overgeneralization

When we look for patterns among the specific things we observe around us, we often assume that a few similar events are evidence of a general pattern. The tendency to overgeneralize is probably greatest when there is pressure to reach a general understanding, yet overgeneralization also occurs in the absence of pressure. Whenever overgeneralization does occur, it can misdirect or impede inquiry.

Imagine you are a rookie police officer newly assigned to foot patrol in an urban neighborhood. Your sergeant wants to meet with you at the end of your shift to discuss what you think are the major law enforcement problems on the beat. Eager to earn favor with your supervisor, you interview the managers of a few stores in a small shopping area. If each mentions vandalism as the biggest concern, you might report that vandalism is the main problem on your beat, even though many residents believe that drug dealing contributes to the neighborhood problems of burglary, street robbery, and vandalism. Overgeneralization leads to misrepresentation and simplification of the problems on your beat.

Criminal justice researchers guard against overgeneralization by committing themselves in advance to a sufficiently large sample of observations and by being attentive to how representative those observations are. The **replication** of inquiry provides another safeguard. Replication means repeating a study, checking to see whether similar results are obtained each time. The study may also be repeated under slightly different conditions or in different locations. The box titled "Arrest and Domestic Violence" describes an example of why replication can be especially important in applied research.

Selective Observation

One danger of overgeneralization is that it may lead to selective observation. Once we have concluded that a particular pattern exists and have developed a general understanding of why, we will be tempted to pay attention to future events and situations that correspond with the pattern and to ignore those that don't. Racial, ethnic, and other prejudices are reinforced by selective observation.

Research plans often specify in advance the number and kind of observations to be made as a basis for reaching a conclusion. For example, if we wanted to learn whether women were more likely than men to support long prison sentences for sex offenders, we would have to make a specified number of observations on that question. We might select a thousand people to be interviewed. Even if the first 10 women supported long sentences and the first 10 men opposed them, we would continue to interview everyone selected for the study and record each observation. We would base our conclusion on an analysis of *all* the observations, not just those first 20.

Illogical Reasoning

People have various ways of handling observations that contradict their judgments about the way things are. Surely one of the most remarkable creations of the human mind is "the exception that proves the rule," an idea that makes no sense at all. An exception can draw attention to a rule or to a supposed rule, but in no system of logic can it prove the rule it contradicts. Yet we often use this pithy saying to brush away contradictions with a simple stroke of illogic.

What statisticians call the "gambler's fallacy" is another illustration of illogic in day-to-day reasoning. According to this fallacy, a consistent run of either good or bad luck is presumed to foreshadow its opposite. Thus, an evening of bad luck at poker may kindle the belief that a winning hand is just around the corner; many a poker player has stayed in a game too long because of that mistaken belief. Conversely, an extended period of good weather may lead us to worry that it is certain to rain on our weekend picnic.

Although we all sometimes use embarrassingly illogical reasoning, scientists avoid this pitfall by using systems of logic consciously and explicitly. Chapters 2 and 4 examine the logic(s) of science in more depth.

Ideology and Politics

Crime is, of course, an important social problem, and a great deal of controversy surrounds policies for dealing with crime. Many people feel strongly one way or another about the death penalty, gun control, and long prison terms for drug users as approaches to reducing crime. There is ongoing concern about racial bias in police practices and sentencing policies. Ideological or political views on such issues can undermine objectivity in the research process. Criminal justice professionals may have particular difficulty separating ideology and politics from a more detached, scientific study of crime.

Criminologist Samuel Walker (1994:16) compares ideological bias in criminal justice research to theology: "The basic problem . . . is that faith triumphs over facts. For both liberals and conservatives, certain ideas are unchallenged articles of faith, almost like religious beliefs that remain unshaken by empirical facts."

Most of us have our own beliefs about public policy, including policies for dealing with crime. The danger lies in allowing such beliefs to distort how research problems are defined and how research results are interpreted. The scientific approach to the study of crime and criminal justice policy guards against, but does not prevent, ideology and theology from coloring the research process. In empirical research, so-called articles of faith are compared with experience.

To Err Is Human

We have seen some of the ways that we can go astray in our attempts to know and understand the world and some of the ways that science protects its inquiries from these pitfalls. Social science differs from our casual, day-to-day inquiry in two important respects. First, social scientific inquiry is a conscious activity. Although we engage in continuous observation in daily life, much of it is unconscious or semiconscious. In social scientific inquiry, in contrast, we make a conscious decision to observe, and we stay alert while we do it. Second, social scientific inquiry is a more careful process than our casual efforts; we are more wary of making mistakes and take special precautions to avoid doing so.

Do social science research methods offer total protection against the errors that people commit in personal inquiry? No. Not only do individuals make every kind of error we've looked at, but social scientists as a group also succumb to the pitfalls and stay trapped for long periods of time.

Foundations of Social Science

Social scientific inquiry generates knowledge through logic and observation.

Science is sometimes characterized as "logico-empirical." This ungainly term carries an important message: The two pillars of science are (1) logic or rationality and (2) observation. A scientific understanding of the world must make sense and must agree with what we observe. Both of these elements are essential to social science and relate to three key aspects of the overall scientific enterprise: theory, data collection, and data analysis.

As a broad generalization, scientific theory deals with the logical aspect of science, data collection deals with the observational aspect, and data analysis looks for patterns in what is observed. This book focuses mainly on issues related to data collection—demonstrating how to conduct empirical research—but social science involves all three elements. With this in mind, Chapter 2 discusses the theoretical context of designing and executing research, and Chapter 13 presents a conceptual introduction to the statistical analysis of data. Figure 1.1 offers a

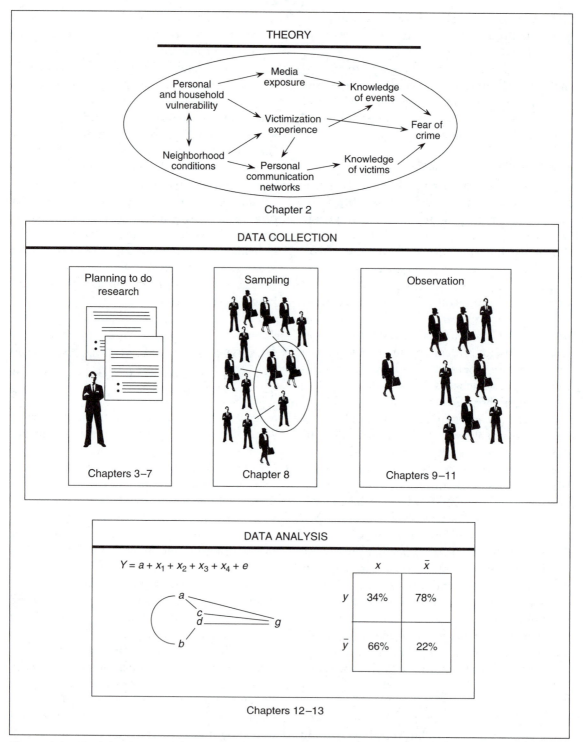

Figure 1.1   Social Science = Theory + Data Collection + Data Analysis

schematic view of how the book addresses these three aspects of social science.

Let's turn now to some of the fundamental issues that distinguish social science from other ways of looking at social phenomena.

Theory, Not Philosophy or Belief

Social scientific theory has to do with what is, not what should be. This means that scientific theory—and, more broadly, science itself—cannot settle debates on value or worth. Social science cannot determine, for example, whether prosecutors who are elected (as in most states) are "better" than prosecutors who are appointed by a state official (as in New Jersey) except in terms of some agreed-on criteria. We can determine scientifically whether elected or appointed prosecutors are more respected by the citizens they serve only if we agree on some measures of citizen respect, and our conclusion will depend totally on the measures we agree on.

By the same token, if we agree that, say, conviction rate or average sentence length is a good measure of a prosecutor's quality, then we will be in a position to determine scientifically whether a prosecutor in one city is better or worse than a prosecutor in another city. Again, however, our conclusion will be inextricably tied to the agreed-on criteria. As a practical matter, however, people are seldom able to agree on criteria for determining issues of value, so science is seldom of any use in settling such debates.

This issue will be considered in more detail in Chapter 12 when we look at evaluation research. Criminal justice research has become increasingly involved in studying whether programs achieve their intended goals. One of the biggest problems faced by evaluation researchers is getting people to agree on the criteria for success and failure. Yet such criteria are essential if social scientific research is to tell us anything useful about matters of value.

As an example, consider the dilemma of how to identify a good parole officer. On the one hand, a parole officer whose clients are rarely cited for violations and returned to prison might be considered a good officer. However, parole officers might attain low violation rates by ignoring transgressions by clients they are supposed to supervise—in effect, by not supervising them at all. Therefore, we might view a parole officer who frequently cites parolees for violations as being especially attentive to his or her job. We might also consider other factors in judging parole officers. Someone who routinely cites parolees for trivial rule infractions would not necessarily be considered a good officer, especially if such actions swell already crowded prison populations.

Thus, social science can assist us in knowing only what is and why. It can be used to address the question of what ought to be only when people agree on the criteria for deciding what makes one thing better than another. But this agreement seldom occurs. With that understanding, let's turn now to some of the fundamentals that social scientists use to develop theories about what is and why.

Regularities

Ultimately, social scientific theory aims to find patterns of regularity in social life. This assumes, of course, that life is "regular," not chaotic or random. That assumption applies to all science, but it is sometimes a barrier for people when they first approach social science.

Certainly, at first glance, the subject matter of the physical sciences appears to be more regular than that of the social sciences. A heavy object, after all, falls to earth every time we drop it. In contrast, a judge may sentence one person to prison and give another probation even though each is convicted of the same offense.

A vast number of norms and rules in society create regularity. For example, only persons who have reached a certain age may obtain a driver's license. In the National Football League, only men participate on the field. Such informal and formal prescriptions, then, regulate, or regularize, social behavior.

In addition to regularities produced by norms and rules, social science is able to identify other types of regularities. For example, teenagers commit more crimes than middle-aged people. When males commit murder, they usually kill another male, but female murderers more often kill a male. On average, white urban residents view police more favorably than nonwhites do. Judges receive higher salaries than police officers. And probation officers have more empathy for the people they supervise than prison guards do.

Science assumes that regularity exists in whatever is to be studied. Therefore, logically, social behavior should be susceptible to scientific analysis. But is that necessarily the case? After all, police officers in large cities often earn more than small-town judges. Or are these kinds of irregularities worthy of scientific study? So males often murder other males, whereas females rarely murder other females. What's the point?

What About Exceptions?

The objection that there are always exceptions to any social regularity misses the point. The existence of exceptions does not invalidate the existence of regularities. Thus, it is not important that a particular police officer earns more money than a particular judge if overall judges earn more than police officers. The pattern still exists. Social regularities represent *probabilistic* patterns, and a general pattern does not have to be reflected in 100 percent of the observable cases to be a pattern.

This rule applies in the physical as well as the social sciences. In genetics, for example, the mating of a blue-eyed person with a brown-eyed person will *probably* result in a brown-eyed offspring. The birth of a blue-eyed child does not challenge the observed regularity, however. Rather, the geneticist states only that the brown-eyed offspring is *more likely* and, furthermore, that a brown-eyed offspring will be born in only a certain percentage of cases. The social scientist makes a similar, probabilistic predic-

tion: that women overall are less likely to murder anybody, but when they do, their victims are most often males.

Aggregates, Not Individuals

Social scientists primarily study social patterns rather than individual ones. All regular patterns reflect the aggregate or combined actions and situations of many individuals. Although social scientists study motivations that affect individuals, **aggregates** are more often the subject of social science research.

A focus on aggregate patterns rather than on individuals distinguishes the activities of criminal justice researchers from the daily routines of many criminal justice practitioners. Consider, for example, the task of processing and classifying individuals newly admitted to a correctional facility. Prison staff administer psychological tests and review the prior record of each new inmate to determine security risks, program needs, and job options. A researcher who is studying whether white inmates tended to be assigned to more desirable jobs than nonwhite inmates would be more interested in patterns of job assignment. The focus would be on aggregates of white and nonwhite persons rather than the assignment for any particular individual.

Social scientific theories, then, typically deal with aggregate, not individual, behavior. Their purpose is to explain why aggregate patterns of behavior are so regular even when the individuals who perform them change over time. In another important sense, social science doesn't even seek to explain people. Rather, it seeks to understand the systems within which people operate, the systems that explain why people do what they do. The elements in such systems are not people but variables.

A Variable Language

Our natural attempts at understanding usually take place at the concrete, idiosyncratic level. That's just the way we think. Suppose someone says to you, "Women are too soft-hearted and weak to be police officers." You are likely to "hear" that comment in terms of what you know about the speaker. If it's your old Uncle Albert, who, you recall, is also strongly opposed to daylight savings time, zip codes, and computers, you are likely to think his latest pronouncement simply fits into his dated views about things in general. If, in contrast, the statement comes from a candidate for sheriff who is trailing a female challenger and who has begun making other statements about women being unfit for public office you may "hear" his latest comment in the context of this political challenge.

In both of these examples, we try to understand the thoughts of a particular, concrete individual. In social science, however, we go beyond that level of understanding to seek insights into classes or types of individuals. In the two preceding examples, we might use terms like *old-fashioned* or *bigoted* to describe the person who made the comment. In other words, we try to identify the actual individual with some set of similar individuals, and that identification operates on the basis of abstract concepts.

One implication of this approach is that it enables us to make sense out of more than one person. In understanding what makes the bigoted candidate think the way he does, we can also learn about other people who are "like him." This is possible because we have not been studying *bigots* as much as we have been studying *bigotry*.

Bigotry is considered a variable in this case because the level of bigotry varies; that is, some people in an observed group are more bigoted than others. Social scientists may be interested in understanding the system of variables that causes bigotry to be high in one instance and low in another. However, bigotry is not the only variable here. Gender, age, and economic status also vary among members of the observed group.

Here's another example: Consider the problem of whether police should make arrests in cases of domestic violence. The object of a police officer's attention in handling a domestic assault is the individual case. Of course, each case includes a victim and an offender, and police are concerned with preventing further harm to the victim. The officer must decide whether to arrest an assailant or to take some other action. The criminal justice researcher's subject matter is different: Does arrest as a general policy prevent future assaults? The researcher may study an individual case (victim and offender), but that case is relevant only as a situation in which an arrest policy might be invoked, which is what the researcher is really studying.

This is not to say that criminal justice researchers don't care about real people. They certainly do. Their ultimate purpose in studying domestic violence cases is to identify ways to protect potential victims from future assaults. But in this example, victims and offenders are most relevant for what they reveal about the effectiveness of the arrest policy. As researchers, our interest centers on variables and aggregates, not on individuals.

Variables and Attributes

Social scientists study variables and the attributes that compose them. Social scientific theories are written in a variable language, and people get involved mostly as the carriers of those variables. Here's what social scientists mean by variables and attributes.

Attributes are characteristics or qualities that describe some object such as a person. Examples are "bigoted," "old-fashioned," "married," "unemployed," and "intoxicated." Any quality we might use to describe ourselves or someone else is an attribute.

Variables are logical groupings of attributes. Thus, for example, "male" and "female" are attributes, and "gender" is the variable composed of the logical grouping of those two attributes. The variable "occupation" is composed of attributes like "dentist," "professor," and "truck driver." "Prior record" is a variable composed of a set of attributes such as "prior convictions," "prior arrests without convictions," and "no prior arrests." It's helpful to think of attributes as the categories that make up a variable. See

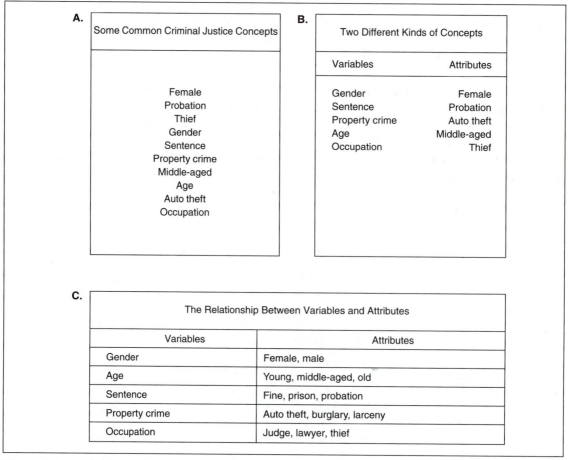

Figure 1.2 Variables and Attributes

Figure 1.2 for a schematic view of what social scientists mean by variables and attributes.

The relationship between attributes and variables lies at the heart of both description and explanation in science. For example, we might describe a prosecutor's office in terms of the variable "gender" by reporting the observed frequencies of the attributes "male" and "female": "The office staff is 60 percent men and 40 percent women." An incarceration rate can be thought of as a description of the variable "incarceration status" of a state's population in terms of the attributes "incarcerated" and "not incarcerated." Even the report of family income for a city is a summary of attributes composing

the income variable: $27,124, $44,980, $76,000, and so forth.

The relationship between attributes and variables becomes more complicated as we try to explain things. Here's a simple example involving two variables: type of defense attorney and sentence. For the sake of simplicity, let's assume that the variable "defense attorney" has only two attributes: "private attorney" and "public defender." Similarly, let's give the variable "sentence" two attributes: "probation" and "prison."

Now let's suppose that 90 percent of people represented by public defenders are sentenced to prison and the other 10 percent are sentenced to probation. And let's suppose that 30 percent

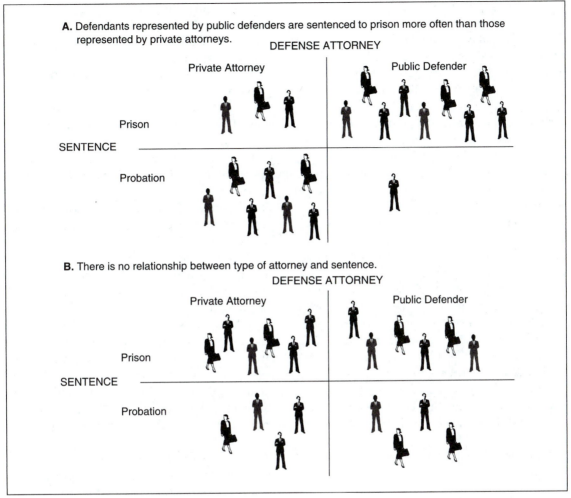

Figure 1.3 Illustration of Relationships Between Two Variables

of people with private attorneys go to prison and the other 70 percent receive probation. This is shown visually in Figure 1.3A.

Figure 1.3A illustrates a relationship between the variables "defense attorney" and "sentence." This relationship can be seen by the pairings of attributes on the two variables. There are two predominant pairings: (1) persons represented by private attorneys who are sentenced to probation, and (2) persons represented by public defenders who are sentenced to prison. But there are two other useful ways of viewing that relationship.

First, imagine that we play a game in which we bet on your ability to guess whether a person is sentenced to prison or probation. We'll pick the people one at a time (not telling you which ones we've picked), and you have to guess which sentence each person receives. We'll do it for all 20 people in Figure 1.3A. Your best strategy in this case is to always guess prison because 12 out of the 20 people are categorized that way. Thus, you'll get 12 right and 8 wrong, for a net success score of 4.

Now suppose that we pick a person from Figure 1.3A and we have to tell you whether the person has a private attorney or a public defender. Your best strategy now is to guess prison for each person with a public defender and probation for each person represented by a private attorney. If you follow that strategy, you will get 16 right and 4 wrong. Your improvement in guessing the sentence based on knowing the type of defense attorney illustrates what it means to say that the variables are related. You would have made a probabilistic statement based on some empirical observations about the relationship between type of lawyer and type of sentence.

Second, let's consider how the 20 people would be distributed if type of defense attorney and sentence were unrelated. This is illustrated in Figure 1.3B. Notice that half the people have private attorneys and half have public defenders. Also notice that 12 of the 20 (60 percent) are sentenced to prison—6 who have private attorneys and 6 who have public defenders. The equal distribution of those sentenced to probation and those sentenced to prison no matter what type of defense attorney each person had allows us to conclude that the two variables are unrelated. Here, knowing what type of attorney a person had would not be of any value to you in guessing whether that person was sentenced to prison or probation.

Variables and Relationships

We will look more closely at the nature of the relationships between variables later in this book. For now, let's consider some basic observations about variables and relationships that illustrate the logic of social scientific theories and their use in criminal justice research.

Theories describe relationships that might logically be expected among variables. This expectation often involves the notion of causation: A person's attributes on one variable are expected to *cause* or encourage a particular attribute on another variable. In the example just given, having a private attorney or a public defender seemed to cause a person to be sentenced to probation or prison, respectively. Apparently,

there is something about having a public defender that leads people to be sentenced to prison more often than if they are represented by a private attorney.

Type of defense attorney and sentence are examples of independent and dependent variables, respectively. These two concepts are implicit in causation, which is the focus of explanatory research. In this example, we assume that criminal sentences are determined or caused by something; the type of sentence depends on something and so is called the **dependent variable.** The dependent variable depends on an **independent variable;** in this case, sentence depends on type of defense attorney.

Notice, at the same time, that type of defense attorney might be found to depend on something else—our subjects' employment status, for example. People who have full-time jobs are more likely to be represented by private attorneys than those who are unemployed. In this latter relationship, the type of attorney is the dependent variable, and the subject's employment status is the independent variable. In cause-and-effect terms, the independent variable is the cause, and the dependent variable is the effect.

How does this relate to theory? Our discussion of Figure 1.3 involved the interpretation of data. We looked at the distribution of the 20 people in terms of the two variables. In constructing a theory, we form an expectation about the relationship between the two variables based on what we know about each. For example, we know that private attorneys tend to be more experienced than public defenders. Many people fresh out of law school gain a few years of experience as public defenders before they enter private practice. Logically, then, we would expect the more experienced private attorneys to be better able to get more lenient sentences for their clients. We might explore this question directly by examining the relationship between attorney experience and sentence, perhaps comparing inexperienced public defenders with public defenders who have been working for a few years. Pursuing this line of reasoning, we could also compare experienced private attorneys with private attorneys fresh out of law school.

Notice that the theory has to do with the variables "defense attorney," "sentence," and "years of experience," not with individual people per se. People are the carriers of those variables. We study the relationship between the variables by observing people. Ultimately, however, the theory is constructed in terms of variables. It describes the associations that might logically be expected to exist between particular attributes of different variables.

Purposes of Research

We conduct criminal justice research to serve different purposes.

Criminal justice research, of course, serves many purposes. Explaining associations between two or more variables is one of those purposes; others include exploration, description, and application. Although a given study can have several purposes, it is useful to examine them separately because each has different implications for other aspects of research design.

Exploration

Much research in criminal justice is conducted to explore a specific problem. A researcher or official may be interested in some crime or criminal justice policy issue about which little is known. Or perhaps an innovative approach to policing, court management, or corrections has been tried in some jurisdiction, and the researcher wishes to determine how common such practices are in other cities or states. An exploratory project might collect data on some measure to establish a baseline with which future changes will be compared.

For example, heightened concern with drug use might prompt efforts to estimate the level of drug abuse in the United States. How many people are arrested for drug sales or possession

each year? How many high school seniors report using marijuana in the past week or the past month? How many hours per day do drug dealers work, and how much money do they make? These are examples of research questions intended to explore different aspects of the problem of drug abuse. Exploratory questions may also be formulated in connection with criminal justice responses to drug problems. How many cities have created special police or prosecutor task forces to crack down on drug sales? What sentences are imposed on major dealers or on casual users? How much money is spent on treatment for drug users? What options exist for treating different types of addiction?

Exploratory studies are also appropriate when a policy change is being considered. Stricter enforcement of laws and longer prison sentences were common policy responses to drug abuse in the 1980s and 1990s, and jails and prisons were soon filled with newly arrested and sentenced drug offenders. This prompted a search for alternatives to incarceration, such as home detention. One of the first questions public officials typically ask when they consider some new policy is, "How have other cities (or states) handled this problem?"

Exploratory research in criminal justice can be simple or complex, using a variety of methods. For example, a mayor anxious to learn about drug arrests in his or her city might simply phone the police chief and request a report. In contrast, estimating how many high school seniors have used marijuana requires more sophisticated survey methods. Since the early 1970s, the National Institute on Drug Abuse has conducted nationwide surveys of students regarding drug use.

Description

A key purpose of many criminal justice studies is to describe the scope of the crime problem or policy responses to the problem. A researcher or public official observes and then describes what was observed. Criminal justice observation and description, methods grounded in the social sciences, tend to be more accurate than the casual observations people may make about how much crime there is or how violent teenagers are today. Descriptive studies are often concerned with counting or documenting observations; exploratory studies focus more on developing a preliminary understanding about a new or unusual problem.

Descriptive studies are frequently conducted in criminal justice. The FBI has compiled Uniform Crime Reports (UCRs) since the 1930s. UCR data are routinely reported in newspapers and widely interpreted as accurately describing crime in the United States. For example, 2001 UCR figures (Federal Bureau of Investigation, 2002) showed that Arizona had the highest rate of auto theft (983.6 per 100,000 residents) in the nation, and South Dakota had the lowest (107.7 per 100,000 residents).

Because criminal justice policy in the United States is almost exclusively under the control of state and local governments, many descriptive studies collect and summarize information from local governments. For example, since 1850 the federal government has conducted an annual census of prisoners in state and local correctional facilities. Like the decennial U.S. census, it gathers basic characteristics of a population—in this case, the population of people in detention (jail or prison) and on probation or parole.

Descriptive studies in criminal justice have other uses. A researcher may attend meetings of neighborhood anticrime groups and observe their efforts to organize block watch committees. These observations form the basis for a case study that describes the activities of neighborhood anticrime groups. Such a descriptive study might present information that officials and residents of other cities can use to promote such organizations themselves. Or consider research by Richard Wright and Scott Decker (1994), in which they describe in detail how burglars search for and select targets, how they gain entry into residences, and how they dispose of the goods they steal.

Explanation

A third general purpose of criminal justice research is to explain things. Recall our earlier example, in which we sought to explain the relationship between type of attorney and sentence length. Reporting that urban residents have generally favorable attitudes toward police is a descriptive activity, but reporting why some people believe that police are doing a good job while other people do not is an explanatory activity. Similarly, reporting why Arizona has the highest auto theft rate in the nation is explanation; simply reporting auto theft rates for different states is description. A researcher has an explanatory purpose if he or she wishes to know why the number of 14-year-olds involved in gangs has increased, as opposed to simply describing changes in gang membership.

Application

Researchers also conduct criminal justice studies of an applied nature. Applied research stems from a need for specific facts and findings with policy implications. Another purpose of criminal justice research, therefore, is its application to public policy. We can distinguish two types of applied research: evaluation and policy analysis.

First, applied research is often used to evaluate the effects of specific criminal justice programs. Determining whether a program designed to reduce burglary actually had that intended effect is an example of evaluation. In its most basic form, evaluation involves comparing the goals of a program with the results. For example, if one goal of increased police foot patrol is to reduce fear of crime, then an evaluation of foot patrol might compare levels of fear before and after increasing the number of police officers on the beat on foot. In most cases, evaluation research uses social science methods to test the results of some program or policy change. Because crime problems persist and seem to change frequently, officials are constantly seeking new approaches, and it is becoming more common for public officials or researchers to conduct evaluations of new programs.

The second type of applied research is policy analysis. What would happen to court backlogs if we designated a judge and prosecutor who would handle only drug-dealing cases? How many new police officers would have to be hired if a department shifted to community policing? These are examples of *what if* questions addressed by policy analysis. Answering such questions is sort of a counterpart to program evaluation. Policy analysis is different from other forms of criminal justice research primarily in its focus on future events. Rather than observing and analyzing current or past behavior, policy analysis tries to anticipate the future consequences of alternative actions.

Our brief discussion of distinct research purposes is not intended to imply that research purposes are mutually exclusive. Many criminal justice studies have elements of more than one purpose. Suppose you want to evaluate a new program to reduce bicycle theft at your university. First, you need some information that describes the problem of bicycle theft on campus. Let's assume your evaluation finds that thefts from some campus locations have declined but that there was an increase in bikes stolen from racks outside dormitories. You might explain these findings by noting that bicycles parked outside dorms tend to be unused for longer periods and that there is more coming and going among bikes parked near classrooms. One option to further reduce thefts would be to purchase more secure bicycle racks. A policy analysis might compare the costs of installing the racks with the predicted savings resulting from a reduction in bike theft.

Differing Avenues for Inquiry

Social science research is conducted in a variety of ways.

There is no one way of doing criminal justice research. If there were, this would be a much shorter book. In fact, much of the power and

potential of social science research lies in the many valid approaches it comprises.

Three broad and interrelated distinctions underlie many of the variations of social science research: (1) ideographic and nomothetic explanations, (2) inductive and deductive reasoning, and (3) quantitative and qualitative data. Although it is possible to see them as competing choices, a good researcher masters each of these orientations.

Idiographic and Nomothetic Explanations

All of us go through life explaining things; we do it every day. You explain why you did poorly or well on an exam, why your favorite team is winning or losing, and why you keep getting speeding tickets. In our everyday explanations, we engage in two distinct forms of causal reasoning—idiographic and nomothetic explanation—although we do not ordinarily distinguish them.

Sometimes, we attempt to explain a single situation exhaustively. Thus, for example, you may have done poorly on an exam because (1) you had forgotten there was an exam that day, (2) it was in your worst subject, (3) a traffic jam caused you to be late to class, and (4) your roommate kept you up the night before with loud music. Given all these circumstances, it is no wonder that you did poorly on the exam.

This type of causal reasoning is **idiographic** explanation. *Idio* in this context means "unique, separate, peculiar, or distinct," as in the word *idiosyncrasy*. When we complete an idiographic explanation, we feel that we fully understand the many causes of what happened in a particular instance. At the same time, the scope of our explanation is limited to the case at hand. Although parts of the idiographic explanation might apply to other situations, our intention is to explain one case fully.

Now consider a different kind of explanation. For example, every time you study with a group, you do better on an exam than if you study alone; or your favorite team does better at home than on the road; or you get more speeding tickets on weekends than during the week. This type of explanation—called **nomothetic**—seeks to explain a class of situations or events rather than a single one. Moreover, it seeks to explain "efficiently," using only one or just a few explanatory factors. Finally, it settles for a partial rather than a full explanation of a type of situation.

In each of the preceding nomothetic examples, you might qualify your causal statements with phrases like "on the whole" or "usually." Thus, you usually do better on exams when you've studied in a group, but there have been exceptions. Similarly, your team has won some games on the road and lost some at home. And last week you got a speeding ticket on the way to Tuesday's chemistry class, but you did not get one over the weekend. Such exceptions are an acceptable price to pay for a broader range of overall explanation.

Both the idiographic and the nomothetic approaches to understanding can be useful in daily life. They are also powerful tools for criminal justice research. Thus, the researcher who seeks an exhaustive understanding of the inner workings of a particular juvenile gang or the rulings of a specific judge is engaging in idiographic research. The aim is to understand that particular group or individual as fully as possible.

In an in-depth study of a group of New York City cocaine dealers, Terry Williams (1989) recognized that the dealers he interviewed and observed were not necessarily typical of dealers in other cities, or even in other parts of New York City. Although Williams gained key insights into how drug rings operate generally, his immediate goal was to understand and describe the activities of a small group of dealers. After spending more than 1200 hours in the field, Williams describes the activities of "Max" and his crew in rich detail.

Sometimes, however, the aim is a more generalized understanding, across a class of events, even though the level of understanding is inevitably more superficial. For example, researchers who seek to uncover the chief factors that lead to juvenile delinquency are pursuing a nomothetic inquiry. They might discover that children who frequently skip school are more likely to have records of delinquency than those who attend school regularly. This explanation would extend well beyond any single juvenile, but it would do so at the expense of a complete explanation.

In contrast to Williams' idiographic study of a cocaine crew, Avshalom Caspi and associates (1994) sought to understand relationships between certain personality traits and delinquency. Although they could not conclusively answer the question of whether there is a criminal personality, Caspi and associates found regularities in personality profiles among research subjects in Dunedin, New Zealand, and Pittsburgh, Pennsylvania. This is an illustration of the nomothetic approach to understanding.

Thus, social scientists have access to two distinct logics of explanation. We can alternate between searching for broad, albeit less detailed, universals (nomothetic) and probing more deeply into more specific cases (idiographic). Both are good science, both are rewarding, and both can be fun.

Inductive and Deductive Reasoning

The distinction between inductive and deductive reasoning exists in daily life, as well as in criminal justice research. You might take two different routes to reach the conclusion that you do better on exams if you study with others. Suppose you find yourself puzzling, halfway through your college career, about why you do so well on exams sometimes and more poorly at other times. You list all the exams you've taken, noting how well you did on each. Then you try to recall any circumstances shared by all the good exams and by all the poor ones. Do you do better on multiple-choice exams or essay exams? Morning exams or afternoon exams? Exams in the natural sciences, the humanities, or the social sciences? After you studied alone or in a group? It suddenly occurs to you that you almost always do better on exams when you studied with others than when you studied alone. This is known as the inductive mode of inquiry.

Inductive reasoning (induction) moves from the specific to the general, from a set of particular observations to the discovery of a pattern that represents some degree of order among the varied events under examination. Notice, incidentally, that your discovery doesn't necessarily tell you *why* the pattern exists—merely that it does.

There is the second, and very different, way you might reach the same conclusion about studying for exams. As you approach your first set of exams in college, you might wonder about the best ways to study. You might consider how much you should review the readings and how much you should focus on your class notes. Should you study at a measured pace over time or pull an all-nighter just before the exam? Among these musings, you might ask whether you should get together with other students in the class or study on your own. You decide to evaluate the pros and cons of both options. On the one hand, studying with others might not be as efficient because a lot of time might be spent on material you already know. Or the group might get distracted from studying. On the other hand, you can understand something even better when you've explained it to someone else. And other students might understand material that you've been having trouble with and reveal perspectives that might have escaped you.

So, you add up the pros and the cons and conclude, logically, that you'd benefit from studying with others. This seems reasonable to you in theory. To see whether it is true in practice, you test your idea by studying alone for half your exams and studying with others for half. This second approach is known as the deductive mode of inquiry.

Deductive reasoning (deduction) moves from the general to the specific. It moves from a pattern that might be logically or theoretically expected to observations that test whether the expected pattern actually occurs in the real world. Notice that deduction begins with "why" and moves to "whether," while induction moves in the opposite direction.

Both inductive and deductive reasoning are valid avenues for criminal justice and other social science research. Moreover, they work together to provide ever more powerful and complete understandings.

Quantitative and Qualitative Data

Simply put, the distinction between quantitative and qualitative data is the distinction between numerical and nonnumerical data. When we say that someone is witty, we are making a qualitative assertion. When we say that that person has appeared three times in a local comedy club, we are attempting to quantify our assessment.

Most observations are qualitative at the outset, whether it is our experience of someone's sense of humor, the location of a pointer on a measuring scale, or a check mark entered in a questionnaire. None of these things is inherently numerical. But it is often useful to convert observations to a numerical form. Quantification often makes our observations more explicit, makes it easier to aggregate and summarize data, and opens up the possibility of statistical analyses, ranging from simple descriptions to more complex testing of relationships between variables.

Quantification requires focusing our attention and specifying meaning. Suppose someone asks whether your friends tend to be older or younger than you. A quantitative answer seems easy. You think about how old each of your friends is, calculate an average, and see whether it is higher or lower than your own age. Case closed.

Or is it? Although we focused our attention on "older or younger" in terms of the number of years people have been alive, we might mean something different with that idea—for example, "maturity" or "worldliness." Thus, your friends may tend to be a little younger than you in age but to act more mature. Or we might have been thinking of how young or old your friends

PUTTING IT ALL TOGETHER

WHY DID CRIME GO DOWN (OR UP) IN NEW YORK CITY?

From the mid-1980s until the early 1990s, crime rates increased in most parts of the country. Homicide in particular peaked at very high levels in virtually all cities. Beginning about 1992, however, this pattern was reversed in many cities. Large urban areas began reporting fewer serious crimes, including murder and other violent offenses. Different measures of crime revealed similar patterns—no matter how (or what) you counted, rates of serious crime were declining.

This changing pattern was strikingly evident in New York City. The nation's largest city also leads with respect to numbers in most crime categories. But starting in 1994, crime in New York began a decline that continued through 2002. In 1993, New York reported over 1900 homicides; by 2002, the number had declined to under 600.

City officials were quick to claim credit for the drop in crime, pointing to fundamental changes in policing as the reason. Criminologists, however, were more cautious in attributing the decline to better policing. Experts cited other possible explanations, such as changes in economic conditions, the age structure of the population, changes in sentencing practices, and the waning popularity of crack cocaine. Besides, said the experts, murder and other serious crime declined in other cities at about the same time. So how could New York City claim that the change was due to innovations in policing?

Some public officials countered by pointing out that, although criminology and criminal justice researchers aspire to be scientific, they aren't very good at predicting or explaining things. Some of these public officials further disparaged criminology and criminal justice researchers by asserting that criminologists offered no conclusive explanations for earlier crime increases for the declining crime rates of the 1990s. As we study research methods and their application in the study of the decline in crime in New York City, keep the public officials' assertions in mind and decide for yourself how accurately criminal justice researchers can predict and explain crime.

This box is the first of a running example that appears throughout the book. We examine the decline in crime through the end of the 1990s, with

---

look or of the variation in their life experiences, their worldliness. All these other meanings are lost in the numerical calculation of average age.

In addition to greater detail, non-numerical observations seem to convey a greater richness of meaning than do quantified data. Think of the cliché "He is older than his years." The meaning of that expression is lost in attempts to specify how much older. In this sense, the richness of meaning is partly a function of ambiguity. If the expression meant something to you when you read it, that meaning came from your own experiences, from people you have known who might fit the description of being "older than their years." Two things are certain: (1) Your understanding of the expression is different from ours, and (2) you don't know exactly what either of us means by the expression.

Earl Babbie has a young friend, Ray Zhang, who was responsible for communications at the 1989 freedom demonstrations at Tiananmen Square in Beijing. Following the army crackdown on the demonstrators, Ray fled south, was arrested, and then was released with orders to return to Beijing. Instead, he escaped from China and made his way to Paris. Eventually, he came to the United States, where he resumed the graduate studies he had to abandon in fleeing his homeland. Ray has had to deal with the difficulties of enrolling in school without any transcripts from China, studying in a foreign language, and meeting his financial needs—on his own, thousands of miles from his family and friends. Through all this, Ray still speaks of one day returning to China to build a system of democracy.

a particular focus on New York City for three reasons. First, New York's declining crime rate was widely publicized, and the city's police department claimed virtually all the credit. Second, the New York Police Department's role in reducing crime has been hotly disputed, with two former police officials claiming credit in recently published books (Bratton, 1998; Maple, 1999). Finally, two researchers at Rutgers University, George Kelling and William Sousa, completed their own study (2001) of the links between policing and crime in New York. These researchers generously shared details of their study with us; Michael Maxfield worked closely with them at all stages of their project.

How Do We Know?

Although it is not logically possible to definitively establish what caused crime to decline in New York and other cities, this topic is a useful vehicle for illustrating how to do research, as well as validating how careful application of the research methods presented in this book can produce reliable results. Accordingly, we apply selected topics from each chapter to the variety of research questions that emerge from the broader question, "Why did crime go down?"

Let's consider what we have covered so far and examine how these general issues in research are reflected in the ongoing controversy about what caused the decline in crime.

- How do we come to believe what caused crime to decline in New York? What evidence supports those beliefs?
- Should we believe the experts? How about the politicians? Why or why not?
- What sorts of errors in personal inquiry might be involved? What about ideology and politics?
- What are the attributes of changes in policing in New York? How are these attributes related to changes in crime rates?
- Maybe we can attribute New York's drop in crime to police action. But does that apply to New York only, or can we generalize to other cities as well?

These are similar to questions we have examined in this chapter, although slightly restated to apply to the case of New York.

In each chapter, we consider how the general principles of that chapter may be used to conduct research on New York's declining crime rate. For example, Chapter 2 examines how theory guides research and how research contributes to the further development of theory. What theory might help us understand changes in policing and changes in crime rates in New York?

We would probably agree that Ray sounds like someone who is both worldly and "older than his years." However, the brief description of Ray's experiences, while it fleshes out the meaning of the phrase, still does not equip us to say how much older or even to compare Ray with someone else without the risk of disagreeing as to which one is more "worldly."

This concept can be quantified to a certain extent, however. For example, we could make a list of life experiences that contribute to what we mean by "worldliness":

Getting married
Getting divorced
Having a parent die
Seeing a murder committed
Being arrested

Being fired from a job
Running away with a rock band

We could quantify people's worldliness by counting how many of these experiences they have had: the more such experiences, the more worldly we say they are. If we think that some experiences are more powerful than others, we can give those experiences more points than others. Once we decide on the specific experiences to be considered and the number of points each warrants, scoring people and comparing their worldliness is fairly straightforward.

To quantify a concept like "worldliness," we must be explicit about what we mean. By focusing specifically on what we will include in our measurement of the concept, as we did here, we also exclude the other possible meanings.

Inevitably, then, quantitative measures will be more superficial than qualitative descriptions. This is the trade-off.

What a dilemma! Which approach should we choose? Which is better? Which is more appropriate to criminal justice research?

The good news is that we don't have to choose. In fact, by choosing to undertake a qualitative or quantitative study, researchers run the risk of artificially limiting the scope of their inquiry. Both qualitative and quantitative methods are useful and legitimate. And some research situations and topics require elements of both approaches.

Ethics and Criminal Justice Research

All criminal justice research must consider basic ethical issues.

Most of this book describes specific techniques of social scientific research in criminal justice and discusses the methods best suited for different situations. Some vital nonscientific concerns also shape the activities of criminal justice researchers. One of the most important of these is ethics. Ethics is especially important in studying crime and criminal justice, because our interest often focuses on human behavior that is illegal.

The foremost ethical rule of social science research is: *Bring no harm to research subjects.* Although no researcher plans to hurt people intentionally, this rule applies to inadvertent or accidental harm as well. Research subjects might be harmed in several ways. For example, a gang member observed talking with a researcher might be physically harmed by other gang members. Victims of crime can suffer psychological harm when asked to describe their experiences. Research subjects engaged in criminal activities may experience legal or economic difficulties if their activities become known to law enforcement officials or employers. Finally, research subjects may suffer embarrassment or violation of privacy. Eliminating the potential for harm to

subjects is not always possible, but researchers use several general strategies to minimize possible harm. Maintaining the confidentiality of data gathered during a criminal justice research project is one of the most widely used.

Another basic ethical rule of research is: *Participation should be voluntary.* Again, in principle, this appears a fairly simple rule to follow. An experimenter who forces people to participate in the experiment will be roundly criticized. When someone calls and asks us to participate in a telephone survey, we are free to refuse. Yet when we go into the field to observe drug transactions on the streets, we don't ask permission of all buyers and sellers who come to our attention. Or, if we trace arrest records for convicted burglars after they are released from prison, we can't really say they are volunteering for our study.

Not harming subjects and ensuring voluntary participation are the most fundamental ethical issues in criminal justice and other social science research. We discuss these ethical issues further in Chapter 3. We'll see that different approaches to criminal justice research often raise different kinds of ethical questions.

Knowing Through Experience: Summing Up and Looking Ahead

Empirical research involves measurement and interpretation.

This chapter introduced the foundation of criminal justice research: empirical research, or learning through experience. Each avenue for inquiry—nomothetic or idiographic description, inductive or deductive reasoning, qualitative or quantitative data—is fundamentally empirical. It's worth keeping that in mind as we examine the various forms criminal justice research can take.

It is also helpful to think of criminal justice research as organized around two basic activities: measurement and interpretation. Researchers measure aspects of reality and then draw conclusions about the meaning of what they have measured. All of us are observing all the time, but measurement refers to something more deliberate and rigorous. Part Two of this book describes ways of structuring observations to produce more deliberate, rigorous measures. Our ability to interpret observations in criminal justice research depends crucially on how those observations are structured. After deciding how to structure observations, we have to actually measure them. Whereas physical scientists sometimes use tensiometers, spectrographs, and other such equipment for measurement, criminal justice researchers use a variety of techniques, examined in Part Three.

The other key to criminal justice research is interpretation. Much of interpretation is based on data analysis, which is introduced in Part Four. More generally, however, interpretation is very much dependent on how observations are structured, a point we will encounter repeatedly.

When we put the pieces together—measurement and interpretation—we are in a position to describe, explain, or predict something. And that is what social science is all about.

✪ *Main Points*

- Knowledge of research methods is valuable to criminal justice professionals as consumers and producers of research.
- The study of research methods is the study of how we know what we know.
- Inquiry is a natural human activity for gaining an understanding of the world around us.
- Much of our knowledge is based on agreement rather than direct experience.
- Tradition and authority are important sources of knowledge.
- Empirical research is based on experience and produces knowledge through systematic observation.
- In day-to-day inquiry, we often make mistakes. Science offers protection against such mistakes.
- Whereas people often observe inaccurately, science avoids such errors by making observation a careful and deliberate activity.
- Sometimes we jump to general conclusions on the basis of only a few observations. Scientists avoid overgeneralizaton through replication.

- Scientists avoid illogical reasoning by being as careful and deliberate in their thinking as in their observations.
- The scientific study of crime guards against, but does not prevent, ideological and political beliefs from influencing research findings.
- Social science involves three fundamental aspects: theory, data collection, and data analysis.
- Social scientific theory addresses what is, not what should be.
- Social scientists are interested in explaining aggregates, not individuals.
- Although social scientists observe people, they are primarily interested in discovering relationships that connect variables.
- Explanations may be idiographic or nomothetic.
- Data may be quantitative or qualitative.
- Theories may be inductive or deductive.
- Two key ethical guidelines in social science research are that no harm should come to research subjects and participation in research should be voluntary.

✪ *Key Terms*

These terms are defined in the chapter where they are set in boldface and can also be found in the Glossary at the end of the book.

Aggregate	Independent variable
Attribute	Inductive reasoning
Dependent variable	Nomothetic
Deductive reasoning	Replication
Empirical	Variable
Idiographic	

✪ *Review Questions and Exercises*

1. Review the common errors of personal inquiry discussed in this chapter. Find a newspaper or magazine article about crime that illustrates one or more of those errors. Discuss how a scientist would avoid making that error.
2. Briefly discuss examples of descriptive research and explanatory research about declining crime rates in New York or some other city.
3. Often, things we think are true and supported by considerable experience and evidence turn out not to be true, or at least not true with the certainty we expected. Criminal justice seems especially vulnerable to this phenomenon, perhaps because crime and criminal justice policy are so often the subjects of mass and popular media attention. If news stories, movies, and TV

shows all point to growing gang- or drug-related violence, it is easy to assume that these are real problems identified by systematic study. Choose a criminal justice topic or claim that's currently prominent in news stories or entertainment. Consult a recent edition of the *Sourcebook of Criminal Justice Statistics* (citation below) for evidence to refute the claim.

✪ *Internet Exercise*

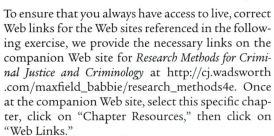

To ensure that you always have access to live, correct Web links for the Web sites referenced in the following exercise, we provide the necessary links on the companion Web site for *Research Methods for Criminal Justice and Criminology* at http://cj.wadsworth.com/maxfield_babbie/research_methods4e. Once at the companion Web site, select this specific chapter, click on "Chapter Resources," then click on "Web Links."

Visit the Web site for *The Washington Post, New York Times, Houston Chronicle,* or *Los Angeles Times*. Use one of these links, or locate a link to the newspaper of your choice, and find one article that provides or seeks an idiographic explanation for some observed action or event and one article that seeks or provides a nomothetic explanation. Provide a copy of each article, and write a paragraph for each explaining why you feel the explanation is idiographic or nomothetic.

✪ *InfoTrac College Edition*

Use the keywords *deductive reasoning* or *inductive reasoning* to find articles that discuss these approaches to scientific thought. Read one article, and compare what you find with what has been discussed in the textbook about scientific reasoning.

✪ *The NEW Companion Web Site for* **Research Methods for Criminal Justice and Criminology,** *Fourth Edition*

http://cj.wadsworth.com/maxfield_babbie/research_methods4e

Supplement your review of this chapter by going to the new companion Web site to take one of the

Tutorial Quizzes, use the flash cards to master key terms, and check out the many other study aids you'll find there. You'll also find special features such as quantitative and qualitative data analysis primers to help you with a special project or do some research on your own.

✪ *Additional Readings*

Babbie, Earl, *The Sociological Spirit* (Belmont, CA: Wadsworth, 1994). The primer in some sociological points of view introduces some of the concepts commonly used in the social sciences.

Hoover, Kenneth R., *The Elements of Social Scientific Thinking* (New York: St. Martin's Press, 1992). This book provides an excellent overview of the key elements in social scientific analysis.

Levine, Robert, *A Geography of Time: The Temporal Misadventures of a Social Psychologist* (New York: Basic Books, 1997). Most of us think of time as absolute. Levine's book is fun and fascinating as he explores how agreement reality plays a major role in how people from different cultures think about time.

Maguire, Kathleen, and Pastore, Ann L. (eds.), *Sourcebook of Criminal Justice Statistics* (Washington, DC: U.S. Department of Justice, Office of Justice Programs, Bureau of Justice Statistics, annual) available at http://www.albany.edu/Sourcebook. For almost 30 years, this annual publication has been a source of basic data on criminal justice. If you're not yet familiar with this compendium, Chapter 1 is a good place to start.

Tilley, Nick, and Laycock, Gloria, *Working Out What to Do: Evidence-Based Crime Reduction* (London: Home Office Policing and Reducing Crime Unit, Crime Reduction Series, no. 11,2002). (http://www.homeoffice.gov.uk/rds/crimreducpubs1.html). One of many excellent publications from the British Home Office, this guide helps justice professionals develop policies based on empirical experience. The guide is clearly written and useful as an illustration of how practitioners use social science.

Chapter 2

Theory and Criminal Justice Research

We'll see what distinguishes scientific theory from everyday reasoning and how the social scientific approach to criminal justice research is linked to theory. We'll also lay a foundation for understanding the research techniques discussed throughout the rest of the book.

Introduction

Criminal justice in particular, and human behavior in general, can be studied scientifically.

The evolution of social science has brought a greater emphasis on systematic explanation and a move away from the previous emphasis on description. For example, political scientists now focus on explaining political behavior rather than describing political institutions. The growth of such subfields as econometrics has had this effect in economics, as has historiography in history. And criminal justice and criminology have followed this same trend. Research on the causes of crime and the effects of criminal justice policy has supplemented a previous emphasis on describing strategies for police investigation or corrections management. Understandably, professionals trained and experienced in the more traditional orientations of these fields sometimes objected to the new directions.

This book is grounded in the position that human social behavior can be subjected to scientific study as legitimately as can the physicist's atoms or the biologist's cells. The study of crime and criminal justice concentrates on particular types of human behavior and so is no less amenable to scientific methods. Our attention now turns to the overall logic of social scientific inquiry as it applies to criminology and criminal justice. That logic is fundamentally rooted in the use of theory to guide inquiry.

The Creation of Social Science Theory

Theory and observation go together in science, but sometimes theory precedes observation, and other times observation comes before theory.

In Chapter 1, we considered some of the foundations of social scientific research as a mode of inquiry involving both logic and observation. Now we'll examine the relationship between **theory** and research in more depth. First, we'll look at "the scientific method" as it is tradition-

ally taught. Next, we'll examine two models for describing how theory and research work together in the practice of social science. Then we'll discuss the important links between theory, research, and policy.

The Traditional Model of Science

Instruction in the scientific method, especially in the physical sciences, tends to create a certain image in students' minds of how science operates. Although this traditional model of science tells only a part of the story, it is important that we have a common understanding of the basic logic of that model. The three main elements in the traditional model of science, which are typically presented in a chronological order of execution, are theory, operationalization, and observation. Let's look at each in turn.

Theory According to the traditional model of science, the scientist begins with an interest in some aspect of the real world. Suppose we are interested in discovering some of the broad social factors that contribute to the concentration of crime in urban areas. What kinds of social problems and characteristics of urban areas are associated with higher levels of crime?

As we think about this question, we might come up with things like population density, crowded housing conditions, poverty, unemployment, limited economic opportunities, weakened family ties, and the absence of appropriate role models. As described by Marvin Krohn (1991), these are some of the ideas that influenced the development of social disorganization theories of crime. In the early 20th century, sociologists began to examine the social disruption produced by rapid population growth in the city of Chicago. What came to be known as the "Chicago School" of criminology began with more general studies of the roots of a broad spectrum of social problems.

Sociologists Ernest Burgess and Robert Park started by describing Chicago's growth as a pattern of concentric zones (Burgess, 1925; Park and Burgess, 1921). At the core was the city's central business district, or downtown area. As Chicago expanded, the city developed in a pattern of circles centered around the core. Each area, from the downtown core to outlying suburbs, displayed particular patterns of land use. Commerce and industry were concentrated in downtown areas, while wealthy families occupied residential areas in outer circles. Lower-income migrants to Chicago settled in transition zones between the core and more distant areas.

Transition zones were so labeled because of the continuous flow of people in and out of the areas. Higher-income residents tended to move outward to avoid the influx of industrial activity expanding from the city's core area. Outward-moving families were replaced by lower-income immigrants from Europe (and later white and black migrants from depressed southern states) who came to the United States to pursue economic opportunity or escape political oppression. Persons moving into transition zones found housing that was deteriorating and crowded but close to the factory jobs that had attracted them to Chicago. As their economic situation improved, they moved outward and were replaced by new in-migrants, thus continuing the cycle of transition.

Burgess argued that these patterns of population movements and neighborhood conditions weakened families, social institutions, and other collective ties, thus producing a general phenomenon he called "social disorganization." Several problems were believed to result from social disorganization, including higher rates of disease, mental illness, and crime. These ideas form the basis of the social disorganization theory of crime.

However, the kinds of social conditions Burgess described as existing in transition zones suggest other possible explanations for the higher rates of crime in these areas. For example, if early-20th-century immigrants from Europe were concentrated in transition zones, such groups might have brought cultural differences to urban areas that contributed to crime and other social ills. In other words, crime in transition zones might have resulted from a concentration of individuals from particular cultural

backgrounds in those areas, rather than being the consequence of social disorganization.

How should we settle the question of whether social disorganization or cultural differences accounted for the concentration of crime in transition zones? The second step in the traditional model of science helps us move toward an answer.

Operationalization   Operationalization means specifying steps, procedures, or operations for actually identifying and measuring the variables we want to observe. In the present example, operationalization involves deciding how to measure things like crime, social disorganization, and cultural background.

While Park and Burgess were developing their general theories of urban growth and its social consequences, sociologists Clifford Shaw and Henry McKay began a series of studies that tested the social disorganization explanation for crime in transition zones. Their landmark study, originally published in 1942, described how important concepts were operationalized (Shaw and McKay, 1969).

First, they chose three indicators of delinquency to measure crime, each obtained from official city records: (1) alleged delinquents brought before juvenile court, (2) juveniles committed to institutions, and (3) alleged delinquents detained by police but not brought before a juvenile court.

Second, social disorganization was measured even less directly, as is often the case in social research. Indicators were constructed from census data and information provided by local agencies. These indicators included families on relief (an earlier version of welfare and unemployment payments), average monthly rent, home ownership, occupational status, and ethnicity. One measure of ethnicity was whether a head of household was born in another country, referred to as "foreign-born"; another was the percentage of black families.

These indicators made it possible to compare delinquency with social disorganization and ethnic background, but how could Shaw and McKay determine which of these two factors was more important in explaining delinquency? Recall the concept of transition zones: People were continuously moving into and out of the neighborhoods between core commercial zones and more wealthy residential areas. The notion of transition implies population movement, and the mobility of urban residents in Chicago offered an answer.

Shaw and McKay compared changes in delinquency rates over time, focusing on three periods: 1900–1906, 1917–1923, and 1927–1933. They also examined delinquency among different ethnic groups within each zone. On the one hand, they suggested, if cultural differences accounted for crime, then delinquency rates in outer zones should increase as people from different cultural backgrounds moved out of transition zones and into more stable residential areas. On the other hand, if social disorganization produced delinquency, then the pattern of lower rates in outer zones and higher rates in transition zones should remain stable despite the outward movement of ethnic groups.

Park and Burgess identified five concentric zones in Chicago: Zones I and II were the inner core and transition areas; farther out, zone III included the homes of working-class families, zone IV was a middle-income residential area, and zone V was a suburban or outer area. Within each zone were several distinct neighborhoods. Shaw and McKay divided the city into 140 areas of approximately one square mile each, so that several areas were included in each of the five zones. These 140 areas represented units of analysis.

Observation   The final step in the traditional model of science involves actual observation—looking at the world and making measurements of what is seen. Having developed theoretical expectations and created a strategy for observation, we next look at the way things are. This step may involve conducting experiments, interviewing people, and visiting what we're interested in and watching it. The observations may

be structured around the testing of specific hypotheses, or the inquiry may be less structured. For Shaw and McKay, it meant poring through published statistics in search of data relevant to their operationalization and then grouping data on delinquency and other indicators according to 140 geographical areas.

Comparing delinquency between ethnic groups, they found that rates were higher for all groups in core areas and transition zones. Although there was wide variation within groups—foreign-born, black, and native white—similar rates for each group were found in similar types of zones. Comparing rates over time, Shaw and McKay (1969:162, 315) found that when foreign-born families moved to outer zones delinquency rates remained lower in those areas than in inner zones. Summarizing these findings, they concluded:

> In the face of these facts it is difficult to sustain the contention that, by themselves, the factors of race, nativity, and nationality are vitally related to the problem of juvenile delinquency. It seems necessary to conclude, rather, that the significantly higher rates of delinquents found among the children of Negroes, the foreign born, and more recent immigrants are closely related to existing differences in their respective patterns of geographical distribution within the city. . . .
>
> Moreover, the fact that in Chicago the rates of delinquents for many years have remained relatively constant in the areas adjacent to centers of commerce and heavy industry, despite successive changes in the nativity and nationality composition of the population, supports emphatically the conclusion that the delinquency-producing factors are inherent in the community.

Although subsequent research has challenged some of the conclusions Shaw and McKay reached, social disorganization theory continues to influence theory and research in criminal justice and other fields. For example, sociologist

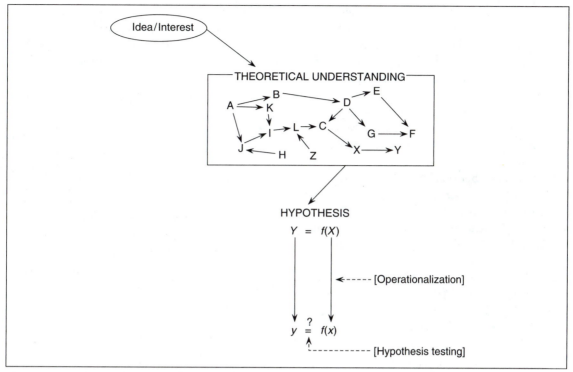

Figure 2.1 The Traditional Image of Science

William Julius Wilson (1987, 1996) argues that limited opportunities for upward economic mobility and outward residential mobility contributed to a host of chronic social problems, including crime, among inner-city residents in the late 20th century. Contemporary environmental theories of crime, which emphasize such concepts as urban form and its influence on human behavior, are rooted in the earlier work of Park and Burgess, and Shaw and McKay (see, for example, Brantingham and Jeffery, 1991).

Notice how Shaw and McKay's research was based on a more general theory of the links between the conditions of urban neighborhoods and a broad class of social ills. They had certain expectations about the patterns they would find in the numbers if a particular theoretical explanation was accurate. Operationalizing delinquency as an example of a social problem, they found higher rates of delinquency in transition zones, regardless of ethnic or cultural composi-

tion. In themselves, of course, these particular data did not *prove* the case; they did not provide definitive evidence that social disorganization produced delinquency. These data, however, were part of a body of evidence that Shaw and McKay amassed.

We have considered this example at some length for three reasons. First, it illustrates the traditional model of scientific research, moving from theory, to operationalization, to observation. Second, it is more realistic than the hypothetical physics experiments you might recall from a science class. Finally, contemporary research in criminal justice continues to build on this theoretical view of the relationship between crime and the urban environment.

Figure 2.1 provides a schematic diagram of the traditional model of scientific inquiry. In it, we see the researcher beginning with an interest in something or an idea about it. Next comes the development of a theoretical understanding of how a number of concepts, represented by the letters A, B, C, and so on, may be related to each other. The theoretical considerations result in a hypothesis, or an expectation about the way things should be in the world if the theoretical expectations are correct. The notation $Y = f(X)$ is a conventional way of saying that Y (for example, delinquency) is a function of or is in some way caused by X (for example, substandard housing). At that level, however, X and Y have general rather than specific meanings.

In the operationalization process, general concepts are translated into specific indicators. Thus, the lowercase x is a concrete indicator of capital X. As an example, census data on the number of housing units that lack indoor plumbing (x) are a concrete indicator of substandard housing (X). This operationalization process results in the formation of a testable hypothesis: For example, did the rate of delinquency among Italian immigrants actually decline as they moved from substandard housing in transition zones to better housing in outer residential areas? Observations aimed at finding out are part of what is typically called **hypothesis testing.**

Although this traditional model of science provides a clear and understandable guide to how we can study something carefully and logically, it presents only a part of the picture. Let's look at the other parts now.

Two Logical Systems

The traditional model of science uses what is called deductive logic, which we introduced in Chapter 1. In this section, we will examine deductive logic as it relates to social science theory, and we will contrast it with inductive logic. W. I. B. Beveridge (1950:113), a philosopher of science, described these two systems of logic as follows:

> Logicians distinguish between inductive reasoning (from particular instances to general principles, from facts to theories) and deductive reasoning (from the general to the particular, applying a theory to a par-

ticular case). In induction one starts from observed data and develops a generalization which explains the relationships between the objects observed. On the other hand, in deductive reasoning one starts from some general law and applies it to a particular instance.

The classic illustration of deductive logic is this familiar syllogism: "All people are mortal; Socrates is a person; therefore, Socrates is mortal." This syllogism, or logical argument, presents a theory and its operationalization. To prove it, we could perform an empirical test of Socrates' mortality. That is essentially the approach of the traditional model.

Using inductive logic, we might begin by noting that Socrates is mortal and observing a number of other people as well. We might then note that all the observed people are mortals, thereby arriving at the tentative conclusion that all people are mortal.

A Deductive Illustration Why is there so much plea bargaining in criminal courts? What accounts for differences in conviction rates and sentence lengths among people convicted of similar offenses? These were among the questions addressed by James Eisenstein and Herbert Jacob (1977) in their classic study of court processing in three U.S. cities. Their research provides a good example of the deductive approach.

They began by identifying the shortcomings of popular views of criminal court outcomes. Differences in defendant and judicial characteristics and in the formal requirements of court procedure were not satisfactory explanations. Furthermore, they argued, previous studies of criminal courts had failed to disentangle the combined influence of differences in judges, lawyers, defendants, and court procedures.

Their novel approach was to view trial courts as organizations and to appeal to various theories of organizational behavior to explain trial court outcomes. Courts in the United States are formal adversarial organizations, meaning that attorneys representing each side are supposed to do battle before a neutral judge. However, said Eisenstein and Jacob, even though prosecutors and defense lawyers are formal adversaries, they work together to achieve the common goal of processing defendants and so have incentives to cooperate with each other. Similarly, judges are supposed to play a neutral role, but they also have to manage their courtrooms and move along large numbers of cases in a timely fashion.

Viewing the judge, prosecutor, and defense attorney as a work group helps explain their mutual interests. In organization theory, work groups are small collections of people who share responsibility for certain tasks. If the work group is stable, with its members working together over time, they come to know one another and develop shared incentives for maintaining group cohesion and harmony. Among the shared goals of courtroom work groups are disposing of caseloads and reducing uncertainty by sharing information about cases and avoiding surprises. Of course, group members also want to do justice, but justice is an elusive concept; other goals are easier to identify and have more immediate relevance to the work group. Finally, like most people who must work together, judges, prosecutors, and defense attorneys find their jobs more pleasant and easier if they get along with one another.

Eisenstein and Jacob drew several hypotheses from this theory, most notably that plea bargaining would be more common in courtrooms with stable work groups. Let's break this hypothesis down into parts to see how it deduces a specific prediction about trial courts from general organization theory. First, the longer people work together in a small group (stability), the better they will come to know one another and pursue common goals in a cooperative way. Second, members of the courtroom work group have a common goal of processing cases. Third, plea bargains are the products of negotiation. Therefore, stable courtroom work groups will more often process cases through negotiated guilty pleas than through formal trials.

Having framed this hypothesis, Eisenstein and Jacob gathered data from felony courts

(those that handle more serious crimes) in Baltimore, Chicago, and Detroit. Their findings generally supported the work group hypothesis by comparing the characteristics of court organization with indicators of case outcomes. However, they found that certain other features of court organization also helped explain case processing.

Plea bargaining was common in Chicago and Detroit for slightly different reasons, each consistent with organizational features. Judges, prosecutors, and public defenders in Chicago were regularly assigned to specific courtrooms for extended periods. This, and the traditional politics of accommodation in Chicago, promoted plea bargaining, which was how 70 percent of convicted offenders were processed.

Detroit courts had less stable work groups but used a system of court administration that played a much stronger role in managing caseloads than in Chicago. Judges and prosecutors took active steps to promote the rapid settlement of cases. As a result, 82 percent of convicted defendants pleaded guilty in plea bargains. The more aggressive management style also resulted in faster processing of cases than in Chicago.

The situation was different in Baltimore. Court management was haphazard, judges were regularly rotated to different courtrooms, and there was a great deal of turnover among prosecutors. As a result, courtroom work groups were less stable, and the informal goals of negotiation gave way to more formal processing of felony cases — only 45 percent were settled by plea bargains. Eisenstein and Jacob also pointed out that in Baltimore, where neither informal work group norms nor formal court management were very strong, there tended to be greater differences in sentences between judges. Where formal and informal organizational controls were weaker, individual differences in sentencing became more common.

This example clearly illustrates the deductive model. Beginning with general, theoretical expectations about the impact of organizational characteristics on court operations, Eisenstein and Jacob derived concrete hypotheses that

GROUNDED THEORY AND COMMUNITY PROSECUTION

by Barbara Boland

Like community policing, community prosecution differs from traditional ways of handling crime in two respects. First, community policing and prosecution involve working with community organizations and ordinary residents. Second, police and prosecutors try to identify patterns of crime and related problems rather than just respond to individual incidents as they occur. "Look for patterns, and look for help" is one way to summarize this approach: Focus on problems rather than incidents; cooperate with community residents and others rather than responding to a crime report or prosecuting a case in isolation of other organizations.

A community prosecutor who worked in a Portland, Oregon, neighborhood initially assumed that the concerns of area residents centered on serious crime problems produced by

repeat offenders. However, conventional notions about crime and appropriate responses were quickly changed once the prosecutor began talking with neighborhood residents. They wanted something done about prostitution, public drinking, drug use, vandalism, littering, assaults, garbage, and thefts from cars—problems that did not match the traditional notions of serious crime.

One particular area in the neighborhood, Sullivan's Gulch, illustrates what troubled residents. A natural depression where two railroad lines intersect, Sullivan's Gulch had long attracted transients who set up illegal camps in the area, sometimes remaining for extended stays. By the late 1980s, the number of illegal campers had exploded. Gulch dwellers wandered into nearby commercial and residential areas to buy and consume liquor, to litter, loiter, urinate, and fight. None of these problems were serious crimes, and such nuisance reports were seldom recorded in crime counts. But they nonetheless troubled neighborhood residents and undermined efforts to revitalize commerce in the area.

---

linked specific measurable variables. The actual empirical data could then be analyzed to determine whether the deductive expectations were supported by empirical reality.

An Inductive Illustration   Often, social scientists begin constructing a theory by observing aspects of social life, seeking to discover patterns that may point to more or less universal principles. Barney Glaser and Anselm Strauss (1967) coined the term **grounded theory** to describe this inductive method of theory construction. Field research—the direct observation of events in progress—is frequently used to develop theories. Or survey research may reveal patterns of attitudes that suggest particular theoretical explanations. Here's an example.

During the 1960s and 1970s, marijuana use on America's college campuses was a subject of considerable discussion in the popular press. Some people were troubled by marijuana's pop-

ularity; others welcomed it. What interests us here is why some students smoked marijuana and others didn't. A survey of students at the University of Hawaii (Takeuchi, 1974) provided the data needed to answer that question.

At the time of the study, countless explanations were being offered for drug use. People who opposed drug use often suggested that marijuana smokers were academic failures who turned to drugs rather than face the rigors of college life. Those in favor of marijuana, in contrast, often spoke of the search for new values: Marijuana smokers, they said, were people who had seen through the hypocrisy of middle-class values.

David Takeuchi's (1974) analysis of the data gathered from University of Hawaii students, however, did not support any of the explanations being offered. Those who reported smoking marijuana had essentially the same academic records as those who didn't smoke it, and both

After talking with area residents and business owners and thinking about the problem, the community prosecutor reasoned that traditional approaches like stepped-up patrol, police visibility, and arrests might work for a time. The increased police presence could not be maintained over a long period, however, and problems would no doubt reappear after police moved on to other areas.

Instead, the prosecutor arranged an initial police sweep to disperse campers from the Gulch. This was accompanied by a city-sponsored clean-up that removed tents, derelict structures, and countless truckloads of debris. The next step was a cooperative effort among police and area residents. Signs reading "No Camping" on one side and listing nearby homeless shelters on the reverse were posted in the area. Citizens were enlisted to patrol the Gulch on a regular basis and to notify police about the appearance of any campsites. Encouraged by the support they had received from police and the prosecutor's office, area residents were diligent in watching for campers and dissuading new arrivals from setting up camp.

Resident concerns about Sullivan's Gulch offer a classic example of the links between disorder and crime, as described in the article "Broken Windows" by James Wilson and George Kelling (1982) and a later book by Wesley Skogan (1990a). The "broken windows" theory of crime holds that: "serious crime flourishes in areas where disorderly behavior goes unchecked" (Wilson and Kelling, 1982:34).

Listening to the concerns of residents and business owners near Sullivan's Gulch and observing the area first-hand, the neighborhood prosecutor "built" a theory. His theory was based on street-level experience, experience that differed from the prevailing suite-level perspective of traditional prosecution. The theory was inductive, grounded in observations that were then used to formulate more general statements about the links between disorder and serious crime in an area of Portland. And these links suggested a theory of action that guided justice policy.

Source: Adapted from Boland (1996:36–37).

---

groups were equally involved in traditional "school spirit" activities. Both groups seemed to feel equally well integrated into campus life.

There were differences, however. First, women were less likely than men to smoke marijuana. Second, Asian students (a large proportion of the University of Hawaii student body) were less likely to smoke marijuana than non-Asians. Finally, students living at home were less likely to smoke marijuana than those living in apartments. These three variables independently affected the likelihood of a student's smoking marijuana. About 10 percent of the Asian women living at home had smoked marijuana, in contrast to about 80 percent of the non-Asian men living in apartments. And the researchers discovered a powerful pattern of drug use before they had an explanation for that pattern.

In this instance, the explanation took a peculiar turn. Instead of explaining why some students smoked marijuana, the researchers explained why some didn't. Assuming that all students had some motivation for trying drugs, the researchers suggested that students differed in the degree of "social constraints" that prevented them from following through on that urge.

American society is, on the whole, more tolerant of men than of women when it comes to deviant behavior. Consider, for example, a group of men getting drunk and boisterous. We tend to dismiss such behavior with references to "camaraderie" and "having a good time," whereas a group of women behaving similarly would be regarded more disapprovingly. The researchers reasoned, therefore, that women would have more to lose by smoking marijuana than men would.

Students who lived at home had obvious constraints against smoking marijuana in comparison with students who lived on their own. Aside from differences in opportunity, those living at home were seen as being more dependent on their parents, and hence more vulnerable to additional punishment for breaking the law.

Finally, the Asian subculture in Hawaii traditionally placed a higher premium on obedience to the law than other subcultures did, so Asian students would have had more to lose if they were caught violating the law by smoking marijuana.

Overall, then, a social constraints theory was offered as the explanation for observed differences in the likelihood of smoking marijuana. The more constraints a student had, the less likely he or she would be to smoke marijuana. It bears repeating that the researchers had no thoughts about such a theory when they began their research. The theory was developed out of an examination of the data—the inductive approach.

Inductive Theory and Criminal Justice Policy Consider a different way of looking at inductive theory building, suggested by Barbara Hart, legal director of the Pennsylvania Coalition Against Domestic Violence.* Speaking on the topic of how to increase the utilization of criminal justice research by justice professionals, Hart argued that the development of grounded theory was commonplace among many practitioners. By this she meant that probation officers, judges, case managers, victim services counselors, and others tend to formulate general explanations to fit the patterns they observe in individual cases. As Hart put it: "Practitioners engage in theory building as they interpret experience." Others refer to a "theory of action" that embraces experience-based theories that guide public officials (Campbell, 1979; Clarke, 1997b).

A theory of action may then guide the future actions of justice professionals, until they discover cases or patterns of cases that don't fit their theory. See the box titled "Grounded Theory and Community Prosecution" for an example.

---

*From remarks at the Family Violence Cluster Conference, National Institute of Justice, Washington, DC, July 12, 1995.

A Graphic Contrast Figure 2.2 shows a graphic comparison of the deductive and inductive methods. In both cases, we are interested in the relationship between the number of hours spent studying for an exam and the grade earned on that exam. Using the deductive method, we begin by examining the matter logically. Doing well on an exam reflects a student's ability to recall and to manipulate information. Both of these abilities should be increased by exposure to the information before the exam. In this fashion, we arrive at a hypothesis suggesting a positive relationship between the number of hours spent studying and the grade earned on the exam. We say *positive* because we expect grades to increase as the hours of studying increase. If increased hours produced lower grades, that would be called a negative relationship. The hypothesis is represented by the graph in part 1(a) of Figure 2.2.

Our next step, using the deductive method, is to make observations relevant to testing our hypothesis. The shaded area in part 1(b) of the figure represents perhaps hundreds of observations of different students, noting how many hours they studied and what grades they got. Finally, in part 1(c) of the figure, we compare the hypothesis and the observations. Because observations in the real world seldom (if ever) match our expectations perfectly, we must decide whether the match is close enough to consider the hypothesis confirmed. Put differently, can we conclude that the hypothesis describes the general pattern that exists, granting some variations in real life?

Now let's address the same research question using the inductive method. In this case, we begin—as in part 2(a) of the figure—with a set of observations. Curious about the relationship between hours spent studying and grades earned, we simply arrange to collect some relevant data. Then we look for a pattern that best represents or summarizes our observations. In part 2(b) of the figure, the pattern is shown as a curved line running through the center of the curving mass of points.

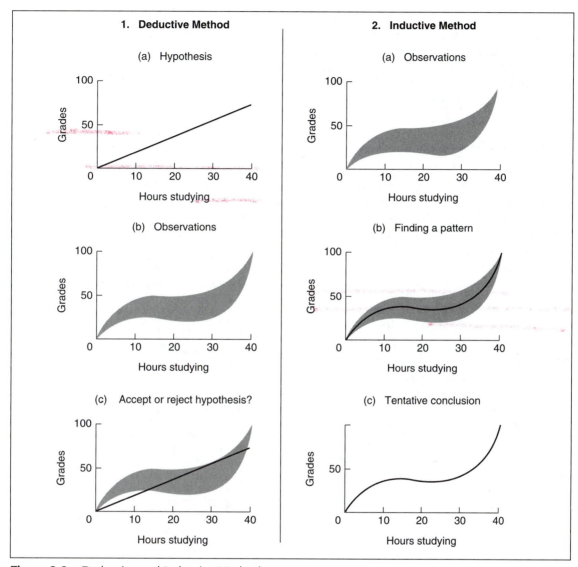

Figure 2.2   Deductive and Inductive Methods

The pattern found among the points in this case—and shown in part 2(c) of the figure—suggests that with 1–15 hours of studying each additional hour generally produces a higher grade on the exam. Studying 15–25 hours actually seems to slightly lower the grade. Studying more than 25 hours, however, results in a return to the initial pattern: More hours produce higher grades. Using the inductive method, then, we end up with a tentative conclusion

about the pattern of the relationship between the two variables. The conclusion is tentative because the observations we have made cannot be taken as a *test* of the pattern; those observations are the *source* of the pattern we've created.

In summary, the scientific norm of logical reasoning provides a bridge between theory and research—a two-way bridge. Scientific inquiry in practice typically involves an alternation between deduction and induction. During the deductive phase, we reason *toward* observations; during the inductive phase, we reason *from* observations. Both logic and observation are essential. In practice, both deduction and induction are routes to the construction of social theories.

Terms Used in Theory Construction

In this section, we will consider some of the terminology used in connection with the creation of scientific theories. We've already been using some of these terms because most people have a general idea of what they mean in everyday language. Now, however, we will examine their meanings more precisely.

Theory   A theory is a systematic explanation for the observed facts and laws that relate to a particular aspect of life—juvenile delinquency, for example, or perhaps social stratification or political revolution. Joseph Maxwell (1996:30) defines theory as "a set of concepts and the proposed relationships among these, a structure that is intended to represent or model something about the world."

Jonathan Turner (1974:3) examined several elements of theory. We consider three of them briefly:

- *Concepts.*   Turner (1974:5) called concepts the "basic building blocks of theory." They are abstract elements that represent classes of phenomena within the field of study. The concepts relevant to a theory of juvenile delinquency, for example, would include "juvenile" and "delinquency" for starters. "Peer group"—the people you hang around with and identify with—would be another relevant concept. "Social disorganization" was a central concept in the theory of delinquency tested by Shaw and McKay. "School performance" might also be relevant to a theory of juvenile delinquency.
- *Variables.*   A variable is a concept's empirical counterpart. Whereas concepts are in the domain of theory, variables can be observed and can take different values; they vary. Thus, variables require more specificity than concepts. For example, as a variable, income might be specified as "annual family income," reported in response to a survey question.
- *Statements.*   A theory comprises several types of statements. Principles or laws are one type. Another type of statement is the axiom, a fundamental assertion—taken to be true—on which the theory is grounded. Propositions are a third type of statement: conclusions drawn about the relationships among concepts, based on the logical interrelationships among the axioms. To clarify, an axiom is an assumption about reality, while a proposition expresses relationships among axioms. For example, in a theory of juvenile delinquency, we might begin with axioms such as "Everyone desires material comforts" and "The ability to obtain material comforts legally is greater for the upper class than for the working class." These axioms might reasonably lead us to the proposition "Working-class youths are more likely to break the law to gain material comforts than upper-class youths are."

Objectivity and Subjectivity   We recognize that some things fall into the realm of attitudes, opinions, and subjective points of view. For example, the question of whether Bach or Beethoven was the better composer is a subjective matter, dependent on the experiences and tastes of the person who is making such a judgment. But the existence of this book in your hands is an objective matter, independent of your experience of it. Objective is typically defined as "independent of mind," but our awareness of what might objectively exist comes to us through our minds. As a working principle, social scientists substitute **intersubjective agreement** for **objectivity:** If several of us agree that something exists, then we treat that thing as though it had objective existence. This view of intersubjective agreement as a working version of objectivity is consistent with our earlier consideration, in Chapter 1, of agreement reality.

Hypotheses A **hypothesis** is a specified expectation about empirical reality, derived from propositions. If we continue the present example, a theory might contain the hypothesis "Working-class youths have higher delinquency rates than upper-class youths." Such a hypothesis could then be tested through research, as we saw in the earlier example of social disorganization and delinquency.

Paradigms No one ever starts out with a completely clean slate to create a theory. When we mentioned juvenile delinquency as an example of a topic for theory construction, you probably already had some implicit ideas about it. If we had asked you to list some concepts relevant to a theory of juvenile delinquency, you would have been able to make suggestions. We might say that you already have a general point of view—a frame of reference or paradigm. A **paradigm** is a fundamental model or scheme that organizes our view of something.

This may strike you as uncomfortably similar to the definition of theory, and this is a natural point of confusion. The primary distinction is based on organization and structure. In Kenneth Hoover's (1992:66) view, "A theory is a collection of hypotheses linked by some kind of logical framework." A paradigm is a much less structured way of viewing things that nonetheless affects how we approach research problems. It may be helpful to think of a paradigm as a pair of tinted glasses; everything we look at reflects the tint, no matter how we structure our observations. A theory serves to structure more carefully what we see through the paradigm's lenses, but what we see is still tinted.

Although a paradigm doesn't necessarily answer important questions, it tells us where, and often how, to look for the answers. And, as we'll see repeatedly, where you look largely determines what you find. Thomas Kuhn (1996:37) describes the importance of paradigms this way:

One of the things a scientific community acquires with a paradigm is a criterion for choosing problems that, while the paradigm is taken for granted, can be assumed to have solutions. To a great extent these are the only problems that the community will admit as scientific or encourage its members to undertake. Other problems, including many that had previously been standard, are rejected as metaphysical, as the concern of another discipline, or sometimes as just too problematic to be worth the time. A paradigm can, for that matter, even insulate the community from those socially important problems that are not reducible to the puzzle form, because they cannot be stated in terms of the conceptual and instrumental tools the paradigm supplies.

Kuhn's chief interest was in how science advances. Although some progress involves the slow, steady, and incremental improvement of established paradigms (Kuhn calls this "normal science"), he suggests that important scientific progress takes the form of paradigm shifts, as established, agreed-on paradigms are discarded in favor of new ones. Thus, for example, Newtonian physics was replaced by Einstein's relativity in what Kuhn calls a "scientific revolution."

We suggest comparing the concept of paradigms with the world of fashion. Just as styles of clothing go in and out of fashion, paradigms that influence criminal justice come and go. We hope some styles and paradigms are gone forever: Contemporary men are free from the powdered wigs of the 18th century, women no longer suffer whalebone corsets (good for whales, too), and Western governments have stopped amputating the hands of thieves. Some good ideas have stood the test of time: Summer shorts are blessings for women and men alike. Similarly, the early research by Park and Burgess and by Shaw and McKay pointed to the role of social disorganization as a cause of crime in the most disadvantaged urban areas, and their insights continue to influence contemporary research.

Theory in Criminal Justice

Theories of law breaking and policy responses guide research and public policy alike.

Because criminal justice draws on many disciplines—such as sociology, economics, geography, political science, psychology, anthropology, and biology—different paradigms, or frames of reference, have influenced criminal justice theory, research, and policy. Let's consider some examples, beginning with a general way of grouping theories in criminal justice. We emphasize that the following section presents *examples* of theories and is not intended to include a complete or even representative inventory.

At the risk of oversimplification, it is useful to consider two broad approaches to criminal justice research: law breaking and policy responses. Studies that focus on law breaking are interested in questions about why people commit crimes. Other studies are interested in how criminal justice institutions respond to crime as a policy problem and how those institutions are managed. Thinking about this distinction for a moment reveals the potential for considerable overlap between the two approaches. Of course, criminal justice policy is interested in why people commit crimes. By the same token, studies that focus on law breaking may suggest ways that public policy encourages or discourages crime.

This distinction, imperfect as it is, still offers a useful way to discuss criminal justice theories and their links to individual disciplines.

Law Breaking

Theories rooted in biology dominated early research on crime, beginning most prominently with the work of an Italian physician, Cesare Lombroso, who in the 19th century tried to identify types of criminals based on their behavior and physical anatomy. Although Lombroso's research and conclusions have long since been discredited and even ridiculed, biological and genetic approaches to the study of criminality continue. For example, Sarnoff Mednick and colleagues conducted studies to compare criminal behavior in persons who are adopted with criminal behavior by their biological and adoptive parents. Finding that adopted males who are criminals were more likely to have a biological father with a criminal record than an adopted father with a criminal record, they conclude that genetic factors influence criminality (Mednick, Gabrielli, and Hutchings, 1984).

In a fascinating study of homicide, Martin Daly and Margo Wilson (1988) drew on Charles Darwin's theory of sexual selection. Beginning with Darwin's principle that a species must reproduce to survive, Daly and Wilson point out that physiological differences between males and females promote conflict among males, but not among females. During their lifetime, females can produce a limited number of offspring. The 9-month gestation period for human females means that through the childbearing years—say, ages 16–46—a woman can produce a maximum of about 30 children. But human males, by mating with more than one female, can produce a hypothetically unlimited number of children. From Darwin's principle of sexual selection, Daly and Wilson argue that an individual human male has incentives to mate with many females and produce a large number of offspring. Because this applies to all human males, they compete for female mates, and their competition may take the form of fatal violence. Daly and Wilson (1988:147–48) present historical homicide statistics from several countries—ranging from 13th-century England to contemporary Miami—to show that males kill males about 100 times more often than females kill females.

Theory from the discipline of psychology also influences studies of law breaking by linking such concepts as intelligence and personality traits to aggressive behavior, drug abuse, and crime. Early studies applying psychological theories showed that delinquent boys, for example, were more likely than nondelinquent boys to have such personality traits as impulsiveness and feelings of resentment (Glueck and Glueck, 1950). More recent research examines how childhood and developmental patterns are related to crime, delinquency, and more general antisocial behavior (Luntz and Widom, 1994).

Research on criminal careers has been one of the most prominent, but controversial, applications of developmental theories. Criminal career studies examine such concepts as when criminal or delinquent behavior begins, how long it continues, how much the number of crimes committed increases, and when a criminal career ends. Alfred Blumstein and colleagues (Blumstein, Cohen, Roth, and Visher, 1986) call these concepts "onset," "persistence," "escalation," and "desistance," respectively.

Theories from the discipline of sociology have had the greatest influence on research on law breaking in the United States in the last half century. Psychologists are more interested in individual behavior, whereas sociologists are concerned with social relationships. In the view of Michael Gottfredson and Travis Hirschi (1990: 75), psychologists see crime as behavior learned by individuals, and sociologists see it as group behavior.

We have already mentioned the early development of theories of social disorganization. Social strain theory begins with the assumption that people in modern society are socialized to pursue success, monetary or otherwise. When they encounter obstacles to achieving success, they experience frustration or strain. Rebellion is one possible reaction to such strain, involving, almost by definition, the rejection of social values. General social values may be replaced with other values that may lead to crime.

Conflict theory is closely associated with sociology but also has roots in political science. Conflict theory rejects absolute definitions of crime and criminality. Instead, crime is a *label* produced by social values and political power, both of which are embodied in criminal law. In connection with crime, politics involves conflict over social and other values. The winners of such conflict define certain behaviors and acts as crimes, and the losers—people whose behavior is rejected—are labeled as criminals.

Political scientist Ted Robert Gurr (1976) advocated a version of conflict theory by focusing not only on crime but also on the more general concept of public order. In Gurr's view, political leaders (and would-be leaders) apply the labels "crime" and "civil strife" to distinguish acts that threaten individuals (crime) from acts that threaten political stability (civil strife). Both types of threats to the public order include violence, but incidents of criminal violence are individual acts, while civil strife represents collective violence. In elaborating this approach, Gurr examined crime and civil strife in Western and Eastern societies from the early 1800s through 1970. For a contemporary example that illustrates Gurr's concept of public order, consider the spread of terrorist acts in the early 21st century. In one sense, suicide bombings and individual attacks on public facilities and ordinary citizens are murders perpetrated by individuals or small groups. In another sense, terroristic violence expresses political opposition to public policy, and thus straddles the fuzzy line between individual and collective violence.

Economists are interested in how people make choices, most often under a fundamental assumption of rationality. People engage in behavior to maximize satisfaction, and such behavior is rational. Rationality, therefore, is the framework through which an economic theory of law breaking would view individual behavior.

In seeking to maximize satisfaction, individuals weigh the costs and benefits of various actions: If benefits outweigh costs, the behavior is rational. Because the calculation of costs and benefits is subjective, and people may have incomplete information about potential costs and benefits, different individuals may have different ideas about what is rational. A burglar, for example, may overestimate how much profit might be made from selling a stolen television or might underestimate the chances of getting caught. Hope Corman and H. Naci Mocan (2000) apply economic theory to study links between numbers of police and crime rates in New York City. The presence of police adds to individual estimates of the cost of offending. As a result, offending is negatively related to numbers of police.

Our final theory of law breaking integrates principles from different social science disciplines. Environmental explanations link criminal behavior to physical and social space. As described by Paul and Patricia Brantingham (1991a: 12–13), the application of social ecology to criminology has two components. First, the physical features of a city—urban form—are partly the results of conflict over a scarce resource, space. Cities are densely populated because land costs are high and many people want to locate near workplaces, stores, and entertainment venues. Second, human behavior is affected by physical form. People behave differently in the downtown areas of large cities, for example, than they do in suburban shopping malls (Wikström, 1995).

Different urban forms present greater or lesser opportunities for crime by bringing potential offenders and victims close to each other. For example, the Brantinghams (1991b: 49) describe how dispersed shopping areas and strip malls are especially vulnerable to high rates of property crime. This is because such shopping areas are designed to provide convenient access to large numbers of people in automobiles. As much as shoppers do, property offenders value ease of access and anonymity and are therefore attracted to dispersed shopping centers and strip developments in large metropolitan areas.

Policy Responses

Each of the disciplines mentioned previously has also influenced studies of how government officials and people in general respond to crime as a policy problem. Organization theory, drawing on psychology and sociology, framed the study of criminal courts by Eisenstein and Jacob (1977).

The disciplines of economics and psychology are evident in most studies of deterrence. Criminal justice policy from law making to corrections

seeks to deter individuals from committing crimes by threatening to punish them. Whether the threat of punishment can deter criminal acts depends on three elements: certainty, severity, and celerity. Deterrence works best when individuals are certain that they will be caught and punished and when their punishment is severe enough to represent a real threat. *Celerity* is another word for swiftness—how quickly punishment follows the crime—and is used primarily because "certainty, severity, and swiftness" does not sound as good. Much deterrence research seeks to find out which of these three factors is most important. Recent research on gun violence in Boston has refined the concept of deterrence in an effort to prevent reoffending by gang members (Kennedy, 1998).

Throughout U.S. history, different paradigms associated with punishment have come and gone. Rehabilitation, retribution, and incapacitation are paradigms in that they represent fundamental frames of reference about the purposes of punishment. Rehabilitation is a paradigm that sees punishment or other sanctions as instruments to change behavior. For many years, research was unable to show much consistent success in rehabilitating wrongdoers. However, some more recent studies, focusing on small, narrowly defined groups of offenders, have shown some success in rehabilitation (Harland, 1996). Partly because of the limited success of rehabilitation, other paradigms have influenced policy approaches to punishment. Retribution, with biblical origins, is the belief that society has a legitimate interest in punishing criminals simply for the sake of expressing disapproval. And incapacitation has long been popular among public officials. This paradigm assumes that society is protected from further harm when criminals are incarcerated; in prison, criminals lack the capacity to commit any more crimes against the general public.

When coupled with research on criminal careers, the principle of incapacitation is potentially interesting to public officials by suggesting that sentencing policy could be more selective. Criminal career research has found that most delinquents and young adult criminals "grow out" of crime; their offending desists as they become older. However, criminal careers for some individuals persist and escalate. These findings suggest that prison sentences should be used more selectively, to incapacitate people who do not grow out of crime or to incapacitate them until they do.

It is not difficult to see that the implications of such selective incapacitation are problematic. In addition to the ethical problem of locking people up until they reach a certain age, there is the prediction problem: Social science methods are not sufficiently accurate to identify who should be incapacitated (Gottfredson and Gottfredson, 1994).

Theory, Research, and Public Policy

Because crime is an important social problem, and not simply a social artifact of interest to researchers, much research in criminal justice is closely linked to public policy. It is interesting and important to determine why some people commit crimes while others do not, but such research takes on added meaning when we consider how new knowledge can be used to formulate policy. Research on criminal justice policy is an example of applied research; research results are applied to specific questions about how government officials and the general public should respond to crime.

Criminal justice theory is just as important in structuring applied research questions as it is in directing basic research. Theory, research, and criminal justice policy are linked in two ways. First, theory is used to guide basic research. The results from this research may point to specific policies. For example, a presiding judge in Phoenix who wishes to process cases faster would be wise to learn about empirical research on trial courts. Eisenstein and Jacob (1977) found that court administrators in Detroit scheduled meetings between prosecutors and defense attorneys in which plea bargains were discussed, and they required that reports

of such meetings be forwarded to judges. The Phoenix presiding judge might then direct all judges to require pretrial meetings between prosecutors and defense attorneys to negotiate the terms of plea bargains.

To understand the second way criminal justice theory and policy are related, consider the similarities between hypotheses and specific programs. Earlier in this chapter, we said that hypotheses are specified expectations about empirical reality. This is also true of public policy programs: They are specified expectations about what empirical reality will result from a particular policy action. Theories of social disorganization include "if-then" statements such as "If an urban neighborhood exhibits signs of social disorder, then crime and delinquency in that neighborhood will be higher compared with neighborhoods having fewer signs of social disorder." This implies a public policy if-then statement: "If we implement a new program to reduce social disorder in an urban neighborhood, then crime and delinquency will decline." Complementary if-then statements such as these underlie the rationale for community policing and the actions taken by Portland's community prosecutor (see the box earlier in this chapter). With community-based crime control strategies, police and prosecutors take action against neighborhood problems of social disorder that may contribute to crime and delinquency.

In summary, theory, research, and policy are related in two similar ways: (1) Theory structures research, which, in turn, is consulted to develop policy, and (2) policies take the form of if-then statements, which implies that they are subject to empirical tests. The second way theory is linked to policy forms the basis for evaluation research—studies that assess whether some program is achieving its intended goals. A program is simply a hypothesis that some specific action will produce some specific result. A program may therefore be empirically evaluated in the same way a research hypothesis can be empirically evaluated.

PUTTING IT ALL TOGETHER

NEW YORK'S SECRET? PURPOSIVE ACTION

As we saw in Chapter 1, findings from the Kansas City Preventive Patrol Experiment appeared to contradict a basic tenet of policing. Simply adding more police patrol officers, and even doubling the number on duty in experimental beats, had no discernible impact on reported crimes, arrests, and people's perceptions of crime problems. However, people commonly misstate these results, claiming that the Kansas City study found that the police have no impact on crime. A more accurate summary, though still something of an oversimplification, is this: *Undirected police patrol has little impact on crime.* One New York police officer put it this way: "Random patrol produces random results."

The most fundamental policing change introduced in New York City in the early 1990s was more direction, or purposive action. Police leaders guided patrol and other department units in two related ways. First, police activities were based on weekly analyses of current crime data, known as Compstat. Crime analysis in New York became the driving force behind monitoring crime problems in different areas and developing new police tactics to address them. Contrast *weekly* sessions, in which the previous week's crime reports in a city of over 7 million people were analyzed by the department's top commanders, to the more common *annual* review of a year's total crime figures. Compare this with one of the key research activities we have considered in this chapter—observation—and think about the difference between annual and weekly observations of crime data.

The second, and more interesting, way New York's police became more purposive was due to the influence of criminological theory. In recent writings, former Police Commissioner William Bratton (1998, 1999) describes how he was attracted to the logic of "broken windows," a theoretical perspective first described by James Q. Wilson and George Kelling (1982). Wilson and

---

This chapter's installment of our running example in New York City illustrates the relationships between theory and public policy. Officials in New York adopted theory-based approaches to reducing crime.

Ecological Theories of Crime and Crime Prevention Policy

In his introduction to a collection of case studies on situational crime prevention, Ronald Clarke (1997b) describes how this approach to criminal justice policy evolved from more general ecological theories of crime.

The word *ecological* is significant: Just as humans and other organisms are affected by environmental forces in nature (weather, global climate change, water quality), human behavior is partially a function of the physical and social environment in which that behavior takes place. This fundamental principle is consistent with social disorganization theory: Crime is more common in urban transition zones where the physical environment (crowded housing) is unpleasant and the social environment (poverty, unemployment, disease) is undesirable.

Ecological theories rooted in research by Shaw and McKay eventually influenced the thinking of architects and city planners, whose work focuses on the design of buildings, streets, parks, and other physical features of the urban landscape. One of the most influential works that blended concepts of urban design and criminal justice was Oscar Newman's (1972) book *Defensible Space*. Newman argued that urban housing should be constructed to enhance the ability of residents to monitor and control

Kelling argued that serious crime was in part a product of low-level crime and disorder. If public drunkenness, rowdy groups of youths, and other signs of disorder were tolerated in a community, offenders would come to believe that they could get away with more serious offending.

How might this theory be useful to a police executive seeking to reduce crime through purposive action? As Bratton and others argue (Kelling and Coles, 1996; Silverman, 1999), if police take action against the relatively minor problems of public drinking, prostitution, and other so-called quality-of-life offenses, then declines in serious crime will follow. As chief of New York's Transit police in the early 1990s, Bratton demanded stricter enforcement against quality-of-life offenses on the city's subway, along with other minor crimes unique to the subway, such as fare evasion. Sharp declines in serious crime on subway trains and platforms followed. After becoming commissioner of police, Bratton again called for stricter enforcement against minor offenses, and again rates of serious crime fell throughout the city.

This example illustrates deductive reasoning by police commanders in New York. But police also develop theories of action inductively. In fact, Hans Toch and J. Douglas Grant (1991) refer to police as street-level social scientists whose job routinely calls for action research. Police observe problems and patterns, develop a tentative explanation for them, and then either propose or take some action in response. That's grounded theory—police action grounded in the inductive accumulation of observations.

In the New York case, the police executive used a compelling theory to develop strategies and tactics for attacking crime in New York. This was purposive action. Empirical results—for example, the number of homicides fell from around 1500 in 1994 to 584 in 2002—seemed to support the theory's predictions. So, not only do we have sharp declines in crime following changes in police actions, we also have a social science theory on which those police actions were based.

Does this prove that crime really went down because of police action? Or does it prove the validity of broken windows theory? Such questions raise issues of cause and effect, which are discussed in Chapter 4.

their environment. Too often, the design of large public housing projects in U.S. cities made it difficult for residents to distinguish threatening strangers from neighbors going about their business.

Around the same time Newman's book appeared, similar ideas about the link between urban design, human behavior, and crime were influencing the development of crime prevention policy in England. Drawing on the economics paradigm of rational choice, researchers in the British Home Office Research Unit extended Newman's ideas about how the physical environment affects potential victims (be they people or places), proposing that decisions made by criminals are also influenced by urban design (Clarke and Mayhew, 1980; Cornish and Clarke, 1986). Offenders may not formally weigh the costs and benefits of committing a crime, but Cornish and Clarke assert that offenders do evaluate potential targets and make choices based at least in part on opportunities.

Such reasoning led Clarke and others to propose crime prevention policies that try to reduce the opportunities for crime. This approach is called "situational crime prevention," defined by Clarke (1997b:4) as "opportunity-reducing measures that are (1) directed at highly specific forms of crime (2) that involve the management, design, or manipulation of the immediate environment in as systematic and permanent a way as possible (3) so as to increase the effort and risks of crime and reduce the rewards as perceived by a wide range of offenders." Clarke describes several examples of situational crime prevention techniques. The effort required to steal cars can be increased by the use of steering wheel locks; rewards of theft from automobiles can be reduced if car owners install removable stereo systems; the risks (to thieves) of auto theft can be increased by more thoughtful design of parking lots.

This example illustrates the deductive approach to moving from theory to policy development. Situational crime prevention policies were deduced, over a period of years, from earlier theories that described the relationships between crime and the physical and social environment of urban areas.

Now consider how Clarke's description of the steps involved in designing specific situational crime prevention programs illustrates the inductive approach to policy development (1997b:5):

1. Collect data about the nature and dimensions of the specific crime problem;
2. analysis of the situational conditions that . . . facilitate the commission of the crimes in question;
3. systematic study of possible means of blocking opportunities for these particular crimes, including analysis of costs;
4. implementation of the most promising, feasible and economic measures; and
5. monitoring of results and dissemination of experience.

Steps 1 and 2 involve collecting data and searching for patterns; steps 3 and 4 are equivalent to formulating a tentative conclusion and operating hypothesis based on the observed patterns. Step 5 is the applied research counterpart to hypothesis testing: Monitor and evaluate results, and then report whether the program achieved its intended objectives.

Throughout this chapter, we have seen various aspects of the links between theory and research in criminal justice inquiry. In the deductive model, research is used to test theories. In the inductive model, theories are developed from the analysis of research data. Although we focused on two logical models for linking theory and research, criminal justice researchers have developed a great many variations on these themes. Sometimes theoretical issues are introduced merely as a background for empirical analyses. Other studies cite selected empirical data to bolster theoretical arguments.

The ground we covered in this chapter reinforces our claim that there is no simple recipe for conducting criminal justice research. It is far more open-ended than the traditional view of science would suggest. Ultimately, science rests on two pillars: logic and observation. As we'll see throughout this book, they can be fit together in many patterns.

✪ *Main Points*

- The traditional image of science includes theory, operationalization, and observation.
- Social scientific theory and research are linked through two logical methods: (1) Deduction involves the derivation of expectations or hypotheses from theories, and (2) induction involves the development of generalizations from specific observations.
- Science is a process involving an alternation of deduction and induction.
- In grounded theory, observations contribute to theory development.
- Although people speak of science as being "objective," it's more a matter of intersubjective agreement—different scientists agree on their observations and conclusions.
- Theory in criminology and criminal justice is frequently adapted from other disciplines in the social and, less often, natural sciences.
- Theories in criminology and criminal justice can be grouped into two general, and often overlapping, categories: law breaking and policy responses.
- Criminal justice theory, research, and policy are linked in two ways: (1) Theory influences basic research, which may suggest new policy developments, and (2) policies are formulated like hypotheses and may therefore be subject to empirical test.

✪ Key Terms

Grounded theory	Objectivity
Hypothesis	Paradigm
Hypothesis testing	Theory
Intersubjective	
agreement	

✪ Review Questions and Exercises

1. Consider the possible relationship between education and deterrence theory. Describe how that relationship might be examined through (a) deductive and (b) inductive reasoning.
2. In his book *Crime and Everyday Life,* Marcus Felson expands on "routine activity theory" as an explanation for why crime occurs. According to this theory, crimes happen when three elements come together: (a) a motivated offender, (b) an attractive victim, and (c) absence of capable guardians. Select one property crime and one violent crime. Apply routine activity theory to explain examples of each. Are you using theory in an inductive or deductive way?
3. Review the relationships between theory and research discussed in this chapter. Select a research article from an academic journal, and classify the relationship between theory and research you find there.

✪ Internet Exercise

To ensure that you always have access to live, correct Web links for the Web sites referenced in the following exercise, we provide the necessary links on the companion Web site for *Research Methods for Criminal Justice and Criminology* at http://cj.wadsworth.com/maxfield_babbie/research_methods4e. Once at the companion Web site, select this specific chapter, click on "Chapter Resources," then click on "Web Links."

Visit Web sites for The Knowledge Base and San Jose State University for some additional information on both inductive and deductive logic. Go to either of the sites (or find one you like better using a search engine and the terms *inductive, deductive, induction and deduction,* or other variations). Compare the information you find with that in the text. Be prepared to share examples, graphics, and any other information you find that will help to clarify these terms.

✪ InfoTrac College Edition

Search using the keyword *grounded theory* to find articles that have made use of this approach in research and theory development. Why do you suppose the authors chose to investigate their topic using this approach?

✪ The NEW Companion Web Site for Research Methods for Criminal Justice and Criminology, *Fourth Edition*

http://cj.wadsworth.com/maxfield_babbie/research_methods4e

Supplement your review of this chapter by going to the new companion Web site to take one of the Tutorial Quizzes, use the flash cards to master key terms, and check out the many other study aids you'll find there. You'll also find special features such as quantitative and qualitative data analysis primers to help you with a special project or do some research on your own.

✪ Additional Readings

Clarke, Ronald V., "Situational Crime Prevention," in Michael Tonry and David Farrington (eds.), *Crime and Justice: An Annual Review of Research* (Chicago: University of Chicago Press, 1995), pp. 91–150. In this essay, Clarke lays out the genesis of situational crime prevention, linking it to past and evolving theories of crime and delinquency. This is an excellent example of synthesizing theory, research, crime prevention policy, and research methods.

Felson, Marcus, *Crime and Everyday Life,* 2nd ed. (Thousand Oaks, CA: Pine Forge, 1998). Felson begins with a simple theory that has nonetheless been embraced by many researchers for its apparent power. Then he deduces explanations for different types of crime. Some explanations make more sense than others; in fact, some explanations border on the strange. Figuring out which is which is fun, and not that difficult.

Gladwell, Malcolm, *The Tipping Point* (Boston: Little, Brown, 2000). Increases and decreases in crime are examples of social epidemics, the focus of

Gladwell's fascinating book. What sorts of social and other forces come together to produce large changes? Gladwell includes an extensive and provocative discussion of New York City. Compare what we have to say about paradigms in this chapter with Gladwell's discussion of tipping points. You can find some basic information on tipping points at Gladwell's Web site: http://www.gladwell.com.

Gottfredson, Michael R., and Hirschi, Travis, *A General Theory of Crime* (Stanford, CA: Stanford University Press, 1990). This book presents a good example of a comprehensive theory, in which the authors argue that crime should be viewed as one type of human behavior that has much in common with other types of behavior. Along the way, the authors comment on how theories from different social and natural science disciplines contribute to theory in criminology and criminal justice.

Kuhn, Thomas, *The Structure of Scientific Revolutions,* 3rd ed. (Chicago: University of Chicago Press, 1996). This book is an exciting and innovative recasting of the nature of scientific development. Kuhn disputes the notion of gradual change and modification in science, arguing instead that established "paradigms" tend to persist until the weight of contradictory evidence brings about their rejection and replacement by new paradigms. This short book is at once stimulating and informative.

Weiss, Carol H., "Nothing As Practical as Good Theory: Exploring Theory-Based Evaluation for Comprehensive Community Initiatives for Children and Families," in James P. Connell, Anne C. Kubisch, Lisbeth B. Schorr, and Carol H. Weiss (eds.), *New Approaches to Evaluating Community Initiatives: Concepts, Methods, and Contexts* (Washington, DC: Aspen Institute, 1995), pp. 65–92. A well-known evaluation researcher, Weiss describes how public officials implicitly use theories to guide their actions. She offers sound advice on how theories can improve research and evaluation in complex policy areas.

Chapter 3

Ethics and Criminal Justice Research

We'll examine some of the ethical considerations that must be taken into account along with the scientific ones in the design and execution of research. We'll consider different types of ethical issues and ways of handling them.

Introduction

Despite our best intentions, we don't always recognize ethical issues in research.

Most of this book focuses on scientific and procedures and constraints. We'll see that the logic of science suggests certain research procedures, but we'll also see that some scientifically "perfect" study designs are not feasible, because they would be too expensive or take too long to execute. Throughout the book, we'll deal with workable compromises.

Before we get to scientific and administrative constraints on research, it's important to explore another essential consideration in doing criminal justice research in the real world — ethics. Just as certain designs or measurement procedures are impractical, others are constrained by ethical problems. We introduce the issue of ethics by quoting from Earl Babbie's book *The Practice of Social Research* (2001:469):

> Several years ago, I was invited to sit in on a planning session to design a study of legal education in California. The joint project was to be conducted by a university research center and the state bar association. The purpose of the project was to improve legal education by learning which aspects of the law school experience were related to success on the bar exam. Essentially, the plan was to prepare a questionnaire that would get detailed information about the law school experiences of individuals. People would be required to answer the questionnaire when they took the bar exam. By analyzing how people with different kinds of law school experiences did on the bar exam, it would be possible to find out what sorts of things worked and what didn't. The findings of the research could be made available to law schools, and ultimately legal education could be improved.
>
> The exciting thing about collaborating with the bar association was that all the normally aggravating logistical hassles would be handled. There would be no problem getting permission to administer questionnaires in conjunction with the exam, for example, and the problem of nonresponse could be eliminated altogether.
>
> I left the meeting excited about the prospects for the study. When I told a colleague about it, I glowed about the absolute handling of the nonresponse problem. Her immediate comment turned everything around completely. "That's unethical. There's no law requiring the questionnaire, and participation in research has to be voluntary." The study wasn't done.

It now seems obvious that requiring participation would have been inappropriate. You may have seen that before you read the comment by Babbie's colleague.

All of us consider ourselves ethical — not perfect perhaps, but more ethical than most of humanity. The problem in criminal justice research — and probably in life — is that ethical considerations are not always apparent to us. As a result, we often plunge into things without seeing ethical issues that may be obvious to others and even to ourselves when they are pointed out. Our excitement at the prospect of a new research project may blind us to obstacles that ethical considerations present.

Any of us can immediately see that a study that requires juvenile gang members to demonstrate how they steal cars is unethical. You'd speak out immediately if we suggested interviewing people about drug use and then publishing what they said in the local newspaper. But, as ethical as we think we are, we are likely to miss the ethical issues in other situations — not because we're bad, but because we're human.

Ethical Issues in Criminal Justice Research

A few basic principles encompass the variety of ethical issues in criminal justice research.

In most dictionaries and in common usage, ethics is typically associated with morality, and both deal with matters of right and wrong. But what is right and what is wrong? What is the source of the distinction? For various individuals, the sources vary from religion, to political ideology, to pragmatic observations of what seems to work and what doesn't.

Webster's New World Dictionary is typical among dictionaries in defining *ethical* as "conforming to the standards of conduct of a given profession or group." Although the relativity embedded in this definition may frustrate those in search of moral absolutes, what we regard as moral and ethical in day-to-day life is no more than a matter of agreement among members of a group. And, not surprisingly, different groups have agreed on different ethical codes of conduct. If someone is going to live in a particular society, then, it is extremely useful to know what that society considers ethical and unethical. The same holds true for the criminal justice research "community."

Anyone preparing to do criminal justice research should be aware of the general agreements shared by researchers about what's proper and improper in the conduct of scientific inquiry. Ethical issues in criminal justice can be especially challenging because our research questions frequently address illegal behavior that people are anxious to conceal. This is true of offenders and, sometimes, people who work in criminal justice agencies.

The sections that follow explore some of the more important ethical issues and agreements in criminal justice research. Our discussion is restricted to ethical issues in criminal justice research, not ethics in criminal justice policy and practice. Thus, we will not consider such issues as the morality of the death penalty, acceptable police practices, the ethics of punishment, or codes of conduct for attorneys and judges. If you are interested in substantive ethical issues in criminal justice policy, consult Jocelyn Pollock (1997) or Richard Hall and associates (1999) for an introduction. Frank Schmalleger (1991) presents a useful annotated bibliography of readings, and the journal *Criminal Justice Ethics* includes a wide range of articles.

No Harm to Participants

Weighing the potential benefits from doing research against the possibility of harm to the people being studied—or harm to other people— is a fundamental ethical dilemma in all research. For example, biomedical research can involve potential physical harm to people or animals. Social research may cause psychological harm or embarrassment in people who are asked to reveal information about themselves. Criminal justice research has the potential to produce both physical and psychological harm, as well as embarrassment. Although the likelihood of physical harm may seem remote, it is worthwhile to consider possible ways it might occur.

Harm to subjects, researchers, or third parties is possible in field studies that collect information from or about persons engaged in criminal activity; this is especially true for field research. Studies of drug crimes may involve locating and interviewing active users and dealers. For example, Bruce Johnson and associates (1985) studied heroin users in New York, recruiting subjects by spreading the word through various means. Other researchers have studied dealers in Detroit (Mieczkowski, 1990), New York (Williams, 1989), and St. Louis (Jacobs and Miller, 1998). Collecting information from active criminals presents at least the possibility of violence against research subjects by other drug dealers.

Potential danger to field researchers should also be considered. For instance, Peter Reuter and associates (Reuter, MacCoun, and Murphy, 1990) selected their drug dealer subjects by consulting probation department records. The researchers recognized that sampling persons from different Washington, DC, neighborhoods would have produced a more generalizable group of subjects, but they rejected that approach because mass media reports of widespread drug-related violence generated concern about the safety of research staff (1990:119). Whether such fears were warranted is unclear, but this example does illustrate how safety issues can affect criminal justice research.

ETHICS AND EXTREME FIELD RESEARCH

by Dina Perrone
Rutgers University

As a female ethnographer studying active drug use in a New York dance club, I have encountered awkward and difficult situations. The main purpose of my research was to study the use of ecstasy and other drugs in rave club settings. I became a participant observer in an all-night dance club (The Plant) where the use of club drugs was common. I covertly observed activities in the club, partly masking my role as a researcher by assuming the role of club-goer.

Though I was required to comply with university institutional review board guidelines, published codes and regulations offered limited guidance for many of the situations I experienced. As a result, I had to use my best judgment, learning from past experiences to make immediate decisions regarding ethical issues. I was forced to make decisions about how to handle drug episodes, so as not to place my research or my informants in any danger. Because my research was conducted in a dance club that is also a place for men to pick up women, I faced problems in getting information from subjects while watching out for my physical safety.

Drug Episodes and Subject Safety
I witnessed many drug episodes—adverse reactions to various club drugs—in my visits to The Plant. I watched groups trying to get their friends out of "K-holes" resulting from Ketamine or "Special K." I even aided a subject throwing up. Being a covert observer made it difficult to handle these episodes. There were times in the club when I felt as though I was the only person not under the influence of a mind-altering substance. This led me to believe that I had better judgment than the other patrons. Getting involved in these episodes, however, risked jeopardizing my research.

During my first observation, I tried to intervene in what appeared to be a serious drug episode but was warned off by an informant. I was new to the club and unsure what would happen if I got involved. If I sought help from club staff or outsiders in dealing with acute drug reactions, patrons as well as the bouncers would begin to question why I kept coming there. I needed to gain the trust of the patrons in order to enlist participants in my research. Furthermore, the bouncers could throw me out of the club, fearing I was a troublemaker who would summon authorities.

As a researcher, I have an ethical responsibility to my participants, and as a human being, I have an ethical responsibility to my conscience. I decided to be extra cautious during my research and to pay close attention to how drug episodes are handled. I would first consult my informants and follow their suggestions. But if I ever felt a person suffering a drug episode was at risk while other patrons were neither able nor inclined to help, I would intervene to the best of my ability.

Sexual Advances in the Dance Club
The Plant is also partly a "meat market." Unlike most bars and dance clubs, the patrons' attire and the dance club entertainment are highly erotic. Most of the males inside the club are shirt-

---

A more sobering example of possible safety concerns is a series of experimental studies of bystander intervention by Bob Latané and John Darley (1970). These researchers staged crimes that, in some instances, could have produced harm to either subjects or research staff. They were interested in circumstances when witnesses to a "crime" would or would not intervene. In one experiment, staging a liquor store holdup, a bystander called police, who responded with drawn guns.

Other researchers acknowledge the potential for harm in the context of respect for ethical principles. The box titled "Ethics and Extreme Field Research" gives examples of subtle and not-so-subtle ethical dilemmas encountered by a Rutgers University researcher in her study of drug use in rave clubs.

less, and the majority of females wear extremely revealing clothes. In staged performances, males and females perform dances with sexual overtones, and clothing is partly shed. This atmosphere promotes sexual encounters; men frequently approach single women in search of a mate. Men had a tendency to approach me—I appeared to be unattached, and because of my research role, I made it a point to talk to as many people as possible. It's not difficult to imagine how this behavior could be misinterpreted.

There were times when men became sexually aggressive and persistent. In most instances, I tended to walk away, and the men usually got the hint. However, some men are more persistent than others, especially when they are on ecstasy. In situations in which men make sexual advances, Terry Williams and colleagues (1992) suggest developing a trusting relationship with key individuals who can play a protective role. Throughout my research, I established a good rapport with my informants who assumed that protective role. Unfortunately, acting in this role has had the potential to place my informants in physically dangerous circumstances.

During one observation, "Tom" grabbed me after I declined his invitation to dance. Tom persisted, grabbed me again, then began to argue with "Jerry," one of my regular informants who came to my aid. This escalated to a fist fight broken up only after two bouncers ejected Tom from the club.

I had placed my informant and myself in a dangerous situation. Although I tried to convince myself that I really had no control over Jerry's actions, I felt responsible for the fight. A basic principle of field research is to not invite harm to participants. In most criminal justice research, harm is associated mainly with the possibility of arrest or psychological harm from discussing private issues. Afterwards, I tried to think about how the incident escalated and how I could prevent similar problems in the future.

Ethical Decision Rules
Evolving from Experience

Academic associations have formulated codes of ethics and professional conduct, but limited guidance is available for handling issues that arise in some types of ethnographic research. Instead, like criminal justice practitioners, those researchers have to make immediate decisions based on experience and training, without knowing how a situation will unfold. Throughout my research, I found myself in situations that I would normally avoid and would probably never confront. Should I help her get through a drug episode? If I don't, will she be okay? If I walk away from this aggressive guy, will he follow me? Does he understand that I wanted to talk to him just for research?

The approach I developed to tackle these issues was mostly gained by consulting with colleagues and reading other studies. An overarching theme regarding all codes of ethics is that ethnographers must put the safety and interests of their participants first, and they must recognize that their informants are more knowledgeable about many situations than they are. Throughout the research, I used my judgment to make the best decisions possible when handling these situations. To decide when to intervene during drug episodes, I followed the lead of my informants. Telling men that my informant was my boyfriend and walking away were successful tactics in turning away sexual advances.

More generally, John Monahan and associates (1993) distinguish three different groups at potential risk of physical harm in their research on violence. First are research subjects themselves. Women at risk of domestic violence, for example, may be exposed to greater danger if assailants learn they have disclosed past victimizations to researchers. Second, researchers might trigger attacks on themselves when they interview subjects who have a history of violent offending. Third, and most problematic, is the possibility that collecting information from unstable individuals might increase the risk of harm to third parties. The last category presents a new dilemma if researchers learn that subjects intend to attack some third party. Should researchers honor a promise of confidentiality to subjects or intervene to prevent the harm?

The potential for psychological harm to subjects exists when interviews are used to collect information. For example, crime surveys that ask respondents about their experiences as victims of crime may remind them of a traumatic, or at least an unpleasant, experience. Surveys may also ask respondents about illegal behaviors such as drug use or crimes they have committed. Talking about such actions with interviewers can be embarrassing.

Some researchers have taken special steps to reduce the potential for emotional trauma in interviews of domestic violence victims (Tjaden and Thoennes, 2000). One of the most interesting examples involves the use of self-completed computer questionnaires in the British Crime Survey (Mirrlees-Black, 1999). Rather than verbally respond to questions from interviewers, respondents read and answer questions on a laptop computer. This procedure affords a greater degree of privacy for research subjects.

Although the fact often goes unrecognized, subjects can also be harmed by the analysis and reporting of data. Every now and then, research subjects read the books published about the studies they participated in. Reasonably sophisticated subjects can locate themselves in the various indexes and tables of published studies. Having done so, they may find themselves characterized — though not identified by name — as criminals, deviants, probation violators, and so forth.

Largely for this reason, information on the city of residence of victims identified in the National Crime Victimization Survey is not available to researchers or the public. The relative rarity of some types of crime means that if crime victimization is reported by city of residence individual victims might recognize the portrayal of their experience or might be identified by third parties.

Recent developments in the use of crime-mapping software have raised similar concerns. Many police departments now use some type of computer-driven crime map, and some have made maps of small areas available to the public on the Web. As Tom Casady (1999) points out, this raises new questions of privacy as individuals might be able to identify crimes directed against their neighbors. Researchers and police alike must recognize the potential for such problems before publishing or otherwise displaying detailed crime maps. See crime maps of New Orleans for an example (http://www.new-orleans.la.us/cnoweb/nopd/maps/basecrimemap.html; accessed 15 January 2003).

By now, it should be apparent that virtually all research runs some risk of harming other people somehow. A researcher can never completely guard against all possible injuries, yet some study designs make harm more likely than others. If a particular research procedure seems likely to produce unpleasant effects for subjects—asking survey respondents to report deviant behavior, for example—the researcher should have firm scientific grounds for doing so. If researchers pursue a design that is essential and also likely to be unpleasant for subjects, they will find themselves in an ethical netherworld, forced to do some personal agonizing.

As a general principle, possible harm to subjects may be justified if the potential benefits of the study outweigh the harm. Of course, this raises a further question of how to determine whether possible benefits offset possible harms. There is no simple answer, but as we will see, the research community has adopted certain safeguards that help subjects to make such determinations themselves.

Not harming people is an easy norm to accept in theory, but it is often difficult to ensure in practice. Sensitivity to the issue and experience in research methodology, however, should improve researchers' efforts in delicate areas of inquiry. Review Dina Perrone's observations in the box "Ethics and Extreme Field Research" for examples.

Voluntary Participation

Criminal justice research often intrudes into people's lives. The interviewer's telephone call or the questionnaire in the mail signals the beginning of an activity that respondents have not requested and that may require a significant portion of their time and energy. Being selected to participate in any sort of research study disrupts subjects' regular activities.

A major tenet of medical research ethics is that experimental participation must be voluntary. The same norm applies to research in criminal justice. No one should be forced to participate. But this norm is far easier to accept in theory than to apply in practice.

For example, prisoners are sometimes used as subjects in experimental studies. In the most rigorously ethical cases, prisoners are told the nature — and the possible dangers — of the experiment; they are told that participation is completely voluntary; and they are further instructed that they can expect no special rewards (such as early parole) for participation. Even under these conditions, volunteers often are motivated by the belief that they will personally benefit from their cooperation. In other cases, prisoners — or other subjects — may be offered small cash payments in exchange for participation. To people with very low incomes, small payments may be an incentive to participate in a study they would not otherwise endure.

When an instructor in an introductory criminal justice class asks students to fill out a questionnaire that she or he plans to analyze and publish, students should always be told that their participation in the survey is completely voluntary. Even so, students might fear that nonparticipation will somehow affect their grade. The instructor should therefore be especially sensitive to the implied sanctions and make provisions to obviate them. For example, students could be asked to return the questionnaires by mail or to drop them in a box near the door prior to the next class.

Notice how this norm of voluntary participation works against a number of scientific concerns or goals. In the most general terms, the goal of generalizability is threatened if experimental subjects or survey respondents are only the people who willingly participate. The same

is true when subjects' participation can be bought with small payments. Research results may not be generalizable to all kinds of people. Most clearly, in the case of a descriptive study, a researcher cannot generalize the study findings to an entire population unless a substantial majority of a scientifically selected sample actually participates — both the willing respondents and the somewhat unwilling.

Field research (the subject of Chapter 10) has its own ethical dilemmas in this regard. Often, a researcher who conducts observations in the field cannot even reveal that a study is being done, for fear that this revelation might significantly affect what is being studied. Imagine, for example, that you are interested in whether the way stereo headphones are displayed in a discount store affects rates of shoplifting. Therefore, you plan a field study in which you will make observations of store displays and shoplifting. You cannot very well ask all shoppers whether they agree to participate in your study.

The norm of voluntary participation is an important one, but it is sometimes impossible to follow. In cases in which researchers ultimately feel justified in violating it, it is all the more important to observe the other ethical norms of scientific research.

Anonymity and Confidentiality

The clearest concern in the protection of the subjects' interests and well-being is the protection of their identity. If revealing their behavior or responses would injure them in any way, adherence to this norm becomes crucial. Two techniques — anonymity and confidentiality — assist researchers in this regard, although the two are often confused.

Anonymity · A research subject is considered anonymous when the researcher cannot associate a given piece of information with the person. **Anonymity** addresses many potential ethical difficulties. Studies that use field observation techniques are often able to ensure that research subjects cannot be identified. Researchers may also gain access to nonpublic records from courts, corrections departments, or other criminal justice agencies in which the names of persons have been removed.

One example of anonymity is a mail survey in which no identification numbers are put on the questionnaires before their return to the research office. Likewise, a telephone survey is anonymous if residential phone numbers are selected at random and respondents are not asked for identifying information. Interviews with subjects in the field are anonymous if the researchers neither ask for nor record the names of subjects.

Assuring anonymity makes it difficult to keep track of which sampled respondents have been interviewed, because researchers did not record their names. Nevertheless, in some situations, the price of anonymity is worth paying. In a survey of drug use, for example, we may decide that the likelihood and accuracy of responses will be enhanced by guaranteeing anonymity.

Respondents in many surveys cannot be considered anonymous because an interviewer collects the information from individuals whose names and addresses are known. Other means of data collection may similarly make it impossible to guarantee anonymity for subjects. If we wished to examine juvenile arrest records for a sample of seventh-grade students, for example, we would need to know their names even though we might not be interviewing them or having them fill out a questionnaire.

Confidentiality **Confidentiality** means that a researcher is able to link information with a given person's identity but essentially promises not to do so publicly. In a survey of self-reported drug use, for example, the researcher is in a position to make public the use of illegal drugs by a given respondent, but the respondent is assured that this will not be done. Similarly, if field interviews are conducted with juvenile gang members, researchers can certify that information will not be disclosed to police or other officials. Studies using court or police records that include individuals' names may protect confidentiality by not including any identifying information.

Some techniques ensure better performance on this guarantee. To begin, field or survey interviewers who have access to respondent identifications should be trained in their ethical responsibilities. As soon as possible, all names and addresses should be removed from data collection forms and replaced by identification numbers. A master identification file should be created linking numbers to names to permit the later correction of missing or contradictory information. This file should be kept under lock and key and be made available only for legitimate purposes.

Whenever a survey is confidential rather than anonymous, it is the researcher's responsibility to make that fact clear to respondents. He or she must never use the term *anonymous* to mean *confidential*. Note, however, that research subjects and others may not understand the difference. For example, a former state-level assistant attorney general once demanded that Maxfield disclose the identities of police officers who participated in an anonymous study. It required repeated explanations of the difference between "anonymous" and "confidential" before the lawyer finally understood. In any event, subjects should be assured that the information they provide will be used for research purposes only and not be disclosed to third parties.

Deceiving Subjects

We've seen that the handling of subjects' identities is an important ethical consideration. Handling our own identity as a researcher can be tricky, too. Sometimes, it's useful and even necessary to identify ourselves as researchers to those we want to study. It would take a master con artist to get people to participate in a laboratory experiment or complete a lengthy questionnaire without letting on that research was being conducted. We should also keep in mind that deceiving people is unethical; in criminal justice research, deception needs to be justified by compelling scientific or administrative concerns.

Sometimes, researchers admit that they are doing research but fudge about why they are doing it or for whom. For example, Cathy Spatz Widom and associates interviewed victims of child abuse some 15 years after their cases had been heard in criminal or juvenile courts (Widom, Weiler, and Cotler, 1999). Widom was interested in whether child abuse victims were more likely than a comparison group of nonvictims to have used illegal drugs. Interviewers could not explain the purpose of the study without potentially biasing responses. Still, it was necessary to provide a plausible explanation for asking detailed questions about personal and family experiences. Widom's solution was to inform subjects that they had been selected to participate in a study of human development. She also prepared a brochure describing her research on human development that was distributed to respondents.

Although we might initially think that concealing our research purpose by deception would be particularly useful in studying active offenders, James Inciardi (1993), in describing methods for sudying "crack houses," makes a convincing case that this is inadvisable. In the first place, concealing our research role when investigating drug dealers and users implies that we are associating with them for the purpose of obtaining illegal drugs. Faced with this situation, a researcher would have the choice of engaging in illegal behavior or offering a convincing explanation for declining to do so. In the second case, which Inciardi faced, masquerading as a crack house patron would have exposed the researcher to the considerable danger of violence that is common in such places. Because the choice of committing illegal acts or becoming a victim of violence is really no choice at all, Inciardi (1993:152) advises researchers who study active offenders in field settings: "Don't go undercover."

Analysis and Reporting

As criminal justice researchers, then, we have ethical obligations to our subjects of study. At the same time, we have ethical obligations to our colleagues in the scientific community; a few comments on those obligations are in order.

In any rigorous study, the researcher should be more familiar than anyone else with the technical shortcomings and failures of the study. Researchers have an obligation to make those shortcomings known to readers. Even though it's natural to feel foolish admitting mistakes, researchers are ethically obligated to do so.

Any negative findings should be reported. There is an unfortunate myth in social scientific reporting that only positive discoveries are worth reporting (and journal editors are sometimes guilty of believing that as well). And this is not restricted to social science. For example, Helle Krogh Johansen and Peter Gotzsche (1999) describe how published research on new drugs tends to focus on successful experiments. Unsuccessful research on new formulations is less often published, which leads pharmaceutical researchers to repeat studies of drugs already shown to be ineffective. Largely because of this bias, researchers at the Johns Hopkins University Medical School have established the *Journal of Negative Observations in Genetic Oncology* (*NOGO*), dedicated to publishing negative findings from cancer research. See the "Internet Exercises" section at the end of this chapter for NOGO's Web address. In social science, as in medical research, it is often as important to know that two things are not related as to know that they are.

Similarly, researchers should avoid the temptation to save face by describing findings as the product of a carefully planned analytic strategy when that is not the case. Many findings are unexpected even though they may seem obvious in retrospect. Suppose you uncover an interesting relationship by accident — so what? Embroidering such situations with descriptions of fictitious hypotheses is dishonest and tends to mislead inexperienced researchers into thinking that all scientific inquiry is rigorously preplanned and organized. Fortunately, evaluation researchers recognize the value of reporting unexpected findings and have developed evaluation approaches that increase the likelihood of discovering unanticipated benefits (Tilley, 2000).

In general, science progresses through honesty and openness, and is retarded by ego defenses and deception. We can serve our fellow researchers — and the scientific community as a whole — by telling the truth about all the pitfalls and problems experienced in a particular line of inquiry. With luck, this will save others from the same problems.

Legal Liability

Two types of ethical problems expose researchers to potential legal liability. First, assume you are making field observations of criminal activity such as street prostitution that is not reported to police. Under criminal law in many states, you might be arrested for obstructing justice or being an accessory to a crime. Potentially more troublesome is the situation in which participant observation of crime or deviance draws researchers into criminal or deviant roles themselves — smuggling cigarettes into a lockup in order to obtain the cooperation of detainees, for example.

The second and more common potential source of legal problems involves knowledge that research subjects have committed illegal acts. Self-report surveys or field interviews may ask subjects about crimes they have committed. If respondents report committing offenses they have never been arrested for or charged with, the researcher's knowledge of them might be construed as obstruction of justice. Or research data may be subject to subpoena by a criminal court. Because disclosure of research data that could be traced to individual subjects violates the ethical principle of confidentiality, a new dilemma emerges.

Fortunately, federal law protects researchers from legal action in most circumstances, provided that appropriate safeguards are used to protect research data. Research plans for 2002 published by organizations in the Office of Justice Programs summarized this protection: "[Research] information and copies thereof shall be immune from legal process, and shall not, without the consent of the person furnishing such information, be admitted as evidence or used for any purpose in any action, suit, or other judicial, legislative, or administrative proceedings" (42 U.S. Code §22.28a). This not only protects researchers from legal action but also can be valuable in assuring subjects that they cannot be prosecuted for crimes they describe to an interviewer or field worker. For example, Bruce Johnson and associates (1985:219) prominently displayed a Federal Certificate of Confidentiality at their research office to assure heroin dealers that they could not be prosecuted for crimes disclosed to interviewers. More savvy than many people about such matters, heroin users were duly impressed.

Note that such immunity requires confidential information to be protected. We have already discussed the principle of confidentiality, so this bargain should be an easy one to keep.

Somewhere between legal liability and physical danger lies the potential risk to field researchers from law enforcement. Despite being up front with crack users about his role as a researcher, Inciardi (1993) points out that police could not be expected to distinguish him from his subjects. Visibly associating with offenders in natural settings brings some risk of being arrested or inadvertently being an accessory to crime. Thus, Inciardi on one occasion fled the scene of a robbery and on another was caught up in a crack-house raid. Another example is the account Bruce Jacobs (1996) gives of his contacts with police while he was studying street drug dealers. Exercises presented at the end of the chapter ask you to think more carefully about the ethical issues involved in Jacobs' contact with police.

Special Problems

Certain types of criminal justice studies present special ethical problems in addition to those we have mentioned. Applied research, for example, may evaluate some existing or new program. Evaluations frequently have the potential to disrupt the routine operations of agencies being studied. Obviously, it is best to minimize such interferences whenever possible.

Staff Misbehavior While conducting applied research, researchers may become aware of irregular or illegal practices by staff in public agencies. They are then faced with the ethical question of whether to report such information. For example, investigators conducting an evaluation of an innovative probation program learned that police visits to the residences of probationers were not taking place as planned. Instead, police assigned to the program had been submitting falsified log sheets and had not actually checked on probationers.[*]

What is the ethical dilemma in this case? On the one hand, researchers were evaluating the probation program and so were obliged to report reasons it did or did not operate as planned. Failure to deliver program treatments (home visits) is an example of a program not operating as planned. Investigators had guaranteed confidentiality to program clients — the offenders assigned to probation — but no such agreement had been struck with program staff. On the other hand, researchers had assured agency personnel that their purpose was to evaluate the probation program, not individuals' job performance. If researchers disclosed their knowledge that police were falsifying reports, they would violate this implied trust.

What would you have done in this situation? We will tell you what the researchers decided at the end of this chapter. You should recognize, however, how applied research in criminal justice agencies can involve a variety of ethical issues.

Research Causes Crime Because criminal acts and their circumstances are complex and imperfectly understood, some research projects have the potential to produce crime or influence its location or target. Certainly, this is a potentially serious ethical issue for researchers.

Most people agree that it is unethical to encourage someone to commit an offense solely for the purpose of a research project. What's more problematic is recognizing situations in which research might indirectly promote offending. Scott Decker and Barrik Van Winkle (1996) discuss such a possibility in their research on gang members. Some gang members offered to illustrate their willingness to use violence by inviting researchers to witness a drive-by shooting. Researchers declined all such invitations (1996:46). Another ethical issue was the question of how subjects used the $20 cash payments they received in exchange for being interviewed (1996:51):

> We set the fee low enough that we were confident that it would not have a criminogenic effect. While twenty dollars is not a small amount of money, it is not sufficient to purchase a gun or bankroll a large drug buy. We are sure that some of our subjects used the money for illegal purposes. But, after all, these were individuals who were regularly engaged in delinquent and criminal acts.

You may or may not agree with the authors' reasoning in the last sentence. But their consideration of how cash payments would be used by active offenders represents an unusually careful recognition of the ethical dilemmas that emerge in studying active offenders.

A different type of ethical problem is the possibility of crime displacement in studies of crime prevention programs. For example, consider an experimental program to reduce street prostitution in one area of a city. Researchers studying such a program might designate experimental target areas for enhanced enforcement, as well as nearby comparison areas that will not receive an intervention. If prostitution is displaced from target areas to adjacent neighborhoods, the evaluation study contributes to an increase in prostitution in the comparison areas.

In a review of more than 50 evaluations of crime prevention projects, René Hesseling (1994) concludes that displacement tended to be associated with programs targeting street

---

[*] Information about this example was provided through personal communication between researchers and one of the authors.

prostitution, bank robbery, and certain combinations of offenses. The type of crime prevention action also made a difference, with displacement more common for target-hardening programs. For example, installing security screens on ground-floor windows in some buildings seemed to displace burglary to less protected structures. Similarly, adding steering column locks to new cars tended to increase thefts of older cars (Felson and Clarke, 1998).

At the same time, Hesseling demonstrates that displacement is by no means inevitable. Furthermore, displacement tends to follow major policy changes not connected with criminal justice research. Researchers cannot be expected to control actions by criminal justice officials that may benefit some people at the expense of others. However, it is reasonable to expect researchers involved in planning an evaluation study to anticipate the possibility of such things as displacement and bring them to the attention of program staff.

Withholding of Desirable Treatments   Certain kinds of research designs in criminal justice can lead to different kinds of ethical questions. Suppose, for example, researchers believe that diverting domestic violence offenders from prosecution to counseling reduces the possibility of repeat violence. Is it ethical to conduct an experiment in which some offenders are prosecuted but others are not?

You may recognize the similarity between this question and those faced by medical researchers who test the effectiveness of experimental drugs. Physicians typically respond to such questions by pointing out that the effectiveness of a drug cannot be demonstrated without such experiments. Failure to conduct research, even at the potential expense of subjects not receiving the trial drugs, would therefore make it impossible to develop new drugs or distinguish beneficial treatments from those that are ineffective and even harmful.

One solution to this dilemma is to interrupt an experiment if preliminary results indicate that a new policy, or drug, does in fact produce improvements in a treatment group. For example, Michael Dennis (1990) describes how such plans were incorporated into a long-term evaluation of enhanced drug treatment counseling. If preliminary results had indicated that the new counseling program reduced drug use, researchers and program staff were prepared to provide enhanced counseling to subjects in the control group. Dennis recognized this potential ethical issue and planned his elaborate research design to accommodate such midstream changes.

Mandatory Reporting   The situation is somewhat murkier for researchers studying certain kinds of family violence. Following the Federal Child Abuse Prevention and Treatment Act of 1974, all states developed child protection agencies and adopted mandatory reporting laws. Specific provisions vary, but in general, people who learn about possible cases of child abuse must report them to designated state agencies. This certainly seems to be a worthwhile goal, but what about researchers who learn about possible child maltreatment in the course of a survey? In most states, such requirements apply only to health professionals and teachers. But in eight states, *anyone* who suspects a case of child maltreatment must report it to designated authorities.

Notice how this is consistent with one ethical principle — protection of human subjects by reporting possible victims — but at odds with another principle — confidentiality. A Bureau of Justice Statistics report on human subjects protection suggests that researchers warn subjects at the beginning of an interview that any information disclosed about child abuse must be reported to authorities (Sieber, 2001). But that threatens researchers' ability to learn about child abuse. Another approach, adopted by Lianne Woodward and David Fergusson (2000), is to interview subjects age 18 and older, asking about experiences of abuse victimization when they were children. This is an imperfect solution, but it illustrates the trade-offs between our interest in protecting research subjects and our interest in studying the phenomenon of child abuse. For more examples and guidance in this vexing research/ethical area, see Seth Kalichman's (2000) book, published by the American Psychological Association.

Research in criminal justice, especially applied research, can pose a variety of ethical dilemmas, only some of which we have mentioned here. See the "Additional Readings" at the end of this chapter for a more complete discussion.

Promoting Compliance with Ethical Principles

Codes of ethics and institutional review boards are two main ways of promoting compliance with ethical principles.

No matter how sensitive they might be to the rights of individuals and possible ways subjects might be harmed, researchers are not always the best judges of whether or not adequate safeguards are used. Recall Babbie's excitement about a project that would have required law students taking the bar exam to complete a questionnaire. He immediately recognized the research benefits of increased response rates but lost sight of the ethical problems such a requirement would have raised.

Codes of Professional Ethics

If the professionals who design and conduct research projects can fail to consider ethical problems, how can such problems be avoided? One approach is for researchers to consult one of the codes of ethics produced by professional associations. Formal codes of conduct describe what is considered acceptable and unacceptable professional behavior. The American Psychological Association (2002) code of ethics is quite detailed, reflecting the different professional roles of psychologists in research, clinical treatment, and educational contexts.

Many of the ethical questions criminal justice researchers are likely to encounter are addressed in the ethics code of the American Sociological Association (1997). Paul Reynolds (1979:442–49) has created a composite code for the use of human subjects in research, drawing on 24 codes of ethics published by national associations of social scientists. The National Academy of Sciences publishes a very useful booklet on a variety of ethical issues, including the problem of fraud and other forms of scientific misconduct (Committee on Science, Engineering, and Public Policy, 1995).

The two national associations representing criminology and criminal justice researchers have one code of ethics between them. The Academy of Criminal Justice Sciences (ACJS) based its code of ethics on that developed by the American Sociological Association. ACJS members are bound by a very general code that reflects the diversity of its membership: "Most of the ethical standards are written broadly, to provide applications in varied roles and varied contexts. The Ethical Standards are not exhaustive—conduct that is not included in the Ethical Standards is not necessarily ethical or unethical" (Academy of Criminal Justice Sciences, 2000:1).

After years of inaction, a committee of the American Society of Criminology (ASC) proposed a draft code of ethics in 1998, one that drew extensively on the code for sociology. But no ethics code had been adopted as of September 2003, and the ASC withdrew its draft code from circulation in 1999. In personal correspondence, a prominent ASC officer expressed doubt that any sort of code would be approved soon; eventually, this person felt, a very brief statement of general principles might be approved.

What can we make of the inability of the largest professional association of criminologists to agree on a code of ethics? The wide variety of approaches to doing research in this area probably has something to do with it. Criminologists also encounter a range of ethical issues and have diverging views on how those issues should be addressed. Finally, we have seen examples of the special problems criminologists face in balancing ethics and research. Not all of these problems have easy solutions that can be embodied in a code.

Even when they exist, professional codes of ethics for social scientists cannot be expected to prevent unethical practices in criminal justice research any more than the American Bar Association's Code of Professional Responsibility eliminates breaches of ethics by lawyers. For this reason, and in reaction to some controversial medical and social science research, the U.S. Department of Health and Human Services (HHS) has established regulations protecting human research subjects. These regulations do not apply to all social science or criminal justice research. It is, however, worthwhile to understand some of their general provisions. Material in the following section is based on the Code of Federal Regulations, Title 45, Chapter 4.6.

Institutional Review Boards

Government agencies and nongovernment organizations (including universities) that conduct research involving human subjects must establish review committees, known as institutional review boards (IRB). These IRBs have two general purposes. First, board members make judgments about the overall risks to human subjects and whether these risks are acceptable, given the expected benefits from actually doing the research. Second, they determine whether the procedures to be used include adequate safeguards regarding the safety, confidentiality, and general welfare of human subjects.

Under HHS regulations, virtually all research that uses human subjects in any way, including simply asking people questions, is subject to IRB review. The few exceptions potentially include research conducted for educational purposes and studies that collect anonymous information only. However, even those studies may be subject to review if they use certain special populations (discussed later) or procedures that might conceivably harm participants. In other words, it's safe to assume that

most research is subject to IRB review if original data will be collected from individuals whose identities will be known. If you think about the various ways subjects might be harmed and the difficulty of conducting anonymous studies, you can understand why this is the case.

Federal regulations and IRB guidelines address other potential ethical issues in social research. Foremost among these is the typical IRB requirement for dealing with the ethical principle of voluntary participation.

Informed Consent   The norm of voluntary participation is usually satisfied through informed consent — informing subjects about research procedures and then obtaining their consent to participate. Although this may seem like a simple requirement, obtaining informed consent can present several practical difficulties. It requires that subjects understand the purpose of the research, possible risks and side effects, possible benefits to subjects, and the procedures that will be used.

If you accept that deception may sometimes be necessary, you will realize how the requirement to inform subjects about research procedures can present something of a dilemma. Researchers usually address this problem by telling subjects at least part of the truth or offering a slightly revised version of why the research is being conducted. In Widom's study of child abuse, subjects were partially informed about the purpose of the research — human development — one component of which is being a victim of child abuse, which the subjects were not told.

Another potential problem with obtaining informed consent is ensuring that subjects have the capacity to understand the descriptions of risks, benefits, procedures, and so forth. Researchers may have to provide oral descriptions to participants who are unable to read. For subjects who do not speak English, researchers should be prepared to describe procedures in their native language. And if researchers use specialized terms or language common in criminal

You and your parents or guardian are invited to participate in a research study of the monitoring program that you were assigned to by the Juvenile Court. The purpose of this research is to study the program and your reactions to it. In order to do this a member of the research team will need to interview you and your parents/guardians when you complete the monitoring program. These interviews will take about 15 minutes and will focus on your experiences with the court and monitoring program, the things you do, things that have happened to you, and what you think. In addition, we will record from the court records information about the case for which you were placed in the monitoring program, prior cases, and other information that is put in the records after you are released from the monitoring program.

Anything you or your parents or guardian tell us will be strictly confidential. This means that only the researchers will have your answers. They *will not* under any conditions (except at your request) be given to the court, the police, probation officers, your parents, or your child!

Your participation in this research is voluntary. If you don't want to take part, you don't have to! If you decide to participate, you can change your mind at any time. Whether you participate or not will have no effect on the program, probation, or your relationship with the court.

The research is being directed by Dr. Terry Baumer and Dr. Robert Mendelsohn from the Indiana University School of Public and Environmental Affairs here in Indianapolis. If you ever have any questions about the research or comments about the monitoring program that you think we should know about, please call one of us at 274-0531.

Consent Statement

We agree to participate in this study of the Marion County Juvenile Monitoring Program. We have read the above statement and understand what will be required and that all information will be confidential. We also understand that we can withdraw from the study at any time without penalty.

Juvenile _____   Date: _____

Parent/Guardian _____

Parent/Guardian _____

Researcher _____

Figure 3.1   Informed Consent Statement for Evaluation of Marion County Juvenile Monitoring Program

justice research, participants may not understand the meaning and thus be unable to grant informed consent. For example, consider this statement: "The purpose of this study is to determine whether less restrictive sanctions such as restitution produce heightened sensitivity to social responsibility among persistent juvenile offenders and a decline in long-term recidivism." Can you think of a better way to describe this study to delinquent 14-year-olds? Figure 3.1 presents a good example of an informed consent statement that was used in a study of juvenile burglars. Notice how the statement describes research procedures clearly and unambiguously tells subjects that participation is voluntary.

Other guidelines for obtaining informed consent include explicitly telling people that their participation is voluntary and assuring them of confidentiality. However, it is more important to understand how informed consent addresses key ethical issues in conducting criminal justice research. First, it ensures that participation is voluntary. Second, by informing subjects of procedures, risks, and benefits, researchers are empowering them to resolve the fundamental ethical dilemma of whether the possible benefits of the research offset the possible risks of participation.

Special Populations   Federal regulations on human subjects include special provisions for certain types of subjects, and two of these are particularly important in criminal justice research—juveniles and prisoners. Juveniles, of course, are treated differently from adults in most aspects of the law. Their status as a special

ETHICS AND JUVENILE GANG MEMBERS

Scott Decker and Barrik Van Winkle faced a range of ethical issues in their study of gang members. Many of these should be obvious given what has been said so far in this chapter. Violence was common among subjects and presented a real risk to researchers. Decker and Van Winkle (1996:252) reported that 11 of the 99 members of the original sample had been killed since the project began in 1990. There was also the obvious need to assure confidentiality to subjects.

Their project was supported by a federal agency and administered through a university, so Decker and Van Winkle had to comply with federal human subjects guidelines as administered by the university institutional review board (IRB). And because many of the subjects were juveniles, they had to address federal regulations concern-

ing that special population. Foremost among these was the normal requirement that informed consent for juveniles include parental notification and approval.

You may immediately recognize the conflicting ethical principles at work here, together with the potential for conflict. The promise of confidentiality to gang members is one such principle that was essential for the researchers to obtain candid reports of violence and other law-breaking behavior. But the need for confidentiality conflicted with initial IRB requirements to obtain parental consent for their children to participate in the research:

> This would have violated our commitment to maintain the confidentiality of each subject, not to mention the ethical and practical difficulties of finding and informing each parent. We told the Human Subjects Committee that we would not, in effect, tell parents that their child was being inter-

population of human subjects reflects the legal status of juveniles, as well as their capacity to grant informed consent. In most studies that involve juveniles, consent must be obtained both from parents or guardians and from the juvenile subjects themselves.

In some studies, however, such as those that focus on abused children, it is obviously not desirable to obtain parental consent. Decker and Van Winkle faced this problem in their study of St. Louis gang members. See the box "Ethics and Juvenile Gang Members" for a discussion of how they reconciled the conflict between two ethical principles and satisfied the concerns of their university's IRB.

Prisoners are treated as a special population for somewhat different reasons. Because of their ready accessibility for experiments and interviews, prisoners have frequently been used in biomedical experiments that produced serious harm (Mitford, 1973). Recognizing this, HHS regulations specify that prisoner subjects may not be exposed to risks that would be consid-

ered excessive for nonprison subjects. Furthermore, undue influence or coercion cannot be used in recruiting prisoner subjects. Informed consent statements presented to prospective subjects must indicate that a decision not to participate in a study will have no influence on work assignments, privileges, or parole decisions. To help ensure that these ethical issues are recognized, if an IRB reviews a project in which prisoners will be subjects, at least one member of that IRB must be either a prisoner or someone specifically designated to represent the interests of prisoners.

Randomization is generally recognized as an ethical procedure for selecting subjects or deciding which subjects will receive an experimental treatment. HHS regulations emphasize this in describing special provisions for using prison subjects: "Unless the principal investigator provides to the [IRB] justification in writing for following some other procedures, control subjects must be selected randomly from the group of available prisoners who meet the characteristics

viewed because they were an active gang member, knowledge that the parents may not have had. (Decker and Van Winkle, 1996:52)

You might think deception would be a possibility—informing parents that their child was selected for a youth development study, for example. This would not, however, solve the logistical difficulty of locating parents or guardians, some of whom had lost contact with their children. Furthermore, it was likely that even if parents or guardians could be located, suspicions about the research project and the reasons their children were selected would prevent many parents from granting consent. Loss of juvenile subjects in this way would compromise the norm of generality as we have described it in this chapter and elsewhere.

Finally, waiving the requirement for parental consent would have undermined the legal principle that the interests of juveniles must be protected by a supervising adult. Remember that researchers are not always the best judges of whether sufficient precautions have been taken to protect subjects. Here is how Decker and Van Winkle (1996:52) resolved the issue with their IRB:

> We reached a compromise in which we found an advocate for each juvenile member of our sample; this person—a university employee—was responsible for making sure that the subject understood (1) their rights to refuse or quit the interview at any time without penalty and (2) the confidential nature of the project. All subjects signed the consent form.

Source: Adapted from Decker and Van Winkle (1996).

needed for that particular research project" (45 CFR 46.305[4]).

Institutional Review Board Requirements and Researcher Rights

Federal regulations contain many more provisions for IRBs and other protections for human subjects. Some researchers believe that such regulations actually create problems by setting constraints on their freedom and professional judgments in conducting research. Recall that potential conflict between the rights of researchers to discover new knowledge and the rights of subjects to be free from unnecessary harm is a fundamental ethical dilemma. It is at least inconvenient to have outsiders review a research proposal. Or a researcher may feel insulted by the implication that the potential benefits of research will not outweigh the potential harm or inconvenience to human subjects.

Much of the original impetus for establishing IRBs had to do with medical experimentation on humans. Many social research study designs are regarded as exempt from IRB review under federal guidelines (45 CFR 46.101[b]). Here are the most relevant for criminal justice research:

(1) Research conducted in established or commonly accepted educational settings, involving normal educational practices.

(2) Research involving the use of educational tests (cognitive, diagnostic, aptitude, achievement), survey procedures, interview procedures or observation of public behavior, unless: (i) information obtained is recorded in such a manner that human subjects can be identified, directly or through identifiers linked to the subjects; and (ii) any disclosure of the human subjects' responses outside the research could reasonably place the subjects at risk of criminal or civil liability or be damaging to the subjects' financial standing, employability, or reputation.

(3) Research involving the use of educational tests (cognitive, diagnostic, aptitude, achievement), survey procedures, interview procedures, or observation of public behavior if: (i) the human subjects are elected or appointed public officials or candidates for public office; or (ii) any personally identifiable information will be maintained as confidential throughout the research and thereafter.

(4) Research involving the collection or study of existing data, documents, records, pathological specimens, or diagnostic specimens, if these sources are publicly available or if the information is recorded by the investigator in such a manner that subjects cannot be identified, directly or through identifiers linked to the subjects.

(5) Research and demonstration projects which are conducted by or subject to the approval of Department or Agency heads, and which are designed to study, evaluate, or otherwise examine: (i) Public benefit or service programs; (ii) procedures for obtaining benefits or services under those programs; (iii) possible changes in or alternatives to those programs or procedures; or (iv) possible changes in methods or levels of payment for benefits or services under those programs.

These exempt categories include quite a number of common models for doing criminal justice research. However, *exempt* means that research proposals do not have to be subject to *full* IRB review. In most cases, researchers who believe that their projects qualify for exemption under these categories must still have IRBs review the research to verify that exemption.

If this strikes you as confusing, you should feel reassured to learn that researchers, IRBs, and federal regulators are often confused as well. Given the unclear language of HHS regulations, many university IRBs have become extremely cautious in reviewing research proposals. See Christopher Shea's (2000) discussion for examples of problems resulting from this. Professional associations and research-oriented federal agencies have tried to offer guidance on what is and is not subject to various levels of IRB approval. Joan Sieber (2001) prepared an analysis of human subjects issues associated with large surveys for the Bureau of Justice Statistics. Always alert for possible restrictions on academic freedom, the American Association of University Professors (2001) published a useful summary of how IRBs have come to regulate social science research.

There is some merit in such concerns; however, we should not lose sight of the reasons IRB requirements and other regulations were created. Researchers are not always the best judges of the potential for their work to harm individuals. In designing and conducting criminal justice research, they may become excited about learning how to better prevent crime or more effectively treat cocaine addiction. That excitement and commitment to scientific advancement may lead researchers to overlook possible harms to individual rights or well-being. You may recognize this as another way of asking whether the ends justify the means. Because researchers are not always disinterested parties in answering such questions, IRBs are established to provide outside judgments. Also recognize that IRBs can be sources of expert advice on how to resolve ethical dilemmas. Decker and Van Winkle shared their university's concern about balancing confidentiality against the need to obtain informed consent from juvenile subjects; together, they were able to fashion a workable compromise.

Another reason for creating regulations to protect human subjects, and IRBs to monitor compliance with those regulations, is the perceived failure of other means, together with ethical controversies raised by some actual studies (Homan, 1991). In the next section, we will describe briefly two research projects that provoked widespread ethical controversy and discussion. These are not the only two controversial projects that have been done; they simply illustrate ethical issues in the real world.

Two Ethical Controversies

Two examples of controversial studies illustrate key issues in ethics.

The first project studied sexual behavior in public rest rooms, and the second examined how "prisoners" and "guards" reacted in a simulated prison setting.

Trouble in the Tearoom

As a graduate student, Laud Humphreys became interested in studying homosexual behavior. He developed a special interest in the casual and fleeting homosexual acts engaged in by some nonhomosexuals. In particular, his research interest focused on male homosexual acts between strangers who met in the public rest rooms in parks, called "tearooms" among homosexuals. The result was the publication of *The Tearoom Trade* (Humphreys, 1975).

What particularly interested Humphreys about the tearoom activity was that the participants seemed to lead otherwise conventional lives as "family men." Thus, it was important to them that they remain anonymous in their tearoom visits. How would you study something like that?

Humphreys approach took advantage of the social structure of the situation. Typically, the tearoom encounter involved 3 people: the 2 men actually engaged in the homosexual act and a lookout, called the "watchqueen." Thus, Humphreys began to show up at public rest rooms, offering to serve as watchqueen whenever it seemed appropriate. Because the watchqueen's payoff was the chance to watch the action, Humphreys was able to observe behavior in natural settings, just as he would if he were studying drug dealers or jaywalking.

To round out his understanding of the tearoom trade, Humphreys needed to know something more about the people who participated. Given that the men probably would not have been thrilled about being interviewed by their watchqueen, Humphreys came up with a different solution. Whenever possible, he noted the license plate numbers of participants' cars and tracked down their names and addresses through the police. Humphreys then visited the men at their homes, disguising himself enough to avoid recognition and claiming that he was conducting a survey. In that fashion, he collected the personal information he was unable to get in the rest rooms.

Humphreys' research provoked considerable controversy, both within and outside the social scientific community. Some critics charged Humphreys with a gross invasion of privacy in the name of science: What men did in public rest rooms was their own business and not Humphreys'. Others were concerned about the deceit involved; Humphreys had lied to the participants by leading them to believe he was only a voyeur. People who believed that the tearoom participants, because they were in a public facility, were fair game for observation nonetheless protested the follow-up survey. They argued that it was unethical for Humphreys to trace the participants to their homes and to interview them under false pretenses. Still others justified Humphreys' research. The topic, they said, was worth studying and couldn't be studied any other way. They regarded the deceit as essentially harmless, noting that Humphreys was careful not to harm his subjects by disclosing their tearoom activities.

The tearoom trade controversy has never been resolved. It remains a topic of debate regarding research ethics and probably always will be because it stirs emotions and reveals ethical issues people disagree about. What do you think? Was Humphreys ethical in doing what he did? Are there parts of the research you feel were acceptable and other parts that were not?

PUTTING IT ALL TOGETHER

CONFIDENTIALITY IN POLICE RESEARCH

Studying the link between police action and crime in the nation's largest city presented Rutgers University researchers with a variety of ethical issues. First, they interacted with human subjects, primarily police officers, supervisors, and command staff. Second, the New York project also required access to confidential department records. Third, observing police on patrol placed researchers in contact with crime victims and offenders. Fourth, accompanying patrol and tactical officers in the field, often on weekend nights, exposed researchers to potential harm. Finally, there was the issue of how voluntary participation by police officers really was.

Police as Human Subjects

Studying police officers as they performed official duties raised ethical issues that are somewhat different from those involving private individuals and their everyday lives. On the one hand, researchers simply observed what public servants are paid to do. Police officers and investigators interact with people as part of their daily routine, and much of

these interactions take place in public view. So, in a sense, researchers became not much different from curious bystanders who are naturally drawn to real-life examples of the stuff of television dramas. But field research observing police is different in several respects. First, researchers accompanied police for an extended time, listening in on their conversations with each other and on messages broadcast over the radio. Riding with police or joining them in surveillance activities also revealed candid actions and comments. And researchers witnessed some actions that were inconsistent with department regulations.

Rutgers researchers also observed high-level command conferences that were not open to public scrutiny. This reflected at least the implicit promise to not report candid comments not intended for public disclosure. That promise was made explicit, along with a pledge not to disclose information that could be attributed to an individual without that person's consent.

Confidential Information

Aggregate crime reports in New York are routinely released to newspapers and published on Web pages available to the general public. In addition to aggregate reports, Rutgers researchers examined a host of other documents used in private, if

---

Whatever your opinion, you are sure to find others who disagree with you.

The Stanford Prison Experiment

The second research controversy differs from the first in many ways. Whereas Humphreys' study involved participant observation, this study setting was in the laboratory. And whereas the first study examined a form of human deviance, this one focused on how people behave in formal institutions.

Few people would disagree that prisons are dehumanizing. Inmates forfeit freedom, of course, but their incarceration also results in a loss of privacy and individual identity. Violence

is among the realities of prison life that people point to as evidence of the failure of prisons to rehabilitate inmates.

Although the problems of prisons have many sources, psychologists Curtis Haney, Craig Banks, and Philip Zimbardo (1973) were interested in two general explanations. The first was the dispositional hypothesis—prisons are brutal and dehumanizing because of the types of people who run them and are incarcerated in them. Inmates have demonstrated their disrespect for legal order and their willingness to use deceit and violence; persons who work as prison guards may be disproportionately authoritarian and sadistic. The second was the situational

not secret, planning sessions. Such data were important for establishing the links between police strategy, actions, and changes in crime levels, but it was equally important to respect the confidentiality of the information.

Contacts with the General Public

Accompanying police on patrol means that researchers witness interactions between the police and the public. For the Rutgers staff, most of these were routine, but other interactions involved police and researchers squarely with elements of human tragedy. The identity of persons arrested is routinely available to the public. However, field observers encountered suspects who were not arrested. Police routinely deal with crime victims, and the identity of victims is routinely protected. Even though researchers did not seek information about individual suspects, arrestees, or victims, they were bound to not reveal the identity of people they encountered as a side effect of their interest in police.

Potential Harm to Researchers

Municipal police departments throughout the country allow researchers and other observers to accompany officers on patrol. Many departments encourage this in connection with citizen police academies that are elements of community policing strategies. In virtually all cases, researchers and other observers are required to sign forms waiving the department's responsibility for injury or other harm.

Departments take other steps to reduce the potential for harm to observers. People accompanying police on patrol are expected to remain in the patrol vehicle during incidents unless instructed otherwise by officers. Rutgers researchers were usually asked to wear body armor. And, recognizing the potential for trouble following the trial in February 2000 of police charged with second-degree murder in shooting an unarmed African immigrant, the department suspended all police ride-alongs for several days following the anticipated verdict announcement.

Informed Consent?

Police departments are often described as paramilitary organizations, with strict provisions for command and control. In situations like this, informed consent is a slippery concept. If a supervisor orders officers to host an observer, that doesn't seem much like voluntary consent. Similarly, individual officers may be reluctant to decline participation if they expect that such a decision would raise the proverbial eyebrows of supervisors. So informed consent is, somewhat paradoxically, important in studying police in much the same way as it is in studying prisoners— police and prisoners may be subject to subtle forms of coercion to participate.

hypothesis—the prison environment itself creates brutal, dehumanizing conditions independent of the kinds of people who live and work in the institutions.

Haney and associates set out to test the situational hypothesis by creating a functional prison simulation in which healthy, psychologically normal male college students were assigned to roles as prisoners and guards. The "prison" was constructed in the basement of a psychology department building: three 6-×-9-foot "cells" furnished with only a cot, a prison "yard" in a corridor, and a 2-×-7-foot "solitary confinement cell." Twenty-one subjects were selected from 75 volunteers after screening to eliminate those with physical or psychological problems. Offered $15 per day for their participation, the 21 subjects were randomly assigned to be either guards or prisoners.

All subjects signed contracts that included instructions about prisoner and guard roles for the planned 2-week experiment. "Prisoners" were told that they would be confined and under surveillance throughout the experiment, and their civil rights would be suspended; they were, however, guaranteed that they would not be physically abused.

"Guards" were given minimal instructions, most notably that physical aggression or physical punishment of "prisoners" was prohibited.

Together with a "warden," however, they were generally free to develop prison rules and procedures. The researchers planned to study how both guards and prisoners reacted to their roles, but guards were led to believe that the purpose of the experiment was to study prisoners.

If you had been a prisoner in this experiment, you would have experienced something like the following after signing your contract: First, you would have been arrested without notice at your home by a real police officer, perhaps with neighbors looking on. After being searched and taken to the police station in handcuffs, you would have been booked, fingerprinted, and placed in a police detention facility. Next, you would have been blindfolded and driven to "prison," where you would have been stripped, sprayed with a delousing solution, and left to stand naked for a period of time in the "prison yard." Eventually, you would have been issued a prison uniform (a loose overshirt stamped with your ID number), fitted with an ankle chain, led to your cell, and ordered to remain silent. Your prison term would then have been totally controlled by the guards.

Wearing mirrored sunglasses, khaki uniforms, and badges and carrying nightsticks, guards supervised prisoner work assignments and held lineups three times per day. Although lineups initially lasted only a few minutes, guards later extended them to several hours. Prisoners were fed bland meals and accompanied by guards on three authorized toilet visits per day.

The behavior of all subjects in the prison yard and other open areas was videotaped; audiotapes were made continuously while prisoners were in their cells. Researchers administered brief questionnaires throughout the experiment to assess emotional changes in prisoners and guards. About 4 weeks after the experiment concluded, researchers conducted interviews with all subjects to assess their reactions.

Haney and associates (1973:88) had planned to run the prison experiment for 2 weeks, but they halted the study after 6 days because subjects displayed "unexpectedly intense reactions." Five prisoners had to be released even before that time because they showed signs of acute depression or anxiety.

Subjects in each group accepted their roles all too readily. Prisoners and guards could interact with each other in friendly ways because guards had the power to make prison rules. But interactions turned out to be overwhelmingly hostile and negative. Guards became aggressive, and prisoners became passive. When the experiment ended prematurely, prisoners were happy about their early "parole," but guards were disappointed that the study would not continue.

Haney and colleagues justify the prison simulation study in part by claiming that the dispositional/situational hypotheses could not be evaluated using other research designs. Clearly, the researchers were sensitive to ethical issues. They obtained subjects' consent to the experiment through signed contracts. Prisoners who showed signs of acute distress were released early. The entire study was terminated after less than half of the planned 2 weeks had elapsed when its unexpectedly harsh impact on subjects became evident. Finally, researchers conducted group therapy debriefing sessions with prisoners and guards and maintained follow-up contacts for a year to ensure that subjects' negative experiences were temporary.

Two related features of this experiment raise ethical questions, however. First, subjects were not fully informed of the procedures. Although we have seen that deception, including something less than full disclosure, can often be justified, in this case deception was partially due to the researchers' uncertainty about how the prison simulation would unfold. This relates to the second and more important ethical problem: Guards were granted the power to make up and modify rules as the study progressed, and their behavior became increasingly authoritarian. Comments by guards illustrate their reactions as the experiment unfolded (Haney, Banks, and Zimbardo, 1973:88):

"They [the prisoners] didn't see it as an experiment. It was real and they were fighting to keep their identity. But we were always there to show them just who was boss."

"During the inspection, I went to cell 2 to mess up a bed which the prisoner had made and he grabbed me, screaming that he had just made it. . . . He grabbed my throat, and although he was laughing, I was pretty scared. I lashed out with my stick and hit him in the chin (although not very hard), and when I freed myself I became angry."

"Acting authoritatively can be fun. Power can be a great pleasure."

How do you feel about this experiment? On the one hand, it provided valuable insights into how otherwise normal people react in a simulated prison environment. Subjects appeared to suffer no long-term harm, in part because of precautions taken by researchers. Paul Reynolds (1979:139) found a certain irony in the short-term discomforts endured by the college student subjects: "There is evidence that the major burdens were borne by individuals from advantaged social categories and that the major benefactors would be individuals from less advantaged social categories [actual prisoners], an uneven distribution of costs and benefits that many nevertheless consider equitable." On the other hand, researchers did not anticipate how much and how quickly subjects would accept their roles. The experiment had to be halted prematurely. In discussing their findings, Haney and associates (1973:90) note: "Our results are . . . congruent with those of Milgram* who most convincingly demonstrated the proposition that evil acts are not necessarily the deeds of evil men, but may be attributable to the operation of powerful social forces." This quote illustrates the fundamental

dilemma—balancing the right to conduct research against the rights of subjects. Is it ethical for researchers to create powerful social forces that lead to evil acts?

Discussion Examples

Research ethics, then, is an important and ambiguous topic. The difficulty of resolving ethical issues cannot be an excuse for ignoring them, however. You need to keep ethics in mind as you read other chapters in this book and whenever you plan a research project.

To further sensitize you to the ethical component of criminal justice and other social research, we've prepared brief descriptions of 10 real and hypothetical research situations. Can you see the ethical issue in each? How do you feel about it? Are the procedures described ultimately acceptable or unacceptable? It would be very useful to discuss these examples with other students in your class.

1. A researcher studies speeding on urban expressways by using a small radar gun to detect speeders, while an assistant records the license plate numbers of cars traveling more than 10 miles per hour over the posted limit. The speeders' addresses are traced, and they receive a mailed questionnaire with a cover letter beginning: "You were observed traveling more than 10 miles per hour over the speed limit on [date and location]."

2. Researchers make field observations of social activities as part of a study of police strategies to reduce certain crimes in specified neighborhoods. While making observations during a weekday afternoon, a researcher witnesses a residential burglary. The incident is recorded in field notes but not reported to police.

3. In a federally funded study of a probation program, a researcher discovers that one participant was involved in a murder while on probation. Public disclosure of this incident might threaten the program that the researcher believes, from all evidence,

---

*Here the authors are referring to controversial research on obedience to authority by Lester Milgram (1965).

is beneficial. Judging the murder to be an anomaly, the researcher does not disclose it to federal sponsors or describe it in published reports.

4. As part of a course on domestic violence, a professor requires students to telephone a domestic violence hotline, pretend to be a victim, and request help. Students then write up a description of the assistance offered by hotline staff and turn it in to the professor.

5. Studying aggression in bars and nightclubs, a researcher records observations of a savage fight in which three people are seriously injured. Ignoring pleas for help from one of the victims, the researcher retreats to a rest room to write up notes from these observations.

6. This quote is from a report on crack dealers by Bruce Jacobs (1996: 364–65, n.5):

> I informed police of my research, realizing that I could not withhold information from authorities if they should subpoena it. This never happened, perhaps because I told police that the research was about street life and urbanism rather than about gangs and crack distribution per se. Although technically this was a violation of the law, many other sociologists studying deviant populations have done the same thing to acquire valid observational data. . . . In addition, my university's Human Subject Review committee approved this research because I obtained written informed consent from all respondents and included safeguards to protect their anonymity and confidentiality.

7. In a study of state police, researchers learn that officers have been instructed by superiors to "not sign anything." Fearing that asking officers to sign informed consent statements will sharply reduce participation, researchers seek some other way to satisfy their university IRB. What should they do?

8. While visiting a police department as part of an evaluation of community policing spon-sored by the National Institute of Justice, two researchers accompany a police captain to a local restaurant for lunch. The captain insists on paying. The tab is less than half the listed price of menu items ordered by the captain and the two researchers.

9. A researcher studying juvenile gangs is asked by a federal funding agency not to publish findings indicating that gang members are less often involved in illegal drug sales than are nongang members.

10. In the example mentioned on page 61, the researchers disclosed to public officials that police were not making visits to probationers as called for in the program intervention. Published reports describe the problem as "irregularities in program delivery."

✪ *Main Points*

- In addition to technical and scientific considerations, criminal justice research projects are shaped by ethical considerations.
- What's ethically "right" and "wrong" in research is ultimately a matter of what people agree is right and wrong.
- Researchers tend not to be the best judges of whether their own work adequately addresses ethical issues.
- Most ethical questions involve weighing the possible benefits of research against the potential for harm to research subjects.
- Criminal justice research may generate special ethical questions, including the potential for legal liability and physical harm.
- Scientists agree that participation in research should, in general, be voluntary. This norm, however, can conflict with the scientific need for generalizability.
- Most scientists agree that research should not harm subjects unless they willingly and knowingly accept the risks of harm.
- Anonymity and confidentiality are two ways to protect the privacy of research subjects.
- Compliance with ethical principles is promoted by professional associations and by regulations issued by the Department of Health and Human Services (HHS).
- HHS regulations include special provisions for two types of subjects of particular interest

to criminal justice researchers: prisoners and juveniles.

- Institutional review boards (IRBs) play an important role in ensuring that the rights and interests of human subjects are protected. But some social science researchers believe that IRBs are becoming too restrictive.

❂ Key Terms

Anonymity   Confidentiality

❂ Review Questions and Exercises

1. Obtain a copy of the Academy of Criminal Justice Sciences' (2000) code of ethics at this Web site: http://www.acjs.org. Read the document carefully. How would the code apply to Laud Humphreys' tearoom research? What about the prison simulation?
2. Discuss the general trade-offs between the requirements of sound scientific research methods and the need to protect human subjects. Where do tensions exist? Cite illustrations of tensions from two or more examples of ethical issues presented in this chapter.
3. Review the box "Ethics and Juvenile Gang Members," noting that Decker and Van Winkle developed an informed consent form for their subjects. Try your hand at preparing such a form, keeping in mind the various ethical principles discussed in this chapter.

❂ Internet Exercises

To ensure that you always have access to live, correct Web links for the Web sites referenced in the following exercises, we provide the necessary links on the companion Web site for *Research Methods for Criminal Justice and Criminology* at http://cj.wadsworth.com/maxfield_babbie/research_methods4e. Once at the companion Web site, select this specific chapter, click on "Chapter Resources," then click on "Web Links."

1. Visit the Web site for the journal *Negative Observations in Genetic Oncology*. Read the "Welcome to NOGO" page from the journal's editor, and browse through a couple of articles. Then present a brief argument in favor of establishing a similar journal dedicated to publishing negative findings—research in which no relationships were found—in criminal justice.
2. The Office for Human Research Protection (OHRP) in the U.S. Department of Health and

Human Services sets standards that provide a basis for university institutional review boards. These guidelines cover a wide array of research situations, but there are specific guidelines for research involving prisoners. Visit the OHRP Web site and click on "Search OHRP" to locate information that addresses research with prisoners. List the primary requirements and safeguards that are mentioned.
3. In the 1970s, the Stanford Prison Experiment was terminated early because of the impact of the experimental situation on the participants. Visit the Stanford University Prison Experiment Web site for an overview of the study and its findings and a discussion of some of the ethical concerns. After reading the information in this site, what do you think of the ethical issues involved? Use the subheadings under "Ethical Issues in Criminal Justice Research" to guide your analysis.
4. Find information about the institutional review board at your college or university or about an IRB at some other institution. Search for terms like "IBR" and "human subjects." Find out what kinds of people serve on the IBR. Summarize procedures for reviewing research proposals.

❂ InfoTrac College Edition

The principles of informed consent vary somewhat when so-called vulnerable populations are involved. These populations include children, prisoners, and the mentally or physically ill. Search InfoTrac College Edition and locate an article that illustrates some of the complexities involved in gaining informed consent from vulnerable populations.

❂ The NEW Companion Web Site for Research Methods for Criminal Justice and Criminology, *Fourth Edition*

http://cj.wadsworth.com/maxfield_babbie/research_methods4e

Supplement your review of this chapter by going to the new companion Web site to take one of the Tutorial Quizzes, use the flash cards to master key terms, and check out the many other study aids you'll find there. You'll also find special features such as quantitative and qualitative data analysis primers to help you with a special project or do some research on your own.

✪ *Additional Readings*

American Association of University Professors, *Protecting Human Beings: Institutional Review Boards and Social Science Research* (Washington, DC: American Association of University Professors/Redbook, 2001) (http://www.aaup.org/statements/Redbook/repirb.htm; accessed 24 January 2003). Largely in response to concern about overly restrictive institutional review boards, the AAUP convened a series of meetings with representatives from major social science professional groups; this report summarizes the discussion. The most interesting sections address the expansion of human subjects' protections in social science and even historical research.

Committee on Science, Engineering, and Public Policy, *On Being a Scientist: Responsible Conduct in Research*, 2nd ed. (Washington, DC: National Academy Press, 1995). This monograph covers a range of issues, including research fraud and other misconduct by researchers. Although many of the issues are specific to the natural sciences, criminologists will find much valuable material.

Homan, Roger, *The Ethics of Social Research* (New York: Longman, 1991). This book provides a thoughtful analysis of ethical issues in social science research.

Inciardi, James A., "Some Considerations on the Methods, Dangers, and Ethics of Crack-House Research," Appendix A in James A. Inciardi, Dorothy Lockwood, and Anne E. Pettieger, *Women and Crack Cocaine* (New York: Macmillan, 1993), pp. 147–57. In this thoughtful essay, Inciardi describes the dangers and depressing realities of field research in a crack house. Should a field researcher intervene when witnessing a gang rape in a crack house? Read this selection for Inciardi's answer.

Kalichman, Seth C., *Mandated Reporting of Suspected Child Abuse: Ethics, Law, and Policy,* 2nd ed. (Washington, DC: American Psychological Association, 2000). This report presents an extensive discussion of legal and ethical issues in conducting research on child abuse.

Sieber, Joan E., *Summary of Human Subjects Protection Issues Related to Large Sample Surveys* (Washington, DC: U.S. Department of Justice, Office of Justice Programs, Bureau of Justice Statistics, 2001). The Bureau of Justice Statistics administers the National Crime Victimization Survey, in which almost 100,000 subjects are interviewed every 6 months. Sieber's report discusses how such large surveys should address a variety of ethical issues, including privacy, information that interviewers are required to report to appropriate authorities, special populations, and special topics in connection with informed consent.

Part Two

Structuring Criminal Justice Inquiry

Posing questions properly is often more difficult than answering them. Indeed, a properly phrased question often seems to answer itself. We sometimes discover the answer to a question in the very process of clarifying the question for someone else.

At base, scientific research is a process for achieving generalized understanding through observation. Part Three of this book will describe some of the specific methods of observation for criminal justice research. But first, Part Two deals with the posing of proper questions, the structuring of inquiry.

Chapter 4 addresses some of the fundamental issues that must be considered in planning a research project. It examines questions of causation, the units of analysis in a research project, the important role of time, and the kinds of things we must consider in proposing to do research projects.

Chapter 5 deals with the specification of what it is we want to study—a process known as conceptualization—and the measurement of the concepts we specify. We'll look at some of the terms that we use casually in everyday life, and we'll see how essential it is to be clear about what we really mean by such terms when we do research. Once we are clear on what we mean when we use certain terms, we are in a position to create measurements of what those terms refer to. The process of devising steps or operations for measuring what we want to study is known as operationalization.

Chapter 6 focuses on a specific, difficult, but important measurement problem: measuring crime. We'll see many different approaches to conceptualization and operationalization and discuss the strengths and weaknesses of each in measuring crime. In doing so, we'll refer to standards of measurement quality described in Chapter 5.

Chapter 7 concentrates on the general design of a criminal justice research project. A criminal justice research design specifies a strategy for finding out something, for structuring a research project. Chapter 7 describes commonly used strategies for experimental and quasi-experimental research. Each is adapted in some way from the classical scientific experiment.

Chapter 4

General Issues in Research Design

Here, we'll examine some fundamental principles about conducting empirical research: causation, and variations on who or what is to be studied, when and how. We'll also take a broad overview of the research process.

(continued)

Introduction

Causation, units, and time are key elements in planning a research study.

Science is an enterprise dedicated to "finding out." No matter what we want to find out, though, there are likely to be a great many ways of doing so. Topics examined in this chapter address how to plan scientific inquiry—how to design a strategy for finding out something. Often, criminal justice researchers want to find out something that involves questions of cause and effect. They may want to find out more about things that make crime more likely to occur or about policies that they hope will reduce crime in some way.

Let's say you are interested in studying corruption in government. That's certainly a worthy and appropriate topic for criminal justice research. But what specifically are you interested in? What do you mean by "corruption"? What kinds of behavior do you have in mind? And

what do you mean by "government"? Whom do you want to study: All public employees? Only sworn police officers? Civilian employees? Elected officials? What is your purpose? Do you want to find out how much corruption there is? Do you want to learn why corruption exists? These are the kinds of questions that need to be answered in research design.

In practice, all aspects of research design are interrelated. They are separated here and in subsequent chapters so that we can explore particular topics in detail. We start with a discussion of causation in social science, the foundation of explanatory research. We then examine units of analysis—the what or whom to study. Deciding on units of analysis is an important part of all research, partly because people sometimes inappropriately use data measuring one type of unit to say something about a different type of unit.

Next, we consider alternative ways of handling time in criminal justice research. It is sometimes appropriate to examine a static cross section of social life, but other studies follow social processes over time. In this regard, researchers must consider the time order of events and processes in making statements about cause.

We then provide a brief overview of the whole research process. This serves two purposes: (1) It provides a map to the remainder of this book, and (2) it conveys a sense of how researchers go about designing a study.

The chapter concludes with guidelines for preparing a research proposal. Often, the actual conduct of research needs to be preceded by a detailed plan of our intentions—perhaps to obtain funding for a major project or to get an instructor's approval for a class assignment. We'll see that preparing a research proposal offers an excellent way to ensure that we have considered all aspects of our research in advance.

Causation in the Social Sciences

Causation is the focus of explanatory research.

Cause and effect are implicit in much of what we have examined so far. One of the chief goals of social science researchers is to explain why things are the way they are. Typically, we do that by specifying the causes for the way things are: Some things are caused by other things.

The general notion of causation is both simple and complex. On the one hand, we could have ignored the issue altogether. We could simply plug in the terms *cause* and *effect* and have little difficulty understanding them. On the other hand, an adequate discourse on causation would require a whole book or even a series of books. We decided to adopt a middle ground, providing more than a commonsense perspective on causation but not attempting to be definitive.

Much of our discussion in this section describes issues of causation and validity for social science in general. Recall from Chapters 1 and 2

that criminal justice research and theory are most strongly rooted in the social sciences. Furthermore, social science research methods are adapted from those used in the physical sciences. Many important and difficult questions about causality and validity occupy researchers in criminal justice, but our basic approach requires stepping back a bit to consider the larger picture of how we can or cannot assert that some cause actually produces some effect.

At the outset, it's important to keep in mind that cause in social science is inherently **probabilistic,** a point we introduced in Chapter 1. We say, for example, that certain factors make delinquency more or less *likely* within groups of people. Thus, teenagers with weak family bonds are *more likely* to commit delinquent acts than teenagers with strong family bonds (Elliott, Huizinga, and Ageton, 1985). Recidivism is *less likely* among offenders who receive more careful assessment and classification at institutional intake (Cullen and Gendreau, 2000).

Criteria for Causality

We begin our consideration of cause by examining what criteria must be satisfied before we can infer that something causes something else. Recall the discussion of idiographic and nomothetic modes of explanation in Chapter 1. Joseph Maxwell (1996:87–88) writes that criteria for assessing an idiographic explanation are (1) how credible and believable it is and (2) whether alternative explanations ("rival hypotheses") were seriously considered and found wanting. The first criterion relates to logic as one of the foundations of science. We demand that our explanations make sense, even if the logic is sometimes complex. The second criterion reminds us of Sherlock Holmes' dictum that when all other possibilities have been eliminated the remaining explanation, however improbable, must be the truth.

Regarding nomothetic explanation, we examine three specific criteria for causality, as described by Thomas Cook and Donald Campbell

(1979). The first requirement in a causal relationship between two variables is that the cause precede the effect in time. It makes no sense to imagine something being caused by something else that happened later on. A bullet leaving the muzzle of a gun does not cause the gunpowder to explode; it works the other way around.

As simple and obvious as this criterion may seem, criminal justice research suffers many problems in this regard. Often, the time order connecting two variables is simply unclear. Which comes first: drug use or crime? And even when the time order seems clear, exceptions may be found. For example, we normally assume that obtaining a master's degree in management is a cause of more rapid advancement in a state department of corrections. Yet corrections executives might pursue graduate education after they have been promoted and recognize that advanced training in management skills will help them do their job better.

The second requirement in a causal relationship is that the two variables be empirically correlated with each other—they must occur together. It makes no sense to say that exploding gunpowder causes a bullet to leave the muzzle of a gun if, in observed reality, a bullet does not come out after the gunpowder explodes.

Again, criminal justice research has difficulties with this requirement. In the probabilistic world of nomothetic models of explanation, at least, we encounter few perfect correlations. Most judges sentence repeat drug dealers to prison, but some don't. We are forced to ask, therefore, how strong the empirical relationship must be for that relationship to be considered causal.

The third requirement for a causal relationship is that the observed empirical correlation between two variables cannot be explained away as being due to the influence of some third variable that causes both of them. For example, we may observe that drug markets are often found near bus stops, but this does not mean that bus stops encourage drug markets. A third variable is at work here: Groups of people naturally congregate in reasonably close proximity at bus stops, and street drug markets are often found where people naturally congregate.

To sum up, most social researchers consider two variables to be causally related—one causes the other—if (1) the cause precedes the effect in time, (2) there is an empirical correlation between them, and (3) the relationship is not found to result from the effects of some third variable on each of the two initially observed. Any relationship that satisfies all these criteria is causal, and these are the only criteria.

Necessary and Sufficient Causes

Recognizing that virtually all causal relationships in criminal justice are probabilistic is central to understanding other points about cause. Within the probabilistic model, it is useful to distinguish two types of causes: necessary and sufficient causes. A *necessary* cause is a condition that, by and large, must be present for the effect to follow. For example, it is necessary for someone to be charged with a criminal offense in order to be convicted, but being charged is not enough; you must plead guilty or be found guilty by the court. Figure 4.1A illustrates that relationship.

A *sufficient* cause, in contrast, is a condition that more or less guarantees the effect in question. Thus, for example, pleading guilty to some criminal charge is a sufficient cause for being convicted, although you could be convicted through a trial as well. Figure 4.1B illustrates this state of affairs.

The discovery of a necessary and sufficient cause is the most satisfying outcome in research. If we are studying juvenile delinquency, we want to discover a single condition that (1) has to be present for delinquency to develop and (2) always results in delinquency. Then we will surely feel that we know precisely what causes juvenile delinquency. Unfortunately, we seldom discover causes that are both necessary and sufficient, nor, in practice, are causes 100 percent

Figure 4.1A   Necessary Cause

Figure 4.1B   Sufficient Cause

necessary or 100 percent sufficient. Most causal relationships that criminal justice researchers work with are probabilistic and partial—we are able to partly explain cause and effect in some percentage of cases we observe.

Molar and Micromediational Causal Statements

Natural scientists and engineers are often interested in making very specific, detailed statements about cause. For example, most of us vaguely understand that lamps come on when switches are flipped because electricity is doing something through plugs and wires. A physicist understands the process differently: Moving a switch closes a circuit that allows electrons to move through a conductor to the element of an incandescent lamp, which glows because electrical resistance slows the flow of electrons and produces heat; this all happens very fast.

Cook and Campbell (1979) referred to such detailed specifications of cause as "micromediational" causal statements. A physicist's explanation of why a light comes on is a micromediational statement about cause. However, most of us get along just fine in life without understanding the micromediational details of excitable electrons, resistance, and heat. We have what Cook and Campbell called a "molar" understanding of the process: Flipping a switch causes a light to come on.

In criminal justice and other social science research, molar statements about cause can be meaningful even when micromediational details are not known. For example, police officers know that consuming large quantities of alcohol inhibits the ability of people to operate motor vehicles safely. They do not have to know the micromediational details of physiology and neurochemical reactions. Corrections officials understand that crowded conditions in prisons cause inmate dissatisfaction and possibly violence, but they cannot specify a micromediational process explaining why this is so.

Molar statements about cause and effect can be just as useful as micromediational statements. For example, if your car will not start on some cold, damp morning, a mechanic's molar explanation—"bad distributor cap"—will be more useful to you than a physicist's micromediational explanation: "An internal combustion engine is based on several principles of thermodynamics and electromechanical resistance. . . ."

Social science research can therefore productively investigate molar questions about cause. This is, of course, consistent with our probabilistic approach. Our statements about cause-and-effect relationships normally describe tendencies rather than infallible laws, and we can propose useful molar statements even when we cannot specify micromediation.

Validity and Causal Inference

Scientists assess the truth of statements about cause by considering threats to validity.

Paying careful attention to cause-and-effect relationships is crucial in criminal justice research. Cause and effect are also key elements of applied studies, in which a researcher may be interested in whether, for example, a new manda-tory sentencing law actually causes an increase in the prison population.

When we are concerned with whether we are correct in inferring that a cause produced some effect, we are concerned with the **validity** of causal inference. In the words of Cook and Campbell (1979:37), validity is "the best available approximation to the truth or falsity of propositions, including propositions about cause." They emphasize that *approximation* is an important word because one can never be absolutely certain about cause.

Our next concern is a number of different **validity threats** in causal inference—reasons we might be incorrect in stating that some cause produced some effect. As Maxwell (1996:87–88) puts it: "The key concept for validity is thus the validity *threat:* a way you might be wrong" (emphasis in original). Here, we will summarize the threats to four general categories of validity: statistical conclusion validity, internal validity, construct validity, and external validity. Chapter 7 discusses each type in more detail, linking the issue of validity to different ways of designing research.

Statistical Conclusion Validity

Statistical conclusion validity refers to our ability to determine whether a change in the suspected cause is statistically associated with a change in the suspected effect. This corresponds with one of the first questions asked by researchers: Are two variables related to each other? For example, if we suspect that using illegal drugs causes people to commit crimes, one of the first things we will be interested in is the common variation between drug use and crime. If drug users and nonusers commit equal rates of crime, and if about the same proportions of criminals and noncriminals use drugs, there will be no statistical relationship between measures of drug use and criminal offending. That seems to be the end of our investigation of the causal relationship between drugs and crime.

Basing conclusions on a small number of cases is a common threat to statistical conclusion validity. For example, suppose a researcher studies 10 drug users and 10 nonusers and compares the numbers of times these subjects are arrested for other crimes over a 6-month period. The researcher might find that the 10 users were arrested an average of three times while nonusers averaged two arrests in 6 months. There is a difference in arrest rates, but is it a significant difference? Statistically, the answer is no because so few drug users were included in the study. Researchers cannot have much confidence in statements about cause if their findings are based on a small number of cases.

Threats to statistical conclusion validity might also have the opposite effect of suggesting that covariation is present when, in fact, there is no cause-and-effect relationship. The reasons for this are again somewhat technical and require a basic understanding of statistical inference. However, some of the superstitious behavior exhibited by gamblers provides a rough-and-ready example.

Let's say you like to play the state lottery; nothing serious, you simply buy a couple of tickets each week. Many people play a system whereby they pick numbers that correspond to their date of birth or their license plate number. Expecting these lucky numbers to influence your chances of winning the lottery is an example of failing to recognize that winning numbers are picked by a random process. If you always pick your favorite uncle's birthday—say, July 7, 1977 (7777)—and buy two tickets per week for 5 years, your lucky number might come up simply by chance in the random system used to pick winning numbers. But there is no statistical conclusion validity to the inference that consistently picking your birthday will cause you to win the lottery. Your winning will be due to the random effects of how numbers are selected.

Internal Validity

Internal validity threats challenge causal statements that are based on some observed relationship. An observed association between two variables has internal validity if the relationship is, in fact, causal and not due to the effects of one or more other variables. Whereas statistical conclusion threats are most often due to random error, internal validity problems result from nonrandom or systematic error. Simply put, threats to the internal validity of a proposed causal relationship between two indicators usually arise from the effects of one or more other variables. Notice how this validity threat relates to the third requirement for establishing a causal relationship: eliminating other possible explanations for the observed relationship.

If, for example, we observe that convicted drug users sentenced to probation are rearrested less often than drug users sentenced to prison, we might be tempted to infer that prison sentences cause recidivism. Although being in prison might have some impact on whether someone commits more crimes in the future, in this case it is important to look for other causes of recidivism. One likely candidate is prior criminal record. Convicted drug users without prior criminal records are more likely to be sentenced to probation, whereas persons with previous convictions more often receive prison terms. Research on criminal careers has found that the probability of reoffending increases with the number of prior arrests and convictions (Chaiken and Chaiken, 1982). In this case, a third variable—prior convictions—may explain some or all of the observed tendency of prison sentences to be associated with recidivism. Prior convictions are associated with both sentence—prison or probation—and subsequent convictions.

Construct Validity

This type of validity is concerned with how well an observed relationship between variables represents the underlying causal process of interest. In a sense, **construct validity** refers to generalizing from what we observe and measure to the real-world things in which we are interested. The concept of construct validity is thus closely related to issues in measurement.

To illustrate construct validity, we adapt an example from Cook and Campbell (1979) on the concept of supervision. They described how a researcher might study the effects of supervision on factory workers, where supervision is defined as standing within speaking distance and watching the work of a machinist. Let's consider the supervision of police officers — specifically, whether close supervision causes police officers to write more traffic tickets. We might define "close supervision" in this way: A police sergeant drives his own marked police car in such a way as to always keep a patrol car in view.

This certainly qualifies as close supervision, but you may recognize a couple of problems. First, two marked patrol cars present a highly visible presence to motorists, who might drive more prudently and thus reduce the opportunities for patrol officers to write traffic tickets. Second, and more central to the issue of construct validity, this represents a narrow definition of the construct "close supervision." Patrol officers may be closely supervised in other ways that cause them to write more traffic tickets. For example, sergeants might closely supervise their officers by reviewing their ticket production at the end of each shift. Supervising subordinates by keeping them in view is only one way of exercising control over their behavior. It may be appropriate for factory workers, but it is not practical for police, representing a very limited version of the construct "supervision."

The well-known Kansas City Preventive Patrol Experiment, discussed in Chapter 1, provides another example of construct validity problems. Recall that the experiment sought to determine whether routine preventive patrol caused reductions in crime and fear of crime and increases in arrests. This causal proposition was tested by comparing measures of crime, fear, and arrests in proactive beats (with twice the normal level of preventive patrol), reactive beats (with no preventive patrol), and control beats (with normal levels of preventive patrol). Researchers found no significant differences in levels of crime, fear, and arrests.

Richard Larson (1975) discussed several difficulties with the experiment's design. One important problem relates to the visibility of police presence, a central concept in preventive patrol. It is safe to assume that the ability of routine patrol to prevent crime and enhance feelings of safety depends crucially on the visibility of police. It makes sense to assume further that withdrawing preventive patrol, as was done in the reactive beats, reduces the visibility of police. But by how much? Larson explored this question in detail and suggested that two other features of police operations during the Kansas City experiment partially compensated for the absence of preventive patrol and produced a visible police presence.

First, the different types of experimental beats were adjacent to one another; one reactive beat shared borders with three control and three proactive beats. This enhanced the visibility of police in reactive beats in two ways: (1) Police in adjoining proactive and control beats sometimes drove around the perimeter of reactive beats, and (2) police often drove through reactive beats on their way to some other part of the city.

Second, many Kansas City police officers were skeptical about the experiment and feared that withdrawing preventive patrol in reactive beats would create problems. Partly as a result, police who responded to calls for service in the reactive areas more frequently used lights and sirens when driving to the location of complaints. A related action was that police units not assigned to the calls for service nevertheless drove into the reactive beats to provide backup service.

Each of these actions produced a visible police presence in the reactive beats. People who lived in these areas were unaware of the experiment and, as you might expect, did not know whether a police car happened to be present because it was on routine patrol, was on its way to some other part of the city, or was responding to a call for assistance. And, of course, the use of lights and sirens makes police cars much more visible.

Larson's point was that the *construct* of police visibility is only partly represented by routine preventive patrol. A visible police presence was produced in Kansas City through other means. Therefore, the researchers' conclusion that routine preventive patrol does not cause a reduction in crime or an increase in arrests suffers from threats to construct validity. Construct validity is a frequent problem in applied studies, in which researchers may oversimplify complex policies and policy goals.

External Validity

Do findings about preventive patrol in Kansas City apply to preventive patrol in, say, San Francisco? Are community crime prevention organizations successful in combating drug use throughout a city, or do they work best in areas with only minor drug problems? Electronic monitoring may be suitable as an alternative sentence for convicted offenders, but can it work as an alternative to jail for defendants awaiting trial? Such questions are examples of issues in **external validity:** Do research findings about cause and effect apply equally to different cities, neighborhoods, and populations?

In a general sense, external validity is concerned with whether research findings from one study can be reproduced in another study, often under different conditions. Because crime problems and criminal justice responses can vary so much from city to city or from state to state, researchers and public officials are often especially interested in external validity. For example, in their evaluation of programs to reduce the fear of crime, Anthony Pate and associates (Pate, Wycoff, Skogan, and Sherman, 1986) conducted experiments in two very different cities—Houston, Texas, and Newark, New Jersey. Houston is physically large and sprawling, reflecting sustained economic and population growth through the 1980s. In contrast, Newark is an older, more densely populated city that had fallen on hard economic times. Pate and associates took account of the physical, social, and economic differences between the two cities in developing specific experimental actions to reduce the fear of crime, thus enhancing the external validity of their study.

The researchers found that certain fear reduction policies had varying effects. For example, neighborhood police storefront offices and foot patrol in Houston had beneficial effects among white residents and homeowners, but these programs had no impact on fear among renters and African American residents (Wycoff, Skogan, Pate, and Sherman, 1985a, 1985b). The extent to which a program intervention caused a desired effect varied across program targets, thus limiting the external validity of certain fear reduction policies.

Validity and Causal Inference Summarized

The four types of validity threats can be grouped into two categories: bias and generalizability. Internal and statistical conclusion validity threats are related to systematic and nonsystematic bias, respectively. Problems with statistical procedures produce nonsystematic bias, while an alternative explanation for an observed relationship is an example of systematic bias. In either case, bias calls into question the inference that some cause produced some effect. Failing to consider the more general cause-and-effect constructs that operate in an observed cause-and-effect relationship results in research findings that cannot be generalized to real-world behaviors and conditions. And a cause-and-effect relationship observed in one setting or at one time may not operate in the same way in a different setting or at a different time.

Cook and Campbell (1979:39) summarized their discussion of these four validity threats by linking them to the types of questions that researchers ask in trying to establish cause and effect. Test your understanding by writing the name of each validity threat after the appropriate question from Cook and Campbell.

1. Is there a relationship between two variables? _____
2. Given that there is a relationship, is it plausibly causal from one operational variable (cause) to the other (effect), or would the

same relationship have been obtained in the absence of any treatment of any kind? _____

3. Given that the relationship is plausibly causal and is reasonably known to be from one variable to another, what particular cause-and-effect constructs are involved in the relationship? _____
4. Given that there is probably a causal relationship from construct A to construct B, how generalizable is this relationship across persons, settings, and times? _____

Does Drug Use Cause Crime?

As a way of illustrating issues of validity and causal inference, we will consider the relationship between drug use and crime. Drug addiction is thought to cause people who are desperate for a fix and unable to secure legitimate income to commit crimes in order to support their habit. In recent decades, researchers with both popular culture and criminal justice policy orientations have explored this issue.

Discussing the validity of causal statements about drug use and crime requires carefully specifying two key concepts—drug use and crime—and considering the different ways these concepts might be related. Jan and Marcia Chaiken (1990) provide unusually careful and well-reasoned insights that will guide our consideration of links between drugs and crime. Let's begin with issues in basic research on the drugs–crime connection and then discuss the implications of this research for criminal justice policy.

First is the question of temporal order: Which comes first, drug use or crime? Research summarized by Chaiken and Chaiken provides no conclusive answer. In an earlier study of prison inmates, Chaiken and Chaiken (1982) found that 12 percent of their adult subjects committed crimes *after* using drugs for at least 2 years, while 15 percent committed predatory crimes 2 or more years *before* using drugs.

Studies of juveniles revealed similar findings: "About 50 percent of delinquent youngsters are delinquent before they start using drugs; about

50 percent start concurrently or after" (Chaiken and Chaiken, 1990:235; based on data from Elliott and Huizinga, 1984).

Many studies have found that some drug users commit crimes and that some criminals use drugs, but Chaiken and Chaiken (1990: 234) conclude that "drug use and crime participation are weakly related as contemporaneous products of factors generally antithetical to traditional United States lifestyles." Stated somewhat differently, drug use and crime (as well as delinquency) are each deviant activities produced by other underlying causes. A statistical association between drug use and crime clearly exists. But the presence of other factors indicates that the relationship is not directly causal, thus bringing into question the internal validity of causal statements about drug use and crime.

To assess the construct validity of research on drugs and crime, let's think for a moment about different patterns of each behavior, rather than assume that drug use and crime are uniform behaviors. Many adolescents in the United States experiment with drugs, just as many—especially males—commit delinquent acts or petty crimes. A large number of adults may be occasional users of illegal drugs as well. Many different patterns of drug use, delinquency, and adult criminality can be found. Because there is no simple way to describe either construct, searching for a single cause-and-effect relationship misrepresents a complex causal process.

Both construct and external validity are concerned with generalizations. Problems with the external validity of research on drugs and crime are similar to those revolving around construct validity. The relationship between occasional marijuana use and delinquency among teenagers is different from that between occasional cocaine use and adult crime; each relationship, in turn, varies from that between heroin addiction and persistent criminal behavior among adults.

The issue of external validity comes into sharper focus when we shift from basic research that seeks to uncover fundamental causal relationships to criminal justice policy. Chaiken

PUTTING IT ALL TOGETHER

CAUSATION AND DECLINING CRIME IN NEW YORK CITY

Did changes in police strategy and tactics in New York City cause a decline in crime? That question is central to what became quite a spirited debate, a debate that centers our attention on causation. In fact, former Police Commissioner William Bratton (1999:17) used language strikingly similar to what you will find in this chapter to argue that crime dropped in New York because of police action:

> As a basic tenet of epistemology . . . we cannot conclude that a causal relationship exists between two variables unless . . . three necessary conditions occur: one variable must precede the other in time, an empirically measured relationship must be demonstrated between the variables, and the relationship must not be better explained by any third intervening variable. Although contemporary criminology's explanations for the decline in New York City meet the first two conditions, they don't explain it better than a third intervening variable.

With these words, Bratton challenged researchers to propose some empirical measure of a variable that better accounted for the crime reduction. A number of researchers have advanced alternative explanations. Let's now consider what some of those variables might be.

Changing Drug Markets

After falling from 1980 through 1984, homicide rates in larger U.S. cities rose sharply through the early 1990s. This corresponded with the emergence of crack cocaine, a low-cost drug sold by loosely organized gangs that settled business disputes with guns instead of lawyers. The decline in crack use in the mid-1990s corresponded with the beginning of decreasing homicide rates. Alfred Blumstein and Richard Rosenfeld (1998) point to changes in crack markets as a plausible explanation—gun homicides and crack markets both increased and decreased together. Other researchers claim changes in crack markets had some effect on violence (Johnson, Golub, and Dunlap, 2000; Karmen, 2000).

Regression

One threat to internal validity is regression to the mean. This refers to a phenomenon whereby social indicators move up and down over time, and abnormally high or low values are eventually followed by a return (regression) to more normal levels. Jeffrey Fagan and associates (Fagan, Zimring, and Kim, 1998) present evidence to suggest that rates of gun homicide in New York were relatively stable from 1969 through the mid-1980s, when they began to increase sharply. Around 1991, rates began to decline, returning to approximate previous levels.

Homicides Declined Everywhere

Fagan and associates (1998) point out that although New York's decline was considerable it was not unprecedented. Many large cities saw

and Chaiken argue that any uniform policy to reduce the use of all drugs among all population groups will have little effect on serious crime.

Basic and applied research on the relationships among drug use and crime readily illustrates threats to the validity of causal inference. It is often difficult to find a relationship because there is so much variation in drug use and crime

participation (statistical conclusion validity threat). A large number of studies have demonstrated that, when statistical relationships are found, both drug use and crime can be attributed to other, often multiple, causes (internal validity threat). Different patterns among different population groups mean that there are no readily identifiable cause-and-effect constructs (construct validity). Because of these dif-

sharp reductions in homicide during the same period, and a few cities had even greater declines. Blumstein and Rosenfeld (1998) cite similar data, pointing out that sharp reductions in homicide rates occurred in cities where no major changes in policing were evident. This suggests that declining crime in New York was simply part of a national trend.

Incapacitation

Homicide declines in the 1990s followed more than a decade of growing rates of incarceration in state and federal correctional facilities. According to the incapacitation argument, rates of homicide and other violent crimes declined because growing numbers of violent criminals were locked up. Some researchers have presented evidence to challenge that claim (Rosenfeld, 2000; Spelman, 2000).

Economic Opportunity

The early 1990s marked the beginning of a sustained period of economic growth in the United States. With greater job opportunities, crime naturally declined. A number of authors have cited this example of how change in one of the "root causes" of crime might have caused changes in rates of homicide and other serious crimes (for example, Karmen, 2000; Silverman, 1999), but none have offered any evidence to support it.

Demographic Change

Because violent and other offenses tend to be committed more by younger people, especially young males, a decline in the number of members in those demographic groups may be responsible

for New York's reduced crime rate. Fagan and associates (1998) present data that show relatively stable numbers of 15- to 19-year-old males in New York, so it seems unlikely that demographic factors account for changes in crime rates. Additional analysis of demographic change has been conducted by Rosenfeld (2000) and James Alan Fox (2000).

Continuation of a Trend

George Kelling and William Bratton (1998) claim that crime declined in New York immediately following the implementation of major changes in policing. But other analysts argue that the beginning of the shift preceded Bratton's changes. Notice that this brings into question another of the three criteria for inferring cause by claiming that the effect—declining crime—occurred *before* the cause—changes in policing. Even more possible explanations have been offered, but those presented here are the most plausible and are most often cited by researchers. Andrew Karmen (2000:263) offers a good summary of different explanations for New York's crime drop.

In our brief summary, we have hinted at some of the ways researchers test for alternative causal explanations. As we work through subsequent chapters in this book, it will be very useful for you to think more systematically about how to test alternative causes. What sorts of measures and data might be needed, and how might they be obtained? What about external validity? If, as Bratton and others claim, New York's decline in crime was due to changes in policing, how might that be tested in other cities? Notice that this is a question of external validity, rather than the internal validity described here.

---

ferences, policies developed to counter drug use among the population as a whole cannot be expected to have much of an impact on serious crime (external validity).

None of the above is to say that there is no cause-and-effect relationship between drug use and crime. However, Chaiken and Chaiken have clearly shown that there is no simple causal connection. See also how questions of cause

and effect emerge in the box, "Causation and Declining Crime in New York City."

Introducing Scientific Realism

In our final consideration of cause and effect in this chapter, we revisit the distinction between idiographic and nomothetic ways of explanation. Doing research to find what causes what most often reflects nomothetic concerns. We wish to find causal explanations that apply generally to situations beyond those we actually study in our research. At the same time, researchers and public officials are often interested in understanding specific causal mechanisms in more narrowly defined situations—what we have described as the idiographic mode of explanation.

Scientific realism bridges idiographic and nomothetic approaches to explanation by seeking to understand how causal *mechanisms* operate in specific *contexts*. Traditional approaches to finding cause and effect usually try to isolate causal mechanisms from other possible influences, something you should now recognize as trying to control threats to internal validity. The scientific realist approach views these other possible influences as contexts in which causal mechanisms operate. Rather than try to exclude or otherwise control possible outside influences, scientific realism studies how such influences are involved in cause-and-effect relationships.

For example, earlier in this chapter, we noted that electronic monitoring as a condition of probation might apply to some populations but not others. We framed this as a question of external validity in the traditional way of considering nomothetic causation. A scientific realist approach would consider the causal mechanism underlying electronic monitoring to be effective in some contexts but not in others. As another example, we reviewed at some length the cause-and-effect conundrum surrounding drug use and crime. That review was framed by traditional nomothetic research to establish cause and effect. A scientific realism approach to the question would recognize that drug use and crime co-occur in some contexts but not in others.

We say that scientific realism bridges idiographic and nomothetic modes of explanation because it exhibits elements of both. Because it focuses our attention on very specific questions, scientific realism seems idiographic: "Will redesigning the Interstate 78 exit in Newark, New Jersey, cause a reduction in suburban residents seeking to buy heroin in this neighborhood?" But this approach is compatible with more general questions of causation: "Can the design of streets and intersections be modified to make it more difficult for street drug markets to operate?" Changing an expressway exit ramp to reduce drug sales in Newark is a specific example of cause and effect that is rooted in the more general causal relationship between traffic patterns and drug markets.

These illustrations of the scientific realist approach to cause and effect are examples of research for the purpose of application, a topic treated at length by British researchers Ray Pawson and Nick Tilley (1997). Application is a type of explanatory research as we indicated in Chapter 1. In later chapters, we call on scientific realism as a strategy for designing explanatory research (Chapter 7) and conducting evaluations (Chapter 12).

Sorting out causes and effects is one of the most difficult challenges of explanatory research. Our attention now turns to two other important considerations that emerge in research for explanation and other purposes: units of analysis and the time dimension.

Units of Analysis

To avoid mistaken inferences, researchers must carefully specify the people or phenomena that will be studied.

In criminal justice research, there is a great deal of variation in what or who is studied—what are technically called **units of analysis.** Individual people are often units of analysis. Researchers may make observations describing certain characteristics of offenders or crime victims, such as age, gender, or race. The descriptions of many individuals are then combined to provide a picture of the population that comprises those individuals.

For example, we may note the age and gender of persons convicted of drunk driving in Fort Lauderdale over a certain period. Aggregating these observations, we might characterize drunk-driving offenders as 72 percent men and 28 percent women, with an average age of

26.4 years. This is a descriptive analysis of convicted drunk drivers in Fort Lauderdale. Although the description applies to the group of drunk drivers as a whole, it is based on the characteristics of individual people convicted of drunk driving.

The same situation could exist in an evaluation study. Suppose we wish to determine whether an alcohol education program reduces repeat arrests of first-time drunk-driving offenders. First, we administer the education program to half the persons convicted of drunk driving in Fort Lauderdale over a period of 2 months; the other half does not receive the program. Next, we observe drunk-driving arrest records for 12 months, keeping track of people who were previously convicted and of whether they received the alcohol education program. Combining our observations, we find that 5 percent of those who received the program were arrested again and that 20 percent of those who did not receive alcohol education were re-arrested within a year. The purpose of the study is to evaluate a *program,* but individual drunk drivers are still the units of analysis.

Units of analysis in a study are typically also the units of observation. Thus, to study what steps people take to protect their homes from burglary, we might observe, perhaps through interviews, individual household residents. Sometimes, however, we "observe" units of analysis indirectly. For example, we might ask individuals about crime prevention measures for the purpose of describing households. We might want to find out whether homes with double-cylinder deadbolt locks are burglarized less often than homes with less substantial protection. In this case, our units of analysis are households, but the units of observation are individual household members who are asked to describe burglaries and home protection to interviewers.

Individuals

Any variety of individuals may be the units of analysis in criminal justice research. This point is more important than it may initially seem. The norm of generalized understanding in social science should suggest that scientific findings are most valuable when they apply to all kinds of people. In practice, however, researchers seldom study all kinds of people. At the very least, studies are typically limited to people who live in a single country, although some comparative studies stretch across national boundaries.

As the units of analysis, individuals may be considered in the context of their membership in different groups. Examples of circumscribed groups whose members may be units of analysis at the individual level are police, victims, defendants in criminal court, correctional inmates, gang members, and active burglars. Note that each of these terms implies some population of individual persons. Descriptive studies having individuals as their units of analysis typically aim to describe the population that comprises those individuals.

Groups

Social groups may also be the units of analysis for criminal justice research. This is not the same as studying the individuals within a group. If we study the members of a juvenile gang to learn about teenagers who join gangs, the individual (teen gang member) is the unit of analysis. But if we study all the juvenile gangs in a city to learn the differences between big gangs and small ones, between gangs selling drugs and gangs stealing cars, and so forth, the unit of analysis is the social group (gang).

Police beats or patrol districts might be the units of analysis in a study. A police beat can be described in terms of the total number of people who live within its boundaries, total street mileage, annual crime reports, and whether the beat includes a special facility such as a park or high school. We can then determine, for example, whether beats that include a park report more assaults than beats without such facilities or whether auto thefts are more common in beats with more street mileage. Here, the individual police beat is the unit of analysis.

Other examples of units at the group level are households, city blocks, census tracts, cities, counties, and other geographic regions. Each of these terms also implies some population of groups. Street gang implies some population that includes all street gangs. The population of street gangs could be described, say, in terms of its geographic distribution throughout a city. An explanatory study of street gangs might discover, for example, whether large gangs are more likely than small ones to engage in inter-gang warfare.

Organizations

Formal political or social organizations may also be the units of analysis in criminal justice research. An example is correctional facilities, which implies, of course, a population of all correctional facilities. Individual facilities might be characterized in terms of their number of employees, status as state or federal prisons, security classification, percentage of inmates who are from racial or ethnic minority groups, types of offenses for which inmates are sentenced to each facility, average length of sentence served, and so forth. We might determine whether federal prisons house a larger or smaller percentage of offenders sentenced for white-collar crimes than do state prisons. Other examples of formal organizations suitable as units of analysis are police departments, courtrooms, probation offices, drug treatment facilities, and victim services agencies.

When social groups or formal organizations are the units of analysis, their characteristics are often derived from the characteristics of their individual members. Thus, a correctional facility might be described in terms of the inmates it houses—gender distribution, average sentence length, ethnicity, and so on. In a descriptive study, we might be interested in the percentage of institutions housing only females. Or, in an explanatory study, we might determine whether institutions housing both males and females report, on the average, fewer or more assaults by inmates on staff compared with male-only institutions. In each example, the correctional facility is the unit of analysis. In contrast, if we ask

whether male or female inmates are more often involved in assaults on staff, then the individual inmate is the unit of analysis.

Some studies involve descriptions or explanations of more than one unit of analysis. Consider, for example, an evaluation of community policing programs in selected neighborhoods of a large city. In such an evaluation, we might be interested in how citizens feel about the program (individuals), whether arrests increased in neighborhoods with the new program compared with those without it (groups), and whether the police department's budget increased more than the budget in a similar city (organizations). In such cases, it is imperative that researchers anticipate what conclusions they wish to draw with regard to what units of analysis.

Social Artifacts

Yet another potential unit of analysis may be referred to as "social artifacts," or the products of social beings and their behavior. One class of social artifacts is stories about crime in newspapers and magazines or on television. A newspaper story might be characterized by its length, placement on front or later pages, size of headlines, and presence of photographs. A researcher could analyze whether television news features or newspaper reports provide the most details about a new police program to increase drug arrests. Or we might examine letters to the editor in a local newspaper to determine whether writers tend to favor or oppose a new program that established roadblocks to deter drunk driving in the area around campus.

Social interactions are also examples of social artifacts suitable for criminal justice research. Police crime reports are an example. We might analyze assault reports to find how many involved three or more people, whether assaults involve strangers or people with some prior acquaintance, or whether they more often occurred in public or private locations.

At first, crime reports may not seem to be social artifacts, but consider for a moment what they represent. When a crime is reported to the police, officers usually record what happened from descriptions by victims or witnesses. For instance, an assault victim may describe how he suffered an unprovoked attack while innocently enjoying a cold beer after work. However, witnesses to the incident might claim that the "victim" started the fight by insulting the "offender." The responding police officer must interpret who is telling the truth in trying to sort out the circumstances of a violent social interaction. The officer's report becomes a social artifact that represents one among the population of all assaults.

Records of different types of social interactions are common units of analysis in criminal justice research. Criminal history records, meetings of community anticrime groups, presentence investigations, and interactions between police and citizens are examples. Notice that each example requires information about individuals but that social interactions between people are the units of analysis.

Units of Analysis in Review

The purpose of this section has been to specify what is sometimes a confusing topic, in part because criminal justice researchers use a variety of different units of analysis. Although individual people are often the units of analysis, that is not always the case. Many research questions can more appropriately be answered through the examination of other units of analysis.

The concept of unit of analysis may seem more complicated than it needs to be. Understanding the logic of units of analysis is more important than memorizing some list of the units. It is irrelevant what we call a given unit of analysis—a group, a formal organization, or a social artifact. It is essential, however, that we be able to identify what our unit of analysis is. We must decide whether we are studying assaults or assault victims, police departments or police officers, courtrooms or judges, and prisons or prison inmates. Without keeping this point in mind, we run the risk of making assertions

about one unit of analysis based on the examination of another.

To test your grasp of the concept of units of analysis, here are some examples of real research topics. See if you can determine the unit of analysis in each. (The answers are given later in the chapter, on page 111.)

1. "Taking into account preexisting traffic fatality trends and several other relevant factors, the implementation of the emergency cellular telephone program resulted in a substantial and permanent reduction in the monthly percentage of alcohol-related fatal crashes" (D'Alessio, Stolzenberg, and Terry, 1999:463–64).

2. "Our analysis provides, at best, extremely weak support for the hypothesis that curfews reduce juvenile crime rates. Of the offense and victimization measures, only burglary, larceny, and simple assault arrests significantly decreased after cities adopted curfew statutes. These decreases occurred only for revised laws, and only the reductions in larceny appeared in both the county and city–county samples" (McDowall, Lofton, and Wiersema, 2000:88).

3. "Despite the record number of homicides in Chicago in 1974, Chicago's murder rate was actually lower than those in Detroit, Cleveland, Washington, DC, and Baltimore" (Wilson, 1987:22).

4. "On average, probationers were 31 years old, African American, male, and convicted of drug or property offenses. Most lived with family, and although they were not married, many were in exclusive relationships (44 percent) and had children (47 percent)" (MacKenzie, Browning, Skroban, and Smith, 1999:433).

5. "Seventy-five percent ($n = 158$) of the cases were disposed at district courts, and 3 percent ($n = 6$) remained pending. One percent of the control and 4 percent of the experimental cases were referred to drug treatment court" (Taxman and Ellis, 1999:42).

6. "The department's eight Field Operations Command substations (encompassing 20 police districts and 100 patrol beats) comprised the study's cross-sectional units. From January 1986 through July 1989, a period of 43 months, data were collected monthly from each substation for a total of 344 cases" (Kessler, 1999:346).

7. For most violent crimes, American rates are among the highest—along with Australia, Canada, Spain, and France—but not the highest. Chances of being robbed, being assaulted, or being the victim of a stranger rape are higher in several other Western countries" (Tonry, 1999:421).

8. "Of all the files opened for Arabs, 32 percent were crimes against the person, whereas of all the files opened for Jews, 30 percent were in that category. Proportionally, more files of property and drug offenses were opened for Jews than for Arabs. In addition, Arabs are overrepresented in public order offenses" (Mesch and Fishman, 1999:184).

9. "An enormous variation of deviant activities was represented in our sample of 1,485 news items. We categorized these deviant activities into five general types for analysis: violence, economic, political, ideological/cultural, and diversionary" (Ericson, Baranek, and Chan, 1991:243–44).

10. "Approximately half of the [burglars] (54 percent) admitted to 50 or more lifetime burglaries. . . . Included in this group are 44 offenders who had committed at least 100 such crimes. At the other extreme are 11 individuals who had participated in nine or fewer residential break-ins" (Wright and Decker, 1994:13).

The Ecological Fallacy

At this point, it is appropriate to introduce two important concepts related to units of analysis: the ecological fallacy and reductionism. The first concept—the **ecological fallacy**—refers to the danger of making assertions about individuals as the unit of analysis based on the ex-amination of groups or other aggregations. Let's consider a hypothetical example of this fallacy.

Suppose we are interested in learning about robbery in different police precincts of a large city. Let's assume that we have information on how many robberies were committed in each police precinct of Chicago for the year 2001. Assume also that we have census data describing some of the characteristics of those precincts. Our analysis of such data might show that a large number of 2001 robberies occurred in the downtown precinct and that the average family income of persons who live in downtown Chicago (the "Loop") was substantially higher than that in other precincts in the city. We might be tempted to conclude that high-income downtown residents are more likely to be robbed than are people who live in other parts of the city—that robbers select richer victims. In reaching such a conclusion, we run the risk of committing the ecological fallacy because lower-income people who did not live in the downtown area were also being robbed there in 2001. Victims might be commuters to jobs in the Loop, people visiting downtown theaters or restaurants, passengers on subway or elevated train platforms, or homeless persons who are not counted by the census. Our problem is that we examined police precincts as our units of analysis, but we wish to draw conclusions about individual people.

The same problem will arise if we discover that incarceration rates are higher in states that have a large proportion of elderly residents. We will not know whether older people are actually imprisoned more often. Or, if we find higher suicide rates in cities with large nonwhite populations, we cannot be sure whether more nonwhites than whites committed suicide.

Don't let these warnings against the ecological fallacy lead you to commit what is called an "individualistic fallacy." Some students approaching criminal justice research for the first time have trouble reconciling general patterns of attitudes and actions with individual exceptions they know of. If, for example, you read a newspaper story about a Utah resident visiting New York who is murdered on a subway platform, the fact remains that most visitors to New York and most subway riders are not at risk of murder. Similarly, mass media stories and popular films about drug problems in U.S. cities frequently focus on drug use and dealing among African Americans. But that does not mean that most African Americans are drug users or that drugs are not a problem among whites.

The individualistic fallacy can be especially troublesome for beginning students of criminal justice. Newspapers, local television news, and television police dramas often present unusual or highly dramatized versions of crime problems and criminal justice policy. These messages may distort the way many people initially approach research problems in criminal justice.

Reductionism

A second concept relating to units of analysis is reductionism. Basically, **reductionism** is an overly strict limitation on the kinds of concepts and variables to be considered as causes in explaining the broad range of human behavior represented by crime and criminal justice policy. Economists may tend to consider only economic variables (marginal value, expected utility); sociologists may consider only sociological variables (values, norms, roles); psychologists may consider only psychological variables (personality types, compulsive personality disorder). For example, why did violent crime by juveniles decline from 1995 through 2002, after an increase from 1985 through about 1994? Was it the result of changes in family structure? Fluctuation in economic opportunities for teenagers? Diminished fascination with images of violence, power, and flashy lifestyles among drug dealers in popular media? Social scientists from different disciplines tend to look at some explanations for crime problems and ignore the others. Explaining crime solely in terms of economic factors is economic reductionism; explaining crime solely in terms of psychological

factors is psychological reductionism. Note how this issue relates to the discussion of theoretical paradigms in Chapter 2.

Reductionism of any type tends to suggest that particular units of analysis or variables are more relevant than others. If we consider the changing family structure as the cause of increased juvenile crime, our unit of analysis will be families. An economist, though, might use the 50 states as the units of analysis and compare juvenile crime rates and economic conditions. A psychologist might choose individual juveniles as the units of analysis to determine how watching violent films affects personality development.

Like the ecological fallacy, reductionism involves the use of inappropriate units of analysis. The appropriate unit of analysis for a given research question is not always clear and is often debated by social scientists, especially across disciplinary boundaries.

The box titled "Units of Analysis in the National Youth Gang Survey" offers several additional examples of using inappropriate units of analysis. It also illustrates that lack of clarity about units of analysis in criminal justice results in part from difficulties in directly measuring the concepts we want to study.

The Time Dimension

Because time order is a requirement for causal inferences, the time dimension of research requires careful planning.

We saw earlier in this chapter how the time sequence of events and situations is a critical element in determining causation. Time is also involved in the generalizability of research findings. Do the descriptions and explanations that result from a particular study accurately represent the situation of 10 years ago or 10 years from now, or do they represent only the present state of affairs? In general, observations may be made more or less at one time point, or they may be deliberately stretched over a longer

Units of Analysis in the National Youth Gang Survey

In 1997, the third annual National Youth Gang Survey was completed for the federal Office of Juvenile Justice and Delinquency Prevention (OJJDP). This survey reflects keen interest in developing better information about the scope of youth gangs and their activities in different types of communities around the country. As important and useful as this effort is, the National Youth Gang Survey—especially reports of its results—illustrates how some ambiguities can emerge with respect to units of analysis.

A variety of attempts, often creative, are used to gather information from or about active offenders. Partly this is because it is difficult to systematically identify offenders for research. Studying youth gangs presents more than the usual share of problems with units of analysis. Are we interested in gangs (groups), gang members (individuals), or offenses (social artifact) committed by gangs?

Following methods developed in earlier years, the 1997 National Youth Gang Survey was based on a sample of law enforcement agencies. The sample was designed to represent different types of communities: rural areas, suburban counties, small cities, and large cities. Questionnaires were mailed to the police chief for municipalities and to the sheriff for counties (National Youth Gang Center, 1999:3). Questions asked respondents to report on gangs and gang activity in their jurisdiction—municipality for police departments, and unincorporated service area for sheriffs' departments. Here are examples of the *types* of questions included in the survey:

1. How many youth gangs were active in your jurisdiction?
2. How many active youth gang members were in your jurisdiction?
3. In your jurisdiction, what percent of street sales of drugs were made by youth gang members? [followed by list: powder cocaine, crack cocaine, marijuana, heroin, methamphetamine, other]
4. Does your agency have the following? [list of special youth gang units]

Notice the different units of analysis embedded in these questions. Seven are stated or implied.

period. Observations made at more than one time point can look forward or backward.

Cross-Sectional Studies

Many criminal justice research projects are designed to study some phenomenon by taking a cross section of it at one time and analyzing that cross section carefully. Exploratory and descriptive studies are often **cross-sectional.** A single U.S. census, for instance, is a study aimed at describing the U.S. population at a given time. A single wave of the National Crime Victimization Survey (NCVS) is a descriptive cross-sectional study that estimates how many people have been victims of crime in a given time.

A cross-sectional exploratory study might be conducted by a police department in the form of a survey that examines what residents believe to be the sources of crime problems in their neighborhood. In all likelihood, the study will ask about crime problems in a single time frame, with the findings used to help the department explore various methods of introducing community policing.

Cross-sectional studies for explanatory or evaluation purposes have an inherent problem. Typically, their aim is to understand causal processes that occur over time, but their conclusions are based on observations made at only one time. For example, a survey might ask respondents whether their home has been burglarized and whether they have any special locks on their doors, hoping to explain whether special locks prevent burglary. Because the questions about burglary victimization and door locks are asked at only one time, it is not possible to determine whether burglary victims installed locks after a burglary or whether special

1. Gangs: item 1
2. Gang members: items 2, 3
3. Jurisdiction (city or part of county area): items 1, 2, 3
4. Street sales of drugs: item 3
5. Drug types: item 3
6. Agency: item 4
7. Special unit: item 4

Now, consider some quotes from a summary report on the 1997 survey (National Youth Gang Center, 1999). Which ones do or do not *reasonably* reflect the actual units of analysis from the survey?

■ "Fifty-one percent of survey respondents indicated that they had active youth gangs in their jurisdictions in 1997." (page 7)
■ "Thirty-eight percent of jurisdictions in the Northeast, and 26 percent of jurisdictions in the Middle Atlantic regions reported active youth gangs in 1997." (extracted from Table 3, page 10)
■ "Results of the 1997 survey revealed that there were an estimated 30,533 youth gangs and 815,986 gang members active in the United States in 1997." (page 13)

■ "The percentage of street sales of crack cocaine, heroin, and methamphetamine conducted by youth gang members varied substantially by region. . . . Crack cocaine sales involving youth gang members were most prevalent in the Midwest (38 percent), heroin sales were most prevalent in the Northeast (15 percent), and methamphetamine sales were most prevalent in the West (21 percent)." (page 27)
■ "The majority (66 percent) of respondents indicated that they had some type of specialized unit to address the gang problem." (page 33)

The youth gang survey report includes a number of statements and tables that inaccurately describe units of analysis. You probably detected examples of this in some of the statements shown here. Other statements accurately reflect units of analysis measured in the survey.

If you read the 1997 survey report and keep in mind our discussion of units of analysis, you will find more misleading statements and tables. This will enhance your understanding of units of analysis.

Source: Information drawn from National Youth Gang Center (1999).

---

locks were already in place but did not prevent the crime. Some of the ways we can deal with the difficult problem of determining time order will be discussed in the section on approximating longitudinal studies.

Longitudinal Studies

Research projects known as **longitudinal studies** are designed to permit observations over an extended period. An example is a researcher who observes the activities of a neighborhood anticrime organization from the time of its inception until its demise. Analysis of newspaper stories about crime or numbers of prison inmates over time are other examples. In the latter instances, it is irrelevant whether the researcher's observations are made over the course of the actual events under study or at one time—for example, examining a year's worth of newspapers

in the library or 10 years of annual reports on correctional populations.

Three special types of longitudinal studies should be noted here: trend, cohort, and panel studies. **Trend studies** look at changes within some general population over time. An example is a comparison of UCR figures over time, showing an increase in reported crime from 1960 through 1993 and then a decline through 2001. Or a researcher might want to know whether changes in sentences for certain offenses were followed by increases in the number of people imprisoned in state institutions. In this case, a trend study might examine annual figures for prison population over time, comparing totals for the years before and after new sentencing laws took effect.

Cohort studies examine more specific populations (cohorts) as they change over time.

Typically, a cohort is an age group, such as those people born during the 1980s, but it can also be based on some other time grouping. Cohorts are often defined as a group of people who enter or leave an institution at the same time, such as persons entering a drug treatment center during July, offenders released from custody in 2002, or high school seniors in March 2003.

In one of the best-known cohort studies, Marvin Wolfgang and associates (Wolfgang, Figlio, and Sellin, 1972) studied all males born in 1945 who lived in the city of Philadelphia from their 10th birthday through age 18 or older. The researchers examined records from police agencies and public schools to determine how many boys in the cohort had been charged with delinquency or arrested, how old they were when first arrested, and what differences there were in school performance between delinquents and nondelinquents.

Panel studies are similar to trend and cohort studies except that observations are made on the same set of people on two or more occasions. The NCVS is a good example of a descriptive panel study. A member of each household selected for inclusion in the survey is interviewed seven times at 6-month intervals. The NCVS serves many purposes, but it was developed initially to estimate how many people were victims of various types of crimes each year. It is designed as a panel study so that persons can be asked about crimes that occurred in the previous 6 months, and two waves of panel data are combined to estimate the nationwide frequency of victimization over a 1-year period.

Panel studies are often used in evaluation research, in which the same persons are interviewed both before and after a new program is introduced. For example, a panel study was used in an evaluation in Joliet, Illinois, of the effects of a new, specialized neighborhood-oriented policing (NOP) unit on police personnel and police organization. Police from all rank levels were surveyed before the implementation of the NOP unit and then twice after the implementation, at 10-month and 22-month intervals (Rosenbaum, Yeh, and Wilkinson, 1994).

Though all longitudinal studies tend to be expensive and difficult to conduct, panel studies face a special problem: panel attrition. Some of the respondents studied in the first wave of a study may not participate in later waves. The danger is that those who drop out of the study may not be typical and may thereby distort the results of the study. Suppose we are interested in evaluating the success of a new drug treatment program by conducting weekly drug tests on a panel of participants for a period of 10 months. Regardless of how successful the program appears to be after 10 months, if a substantial number of people drop out of our study, we can expect that treatment was less effective in keeping them off drugs.

Approximating Longitudinal Studies

It may be possible to draw conclusions about processes that take place over time even when only cross-sectional data are available. It is worth noting some of the ways to do that.

Sometimes, cross-sectional data imply processes that occur over time on the basis of simple logic. Consider, for example, a study of gun ownership and violence by Swiss researcher Martin Killias (1993). Killias compared rates of gun ownership as reported in an international crime survey to rates of homicide and suicide committed with guns. He was interested in the possible effects of gun availability on violence: Do nations with higher rates of gun ownership also have higher rates of gun violence?

Killias reasoned that inferring causation from a cross-sectional comparison of gun ownership and homicides committed with guns would be ambiguous. Gun homicide rates could be high in countries with high gun ownership rates because the availability of guns was higher. Or people in countries with high gun ownership rates could have bought guns to protect themselves, in response to rates of homicide. Cross-sectional analysis would not make it possible to sort out the time order of gun ownership and gun homicides.

But does that reasoning hold for gun suicides? Killias argues that the time order in a relationship between gun ownership and gun suicides is less ambiguous. It makes much more sense that suicides involving guns are at least partly a result of gun availability. But it is not reasonable to assume that people might buy guns in response to high gun suicide rates.

Logical inferences may also be made whenever the time order of variables is clear. For example, if we discover in a cross-sectional study of high school students that men are more likely than women to smoke marijuana, we can conclude that gender affects the propensity to use marijuana, not the other way around. Thus, even though our observations are made at only one time, we are justified in drawing conclusions about processes that take place across time.

Retrospective Studies

Retrospective research, which asks people to recall their pasts, is another common way of approximating observations over time. In a study of recidivism, for example, we might select a group of prison inmates and analyze their history of delinquency or crime. Or suppose we are interested in whether college students convicted of drunk driving are more likely to have parents with drinking problems than college students with no drunk-driving record. Such a study is retrospective because it focuses on the histories of college students who have or have not been convicted of drunk driving.

The danger in this technique is evident. Sometimes, people have faulty memories; sometimes, they lie. Retrospective recall is one way of approximating observations across time, but it must be used with caution. Retrospective studies that analyze records of past arrests or convictions suffer from different problems: Records may be unavailable, incomplete, or inaccurate.

A more fundamental issue in retrospective research hinges on how subjects are selected and how subject selection affects the kinds of questions such studies can address.

Imagine that you are a juvenile court judge, and you're troubled by what appears to be a large number of child abuse cases in your court. Talking with a juvenile caseworker, you wonder whether the parents of these children were abused or neglected during their own childhood. Together, you formulate a hypothesis about the intergenerational transmission of violence: Victims of childhood abuse later abuse their own children. How might you go about investigating that hypothesis?

Given your position as a judge who regularly sees abuse victims, you will probably consider a retrospective approach that examines the backgrounds of families appearing in your court. Let's say you and the caseworker plan to investigate the family backgrounds of 20 abuse victims who appear in your court during the next 3 months. The caseworker consults with a clinical psychologist from the local university and obtains copies of a questionnaire, or "protocol," that has been used by researchers to study the families of child abuse victims. After interviewing the families of 20 victims, the caseworker reports to you that 18 of the 20 child victims have a mother or father who was abused as a child. It seems safe to conclude that your hypothesis about the intergenerational transmission of violence is strongly supported, because 90 percent (18 out of 20) of abuse/neglect victims brought before your court come from families with a history of child abuse.

Think for a moment about how you approached the question of whether child abuse breeds child abuse. You began with abuse victims and retrospectively established that many of their parents had been abused. However, this is different from the question of how many victims of childhood abuse later abuse their own children. That question requires a **prospective** approach, in which you begin with childhood victims and then determine how many of them later abuse their own children.

To clarify this point, let's shift from the hypothetical study to actual research that illustrates the difference between prospective and retrospective approaches to the same question. Rosemary Hunter and Nancy Kilstrom (1979) conducted a study of 255 infants and their parents.* The researchers began by selecting families of premature infants in a newborn intensive care unit. Interviews with the parents of 255 infants revealed that either the mother or the father in 49 of the families had been the victim of abuse or neglect; 206 families revealed no history of abuse. In a prospective follow-up study, Hunter and Kilstrom found that within 1 year 10 of the 255 infants had been abused. Nine of those 10 infant victims were from the 49 families with a history of abuse, while 1 abused infant was from the 206 families with no background of abuse.

Figure 4.2A illustrates these prospective results graphically. Infants in 18 percent (9 out of 49) of families with a history of abuse showed signs of abuse within 1 year of birth, while less than 1 percent of infants born to parents with no history of abuse were themselves abused within 1 year. Although that is a sizable difference, notice that the 18 percent figure for continuity of abuse is very similar to the 19 percent rate of abuse discovered in the histories of all 255 families.

Now consider what Hunter and Kilstrom would have found if they had begun with the 10 abused infants at time 2 and then checked their family backgrounds. Figure 4.2B illustrates this retrospective approach. A large majority of the 10 infant victims (90 percent) had parents with a history of abuse.

You probably realize by now that the prospective and retrospective approaches address fundamentally different questions, even though the questions may appear similar on the surface:

> Prospective: What percentage of abuse victims later abuse their children? (18 percent; Figure 4.2A)
>
> Retrospective: What percentage of abuse victims have parents who were abused? (90 percent; Figure 4.2B)

---

*This example was suggested by Cathy Spatz Widom (1989b) in a comprehensive review and critique of research on the intergenerational transmission of child abuse.

In a study of how child abuse and neglect affect drug use, Cathy Spatz Widom and associates (Widom, Weiler, and Cotler, 1999) present a similar contrast of prospective and retrospective analysis. Looking backward, 75 percent of subjects with a drug abuse diagnosis in semiclinical interviews were victims of childhood abuse or neglect. Looking forward, 35 percent of childhood victims and 34 percent of nonvictims had a drug abuse diagnosis.

More generally, Robert Sampson and John Laub (1993:14) comment on how retrospective and prospective views yield different interpretations about patterns of criminal offending over time:

> Looking *back* over the careers of adult criminals exaggerates the prevalence of stability. Looking *forward* from youth reveals the success and failures, including adolescent delinquents who go on to be normal functioning adults. This is the paradox noted [by Lee Robins] earlier: adult criminality seems to be always preceded by childhood misconduct, but most conduct-disordered children do not become antisocial or criminal adults (Robins, 1978). (emphasis in original)

Our intention here is not to suggest that retrospective studies have no value. Rather, we want to point out how the time dimension is linked to the framing of research questions. A retrospective approach is limited in its ability to reveal how causal processes unfold over time. A retrospective approach is therefore not well suited to answer questions such as how many childhood victims of abuse or neglect later abuse their own children. A retrospective study can be used, however, to compare whether childhood victims are more likely than nonvictims to have a history of abuse in their family background.

The Time Dimension Summarized

Joel Devine and James Wright (1993:19) offer a clever metaphor that distinguishes longitudinal studies from cross-sectional ones. Think of a

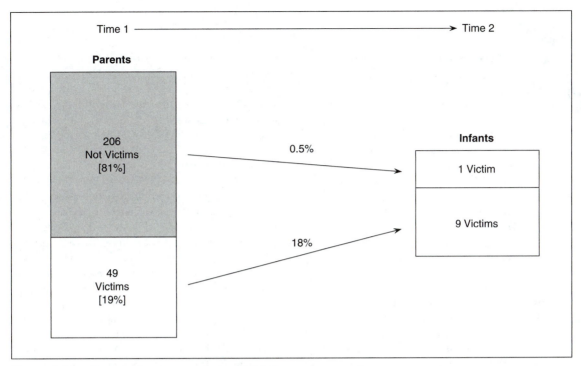

Figure 4.2A   Prospective Approach to a Subject

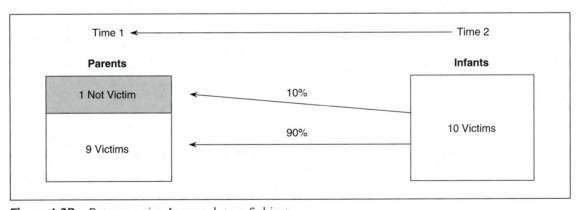

Figure 4.2B   Retrospective Approach to a Subject

Source: Adapted from Hunter and Kilstrom (1979), as suggested by Widom (1989b).

cross-sectional study as a snapshot, a trend study as a slide show, and a panel study as a motion picture. A cross-sectional study, like a snapshot, produces an image at one point in time. This can provide useful information about crime—burglary, for example—at a single time, perhaps in a single place. A trend study is akin to a slide show—a series of snapshots, in sequence over time. By viewing a slide show, we can tell how some indicator—change in burglary rates—varies over time. But a trend study is usually based on aggregate information. It can tell us something about aggregations of burglary over time, but not, for instance, whether the same

PUTTING IT ALL TOGETHER

UNITS AND TIME IN NEW YORK CITY

The Rutgers study of changes in policing in New York City, and the relationship between policing and crime rates, offers a good example of three main concepts discussed in this chapter.

Designing a Research Project

Researchers at Rutgers worked through all the research design steps described in this chapter. So far, one report has been issued—*Do Police Matter? An Analysis of the Impact of New York City's Police Reforms* (Kelling and Sousa, 2001). Conceptualization was an issue from the outset. At a general level, it was clear that the project would obtain measures of crime and police action. But each of those required further specification. Eventually, researchers operationalized many measures of crime and arrests by using data already prepared

for publication in Compstat reports. Compstat stands for "compare statistics"—department jargon for the publication of weekly crime and arrests reports throughout the city. Several different research methods were used, including interviews, field observation, and analysis of existing data.

Units of Analysis

Different units of analysis were studied for different phases of the project. One focus was changes in crime rates for the city as a whole, so New York was the unit. In addition, six of the city's 76 precincts were selected for more detailed study. For the most part, aggregations of crime reports were analyzed at the precinct level, so police precincts were units of analysis.

Studying the independent variable—changes in police strategy and tactics—requires different, and sometimes confusing, units of analysis. At one level, the entire department was a unit, because changes in policing were fundamental and permeated this complex organization. At another level,

---

people are committing burglaries at an increasing or decreasing rate, or whether there are more or fewer burglars with a relatively constant rate of crime commission. A panel study, like a motion picture, can capture moving images of the same individuals and give us information about individual rates of offending over time.

These, then, are some of the ways time figures in criminal justice research and some of the ways researchers have learned to cope with it. In designing any study, you need to look at both the explicit and implicit assumptions they are making about time. Are you interested in describing some process that occurs over time, such as whether mandatory jail sentences reduce drunk driving? Or are you simply going to describe how many people were arrested for drunk driving in the past year? If you want to describe a process that occurs over time, will you be able to make observations at different points in the process, or will you have to approximate such observations, drawing logical

inferences from what you can observe now? See the box titled "Units and Time in New York City" for information on how Rutgers researchers defined units and time.

How to Design a Research Project

Designing research requires planning several stages, but the stages do not always occur in the same sequence.

We've now seen some of the options available to criminal justice researchers in designing projects, but what if you were to undertake research? Where would you start? Then where would you go? How would you begin planning your research?

Although research design occurs at the beginning of a research project, it involves all the steps of the subsequent project. The comments that follow, then, should give you some guid-

changes in policing were implemented by individual officers, detectives, supervisors, and commanders; so information was obtained from individual people as units. Considering "units" in a different sense, one policing innovation called for special groups of officers to target drug, weapons, and other specific types of crime in different neighborhoods; that adds special subgroups and neighborhoods as possible units of analysis.

Sorting out all these units of analysis was difficult. Rutgers University researchers had to conceptualize and ultimately analyze a variety of units.

The Time Dimension

Time order is an absolute requirement for causal inference. If it can't be established that changes in policing occurred before declines in crime, that key requirement for inferring cause cannot be met.

Researchers studied longitudinal data on crime to see when the crime decrease began and how much could be attributed to changes in policing. Longitudinal data on crime are readily available in New York; dates of incidents and arrests are recorded on computer files, a practice that preceded changes in policing by several years. But information on changes in police tactics was much more difficult to obtain. Some changes are documented in department files. However, the implementation of specific anticrime actions by officers and special units was not systematically captured on paper. So Rutgers researchers conducted interviews (in 1999 and 2000) with officers and commanders, asking them to document changes in policing that occurred as many as 6 years earlier. But this retrospective approach to establishing time order is imperfect. With the passage of time, people forget. Subjects might also exaggerate their description of changes in policing in New York to place their own actions in a better historical light.

In practice, this project was more complex than we can summarize here. But you should be able to recognize how time played a role, what units of analysis were involved, and why conceptualization and operationalization were important. Our discussion of the New York City project in the next chapter presents an example of difficulty in specifying a key concept in the project.

ance on how to start a research project, as well as provide an overview of the topics addressed in subsequent chapters of the book.

Every project has a starting point, but it is important to think through later stages even at the beginning. Figure 4.3 presents a schematic view of the social science research process. We present this view reluctantly because it may suggest more of a "cookbook" approach to research than is the case in practice. Nonetheless, it's important to have an overview of the whole process before we launch into the details of particular components of research. Essentially, this figure presents another and more detailed picture of the scientific process discussed in Chapter 2.

The Research Process

At the top of the diagram in Figure 4.3 are interests, ideas, theories, and new programs—the possible beginning points for a line of research. The letters (A, B, X, Y, and so forth) represent variables or concepts such as deterrence or child abuse. Thus, you might have a general interest in finding out why the threat of punishment deters some, but not all, people from committing crimes, or you might want to investigate how burglars select their targets. Alternatively, your inquiry might begin with a specific idea about the way things are. You might have the idea that aggressive arrest policies deter drug use, for example. Question marks in the diagram indicate that you aren't sure things are the way you suspect they are. We have represented a theory as a complex set of relationships among several variables (A, B, E, and F).

The research process might also begin with an idea for a new program. Imagine that you are the director of a probation services department, and you want to develop a new program to require weekly drug tests for people on probation. Because you have taken a course on criminal justice research methods, you decide to design an evaluation of the new program before trying

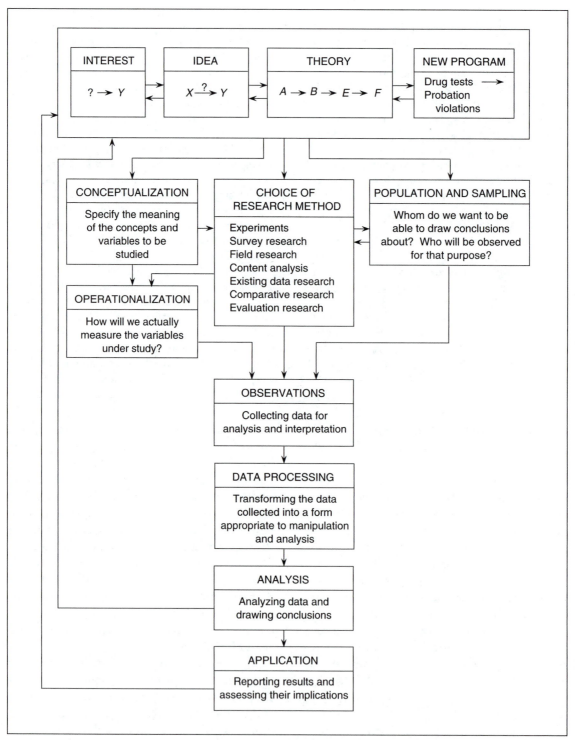

Figure 4.3   The Research Process

it out. The research process begins with your idea for the new drug-testing program.

Notice the movement back and forth among these several possible beginnings. An initial interest may lead to the formulation of an idea, which may be fit into a larger theory, and the theory may produce new ideas and create new interests. Or your understanding of some theory may encourage you to consider new policies.

To make this discussion more concrete, let's take a specific research example. Suppose you are concerned about the problem of crime on your campus, and you have a special interest in learning more about how other students view the issue and what they think should be done about it. Going a step further, let's say you have the impression that students are especially concerned about violent crimes such as assault and robbery, and that many students feel the university should be doing more to prevent violent crime. The source of this idea might be your own interest after being a student for a couple of years. You might develop the idea while reading about theories of crime in a course you are taking. Perhaps you recently read stories about a "crime wave" on campus. Or maybe some combination of things makes you want to learn more about campus crime.

Considering the research purposes discussed earlier in this chapter, your research will be mainly exploratory. You probably have descriptive and explanatory interests as well: How much of a problem is violent crime on campus? Are students especially concerned about crime in certain areas? Why are some students more worried about crime than others? What do students think would be effective changes to reduce campus crime problems?

At this point, you should begin to think about units of analysis and the time dimension. Your interest in violent crime might suggest a study of crimes reported to campus police in recent years. In this case, the units of analysis will be social artifacts (crime reports) in a longitudinal study (crime reports in recent years). Or, after thinking a bit more, you may be interested in current student attitudes and opinions about violent crime. Here, the units of analysis will be individuals (college students), and a cross-sectional study will suit your purposes nicely.

Getting Started

To begin pursuing your interest in student concerns about violent crime, you undoubtedly will want to read something about the issue. You might begin by finding out what research has been done on fear of crime and on the sorts of crime that concern people most. Newspaper stories should provide information on the violent crimes that occurred recently on campus. Appendix A on the web site for this book will give you some assistance in using your college library. In addition, you will probably want to talk to people—other students or campus police officers, for example. These activities will prepare you to handle the various research design decisions we are about to examine. As you review the research literature, you should make note of the designs used by other researchers, asking whether the same designs will meet your research objective.

What is your objective, by the way? It's important that you are clear about that before you design your study. Do you plan to write a paper based on your research to satisfy a course requirement or as an honors thesis? Is your purpose to gain information that will support an argument for more police protection or better lighting on campus? Do you want to write an article for the campus newspaper or an academic journal?

Usually, your objective for undertaking research can be expressed in a report. Appendix C on the web site for this book will help you with the organization of research reports, and we recommend that you outline such a report as the first step in the design of any project. You should be clear about the kinds of statements you will want to make when the research is complete. Here are two examples of such statements: "x percent of State U students believe that sexual assault is a big problem on campus," and

"Female students living off campus are more likely than females living in dorms to feel that emergency phones should be installed near buildings where evening classes are held." Although your final report may not look much like your initial image of it, outlining the planned report will help you make better decisions about research design.

Conceptualization

We often talk casually about criminal justice concepts such as deterrence, recidivism, crime prevention, community policing, and child abuse, but it's necessary to specify what we mean by these concepts in order to do research on them. Chapter 5 will examine this process of **conceptualization** in depth. For now, let's see what it might involve in our hypothetical example.

If you are going to study student concerns about violent crime, you must first specify what you mean by "concern about violent crime." This ambiguous phrase can mean different things to different people. Campus police officers are concerned about violent crime because that is part of their job. On the one hand, students might be concerned about crime in much the same way they are concerned about other social problems, such as homelessness, animal rights, and the globalized economy. They recognize these issues as problems society must deal with, but they don't feel that the issues affect them directly; we could specify this concept as "general concern about violent crime." On the other hand, students may feel that the threat of violent crime does affect them directly, and they express some fear about the possibility of being a victim; let's call this "fear for personal safety."

Obviously, you need to specify what you mean by the term in your research, but this doesn't necessarily mean you have to settle for a single definition. In fact, you might want to define the concept of "concern about violent crime" in more than one way and see how students feel about each.

Of course, you need to specify all the concepts you wish to study. If you want to study the possible effect of concern about crime on student behavior, you'll have to decide whether you want to limit your focus to specific precautionary behavior such as keeping doors locked or general behavior such as going to classes, parties, and football games.

Choice of Research Method

A variety of methods are available to the criminal justice researcher. Each method has strengths and weaknesses, and certain concepts are more appropriately studied by some methods than by others.

A survey is the most appropriate method for studying both general concern and fear for personal safety. You might interview students directly or ask them to fill out a questionnaire. As we'll see in Chapter 9, surveys are especially well suited to the study of individuals' attitudes and opinions. Thus, if you wish to examine whether students who are afraid of crime are more likely to believe that campus lighting should be improved than students who are not afraid, a survey is a good method.

This is not to say that you can't make good use of other methods presented in Part Three. Through content analysis (discussed in Chapter 11), for example, you might examine letters to the editor in your campus newspaper and analyze what the writers believe should be done to improve campus safety. Field research (see Chapter 10), in which you observe whether students tend to avoid dark areas of the campus, will help you understand student behavior in avoiding certain areas of the campus at night. Or you might study official complaints made to police and college administrators about crime problems on campus. As you read Part Three, you'll see ways other research methods might be used to study this topic. Usually, the best study design is one that uses more than one research method, taking advantage of their different strengths.

Operationalization

Having specified the concepts to be studied and chosen the research method, you now must create concrete measurement techniques. **Operationalization,** discussed in detail in Chapter 5, refers to the concrete steps or operations used to measure specific concepts.

If you decide to study concern about violent crime by a survey, your operationalization will take the form of questionnaire items. You might operationalize fear for personal safety with the question "How safe do you feel alone on the campus after dark?" This could be followed by boxes indicating the possible answers "Safe" and "Unsafe." Student attitudes about ways of improving campus safety could be operationalized with the item "Listed below are different actions that might be taken to reduce violent crime on campus. Beside each description, indicate whether you favor or oppose the actions described." This could be followed by several different actions, with "Favor" and "Oppose" boxes beside each.

Population and Sampling

In addition to refining concepts and measurements, decisions must be made about whom or what to study. The population for a study is that group (usually of people) about whom we want to be able to draw conclusions. We are almost never able to study all the members of the population that interests us, however. In virtually every case, we must sample subjects for study. Chapter 8 describes methods for selecting samples that adequately reflect the whole population that interests us. Notice in Figure 4.3 that decisions about population and sampling are related to decisions about the research method to be used.

In the study of concern about violent crime, the relevant population is the student population of your college. As you'll discover in Chapter 8, however, selecting a sample requires you to get more specific than that. Will you include part-time as well as full-time students? Only degree candidates or everyone? Students who live on campus, off campus, or both? There are many such questions, and each must be answered in terms of your research purpose. If your purpose is to study concern about sexual assault, you might consider limiting your population to female students. If hate crimes are of special interest, you will want to be sure that your study population included minorities and others who are thought to be particularly targeted by hate crimes.

Observations

Having decided what to study, among whom, and by what method, you are ready to make observations—to collect empirical data. The chapters of Part Three, which describe various research methods, discuss the different observation methods appropriate to each.

For a survey of concern about violent crime, you might prepare an electronic questionnaire and e-mail it to a sample selected from the student body, or you could have a team of interviewers conduct the survey over the telephone. The relative advantages and disadvantages of these and other possibilities are discussed in Chapter 9.

Data Processing

Depending on the research method chosen, you will amass a volume of observations in a form that probably isn't easily interpretable. In the case of a survey, the "raw" observations are typically in the form of questionnaires with boxes checked, answers written in spaces, and the like. The data-processing phase for a survey typically involves classifying (coding) the written-in answers and transforming all information to some computer format.

Analysis

Finally, we manipulate the collected data for the purpose of drawing conclusions that reflect on the interests, ideas, and theories that initiated the inquiry. Chapter 13 describes a few of the many options available to you in analyzing data. Notice in Figure 4.3 that the results of your analyses feed back into your initial interests, ideas, and theories. In practice, this feedback may initiate another cycle of inquiry. In the study of student concern about violent crime, the analysis phase will have both descriptive and explanatory purposes. You might begin by calculating the percentage of students who feel afraid to use specific parking facilities after dark and the percentage who favor or oppose each of the different things that might be done to improve campus safety. Together, these percentages will provide a good picture of student opinion on the issue.

Moving beyond simple description, you might examine the opinions of different subsets of the student body: men versus women; freshmen, sophomores, juniors, seniors, and graduate students; and students who live in dorms versus off-campus apartments. You might then conduct some explanatory analysis to make the point that students who are enrolled in classes that meet in the evening hours are most in favor of improved campus lighting.

Application

The final stage of the research process involves using the research you've conducted and the conclusions you've reached. To start, you will probably want to communicate your findings so that others will know what you've learned. It may be appropriate to prepare—and even publish—a written report. Perhaps you will make oral presentations in class or at a professional meeting. Or you might prepare a Web page that presents your results. Other students will be interested in hearing what you have learned about their concerns about violent crime on campus.

Your study might also be used to actually do something about campus safety. If you find that a large proportion of students you interviewed believe that a parking lot near the library is poorly lighted, university administrators could add more lights, or campus police might patrol the area more frequently. Crime prevention programs might be launched in dormitories if residents are more afraid of violent crime than students who live in other types of housing. Students in a Rutgers University class on crime prevention focused on car thefts and break-ins surrounding the campus in Newark, New Jersey. Their semester project presented specific recommendations on how university and city officials could reduce the problem.

Finally, you should consider what your research suggests with regard to further research on your subject. What mistakes should be corrected in future studies? What avenues, opened up slightly in your study, should be pursued further in later investigations?

Research Design in Review

As this overview shows, research design involves a set of decisions regarding what topic is to be studied, among what population, with what research methods, and for what purpose. Whereas the earlier sections of this chapter on cause and effect, units of analysis, and the time dimension aimed at broadening your perspective in all these regards, research design is the process of narrowing, of focusing, your perspective for purposes of a particular study.

If you are doing a research project for a course you are taking, many aspects of research design may be specified for you in advance. For a project in a course on experimental methods in criminal justice, the design for selecting subjects will be specified for you. For a project in a course on corrections policy, the research topic will be somewhat specified. Because it is not feasible for us to anticipate all such constraints, the following discussion will assume there are none.

In designing a research project, you will find it useful to begin by assessing three things: (1) your interests, (2) your abilities, and (3) the resources available to you. Each of these considerations will suggest a number of possible studies.

What are you interested in understanding? Surely, you have several questions about crime and possible policy responses. Why do some juvenile gangs sell drugs while others steal cars? Why do particular neighborhoods near campus seem to have higher rates of burglary? What types of community groups are more active in neighborhood anticrime programs? Do sentencing policies discriminate against minorities? Do cities with gun control laws have lower murder rates? Are sentences for rape more severe in some states than in others? Are mandatory jail sentences more effective than license suspension in reducing repeat drunk-driving offenses? Think for a while about the kinds of questions that interest and concern you.

Once you have a few questions you are interested in answering, think about the kind of information you will need to answer them. What research units of analysis will provide the most relevant information: gangs, burglary victims, drunk drivers, households, community groups, police departments, cities, or states? This question should be inseparable from the question of research topics. Then ask which aspects of the units of analysis will provide the information you need to answer your research question.

Your next consideration is how to obtain that information. Are the relevant data likely to be already available somewhere (say, in a government publication), or will you have to collect them yourself? If you think you will have to collect them, how will you do that? Will it be necessary to observe juvenile gangs, interview a large number of burglary victims, or attend meetings of community crime prevention groups? Or will you have to design an experiment to study sentences for drunk driving?

As you answer these questions, you are well into the process of research design. Keep in mind, however, your own research abilities, the resources available to you, and the time required to complete your research project. Do not design the perfect study if you will be unable to carry it out in a reasonable time. You may want to try a research method you have not used before because research should be a learning experience in many ways, but you should not put yourself at too great a disadvantage.

Once you have a general idea of what you want to study and how, carefully review previous research in journals, books, and government reports to see how other researchers have addressed the topic and what they have learned about it. Your review of the literature may lead you to revise your research design; perhaps you will decide to use another researcher's method or even replicate an earlier study. The independent replication of research projects is a standard procedure in the physical sciences, and it is just as important in criminal justice research. Or you might want to go beyond replication and study some aspect of the topic that you feel other researchers have overlooked.

Here's another approach you might take. Suppose a topic has been studied previously using survey methods. Can you design an experimental study to test the findings of those earlier researchers? Or can you think of how a field study might supplement information gained from a survey? The use of several different research methods to test the same finding is sometimes called "triangulation," and you should keep it in mind as a valuable research strategy. Because each research method has particular strengths and weaknesses, there is always a danger that research findings will reflect, at least in part, the method of inquiry. In the best of all worlds, your own research design should bring more than one research method to bear on the topic.

The Research Proposal

Research proposals describe planned activities and include a budget and time line.

If you undertake a research project—an assignment for this course, perhaps, or even a major study funded by the government or a research foundation—you will probably have to provide a research proposal describing what you intend to accomplish and how. We'll conclude this chapter with a discussion of how you might prepare such a proposal.

Elements of a Research Proposal

Some funding agencies have specific requirements for a proposal's elements, structure, or both. For example, in its research solicitation announcements for the 2003–04 fiscal year, the National Institute of Justice (NIJ) describes what should be included in research proposals on such topics as domestic violence and school safety technology (http://www.ojp.usdoj.gov/nij/funding.html). Your instructor may have certain requirements for a research proposal you are to prepare in this course. Here are some basic elements that should be included in almost any research proposal.

Problem or Objective   What exactly do you want to study? Why is it worth studying? Does the proposed study contribute to our general understanding of crime or policy responses to crime? Does it have practical significance? If your proposal describes an evaluation study, then the problem, objective, or research questions may already be specified for you. For example, in its request for evaluation proposals issued in 2003, the NIJ asked that research proposals address three specific issues for programs that would be evaluated:

> 1) effectiveness—attribution of project outcomes to project activities; 2) transferability, or feasibility for adoption by other organizations; and, 3) return on investment—whether the projects are cost-effective or . . . cost-beneficial. (National Institute of Justice, 2003b: 1)

Literature Review   What have others said about this topic? What theories address it, and what do they say? What research has been done? Are the findings consistent, or do past studies disagree? Are there flaws in the body of existing research that you feel you can remedy?

Subjects for Study   Whom or what will you study in order to collect data? Identify the subjects in general terms, and then specifically identify who (or what) is available for study and how you will reach them. Is it appropriate to select a sample? If so, how will you do that? If there is any possibility that your research will have an impact on those you study, how will you ensure that they are not harmed by the research?

Measurement   What are the key variables in your study? How will you define and measure them? Do your definitions and measurement methods duplicate (that's okay, incidentally) or differ from those of previous research on this topic? If you have already developed your measurement device (a questionnaire, for example), or if you are using something developed by others, you should include a copy in an appendix to your proposal.

Data Collection Methods   How will you actually collect the data for your study? Will you observe behavior directly or conduct a survey? Will you undertake field research, or will you focus on the reanalysis of data already collected by others?

Analysis   Give some indication of the kind of analysis you plan to conduct. Spell out the purpose and logic of your analysis. Are you interested in precise description? Do you intend to explain why things are the way they are? Will you analyze the impact of a new program? What possible explanatory variables will your analysis consider, and how will you know whether you've explained program impact adequately?

Schedule   It is often appropriate to provide a schedule for the various stages of research. Even if you don't do this for the proposal, do it for yourself. Unless you have a time line for accomplishing the several stages of research and keeping track of how you're doing, you may end up in trouble.

Budget   If you are asking someone to give you money to pay the costs of your research, you will need to provide a budget that specifies where the money will go. Large, expensive projects include budgetary categories such as personnel, equipment, supplies, and expenses (for example, travel, copying, and printing). Even for a more modest project you will pay for yourself, it's a good idea to spend some time anticipating any expenses involved: office supplies, photocopying, computer disks, telephone calls, transportation, and so on.

As you can see, if you are interested in conducting a criminal justice research project, it is a good idea to prepare a research proposal for your own purposes, even if you aren't required to do so by your instructor or a funding agency. If you are going to invest your time and energy in such a project, you should do what you can to ensure a return on that investment.

Answers to the Units-of-Analysis Exercise

1. Social artifacts (alcohol-related fatal crashes)
2. Groups (cities and counties)
3. Groups (cities)
4. Individuals (probationers)
5. Social artifacts (court cases)
6. Organizations (police substations)
7. Groups (countries)
8. Social artifacts (offense files)
9. Social artifacts (news items)
10. Individuals (burglars)

✪ Main Points

- Explanatory scientific research centers on the notion of cause and effect.
- Most explanatory social research uses a probabilistic model of causation. X may be said to cause Y if it is seen to have some influence on Y.
- X is a necessary cause of Y if Y cannot happen without X having happened. X is a sufficient cause of Y if Y always happens when X happens.
- Three basic requirements determine a causal relationship in scientific research: (1) The independent variable must occur before the dependent variable, (2) the independent and dependent variables must be empirically related to each other, and (3) the observed relationship cannot be explained away as the effect of another variable.
- When scientists consider whether causal statements are true or false, they are concerned with the validity of causal inference.
- Four classes of threats to validity correspond to the types of questions researchers ask in trying to establish cause and effect. Threats to statistical conclusion validity and internal validity arise from bias. Construct and external validity threats may limit our ability to generalize from an observed relationship.
- A scientific realist approach to examining mechanisms in context bridges idiographic and nomothetic approaches to causation.
- Units of analysis are the people or things whose characteristics researchers observe, describe, and explain. The unit of analysis in criminal justice research is often the individual person, but it may also be a group, organization, or social artifact.
- Researchers sometimes confuse units of analysis, resulting in the ecological fallacy or the individualistic fallacy.
- Cross-sectional studies are those based on observations made at one time. Although such studies are limited by this characteristic, inferences can often be made about processes that occur over time.
- Longitudinal studies are those in which observations are made at many times. Such observations may be made of samples drawn from general populations (trend studies), samples drawn from more specific subpopulations (cohort studies), or the same sample of people each time (panel studies).
- Retrospective studies can sometimes approximate longitudinal studies, but retrospective approaches must be used with care.
- The research process is flexible, involving different steps that are best considered together. The process usually begins with some general interest or idea.
- A research proposal provides an overview of why a study will be undertaken and how it will be conducted. It is a useful device for planning and is required in some circumstances.

✪ Key Terms

Cohort study
Conceptualization
Construct validity
Cross-sectional study
Ecological fallacy
External validity
Internal validity
Longitudinal study
Operationalization
Panel study
Probabilistic

Prospective
Reductionism
Retrospective
Scientific realism
Statistical conclusion
    validity
Trend study
Units of Analysis
Validity
Validity threats

✪ Review Questions and Exercises

1. Discuss one of the following statements in terms of what you have learned about the criteria of causation and threats to the validity of causal inference. What cause-and-effect relationships are implied? What are some alternative explanations?

    a. Guns don't kill people; people kill people.
    b. Capital punishment prevents murder.
    c. Marijuana is a gateway drug that leads to the use of other drugs.

2. Several times, we have discussed the relationship between drug use and crime. Describe the conditions that would lead us to conclude that drug use is:

    a. A necessary cause
    b. A sufficient cause
    c. A necessary and sufficient cause

3. In describing different approaches to the time dimension, criminologist Lawrence Sherman (1995) claims that cross-sectional studies can show differences and that longitudinal studies can show change. How does this statement relate to the three criteria for inferring causation?

4. William Julius Wilson (1996:167) cites the following example of why it's important to think carefully about units and time. Imagine a 13-bed hospital, in which 12 beds are occupied by the same person for 1 year. The other hospital bed is occupied by 52 people, each staying 1 week. At any given time, 92 percent of beds are occupied by long-term patients (12 out of 13); but over the entire year, 81 percent of patients are short-term patients (52 out of 64). Discuss the implications of a similar example, in which "jail cell" is substituted for "hospital bed."

✪ Internet Exercises

To ensure that you always have access to live, correct Web links for the Web sites referenced in the following exercises, we provide the necessary links on the companion Web site for *Research Methods for Criminal Justice and Criminology* at http://cj.wadsworth.com/maxfield_babbie/research_methods4e. Once at the companion Web site, select this specific chapter, click on "Chapter Resources," then click on "Web Links."

1. Visit the home page of "The Nun Study." Explore the site, beginning with the FAQ link, which presents a brief description of the Nun Study. Be sure to read the sections "What Is the Nun Study?" and "Why Study Nuns?" Browse through other links about the Nun Study, and describe how it illustrates some of the key concepts discussed in this chapter. Think especially about internal and external validity, causation, and different types of longitudinal studies.

2. The Web page maintained by the Texas Criminal Justice Policy Council includes several reports relevant to criminal justice researchers and policy makers. Download and read one of these reports, and provide the following information: the primary purpose of the research (exploration, description, explanation, or application), the units of analysis (individuals, groups, organizations, or social artifacts), and the use of time in the study (cross-sectional, trend, cohort, or panel study).

✪ InfoTrac College Edition

Several types of longitudinal studies were described in this chapter: *cross-sectional, cohort,* and *panel.* Search InfoTrac College Edition to combine one of these terms with *criminology,* or *recidivism,* or *delinquency,* and locate an article that uses a longitudinal design. Why do you suppose the author chose this particular method to investigate his or her issue?

In addition, this chapter describes four general ways to think about validity: *statistical conclusion validity, internal validity, construct validity,* and *external validity.* Search InfoTrac College Edition and choose one of these terms to locate an article that considers this concept as described in the text. Describe what you find and how the article provides an example of your chosen concept. Were there any terms that you could not find or that had different meanings in the article from the one presented in the text?

✪ *The NEW Companion Web Site for* Research Methods for Criminal Justice and Criminology, *Fourth Edition*

http://ci.wadsworth.com/maxfield_babbie/ research_methods4e

Supplement your review of this chapter by going to the new companion Web site to take one of the Tutorial Quizzes, use the flash cards to master key terms, and check out the many other study aids you'll find there. You'll also find special features such as quantitative and qualitative data analysis primers to help you with a special project or do some research on your own.

✪ *Additional Readings*

Cook, Thomas D., and Campbell, Donald T., *Quasi-experimentation: Design and Analysis Issues for Field Settings* (Boston: Houghton Mifflin, 1979). This book is considered by many social science researchers to be a definitive discussion of cause and threats to the validity of causal inference. See especially Chapters 1 and 2.

Farrington, David P., Ohlin, Lloyd E., and Wilson, James Q., *Understanding and Controlling Crime: Toward a New Research Strategy* (New York: Springer-Verlag, 1986). Three highly respected criminologists describe the advantages of longitudinal studies and policy experiments for criminal justice research. The book also presents a research agenda for studying the causes of crime and the effectiveness of policy responses.

Gottfredson, Michael R., and Hirschi, Travis, "The Methodological Adequacy of Longitudinal Research on Crime," *Criminology*, Vol. 25 (1987), pp. 581–614. Two other highly respected criminologists point to some of the shortcomings of longitudinal studies.

Maxwell, Joseph A., *Qualitative Research Design: An Interactive Approach* (Thousand Oaks, CA: Sage, 1996). Despite the word *qualitative* in the title, this book offers excellent advice in progressing from general interests or thoughts to more specific plans for actual research. Each chapter concludes with exercises that incrementally help readers develop research plans.

Pawson, Ray, and Tilley, Nick, *Realistic Evaluation* (Thousand Oaks, CA: Sage, 1997). The authors propose an alternative way of thinking about cause, in the context of what they call "scientific realism." Although they criticize traditional social science approaches to inferring cause, Pawson and Tilley supplement the classic insights of Cook and Campbell.

Sampson, Robert J., and Laub, John H., *Crime in the Making: Pathways and Turning Points Through Life* (Cambridge, MA: Harvard University Press). This highly acclaimed study illustrates the longitudinal approach to explanatory research. Sampson and Laub are also attentive to possible validity threats to their findings.

Weisburd, David, *Reorienting Crime Prevention Research and Policy: From the Causes of Criminality to the Context of Crime* (Washington, DC: U.S. Department of Justice, Office of Justice Programs, National Institute of Justice, 1997) (http://www .ncjrs.org/txtfiles/165041.txt). Much criminological research examines people or organizations as units of analysis. Weisburd argues that we should also examine places and contexts of crime, raising interesting questions about units of analysis.

Chapter 5

Concepts, Operationalization, and Measurement

It's essential to specify exactly what we mean (and don't mean) by the terms we use. This is the first step in the measurement process, and we'll cover it in depth.

Introduction

Because measurement is difficult and imprecise, researchers try to describe the measurement process explicitly.

This chapter describes the progression from having a vague idea about what we want to study to being able to recognize it and measure it in the real world. We begin with the general issue of conceptualization, which sets up a foundation for our examination of operationalization and measurement. We then turn to different approaches to assessing measurement quality. The chapter concludes with an overview of strategies for combining individual measures into more complex indicators. Our examination of measurement continues in the next chapter, where we'll focus on different strategies for measuring crime.

As you read this chapter, keep in mind a central theme: communication. Ultimately, criminal justice and social scientific research seeks to communicate findings to an audience—professors, classmates, journal readers, or co-workers in a probation services agency, for example. Moving from vague ideas and interests to a completed research report, as we described in Chapter 4, involves communication at every step—from general ideas to more precise definitions of critical terms. With more precise definitions, we can begin to develop measures to apply in the real world.

Conceptions and Concepts

Clarifying abstract mental images is an essential first step in measurement.

If you hear the word *recidivism,* what image comes to mind? You might think of someone who has served time for burglary and who breaks into a house soon after being released from prison. Or, in contrast to that rather specific image, you might have a more general image of the habitual criminal. Someone who works in a criminal justice agency might have a different mental image. Police officers might think of a specific individual they have arrested repeatedly for a variety of offenses, and a judge might think of a defendant who has three prior convictions for theft.

Ultimately, *recidivism* is simply a term we use in communication—a word representing a collection of related phenomena that we have either observed or heard about somewhere. It's as though we have file drawers in our minds containing thousands of sheets of paper, and each sheet has a label in the upper right-hand corner. One sheet of paper in your file drawer has the term *recidivism* on it, and the person who sits next to you in class has one, too.

The technical name for those mental images, those sheets of paper in our file drawers, is **conception.** Each sheet of paper is a conception—a subjective thought about things that we encounter in daily life. But those mental images cannot be communicated directly. There is no way we can directly reveal what's written on our mental images. Therefore, we use the terms written in the upper right-hand corners as a way of communicating about our conceptions and the things we observe that are related to those conceptions.

For example, the word *crime* represents our conception about certain kinds of behavior. But individuals have different conceptions; they may think of different kinds of behavior when they hear the word *crime.* For example, police officers in most states would include possession of marijuana among their conceptions of crime, whereas members of the advocacy group NORML would not. Recent burglary victims might recall their own experiences in their conceptions of crime, whereas more fortunate neighbors might think about the murder story in yesterday's newspaper.

Because conceptions are subjective and cannot be communicated directly, we use the words and symbols of language as a way of communicating about our conceptions and the things we observe that are related to those conceptions.

Concepts are the words or symbols in language that we use to represent these mental images. We use concepts to communicate with one another, to share our mental images. Although a common language enables us to communicate, it is important to recognize that the words and phrases we use represent abstractions. Concepts are abstract because they are independent of the labels we assign to them. Crime as a concept is abstract, meaning that in the English language this label represents mental images of illegal acts. Of course, actual crimes are real events, and our mental images of crime may be based on real events (or the stuff of TV drama). However, when we talk about crime, without being more specific, we are talking about an abstraction. Thus, for example, the concept of crime proposed by Michael Gottfredson and Travis Hirschi (1990:15)—using force or fraud in pursuit of self-interest—is abstract. "Crime" is the symbol or label they have assigned to this concept.

Let's discuss a specific example. What is your conception of "serious crime"? What mental images come to mind? Most people agree that airplane hijacking, rape, bank robbery, and murder are serious crimes. What about a physical assault that results in a concussion and facial injuries? Many of us would classify it as a serious crime, but not if the incident took place in a boxing ring. Is burglary a serious crime? It doesn't rank up there with drive-by shooting, but we would probably agree that it is more serious than shoplifting. What about drug use or drug dealing?

Our mental images of serious crime may vary depending on our backgrounds and experiences. If your home has ever been burglarized, you might be more inclined than someone who has not suffered that experience to rate it as a serious crime. If you have been both burglarized and robbed at gunpoint, you would probably think the burglary was less serious than the robbery. There is much disagreement over the seriousness of drug use. Younger people, whether or not they have used drugs, may be less inclined to view drug use as a serious crime, whereas police and other public officials might rank drug use as very serious. In 1996, a majority of California residents approved a state referendum that legalized the use of marijuana for medical purposes even as officials in the Department of Justice continued to view any marijuana use as a crime.

"Serious crime" is an abstraction, a label we use to represent a concept. However, we must be careful to distinguish the label we use for a concept from the reality that the concept represents. There are real robberies, and robbery is a serious crime, but the concept of crime seriousness is not real.

In order to link conceptions, concepts, and measurement, consider Abraham Kaplan's (1964) discussion of three classes of things that scientists measure: direct observables, indirect observables, and constructs. The first class, direct observables, includes those things that we can observe simply and directly, such as the color of an apple or the words in a crime report. Indirect observables require "relatively more subtle, complex, or indirect observations" (1964:55). We note that a police officer has written "robbery" in the place for "offense type" on a crime report and has thus indirectly observed what crime has occurred. Newspaper stories, court transcripts, and criminal history records provide indirect observations of past actions. Finally, constructs are theoretical creations based on things that cannot be observed directly or indirectly. IQ is a good example: It is constructed mathematically from observations of the answers to questions on an IQ test.

Kaplan (1964:49) defined *concept* as a "family of conceptions." A concept is, as Kaplan noted, a construct. The concept of serious crime, then, is a construct created from your conception of it, our conception of it, and the conceptions of all those who have ever used the term. The concept of serious crime cannot be observed directly or indirectly. We can, however, meaningfully discuss the concept, observe examples of serious crime, and measure it indirectly.

Conceptualization

Day-to-day communication is made possible through general but often vague and unspoken agreements about the use of terms. Usually, other people do not understand exactly what we wish to communicate, but they get the general drift of our meaning. For example, although we may not fully agree about the meaning of the term *serious crime,* it's safe to assume that the crime of bank robbery is more serious than the crime of bicycle theft. A wide range of misunderstandings is the price we pay for our imprecision, but somehow we muddle through. Science, however, aims at more than muddling, and it cannot operate in a context of such imprecision.

Conceptualization is the process by which we specify precisely what we mean when we use particular terms. Suppose we want to find out whether violent crime is more serious than nonviolent crime. Most of us would probably assume that is true, but it might be interesting to find out whether it's really so. Notice that we can't meaningfully study the issue, let alone agree on the answer, without some precise working agreements about the meanings of the terms we are using. They are working agreements in the sense that they allow us to work on the question.

We begin by clearly differentiating violent and nonviolent crime. In violent crimes, an offender uses force or threats of force against a victim. Nonviolent crimes either do not involve any direct contact between a victim and an offender or involve contact but no force. For example, pickpocketing involves direct contact but no force. In contrast, robbery involves at least the threat to use force on victims. Burglary, auto theft, shoplifting, and the theft of unattended personal property such as bicycles are examples of nonviolent crimes. Assault, rape, robbery, and murder are violent crimes.

Indicators and Dimensions

The end product of the conceptualization process is the specification of a set of indicators of what we have in mind, indicating the presence or absence of the concept we are studying. To illustrate this process, let's discuss the more general concept of crime seriousness. This concept is more general than serious crime because it implies that some crimes are more serious than others.

One good indicator of crime seriousness is harm to the crime victim. Physical injury is an example of harm, and physical injury is certainly more likely to result from violent crime than from nonviolent crime. What about other kinds of harm? Burglary victims suffer economic harm from property loss and perhaps damage to their homes. Is the loss of $800 in a burglary an indicator of more serious crime than a $10 loss in a robbery in which the victim was not injured? Victims of both violent crime and nonviolent crime may suffer psychological harm. Charles Silberman (1978:18–19) described how people feel a sense of personal violation after discovering that their home has been burglarized. Other types of victim harm can be combined into groups and subgroups as well.

The technical term for such groupings is **dimension**—some specifiable aspect of a concept. Thus, we might speak of the "victim harm dimension" of crime seriousness. This dimension could include indicators of physical injury, economic loss, or psychological consequences. And we can easily think of other indicators and dimensions related to the general concept of crime seriousness. If we consider the theft of $20 from a poor person to be more serious than the theft of $2000 from a wealthy oil company CEO, victim wealth might be another dimension. Also consider a victim identity dimension. Killing a burglar in self-defense would not be as serious as threatening to kill the president of the United States.

Thus, it is possible to subdivide the concept of crime seriousness into several dimensions. Specifying dimensions and identifying the various indicators for each of those dimensions are both parts of conceptualization.

Specifying the different dimensions of a concept often paves the way for a more sophisticated understanding of what we are studying.

We might observe, for example, that fistfights among high school students result in thousands of injuries per year but that the annual costs of auto theft cause direct economic harm to hundreds of insurance companies and millions of auto insurance policyholders. Recognizing the many dimensions of crime seriousness, we cannot say that violent crime is more serious than nonviolent crime in all cases.

As it happens, defining and measuring crime seriousness is an important issue in criminal justice policy and research. Domestic assaults and acquaintance rape are examples of violent crimes that are often treated differently than physical or sexual violence among strangers, suggesting a victim–offender relationship dimension. For instance, the battered-woman defense has been used in trials of women who kill a spouse or lover following an extended period of violence (Williams, 1991). Such mitigating circumstances mean that some types of murder are treated differently than others, based in part on motivation and the relationship between victim and offender. The tendency of courts to punish rapists less harshly if they had some prior relationship with their victims has led to growing protests (Lopez, 1992). Studies have shown that death penalties were more often imposed on blacks convicted of killing whites, which indicates that victim race is related to sentencing and might therefore be considered an indicator of crime seriousness (Baldus, Pulaski, and Woodworth, 1983). Later in this chapter, we will discuss specific attempts to develop measures of crime seriousness.

Confusion over Definitions and Reality

To review briefly, our concepts are derived from the conceptions (mental images) that summarize collections of seemingly related observations and experiences. Although the observations and experiences are real, our concepts are mental creations. The terms associated with concepts are merely devices created for communication. The term *crime seriousness* is an ex-

ample. Ultimately, that phrase is only a collection of letters and has no intrinsic meaning. We could have as easily and meaningfully created the term *crime pettiness* to serve the same purpose.

Often, however, we fall into the trap of believing that terms have real meanings. That danger seems to grow stronger when we begin to take terms seriously and attempt to use them precisely. And the danger is all the greater in the presence of experts who appear to know more about what the terms really mean. It's easy to yield to the authority of experts in such a situation.

Once we have assumed (mistakenly) that terms have real meanings, we begin the task of discovering what those real meanings are and what constitutes a genuine measurement of them. Figure 5.1 illustrates this process. We make up conceptual summaries of real observations because the summaries are convenient— so convenient, however, that we begin to think they are real. The process of regarding as real things that are not is called **reification.** The reification of concepts in day-to-day life is very common.

Creating Conceptual Order

The design and execution of criminal justice research requires that we clear away the confusion over concepts and reality. To this end, logicians and scientists have found it useful to distinguish three kinds of definitions: real, conceptual, and operational. The first of these reflects the reification of terms, and as Carl G. Hempel (1952:6) has cautioned:

> A "real" definition, according to traditional logic, is not a stipulation determining the meaning of some expression but a statement of the "essential nature" or the "essential attributes" of some entity. The notion of essential nature, however, is so vague as to render this characterization useless for the purposes of rigorous inquiry.

A "real" or "essential nature" definition is inherently subjective. The specification of concepts

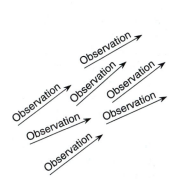

1. Many of our observations in life seem to have something in common. We get the sense that they represent something more general than the simple content of any single observation. We find it useful, moreover, to communicate about the general concept.

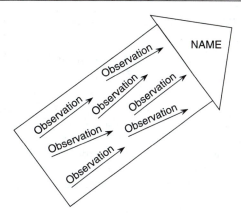

2. It is inconvenient to keep describing all the specific observations whenever we want to communicate about the general concept they seem to have in common, so we give a name to the general concept—to stand for whatever it is the specific observations have in commmon.

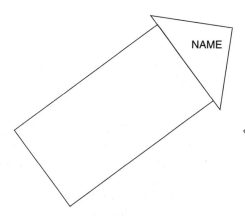

3. As we communicate about the general concept, using its term, we begin to think that the concept is some *thing* that really exists, not just a summary reference for several concrete observations in the world.

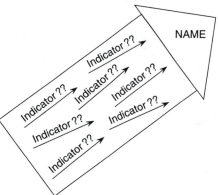

4. The belief that the concept itself is real results in irony. We now begin discussing and debating whether specific observations are "really" sufficient indicators of the concept.

Figure 5.1   Process of Conceptual Entrapment

WHAT IS RECIDIVISM?

by Tony Fabelo
Executive Director, Texas Criminal
Justice Policy Council

The Senate Criminal Justice Committee will be studying the record of the corrections system and the use of recidivism rates as a measure of performance for the system. The first task for the committee should be to clearly define recidivism, understand how it is measured, and determine the implications of adopting recidivism rates as measures of performance.

Defining Recidivism

Recidivism is the reoccurrence of criminal behavior. The rate of recidivism refers to the proportion of a specific group of offenders (for example, those released on parole) who engage in criminal behavior within a given period of time. Indicators of criminal behavior are re-arrests, reconvictions, or reincarcerations.

Each of these indicators depends on contact with criminal justice officials, and will therefore underestimate the reoccurrence of criminal be-

havior. However, criminal behavior that is unreported and not otherwise known to officials in justice agencies is difficult to measure in a consistent and economically feasible fashion.

In 1991 the Criminal Justice Policy Council recommended to the legislature and state criminal justice agencies that recidivism be measured in the following way:

> Recidivism rates should be calculated by counting the number of prison releases or number of offenders placed under community supervision who are reincarcerated for a technical violation or new offense within a uniform period of at-risk street time.

> The at-risk street time can be one, two, or three years, but it must be uniform for the group being tracked so that results are not distorted by uneven at-risk periods.

> Reincarceration should be measured using data from the "rap sheets" collected by the Texas Department of Public Safety in their Computerized Criminal History system. A centralized source of information reduces reporting errors.

in scientific inquiry depends instead on conceptual and operational definitions. A **conceptual definition** is a working definition specifically assigned to a term. In the midst of disagreement and confusion over what a term really means, the scientist specifies a working definition for the purposes of the inquiry. Wishing to examine socioeconomic status (SES), for example, we may simply specify that we are going to treat it as a combination of income and educational attainment. With that definitional decision, we rule out many other possible aspects of SES: occupational status, money in the bank, property, lineage, lifestyle, and so forth.

The specification of conceptual definitions does two important things. First, it serves as a specific working definition we present so that readers will understand exactly what we mean by a concept. Second, it focuses our observational strategy. Notice that a conceptual defini-

tion does not directly produce observations; rather, it channels our efforts to develop actual measures.

As a next step, we must specify exactly what we will observe, how we will do it, and what interpretations we will place on various possible observations. These further specifications make up the **operational definition** of the concept— a definition that spells out precisely how the concept will be measured. Strictly speaking, an operational definition is a description of the "operations" undertaken in measuring a concept.

Pursuing the definition of SES, we might decide to ask the people we are studying three questions:

1. What was your total household income during the past 12 months?
2. How many persons are in your household?

Systemwide Recidivism Rates

Recidivism rates can be reported for all offenders in the system—for all offenders released from prison or for all offenders placed on probation. This I call *systemwide recidivism rates.* Approximately 48 percent of offenders released from prison on parole or mandatory supervision, or released from county jails on parole, in 1991 were reincarcerated by 1994 for a new offense or a parole violation.

For offenders released from prison in 1991 the reincarceration recidivism rate three years after release from prison by offense of conviction is listed below:

Burglary	56%	Assault	44%
Robbery	54%	Homicide	40%
Theft	52%	Sexual assault	39%
Drugs	43%	Sex offense	34%

For the same group, the reincarceration recidivism rate three years after release by age group is listed below:

17–25	56%
26–30	52%
31–35	48%
36–40	46%
41 or older	35%

The Meaning of Systemwide Recidivism Rates

The systemwide recidivism rate of prison releases should not be used to measure the performance of institutional programs. There are many socioeconomic factors that can affect systemwide recidivism rates.

For example, the systemwide recidivism rate of offenders released from prison in 1995 declined because of changes in the characteristics of the population released from prison. Offenders are receiving and serving longer sentences, which will raise the average age at release. Therefore, "performance" in terms of systemwide recidivism will improve but not necessarily due to improvements in the delivery of services within the prison system.

On the other hand, the systemwide recidivism rate of felons released from state jail facilities should be expected to be relatively high, since state jail felons are property and drug offenders who tend to have high recidivism rates.

---

3. What is the highest level of school you have completed?

Next, we need to specify a system for categorizing the answers people give us. For income, we might use the categories "under $25,000" and "$25,000–$35,000." Educational attainment might be similarly grouped into categories, and we might simply count the number of people in each household. Finally, we need to specify a way to combine each person's responses to these three questions to create a measure of SES.

The end result is a working and workable definition of SES. Others might disagree with our conceptualization and operationalization, but the definition has one essential scientific virtue: It is absolutely specific and unambiguous. Even if someone disagrees with our definition, that person will have a good idea of how to interpret our research results because what we mean by the term SES—reflected in our analyses and conclusions—is clear.

Here is a diagram showing the progression of measurement steps from our vague sense of what a term means to specific measurements in a scientific study:

Conceptualization

↓

Conceptual definition

↓

Operational definition

↓

Measurements in the real world

To test your understanding of these measurement steps, return to the beginning of the chapter, where we asked you what image comes to mind in connection with the word *recidivism.*

Recall your own mental image, and compare it with Tony Fabelo's discussion in the box titled "What Is Recidivism?"

Operationalization Choices

Describing how to obtain actual empirical measures begins with operationalization.

Recall from Chapter 4 that the research process is not usually a set of steps that proceed in order from first to last. This is especially true of operationalization, the process of developing operational definitions. Although we begin by conceptualizing what we wish to study, once we start to consider operationalization, we may revise our conceptual definition. Developing an operational definition also moves us closer to measurement, which requires that we think about selecting a data collection method as well. In other words, operationalization does not proceed according to a systematic checklist.

To illustrate this fluid process, let's return to the issue of crime seriousness. Suppose we want to conduct a descriptive study that shows which crimes are more serious and which crimes are less serious.

One obvious dimension of crime seriousness is the penalties that are assigned to different crimes by law. Let's begin with this conceptualization. Our conceptual definition of crime seriousness is therefore the level of punishment that a state criminal code authorizes for different crimes. Notice that this definition has the distinct advantage of being unambiguous, a point noted by Ronald Farrell and Victoria Lynn Swigert (1978:440), who argued that the legislated maximum sentence is "the most objective determination of the severity of an offense." We're making progress, which leads us to an operational definition something like this:

> Consult the Texas Criminal Code. (1) Those crimes that may be punished by death will be judged most serious. (2) Next will be crimes that may be punished by a prison sentence of more than 1 year. (3) The least

serious crimes are those with jail sentences of less than a year and/or fines.

The operations undertaken to measure crime seriousness are specific. Our data collection strategy is also clear: Go to the library, make a list of crimes described in the Texas Code, and classify each crime into one of the three groups.

Note that we have produced rather narrow conceptual and operational definitions of crime seriousness. We might presume that penalties in the Texas Code take into account additional dimensions like victim harm, offender motivation, and other circumstances of individual crimes. However, the three groups of crimes include very different types of incidents and so do not tell us much about crime seriousness.

An alternative conceptualization of crime seriousness might center on what people think of as serious crime. In this view, crime seriousness is based on people's beliefs, which may reflect their perceptions of harm to victims, offender motivation, or other dimensions. Conceptualizing crime seriousness in this way suggests a different approach to operationalization: You will present descriptions of various crimes to other students in your class and ask them to indicate how serious they believe the crimes are. If crime seriousness is operationalized in this way, a questionnaire is the most appropriate data collection method.

We must make many other decisions before actually taking measurements of crime seriousness. How should crimes be described, and how should students indicate whether a crime is serious or not serious? Will crime descriptions simply be ranked from most to least serious, or will we try to make more precise measurements about how, for example, rape compares with smoking marijuana.

Measurement as "Scoring"

Operationalization involves describing how actual measurements will be made. The next step, of course, is making the measurements. Royce Singleton and associates (Singleton, Straits, and Straits, 1993:100) define *measurement* as "the process of assigning numbers or labels to units of analysis in order to represent conceptual properties. This process should be quite familiar to the reader even if the definition is not." You should be able to think of examples of the process. Your instructor assigns number or letter grades to exams and papers to represent your mastery of course material. You count the number of pages in this week's history assignment to represent how much time you will have to spend studying. The American Bar Association rates nominees to the U.S. Supreme Court as qualified, highly qualified, or not qualified. You might rank last night's date on the proverbial scale of 1 to 10, reflecting whatever conceptual properties are important to you.

Another way to think of measurement is in terms of scoring. Your instructor scores exams by counting the right answers and assigning some point value to each answer. Referees keep score at basketball games by counting the number of 1-point free throws and 2- and 3-point field goals for each team. Judges or juries score persons charged with crime by pronouncing "guilty" or "not guilty." City murder rates are scored by counting the number of murder victims and dividing by the number of city residents.

Measurement is distinct from operationalization in that measurement involves actually making observations and assigning scores—numbers or other labels—to those observations. Making observations, of course, is related to the data collection method, which, in turn, is implied by operationalization. However, the measurement process begins much earlier, usually with conceptualization.

Many people consider measurement to be the most important and difficult phase of criminal justice research. It is difficult, in part, because so many basic concepts in criminal justice are not easy to define as specifically as we would like. Without being able to settle on a conceptual definition, we find operationalizing and measuring things challenging. This is illustrated by the box titled "Jail Stay."

In addition to being challenging, different operationalization choices can produce different results. Here are three brief examples, developed with the excellent assistance of students in a research methods class at John Jay College of Criminal Justice in New York City (CRJ 715-03, 9 October 2003).

First, in comparing a general-purpose survey of crime victimization with specialized studies of family conflict, Murray Straus (1999) reports that domestic assault rates are over 16 times higher in surveys of family conflict. He attributes this to an explicit focus on *crime* in crime surveys, whereas studies of family conflict do not cue respondents with the keyword *crime*. As a result, physical violence among family members appears to be much more prevalent in Straus's research than in general crime surveys. The opposite is true of injuries—Straus reports that less than 4 percent of family violence incidents produced an injury, compared with 75 percent in the National Crime Victimization Survey (NCVS). These divergent findings make sense. Straus finds higher rates of less severe violence, while crime surveys reveal lower rates of more severe violence.

Second, according to the FBI Uniform Crime Report (UCR) about 7 million larcenies were reported in 2001 (Federal Bureau of Investigation, 2002), while the NCVS estimated over 14 million larcenies nationwide for the same year (Rennison, 2002). FBI data count only crimes reported to police, while the NCVS includes incidents not reported. Less than half of larcenies are reported, accounting for most of the difference. But for motor vehicle theft, the patterns are reversed: Over 1,226,000 vehicle thefts were recorded for the 2001 UCR, compared with under 1,009,000 for the NCVS. A different operationalization rule is at work here: The NCVS measures crimes against households and cannot count thefts of vehicles owned by businesses or other organizations; these crimes do appear in UCR counts.

Third, in the box titled "What Is Recidivism?" Tony Fabelo argues that the at-risk period for comparing recidivism for different groups of

JAIL STAY

Recall from Chapter 1 that two of the general purposes of research are description and explanation. The distinction between them has important implications for the process of definition and measurement. If you have formed the opinion that description is a simpler task than explanation, you may be surprised to learn that definitions can be more problematic for descriptive research than for explanatory research. To illustrate this, we present an example based on an attempt by one of the authors to describe what he thought was a simple concept.

In the course of an evaluation project, Maxfield wished to learn the average number of days people stayed in the Marion County (Indiana) jail. This concept was labeled "jail stay." People can be in the county jail for three reasons: (1) They are serving a sentence of 1 year or less, (2) they are awaiting trial, or (3) they are being held temporarily while awaiting transfer to another county or state or to prison. The third category includes people who have been sentenced to prison and are waiting for space to open up, or those who have been arrested and are wanted for some reason in another jurisdiction.

Maxfield vaguely knew these things but did not recognize how they complicated the task of defining and ultimately measuring jail stay. So the original question—"What is the average jail stay?"—was revised to "What is the average jail stay for persons serving sentences and for persons awaiting trial?"

Just as people can be in jail for different reasons, an individual can be in jail for more than one reason. For example, let's consider a hypothetical jail resident we'll call Allan. He was convicted of burglary in July 2002 and sentenced to a year in jail. All but 30 days of his sentence were suspended, meaning that he was freed but could be required to serve the remaining 11 months if he got into trouble again. It did not take long. Two

months after being released, Allan was arrested for robbery and returned to jail.

Now it gets complicated. A judge imposes the remaining 11 months of Allan's suspended sentence. Allan is denied bail and must wait for his trial in jail. It is soon learned that Allan is wanted by police in Illinois for passing bad checks. Many people would be delighted to send Allan to Illinois; they tell officials in that state they can have him, pending resolution of the situation in Marion County. Allan is now in jail for three reasons: (1) serving his sentence for the original burglary, (2) awaiting trial on a robbery charge, and (3) waiting for transfer to Illinois.

Is this one jail stay or three? In a sense, it is one jail stay because one person, Allan, is occupying a jail cell. But let's say Allan's trial on the robbery charge is delayed until after he completes his sentence for the burglary. He stays in jail and begins a new jail stay. When he comes up for trial, the prosecutor asks to waive the robbery charges against Allan in hopes of exporting him to the neighboring state, and a new jail stay begins as Allan awaits his free trip to Illinois.

You may recognize this as a problem with units of analysis. Is the unit the person who stays in jail? Or are the separate reasons Allan is in jail—which are social artifacts—the units of analysis? After some thought, Maxfield decided that the social artifact was the more appropriate unit because he was interested in whether jail cells are more often occupied by people serving sentences or people awaiting trial. But that produced a new question of how to deal with people like Allan. Do we double-count the overlap in Allan's jail stays, so that he accounts for two jail stays while serving his suspended sentence for burglary and waiting for the robbery trial? This seemed to make sense, but then Allan's two jail stays would count the same as two other people with one jail stay each. In other words, Allan would appear to occupy two jail beds at the same time. This was neither true nor helpful in describing how long people stay in jail for different reasons.

offenders should be uniform. It's possible to examine 1-, 2-, or 3-year rates, but comparisons should use standard at-risk periods. Varying the at-risk period produces, as we might expect,

differences in recidivism rates. Evaluating a Texas program that provided drug abuse treatment, Michael Eisenberg (1999:8) reports rates for different at-risk periods:

	1-Year	2-Year	3-Year
All participants	14%	37%	42%

Note that the difference between 1- and 2-year rates is much larger than that between 2- and 3-year rates. Operationalizing "recidivism" as a 1-year failure rate would be much less accurate than operationalizing the concept as a 2-year rate, because recidivism rates seem to stabilize at the 2-year point.

Exhaustive and Exclusive Measurement

Briefly revisiting terms introduced in Chapter 1, an attribute is a characteristic or quality of something. "Female" is an example, as are "old" and "student." Variables, in contrast, are logical sets of attributes. Thus, "gender" is a variable composed of the attributes "female" and "male." The conceptualization and operationalization processes can be seen as the specification of variables and the attributes composing them. Thus, "employment status" is a variable that has the attributes "employed" and "unemployed," or the list of attributes could be expanded to include other possibilities such as "employed part-time," "employed full-time," and "retired."

Every variable should have two important qualities. First, the attributes composing it should be *exhaustive*. If the variable is to have any utility in research, researchers must be able to classify every observation in terms of one of the attributes composing the variable. We will run into trouble if we conceptualize the variable "sentence" in terms of the attributes "prison" and "fine." After all, some convicted persons are assigned to probation, some have a portion of their prison sentence suspended, and others may receive a mix of prison terms, probation, suspended sentences, or perhaps community service. Notice that we could make the list of attributes exhaustive by adding "other" and "combination." Whatever approach we take, we must be able to classify every observation.

At the same time, attributes composing a variable must be *mutually exclusive*. Researchers

must be able to classify every observation in terms of one and only one attribute. Thus, for example, we need to define "prison" and "fine" in such a way that nobody can be both at the same time. That means we must be able to handle the person whose sentence includes both a prison term and a fine. In this case, attributes could be defined more precisely by specifying "prison only," "fine only," and "both prison and fine."

Levels of Measurement

Attributes composing any variable must be mutually exclusive and exhaustive. Attributes may be related in other ways as well. Of particular interest is that variables may represent different levels of measurement: nominal, ordinal, interval, and ratio. Levels of measurement tell us what sorts of information we can gain from the "scores" assigned to the values of a variable.

Nominal Measures Variables whose attributes have only the characteristics of exhaustiveness and mutual exclusiveness are **nominal measures.** Examples are gender, race, city of residence, college major, Social Security number, and marital status. Although the attributes composing each of these variables—"male" and "female" for the variable "gender"—are distinct from one another and more or less exhaust the possibilities among people, they have none of the additional structures mentioned later. Nominal measures merely offer names or labels for characteristics.

Imagine a group of people being characterized in terms of a nominal variable and physically grouped by the appropriate attributes. Suppose we are at a convention attended by hundreds of police chiefs. At a social function, we ask them to stand together in groups according to the states in which they live: all those from Vermont in one group, those from California in another, and so forth. (The variable is "state of residence"; the attributes are "live in Vermont," "live in California," and so on.) All the people standing in a given group have at least one thing in common; the people in any one group differ from the people in all other groups in that same regard. Where the individual groups are formed, how close they are to one another, and how they are arranged in the room is irrelevant. All that matters is that all the members of a given group share the same state of residence and that each group has a different shared state of residence.

Ordinal Measures Variables whose attributes may be logically rank ordered are **ordinal measures.** The different attributes represent relatively more or less of the variable. Examples of variables that can be ordered in some way are opinion of police, occupational status, crime seriousness, and fear of crime.

Let's pursue the earlier example of grouping police chiefs at a social gathering and imagine that we ask all those who have graduated from college to stand in one group, all those with a high school diploma (but who were not also college graduates) to stand in another group, and all those who have not graduated from high school to stand in a third group. This manner of grouping people satisfies the requirements for exhaustiveness and mutual exclusiveness. In addition, however, we might logically arrange the three groups in terms of their amount of formal education (the shared attribute). We might arrange the three groups in a row, ranging from most to least formal education. This arrangement provides a physical representation of an ordinal measure. If we know which groups two individuals are in, we can determine that one has more, less, or the same formal education as the other.

Note that in this example it is irrelevant how close or far apart the educational groups are from one another. They might stand 5 feet apart or 500 feet apart; the college and high school groups could be 5 feet apart, and the less-than-high-school group might be 500 feet farther down the line. These actual distances have no meaning. The high school group, however, should be between the less-than-high-school group and the college group, or else the rank order is incorrect.

Interval Measures When the actual distance that separates the attributes composing some variables does have meaning, the variables are **interval measures.** The logical distance between attributes can then be expressed in meaningful standard intervals.

Interval measures commonly used in social scientific research are constructed measures such as standardized intelligence tests. The interval that separates IQ scores of 100 and 110 is the same as the interval that separates scores of 110 and 120 by virtue of the distribution of the observed scores of the many thousands of people who have taken the test over the years. Criminal justice researchers often combine individual nominal and ordinal measures to produce a composite interval measure. We'll see examples at the end of this chapter.

Ratio Measures Most of the social scientific variables that meet the minimum requirements for interval measures also meet the requirements for **ratio measures.** In ratio measures, the attributes that compose a variable, besides having all the structural characteristics mentioned previously, are based on a true zero point. Examples from criminal justice research are age, dollar value of property loss from burglary, number of prior arrests, blood alcohol content, and length of incarceration.

Returning to the example of various ways to classify police chiefs, we might ask the chiefs to group themselves according to years of experience in their present position. All those new to their job would stand together, as would those with 1 year of experience, those with 2 years on the job, and so forth. The facts that members of each group share the same years of experience and that each group has a different shared length of time satisfy the minimum requirements for a nominal measure. Arranging the several groups in a line from those with the least to those with the most experience meets the additional requirements for an ordinal measure and permits us to determine whether one person is more experienced, is less experienced, or has the same level of experience as another. If we arrange

Table 5.1   Crime Seriousness and Levels of Measurement

Crime	Victim	Seriousness Score	Rank	Value of Property Loss
Accepting a bribe	Society	9.0	9	0
Arson	Business	12.7	6	$10,000
Auto theft	Home	8.0	10	$12,000
Burglary	Business	15.5	5	$100,000
Burglary	Home	9.6	8	$1,000
Buying stolen property	Society	5.0	12	0
Heroin sales	Society	20.6	4	0
Heroin use	Society	6.5	11	0
Murder	Person	35.7	1	0
Obstructing justice	Society	10.0	7	0
Public intoxication	Society	0.8	15	0
Rape and injury	Person	30.0	2	0
Robbery and injury	Person	21.0	3	$1,000
Robbery attempt	Person	3.3	13	0
Robbery, no injury	Person	8.0	10	$1,000
Shoplifting	Business	2.2	14	$10
Trespassing	Home	0.6	16	0

Source: Adapted from Wolfgang, Figlio, Tracy, and Singer (1985).

the groups so that there is the same distance between each pair of adjacent groups, we satisfy the additional requirements of an interval measure and can say how much more experience one chief has than another. Finally, because one of the attributes included — experience — has a true zero point (police chiefs just appointed to their job), the phalanx of hapless convention-goers also meets the requirements for a ratio measure, permitting us to say that one person is twice as experienced as another.

Implications of Levels of Measurement

To review this discussion and to understand why level of measurement may make a difference, consider Table 5.1. It presents information on crime seriousness adapted from a survey of crime severity conducted for the Bureau of Justice Statistics (Wolfgang, Figlio, Tracy, and Singer, 1985). The survey presented brief descriptions of more than 200 different crimes to a sample of 60,000 people. Respondents were

asked to assign a score to each crime based on how serious they thought the crime was compared with bicycle theft (scored at 10).

The first column in Table 5.1 lists some of the crimes described. The second column shows a nominal measure that identifies the victim in the crime: home, person, business, or society. Type of victim is an attribute of each crime. The third column lists seriousness scores computed from survey results, ranging from 0.6 for trespassing to 35.7 for murder. These seriousness scores are interval measures because the distance between, for example, auto theft (at 8.0) and accepting a bribe (at 9.0) is the same as that between accepting a bribe (at 9.0) and obstructing justice (at 10.0). Seriousness scores are not ratio measures; there is no absolute zero point, and three instances of obstructing justice (at 10.0) do not equal one rape with injury (at 30.0).

The fourth column shows the ranking for each of the 17 crimes in the table; the most serious crime, murder, is ranked 1, followed by rape with injury, and so on. The rankings express only the order of seriousness, however, because the difference between murder (ranked 1) and rape (ranked 2) is smaller than the distance between rape and robbery with injury (ranked 3).

Finally, the crime descriptions presented to respondents indicated the value of property loss for each offense. This is a ratio measure with a true zero point, so that ten burglaries with a loss of $1000 each have the same property value as one arson offense with a loss of $10,000.

Specific analytic techniques require variables that meet certain minimum levels of measurement. For example, we could compute the average property loss from the crimes listed in Table 5.1 by adding up the individual numbers in the fifth column and dividing by the number of crimes listed (17). However, we would not be able to compute the average victim type because that is a nominal variable. In that case, we could report the modal—the most common—victim type, which is society in Table 5.1.

You may treat some variables as representing different levels of measurement. Ratio measures are the highest level, followed by interval, ordinal, and nominal. A variable that represents a given level of measurement—say, ratio—may also be treated as representing a lower level of measurement—say, ordinal. For example, age is a ratio measure. If we wish to examine only the relationship between age and some ordinal-level variable, such as delinquency involvement (high, medium, or low), we might choose to treat age as an ordinal-level variable as well. We might characterize the subjects of our study as being young, middle-aged, and old, specifying the age range for each of those groupings. Finally, age might be used as a nominal-level variable for certain research purposes. Thus, people might be grouped together as baby boomers if they were born between 1945 and 1955.

The analytic uses planned for a given variable, then, should determine the level of measurement to be sought, with the realization that some variables are inherently limited to a certain level. If a variable is to be used in a variety of ways that require different levels of measure-

ment, the study should be designed to achieve the highest level possible. Although ratio measures such as number of arrests can later be reduced to ordinal or nominal ones, it is not possible to convert a nominal or ordinal measure to a ratio one. More generally, you cannot convert a lower-level measure to a higher-level one. That is a one-way street worth remembering.

Criteria for Measurement Quality

The key standards for measurement quality are reliability and validity.

Measurements can be made with varying degrees of precision, which refers to the fineness of the distinctions made between the attributes that compose a variable. Saying that a woman is "43 years old" is more precise than that she is "in her forties." Describing a felony sentence as "18 months" is more precise than "over 1 year."

As a general rule, precise measurements are superior to imprecise ones, as common sense would suggest. Precision is not always necessary or desirable, however. If knowing that a felony sentence is over 1 year is sufficient for your research purpose, then any additional effort invested in learning the precise sentence would be wasted. The operationalization of concepts, then, must be guided partly by an understanding of the degree of precision required. If your needs are not clear, be more precise rather than less.

But don't confuse precision with accuracy. Describing someone as "born in Stowe, Vermont" is more precise than "born in New England," but suppose the person in question was actually born in Boston? The less precise description, in this instance, is more accurate; it's a better reflection of the real world. This is a point worth keeping in mind. Many criminal justice measures are imprecise, so reporting approximate values is often preferable.

Precision and accuracy are obviously important qualities in research measurement, and they probably need no further explanation. When criminal justice researchers construct and evaluate measurements, they pay special attention to two technical considerations: reliability and validity.

Reliability

In the abstract, **reliability** is a matter of whether a particular measurement technique, applied repeatedly to the same thing, will yield the same result each time. In other words, measurement reliability is roughly the same as measurement consistency or stability. Imagine, for example, a police officer standing on the street, guessing the speed of cars that pass by, and issuing speeding tickets based on that judgment. If you received a ticket from this officer and went to court to contest if, you would almost certainly win your case. The judge would no doubt reject this way of measuring speed, regardless of the police officer's experience. The reliability or consistency of this method of measuring vehicle speed is questionable at best. If the same police officer used a radar speed detector, however, it is doubtful that you would be able to beat the ticket. The radar device is judged a much more reliable way of measuring speed.

Reliability, though, does not ensure accuracy any more than precision does. The speedometer in your car may be a reliable instrument for measuring speed, but it is common for speedometers to be off by a few miles per hour, especially at higher speeds. If your speedometer shows 55 miles per hour when you are actually traveling at 60, it gives you a consistent but inaccurate reading that might attract the attention of police officers with more accurate radar guns.

Measurement reliability is often a problem with indicators used in criminal justice research. Numerous studies have shown that measures of crime based on police records often suffer from reliability problems. For example, Richard McCleary and associates (McCleary, Nienstedt, and Erven, 1982:362) analyzed changes in police records of burglary following a change in how burglary reports were investigated in a large city. Under the new system, detectives formally investigated burglaries that previously had been examined only by patrol officers. Burglaries declined sharply as soon as the new investigation procedures were implemented. The reason for the decline was that some patrol officers counted some crimes as burglaries that did not meet the official definition of burglary. When a smaller number of detectives began to investigate burglaries, they were more consistent in applying the official definition.

Other examples of reliability problems can be found in criminal justice research and policy settings. How accurate are the evaluations of judges in determining which defendants are at risk of fleeing before trial? A study by Sheila Royo Maxwell (1999) found that the factors used by judges in deciding whether to release defendants on their own recognizance were neither reliable nor effective predictors of the likelihood that defendants would fail to appear in court. Inconsistency in the administration of blood alcohol tests in certain states has forced researchers to search for new measures of drunk driving (Heeren, Smith, Morelock, and Hingson, 1985). Forensic DNA evidence is increasingly being used in violent crime cases. A National Research Council (1996) study found a variety of errors in laboratory procedures—including sample mishandling, evidence contamination, and analyst bias. These are measurement reliability problems that can lead to unwarranted exclusion of evidence or to the conviction of innocent people. For example, irregularities in DNA tests by a Texas crime lab led to the exoneration of at least one previously convicted defendant and prompted reviews of hundreds of additional cases (McVicker and Khanna, 2003).

Reliability problems crop up in many forms. Reliability is a concern every time a single observer is the source of data because we have no way to guard against that observer's subjectivity. We can't tell for sure how much of what's reported represents true variation and how much is due to the observer's unique perceptions.

Reliability can also be an issue when more than one observer makes measurements. Survey researchers have long known that different interviewers get different answers from respondents as a result of their own attitudes and demeanor. Suppose we want to conduct a study of editorial opinions about work release centers. We could create a team of coders to read hundreds of newspaper editorials and classify them in terms of their position on the issue, but different coders might code the same editorial differently. Or we may want to classify a few hundred community anticrime groups in terms of some standard coding scheme, such as a set of categories created by the National Institute of Justice. However, a police officer and a neighborhood activist are unlikely to code all those groups into the same categories.

These examples illustrate problems of reliability. Similar problems arise when we ask people for information about themselves. Sometimes we ask questions that people don't know the answers to ("How many times have you seen a police officer in the last month?"). Sometimes we ask people about things that are totally irrelevant to them ("Are you satisfied with the FBI's guidelines on the purchase of office supplies?"). And sometimes we ask questions that are so complicated that a person who has a clear opinion on the matter might have a different interpretation of the question when asked a second time.

How do we create reliable measures? Because the problem of reliability is a basic one in criminal justice measurement, researchers have developed a number of techniques for dealing with it.

The Test–Retest Method   Sometimes it is appropriate to make the same measurement more than once. If there is no reason to expect the information to change, we should expect the same response both times. If answers vary, however, then the measurement method is, to the extent of that variation, unreliable. Here's an illustration.

In their classic research on delinquency in England, Donald West and David Farrington (1977) interviewed a sample of 411 males from a working-class area of London at age 16 and again at age 18. The subjects were asked to describe a variety of aspects of their lives, including educational and work history, leisure pursuits, drinking and smoking habits, delinquent activities, and experience with police and courts.

Because many of these topics involve illegal or at least antisocial activity, West and Farrington were concerned about the accuracy of information obtained in their interviews. They assessed reliability in several ways. One was to compare responses from the interview at age 18 with those from the interview at age 16. For example, in each interview, the youths were asked at what age they left school. In most cases, there were few discrepancies in stated age from one interview to the next, which led the authors to conclude: "There was therefore no systematic tendency for youths either to increase or lessen their claimed period of school attendance as they grew older, as might have occurred if they had wanted either to exaggerate or to underplay their educational attainments" (1977:76–77). If West and Farrington had found less consistency in answers to this and other items, they would have had good reason to doubt the truthfulness of responses to more sensitive questions. The test–retest method suggested to the authors that memory lapses were the most common source of minor differences.

Although this method can be a useful reliability check, it is limited in some respects. Faulty memory may produce inconsistent responses if there is a lengthy gap between the initial interview and the retest. A different problem can arise in trying to use the test–retest method to check the reliability of attitude or opinion measures. If the test–retest interval is short, then answers given in the second interview may be affected by earlier responses if subjects try to be consistent.

Interrater Reliability   It is also possible for measurement unreliability to be generated by research workers—for example, interviewers and coders. To guard against interviewer unreliability, it is common practice in surveys to have a supervisor call a subsample of the respondents on the telephone and verify selected information. West and Farrington (1977:173) checked interrater reliability in their study of London youths and found few significant differences in results obtained from different interviewers.

Comparing measurements from different raters works in other situations as well. For example, Michael Geerken (1994) presents an important discussion of reliability problems that researchers are likely to encounter in measuring prior arrests through police "rap sheets." Duplicate entries, the use of aliases, and the need to transform official crime categories into a smaller number of categories for analysis are among the problems Geerken cites. One way to increase consistency in translating official records into research measures, a process often referred to as coding, is to have more than one person code a sample of records and then compare the consistency of coding decisions made by each person. This approach was used by Michael Maxfield and Cathy Spatz Widom (1996) in their analysis of adult arrests of child abuse victims.

In general, whenever researchers are concerned that measures obtained through coding may not be classified reliably, they should have each independently coded by different people. In the hypothetical study of newspaper editorials about a proposed work release center, coding decisions that generate disagreement should be evaluated more carefully and resolved. If we find a great deal of disagreement, our operational definitions of how to code newspaper editorials should be carefully reviewed and made more specific.

Split-Half Method   As a general rule, it is always a good idea to make more than one measurement of any subtle or complex social concept, such as prejudice or fear of crime. This procedure lays the groundwork for another check on reliability. Suppose you've created a questionnaire that contains 10 items you believe measure prejudicial beliefs about African Americans and delinquency. Using the split-half technique, you randomly assign those 10 items to two sets of five items. Each set should provide

a good measure of prejudice, and the sets should agree in the way they classify the respondents. If the two sets of items measure people differently, then that, again, points to a problem in the reliability of how you are measuring the variable.

The reliability of measurements is a fundamental issue in criminal justice research, and we'll return to it in the chapters to come. For now, however, we hasten to point out that even total reliability doesn't ensure that our measures actually measure what we think they measure. That brings us to the issue of validity.

Validity

In conventional usage, the term **validity** means that an empirical measure adequately reflects the meaning of the concept under consideration. Put another way, measurement validity involves whether you are really measuring what you say you are measuring. Recall that an operational definition specifies the operations you will perform to measure a concept. Does your operational definition accurately reflect the concept you are interested in? If the answer is yes, you have a valid measure. A radar gun is a valid measure of vehicle speed, but a wind velocity indicator is not because the volume of air displaced by a slow-moving truck will register higher than that displaced by a fast-moving sports car.

Although methods for assessing reliability are relatively straightforward, it is more difficult to demonstrate that individual measures are valid. Because concepts are not real, but abstract, we cannot directly demonstrate that measures, which are real, are actually measuring an abstract concept. Nevertheless, researchers have some ways of dealing with the issue of validity.

Face Validity   First, there's something called **face validity.** Particular empirical measures may or may not jibe with our common agreements and our individual mental images about a particular concept. We might debate the adequacy of measuring satisfaction with police services by counting the number of citizen complaints registered by the mayor's office, but we'd surely agree that the number of citizen complaints has something to do with levels of satisfaction. If someone suggested that we measure satisfaction with police by finding out whether people like to watch police dramas on TV, we would probably agree that the measure has no face validity; it simply does not make sense.

Second, there are many concrete agreements among researchers about how to measure certain basic concepts. The Census Bureau, for example, has created operational definitions of such concepts as family, household, and employment status that seem to have a workable validity in most studies using those concepts.

Criterion-Related Validity **Criterion-related validity** involves comparing a measure with some external criterion. A measure can be validated by showing that it predicts scores on another measure that is generally accepted as valid; this is sometimes referred to as convergent validity. The validity of College Board exams, for example, is shown in their ability to predict the success of students in college.

Timothy Heeren and associates (Heeren, Smith, Morelock, and Hingson, 1985) offer a good example of criterion-related validity in their efforts to validate a measure of alcohol-related auto fatalities. Of course, conducting a blood alcohol laboratory test on everyone killed in auto accidents would be a valid measure. Not all states regularly do this, however, so Heeren and colleagues tested the validity of an alternate measure: single-vehicle fatal accidents involving male drivers occurring between 8:00 P.M. and 3:00 A.M. The validity of this measure was shown by comparing it with the blood alcohol test results for all drivers killed in states that reliably conducted such tests in fatal accidents. Because the two measures agreed closely, Heeren and associates claimed that the proxy or surrogate measure would be valid in other states.

Another approach to criterion-related validity is to show that our measure of a concept is different from measures of similar but distinct concepts. This is called discriminant validity,

meaning that measures can discriminate different concepts. For example, Wesley Skogan and Michael Maxfield (1981:56–57) described how "crime" may sometimes be considered a code word for "race" among white Americans. Measures of fear of crime for some people may therefore be contaminated by racist fears about African Americans and crime. They established the discriminant validity of their measure by showing that it was not related to an index of racial intolerance.

Sometimes, it is difficult to find behavioral criteria that can be used to validate measures as directly as in the examples described here. In those instances, however, we can often approximate such criteria by considering how the variable in question ought, theoretically, to relate to other variables.

Construct Validity **Construct validity** is based on the logical relationships among variables. Let's suppose, for example, that we are interested in studying fear of crime—its sources and consequences. As part of our research, we develop a measure of fear of crime, and we want to assess its validity.

In addition to our measure, we will also develop certain theoretical expectations about the way the variable "fear of crime" relates to other variables. For instance, it's reasonable to conclude that people who are afraid of crime are less likely to leave their homes at night for entertainment than people who are not afraid of crime. If our measure of fear of crime relates to how often people go out at night in the expected fashion, that constitutes evidence of our measure's construct validity. However, if people who are afraid of crime are just as likely to go out at night as people who are not afraid, that challenges the validity of our measure.

Tests of construct validity, then, can offer a weight of evidence that our measure either does or doesn't tap the quality we want it to measure, without providing definitive proof. We have suggested here that tests of construct validity are less compelling than tests of criterion validity. However, there is room for disagreement

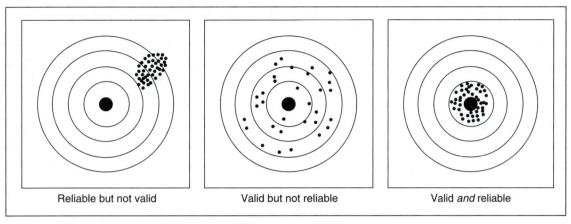

| Reliable but not valid | Valid but not reliable | Valid *and* reliable |

Figure 5.2 Analogy to Validity and Reliability

about which kind of test should be done in a given situation. It is less important to distinguish these two types than to understand the logic of validation that they have in common: If we are successful in measuring some variable, then those measurements should relate to other measures in some logical fashion.

Content Validity Finally, **content validity** refers to the degree to which a measure covers the range of meanings included within the concept. For instance, this question has frequently been used in surveys to measure fear of crime:

> How safe do you feel (or would you feel) walking alone in this area after dark? Would you say very safe, fairly safe, fairly unsafe, or very unsafe?

Although this question may provide a valid measure of fear in connection with street crime, it is not a good measure of fear of burglary, auto theft, or airplane hijacking. The concept of fear of crime is broader than the concept represented in the question.

Multiple Measures Another approach to validation of an individual measure is to compare it with alternative measures of the same concept. The use of multiple measures is similar to establishing criterion validity. However, the use of multiple measures does not necessarily as-

sume that the criterion measure is always more accurate. For example, many crimes that are committed never result in an arrest, so arrests are not good measures of how many crimes are committed by individuals. Self-report surveys have often been used to measure delinquency and criminality. But how valid are survey questions that ask people how many crimes they have committed?

The approach used by West and Farrington (and by others) is to ask, for example, how many times someone has committed robbery and how many times someone has been arrested for that crime. Those who admit having been arrested for robbery are asked when and where the arrest occurred. Self-reports can then be validated by checking police arrest records. This works two ways: (1) It is possible to validate individual reports of being arrested for robbery, and (2) researchers can check police records for all persons interviewed to see if there are any records of robbery arrests that subjects do not disclose to interviewers.

Figure 5.2 illustrates the difference between validity and reliability. Think of measurement as analogous to hitting the bull's-eye on a target. A reliable measure produces a "tight pattern," regardless of where it hits, because reliability is a function of consistency. Validity, in contrast, relates to the arrangement of shots around the bull's-eye. The failure of reliability in the figure can be seen as a random error; the failure of validity is a systematic error. Notice that neither an unreliable nor an invalid measure is likely to be very useful.

Composite Measures

Combining individual measures often produces more valid and reliable indicators.

Sometimes it is possible to construct a single measure that captures the variable of interest. For example, asking auto owners whether their car has been stolen in the previous 6 months is a straightforward way to measure auto theft victimization. But other variables may be better measured by more than a single indicator. To begin with a simple and well-known example, the FBI crime index is a composite measure of crime that combines police reports for seven different offenses into one indicator.

Composite measures are frequently used in criminal justice research for three reasons. First, despite carefully designing studies to provide valid and reliable measurements of variables, the researcher is often unable to develop single indicators of complex concepts. That is especially true with regard to attitudes and opinions that are measured through surveys. For example, we saw that measuring fear of crime through a question that asks about feelings of safety on neighborhood streets measures some dimensions of fear but certainly not all of them. This leads us to question the validity of using that single question to measure fear of crime.

Second, we may wish to use a rather refined ordinal measure of a variable, arranging cases in several ordinal categories from very low to very high on a variable such as degree of parental supervision. A single data item might not have enough categories to provide the desired range of variation, but an index or scale formed from several items would.

Finally, indexes and scales are *efficient* devices for data analysis. If a single data item gives only a rough indication of a given variable, considering several data items may give us a more comprehensive and more accurate indication. For example, the results of a single drug test would give us some indication of drug use by a probationer. Examining results from several drug tests would give us a better indication, but the manipulation of several data items simultaneously can be very complicated. In contrast, composite measures are efficient data reduction devices. Several indicators may be summarized in a single numerical score, even while perhaps very nearly maintaining the specific details of all the individual indicators.

Typologies

Researchers combine variables in different ways to produce different composite measures. The simplest of these is a **typology,** sometimes called a "taxonomy." Typologies are produced by the intersection of two or more variables to create a set of categories or types. We may, for example, wish to classify people according to the range of their experience in criminal court. Assume we have asked a sample of people whether they have ever served as a juror and whether they have ever testified as a witness in criminal court. Table 5.2 shows how the yes/no responses to these two questions can be combined into a typology of experience in court.

Typologies can be more complex—combining scores on three or more measures or combining scores on two measures that take many different values. For an example of a complex typology, consider research by Rolf Loeber and associates (Loeber, Stouthamer-Loeber, von Kammen, and Farrington, 1991) on patterns of delinquency over time. The researchers used a longitudinal design in which a sample of boys was selected from Pittsburgh public schools and interviewed many times. Some questions asked about their involvement in delinquency and criminal offending. This approach made it possible to distinguish boys who reported different types of offending at different times.

Table 5.2 Typology of Court Experience

		Serve on Jury?	
		No	Yes
Testify as Witness?	No	A	B
	Yes	C	D

Typology
  A: No experience with court
  B: Experience as juror only
  C: Experience as witness only
  D: Experience as juror and witness

Table 5.3 Typology of Change in Juvenile Offending

Typology	Juvenile Offending	
	Screening (Time 1)	Follow-Up (Time 2)
A. Nondelinquent	0	0
B. Starter	0	1, 2, or 3
C. Desistor	1, 2, or 3	0
D. Stable	1	1
D. Stable	2	2
D. Stable	3	3
E. Deescalator	3	2
E. Deescalator	2 or 3	1
F. Escalator	1	2 or 3
F. Escalator	2	3

Juvenile Offending Typology
  0: None
  1: Minor
  2: Moderate
  3: Serious
Source: Adapted from Loeber and associates (1991:43–46).

Loeber and associates first classified delinquent and criminal acts into these ordinal seriousness categories (1991:44):

None: No self-reported delinquency
Minor: Theft of items worth less than $5, vandalism, fare evasion
Moderate: Theft over $5, gang fighting, carrying weapons
Serious: Car theft, breaking and entering, forced sex, selling drugs

Next, to measure changes in delinquency over time, the researchers compared reports of delinquency from the first screening interview with reports from follow-up interviews. These two measures—delinquency at time 1 and delinquency at time 2—formed the typology, which they referred to as a "dynamic classification of offenders" (1991:44). Table 5.3 summarizes this typology.

The first category in the table, "nondelinquent," includes those boys who reported committing no offenses at both the screening and follow-up interviews. "Starters" reported no offenses at screening and then minor, moderate, or serious delinquency at follow-up, while "desistors" were just the opposite. Those who committed the same types of offenses at both times were labeled "stable"; "deescalators" reported committing less serious offenses at follow-up; and "escalators" moved on to more serious offenses.

Notice the efficiency of this typology. Two variables (delinquency at screening and follow-up) with four categories each are reduced to a single variable with six categories. Furthermore, the two measures of delinquency are themselves composite measures, produced by summarizing self-reports of a large number of individual offenses. Finally, notice also how this efficiency is reflected in the clear meaning of the new composite measure. This dynamic typology summarizes information about time, offending, and offense seriousness in a single measure.

An Index of Disorder

"What is disorder, and what isn't?" asks Wesley Skogan (1990:4) in his book on the links between crime, fear, and social problems such as public drinking, drug use, litter, prostitution, panhandling, dilapidated buildings, and groups of boisterous youths. In an influential article titled "Broken Windows," James Wilson and George Kelling (1982) describe disorder as a sign of crime that may contribute independently to fear and crime itself. The argument goes something like this: Disorder is a symbol of urban decay that people associate with crime. Signs of disorder can produce two related problems. First, disorder may contribute to fear of crime, as urban residents believe that physical decay and "undesirables" are symbols of crime. Second, potential offenders may interpret evidence of disorder as a signal that informal social control mechanisms in a neighborhood have broken down and that the area is fair game for mayhem and predation.

We all have some sort of mental image (conception) of disorder, but, to paraphrase Skogan's question: How do we measure it? Let's begin by distinguishing two conceptions of disorder. First, we can focus on the *physical presence* of disorder—whether litter, public drinking, public drug use, and the like are actually evident in an urban neighborhood. We might measure the physical presence of disorder through a series of systematic observations. This is the approach used by Robert Sampson and Stephen Raudenbush (1999) in their study of links between disorder and crime in Chicago. Unfortunately, these authors observed very few examples of disorder and altogether ignored the question of whether such behaviors were perceived as problematic by residents of Chicago neighborhoods.

That brings us to the second conception, one focusing on the *perception* of disorder. Thus, some people might view public drinking as disorderly, while others (New Orleans residents, for example) consider public drinking to be perfectly acceptable. Questionnaires and survey methods are the best suited for measuring perceived disorder.

Having settled on perceptions of disorder that we will measure through a survey, we must make some more decisions. Consider two versions of a question asking about people loitering on the street. The first is from a series of surveys conducted in three U.S. cities; the second is from a nationwide survey conducted in En-

gland and Wales in 1984. Each question is paraphrased from the original questionnaire.

1. Are groups of loiterers hanging out on the streets a big problem, some problem, or almost no problem in your neighborhood? (See Skogan and Maxfield, 1981.)
2. In your area, how common are loiterers hanging around on the street: very common, fairly common, not very common, or not at all common? (See Maxfield, 1987b.)

The first question asks about perceptions of loiterers hanging out as a *problem;* the second question asks about perceptions of the *frequency* of people hanging out. Notice also that the first question requires two rather different things of respondents: They must perceive loiterers hanging around, and they must judge that to be a problem. Skogan used the first formulation of the question, reasoning that perception of behavior as a problem is required for it to be perceived as disorder.

Is this a good measure of disorder? The belief that loiterers hanging around is a problem surely has something to do with perceptions of disorder, but there is more to it than that. As it stands, we have a measure of one dimension of disorder, but our measure is quite narrow. In order to represent the concept of disorder more completely, we should measure additional behaviors or characteristics that represent other examples of disorder.

Skogan used questions about nine different examples of disorder and classified them into two groups representing what he calls social and physical disorder (Skogan, 1990:51, 191):

Social Disorder	**Physical Disorder**
Groups of loiterers	Abandoned buildings
Drug use and sales	Garbage and litter
Vandalism	Junk in vacant lots
Gang activity	
Public drinking	
Street harassment	

Introduction:

Now I'm going to read you a list of crime-related problems that may be found in some parts of the city. For each one, please tell me how much of a problem it is in your neighborhood. Is it a big problem, some problem, or almost no problem?

	Big problem	Some problem	No problem
(S) Groups of people loitering	②	1	0
(S) People using or selling drugs	2	①	0
(P) Abandoned buildings	2	1	⓪
(S) Vandalism	2	①	0
(P) Garbage and litter on street	②	1	0
(S) Gangs and gang activity	2	1	⓪
(S) People drinking in public	②	1	0
(P) Junk in vacant lots	2	1	⓪
(S) People making rude or insulting remarks	2	①	0

(S) Social = 2 + 1 + 1 + 0 + 2 + 1 = 7
    Index score = $7/8$ = 1.16

(P) Physical = 0 + 2 + 0 = 2
    Index score = $2/3$ = 0.67

Figure 5.3 Index of Disorder

Questions corresponding to each of these examples of disorder asked respondents to rate them as big problems (scored 2), some problem (scored 1), or almost no problem (scored 0) in their neighborhood. Together, these nine items measure different types of disorder and appear to have reasonable face validity. However, examining the relationship between each individual item and respondents' fear of crime or experience as a crime victim would be unwieldy at best. So Skogan created two indexes, one for social disorder and one for physical disorder, by adding up the scores for each item and dividing by the number of items in each group. Figure 5.3 shows a hypothetical sample questionnaire for these nine items, together with the scores that would be produced for each index.

This example illustrates how several related variables can be combined to produce an index

that has three desirable properties. First, a composite index is a more valid measure of disorder than is an single question. Second, computing and averaging across all items in a category create more variation in the index than we could obtain in any single item. Finally, two indexes are more parsimonious than nine individual variables; data analysis and interpretation can be more efficient.

Measurement Summary

We have covered substantial ground in this chapter but still have introduced only the important and often complex issue of measurement in criminal justice research. The box "What's a Police Activity?" presents an illustration from our running example. More than a step in the research process, measurement involves continuous thinking about what

PUTTING IT ALL TOGETHER

WHAT'S A POLICE ACTIVITY?

As described in this chapter, measurement involves a series of steps: (1) conceptualization, (2) conceptual definition, (3) operational definition, and (4) actual measurements. But, like the research process summarized in Chapter 4, measurement steps do not always proceed one after another. Efforts by researchers at Rutgers University to develop a measure of police activity offer examples of challenges in executing these four steps.

Conceptualization

"Police activity" can generate a wide variety of mental images. In the famous Kansas City Preventive Patrol Experiment, "police activity" generally meant that officers drove around their assigned beats in patrol cars. But changes to policing in New York centered around more purposive action, as described in Chapter 2. So researchers framed their conceptualization of police activity as follows: *specific actions by patrol officers and detectives undertaken as part of a planned field tactic.* The key here was linking actions to plans—the *purposive* part of purposive action.

Conceptual Definition

Researchers seldom (if ever) produce simple, unambiguous definitions of key concepts. In the New York City project, the conceptual definition evolved after members of the research team attended several meetings and observed police operations in different precincts. Here is what became a working conceptual definition:

> Our interest in police activity centers on activities that follow meetings to plan tactical field operations. These meetings take place weekly, usually following the release of the previous week's crime data. So police activity is conceptually defined as "actions of police officers and detectives that are implied by specific tactics developed in planning sessions conducted by precinct commanders and whomever they choose to involve in the planning process."

This was not an entirely satisfactory definition given the various ambiguities. But the pressures of time, a general eagerness to get on with the project, and a recognition that the definition might be revised later prompted researchers to move on.

Operational Definition

It tends to be easier to develop operational definitions if conceptual definitions are clearly specified. Starting with the somewhat general conceptual definition stated previously, the New York study produced an even less restrictive operational definition:

conceptual properties we wish to study, how we will operationalize those properties, and how we will develop measures that are reliable and valid. Often, some type of composite measure better represents underlying concepts and thus enhances validity.

Subsequent chapters will pursue issues of measurement further. Part Three of this book will describe data collection—how we go about making actual measurements. And the next chapter will focus on different approaches to measuring crime.

✪ *Main Points*

- Concepts are mental images we use as summary devices for bringing together observations and experiences that seem to have something in common.
- Our concepts do not exist in the real world, so they can't be measured directly.
- In operationalization, we specify concrete empirical procedures that will result in measurements of variables.
- Operationalization begins in study design and continues throughout the research project, including the analysis of data.

A police activity is any action by officers that deviates from general, random patrol that: (1) involves an encounter with another individual beyond casual communication with officers, and (2) lasts more than 30 seconds. (Sousa, 2003:119)

This definition guided observations of police on duty. Notice that, although the operational definition potentially encompasses a broader range of police actions, it does offer specific directions as to what types of police behavior to record.

Observations in the Field

In planning field observations, a researcher attended meetings at precincts where tactics were developed. The researcher recorded the tactics, together with information about the anticipated results. The researcher then consulted with precinct staff to identify patrol or special units that were designated to implement the tactics. With this knowledge, the researcher accompanied these units, making field observations of their activities. These observations were recorded on data collection forms and later coded to tabulate measures of activity.

Certain logistical problems had to be solved in planning and executing specific observations. Compstat reports were issued each Monday and usually were followed by precinct planning sessions later that day or on Tuesday. Because researchers were studying six precincts in widely separated areas of the nation's largest city, the logistics of physically getting to different precinct stations within one day presented a major obstacle. This problem was addressed by attending meetings and making observations at one precinct after another. But this solution provoked further a question: What if Precinct A was selected for a particular week, but the weekly crime reports showed little activity and therefore no need to plan new tactics?

Researchers ended up selecting precincts for observation based on a review of their Compstat reports. Researchers would receive Compstat reports at about the same time precinct commanders did. If Compstat data indicated what appeared to be a new crime problem in the precinct, that precinct would be selected for measurement—observing planning sessions and field operations. But that, of course, required researchers to anticipate what sorts of problems would generate attention and tactical planning in a precinct. This issue was addressed by telephoning precinct contacts and asking about whether any special tactics were planned. Timing became very important.

Observations began. A researcher attended precinct planning meetings, recorded descriptions of specific tactics, and set out for field observations with officers and special units. The decision was made to conduct observations during Friday or Saturday night shifts, which had the greatest density of incidents and thus activities. This strategy paid off. Researchers accompanied police units on 40 tours of duty. Applying the operational definition resulted in a total of 429 observed activities.

- Categories in a measure must be mutually exclusive and exhaustive.
- Higher levels of measurements specify categories that have ranked order or more complex numerical properties.
- A given variable can sometimes be measured at different levels of measurement. The most appropriate level of measurement used depends on the purpose of the measurement.
- Precision refers to the exactness of the measure used in an observation or description of an attribute.

- Reliability and validity are criteria for measurement quality. Valid measures are truly indicators of underlying concepts. A reliable measure is consistent.
- The creation of specific, reliable measures often seems to diminish the richness of meaning our general concepts have. A good solution is to use multiple measures, each of which taps different aspects of the concept.
- Composite measures, formed by combining two or more variables, are often more valid measures of complex criminal justice concepts.

✪ *Key Terms*

Concept	Interval measures
Conception	Nominal measures
Conceptual definition	Operational definition
Conceptualization	Ordinal measures
Construct validity	Ratio measures
Content validity	Reification
Criterion-related	Reliability
validity	Typology
Dimension	Validity
Face validity	

✪ *Review Questions and Exercises*

1. Review the box titled "What Is Recidivism?" From that discussion, write conceptual and operational definitions for *recidivism*. Summarize how Fabelo proposes to measure the concept. Finally, discuss possible reliability and validity issues associated with Fabelo's proposed measure.

2. Each year publications such as the *Places Rated Almanac* attract praise from residents of highly rated cities and protests from those who live in lower-rated areas. The 1997 edition rated Orange County, California (where Babbie lives), first and Newark, New Jersey (where Maxfield works), last. Find a recent edition of this or a similar rating guide, and discuss the measurement procedures used for developing the ratings. If appropriate, criticize how various dimensions of the ratings have been operationalized. Can you spot and explain any apparent anomalies in the ratings? For example, the 1997 edition rated Gary, Indiana, higher than Santa Fe, New Mexico.

3. We all have some sort of mental image of the pace of life. In a fascinating book titled *A Geography of Time,* Robert Levine (1997) operationalized the pace of life in cities around the world with a composite measure of the following:
   a. How long it took a single pedestrian to walk 60 feet on an uncrowded sidewalk
   b. What percentage of public clocks displayed the correct time
   c. How long it took to purchase the equivalent of a first-class postage stamp with the equivalent of a $5 bill

Discuss possible reliability and validity issues with these indicators of pace of life. Be sure to specify a conceptual definition for pace of life.

✪ *Internet Exercises*

To ensure that you always have access to live, correct Web links for the Web sites referenced in the following exercises, we provide the necessary links on the companion Web site for *Research Methods for Criminal Justice and Criminology* at http://cj.wadsworth. com/maxfield_babbie/research_methods4e. Once at the companion Web site, select this specific chapter, click on "Chapter Resources," then click on "Web Links."

1. Race is a concept that has been categorized in many ways over the years. The U.S. census in 2000 dramatically altered how race is quantified and measured for purposes of counting the population of the United States. Visit the Revisions to the Standards for the Classification of Federal Data on Race and Ethnicity Web site to investigate how race is operationalized in this recent census and explore the reasons for the change. Then the United States Historical Census site to look at some of the categories of race used in the census in the past.

2. The concepts of reliability and validity are essential to measurement and operationalization of constructs. Use the Learning Maze for Reliability Theory and Validity Theory Web sites to gain a deeper understanding of these concepts. Summarize what you learn in two short paragraphs — one for reliability and one for validity.

3. For several years, staff in the New York City Office of the Mayor have compiled detailed performance measures for city agencies. In 2002, detailed statistics became available for large neighborhood areas throughout New York. Visit the NYC Web site, click on "Continue," and then enter either a street address or intersection. Try "42nd st," "Broadway," and "Manhattan," for example, to get information on the Times Square area. You will then see a series of indicators organized into several categories. Scroll down these figures and click on a few measures that seem especially interesting. You will then see an operational definition of the indicator. Note that these indicators together reveal a number of dimensions of life in New York. Dis-

cuss how different indicators illustrate key concepts in this chapter.

✪ *InfoTrac College Edition*

Use InfoTrac College Edition to locate, print, and read a research article on a topic of interest to you. Describe the level of measurement associated with each of the measures described in the article.

✪ *The NEW Companion Web Site for* Research Methods for Criminal Justice and Criminology, *Fourth Edition*

http://cj.wadsworth.com/maxfield_babbie/
research_methods4e

Supplement your review of this chapter by going to the new companion Web site to take one of the Tutorial Quizzes, use the flash cards to master key terms, and check out the many other study aids you'll find there. You'll also find special features such as quantitative and qualitative data analysis primers to help you with a special project or do some research on your own.

✪ *Additional Readings*

Best, Joel, *Damned Lies and Statistics: Untangling Numbers from the Media, Politicians, and Activists* (Berkeley: University of California Press, 2001). Despite the title, much of this entertaining and informative book describes problems with measurement. For example, page 45 tells us: "Measuring involves deciding how to go about counting." Best emphasizes how ambiguity in measures of social problems make it easy for advocates to exaggerate the frequency of such problems. Mass media often report and perpetuate errorful measures. What results, Best informs us, are *mutant statistics.*

Bonta, James, "Risk-Needs Assessment and Treatment," in Alan Harlan (ed.), *Choosing Correctional Options That Work* (Thousand Oaks, CA: Sage, 1996). Measuring the security risks of and programming needs for convicted offenders has long been of interest to corrections officials. Largely because of a growth in persons sentenced to incarceration, developing better measures has attracted new interest. Bonta presents a thoughtful discussion of this important and difficult measurement problem.

Bureau of Justice Statistics, *Performance Measures for the Criminal Justice System* (Washington, DC: U.S. Department of Justice, Office of Justice Programs, Bureau of Justice Statistics, 1993). This collection of essays by prominent criminal justice researchers focuses on developing measures for evaluation uses. The discussion of general measurement issues as encountered in different types of justice agencies is uncommonly thoughtful. You will find this a provocative discussion of how to measure important constructs in corrections, trial courts, and policing. See especially the general essays by John DiIulio and James Q. Wilson.

Langworthy, Robert (ed.), *Measuring What Matters: Proceedings from the Policing Research Institute Meetings* (Washington, DC: U.S. Department of Justice, Office of Justice Programs, National Institute of Justice, 1999). With the spread of community policing, researchers and officials alike have struggled with the question of how to measure police performance. Most people agree that simply counting crimes is not enough, but no one knows how to measure other dimensions of police performance. This document presents papers and discussions from a series of meetings in which police, researchers, reporters, and others discussed what matters in policing and how to measure it.

Chapter 6

Measuring Crime

How do you measure crime? How much crime is there? Researchers and policy makers have developed several different approaches to measuring crime. Nevertheless, there's no definitive answer to the second question. We'll examine a variety of strategies for measuring crime and discuss the strengths and weaknesses of each.

(continued)

Introduction

*Measures of crime are important for many criminal
justice research purposes.*

Having discussed the principles of measurement and measurement quality at some length,
we now turn to a basic task for criminal justice
researchers: measuring crime. Crime is a fundamental dependent variable in criminal justice and criminology. Explanatory studies frequently seek to learn what causes crime, while
applied studies often focus on what actions
might be effective in reducing crime. Descriptive and exploratory studies may simply wish to
count how much crime there is in some specific
area, a question of obvious concern to criminal
justice officials as well as researchers.

Crime can also be an independent variable—
for example, in a study of how crime affects fear
or other attitudes, or whether people who live in
high-crime areas are more likely than others to
favor long prison sentences for drug dealers.
Sometimes crime can be both an independent
and a dependent variable, as in a study about
the relationship between drug use and other
offenses.

Whatever our research purpose, and whether
we're interested in what causes crime or what
crime causes, measuring crime clearly is important. It's also difficult; how to measure crime
has long been a key research issue in criminology and criminal justice.

We have three objectives in this chapter.
First, we'll use the challenge of measuring crime
to illustrate the more general measurement issues we considered in Chapter 5. Second, we'll
examine a range of available measures of crime
and compare the strength and weaknesses of
each. Finally, we'll briefly consider some independent measures of crime developed for specific research or policy purposes.

General Issues
in Measuring Crime

*Researchers must decide on offenses, units of analy-
sis, and purposes before specifying measures of crime.*

At the outset, we must acknowledge some
broad questions that influence all measures of
crime: (1) What offenses should be measured?
(2) What units of analysis should be used? and

(3) What is the research or policy purpose in measuring crime?

What Offenses?

Let's begin by proposing a conceptual definition of crime—one that will enable us to decide what specific types of crime we'll measure. Recall a definition from Michael Gottfredson and Travis Hirschi (1990:15), mentioned in Chapter 5: "Acts of force or fraud undertaken in pursuit of self-interest." This is an interesting definition, but it is better suited to an extended discussion of *theories* of crime than to our purposes in this chapter. For example, we would have to clarify what was meant by *self-interest*, a term that has engaged philosophers and social scientists for centuries.

James Q. Wilson and Richard Herrnstein (1985:22) propose a different definition that should get us started: "A crime is any act committed in violation of a law that prohibits it and authorizes punishment for its commission." Although other criminologists (Gottfredson and Hirschi, for example) might not agree with this conceptual definition, it has the advantage of being reasonably specific. We could be even more specific by consulting a state or federal code and listing the type of acts for which the law provides punishment.

Our list would be very long. For example, the Indiana Code (IC) includes harvesting ginseng root out of season (IC 14-31-3-16)* and selling a switchblade knife (IC 35-47-5-2) as acts punishable by 6 months' incarceration and a $1000 fine. Taking Indiana ginseng out of the state without permission (IC 14-31-3-20) and assault resulting in nonserious bodily injury to an adult (IC 35-42-2-1) are equivalent crimes that could bring a year's incarceration and a fine of $5000. However we decide to measure crime, we certainly want to distinguish acts of violence and the sale of illegal weapons from irregularities concerning rare herbs.

One of the principal difficulties we encounter when we try to measure crime is that many different types of behaviors and actions are included in our conceptualization of crime as an "act committed in violation of a law that prohibits it and authorizes punishment for its commission." Different measures tend to focus on different types of crime, primarily because not all crimes can be measured the same way with any degree of reliability or validity. Therefore, one important step in selecting a measure is deciding what crimes will be included.

What Units of Analysis?

Recall that units of analysis are the specific entities researchers collect information about. Chapter 4 considered individuals, groups, social artifacts, and other units of analysis. Deciding how to measure crime requires that we once again think about these units.

Crimes involve four elements that are often easier to recognize in the abstract than they are to actually measure. The most basic of these elements is the offender. Without an offender, there's no crime, so a crime must, at a minimum, involve an offender. The offender is therefore one possible unit of analysis. We might decide to study burglars, auto thieves, bank robbers, child molesters, drug dealers, or people who have committed many different types of offenses.

Crimes also require some sort of victim, the second possible unit of analysis. We could study victims of burglary, auto theft, bank robbery, or assault. Notice that this list of victims includes different types of units: households or businesses for burglary, car owners for auto theft, banks for bank robbery, and individuals for assault. Some of these units are organizations (banks, businesses), some are individual people, some are abstractions (households), and some are ambiguous (individuals or organizations can own automobiles).

What about so-called victimless crimes like

---

* This citation reflects the standard form of references to a "code"—the body of all laws in effect for a jurisdiction, organized by subject. In this case, "IC" is the abbreviation for Indiana Code; the numbers cite title, article, chapter, and section. So this citation refers to Title 14, article 31, chapter 3, section 16 of the Indiana Code. "USC" refers to the United States Code, that body of federal laws in effect for the United States.

drug use, bookmaking, or prostitution? In a legal sense, victimless crimes do not exist because crimes are acts that injure society, organizations, and/or individuals. But studying crimes in which only society is the victim—prostitution, for example—presents special challenges, and specialized techniques have been developed to measure certain types of victimless crimes. In any event, it's crucial to think about units of analysis in advance. Later, we will examine surveying victims as one approach to counting crime. But surveying individuals, organizations, and society involves fundamentally different tasks.

The final two elements of crimes—offense and incident—are closely intertwined and so will be discussed together. An offense is defined as an individual act of burglary, auto theft, bank robbery, and so on. The Federal Bureau of Investigation (FBI) defines incident as "one or more offenses committed by the same offender, or group of offenders *acting in concert, at the same time and place*" (Federal Bureau of Investigation, 2000:17; emphasis in original).

Think about the difference between offense and incident for a moment. A single incident can include multiple offenses, but it's not possible to have one offense and multiple incidents. Of course, a single incident could include multiple victims.

To illustrate the different units of analysis—offenders, victims, offenses, and incidents—consider the examples in the box titled "Units of Analysis and Measuring Crime." These examples help distinguish units from each other and illustrate the links among different units.

Notice that we have said nothing about aggregate units of analysis, a topic we examined in Chapter 4. We have considered only individual units, even though measures of crime are often based on aggregate units of analysis—neighborhoods, cities, counties, states, and so on.

What Purpose?

Different strategies for measuring crime can be distinguished by their general purpose. Measuring crime has at least one of three general purposes: (1) monitoring, (2) agency accountability, and (3) research.

We measure crime for the purpose of monitoring in much the same way that we measure consumer prices, stock market activity, traffic fatalities, birthrates, population, unemployment, and HIV infection rates. This reflects more than merely a compulsion for counting things, however. We measure a variety of social, economic, demographic, and public health indicators to keep track of social and economic conditions, the size and age distribution of the population, and threats to public health. By the same token, one purpose for measuring crime is to monitor potential threats to public safety and security.

At the national level, two series of crime measures seek to assess "the magnitude, nature, and impact of crime in the Nation [sic]" (U.S. Department of Justice, 1995:1). We'll examine the Uniform Crime Reports (UCR) and the National Crime Victimization Survey (NCVS) in detail later in this chapter. Here, we point out that the fundamental purpose for these two measures is monitoring. In the field of public health, this is referred to as a **surveillance system** (Wilt and Gabrel, 1998). Just as a variety of statistical series administered by the U.S. Public Health Service monitor the incidence of disease and death rates from various causes, the U.S. Department of Justice oversees two nationwide surveillance systems for measuring crime.

The second measurement purpose is agency accountability. Government agencies are obliged to keep records that document their actions and areas of responsibility. Such accountability is a basic principle of the U.S. version of democratic government and is one reason individual police departments measure crime. "You can't manage what you can't measure," states the title page on Idaho's 2001 state crime report, underscoring the significance of accountability (Idaho State Police, 2002).

The final purpose is research; measures of crime are made for research purposes that are distinct from the purpose of surveillance or accountability. We emphasize these different purposes for a reason we'll encounter throughout

Units of Analysis and Measuring Crime

Figuring out the different units of analysis in counting crimes can be difficult and confusing at first. Much of the problem comes from the possibility of what database designers call one-to-many and many-to-many relationships. The same incident can have multiple offenses, offenders, and victims, or just one of each. Fortunately, thinking through some examples usually clarifies the matter. Our two examples are adapted from an FBI publication (2000:18).

Example 1

Two males entered a bar. The bartender was forced at gunpoint to hand over all money from the cash register. The offenders also took money and jewelry from three customers. One of the offenders used his handgun to beat one of the customers, thereby causing serious injury. Both offenders fled on foot.

> 1 incident
>> 1 robbery offense
>>> 2 offenders
>>> 4 victims (bar cash, 3 patrons)
>> 1 aggravated assault offense
>>> 2 offenders
>>> 1 victim

Even though only one offender actually assaulted the bar patron, the other offender would be charged with assisting in the offense because he prevented others from coming to the aid of the assault victim.

Example 2

Two males entered a bar. The bartender was forced at gunpoint to hand over all money from the cash register. The offenders also took money and jewelry from two customers. One of the offenders, in searching for more people to rob, found a female customer in a back room and raped her there, outside of the view of the other offender. When the rapist returned, both offenders fled on foot.

This example includes two incidents because the rape occurred in a different place and the offenders were not acting in concert. And because they were not acting in concert in the same place, only one offender was associated with the rape incident.

> Incident 1
>> 1 robbery offense
>>> 2 offenders
>>> 3 victims (bar cash, 2 patrons)
> Incident 2
>> 1 rape offense
>>> 1 offender
>>> 1 victim

---

this and subsequent chapters. Criminal justice research often uses measures of crime that are collected for surveillance or accountability purposes, not for research. It's worth keeping that point in mind when planning a research project that will measure crime with one or more existing data series.

Crimes Known to Police

Police-based crime measures are the most widely used, but they are subject to certain types of error.

The most widely used measures of crime are based on police records and are commonly referred to as "crimes known to police." This phrase has important implications for understanding what police records do and do not measure. One obvious implication is that crimes not known to police cannot be measured by consulting police records. We can better understand the significance of this by considering the two ways police come to know about crime: observation and reports from other people.

Certain types of crimes are detected almost exclusively by observation—for example, traffic offenses and so-called victimless crimes. Police count drug sales because they observe the transaction; they count incidents of prostitution because they witness solicitions. Obviously, police detect traffic offenses through observation. Most other crimes, however, are detected and counted because they are reported to police by other people—victims or witnesses. Victims report burglaries, robberies, assaults, purse snatchings, and other offenses to police; witnesses also report crimes.

Recognizing that police measure crime in these two ways—observation and reports by others—we can readily think of crimes that are not well measured by police records. Consider shoplifting, for example. Many instances of shoplifting are observed neither by police nor by other people who might report them to police. Those instances are not detected and therefore not measured. Shoplifting certainly is included in our conceptual definition of an act committed in violation of a law that prohibits it and that authorizes punishment. However, measuring shoplifting by counting crimes known to police would omit many offenses.

Thinking about crime measured almost exclusively by police observation—victimless crimes and traffic offenses—should make you realize that crimes known to police are not a good measure of these types of offenses either. Most of us have committed traffic offenses and not been caught. Similarly, most instances of drug sales, not to mention drug possession, are not detected.

The other way police measure crime is also imperfect. Many crimes are not reported to police, especially minor thefts and certain types of assaults. People don't report crimes for several reasons, which tend to vary by type of crime. Attempted thefts may not be reported because no property was lost. Many minor assaults or other personal crimes are considered by victims to be private matters that they will settle themselves without involving the police. Other victims may believe that minor losses are not important enough to trouble police or that reporting a crime would make no difference because police could neither capture the offender nor recover the stolen property (Bureau of Justice Statistics, 1996).

Another problem with police measurement of crime undermines the meaning of the phrase "crimes known to police." Research has shown

what some people may have personally experienced: Police do not always make official records of crimes they observe or crimes reported to them. Donald Black (1970) and Albert Reiss (1971) described a number of factors that influence police decisions on whether to officially record crimes they know about. Assaults, for example, between people who know each other well or are related to each other are less likely to be recorded as assaults than are fights between strangers. If a victim urges a police officer not to arrest someone or not to press charges against an offender, the officer is less likely to treat the incident as a crime. Black also found that police more often made official crime reports for incidents that involved victims of higher socioeconomic status. Finally, Richard and Carolyn Rebecca Block (1980) found that robberies in Chicago were less often recorded if no weapon was used, if victims resisted the offender, or if the attempt was unsuccessful. They concluded that robberies are counted by police if they are "based on a stereotypical idea of robbery—a helpless victim attacked by a gun-wielding thug. The more an incident approximates this ideal robbery, the more likely it will become a robbery statistic" (1980:636).

Uniform Crime Reports

Police measures of crime form the basis for the FBI's Uniform Crime Reports (UCR), a data series that has been collected since 1930 and has been widely used by criminal justice researchers. But certain characteristics and procedures related to the UCR affect its suitability as a measure of crime. Most of our discussion highlights shortcomings in this regard, but keep in mind that the UCR will continue to be a very useful measure for researchers and public officials.

Because UCR data are based on crimes reported to police, they share the measurement problems mentioned earlier. However, the FBI crime counts include three additional sources of measurement error.

First, the UCR does not even try to count all crimes reported to police. What are referred to as index offenses—also called Part I crimes—

are counted if these offenses are reported to police (and recorded by police). Index offenses include murder and nonnegligent manslaughter, forcible rape, robbery, aggravated assault, burglary, larceny-theft, and motor vehicle theft (Federal Bureau of Investigation, 1999). Other offenses, referred to as Part II crimes, are counted only if a person has been arrested and charged with a crime. The UCR therefore does not include such offenses as shoplifting, drug sale or use, fraud, prostitution, simple assault, vandalism, receiving stolen property, and all other nontraffic offenses unless someone is arrested. This means that a large number of crimes reported to police are not measured in the UCR.

Second, one of the reasons Part II offenses are counted only if an arrest is made is that individual states have different definitions of crimes. The operational definition of crime can vary from state to state, and this introduces another source of measurement error into the FBI data. For example, the state of Louisiana includes verbal threats in its counts of assaults, but most other states do not (Justice Research and Statistics Association, 1996:20).

The FBI compiles its UCR figures from data submitted by individual states or local law enforcement agencies. In some states, local police and sheriffs' departments send their crime reports to a state agency, which forwards the data to the FBI. In other states, local law enforcement agencies send crime data directly to the FBI. However, not all local police and sheriffs' departments send complete crime report data to either their state agency or the FBI. Inconsistency also exists in the quality of data submitted. In other words, individual states, cities, and counties vary in the quality and completeness of crime data sent to the FBI and reported in the annual UCR publication, *Crime in the United States*. Just as the decennial census cannot count everyone who lives in the United States, the FBI is not able to reliably count all crimes—either Part I or Part II offenses—that occur in the United States. In some cases, especially since the early 1990s, only a small fraction of law en-

forcement agencies in a state report under the UCR program. Michael Maltz (1999) describes the scope of this problem (greater than most people realize) and efforts to estimate the amount of missing reports.

UCR data can also suffer from clerical, data-processing, and, in some cases, political problems. For example, Henry Brownstein (1996) describes his experience as a senior analyst in the New York Division of Criminal Justice Services, a state agency that compiles local crime reports for submission under the UCR program. The accuracy of data from cities and counties in New York is affected by staff shortages that undermine efforts to verify local reports, maintenance of an aging computer program that compiles UCR reports, and what Brownstein calls the "New York City reconciliation." Here is how he describes that problem (1996:22–23):

> As localities and agencies within localities compete amongst themselves for a greater share of State resources, they all compete to show that they are responsible for a greater share of the problem that the resources will be used to solve. Consequently, everyone wants credit for reported crimes and arrests. In New York City, where there are so many competing jurisdictions and agencies, this translates as a problem of duplicate reporting. So every summer a senior data entry clerk conducts the reconciliation, separating out by hand and by assumption the duplicate reports of the same crimes and arrests submitted by different jurisdictions and agencies.

The third source of measurement error in the UCR is produced by the hierarchy rule used by police agencies and the FBI to classify crimes. Under the hierarchy rule, if multiple crimes are committed in a single incident, only the most serious is counted in the UCR. For example, if a burglar breaks into a home, rapes one of the occupants, and flees in the homeowner's car, at least three crimes are committed—burglary, rape, and vehicle theft. Under the FBI hierarchy rule, however, only the most serious crime, rape, is counted in the UCR, even though if captured, the offender could be charged with all three offenses. In the examples described in tthe box "Units of Analysis and Measuring Crime," the UCR would count one offense in each incident: a single robbery in the first example and rape in the second.

The UCR and Criteria for Measurement Quality

Let's now consider how using the UCR to operationalize and measure crime satisfies the criteria for measurement quality we discussed in Chapter 5. Are the UCR data exclusive, exhaustive, valid, and reliable? First, the UCR clearly is neither an exclusive nor an exhaustive measure. Many crimes are not counted (nonexhaustive), and the hierarchy rule means that crime definitions are not strictly exclusive, because only the most serious crime in an incident in which multiple crimes are committed is counted. It does not help us if, for example, we are especially interested in burglary because burglaries are not counted if a rape, robbery, or murder is committed in the same incident.

Because the UCR does not count all crimes, we can rightly question its validity. The UCR does not really measure the concept of crime as we have defined it: any act committed in violation of a law that prohibits it and authorizes punishment for its commission.

Finally, is the UCR a reliable measure? Not all law enforcement agencies submit complete reports to the FBI, and the quality of the data submitted varies. Inconsistencies in reporting, such as those Brownstein describes for New York, produce problems with the reliability of UCR data. Also recall the Blocks' study and other research findings that police do not always make records of crimes that come to their attention. When individual police officers exercise discretion in making crime reports, the reliability of measuring crime through the UCR is further undermined.

Recognizing these and other problems with UCR data, the FBI has been pursuing two initiatives to enhance the validity and reliability of crimes known to police. First, under its Quality Assurance Review program, staff from the FBI Criminal Justice Information Services Division audit crime data submitted by samples of reporting agencies. Results from this data quality review are shared with staff from state agencies; 11 states participated in audits conducted in 2001 (Federal Bureau of Investigation, 2002:5). The second FBI initiative is actually a from-the-ground-up overhaul of crime reporting, a topic we will examine in the following section.

Before we move on to other approaches to measuring crime, consider how units of analysis figure into UCR data. The UCR system produces what is referred to as a **summary-based measure** of crime. This means that UCR data include summary, or total, crime counts for reporting agencies—cities or counties. UCR data therefore represent groups as units of analysis. Crime reports are available for cities or counties, and these may be aggregated upward to measure crime for states or regions of the United States. But UCR data available from the FBI cannot represent individual crimes, offenders, or victims as units.

Recall that it is possible to aggregate units of analysis to higher levels, but it is not possible to disaggregate grouped data to the individual level. Because UCR data are aggregates, they cannot be used in descriptive or explanatory studies that focus on individual crimes, offenders, or victims. UCR data are therefore restricted to the analysis of such units as cities, counties, states, or regions.

Incident-Based Police Records

The U.S. Department of Justice sponsors two series of crime measures that are based on incidents as units of analysis. The first of these **incident-based measures,** Supplementary Homicide Reports (SHR), was begun in 1961 and is actually part of the UCR program, as implied by the word *supplementary*.

Local law enforcement agencies submit detailed information about individual homicide incidents under the SHR program. This includes information about victims and, if known, offenders (age, gender, race); the relationship between victim and offender; the weapon used; the location of the incident; and the circumstances surrounding the killing.

Notice how the SHR relates to our discussion of units of analysis. Incidents are the basic unit and can include one or more victims and offenders; because the series is restricted to homicides, offense is held constant.

Because the SHR is an incident-based system, investigators can use SHR data to conduct descriptive and explanatory studies of individual events. For example, it's possible to compare the relationship between victim and offender for male victims and female victims or to compare the types of weapons used in killings by strangers and killings by nonstrangers. Such analyses are not possible if we are studying homicide using UCR summary data. If our unit of analysis is jurisdiction—city or county, for example—we can examine only the aggregate number of homicides in each jurisdiction for a given year; it will not be possible to say anything about individual homicide incidents.

Crime measures based on incidents as units of analysis therefore have several advantages over summary measures. It's important to keep in mind, however, that SHR data still represent crimes known to police and recorded by police. Of course, records of homicides will be better represented in police records than will, say, records of shoplifting, but clerical and other errors can still be a factor. Brownstein (1996) describes some of these problems, and Maxfield (1989) discusses some validity concerns with respect to the SHR. Most potential errors in the SHR are due to recording and record-keeping practices, topics we will discuss in Chapter 11.

The National Incident-Based Reporting System

The most recent development in police-based measures at the national level is the ongoing effort by the FBI and the Bureau of Justice Statistics (BJS) to convert the UCR to a National Incident-Based Reporting System (NIBRS, pronounced ny-bers). Planning for replacement of

the UCR began in the mid-1980s, but because NIBRS represents major changes, law enforcement agencies have shifted only gradually to the new system.

Briefly, NIBRS is a Very Big Deal. We'll first put things in perspective by comparing NIBRS and the UCR for a single state, Idaho, that currently reports incident-level measures. Then we'll discuss some of the specific features of NIBRS, concluding with comments on progress in implementing the system.

About 17,000 law enforcement agencies report UCR summary data each year; that's 17,000 annual observations, one for each reporting agency. Idaho has 109 UCR-reporting agencies, so Idaho submits a maximum of 109 annual observations. Under NIBRS, Idaho reported over 88,000 incidents in 2001. So, for Idaho, shifting from the summary UCR system for measuring crime to the incident-based NIBRS system meant shifting from 109 units (UCR-reporting jurisdictions) to more than 88,000 units. In other words, rather than reporting 109 summary crime counts for seven UCR Part I offenses, Idaho reported detailed information on 88,798 individual incidents. And this is Idaho, which ranks 39th among the states in 2000 resident population!

These numbers illustrate the main difference between NIBRS and the UCR system: reporting each crime incident rather than reporting the total number of certain crimes for each law enforcement agency. But the significance of shifting from reporting *aggregate numbers* to reporting *individual incidents* lies in the type of information that is available about each incident. In essence, NIBRS measures many features of each incident, and each of these features is reported individually. Table 6.1 lists most of the "segments" or categories of information recorded for each incident, together with examples of the information recorded within each segment.

As Table 6.1 shows, NIBRS includes much more detailed information about individual incidents, together with the offenses, offenders, and victims within each incident. Referring

Table 6.1 Selected Information in National Incident-Based Reporting System Records

Administrative Segment
  Incident date and time
  Reporting agency ID
  Other ID numbers

Offense Segment
  Offense type
  Attempted or
    completed
  Offender drug/
    alcohol use
  Location type
  Weapon use

Victim Segment
  Victim ID number
  Offense type
  Victim age, gender, race
  Resident of jurisdiction?
  Type of injury
  Relationship to offender
  Victim type:
    Individual person
    Business
    Government
    Society/public

Offender Segment
  Offender ID number
  Offender age,
    gender, race

Source: Adapted from Federal Bureau of Investigation (2000: 6–8, 90).

Table 6.2 Crime in Idaho, 2001

Summary UCR Index Offenses	
Murder	30
Rape	424
Robbery	246
Aggravated assault	2,492
Burglary	7,219
Larceny	28,070
Motor vehicle theft	2,320
Arson	289
Subtotal	41,090

Additional NIBRS Group A Offenses	
Simple assault	13,525
Intimidation	1,515
Bribery	4
Counterfeit/forgery	2,066
Destruction of property	14,027
Drug violations	5,780
Drug equipment violations	5,229
Embezzlement	317
Extortion/blackmail	16
Fraud	2,036
Gambling	2
Kidnapping/abduction	196
Pornography/obscene material	40
Prostitution	7
Forcible sex offenses	1,167
Nonforcible sex offenses	176
Stolen property	461
Weapons violations	1,139
Subtotal	47,703
NIBRS total	88,793

Source: Adapted from Idaho State Police (2002).

back to our earlier discussion of the elements of crime—incidents, offenders, offenses, and victims—notice how the information in Table 6.1 is organized around each incident. Each incident can include one or more offenses, offenders, and victims, as we described in the box on units of analysis.

In addition, NIBRS guidelines call for gathering information about a much broader array of offenses. Whereas the UCR reports information about seven Part I offenses (plus arson), NIBRS is designed to collect detailed information on 46 "Group A" offenses. Table 6.2 demonstrates the significance of this by showing NIBRS crime data for Idaho in 2001. Compare the top part of the table, reporting crime counts for UCR index offenses, to the bottom part. Additional NIBRS Group A offenses more than double the number of crimes "known to police" in Idaho (41,090 UCR index plus 47,703 Group A). Simple assault and vandalism are by far the most common of these additional offenses, but drug violations accounted for about 11,000 offenses in 2001 (drug violations plus drug equipment violations).

Collecting detailed information on each incident for each offense, victim, and offender, and doing so for a large number of offense types, represents the most significant changes in NIBRS compared with the UCR. Dropping the hierarchy rule is also a major change, but that is a consequence of incident-based reporting. NIBRS incorporates six other revisions (Federal Bureau of Investigation, 2000:12–15):

1. *Victim type.* Table 6.1 lists most categories for victim type; the most notable of these is "society/public," a category that has the effect of annulling the phrase "victimless crime." Whereas UCR summary data combine all types of victims (individuals, businesses, others) into one summary measure, NIBRS makes it possible to distinguish different categories of victims.

2. *Attempted/completed.* UCR summary reports include both attempted and completed offenses, but it's not possible to distinguish them. NIBRS adds a category to indicate whether each offense within each incident was attempted or completed.

3. *Computer-base submission.* UCR reports could be sent to the FBI on paper forms, but NIBRS data must be submitted on computer tape or disks.

4. *Drug-related offenses.* Because the 1980s witnessed a growing public concern with illegal drug use, NIBRS includes provisions to assess offender drug use in nondrug offenses and to record whether drugs or drug paraphernalia were seized.

5. *Computers and crime.* The 1980s also witnessed an explosion of computer use, including computers as instruments and targets of crime. Categories to record the involvement of computers are included.

6. *Quality control.* Complexity increases the potential for error, but requiring computerized submission makes it easier to check for patterns of problems in NIBRS data. The FBI is also developing audit procedures and standards for reviewing NIBRS data.

NIBRS and Criteria for Measurement Quality

You now have some idea about the potential wealth of information available from NIBRS and the ways in which this new system represents major changes from the summary-based UCR. How does incident-based reporting fare on our criteria for measurement quality? After considering NIBRS in light of our earlier comments on the UCR, some improvements are clearly evident. Eliminating the hierarchy rule means offense classifications are mutually exclusive. Is NIBRS exhaustive? Table 6.2 lists more offenses compared with the UCR, but additional offenses are recorded only for crimes that result in arrest; not all crimes are counted.

In at least one sense, NIBRS data hold the promise of being more reliable. The FBI has produced very thorough documentation on how to record and classify incidents and their component records. Creating auditing standards and requiring submission of data on computer-readable media also enhance reliability. Finally, the FBI requires that state records systems be certified before the state can submit incident-based reports.

The production of NIBRS data is, however, still a selective process: Crimes are selectively reported to police and selectively recorded by police. And researchers are likely to encounter three practical problems in using NIBRS data to measure crime.

First, law enforcement agencies using NIBRS report huge amounts of data. For example, data files available for analysis include over 3 million incidents for the year 2000. Data on just the offense and victim parts of NIBRS for those 3 million incidents occupy over 500 megabytes of disk space. And those 3 million incidents represent less than 15 percent of all reported crime in the United States. Researchers accustomed to working with a few hundred summary reports must now analyze hundreds of thousands of incident reports.

Second, implementing NIBRS requires enormous effort by individual law enforcement agencies to comply with the FBI's detailed specifications on record keeping and reporting. Because it is a computer-based system, individual agencies must either develop the necessary data-processing capability or adapt existing systems to NIBRS specifications. The FBI and BJS have promoted the shift to NIBRS with technical and financial assistance for state and local agencies. Somewhat paradoxically, this has meant that smaller states and smaller police and sheriffs' departments within states have been more readily able to develop NIBRS-compliant systems from the ground up (Maxfield, 1999). Most larger agencies developed customized records management systems some years ago, and adapting those systems to NIBRS standards has proved to be difficult and costly (MEGG Associates, 1996).

Third, like UCR reporting, NIBRS is voluntary; no agency is required to submit crime reports to the FBI in any form. Given the major expense and effort involved in shifting to NIBRS, the conversion process has been slow. In 1988, the FBI published the first extensive guidelines on developing and implementing NIBRS. At the end of 2002, 23 states were certified to report NIBRS data to the FBI (Justice Research and Statistics Association, 2003). Though this is close to half of all states, most were smaller states, and only some agencies in each state reported NIBRS data.

In the future, incident-based police records will become more readily available and will cover a larger number of law enforcement agencies. In fact, many agencies have developed their own incident-based records systems independent of NIBRS, largely because of major advances in computing technology (Maxfield, 1999). Furthermore, researchers are beginning to analyze NIBRS data, something that is certain to prompt other researchers to do the same. For example, see studies of child abuse (Finkelhor and Ormond, 2001; Snyder, 2000) and hate crimes (Nolan, Akiyama, and Berhanu, 2002; Strom, 2001).

Measuring Crime Through Victim Surveys

Victim surveys are alternative measures of crime but are still subject to error.

Recognizing the shortcomings associated with using measures of crime known to police, we should consider alternative approaches. Conducting a **victim survey** that asks people whether they have been the victim of a crime is one alternative. Survey research methods will be described in detail in Chapter 9. For now, we assume that you have a general understanding of what a survey involves—presenting a sample of people with carefully worded questions and recording their responses.

In principle, measuring crime through surveys has several advantages. Surveys can obtain information on crimes that were not reported to police. Asking people about victimizations can also measure incidents that police may not have officially recorded as crimes. Finally, asking people about crimes that may have happened to them provides data on victims and offenders (individuals) and on the incidents themselves (social artifacts). Like an incident-based reporting system, a survey can therefore provide more disaggregated units of analysis. When conducted in a rigorous, systematic fashion, surveys can yield reliable measures.

The National Crime Victimization Survey

Since 1972, the U.S. Census Bureau has conducted the National Crime Victimization Survey (NCVS). The NCVS was launched following pilot studies in the mid-1960s by President Lyndon Johnson's Commission on Law Enforcement and Administration of Justice, commonly known as the President's Crime Commission. One of the primary reasons for conducting crime surveys was to illuminate what came to be referred to as the "dark figure of unreported crime." The NCVS is based on a nationally representative sample of households and uses uniform procedures to select and interview respondents, which enhances the reliability of crime measures. Because individual people living in households are interviewed, the NCVS can be used in studies in which individuals or households are the unit of analysis.

The NCVS cannot measure all crimes, however, in part because of the procedures used to select victims. Because the survey is based on a sample of households, it cannot count crimes in which businesses or commercial establishments are the victims. Bank robberies, gas station holdups, shoplifting, embezzlement, and securities fraud are examples of crimes that cannot be systematically counted by interviewing household members. Samples of banks, gas stations, retail stores, business establishments, or stockbrokers would be needed to measure those crimes. In much the same fashion, crimes directed at homeless victims cannot be counted by surveys of households like the NCVS.

What about "victimless" crimes? For example, think about how you would respond to a Census Bureau interviewer who asked whether you had been the victim of a drug sale. If you have bought drugs from a dealer, you might think of yourself as a customer rather than as a victim. Or if you lived near a park where drug sales were common, you might think of yourself as a victim even though you did not participate in a drug transaction. The point is that victim surveys are not good measures of victimless crimes because the respondents can't easily be conceived as victims.

Measuring certain forms of delinquency through victim surveys presents similar problems. Status offenses such as truancy and curfew violations do not have identifiable victims who can be included in samples based on households. Homicide and manslaughter are other crimes that are not well measured by victim surveys, for obvious reasons.

Because the NCVS, by design, excludes many types of crimes, you should recognize potential validity problems. But what about the reliability of crime surveys in general and the NCVS in particular? Because it is a survey, the NCVS is subject to the errors and shortcomings associated with that method of measuring concepts. In the following paragraphs, we will consider some reliability problems that are particularly troublesome in using surveys as a technique to count crime.

For many years, NCVS interviewers began the section of the survey on victimization with this introduction: "Now I'd like to ask some questions about crime. They refer only to the last six months—between [date 6 months before interview] and [date of interview]. During the last six months, did anyone [crime description]?" (Bureau of Justice Statistics, 1994:122). Respondents were then asked a series of screening questions to determine whether they might have been a crime victim in the previous 6 months. Those who answered yes to screening questions were next presented with detailed questions about the incident.

Asking people about crime in this way brings up the possibility of different types of recall error. First, respondents may simply not remember some incidents. This problem is particularly acute for minor crimes such as theft and for people who may have been the victim of more than one crime in the 6-month recall period.

The second recall problem, known as telescoping, involves respondents not accurately recalling when an incident occurred. Forward telescoping means that people may respond to questions by mentioning crimes that occurred more than 6 months ago, thus bringing past incidents forward into the recall period. In contrast, backward telescoping means that respondents inaccurately recall recent crimes as occurring in the more distant past. Because the NCVS tries to count crimes that occur every 6 months, forward or backward telescoping can produce unreliable counts. However, the NCVS is designed to reduce the possibility of telescoping, in part by specifying the relatively short recall window of 6 months.

A different type of recall problem affects people who have been victimized several times during the 6-month reference period. The Bureau of Justice Statistics (BJS) (1997) describes this as a problem with series victimizations, which are defined as six or more similar but separate crimes that the respondent cannot describe individually to an interviewer. Series victimizations constitute a problem for surveys because it is not clear how they should be counted or combined with individual crimes that the respondent can describe separately. The potential impact of series victimizations is substantial, especially for violent crimes. For example, Callie Marie Rennison (2001) estimates that series crimes account for 6–7 percent of all violent crimes measured by the NCVS.

Finally, the NCVS underestimates incidents in which the victim and offender know each other — domestic violence or other assaults involving friends or acquaintances, for example. Respondents may not tell interviewers about nonstranger crimes for various reasons. Some domestic violence victims view the assaults as a personal problem, not as a crime, and so may not mention the incidents. Other persons — victims of rape or domestic violence, for example — may feel shame or embarrassment and not wish to talk about their experiences. In addition, respondents who have been victimized by a family member may fear some further assault if they discuss a past incident.

NCVS Redesign

To address these and other concerns about the ability of the NCVS to measure different types of crime, the BJS substantially revised the survey in the 1990s. Victimization estimates from interviews conducted in 1993 reflect the full scope of the redesign effort after various changes in survey procedures were gradually incorporated. For the most part, the redesign effort focused on obtaining better measures of domestic violence and sexual assault, together with methods to help respondents recall a broader range of incidents. Here is a brief summary of major changes undertaken to produce better measures of victimization (Bureau of Justice Statistics, 1996; U.S. Bureau of the Census, 1994):

- Revised screening questions and added cues throughout the interview to help respondents recall and distinguish minor incidents
- More direct questions on rape and other sexual crimes, reflecting the belief that people's willingness to discuss such incidents has increased in recent years

- Greater attention to measuring victimizations by someone the respondent knows, including incidents of domestic violence
- Gradual increase in the use of telephone interviews to replace in-person interviews
- An increase in the threshold for series victimizations from three to six, consistent with other efforts to help respondents distinguish individual victimizations

Recent crime counts indicate that the redesign captured a greater number of incidents, especially crimes of violence.

Before taking a look at the victimization rates from the redesigned NCVS, let's consider the changes in survey screening questions. These are summarized in Table 6.3. The redesigned NCVS presents more specific questions and cues, in effect encouraging respondents to think about specific types of incidents. Notice in particular the explicit reference to "forced or unwanted sexual acts" in the redesigned survey; the old NCVS made no direct reference to rape or other sexual assaults, implicitly including them in the general categories of "attack you" and "try to attack you." Redesigned NCVS questions also refer more directly to offenses committed by someone known to the respondent:

> People often don't think of incidents committed by someone they know. Did you have something stolen from you OR were you attacked or threatened by-
> (a) Someone at work or at school-
> (b) A neighbor or friend-
> (c) A relative or family member-
> (d) Any other person you've met or known?

Table 6.4 compares estimates of victimization rates from the first years of the redesigned NCVS with rates from pre-redesign versions. Panel A, reproduced from a study examining violence against women (Bachman and Saltzman, 1995), shows rates of violent crime victimization by victim–offender relationship for males and females. Notice that the redesigned survey yields higher rates for all categories of

Table 6.3   Comparison of Old and Redesigned NCVS Screening Questions

General Screening Question	
Old NCVS	**Redesigned NCVS**
Was anything stolen from you while you were away from home—for instance, at work, in a theater or restaurant, or while traveling?	Were you attacked or threatened OR did you have something stolen from you a. At home including the yard or porch b. At or near a friend's or neighbor's home c. At work or school d. In a place such as a shopping mall, laundry room, restaurant, bank, or airport e. While riding in any vehicle f. On the street or in a parking lot g. At such places as a party, theater, gym, picnic area, or while fishing or hunting OR h. Did anyone ATTEMPT to attack or attempt to steal anything belonging to you from any of these places?

Screening Questions for Violent Crimes	
Old NCVS	**Redesigned NCVS**
Did anyone take something from you by using force, such as by a stickup, mugging, or threat? Did anyone TRY to rob you by using force or threatening to harm you? Did anyone beat you up, attack you, or hit you with something such as a rock or bottle? Were you knifed, shot at, or attacked with some other weapon by anyone at all? Did anyone THREATEN to beat you up or threaten you with a knife, gun, or some other weapon, NOT including telephone threats? Did anyone TRY to attack you in some other way?	Has anyone attacked or threatened you in any of these ways a. With any weapon such as a gun or knife b. With anything like a baseball bat, frying pan, scissors, or stick c. By something thrown, such as a rock d. Include any grabbing, punching, or kicking e. Any rape, attempted rape, or other type of sexual assault f. Any face-to-face threats OR g. Any attack or threat or use of force by anyone at all? Please mention it even if you were not certain it was a crime. Incidents involving forced or unwanted sexual acts are often difficult to talk about. Have you ever been forced or coerced to engage in unwanted sexual activity by a. Someone you didn't know before b. A casual acquaintance OR c. Someone you know well?

Source: Adapted from Bachman and Saltzman (1995:8).

relationship but that the increase tends to be greater for nonstranger offenses. The category "intimate" includes both married persons and those in a quasi-marital or other intimate relationship. Redesigned survey results indicate that just less than 1 percent (9.3 per 1000) of female respondents reported being the victim of a violent offense by an intimate partner or former partner. It therefore appears that efforts to uncover more incidents of violence perpetrated by nonstrangers have been successful.

Similarly, Panel B in Table 6.4 compares victimization rates for specific violent offenses; estimates of rape and sexual assault victimization

Table 6.4   Comparison of Violent Victimization Rate, Old and Redesigned NCVS

Panel A: Average Annual Rate of Violent Victimizations per 1000 Persons

Victim–Offender Relationship	Female	Male
Old NCVS (1987–91)		
Intimate	5.4	0.5
Other relative	1.1	0.7
Acquaintance/friend	7.6	13.0
Stranger	5.4	12.2
Redesigned NCVS (1992–93)		
Intimate	9.3	1.4
Other relative	2.8	1.2
Acquaintance/friend	12.9	17.2
Stranger	7.4	19.0

Source: Bachman and Saltzman (1995:8).

Panel B: Rate of Violent Victimizations per 1000 Persons

Offense	Female	Male
1991 NCVS		
Rape	1.4	0.2
Robbery	3.5	7.8
Aggravated assault	4.4	11.5
Simple assault	13.4	20.9
1994 NCVS		
Rape and sexual assault	3.7	0.2
Robbery	4.1	8.1
Aggravated assault	8.1	15.3
Simple assault	26.6	35.9

Source: Bureau of Justice Statistics (1992b:22) (1991 rates); Bureau of Justice Statistics (1996a:4) (1994 rates).

rates for females were about 2.5 times higher in 1994 than in 1991. Notice, however, that the redesigned NCVS includes "sexual assault other than rape," so the estimates are not directly comparable. Males are more likely to be victims of both aggravated and simple assault, but as the redesigned NCVS shows, estimates of assault victimization rates increased more for females than for males. This is consistent with redesign efforts to obtain better estimates of violent offenses.

At this point, we want to underscore two general points about the redesign in particular and the NCVS in general. First, what we learn about crime from the NCVS or any other survey depends on *what* we ask and *how* we ask it. Keep in mind that measures of crime are affected in part by the procedures we use to make those measures. This is another example of an important point from Chapter 5: Changing how we operationalize measures can change the values we obtain for those measures. Presenting respondents with rather general questions about being attacked by someone discloses fewer crimes of violence than asking questions about specific kinds of violence. Likewise, when we specifically ask respondents to think of acts committed by someone they know, we will uncover more offenses than if we do not include such cues and prompts.

The second point is a consequence of the first: Because of the redesigned NCVS, any effort to compare trends and changes in crime over time must take account of changes in measurement. BJS analysts are attentive to this and caution readers of their reports to be aware of changes in survey methods: "Data based on the redesign are not comparable to data before 1993. . . . A number of fundamental changes were introduced when the survey was redesigned. These changes were phased into the sample over several years" (Bureau of Justice Statistics, 1996:8).

We emphasize these two points because beginning researchers are often less critical users of data such as the NCVS than are more experienced researchers; after all, the survey is sponsored by the U.S. Department of Justice and conducted by the Census Bureau. Examining Table 6.4 without being aware of survey changes would suggest that violent victimization rates had increased sharply from 1991 to 1994, a conclusion that would be misleading.

Community Victimization Surveys

Following the initial development of victim survey methods in the late 1960s, the Census Bureau completed a series of city-level surveys. These were discontinued for a variety of reasons, but researchers and officials in the BJS occasionally conducted city-level victim surveys in specific communities. More recently, in 1998, the BJS and the Office of Community Oriented Policing Services (COPS) launched pilot surveys in 12 large and medium-sized cities (Smith, Steadman, Minton, and Townsend, 1999).

The new city-level initiative underscores one of the chief advantages of measuring crime through victim surveys—obtaining counts of incidents not reported to police. In large part, city-level surveys were promoted by BJS and COPS to enable local law enforcement agencies to better understand the scope of crime—reported and unreported—in their communities. Notice also the title of the first report: "Criminal Victimization and *Perceptions* of Community Safety in 12 Cities, 1998." We emphasize *perceptions* to illustrate that city-level surveys can be valuable tools for implementing community policing, a key component of the 1994 Crime Bill that provided billions of dollars to hire new police officers nationwide. It is significant that the Department of Justice recognized the potential value of survey measures of crime and perceptions of community safety to develop and evaluate community policing.

Furthermore, the initial BJS/COPS effort was a pilot test of new methods for conducting city-level surveys. These bureaus jointly developed a guidebook and software so that local law enforcement agencies and other groups can conduct their own community surveys (Weisel, 1999). These tools also promise to be useful for researchers who wish to study local patterns of crime and individual responses.

Comparing Victim Surveys and Crimes Known to Police

Before moving on to the next section, let's briefly compare the different ways of measuring crime we have discussed so far.

Researchers have devoted special attention to comparing data from the UCR and the NCVS in efforts to determine how the two measures differ and what the strengths and weaknesses of each method are for measuring crime. In fact,

Alfred Blumstein, Jacqueline Cohen, and Richard Rosenfeld (1991:237) claim that "criminal justice researchers and policy analysts are fortunate in having two independent data series." An early study by Wesley Skogan (1974) recognized that crime surveys and police data take fundamentally different approaches to measuring crime but that UCR and NCVS counts of robbery and auto theft are moderately related. More recently, Blumstein and associates (1991) report that, once appropriate statistical adjustments are made, UCR and NCVS data for robbery and burglary exhibit similar trends from 1972 through 1986.

Whereas the UCR provides only summary measures of aggregate units, the NCVS yields more disaggregated data on individual victims, offenders, and incidents. This means that the NCVS is better suited to studies of individual factors in the types of incidents covered by the survey.

SHR and NIBRS data are incident-based systems and can be used to study individual incidents, victims, and offenders. However, the SHR measures one type of crime only. NIBRS holds great promise for the future, but its limited coverage means that it cannot yet serve as a measure of nationwide incidents known to police. For the present, NIBRS data can be used only for those states that currently participate in the program.

By the way, this feature of NIBRS—its availability from only certain local agencies and states—highlights another characteristic of the NCVS worth emphasizing: It is not possible to use survey data to study victimization at the local level. This is because the National Crime Victimization Survey is just that: a *national* survey. It is designed to represent nationwide levels of crime (subject to the limitations we have discussed), but it cannot provide estimates of crime for cities, counties, or most states. Michael Maltz (1998) reports the little-known fact that the NCVS can be used to estimate victimization for more common incidents in the 10 largest states. In addition, as officials gain more experience with the BJS/COPS community victim surveys, resultant data will provide detailed information about victimization at the local level for participating cities. The nation's three largest cities—New York, Los Angeles, and Chicago—were included in the first wave described by Smith and associates (1999).

Despite the limited coverage of NIBRS, incident-based measures have great potential for criminal justice research. Like the NCVS, NIBRS yields details about individual incidents. Unlike the NCVS, NIBRS data can be examined for specific geographic areas at the local level and, eventually, for all states. A series of articles in the *Journal of Quantitative Criminology* presents the first published analysis of NIBRS data. Michael Maxfield (1999) summarizes many of the additional applications of NIBRS data for research and policy. We conclude this section by briefly discussing one area in which NIBRS data measure a type of offense not counted by other annual data series at the national level.

Despite improvements following the NCVS redesign, its sampling plan is still restricted to household residents ages 12 and over. We have discussed the significance of a household-based sample. What kinds of offenses might the NCVS miss by not counting victimizations for individuals younger than 12?

Howard Snyder's (2000) analysis of NIBRS sexual assault data from 12 states provides a clue. About 34 percent of some 61,000 victims of sexual assault were under age 12; that means that over 20,000 sexual assault victims would not have been counted by the NCVS (Snyder, 2000:1–2). Furthermore, the expanded information available under NIBRS reveals that over 40 percent of sexual assault victims under age 12 were assaulted by a family member; an additional 50 percent of the offenders were known by the victims. Only about 5 percent of female victims under age 12 were assaulted by strangers.

These figures should make you think of child abuse, or at least child sexual abuse, as an offense type not measured by the NCVS. Of course, child abuse is undercounted by the UCR and NIBRS as well because much child abuse is not reported to police. NIBRS data represent new sources of information about this type of crime and other offenses that affect young victims.

Surveys of Offending

Delinquency, "victimless" crimes, and crimes rarely observed may be measured by self-report surveys.

Just as survey techniques can measure crime by asking people to describe their experiences as victims, **self-report surveys** ask people about crimes they may have committed. We might initially be skeptical of this technique: How truthful are people when asked about crimes they may have committed? Our concern is justified. Many people do not wish to disclose illegal behavior to interviewers even if they are assured of confidentiality. Others might deliberately lie to interviewers and exaggerate the number of offenses they have committed.

Self-report surveys, however, are probably the best method for trying to measure certain crimes that are poorly represented by other techniques. Thinking about the other methods we have discussed—crimes known to police and victimization surveys—suggests several examples. Crimes such as prostitution and drug abuse are excluded from victimization surveys and underestimated by police records of people arrested for these offenses. Public order crimes and delinquency are other examples. A third class of offenses that might be better counted by self-report surveys are crimes that are rarely reported to or observed by police. Shoplifting and drunk driving are examples.

Think of it this way: As we saw earlier, all crimes require an offender. Not all crimes have clearly identifiable victims who can be interviewed, however, and not all crimes are readily observed by police, victims, or witnesses. If we can't observe the offense and can't interview a victim, what's the next logical step?

There are no nationwide efforts to systematically collect self-report measures of all types of crimes. Instead, periodic surveys yield information either on specific types of crime or on crimes committed by a specific target population. We will consider two ongoing self-report surveys here and comment on the validity and reliability of this method for measuring crime.

National Household Survey on Drug Abuse*

Like the NCVS, the National Household Survey on Drug Abuse (NHSDA) is based on a national sample of households. Both surveys are designed to monitor nationwide patterns. Unlike the victimization survey, however, the central purpose of the NHSDA is to obtain self-reports of drug use.

The survey has been conducted since 1971, with sampling and questioning procedures having been revised several times. The survey is currently sponsored by the Substance Abuse and Mental Health Services Administration in the U.S. Department of Health and Human Services. Persons ages 12 and over who live in households are the target population. In the 2001 sample, about 69,000 individuals responded to questions regarding their use of illegal drugs, alcohol, and tobacco (Substance Abuse and Mental Health Services Administration, 2002a). Because it has been conducted for over 3 decades, the NHSDA provides information on trends and changes in drug use among respondents.

Think for a moment about what sorts of questions we would ask to learn about people's experience in using illegal drugs. Among other things, we would probably want to distinguish someone who tried marijuana once from daily users. The drug use survey does this by including questions to distinguish *lifetime* use (ever used) of different drugs from *current* use (used within

the past month). You may or may not agree that, for example, use in the past month represents current use, but it is the standard used in regular reports on NHSDA results. That's the operational definition of "current use."

Two potential sources of measurement problems with the NHSDA should come to mind. We have already touched on the first concern: Do people tell the truth when asked about drug use? The NHSDA incorporates certain procedures to encourage candid, truthful responses from individuals. After obtaining basic demographic information about all household residents, interviewers conduct the rest of the interviews in a private area away from other household members. Interviewers do not directly ask about drug use. Instead, these questions, and questions about other illegal behaviors, are administered through computer-assisted self-interviewing. Respondents read questions on a computer screen or listen to questions through earphones and key in their responses. Beginning in 1999, the NHSDA instituted major changes in the question format and questionnaire design in an effort to improve the validity of self-report measures.

Although these procedures produce better measures of drug use than interviews conducted by telephone, the NHSDA still underreports drug use (Gfroerer, Eyerman, and Chromy, 2002). In fact, the circumstances of the NHSDA interview appear to especially affect reporting by adolescents. Joseph Gfroerer (1993) found higher reported rates of drug use by youths from surveys administered in the classroom compared with surveys administered at home. We will discuss an example of school-based surveys shortly, but let's first briefly consider the second source of concern in using the NHSDA as a measure of drug use.

Recall the earlier point about how the household sample design of the NCVS measures only victimizations that affect households or household residents. Commercial establishments, people in institutional quarters—military housing or work-release community corrections cen-

---

*Descriptive information about the National Household Survey on Drug Abuse was obtained from Mieczkowski (1996) and Substance Abuse and Mental Health Services Administration (2002).

ters, for example—and homeless people are not eligible for inclusion in a household sample. Although the NHSDA makes special efforts to include people living in such facilities as shelters or migrant worker camps, a household survey on drug use excludes many people who do not live in traditional households.

Monitoring the Future*

Our second example is different in two respects: (1) It targets a specific population, and (2) it asks sampled respondents a broader variety of questions.

Since 1975, the National Institute on Drug Abuse has sponsored an annual survey of high school seniors, Monitoring the Future: A Continuing Study of the Lifestyles and Values of Youth, or Monitoring the Future (MTF) for short. As its long title implies, the MTF survey is intended to monitor the behaviors, attitudes, and values of young people. In recent years, researchers and policy makers have become especially interested in drug, alcohol, and tobacco use among youths, and the MTF has been used as something of a sentinel to measure such behaviors.

The MTF actually includes several samples of high school students and others groups, totaling about 43,700 respondents in 2002 (Johnston et al., 2003). We'll begin with the high school sample and then briefly mention the others.

Each spring, about 420 high schools are sampled within particular geographic areas. In larger high schools, samples of up to 350 seniors are selected; in smaller schools, all seniors may participate. The students fill out computer scan sheets containing batteries of questions that include self-reported use of alcohol, tobacco, and illegal drugs. In most cases, students record their answers in classrooms during normal school hours, although in some

circumstances students complete the questionnaires in larger groups.

The core sample of the MTF—surveys of high school seniors—thus provides a cross section for measuring annual drug use and other illegal acts. In addition, the MTF has expanded its samples over the years to include public school students in the 8th and 10th grades (since 1991). A subset of about 2400 MTF respondents from the high school samples is selected each year to receive a follow-up questionnaire in the mail. The follow-up samples provide MTF data from college students—those high school seniors who went on to college—and from adults. Data from the oldest follow-up group were first collected in 1976, so, assuming most high school seniors are age 18, respondents in the 2001 follow-up sample could have been up to 43 years old.

Now recall our discussion of the time dimension in Chapter 4. Each year, both the MTF and the NHSDA measure drug use for a cross section of high school seniors and adults in households, thus providing a snapshot of annual rates of self-reported drug use. Examining annual results from the MTF and the NHSDA over time provides a time series or trend study that enables researchers and policy makers to detect changes in drug use among high school seniors, college students, and adults. Finally, the follow-up samples of MTF respondents constitute a series of panel studies whereby changes in drug use among individual respondents can be studied over time. Thomas Mieczkowski (1996) presents an excellent discussion of these two surveys and compares self-reported drug use from each series over time.

Because MTF measures for all samples are collected through self-reports, these data share the potential problems we mentioned in connection with the NHSDA. We noted that at least one study (Gfroerer, 1993) suggests that young people self-report drug use more frequently in school settings than in their homes. However, Mieczkowski (1996:378) points out that students are asked to provide their names to survey

---

*Descriptive information about Monitoring the Future is drawn primarily from Johnston, O'Malley, and Bachman (2003) and Mieczkowski (1996).

staff, something that's necessary for later follow-ups but that might undermine the truthfulness of their responses.

What about sampling procedures for the MTF? In one sense, selecting schools and then students within schools is a sound procedure for sampling high school seniors. But you should be able to think of at least one problem with this approach. Students who are absent on the day the survey is administered are not included and are not eligible for the follow-up sample. We might reasonably expect that students with poor attendance records are absent more often and thus less represented in the sample. And because our interest in the MTF is as a measure of drug use and offending, we might suspect that students with poor attendance records might have higher rates of drug use and offending.

Validity and Reliability of Self-Report Measures

This chapter cannot supply the final word on efforts to validate self-report measures. On the one hand, the final word has not yet been written; on the other, a small number of researchers have examined the issue in some detail. In most cases, the latter studies compare self-reported offending with other measures—usually, records of offending from law enforcement and juvenile justice agencies. You may recognize this as an example of convergent validity, a topic from Chapter 5.

For example, in their study of London delinquents (mentioned in Chapter 5), Donald West and David Farrington (1977:22) compared official criminal records to self-reported delinquent convictions disclosed in interviews with their subjects. Only a small proportion of subjects failed to mention one or more delinquent acts that appeared in criminal records. After further study, West and Farrington concluded that these omissions were due more to memory lapses than to untruthful responses, because most inconsistencies between the sources occurred for high-rate delinquents.

In a more recent longitudinal study of a sample of Pittsburgh youths, Farrington and associates (1996) examined convergent validity by again comparing self-reported offending and arrests with official records of arrests and juvenile petitions. Because it was a longitudinal panel study, interviewing the sample at multiple time points, the authors were able to estimate predictive validity by comparing self-reported delinquency at one time period with arrests and juvenile petitions at later times. As you might expect, the relationship is imperfect, but the researchers did find that subjects who self-reported higher levels of more serious offenses at time 1 were much more likely to have official arrest or delinquency records at time 2.

Three additional studies of self-report validity lead us into a summary of this method of measuring crime. Joseph Weis (1986) presents a thorough discussion of the strengths and weaknesses of self-report and official arrest records as measures of offending. Validity and reliability of self-reports are discussed in unusual detail by David Huizinga and Delbert Elliott (1986) as they draw on data from a long-term panel study. Among other things, Huizinga and Elliott make some important comments about the self-interests of researchers in too readily accepting the validity of whatever measure of crime they happen to be using. Finally, Michael Maxfield and associates (Maxfield, Weiler, and Widom, 2000) show that the convergence of self-reported and official records of arrests varies by gender, ethnicity, and type of offense. In a study of the long-term consequences of child abuse, the authors show that female and nonwhite subjects less often report known arrests. All subjects were more likely to self-report offenses that are more common—most notably, drug use.

Self-Report Surveys Summarized

Researchers and policy makers are best advised to be *critical users* of measures obtained from self-report surveys. Self-reports can and should be used to measure offending, but researchers, public officials, and others who use such measures should be aware of their strengths and limitations. For example, because MTF and NHSDA sampling and interviewing procedures have remained relatively constant, the surveys provide reasonably consistent information on trends in drug use or offending over time. These two surveys are better as measures of change than as measures of absolute levels.

Our consideration of these two surveys also highlighted the importance of sampling procedures. Samples based on households may not be readily generalized to other populations, and data obtained from high school seniors in class may be different from data obtained from dropouts or chronic truants.

Also consider that alternative measures of offenses like drug use and delinquency are not readily available for general populations. This leaves three alternatives: (1) carefully using imperfect measures, (2) having no measures of certain types of offenses, or (3) developing new measures. Our strong preference is to pursue both the first and the third alternatives. Having read Chapter 5 and worked your way through most of this chapter, you are becoming better equipped to carefully interpret measures of all kinds. We now consider some different measures of drug use that have been less widely used in criminal justice research.

Drug Surveillance Systems

Surveillance systems have been developed to obtain alternative measures of drug use.

The challenge of developing reliable and valid measures of such offenses as drug use has prompted researchers and policy makers to search for alternative approaches. We will briefly consider examples of focused efforts to monitor drug use and its consequences among specialized populations.

Arrestee Drug Abuse Monitoring

The National Institute of Justice (NIJ) has conducted the Arrestee Drug Abuse Monitoring (ADAM) program since 1997. Prior to that, a substantially similar program, Drug Use Forecasting (DUF), had been in place for about 10 years. Four times per year, cities that participate in ADAM select samples of persons arrested for a variety of offenses. Anonymous interviews and urine specimens are obtained from those who agree to take part in the voluntary study. In 2001, more than 25,000 arrestees participated in ADAM. About 630 adult males were sampled in each of 33 participating cities; about 120 adult females were also selected in most sites (National Institute of Justice, 2002). For the year 2000, ADAM collected data from 2100 male and 420 female juvenile detainees in 9 cities (National Institute of Justice, 2003a).

The main purpose of ADAM is to provide an ongoing assessment of the prevalence of drug use among persons arrested for criminal offenses. Results for 2000 showed that about 63 percent of adult arrestees and more than half of male juveniles tested positive for at least one drug (National Institute of Justice, 2003a).

Annual ADAM results are widely distributed by the NIJ and have come to be viewed as a rough-and-ready indicator of drug use among criminal offenders. More importantly, samples from ADAM (and its predecessor) have been collected four times per year since 1987 and so can indicate trends in drug use among arrestees. Trends vary by city, but rates of positive tests for any drug have remained fairly high, showing some fluctuation in different cities. Greater changes are exhibited for specific drugs, with fluctuations in the use of cocaine, opiates, and methamphetamine.

For our purposes, one of the most interesting aspects of ADAM is that it combines urinalysis and self-report measures of drug use. Interviews with arrestees include self-report items, so responses can be compared with urine test results. Beginning in 2000, a new interview instrument was introduced, adding questions that focus on drug-related policy issues such as perceived dependency and treatment needs, along with respondents' assessment of local drug markets.

Unfortunately, few comparisons of urinalysis and self-report measures have been made, and researchers reach different conclusions about how well self-reports stand up to urinalysis results. Richard Rosenfeld and Scott Decker (1993) conclude that subjects substantially underreport drug use. More recently, Julie Yun Soo Kim and associates (Kim, Fendrich, and Wislar, 2000) found that juveniles who tested positive for marijuana use more often self-reported lifetime marijuana use or use in the past 30 days than in the past 3 days. And juveniles were much more likely to self-report marijuana use than cocaine use. Together, these findings suggest that something called "social desirability" is at work: Using marijuana is seen as more socially desirable than using cocaine, and using either drug in the more distant past is more desirable than having used it in the past 3 days. This is consistent with a comment by Mieczkowski (1990) that arrestees who may have recently used drugs are not the best persons to verify the truthfulness of self-reports. This quote from the 1995 NIJ annual report illustrates this point clearly:

> At times, obtaining valid self-reported data in a jail or lockup [where interviews are conducted] can be difficult. The sensitivity of the topic, the proximity of jail staff, the confidence arrestees have in the guarantee of anonymity, and the lucidness of respondents all affect the data collection process. (National Institute of Justice, 1996:9)

Any measure of crime is selective; neither all crimes nor all people are included. In what ways is the ADAM program selective as a measure of drug use? Based on what we have covered so far, three ways should be evident. First, ADAM operates in a maximum of 35 cities (in 2000). Because participation requires a substantial effort from police departments, we can't assume that participating cities are representative of other cities. Second, and perhaps most importantly, ADAM includes only arrested persons. It's obvious that we cannot generalize from people who are arrested to the population at large. It's less obvious that arrest is a selective process. Police exercise discretion in deciding whether to make an arrest, and their priorities can change over time. Third, ADAM interviews and testing are voluntary, although this has not had much impact on participation. Perhaps surprisingly, a large proportion of 1998 arrestees agreed to participate: More than 80 percent consented to the interview, and between 75 and 98 percent provided a urine specimen (National Institute of Justice, 2003a:9).

Even though ADAM is limited as a measure of drug use, it represents an imaginative attempt to obtain a different type of measure. Data from ADAM can provide information about gross trends in drug use among arrestees. Additional data collected through the interview may be used to analyze drug use by offense, age, gender, and other variables.

The Drug Abuse Warning Network

The ADAM system implicitly assumes that at least some drug users will be involved in other offenses. Our next specialized measure assumes that drug use can produce acute health problems that cause users to seek treatment in hospital emergency rooms. The Drug Abuse Warning Network (DAWN) collects emergency medical treatment reports for "drug episodes" from samples of hospitals and medical examiners nationwide. In 2001, the DAWN sample included 470 hospitals in 21 major metropolitan areas. Participating hospitals submitted information on over 267,000 drug abuse episodes for the year 2001 (Substance Abuse and Mental Health Services Administration, 2002b).

Drug episodes are defined as visits to a hospital emergency room that are produced by or directly related to use of illegal drugs or nonmedical use of legal drugs. Included under this definition are direct effects of drug ingestion (overdoses, other physical or psychic reactions), as well as injuries or deaths in which drug intoxication was a contributing factor. Nonfatal episodes are drawn from emergency rooms, while drug-related deaths are recorded by medical examiners. Notice that DAWN is based on units of analysis that are only indirectly linked to criminal offenses. The concept of drug episodes is most relevant for studies of public health, and, in fact, DAWN was designed as a data system for health surveillance.

Because it was begun in the early 1970s, DAWN is a comparatively long-term time series that monitors the most serious medical consequences of drug use. Like ADAM, DAWN is best suited to measuring trends. For example, learning that the participating hospitals in Baltimore mentioned opiates (heroin or morphine) in 1667 drug episodes for 1990 is not especially meaningful. Comparing Baltimore with San Francisco, a city with about the same population in 1990, helps a little. San Francisco had 3954 opiate drug episodes in 1990, which suggests that heroin and morphine were a greater medical problem in that California city. In 1994, however, DAWN recorded 3123 opiate drug episodes for San Francisco and 8882 for Baltimore (McCaig and Greenblatt, 1996). By 2001, both Baltimore and San Francisco were among the top four cities in heroin use. In addition, San Francisco rated as the top city for methamphetamine episodes, while none were recorded in Baltimore (Substance Abuse and Mental Health Services Administration, 2002b).

Like ADAM, DAWN records include demographic and other information about the individuals whose drug use brings them to hospitals and morgues. But the unusual unit of analysis for DAWN means that one individual can account for multiple drug episodes. This makes it difficult to use DAWN data for research in which individual people are the unit of analysis.

Mieczkowski (1996:387) points out that DAWN data for a single metropolitan area might serve as indicators of the impact of anti-drug programs. For example, examining trends in drug episodes involving teenagers might be used in an evaluation of high school education and prevention programs. Or measures of police cocaine seizures might be compared with changes in cocaine drug emergencies.

Pulse Check

Our examination of different measures has so far described systematic attempts to count crime and drug use through surveys, tabulations of crime reports, arrest records, and emergency room episodes. A recent addition to the battery of systems that monitor drug problems is completely different. Since 1992, the Office of National Drug Control Policy (ONDCP) has published a quarterly or semiannual report based on qualitative information obtained from selected cities.

Pulse Check reports efforts by researchers to collect information from three sources: ethnographers, local and federal law enforcement officers, and drug treatment service providers (Office of National Drug Control Policy, 2003). All sources are in or near the cities for which they provide information. Researchers conduct semistructured interviews by telephone, asking about trends in the availability and use of different types of drugs.

Ethnographers are usually local researchers who have extensive experience in qualitative field methods, a topic we will examine in Chapter 10. The basic premise of ethnographic research is that researchers can learn much about social phenomena by immersing themselves in the field: "The ethnographer, who is fully revealed as a social science researcher, enters the drug user's world to record and describe it" (Office of National Drug Control Policy, 1996:3). Wright and Decker (1994) studied burglars in the field and active robbers (Wright and Decker, 1997). Tracey Bush reported on domestic violence in a London public housing project after living there for 5 years (Hood-Williams and Bush, 1995). Other criminal justice researchers have studied other dimensions of crime and criminal justice agencies through ethnographic research.

Table 6.5   Pulse Check: Heroin

	Incidence	Who's Using?	Change in Users	Price and Purity	Who's Selling
Ethnographers					
Bridgeport, CT	Stable at high level	All ethnicities; older users	Increase in usage by 20- to 29-year-olds; increased snorting by 16- to 20-years olds	$10 per bag; high purity	Gangs; 15- to 25-year-olds; sold and home delivered via beeper use
San Antonio, TX	Up	Young users; mostly Mexican American	More women; more youths	$10–40 per gram	Mexican mafia; Texas syndicate; more young sellers
Police					
Bridgeport, CT	Up	All ethnicities; often used by prostitutes	More males than females	$10 units; usually 28–30% pure	Mostly minorities; all in inner city
San Antonio, TX	Up	Mostly older Hispanic males	Younger males of all ethnicities	$10–20 per bag	Mostly older Hispanic males selling at street and mid-level

Source: Adapted from Office of National Drug Control Policy (1996: Tables 1, 2).

Semistructured telephone interviews are also conducted with police officers who are active in drug law enforcement. Police know quite a bit about what goes on in the streets—knowledge that is not reflected in crime or arrest reports. Because drug law enforcement requires a great deal of information gathering, police who work on special drug squads or task forces have considerable knowledge about the drug scene in their jurisdiction.

By the same token, drug treatment professionals have regular contact with drug users and former users. They are in a position to learn about new drugs on the street, the strength or purity of different drugs, and the emergence or decline of particular dealing networks.

Table 6.5 gives you an idea of what sort of information is available from Pulse Check. Ethnographers and police are asked similar types of questions about drug users, sellers, prices, and so on. Table 6.5 shows how these two sources of information responded to questions about heroin in two cities. You will see some differences in ratings by the two types of observers in each city, but notice the general agreement on user profiles.

Information from drug treatment providers cannot be compared with that from police and ethnographer sources quite so easily. Treatment provider responses are organized by region, not by individual city, and records on treatment clients are tabulated by age, gender, race, and type of drug use.

Measuring Crime for Specific Purposes

Sometimes, alternative measures of crime are collected for research or policy purposes.

Each of the crime measures discussed so far can be used for a variety of research purposes—exploration, description, explanation, and applied research. However, each has the primary purpose of providing some type of crime count—crimes known to police, victimizations of households and people who live in households, self-reported drug use and other offending, drug use among arrestees and emergency room patients, or qualitative assessments of drug use and availability in specific urban areas.

Such measures are useful for criminal justice and public health professionals. Researchers have also made extensive use of data from standard series such as the UCR, SHR, and NCVS.

Often, however, none of these regular series of crime measures meets the needs of researchers, public officials, or others looking for specialized information about crime. At this point, we want to call your attention to examples of crime measures developed for specific research and policy purposes.

Local Crime Surveys

We have seen that victimization surveys have certain advantages over other measures of crime. Surveys are especially useful for learning about crimes not reported to police. Because the NCVS is a national survey, one drawback is that it cannot be used to estimate victimizations for individual cities or for all but the largest states. Because of their potential strengths, victimization surveys are more often being conducted in specific states, cities, or even neighborhoods. Sometimes, local surveys are conducted by researchers; other times, local governments, police departments, and even community organizations conduct them. Cities or counties that have shifted to community policing often do victimization surveys to learn more about crime problems that affect people in particular areas.

For example, the Kansas City, Missouri, police department conducts community safety surveys before implementing new programs in a specific area. Officials ask questions about crime problems, victimization experiences, and feelings of neighborhood safety. After neighborhood initiatives have been in effect for approximately one year, police conduct another survey to assess change. Similarly, certain community groups in Kansas City periodically survey neighborhood residents about local crime problems. Results are shared with police officers assigned to the community and used to direct targeted anticrime initiatives.

Such surveys are rarely up to the standards required by researchers or those that guide such efforts as the NCVS. They usually do not employ probability samples (we'll discuss these in Chapter 8), and questionnaires can be casual affairs at best. Nevertheless, local crime surveys are useful tools for public officials and citizens in many communities.

In recent years, a variety of publications have been issued to guide such survey applications. A book by John Eck and Nancy LaVigne (1994) and an excellent handbook by the Bureau of Justice Assistance (1993) are examples of publications prepared for use by law enforcement agencies. As described earlier in this chapter, the BJS and COPS recently collaborated to produce guidelines and software for conducting community victimization surveys (Weisel, 1999). This new tool has the potential to improve the quality and expand the use of local crime surveys.

We noted some of the validity and reliability problems of the NCVS in measuring certain kinds of offenses, such as domestic violence. These shortcomings have led other researchers to develop surveys that focus more narrowly on domestic violence and other topics. One of the best recent examples is the National Violence Against Women Survey (NVAWS), sponsored by the National Institute of Justice and the Centers for Disease Control and Prevention. Conducted in 1995 and 1996, the survey employed special procedures to produce better measures of sexual assault and family violence. These included screening questions that were even more specific than those noted earlier for the revised NCVS and provisions for ensuring the privacy of interviews. As a result, the NVAWS produced estimates of rape victimization and assault by a family member that were substantially higher than NCVS estimates. Patricia Tjaden and Nancy Thoennes, authors of the most comprehensive report on the NVAWS, provide a very useful discussion of how differences between the two surveys produce different counts of crime victimization (2000:15–16). Their discussion supports one important theme in this chapter: Different procedures for measuring a concept will produce different results.

PUTTING IT ALL TOGETHER

MEASURING CRIME IN NEW YORK CITY

Measuring crime is a key element of policing in New York City, and Compstat is at the heart of innovative crime measurement.

Each Monday, several types of indicators are compiled and distributed to commanders of the city's 76 precincts and to police executives throughout the department. Each week, Rutgers University researchers received the same Compstat reports distributed to precinct commanders. These Compstat reports present measures of crime and police activity for the previous week. Considering what sort of information is included in the weekly reports illustrates some variations in crime measures known to police.

First, reported crimes—termed "crime complaints" by the department—for the Part I UCR categories are listed in each precinct report. Second, recorded arrests for the Part I categories are listed. This is followed by data on arrests for a variety of other types of incidents, including drugs, driving while intoxicated, and incidents involving

guns. Finally, weekly reports of "summons activity" list citations issued for traffic violations and "quality of life" incidents. This last category includes things like public intoxication, public drinking, and other minor offenses. In later observations of police tactics, Rutgers researchers learned first-hand how police discretion affected citations for quality-of-life incidents.

Measures of arrests are traditionally important performance indicators for police, especially arrests for serious crimes. But Compstat includes arrests for some offenses in part to measure so-called victimless crime. Recall that these offenses are not reliably measured by crime reports, so arrests are something of a proxy indicator for minor offenses. Consider some of the advantages and disadvantages of measuring victimless crime in this way.

Compstat reports of crimes known to police are timely and much more detailed than we can consider here. But it's worth noting two general features of Compstat reports. First, the department's purpose in measuring crime is to support strategy and tactics development, operations monitoring, and general accountability. In a sense, Compstat data are collected and dissemi-

What about self-report surveys? The Kansas City–based Kauffman Foundation sponsors an annual survey of students in local high schools that is modeled after the MTF surveys. Information about drug and alcohol use by Kansas City youths helps local officials plan and evaluate programs to reduce substance abuse (Maxfield, 2001).

Incident-Based Crime Records

We mentioned earlier that larger jurisdictions have been slow to convert from UCR reporting to NIBRS, largely because police departments in large cities have tailored data management systems to their own particular needs. Advances in geographic information systems and the development of computer software to produce maps of crime patterns have spurred the creation of

highly sophisticated incident-based crime data systems in some agencies.

Chicago offers one of the best examples among U.S. cities. Under the leadership of researchers at the Illinois Criminal Justice Information Authority and Loyola University of Chicago, detailed information about crimes reported to police can be linked to a variety of other information to reveal space-based patterns of crime (C. Block, 1995; R. Block, 1995). Chicago's system is powerful, timely (updated daily), and easy to use. Community police officers in the city regularly produce maps of crime patterns for their own use and for neighborhood residents. Researchers have also used these data to examine, for example, the clustering of crime around Chicago mass transit stations (Davis, 1996).

nated for a research purpose, but it is very much applied research. These data are compiled for the department's use, not for researchers' benefit or for periodic reporting to a state or federal agency. Nonetheless, Compstat data were invaluable sources for Rutgers researchers.

Second, the precinct-level reports present decentralized data for relatively small areas, but these are still *summary data* that do not include details for individual incidents. Incident-level crime data are available, and they are used to analyze crimes by location, time of day, and related features. However, incident-level NYPD reports are not readily available for analysis by researchers, and New York City does not report data for NIBRS.

Measurement Quality

What about the quality of Compstat data? Given the importance of Compstat for accountability, precinct commanders have powerful incentives to reduce crime and might be expected to tinker with crime reports in an effort to keep their numbers down. In the early stages of Compstat implementation, some manipulation of crime reports was discovered, and precinct commanders lost their jobs as a result. More important is how the falsified crime reports were discovered. The department created a headquarters-level office known as the Data Integrity Unit to systematically audit crime reporting from all precincts (Maple, 1999; Silverman, 1999). Of course, such audits cannot guarantee that police records of crime are completely reliable. Conducting regular audits does, however, foster more confidence in the accuracy of New York's crime statistics. Their extended access to planning and analysis staff in the NYPD enabled researchers to witness examples of data quality control. Among other things, this undermines one alternative explanation for the decline in crime—systematic manipulation of crime data by police.

Local Victim Surveys

New York was among the 12 cities included in the initial BJS/COPS wave of city-level victim surveys. At this point, it is not known whether the local survey in New York will be continued on a regular basis. If annual citywide surveys were conducted, they would be useful in two respects. First, a city-level survey would provide measures of unreported crime, something that would be important to gauge in assessing the impact of police action on crime. Second, comparing annual changes in survey-based measures to annual change in police records would be a very useful application of the principle of multiple measures in social science.

Cities and other jurisdictions vary in the quality of their records systems, but many police departments are making rapid advances. Local measures of crimes known to police may be more current, complete, and detailed than measures submitted to the FBI under its UCR, SHR, or NIBRS data series. Our running example of New York City illustrates this nicely.

Observing Crime

We have seen that police learn about certain types of crime primarily through observation—for example, drug use and sales, prostitution, public order offenses, and drunk driving. Researchers may face situations in which they need to make independent observations of crime.

For example, we have pointed out that shoplifting is poorly measured by police rec-ords. Victim surveys might reveal some instances of shoplifting, but only if we sampled shops, and then we would learn only about those incidents detected by shop staff. Self-report surveys could tell us something about *shoplifters,* but it would be difficult to use this method to measure *shoplifting* incidents. Terry Baumer and Dennis Rosenbaum (1982) conducted systematic observations of a large department store in Chicago for descriptive and applied purposes. Using ingenious methods, they sought to estimate the frequency of shoplifting and to evaluate the effectiveness of different store security measures. Chapter 10, on field research, describes this study and its findings in detail.

What about assault? Again, police measure assaults that are reported to them, usually by victims or witnesses. The NCVS was redesigned in part to get better counts of assault, but for some research purposes, independent observations may yield better measures.

Ross Homel and associates (Homel and Clark, 1994; Macintyre and Homel, 1997) were interested in the links between drinking and violence in bars and nightclubs. Specifically, they sought to learn what sorts of physical features and situations in bars tended to either discourage or facilitate violence. Their explanatory studies required selecting samples of public drinking establishments in Sydney, Australia, and dispatching pairs of observers to each site. Observers recorded information about violent incidents they witnessed, together with details about each bar's physical layout, entertainment, and procedures for controlling access and regulating conduct. Researchers were able to make general explanatory statements about how the physical environment and management practices were related to violence.

Police normally learn about drug use or sales only if they witness the acts. Constraints on the ability of police to make such observations are often cited as obstacles to the enforcement of drug laws. In many communities, however, neighborhood organizations supplement law enforcement through patrols and targeted surveillance of drug activity in specific neighborhoods. If such citizen patrols witness suspected drug activity, they inform police, community prosecutors, or other justice officials who may launch further investigations. Neighborhood organizations in Kansas City, Albuquerque, Philadelphia, and many other cities use directed observations in this way (Maxfield, 2001).

These examples of directed observation have three common characteristics. First, each has a fairly specific research or policy purpose. Baumer and Rosenbaum wanted to obtain estimates of shoplifting frequency and to evaluate the effectiveness of certain security measures; Homel and associates wished to learn more about the association between public drinking and violence; members of community organizations participate in neighborhood sur-

veillance to take action against drug and other problems. Second, the three examples focus on relatively small areas—a single department store, a sample of bars and nightclubs, or a specific neighborhood. Finally, the expected density of incidents made observation an appropriate way to measure crime. Shoplifting happens in shops, and large department stores offer opportunities to observe many incidents; it's well known that public violence is relatively common in bars, and police records can be used to select bars with a history of violence; finally, citizen patrols and neighborhood surveillance programs are launched because residents are troubled by local drug problems.

Measuring Crime Summary

Each measure of crime has strengths and weaknesses.

Table 6.6 summarizes some of what we have considered in this chapter by comparing different measures of crime. Each method has its own strengths and weaknesses. The UCR and SHR provide the best counts for murder and crimes in which the victim is either a business or a commercial establishment. Crimes against persons or households that are not reported to police are best counted by the NCVS. Usually, these are less serious crimes, many of them UCR Part II incidents that are counted only if a suspect is arrested. Recent changes in NCVS procedures have increased the counts of sexual assault and other violent victimizations. Compared with the UCR, NIBRS potentially provides much greater detail for a broader range of offenses. NIBRS complements the NCVS by including disaggregated incident-based reports for state and local areas and by recording detailed information on crimes against children under age 12.

Self-report surveys are best at measuring crimes that do not have readily identifiable victims and that are less often observed by or reported to police. The two self-report surveys listed in Table 6.6 sample different populations and use different interview procedures.

Table 6.6   Measuring Crime Summary

	Units	Target Population	Crime Coverage	Best Count For
Known to Police				
UCR	Aggregate: reporting agency	All law enforcement agencies; 98% reporting	Limited number reported and recorded crimes	Commercial and business victims
SHR	Incident	All law enforcement agencies; 98% reporting	Homicides only	Homicides
NIBRS	Incident	All law enforcement agencies; limited reporting	Extensive	Details on local incidents; victims under age 12
Surveys				
NCVS	Victimization, individuals and households	Individuals in households	Household and personal crimes	Household and personal crimes not reported to police
NHSDA	Individual respondent, offender	Individuals in households	Drug use	Drug use by adults in households
MTF	Individual respondent, offender	High school seniors; follow-up on sample	Substance use, delinquency, offending	Drug use by high school seniors
Sentinel				
ADAM	Arrested offenders	Quarterly samples of arrestees, 35 cities	Drug use	Changes in drug use among arrestees
DAWN	Medical emergency: drug episodes	National sample of hospitals	Drug-related medical emergencies	Changes in acute drug use problems
Pulse Check	Aggregate: ethnographer, police, treatment report	Selected cities (number varies)	Qualitative assessments drug use, price, user profiles	Comparative profile of drug use, price, use patterns

Sentinel measures target more narrowly defined populations for the purposes of monitoring and are best seen as measures of change. The two quantitative series in Table 6.6 measure drug use in the context of medical and legal crises, while the qualitative Pulse Check depends on judgments from street-level experts.

Be aware that Table 6.6 and our discussions throughout this chapter include only a partial listing of crime measures used by researchers and public officials. Each local and state law enforcement agency maintains its own records, which often provide the best measures for research in specific geographic areas. Finally, a specific research purpose may require collecting independent measures of crime.

Don't forget that all crime measures are selective, so it's important to understand the selection process. Despite their various flaws, the measures of crime available to you can serve many research purposes. Researchers are best advised to be critical and careful users of whatever measure of crime best suits their research purpose.

✪ *Main Points*

- Crime is a fundamental concept in criminal justice research. Different approaches to measuring crime illustrate general principles of conceptualization, operationalization, and measurement.
- Before using any measure of crime, researchers should understand what types of offenses it does and does not include.

- Different measures of crime are based on different units of analysis. The UCR is a summary measure that reports totals for individual agencies. Other measures use offenders, victims, incidents, or offenses as the units of analysis.
- Crime data are collected for one or more general purposes: monitoring, agency accountability, and research.
- Crimes known to police have been the most widely used measures. UCR data have been available since the early 20th century; more detailed information about homicides was added to the UCR in 1961. Most recently, the FBI has developed an incident-based reporting system that is gradually being adopted.
- Surveys of victims reveal information about crimes that are not reported to police. The NCVS includes very detailed information about personal and household incidents but does not count crimes against businesses or individual victims under age 12. Although the NCVS is a nationally representative measure, it cannot estimate victimizations for states or local areas.
- Self-report surveys were developed to measure crimes with unclear victims that are less often detected by police. Two such surveys estimate drug use among high school seniors and adults.
- Self-report surveys do not measure all drug use because of incomplete reporting by respondents and procedures for selecting survey respondents.
- ADAM and DAWN provide measures of drug use among special populations but are best suited to monitoring changes in drug use. A qualitative monitoring system reflects the perceptions and judgments of selected experts in specific cities.
- Different measures of crime are also developed for specific research and policy purposes. Many police departments do crime analysis with their own incident-based records. The NVAWS measures specific types of crime for specific purposes.
- We have many different measures of crime because each measure is imperfect. Each measure has its own strengths and weaknesses.

✪ Key Terms

Incident-based measure	Summary-based measure
Self-report survey	Surveillance system
	Victim survey

✪ Review Questions and Exercises

1. Los Angeles police consider a murder to be gang-related if either the victim or the offender is known to be a gang member, whereas Chicago police record a murder as gang-related only if the killing is directly related to gang activities (Spergel, 1990). Describe how these different operational definitions illustrate general points about measuring crime discussed in this chapter.
2. Measuring gang-related crime is an example of trying to measure a particular dimension of crime: motive. Other examples are hate crimes, terrorist acts, and drug-related crimes. Specify conceptual and operational definitions for at least one of these types. Find one newspaper story and one research report that presents an example.
3. How would you measure crime in a specific city if you wanted to evaluate a community policing program that encourages neighborhood residents to report incidents to police?

✪ Internet Exercises

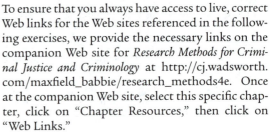

To ensure that you always have access to live, correct Web links for the Web sites referenced in the following exercises, we provide the necessary links on the companion Web site for *Research Methods for Criminal Justice and Criminology* at http://cj.wadsworth. com/maxfield_babbie/research_methods4e. Once at the companion Web site, select this specific chapter, click on "Chapter Resources," then click on "Web Links."

1. A growing number of cities and other jurisdictions are using measures of local crime to produce crime maps and other analytic tools. The National Institute of Justice (NIJ) maintains a crime-mapping resource center that provides assistance in crime analysis and links to individual agencies. Visit the NIJ Website, link to a site of your choice, and then examine available crime maps and data. Use the information you find to provide a summary statement about crime trends over the past few years in the city you selected. To do this, you might want to limit your discussion to one or two index crimes.
2. Published reports and actual data from various measures of crime we have discussed are increasingly available on the Web. Visit one of the following Web sites: Arrestee Drug Abuse Monitoring (ADAM), Monitoring the Future (MTF), National Household Survey on Drug Abuse

(NHSDA), New York City Police Department, or Uniform Crime Reports. Using one of these links, download or record data on at least two offenses (or, in the case of the MTF and the NHSDA, data on drug use for two specific drugs) in two cities over a 5-year period. Bring your data to class and discuss what you have found.

3. In this chapter and Chapter 5, we pointed out that different ways of operationalizing concepts can produce different results. The Bureau of Justice Statistics Web site presents another example of this in a graph displaying trends for four measures of violent crime over a 30-year period. Visit the BJS Web site, and review the graph and accompanying explanations. Then discuss how the four series of data are different and how they are similar. What do you think is the most important single factor explaining why the measures are different?

4. The Justice Research and Statistics Association (JRSA) assists state-level statistical analysis centers in using a variety of criminal justice data and in conducting evaluations. The JRSA has established a Web page to help states shift to NIBRS. Visit the JRSA site, and then find a Web page that presents state-level NIBRS data. Bring the results to class.

✪ InfoTrac College Edition

Several different sources of data for measuring crime were discussed in this chapter. Choose one source (for example, the NCVS, NIBRS, or the MTF), and search InfoTrac College Edition for an article that uses that source. Summarize the article and be prepared to discuss it in class.

✪ The NEW Companion Web Site for Research Methods for Criminal Justice and Criminology, *Fourth Edition*

http://cj.wadsworth.com/maxfield_babbie/research_methods4e

Supplement your review of this chapter by going to the new companion Web site to take one of the Tutorial Quizzes, use the flash cards to master key terms, and check out the many other study aids you'll find there. You'll also find special features such as quantitative and qualitative data analysis primers to help you with a special project or do some research on your own.

✪ Additional Readings

Blumstein, Alfred, Cohen, Jacqueline, and Rosenfeld, Richard, "Trend and Deviation in Crime Rates: A Comparison of UCR and NCS Data for Burglary and Robbery," *Criminology*, Vol. 29 (1991), pp. 237–63. This article is an excellent discussion of how the UCR and NCVS yield similar counts for these two offenses after taking account of the different designs of the two measuring systems.

Fendrich, Michael, Johnson, Timothy P., Sudman, Seymour, Wislar, Joseph S., and Spiehler, Vina, "Validity of Drug Use Reporting in a High-Risk Community Sample: Comparison of Cocaine and Heroin Survey Reports with Hair Tests," *American Journal of Epidemiology*, Vol. 149, no. 10 (1999), pp. 955–62. Tackling the question of how valid self-reports are, the authors compare survey measures with laboratory tests of drug use from hair samples. Among other things, tests of hair samples can show drug use over time, making it possible to validate self-reported use over a period of several months.

Maxfield, Michael G., "The National Incident-Based Reporting System: Research and Policy Implications," *Journal of Quantitative Criminology*, Vol. 15, no. 2 (1999), pp. 119–49. This article describes NIBRS in detail and compares this source of crime data with the UCR and the NCVS. See also other articles in this issue for the first published examples of NIBRS data being used in research and policy analysis.

National Research Council, *Informing America's Policy on Illegal Drugs: What We Don't Know Keeps Hurting Us* (Washington, DC: National Academy Press, 2001). The title of this volume underscores the need for better measures of drug use. This report describes and compares four sources of information on drug use: ADAM, DAWN, the MTF, and the NHSDA.

Zimring, Franklin E., *American Youth Violence* (New York: Oxford University Press, 1998). The author compares police reports and data from the NCVS to argue that the increase in youth violence of the late 1980s and early 1990s was misrepresented by those warning about a coming "bloodbath" of violence in the early 21st century. Read this provocative book for an example of how measures of crime can support different interpretations.

Chapter 7

Experimental and Quasi-Experimental Designs

We'll learn about the experimental approach to social science research. We'll consider a wide variety of experimental and other designs available to criminal justice researchers.

Introduction

Experimentation is an approach to research best suited for explanation and evaluation.

Research design in the most general sense involves devising a strategy for finding out something. We'll first discuss the experiment as a mode of scientific observation in criminal justice research. Abraham Kaplan (1964:144) described experimentation as "a process of observation, to be carried out in a situation expressly brought about for that purpose." At base, experiments involve (1) taking action and (2) observing the consequences of that action. Social science researchers typically select a group of subjects, do something to them, and observe the effect of what was done.

It is worth noting at the outset that experiments are often used in nonscientific human inquiry as well. We experiment copiously in our attempts to develop a more generalized understanding about the world we live in. We learn many skills through experimentation: riding a bicycle, driving a car, swimming, and so forth. Students discover how much studying is required for academic success through experimentation. Professors learn how much preparation is required for successful lectures through experimentation.

Returning to social science applications, experiments are especially well suited to research projects that involve relatively well-defined concepts and propositions. A further requirement is the ability to control the conditions under which research is conducted. The traditional model of science, discussed in Chapter 2, and the experimental model are closely related.

Experimentation is especially appropriate for hypothesis testing—it is better suited to explanation and evaluation than to descriptive purposes. Suppose we are interested in studying alcohol abuse among college students and in discovering ways to reduce it. We might hypothesize that acquiring an understanding about the health consequences of binge drinking and long-term alcohol use will have the effect of reducing alcohol abuse. We can test this hypothesis experimentally. To begin, we might ask a group of experimental subjects how much beer, wine, or spirits they drank on the previous day and how frequently, in an average week, they consume alcohol for the specific purpose of getting drunk. Next, we might show these subjects a video depicting the various physiological effects of chronic drinking and binge drinking. Finally—say, 1 month later—we might again ask the subjects about their use of alcohol in the previous week to determine whether watching the video actually reduced alcohol use.

Because experiments are best suited for hypothesis testing, they may also be appropriate in the study of criminal justice policy. In Chapter 2, we discussed the logical similarity between hypotheses and criminal justice policies, noting that evaluation research is conceptually equivalent to hypothesis testing. The experimental model therefore can be a useful design for evaluating criminal justice policy.

You might typically think of experiments as being conducted in laboratories under carefully controlled conditions. Although this may be true in the natural sciences, few social scientific experiments take place in laboratory settings. The most notable exception to this occurs in the discipline of psychology, in which laboratory experiments are common. Criminal justice experiments are almost always conducted in field settings outside the laboratory.

The Classical Experiment

Variables, time order, measures, and groups are the central features of the classical experiment.

Like much of the vocabulary of research, the word *experiment* has acquired both a general and a specialized meaning. So far, we have referred to the general meaning, defined by David Farrington, Lloyd Ohlin, and James Q. Wilson (1986: 65) as "a systematic attempt to test a causal hypothesis about the effect of variations in one factor (the independent variable) on another (the dependent variable). . . . The defining feature of an experiment lies in the control of the independent variable by the experimenter." In a narrower sense, the term *experiment* refers to a specific way of structuring research, usually called the **classical experiment.** In this section, we examine the requirements and components of the classical experiment. Later in the chapter, we will consider designs that can be used when some of the requirements for classical experiments cannot be met.

The most conventional type of experiment, in the natural and the social sciences, involves three major pairs of components: (1) independent and dependent variables, (2) pretesting and posttesting, and (3) experimental and control groups. We will now consider each of those components and the way they are put together in the execution of an experiment.

Independent and Dependent Variables

Essentially, an experiment examines the effect of an **independent variable** on a **dependent variable.** Typically, the independent variable takes the form of an experimental stimulus that is either present or absent—that is, a *dichotomous* variable, having two attributes. That need not be the case, however, as subsequent sections of this chapter will show. In the example concerning alcohol abuse, how often subjects used alcohol is the dependent variable, and exposure to a video about alcohol's effects is the independent variable. The researcher's hypothesis suggests that levels of alcohol use depend, in part, on understanding its physiological and health effects. The purpose of the experiment is to test the validity of this hypothesis.

The independent and dependent variables appropriate to experimentation are nearly limitless. It should be noted, moreover, that a given variable might serve as an independent variable in one experiment and as a dependent variable in another. For example, alcohol abuse is the dependent variable in our example, but it might be the independent variable in an experiment that examines the effects of alcohol abuse on academic performance.

In the terms of our discussion of cause and effect in Chapter 4, the independent variable is the cause and the dependent variable is the effect. Thus, we might say that watching the video *causes* a change in alcohol use or that reduced alcohol use is an *effect* of watching the video.

It is essential that both independent and dependent variables be operationally defined for the purposes of experimentation. Such operational definitions might involve a variety of observation methods. Responses to a questionnaire, for example, might be the basis for defining self-reported alcohol use on the previous day. Alternatively, alcohol use by subjects could be measured with Breathalyzer or blood alcohol tests.

Conventionally, in the experimental model, the dependent and independent variables are operationally defined before the experiment begins. However, as we will see in connection with survey research and other methods, it is sometimes appropriate to first make a variety of observations during data collection and then determine the most useful operational definitions of variables during later analyses. Ultimately, however, experimentation requires specific and standardized measurements and observations.

Pretesting and Posttesting

In the simplest experimental design, subjects are measured on a dependent variable (pretested), exposed to a stimulus that represents an independent variable, and then remeasured on the dependent variable (posttested). Differences noted between the first and second measurements on the dependent variable are then attributed to the influence of the independent variable.

In our example of alcohol use, we might begin by pretesting the extent of alcohol use among our experimental subjects. Using a questionnaire, we measure the extent of alcohol use reported by each individual and the average level of alcohol use for the whole group. After showing subjects the video on the effects of alcohol, we administer the same questionnaire again. Responses given in this posttest permit us to measure the subsequent extent of alcohol use by each subject and the average level of alcohol use of the group as a whole. If we discover a lower level of alcohol use on the second administration of the questionnaire, we might conclude that the video indeed reduced the use of alcohol among the subjects.

In the experimental examination of behaviors such as alcohol use, we face a special practical problem relating to validity. As you can imagine, the subjects might respond differently to the questionnaires the second time, even if their level of drinking remained unchanged. During the first administration of the questionnaire, the subjects may have been unaware of its purpose. By the time of the second measurement, however, they may have figured out the purpose of the experiment, become sensitized to the questions about drinking, and changed their answers. Thus, the video might *seem* to have reduced alcohol abuse although, in fact, it did not.

This is an example of a more general problem that plagues many forms of criminal justice research: The very act of studying something may change it. Techniques for dealing with this problem in the context of experimentation are covered throughout the chapter.

Experimental and Control Groups

The traditional way to offset the effects of the experiment itself is to use a **control group.** Social scientific experiments seldom involve only the observation of an **experimental group** to which a stimulus has been administered. Researchers also observe a control group to which the experimental stimulus has not been administered.

In our example of alcohol abuse, two groups of subjects are examined. To begin, each group is administered a questionnaire designed to measure their alcohol use in general and binge drinking in particular. Then only one of the groups—the experimental group—is shown the video. Later, the researcher administers a posttest of alcohol use to both groups. Figure 7.1 illustrates this basic experimental design.

Using a control group allows the researcher to control for the effects of the experiment itself. If participation in the experiment leads the subjects to report less alcohol use, that should occur in both the experimental and the control groups. If, on the one hand, the overall level of drinking exhibited by the control group decreases between the pretest and posttest as much as for the experimental group, then the apparent reduction in alcohol use must be a function of the experiment or of some external factor, not a function of watching the video specifically. In this situation, we can conclude that the video did not cause any change in alcohol use.

If, on the other hand, drinking decreases only in the experimental group, then we can be more confident in saying that the reduction is a consequence of exposure to the video

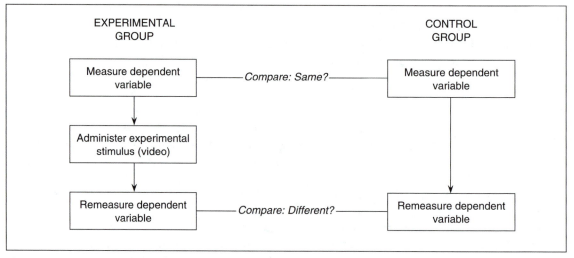

Figure 7.1   Basic Experimental Design

(because that's the only difference between the two groups). Or, alternatively, if drinking decreases more in the experimental group than in the control group, then that, too, is grounds for assuming that watching the video reduced alcohol use.

The need for control groups in social scientific research became clear in a series of employee satisfaction studies conducted by Fritz J. Roethlisberger and William J. Dickson (1939) in the late 1920s and early 1930s. They studied working conditions in the telephone "bank wiring room" of the Western Electric Works in Chicago, attempting to discover what changes in working conditions would improve employee satisfaction and productivity.

To the researchers' great satisfaction, they discovered that making working conditions better consistently increased satisfaction and productivity. When the workroom was brightened by better lighting, for example, productivity went up. Lighting was further improved, and productivity went up again. To substantiate their scientific conclusion, the researchers then dimmed the lights: *Productivity again improved!*

It became evident then that the wiring room workers were responding more to the attention given them by the researchers than to improved working conditions. As a result of this phenomenon, often called the "Hawthorne effect," so-

cial researchers have become more sensitive to and cautious about the possible effects of experiments themselves. The use of a proper control group—studied intensively, with the working conditions otherwise unchanged—would have revealed this effect in the wiring room study.

The need for control groups in experimentation has been most evident in medical research. Time and again, patients who participated in medical experiments appeared to improve, but it was unclear how much of the improvement came from the experimental treatment and how much from the experiment. Now, in testing the effects of new drugs, medical researchers frequently administer a placebo (for example, sugar pills) to a control group. Thus, the control-group patients believe that they, like members of the experimental group, are receiving an experimental drug—and they often improve! If the new drug is effective, however, those who receive that drug will improve more than those who received the placebo.

In criminal justice experiments, control groups are important as a guard against the effects not only of the experiments themselves but also of events that may occur outside the laboratory during the course of experiments. Suppose the alcohol use experiment was being conducted on your campus, and at that time a popular athlete was hospitalized for acute alcohol poisoning after he and a chum drank a bottle of rum. This event might shock the experimental subjects and thereby decrease their reported drinking. Because such an effect should happen about equally for members of the control and experimental groups, lower levels of reported alcohol use in the experimental group than in the control group would again demonstrate the impact of the experimental stimulus: watching the video that describes the health effects of alcohol abuse.

Sometimes, an experimental design requires more than one experimental or control group. In the case of the alcohol video, for example, we might also want to examine the impact of participating in group discussions about why college students drink alcohol, with the intent of demonstrating that peer pressure may promote drinking by people who would otherwise abstain. We might design our experiment around three groups. One group would see the video and participate in the group discussions, another would only see the video, and still another would only participate in group discussions; the control group would do neither. With this kind of design, we could determine the impact of each stimulus separately, as well as their combined effect.

Double-Blind Experiments

As we saw in medical experimentation, patients sometimes improve when they think they are receiving a new drug; thus, it is often necessary to administer a placebo to a control group.

Sometimes, experimenters have this same tendency to prejudge results. In medical research, the experimenters may be more likely to "observe" improvements among patients who receive the experimental drug than among those receiving the placebo. That would be most likely, perhaps, for the researcher who developed the drug. A double-blind experiment eliminates this possibility because neither the subjects nor the experimenters know which is the experimental group and which is the control. In medical experiments, those researchers who are responsible for administering the drug and for noting improvements are not told which subjects receive the drug and which receive the placebo. Thus, both researchers and subjects are "blind" with respect to who is receiving the experimental drug and who is getting the placebo. Another researcher knows which subjects are in which group, but that person is not responsible for administering the experiment.

An example of a double-blind experiment is the study of the Domestic Violence Reduction Unit in Portland, Oregon, by Annette Jolin and associates (Jolin, Feyerhorn, Fountain, and Friedman, 1998). The researchers evaluated an intervention designed to reduce repeat offenses against victims of domestic violence by instructing them in strategies for "keeping safe" and putting more resources into the investigation of domestic violence incidents.

In the experimental evaluation, after misdemeanor offenses for which male offenders had been arrested and taken to jail, their female victims were randomly assigned to a treatment group that received supplementary services or to a control group that did not receive the intervention. Cases in the treatment group were more intensively investigated, including more thorough efforts to collect evidence. Victims in the treatment group received additional services including assistance in developing safety plans, information on how to access a variety of services, and transportation to service providers when necessary. Staff randomly assigned cases to the treatment or control groups, but assignment was coded so the staff were not aware which victims were to receive supplementary services and which were not. Likewise, victims were not informed whether they were in the treatment or the control group. This double-blind experiment was therefore able to test the effects of supplementary domestic violence services without being contaminated by the expectations of victims or researchers.

In social scientific experiments, as in medical experiments, the danger of experimenter bias is further reduced to the extent that the operational definitions of the dependent variables are clear and precise. Thus, in the domestic violence experiment, researchers were less likely to unconsciously bias their interpretation of reports of repeat domestic violence than they were to unconsciously bias their subjective assessment of how satisfied victims were with services provided to them.

Selecting Subjects

Before beginning an experiment, we must make two basic decisions about who will participate. First, we must decide on the target population—the group to which the results of our experiment will apply. If our experiment is designed to determine, for example, whether restitution is more effective than probation in reducing recidivism, our target population is some group of persons convicted of crimes. In our hypothetical experiment about the effects of watching a video on the health consequences of alcohol abuse, the target population might be college students.

Second, we must decide how particular members of the target population will be selected for the experiment. In most cases, the methods used to select subjects must meet the scientific norm of generalizability; it should be possible to generalize from the sample of subjects actually studied to the population those subjects represent.

Aside from the question of generalizability, the cardinal rule of subject selection and experimentation is the comparability of the experimental and control groups. Ideally, the control group represents what the experimental group would have been like if it had not been exposed to the experimental stimulus. It is essential, therefore, that the experimental and control groups be as similar as possible.

Randomization

Having recruited, by whatever means, a group of subjects, we randomly assign those subjects to either the experimental or the control group. This might be accomplished by numbering all the subjects serially and selecting numbers by means of a random-number table. Or we might assign the odd-numbered subjects to the experimental group and the even-numbered subjects to the control group.

Randomization is a central feature of the classical experiment. The most important characteristic of randomization is that it produces experimental and control groups that are *statistically equivalent*. Put another way, randomization reduces possible sources of systematic bias in assigning subjects to groups. The basic principle is simple: If subjects are assigned to experimental and control groups through a random process such as flipping a coin, the assignment process is said to be unbiased, and the resultant groups are equivalent.

Although the rationale underlying this principle is a bit complex, understanding how randomization produces equivalent groups is a key point. Farrington and associates (Farrington, Ohlin, and Wilson, 1986:66) compare randomization in criminal justice research to laboratory controls in the natural sciences:

> The control of extraneous variables by randomization is similar to the control of extraneous variables in the physical sciences by holding physical conditions (e.g., temperature, pressure) constant. Randomization insures that the average unit in [the] treatment group is approximately equivalent to the average unit in another [group] before the treatment is applied.

You've surely heard the expression "All other things being equal." Randomization makes it possible to assume that all other things are equal.

Experiments and Causal Inference

Experiments potentially control for many threats to the validity of causal inference, but researchers must remain aware of these threats.

The central features of the classical experiment are independent and dependent variables, pretesting and posttesting, and experimental and control groups created through random assign-

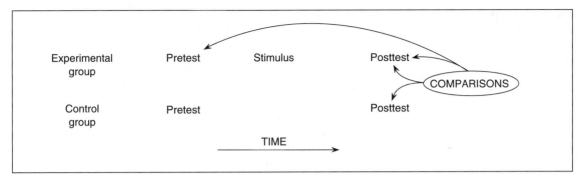

Figure 7.2   Another Look at the Classical Experiment

ment. Think of these features as building blocks of a research design to demonstrate a cause-and-effect relationship. This point will become clearer by comparing the criteria for causality, discussed in Chapter 4, to the features of the classical experiment, as shown in Figure 7.2.

The experimental design ensures that the cause precedes the effect in time by taking post-test measurements of the dependent variable after introducing the experimental stimulus. The second criterion for causation—an empirical correlation between the cause-and-effect variables—is determined by comparing the pretest (in which the experimental stimulus is not present) to the posttest for the experimental group (after the experimental stimulus is administered). A change from pretest to posttest measures demonstrates correlation.

The final requirement is to show that the observed correlation between cause and effect is not due to the influence of some third variable. The classical experiment makes it possible to satisfy this criterion for cause in two ways. First, the posttest measures for the experimental group (stimulus present) are compared with those for the control group (stimulus not present). If the observed correlation between the stimulus and the dependent variable is due to some other factor, then the two posttest scores will be similar. Second, random assignment produces experimental and control groups that are equivalent and will not differ on some other variable that could account for the empirical correlation between cause and effect.

Experiments and Threats to Validity

The classical experiment is designed to satisfy the three requirements for demonstrating cause-and-effect relationships. But what about threats to the validity of causal inference discussed in Chapter 4? In this section, we consider each of those threats in more detail and describe how the classical experiment reduces many of them. The book by Donald Campbell and Julian Stanley (1966) is the most frequently cited authority on threats to validity. For a fuller discussion, on which we draw heavily, see the book by Thomas Cook and Donald Campbell (1979). We present these threats in a slightly different order, beginning with threats to internal validity.

Threats to Internal Validity

The problem of threats to internal validity refers to the possibility that conclusions drawn from experimental results may not accurately reflect what went on in the experiment itself. As we stated in Chapter 4, conclusions about cause and effect may be biased in some systematic way. Cook and Campbell (1979:51–55) pointed to several sources of the problem. As you read about these different threats to internal validity, keep in mind that each is an example of a simple point: possible ways researchers might be wrong in inferring causation.

History   Historical events may occur during the course of the experiment that confound the experimental results. The hospitalization of a popular athlete for acute alcohol poisoning during an experiment on reducing alcohol use is an example.

Maturation   People are continually growing and changing, whether in an experiment or not, and those changes affect the results of the experiment. In a long-term experiment, the fact that the subjects grow older (and wiser?) may have an effect. In shorter experiments, they may become tired, sleepy, bored, or hungry, or change in other ways that affect their behavior in the experiment. A long-term study of alcohol abuse might reveal a decline in binge drinking as the subjects mature.

History and maturation are similar in that they represent a correlation between cause and effect that is due to something other than the independent variable. They're different in that history represents something that's outside the experiment altogether, whereas maturation refers to change within the subjects themselves.

Testing   Often, the process of testing and retesting influences people's behavior and thereby confounds the experimental results. Suppose we administer a questionnaire to a group as a way of measuring their alcohol use. Then we administer an experimental stimulus and remeasure their alcohol use. By the time we conduct the posttest, the subjects may have gotten more sensitive to the issue of alcohol use and so provide different answers. In fact, they may have figured out that we are trying to determine whether they drink too much. Because excessive drinking is frowned on by university authorities, our subjects will be on their best behavior and give answers that they think we want or that will make them look good.

Instrumentation   Thus far, we haven't said much about the process of measurement in pretesting and posttesting, and it's appropriate to keep in mind the problems of conceptualization and operationalization discussed in Chapter 5. If we use different measures of the dependent variable (say, different questionnaires about alcohol use), how can we be sure that they

are comparable? Perhaps alcohol use seems to have decreased simply because the pretest measure was more sensitive than the posttest measure. Or if the measurements are being made by the experimenters, their procedures may change over the course of the experiment. This is a problem of reliability.

Instrumentation is always a potential problem in criminal justice research that uses secondary sources of information such as police records about crime or court records about probation violations. There may be changes in how probation violations are defined or changes in the record-keeping practices of police departments.

The differences between testing and instrumentation threats to internal validity may seem unclear. In general, testing refers to changes in how subjects respond to measurement, whereas instrumentation is concerned with changes in the measurement process itself. If police officers respond differently to pretest and posttest questionnaires about prejudice, for example, that is a testing problem. However, if different questionnaires about prejudice are used in pretest and posttest measurements, instrumentation is a potential threat.

Statistical Regression   Sometimes, it's appropriate to conduct experiments on subjects who start out with extreme scores on the dependent variable. Many sentencing policies, for example, target chronic offenders. Charles Murray and L. A. Cox (1979) examined a program to incarcerate high-rate male juvenile offenders. They found that re-arrest rates for subjects who had served sentences averaging 11 months were substantially lower than those for other offenders who were not incarcerated. These findings were questioned by Michael Maltz and associates (Maltz, Gordon, McDowall, and McCleary, 1980), who pointed out that the number of crimes committed by any given offender fluctuates over time. They argued that subjects in the experimental group—chronic offenders—were jailed following a period when their offense rates were abnormally high and that the decline in posttest arrests simply reflected a natural return to less extreme rates of offending. Even without any experimental stimulus, then, the group as a whole was likely to show some improvement over time.

Commonly referred to as "regression to the mean," this threat to validity can emerge whenever researchers are interested in cases that have extreme scores on some variable. As a simple example, statisticians often point out that extremely tall people as a group are likely to have children shorter than themselves, and extremely short people as a group are likely to have children taller than themselves. The danger, then, is that changes occurring by virtue of subjects starting out in extreme positions will be attributed erroneously to the effects of the experimental stimulus.

Selection Biases Randomization eliminates the potential for systematic bias in selecting subjects, but subjects may be chosen in other ways that threaten validity. Volunteers are often solicited for experiments conducted on college campuses. Students who volunteer for an experiment may not be typical of students as a whole, however. Volunteers may be more interested in the subject of the experiment and more likely to respond to a stimulus. Or, if experimental subjects are paid some fee, students in greater financial need may participate, although they may not be representative of other students.

A common type of selection bias in applied criminal justice studies results from the natural caution of public officials. Let's say you are a bail commissioner in a large city, and the mayor wants to try a new program to increase the number of arrested persons who are released on bail. The mayor asks you to decide what kinds of defendants should be eligible for release and informs you that staff from the city's criminal justice services agency will be evaluating the program. In establishing eligibility criteria, you will probably try to select defendants who will not be arrested again while on bail and defen-

dants who will most likely show up for scheduled court appearances. In other words, you will try to select participants who are least likely to fail. This common and understandable caution is sometimes referred to as "creaming"—skimming the best risks off the top. Creaming is a threat to validity because the low-risk persons selected for release, although most likely to succeed, do not represent the jail population as a whole.

Experimental Mortality Experimental subjects often drop out of an experiment before it is completed, and that can affect statistical comparisons and conclusions. This is termed "experimental mortality." In the classical experiment involving an experimental and a control group, each with a pretest and a posttest, suppose that the heavy drinkers in the experimental group are so turned off by the video on the health effects of binge drinking that they tell the experimenter to forget it and leave. Those subjects who stick around for the posttest were less heavy drinkers to start with, and the group results will thus reflect a substantial "decrease" in alcohol use.

In this example, mortality is related to the experimental stimulus itself: Subjects who score highest on the pretest are the most likely to drop out after viewing the video. Mortality may also be a problem in experiments that take place over a long period (people may move away) or in experiments that require a substantial commitment of effort or time by subjects; they may become bored with the study or simply decide it's not worth the effort.

Causal Time Order In criminal justice research, there may be ambiguity about the time order of the experimental stimulus and the dependent variable. Whenever this occurs, the research conclusion that the stimulus caused the dependent variable can be challenged with the explanation that the "dependent" variable actually caused changes in the stimulus. Many early studies of the relationship between different types of punishments and rates of offending exhibited this threat to validity by relying on single interviews with subjects who were asked how they viewed alternative punishments and whether they had committed any crimes.

Diffusion or Imitation of Treatments   In the event that experimental- and control-group subjects are in communication with each other, it's possible that experimental subjects will pass on some elements of the experimental stimulus to the control group. David Weisburd and Lorraine Green (1995) studied police interventions in high-crime areas by randomly assigning 56 drug "hot spots" to receive either intensive narcotics interventions (experimental condition) or traditional enforcement (control condition). Narcotics squads from the Jersey City, New Jersey, police department were then randomly assigned to experimental or control conditions. Three squads used intensive investigative techniques in the experimental hot spots, while three other squads used traditional methods in the control hot spots. The researchers were aware that the integrity of the treatment would be threatened if the officers in the control squads attempted to "mimic" the experimental squad. To guard against this, squads working in experimental and control areas were physically separated.

Critics of highly localized crime prevention argue that reducing crime in one location simply displaces it to another. To test for this, Weisburd and Green (1995) examined measures of crime in two-block areas surrounding the hot spots. They found no evidence of displacement, but they did observe a reduction in some crime measures in areas adjacent to the experimental hot spots. This suggests that some treatment effects "spilled over" into areas not subject to experimental conditions.

Compensatory Treatment   In many criminal justice experiments—such as a special job-training program for incarcerated felons—subjects in the control group may be deprived of something of value to them. In such cases, there may be pressures to offer some form of compensation. Recall the discussion in Chapter 4 of how police in the Kansas City Preventive Patrol Experiment patrolled the perimeter of reactive beats—those with no preventive patrol. As we noted, they more often used lights and sirens when responding to calls for service in the reactive beats. Some police officers compensated for the absence of preventive patrol in a way that reduced the differences among proactive, reactive, and control beats.

It's helpful to think of treatment diffusion as the accidental spillover of an experimental stimulus, in contrast to the more intentional compensatory treatment by public officials that occurred in the Kansas City case. In applied criminal justice research, such treatment is probably more common, and researchers often take steps to prevent it. For example, in an evaluation of intensive supervision probation (ISP) programs in 11 sites, researchers from the RAND Corporation recognized that probation officers might provide enhanced supervision to clients in the control group, under the assumption that the experimental program (ISP) was better than traditional probation (Petersilia, 1989). This potential for compensation was reduced in two ways. First, researchers explained to program staff why the experimental and control groups should receive different types of services. Second, a type of double-blind procedure was used whereby researchers tried to disguise the records of subjects in the control group so probation staff could not distinguish subjects who were participating in the experiment from their regular probation caseload.

Compensatory Rivalry   In real-life experiments, subjects deprived of the experimental stimulus may try to compensate by working harder. Suppose an experimental career development program for corrections officers is the experimental stimulus; the control group may work harder than before in an attempt to keep pace with the "special" experimental subjects.

Demoralization   Feelings of deprivation among the control group may also result in subjects giving up. A career development program for corrections officers may prompt demoralization among control-group subjects who believe their opportunities for advancement will suffer. As a result, it may not be clear whether posttest differences between experimental and control groups in, say, job performance actually reflected program impacts or were due to demoralization among the control group.

Notice that the possibilities of compensatory rivalry and demoralization are based on subjects' reactions to the experiment, while diffusion and compensatory treatment are accidental or intentional extensions of the experimental stimulus to the control group. In studies in which agency staff, not researchers, administer an experimental treatment to subjects, there is a greater potential for intentional compensation. In studies in which subjects in a control group are aware that other subjects are receiving a desirable treatment, compensatory rivalry or demoralization is possible.

Ruling Out Threats to Internal Validity

These, then, are the threats to internal validity cited by Campbell, Stanley, and Cook. The classical experiment, coupled with proper subject selection and assignment, can *potentially* handle each of the 12 threats to internal validity.

How do researchers determine whether a particular design rules out threats to internal validity? Cook and Campbell (1979:55) provided an excellent rule of thumb: "Estimating the internal validity of a relationship is a deductive process in which the investigator has to systematically think through how each of the internal validity threats can be ruled out." Let's look again at the classical experiment, presented graphically in Figure 7.2.

Pursuing the example of the educational video as an attempt to reduce alcohol abuse, if we use the experimental design shown in Figure 7.2, we should expect two findings. For the experimental group, the frequency of drinking measured in their posttest should be less than in their pretest. In addition, when the two

posttests are compared, the experimental group should have less drinking than the control group.

This design guards against the problem of history because anything occurring outside the experiment that might affect the experimental group should also affect the control group. There should still be a difference in the two posttest results. The same comparison guards against problems of maturation as long as the subjects have been randomly assigned to the two groups. Testing and instrumentation should not be problems because both the experimental and the control groups are subject to the same tests and experimenter effects. If the subjects have been assigned to the two groups randomly, statistical regression should affect both equally, even if people with extreme scores on drinking (or whatever the dependent variable is) are being studied. Selection bias is ruled out by the random assignment of subjects.

Experimental mortality can be more complicated to handle because dropout rates may be different between the experimental and control groups. The experimental treatment itself may increase mortality in the group exposed to the video. As a result, the group of experimental subjects that received the posttest will differ from the group that received the pretest. In our example of the alcohol video, it would probably not be possible to handle this problem by administering a placebo, for instance. In general, however, the potential for mortality can be reduced by shortening the time between pretest and posttest, by emphasizing to subjects the importance of completing the posttest, or perhaps by offering cash payments for participating in all phases of the experiment.

The remaining problems of internal invalidity can be avoided through the careful administration of a controlled experimental design. The experimental design we've been discussing facilitates the clear specification of independent and dependent variables. Experimental and control subjects can be kept separate to reduce the possibility of diffusion or imitation of treatments.

Administrative controls can be applied to avoid compensations given to the control group, and compensatory rivalry can be watched for and taken into account in evaluating the results of the experiment, as can the problem of demoralization.

We emphasize careful administration here. Random assignment, pretest and posttest measures, and use of control and experimental groups do not automatically rule out threats to validity. This caution is especially true in field studies and evaluation research, in which subjects participate in natural settings, and uncontrolled variation in the experimental stimulus may be present. Control over experimental conditions is the hallmark of this approach, but conditions in field settings are usually more difficult to control. In fact, David Weisburd and associates (Weisburd, Petrosino, and Mason, 1993) argue convincingly that field experiments involving a larger number of subjects become more difficult to manage, which offsets the advantages of random assignment and a large number of subjects.

Compare, for example, our hypothetical study of alcohol use among college students with the field experiment on ISP described by Joan Petersilia (1989). In Petersilia's study, more intensive probation was the independent variable, and recidivism the dependent variable. Subjects were randomly assigned to the experimental group (ISP) or the control group (regular probation).

The alcohol use study could conceivably be completed in about 1 week, using subjects from a class, dormitory, or house on a single campus. ISP programs were evaluated in 11 sites over 4 years, using probation clients as subjects. The video on the health effects of alcohol use is a well-defined treatment that is readily standardized and can easily be controlled by researchers. The experimental treatment in the ISP programs was a reduced caseload for probation workers, together with an increased number of regular contacts with each probation client; program staff, not researchers, administered

the experimental treatment. There was a great potential for uncontrolled variation in the delivery of ISP treatments; ISP is not a simple dichotomous treatment as is the video/no-video treatment in the alcohol use experiment.

Finally, the alcohol use questionnaire can easily be administered by researchers, providing reliable measures of alcohol use. Data on recidivism for the ISP study were collected by probation staff in each of the 11 sites. Although recidivism can be readily defined as the number of new arrests after beginning probation, there may have been wide variation in the ability of staff in the 11 sites to reliably detect new arrests.

These remarks are not intended as criticism of the ISP study. In her description of the evaluation, Petersilia (1989) documents the extensive steps taken by RAND Corporation researchers to control possible validity threats. The important point is that field experiments and evaluations can present many obstacles that are not eliminated simply by adopting a randomized experimental design. Careful administration and control throughout the experiment are necessary to reduce potential threats to internal validity.

Generalizability and Threats to Validity

Potential threats to internal validity are only some of the complications faced by experimenters. They also have the problem of generalizing from experimental findings to the real world. Even if the results of an experiment are an accurate gauge of what happened during that experiment, do they really tell us anything about life in the wilds of society? With our examination of cause and effect in Chapter 4 in mind, we consider two dimensions of **generalizability:** construct validity and external validity.

Threats to Construct Validity

In the language of experimentation, construct validity is the correspondence between the empirical test of a hypothesis and the underlying causal process that the experiment is intended to represent. Construct validity is thus concerned with generalizing from our observations in an experiment to actual causal processes in the real world. In our hypothetical example, the educational video is how we operationalize the construct of understanding the health effects of alcohol abuse. Our questionnaire represents the dependent construct of actual alcohol use.

Are these reasonable ways to represent the underlying causal process in which understanding the effects of alcohol use causes people to reduce excessive or abusive drinking? It's a reasonable representation, but also one that is certainly incomplete. People develop an understanding of the health effects of alcohol use in many ways. Watching an educational video is one way; having personal experience, talking to friends and parents, taking other courses, and reading books and articles are others. Our video may do a good job of representing the health effects of alcohol use, but it is an incomplete representation of that construct. Alternatively, the video may be poorly produced, too technical, or incomplete. Then the experimental stimulus may not adequately represent the construct we are interested in — educating students about the health effects of alcohol use. There may also be problems with our measure of the dependent variable: questionnaire items on self-reported alcohol use.

By this time, you should recognize a similarity between construct validity and some of the measurement issues discussed in Chapter 5. Almost any empirical example or measure of a construct is incomplete. Part of construct validity involves how completely an empirical measure can represent a construct or how well we can generalize from a measure to a construct.

A related issue in construct validity is whether a given level of treatment is sufficient. Perhaps showing a single video to a group of subjects would have little effect on alcohol use, but administering a series of videos over several weeks would have a greater impact. We could test this experimentally by having more than one experimental group and varying the number of videos seen by different groups.

Threats to construct validity are problematic in criminal justice experiments, often because researchers do not clearly specify precisely what constructs are to be represented by particular measures or experimental treatments. For example, Anne Schneider (1990) points out that many studies of probation policies do not specify whether an innovative probation program represents a punishment or an attempt to reform offenders through counseling or other treatments. As a consequence, it is not clear what specific components of an effective probation program might be. Do the punitive components of probation reduce subsequent offending, or does enhanced counseling have a greater impact?

Farrington and associates (Farrington, Ohlin, and Wilson, 1986:92) make a related point: "Most treatments in existing experiments are not based on a well-developed theory but on a vague idea about what might influence offending. The treatments given are often heterogeneous, making it difficult to know which element was responsible for any observed effect." These authors also note the importance of thinking about levels of constructs. The RAND Corporation evaluation of intensive supervision provides a good example of why this is important. The ISP program explicitly defined enhanced probation as punitive. This leads to the question of how enhanced probation must be. If a typical probation officer carries an average caseload of 100 clients and sees each an average of twice per month, what workload and contact levels are sufficiently intensive to reduce recidivism? Cutting the workload in half and doubling the number of contacts would be more intensive, but would it be intensive enough to produce a decline in recidivism? Again, an experiment could test this question by including more than one experimental group and giving each a different level of probation supervision.

In sum, three elements in enhancing construct validity, therefore, are (1) linking constructs and measures to theory, (2) clearly indicating what constructs are represented by specific measures, and (3) thinking carefully about what levels of treatment may be necessary to produce some level of change in the dependent measure.

Threats to External Validity

Will an experimental study, conducted with the kind of control we have emphasized here, produce results that would also be found in more natural settings? Can an intensive probation program shown to be successful in Minneapolis achieve similar results in Miami? External validity represents a slightly different form of generalizability, one in which the question is whether results from experiments in one setting (time and place) will be obtained in other settings, or whether a treatment found to be effective for one population will have similar effects on a different group.

Threats to external validity are greater for experiments conducted under carefully controlled conditions. If the alcohol education experiment reveals that drinking decreased among students in the experimental group, then we can be confident that the video actually reduced alcohol use among our experimental subjects. But will the video have the same effect on high school students or adults if it is broadcast on television? We cannot be certain because the carefully controlled conditions of the experiment might have had something to do with the video's effectiveness.

In contrast, criminal justice field experiments are conducted in more natural settings. Real probation officers in 11 different local jurisdictions delivered intensive supervision to real probationers in the RAND ISP experiment. Because of the real-world conditions and multiple sites, there were fewer potential threats to external validity. This is not to say that external validity is never a problem in field experiments. The 11 probation agencies that participated in this evaluation may not be typical of probation agencies in other areas. The simple fact that they were willing to participate in the study

suggests that staff could be more dedicated or more amenable to trying new approaches to probation. One of the advantages of field experiments in criminal justice is that, because they take place under real-world conditions, results are more likely to be valid in other real-world settings as well.

You may have detected a fundamental conflict between internal and external validity. Threats to internal validity are reduced by conducting experiments under carefully controlled conditions. But such conditions do not reflect real-world settings, and this restricts our ability to generalize results. Field experiments generally have greater external validity, but their internal validity may suffer because such studies are more difficult to monitor than those taking place in more controlled settings.

Cook and Campbell (1979:83) offered some useful advice for resolving the potential for conflict between internal and external validity. Explanatory studies that test cause-and-effect theories should place greater emphasis on internal validity, while applied studies should be more concerned with external validity. This is not a hard and fast rule because internal validity must be established before external validity becomes an issue. That is, applied researchers must have confidence in the internal validity of their cause-and-effect relationships before they ask whether similar relationships would be found in other settings.

Threats to Statistical Conclusion Validity

The basic principle of *statistical conclusion validity* is simple. Virtually all experimental research in criminal justice is based on samples of subjects that represent a target population. Larger samples of subjects, up to a point, are more representative of the target population than are smaller samples. Statistical conclusion validity becomes an issue when findings are based on small samples of cases. Because experiments can be costly and time consuming, they are frequently conducted with relatively small numbers of subjects. In such cases, only large differences between experimental and control groups on posttest measures can be detected with any degree of confidence.

In practice, this means that finding cause-and-effect relationships through experiments depends on two related factors: (1) the number of subjects and (2) the magnitude of posttest differences between the experimental and control groups. Experiments with large numbers of cases may be able to reliably detect small differences, but experiments with smaller numbers can detect only large differences.

Threats to statistical conclusion validity can be magnified by other difficulties in field experiments. If treatment spillover or compensation is a problem, then smaller differences in the experimental stimulus will be delivered to each group. More generally, Weisburd and associates (1993) concluded, after reviewing a large number of criminal justice experiments, that failure to maintain control over experimental conditions reduces statistical conclusion validity even for studies with large numbers of subjects. Furthermore, these authors found that as sample size increases, so do implementation difficulties, which undermines experimental results in a variety of ways.

	Classical Experiment		
Experimental group	*O*	*X*	*O*
Control group	*O*		*O*
	t_1	t_2	t_3
		Time →	

O = observation or measurement
X = experimental stimulus
t = time point

	Posttest Only	
Experimental group	*X*	*O*
Control group		*O*
	t_1	t_2

	Factorial		
Experimental treatment 1	*O*	X_1	*O*
Experimental treatment 2	*O*	X_2	*O*
Control	*O*		*O*
	t_1	t_2	t_3

Figure 7.3 Variations in the Experimental Design

Variations in the Classical Experimental Design

The basic experimental design is adapted to meet different research applications.

We now turn to a more systematic consideration of variations on the classical experiment that can be produced by manipulating the building blocks of experiments.

Slightly restating our earlier remarks, four basic building blocks are present in experimental designs: (1) the number of experimental and control groups, (2) the number and variation of experimental stimuli, (3) the number of pretest and posttest measurements, and (4) the procedures used to select subjects and assign them to groups. By way of illustrating these building blocks and the ways they are used to produce different designs, we adopt the system of notation used by Campbell and Stanley (1966). Figure 7.3 presents this notation and shows how it is used to represent the classical experiment and examples of variations on this design.

In Figure 7.3, the letter *O* represents observations or measurements, and *X* represents an experimental stimulus or treatment. Different time points are displayed as *t* with a subscript to represent time order. Thus, for the classical experiment shown in Figure 7.3, *O* at t_1 is the pretest, *O* at t_3 is the posttest, and the experimental stimulus, *X*, is administered to the experimental group at t_2, between the pretest and posttest. Measures are taken for the control group at times t_1 and t_3, but the experimental stimulus is not administered to the control group.

Now consider the design labeled "Posttest Only." As implied by its name, no pretest measures are made on either the experimental or the control group. Thinking for a moment about the threats to internal validity, we can imagine situations in which a posttest-only design is appropriate. Testing and retesting might especially influence subjects' behavior if measurements are made by administering a questionnaire, with subjects' responses to the posttest potentially affected by their experience in the pretest. A posttest-only design can reduce the possibility of testing as a threat to validity by eliminating the pretest.

Without a pretest, it is obviously not possible to detect *change* in measures of the dependent variable, but we can still test the effects of the experimental stimulus by comparing posttest measures for the experimental group with posttest measures for the control group. For example, if we are concerned about the possibility of sensitizing subjects in a study of an alcohol education video, we might eliminate the pretest and examine the posttest differences between the experimental and control groups. Randomization is the key to the posttest-only design. If subjects are randomly assigned to experimental and control groups, we expect them to be equivalent. Any posttest differences between the two groups on the dependent variable can then be attributed to the influence of the video.

In general, posttest-only designs are appropriate when researchers suspect that the process of measurement may bias subjects' responses to a questionnaire or other instrument. This is more likely when only a short time elapses between pretest and posttest measurements. The number of observations made on subjects is a design building block that can be varied as needed. We emphasize here that random assignment is essential in a posttest-only design.

Figure 7.3 also shows a factorial design, which has two experimental groups that receive different treatments, or different levels of a single treatment, and one control group. This design is useful for comparing the effects of different interventions or different amounts of a single treatment. In evaluating an ISP program, we might wish to compare how different levels of contact between probation officers and probation clients affect recidivism. In this case, subjects in one experimental group might receive weekly contact (X_1), the other experimental group be seen by probation officers twice each week (X_2), and control-group subjects have normal contact (say, monthly) with probation officers. Because more contact is more expensive than less contact, we would be interested in seeing how much difference in recidivism was produced by monthly, weekly, and twice-weekly contacts.

Thus, an experimental design may have more than one group receiving different versions or levels of experimental treatment. We can also vary the number of measurements made on dependent variables. No hard and fast rules exist for using these building blocks to design a given experiment. A useful rule of thumb, however, is to keep the design as simple as possible to control for potential threats to validity. The specific design for any particular study depends on the research purpose, available resources, and unavoidable constraints in designing and actually carrying out the experiment.

One very common constraint is how subjects or units of analysis are selected and assigned to experimental or control groups. This building block brings us to the subject of quasi-experimental designs.

Quasi-Experimental Designs

When randomization is not possible, researchers can use different types of quasi-experimental designs.

By now, the value of random assignment in controlling threats to validity should be apparent. However, it is often impossible to randomly select subjects for experimental and control groups. There may be legal or ethical reasons randomization cannot be used in criminal justice experiments. More often, there may be practical or administrative obstacles.

When randomization is not possible, the next-best choice is often a **quasi-experiment.**

The prefix *quasi-*, meaning "to a certain degree," is significant—a quasi-experiment is, to a certain degree, an experiment. In most cases, quasi-experiments do not randomly assign subjects and therefore may suffer from the internal validity threats that are so well controlled in true experiments. Without random assignment, the other building blocks of experimental design must be used creatively to reduce validity threats. Following Cook and Campbell, we will group quasi-experimental designs into two categories: (1) nonequivalent-groups designs and (2) time-series designs. Each can be represented with the same *O*, *X*, and *t* notation used to depict experimental designs.

Nonequivalent-Groups Designs

The name for this family of designs is also meaningful. The main strength of random assignment is that it allows us to assume equivalence in experimental and control groups. When it is not possible to create groups through randomization, we must use some other procedure, one that is not random. If we construct groups through some nonrandom procedure, however, we cannot assume that the groups are equivalent—hence, the label *nonequivalent-groups design*.

Whenever experimental and control groups are not equivalent, we should select subjects in some way that makes the two groups as comparable as possible. Often, the best way to achieve comparability is through a matching process in which subjects in the experimental group are matched with subjects in a comparison group. The term *comparison group* is commonly used, rather than *control group*, to highlight the nonequivalence of groups in quasi-experimental designs. A comparison group does, however, serve the same function as a control group.

Some examples of research that use nonequivalent-group designs illustrate various approaches to matching and the creative use of experimental design building blocks. Examples include studies of child abuse (Widom, 1989a), obscene phone calls (Clarke, 1997a), and an instrument to predict parole risk (Bonta and

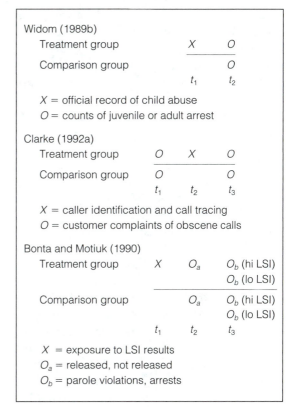

Figure 7.4   Quasi-Experimental Design Examples

Motiuk, 1990). Figure 7.4 shows a diagram of each design using the *X*, *O*, and *t* notation. The solid line that separates treatment and comparison groups in the figure signifies that subjects have been placed in groups through some nonrandom procedure.

Child Abuse and Later Arrest   Cathy Spatz Widom (1989b) studied the long-term effects of child abuse—whether abused children are more likely to be charged with delinquent or adult criminal offenses than children who were not abused. Child abuse was the experimental stimulus, and the number of subsequent arrests was the dependent variable.

Of course, it is not possible to assign children randomly to groups in which some are abused and others are not. Widom's design called for selecting a sample of children who, according to court records, had been abused. She then matched each abused subject with a comparison subject—of the same gender, race, age, and approximate socioeconomic status (SES)—who had not been abused. The assumption with these matching criteria was that age at the time of abuse, gender, race, and SES differences might confound any observed relationship between abuse and subsequent arrests.

You may be wondering how a researcher selects important variables to use in matching experimental and comparison subjects. We cannot provide a definitive answer to that question, any more than we can specify what particular variables should be used in a given experiment. The answer ultimately depends on the nature and purpose of the experiment. As a general rule, however, the two groups should be comparable in terms of variables that are likely to be related to the dependent variable under study. Widom matched on gender, race, and SES because these variables are correlated with juvenile and adult arrest rates. Age at the time of reported abuse was also an important variable because children abused at a younger age had a longer "at-risk" period for delinquent arrests.

Widom produced experimental and comparison groups matching individual subjects. It is also possible to construct experimental and comparison groups through aggregate matching, the average characteristics of each group are comparable. This is illustrated in our next example.

Predicting Parole Risk Deciding which inmates should be paroled and which present too great a risk for parole is a fundamental problem in corrections policy. Two corrections officials in Canada, James Bonta and Laurence Motiuk (1990), tested a prediction tool, the level of supervision inventory (LSI), as an aid in deciding which inmates could be released to parole and halfway houses. Low scores on the LSI were intended to indicate that the inmate presented a low risk for parole or release to a halfway house.

Bonta and Motiuk were interested in the answers to two questions: (1) Do inmates who

score low on the LSI have fewer parole violations and re-arrests than inmates who score high? and (2) Does the use of the LSI increase the number of inmates released to parole and halfway houses? The first question is relatively straightforward; a prediction instrument is not helpful if it cannot discriminate between inmates who present greater or lesser risks on release.

The second question requires a bit more explanation. Recall the earlier discussion of "creaming" as a selection bias—the natural tendency of public officials to choose experimental subjects who are least likely to fail. Parole boards are understandably cautious in deciding whom to release or place in some experimental program. A measure such as the LSI can provide a more objective indicator of an inmate's risk and might result in parole for more people. Bonta and Motiuk developed an ingenious double-blind procedure to test both whether the LSI was a good measure of parole risk and whether officials who used the LSI released more inmates than officials who did not use it.

The corrections staff administered the LSI to all inmates who were serving sentences of 4 months or more in three Canadian jails. But the LSI was used to make release decisions in only two of the jails; inmates released from those facilities were in the treatment group. Staff in the third jail were not informed of LSI scores; they selected inmates for release using existing procedures. Persons released from the third jail made up the comparison group. This design made it possible for the researchers to address their two questions directly.

First, the two jails using the LSI did, in fact, release more inmates to parole and halfway houses compared with the jail where the LSI was not used. Because LSI scores for inmates in all three jails were known to researchers, they were able to determine that many low-scoring inmates from the "blind" jail were not released. Comparing measures of misconduct while incarcerated, Bonta and Motiuk found that the low-LSI group encountered fewer problems than the high-LSI group.

All inmates were eventually released, which enabled the researchers to compare postparole performance for the low- and high-LSI inmates. Those inmates who scored low on the LSI, whether they were released early or stayed in jail, had fewer parole violations and fewer re-arrests than inmates who scored higher on the LSI. Bonta and Motiuk were therefore able to conclude that (1) the LSI was a good predictor of parole risk and (2) officials who used the LSI approved more inmates for release compared with officials who did not use the LSI. Notice how these two findings indicate that the LSI helped corrections officials make better decisions: Low-scoring inmates performed better on release, and more low-risk inmates were released.

Let's briefly summarize how this study used the building blocks of experimental design. First, officials' exposure to LSI results was the experimental treatment. Second, the treatment was administered to officials who rated the inmates in two jails—the experimental group—but not to officials in the third jail—the comparison group. Third, it was not practical to randomly assign corrections officials to treatment and comparison groups because a single board in each jail made release decisions. Therefore, Bonta and Motiuk created treatment and comparison groups through aggregate matching. Aggregate characteristics of inmates in the two treatment jails were matched against the same characteristics of inmates in the comparison jail. Although the two groups were not technically equivalent because they had not been created through random assignment, aggregate indicators of prior and current offenses, average sentence length, and LSI scores were very similar for the two groups (Bonta and Motiuk, 1990:501).

Finally, two different dependent variables were measured: whether inmates were released to parole or halfway houses, and how inmates performed after release. Release/no release, measured at t_2 in Figure 7.4, addressed whether using the LSI increased the number of inmates paroled and placed in halfway houses. Frequency counts of parole violations and arrests

1 year after release—at t_3—measured the predictive accuracy of the LSI.

Deterring Obscene Phone Calls   In 1988, the New Jersey Bell telephone company introduced caller identification (ID) and instant call tracing in a small number of telephone exchange areas. Caller ID displays the phone number of the person who is placing a call on the telephone of the call recipient. Instant call tracing allows the recipient of an obscene or threatening call to automatically initiate a procedure to trace the source of the call.

Ronald Clarke (1997a) studied the effects of these new technologies in deterring obscene phone calls. Clarke expected that obscene calls would decrease in areas where the new services were available. To test this, he compared records of formal customer complaints about annoying calls in the New Jersey areas that had the new services to formal complaints in other New Jersey areas where caller ID and call tracing were not available. One year later, the number of formal complaints had dropped sharply in areas serviced by the new technology; no decline was found in other New Jersey Bell areas.

In this study, telephone service areas with new services were the treatment group, and areas without the services were the comparison group. Clarke's matching criterion was a simple one: telephone service by New Jersey Bell, assuming the volume of obscene phone calls was relatively constant within a single phone service area. Of course, matching on telephone service area cannot eliminate the possibility that the volume of obscene phone calls varies from one part of New Jersey to another, but Clarke's choice of a comparison group was straightforward and certainly more plausible than comparing New Jersey to, say, Nebraska.

Clarke's study is a good example of a natural field experiment. The experimental stimulus—caller ID and call tracing—was not specifically introduced by Clarke, but he was able to obtain measures for the dependent variable before and after the experimental stimulus was introduced. He then compared the levels of change from pretest to posttest measures for the treatment and comparison groups. Randomization could not be used, but Clarke's design made it possible to infer with reasonable confidence that caller ID and call tracing reduced the number of formal complaints about obscene phone calls.

Together, these three studies illustrate different approaches to research design when it is not possible to randomly assign subjects to treatment and control groups. Lacking random assignment, researchers must use creative procedures for selecting subjects, constructing treatment and comparison groups, measuring dependent variables, and exercising other controls to reduce possible threats to validity.

Cohort Designs

Chapter 4 mentioned cohort studies as examples of longitudinal designs. We can also view cohort studies as nonequivalent-control-group designs. Recall from Chapter 4 that a cohort may be defined as a group of subjects who enter or leave an institution at the same time. For example, a class of police officers who graduate from a training academy at the same time could be considered a cohort. Or we might view all persons who were sentenced to probation in May as a cohort.

Now think of a cohort that is exposed to some experimental stimulus. The May probation cohort might be required to complete 100 hours of community service in addition to meeting other conditions of probation. If we are interested in whether probationers who receive community service sentences are charged with fewer probation violations, we can compare the performance of the May cohort with that of the April cohort, or the June cohort, or some other cohort not sentenced to community service. Cohorts that do not receive community service sentences serve as comparison groups. The groups are not equivalent because they were not created by random assignment. But if we assume that a comparison cohort does not systematically differ from a treatment cohort on important variables, we can use this design to determine whether community service sentences reduce probation violations.

That last assumption is very important, but it may not be viable. Perhaps a criminal court docket is organized to schedule certain types of cases at the same time, so a May cohort would be systematically different from a June cohort. But if the assumption of comparability can be met, cohorts may be used to construct nonequivalent comparison and experimental groups by taking advantage of the natural flow of cases through some institutional process.

A study by Edmund Risler and associates (Risler, Sweatman, and Nackerud, 1998) on the effectiveness of a judicial waiver law in deterring juvenile crime is a good example of a cohort design. Judicial waiver laws signaled a shift in juvenile justice philosophy, largely because of a perceived increase in violent crime by juveniles and a growing sentiment that juvenile courts were not tough enough on young violent offenders. A judicial waiver law in Georgia required that anyone between the ages of 13 and 17 be tried as an adult if charged with one of several violent crimes: murder, voluntary manslaughter, rape, aggravated sexual battery, aggravated child molestation, aggravated sodomy, or robbery with a firearm. Risler and associates were interested in whether the law achieved its goal of deterrence.

The Georgia law—the experimental stimulus—became effective in 1994. Two samples of juveniles were studied: (1) a preintervention cohort, juveniles processed during the 2-year period prior to the law's enactment (1992–93), and (2) a postintervention cohort, juveniles processed during the 2-year period after the law took effect (1994–95). Mean arrest rates for juveniles for the seven offenses covered under the judicial waiver law were compared across these two samples. Arrest rates for 1992 and 1993 served as observations for the pretest cohort; those for 1994 and 1995 served as posttest observations.

The two cohorts could not be considered equivalent because they were not produced by random assignment. However, they were assumed to be sufficiently similar for the purpose of the authors' study.

Risler and associates found that the mean arrests rate for crimes covered under the judicial waiver law actually increased slightly for the postintervention cohort. The authors therefore concluded that the law did not act as a deterrent to reduce violent offending by juveniles.

Time-Series Designs

Time-series designs are common examples of longitudinal studies in criminal justice research. As the name implies, a time-series design involves examining a series of observations on some variable over time. A simple example is examining trends in arrests for drunk driving over time to see whether the number of arrests is increasing, decreasing, or staying constant. A police executive might be interested in keeping track of arrests for drunk driving, or for other offenses, as a way of monitoring the performance of patrol officers. Or state corrections officials might want to study trends in prison admissions as a way of predicting the future need for correctional facilities.

An interrupted time series is a special type of time-series design that can be used in cause-and-effect studies. A series of observations is compared before and after some intervention is introduced. For example, a researcher might want to know whether roadside sobriety checkpoints cause a decrease in fatal automobile accidents. Trends in accidents could be compared before and after the roadside checkpoints are established.

Interrupted time-series designs can be very useful in criminal justice research, especially in applied studies. They do have some limitations, however, just like other ways of structuring research. Cook and Campbell (1979) described the strengths and limitations of different approaches to time-series designs. We will introduce these approaches with a hypothetical example and then describe some specific criminal justice applications.

Continuing with the example of sobriety checkpoints, Figure 7.5 presents four possible patterns of alcohol-related automobile accidents. The vertical line in each pattern shows the time when the roadside checkpoint program is introduced. Which of these patterns indicates that the new program caused a reduction in car accidents?

If the time-series results looked like pattern 1 in Figure 7.5, we might think initially that the checkpoints caused a reduction in alcohol-related accidents, but there seems to be a general downward trend in accidents that continues after the intervention. It's safer to conclude that the decline would have continued even without the roadside checkpoints.

Pattern 2 shows that an increasing trend in auto accidents has been reversed after the intervention, but this appears to be due to a regular pattern in which accidents have been bouncing up and down. The intervention was introduced at the peak of an upward trend, and the later decline may be an artifact of the underlying pattern rather than of the new program.

Patterns 1 and 2 exhibit some outside trend, rather than an intervention, that may account for a pattern observed over time. We may recognize this as an example of *history* as a validity threat to the inference that the new checkpoint program caused a change in auto accidents. The general decline in pattern 1 may be due to reduced drunk driving that has nothing to do with sobriety checkpoints. Pattern 2 illustrates what is referred to as *seasonality* in a time series — a regular pattern of change over time. Cook and Campbell (1979) described seasonality as a special case of history. In our example, the data might reflect seasonal variation in alcohol-related accidents that occurs around holidays or maybe on football weekends near a college campus.

Patterns 3 and 4 lend more support to the inference that sobriety checkpoints caused a decline in alcohol-related accidents, but the two patterns are different in a subtle way. In pattern 3, accidents decline more sharply from

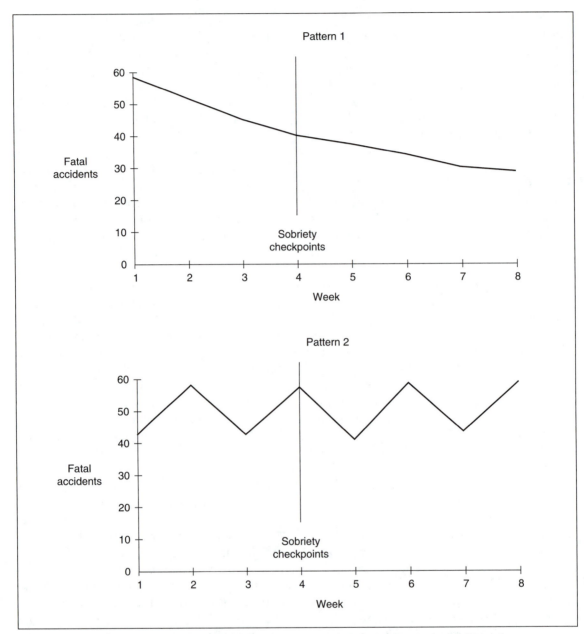

Figure 7.5   Four Patterns of Change in Fatal Automobile Accidents (Hypothetical Data)

a general downward trend immediately after the checkpoint program was introduced, while pattern 4 displays a sharper decline some time after the new program was established. Which pattern provides stronger support for the inference?

In framing your answer, recall what we have said about construct validity. Think about the underlying causal process these two patterns represent, or consider possible mechanisms that might be at work. Pattern 3 suggests that the program was immediately effective and sup-

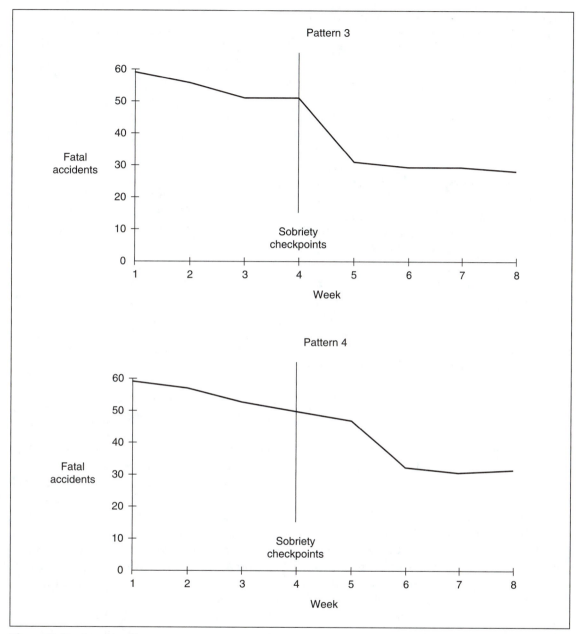

Figure 7.5   (*continued*)

ports what we might call an incapacitation mechanism: Roadside checkpoints enabled police to identify and arrest drunk drivers, thereby getting them off the road and reducing accidents. Pattern 4 suggests a deterrent mechanism: As drivers learned about the checkpoints, they less often drove after drinking, and accidents eventually declined. Either explanation is possible given the evidence presented. This illustrates an important limitation of interrupted time-series designs: They operationalize complex causal constructs in simple ways. Our interpretation depends in large part on how we understand this causal process.

Research by Richard McCleary and associates (McCleary, Neinstedt, and Erven, 1982), mentioned in Chapter 5, illustrates the need to think carefully about how well time-series results reflect underlying causal patterns. Recall that McCleary and colleagues reported a sharp decline in burglaries immediately after a special burglary investigation unit was established in a large city. This finding was at odds with their understanding of how police investigations could reasonably be expected to reduce burglary. A special unit might eventually be able to reduce the number of burglaries, after investigating incidents over a period of time and making arrests. But it is highly unlikely that changing investigative procedures would have an immediate impact. This discrepancy prompted McCleary and associates to look more closely at the policy change and led to their conclusion that the apparent decline in burglaries was produced by changes in record-keeping practices. No evidence existed of any decline in the actual number of burglaries.

This example illustrates our discussion of instrumentation earlier in this chapter. Changes in the way police counted burglaries produced what appeared to be a reduction in burglary. Instrumentation can be a particular problem in time-series designs for two reasons. First, observations are usually made over a relatively long time period, which increases the likelihood of changes in measurement instruments. Second, time-series designs often use measures that are produced by an organization such as a police department, criminal court, probation office, or corrections department. There may be changes or irregularities in the way data are collected by these agencies that are not readily apparent to researchers and that are, in any case, not subject to their control.

Variations in Time-Series Designs

If we view the basic interrupted time-series design as an adaptation of basic design building

Simple Interrupted Time Series

O	O	O	O	X	O	O	O	O
t_1	t_2	t_3	t_4		t_5	t_6	t_7	t_8

Interrupted Time Series with Nonequivalent Comparison Group

O	O	O	O	X	O	O	O	O
O	O	O	O		O	O	O	O
t_1	t_2	t_3	t_4		t_5	t_6	t_7	t_8

Interrupted Time Series with Removed Treatment

O	O	X	O	O	O	$-X$	O	O	O
t_1	t_2		t_3	t_4	t_5		t_6	t_7	t_8

Interrupted Time Series with Switching Replications

O	O	O	X	O	O	O	O	O
O	O	O	O	O	X	O	O	O
t_1	t_2	t_3	t_4		t_5	t_6	t_7	t_8

Figure 7.6   Interrupted Time-Series Designs

blocks, we can consider how modifications can help control for many validity problems. The simplest time-series design studies one group— the treatment group—over time. Rather than making one pretest and one posttest observation, the interrupted time-series design makes a longer series of observations before and after introducing an experimental treatment.

What if we considered the other building blocks of experimental design? Figure 7.6 presents the basic design and some variations using the familiar O, X, and t notation. In the basic design, shown at the top of Figure 7.6, many pretest and posttest observations are made on a single group that receives some treatment.

We could strengthen this design by adding a comparison series of observations on some group that does not receive the treatment. If, for example, roadside sobriety checkpoints were introduced all over the state of Ohio but were not used at all in Michigan, then we could compare auto accidents in Ohio (the treatment series) with auto accidents in Michigan (the comparison series). If checkpoints caused a reduction in alcohol-related accidents, we would expect to see a decline in Ohio following the intervention, but there should be no change or a lesser decline in Michigan over the same time period. The second part of Figure 7.6 shows this design—an interrupted time series with a nonequivalent comparison group. The two series are not equivalent because we did not randomly assign drivers to Ohio or Michigan. So Young Kim and Wesley Skogan (2003) present a good example of this design in their analysis of police problem solving in Chicago. They examined changes in crime for police beats where specific problems were identified and addressed to comparison beats where no crime-specific interventions were developed.

A single-series design may be modified by introducing and then removing the intervention, as shown in the third part of Figure 7.6. We might test sobriety checkpoints by setting them up every weekend for a month and then not setting them up for the next few months. If the checkpoints caused a reduction in alcohol-related accidents, we might expect an increase after they were removed. Or the effects of weekend checkpoints might persist even after we removed them.

Because different states or cities sometimes introduce new drunk-driving programs at different times, we might be able to use what Cook and Campbell (1979:223) called a "time-series design with switching replications." The bottom of Figure 7.6 illustrates this design. For example, assume that Ohio begins using checkpoints in May 1998 and Michigan introduces them in July of the same year. A switching replications design could strengthen our conclusion that checkpoints reduce accidents if we saw that a decline in Ohio began in June and a similar pattern was found in Michigan beginning in August. The fact that similar changes occurred in the dependent variable in different states at different times, corresponding to when the program was introduced, would add to our confidence in stating that sobriety checkpoints actually reduced auto accidents.

Variable-Oriented Research and Scientific Realism

Another way to think about a time-series design is as a study of one or a few cases with many observations. If we design a time-series study of roadside checkpoints in Ohio, we will be examining one case (Ohio) with many observations of auto accidents. Or a design that compares Ohio and Michigan will examine many observations for two cases. Thinking once again about design building blocks, notice how we have slightly restated one of those building blocks. Instead of considering the number of experimental and control *groups,* our attention centers on the number of subjects or *cases* in our study. In Figure 7.6, the first and third time-series designs have one case each, while the second and fourth designs examine two cases each.

Classical experiments and quasi-experiments with large numbers of subjects are examples of what Charles Ragin (2000) terms **case-oriented research,** in which many cases are examined to understand a small number of variables. Time-series designs and case studies are examples of **variable-oriented research,** in which a large number of variables are studied for a small number of cases or subjects. Suppose we wish to study inmate-on-inmate assaults in correctional facilities. With case-oriented approach, we might send a questionnaire to a sample of 500 correctional facilities, asking facility staff to provide information about assaults, facility design, inmate characteristics, and housing conditions. Here, we are gathering information on a few variables from a large number of correctional facilities. Using a variable-oriented approach, we might visit one or a few facilities to conduct in-depth interviews with staff, observe the condition of facilities, and gather information from institutional records. Here, we are collecting information on a wide range of variables from a small number of institutions.

The **case-study** design is an example of variable-oriented research. Here, the researcher's

PUTTING IT ALL TOGETHER

A VARIETY OF DESIGNS IN NEW YORK CITY

The Rutgers University research on links between changes in police action and crime could not be conducted as a classical experiment for a couple of reasons. First, the research project was conceived and planned some years after the most significant policing changes were introduced in 1994. Second, management and strategic changes in New York were introduced citywide; there was no opportunity to randomly assign some areas of the city to receive different types of policing. For these and other reasons, researchers devised a variety of quasi-experimental approaches.

Precincts as Nonequivalent Groups

First, 6 of the city's 76 precincts were selected for particularly intensive study. Because each precinct faced different kinds of crime problems and adopted correspondingly different tactics in policing, researchers could compare police actions and changes in crime across different precincts. Clearly, precincts are "nonequivalent" groups in this regard, but not in the traditional research sense that one or more groups receive a treatment while one or more other groups do not. Policing changed in *all* precincts, but it changed in different ways and at different times. It's also possible to view the six precincts as multiple case studies, an example of variable-oriented research in which a lot of data are gathered for each case.

So Rutgers researchers were able to do the following: (1) examine measures of crime in different precincts at different times, (2) study what spe-

attention centers on an in-depth examination of one or a few cases on many dimensions. Charles Ragin and Howard Becker (1992) point out that the term *case* is used broadly. Cases can be individual people, neighborhoods, correctional facilities, courtrooms, or other aggregations. Our running example of policing and crime reduction in New York City has some elements of a case study. Researchers gathered information from different sources to measure several types of variables for one case (New York) and a small number of other cases (precincts) in the city.

Robert Yin (1994) cautions that the case-study design is often misunderstood as representing "qualitative" research or participant observation study. Instead, Yin advises that the case study is a design strategy and that the labels *qualitative* and *quantitative* are not useful ways to distinguish design strategies. Case studies appear qualitative in focusing on one or a small number of units, but many case studies employ sophisticated statistical techniques to examine

many variables for those units. An example illustrates how misleading it can be to associate case studies with qualitative research.

In what has come to be known as the "Boston Gun Project," Anthony Braga and associates (Braga, Kennedy, Waring, and Piehl, 2001) studied violence by youth gangs in Boston neighborhoods. Theirs was an applied explanatory study. They worked with local officials to better understand gang violence, develop ways to reduce it, and eventually assess the effects of their interventions. Neither a classical experiment nor a nonequivalent-groups design was possible. Researchers sought to understand and reduce violence by all gangs in the city. Their research centered on gangs, not individuals, though some interventions targeted particular gang members.

Researchers collected a large amount of information about gangs and gang violence from several sources. Earlier reports (Kennedy, Piehl, and Braga, 1996) described something called "network analysis," in which researchers exam-

cific strategies were developed and implemented to reduce specific types of crime, and (3) analyze subsequent measures of crime to look for reductions. In the language used in this chapter, pre-intervention measures were made, an intervention was developed, and then postintervention measures were examined. This process was repeated in each of six precincts.

A Series of Interrupted Time Series

Researchers were fortunate in having access to New York crime and arrest data dating to the late 1980s. And New Yorkers' misfortune in having a great deal of crime was a windfall for researchers. Throughout the nation's largest city, and in the precincts most plagued by crime, enough incidents occurred to examine weekly trends. This means that researchers had access to more than 570 weekly observations (11 years [1989–2000] × 52 weeks + 3 weeks for leap years [1992, 1996, 2000]). The year 1994 marked the beginning of

changes in New York's policing strategy citywide, so researchers compared pre-1994 crime trends to post-1994 changes.

More importantly, researchers use individual series in the six precincts selected for closer study. At weekly planning meetings, precinct staff devised tactics for dealing with particular crime problems in the area. These tactics were interventions, and researchers examined changes from pre- to postintervention measures of crimes. Having multiple precincts implementing tactics at different times offered a type of switching-replications time-series design.

Of course, researchers had to deal with a variety of validity threats in this variety of designs. What might some of these be? In considering this question, think about measurement (Chapters 5 and 6) and about the quasi-experimental designs that were used. It will also be useful to sketch out representations of your understanding of these designs using the *X, O,* and *t* notation.

---

ined relationships between gangs in different neighborhoods and conflicts over turf within neighborhoods. Police records of homicides, assaults, and shootings were studied. Based on extensive data on a small number of gangs, researchers collaborated with public officials, neighborhood organizations, and a coalition of religious leaders—the "faith community." A variety of interventions were devised, but most were crafted from a detailed understanding of the specific nature of gangs and gang violence as they existed in Boston neighborhoods. David Kennedy (1998) summarizes these using the label "pulling levers," signifying that key gang members were vulnerable to intensive monitoring via probation or parole. The package of strategies was markedly successful: Youth homicides were reduced from about 35–40 each year in the 20 years preceding the program to about 15 per year in the first 5 postintervention years (Braga, 2002:70).

The Boston research is also a good example of the scientific realist approach of Ray Pawson

and Nick Tilley (1997). Researchers examined a small number of subjects—gangs and gang members—in a single city and in the context of specific neighborhoods where gangs were active. Extensive data were gathered on the mechanisms of gang violence. Interventions were tailored to those mechanisms in their context.

Braga and associates (2001) emphasize that the success of the Boston efforts was due to the *process* by which researchers, public officials, and community members collaboratively studied gang violence and then developed appropriate policy actions based on their analyses. Other jurisdictions mistakenly tried to reproduce Boston's interventions, with limited or no success, failing to recognize that the interventions were developed specifically for Boston. In case-study language, researchers examined many variables for one site and based policy decisions on that analysis. In the words of scientific realism, researchers studied the gang violence mechanism in the Boston context. In other contexts (Baltimore, or Minneapolis, for example), gang violence operated as a different mechanism; the "levers" pulled in Boston did not work elsewhere. Braga and associates emphasize that the problem-solving process is exportable to other settings but that the interventions used in Boston are not (2001:220).

How do case studies address threats to validity? In the most general sense, case studies attempt to isolate causal mechanisms from possible confounding influences by studying very precisely defined subjects. Donald Campbell (1994:x) likens this to laboratory experiments in the natural sciences, in which researchers try to isolate causal variables from outside influences. Case-study research takes place in natural field settings, not in laboratories. But the logic of trying to isolate causal mechanisms by focusing on one or a few cases is a direct descendant of the rationale for experimental isolation in laboratories.

Figure 7.7 summarizes advice from Yin (1994:32–36) on how to judge the quality of case-study designs in language that should now be familiar. Construct validity is established through multiple sources of evidence, the establishment of chains of causation that connect independent and dependent variables, and what are termed "member checks"—asking key informants to review tentative conclusions about causation. Examples of techniques for strengthening internal validity are theory-based pattern matching and time-series analysis. The first criterion follows Cook and Campbell, calling on researchers to make specific theory-based predictions about what pattern of results will support hypothesized causal relationships. Alternative explanations, also termed "rival hypotheses," are less persuasive when specific predictions of results are actually obtained. For example, Braga and associates (2001) predicted that gun killings among male Boston residents under age 25 would decline following implementation of the package of interventions in the Boston gun strategy. Although other explanations are possible for the sharp observed declines, the specific focus of the researchers' interventions

Case Study Approach	
Construct Validity	Multiple sources of evidence
	Establishment of chain of causation
	Member checks
Internal Validity	Pattern matching
	Time-series analysis
External Validity	Replication through multiple case studies

Figure 7.7   Case Studies and Validity
Source: Adapted from Yin (1994:33).

and the concomitant results undermine the credibility of rival hypotheses. Having many measures of variables over time strengthens internal validity if observations support our predicted expectations about cause. We saw earlier how nonequivalent time-series comparisons and switching replications can enhance findings. This is also consistent with pattern matching—we make specific statements about what patterns of results we expect in our observations over time.

Finally, a single case study is vulnerable to external validity threats because it is rooted in the context of a specific site. Conducting multiple case studies in different sites illustrates the principle of replication. By replicating research findings, we accumulate evidence. We may also find that causal relationships are different in different settings, as did researchers who tried to transplant specific interventions from the Boston Gun Project. Although such findings can undermine the generalizability of causality, they also help us understand how causal mechanisms can operate differently in different settings.

Time-series designs and case studies are examples of variable-oriented research. A case study with many observations over time can be an example of a time-series design. Adding one or more other cases offers opportunities to create nonequivalent comparisons. Time-series designs, case studies, and nonequivalent comparisons are quasi-experimental designs—they are conducted in the manner of experiments, using design building blocks in different ways.

Experimental and Quasi-Experimental Designs Summarized

Understanding the building blocks of research design and adapting them accordingly works better than trying to apply the same design to all research questions.

By now, it should be clear that there are no simple formulas or recipes for designing an experimental or quasi-experimental study. Researchers have an almost infinite variety of ways of varying the number and composition of groups of subjects, selecting subjects, determining how many observations to make, and deciding what types of experimental stimuli to introduce or study.

Variations on the classical experimental designs are especially useful for explanatory research and in evaluation studies, but exploratory and descriptive studies usually use other methods. Surveys conducted at one point in time, for example, may be used to explore or describe such phenomena as fear of crime or public attitudes toward punishment. Longitudinal studies of age cohorts are often the best ways to examine criminal careers or developmental causes of delinquency.

Even when experimental designs might be the best choice, it is not always possible to construct treatment and control groups, to use random assignment, or even to analyze a series of observations over time. For instance, Dennis Rosenbaum and associates (1992) conducted an extensive study of community organizations and their potential for addressing problems of drug abuse. The researchers conducted community surveys, interviewed members of neighborhood groups, observed group meetings, participated in planning sessions, and investigated physical and social conditions in project neighborhoods. Antidrug activity by groups in eight sites was the experimental treatment, but this treatment was neither introduced nor controlled by the researchers. The large and varying scope of group activities, combined with limited funding for research, made it impossible to construct anything like comparison groups. Nevertheless, Rosenbaum and associates were able to conduct what amounted to eight case studies and to provide valuable insights into the kinds of group actions that were more or less effective in combating neighborhood drug problems.

As we stated early in this chapter, experiments are best suited to topics that involve well-defined concepts and propositions. Experiments and quasi-experiments also require that researchers be able to exercise, or at least approximate, some degree of control over an experimental stimulus. Finally, these designs depend on the ability to unambiguously establish the time order of experimental treatments and observations on the dependent variable. Often, it is not possible to achieve the necessary degree of control.

In designing research projects, researchers should be alert to opportunities for using experimental designs. Researchers should also be aware of how quasi-experimental designs can be developed when randomization is not possible. Experiments and quasi-experiments lend themselves to a logical rigor that is often much more difficult to achieve in other modes of observation. The building blocks of research design can be used in creative ways to address a variety of criminal justice research questions. Careful attention to design issues, and to how design elements can reduce validity threats, is essential to the research process.

✪ *Main Points*

- Experiments are an excellent vehicle for the controlled testing of causal processes. Experiments may also be appropriate for evaluation studies.
- The classical experiment tests the effect of an experimental stimulus on some dependent variable through the pretesting and posttesting of experimental and control groups.

- It is less important that a group of experimental subjects be representative of some larger population than that experimental and control groups be similar to each other.
- Randomization is the best way to achieve comparability in the experimental and control groups.
- The classical experiment with random assignment of subject guards against most of the threats to internal invalidity.
- Because experiments often take place under controlled conditions, results may not be generalizable to real-world constructs. Or findings from an experiment in one setting may not apply to other settings.
- The classical experiment may be modified to suit specific research purposes by changing the number of experimental and control groups, the number and types of experimental stimuli, and the number of pretest or posttest measurements.
- Quasi-experiments may be conducted when it is not possible or desirable to use an experimental design.
- Nonequivalent-groups and time-series designs are two general types of quasi-experiments.
- Time-series designs and case studies are examples of variable-oriented research, in which a large number of variables are examined for one or a few cases.
- Both experiments and quasi-experiments may be customized by using design building blocks to suit particular research purposes.
- Not all research purposes and questions are amenable to experimental or quasi-experimental designs because researchers may not be able to exercise the required degree of control.

✪ Key Terms

Case-oriented research	Generalizability
Case study	Independent variable
Classical experiment	Quasi-experiment
Control group	Randomization
Dependent variable	Variable-oriented
Experimental group	research

✪ Review Questions and Exercises

1. If you do not remember participating in D.A.R.E.—Drug Abuse Resistance Education—you have probably heard or read something about it. Describe an experimental design to test the causal hypothesis that D.A.R.E. reduces re-

cidivism. Is your experimental design feasible? Why or why not?

2. Experiments are often conducted in public health research, where a distinction is made between an efficacy experiment and an effectiveness experiment. Efficacy experiments focus on whether some new health program works under ideal conditions; effectiveness experiments test the program under typical conditions that health professionals encounter in their day-to-day work. Discuss how efficacy experiments and effectiveness experiments reflect concerns about internal validity threats on the one hand and generalizability on the other.

3. Crime hot spots are areas where crime reports, calls for police service, or other measures of crime are especially common. Police in departments with a good analytic capability routinely identify hot spots and launch special tactics to reduce crime in these areas. What kinds of validity threats should researchers be especially attentive to in studying the effects of police interventions on hot spots?

4. David Weisburd and associates (Weisburd, Lum, and Petrosino, 2001) studied relationships between the types of research designs and the findings of applied research projects. The authors report that experimental designs are more likely to find no relationship between independent and dependent variables, while quasi-experimental designs are more likely to support hypothesized relationships between independent and dependent variables. Given your understanding of threats to validity, present at least two alternative explanations for the findings by Weisburd and associates.

✪ Internet Exercises

To ensure that you always have access to live, correct Web links for the Web sites referenced in the following exercises, we provide the necessary links on the companion Web site for *Research Methods for Criminal Justice and Criminology* at http://cj.wadsworth.com/maxfield_babbie/research_methods4e. Once at the companion Web site, select this specific chapter, click on "Chapter Resources," then click on "Web Links."

1. Researchers at the University of Maryland published a summary report on crime prevention research in 1997 titled *Preventing Crime: What Works, What Doesn't, What's Promising.* One of its

most interesting features is a measure of the strength of research methods used by various crime prevention studies. Go to the NCJRS Web site and review Chapter 2, "Thinking About Crime Prevention," by Lawrence Sherman, and the appendix on research methods by Sherman and Denise Gottfredson. Pay particular attention to the "scale of evidentiary strength for cause and effect." Then discuss these two sections of the report using the language of research design and validity threats from this chapter of your text.

2. Randomization is one of the hallmarks of a true experimental design. Visit William Trochmin's Knowledge Base Web site to help you to understand and summarize the difference between random assignment and random sampling. If you are ready to randomly assign subjects to conditions, visit the Research Randomizer Web site.

✪ *InfoTrac College Edition*

Use the keyword *time-series analysis* to find a criminal justice article that uses this quasi-experimental method. Read the article and note why the author(s) chose to use this particular method rather than an experimental design.

✪ *The NEW Companion Web Site for* **Research Methods for Criminal Justice and Criminology,** *Fourth Edition*

http://cj.wadsworth.com/maxfield_babbie/ research_methods4e

Supplement your review of this chapter by going to the new companion Web site to take one of the Tutorial Quizzes, use the flash cards to master key terms, and check out the many other study aids you'll find there. You'll also find special features such as quantitative and qualitative data analysis primers to help you with a special project or do some research on your own.

✪ *Additional Readings*

Campbell, Donald T., and Stanley, Julian, *Experimental and Quasi-Experimental Designs for Research* (Chicago: Rand McNally, 1966). This short book provides an excellent analysis of the logic and methods of experimentation in social research

and is widely cited as the classic discussion of validity threats.

Cook, Thomas D., and Campbell, Donald T., *Quasi-Experimentation: Design and Analysis Issues for Field Settings* (Boston: Houghton Mifflin, 1979). The authors update and substantially expand issues introduced by Campbell and Stanley. Although Cook and Campbell can be difficult reading, this book remains the definitive treatment of the principles of experimental and quasi-experimental designs for social science.

Kim, So Young, and Skogan, Wesley G., "Statistical Analysis of Time Series Data on Problem Solving," Community Policing Working Paper #27 (Center for Policy Research, Northwestern University, 2003) (http://www.northwestern.edu/ ipr/publications/policing.html). Kim and Skogan present a number of time-series studies to examine the effects of problem solving by Chicago police. This is a good example of switching-replications time-series designs by researchers at the university where Campbell and Cook did their pioneering work on quasi-experimental designs.

Pawson, Ray, and Tilley, Nick, *Realistic Evaluation* (Thousand Oaks, CA: Sage, 1997). We mentioned this book in Chapter 4. Pawson and Tilley argue that experiments and quasi-experiments focus too narrowly on threats to internal validity. Instead, they propose a different view of causation and different approaches to assessing cause.

Weisburd, David, Lum, Cynthia M., Petrosino, Anthony, "Does Research Design Affect Study Outcomes in Criminal Justice?" *The Annals,* Vol. 578 (2001), pp. 50–70. The authors make the intriguing claim that stronger experimental designs are more likely to find no causal relationships, while quasi-experimental designs more often find relationships. Read this article carefully (whether or not you complete the exercise described above), and decide whether you agree with the authors' conclusions.

Yin, Robert K., *Case Study Research: Design and Methods,* 2nd ed. (Thousand Oaks, CA: Sage Publications, 1994). Many people incorrectly associate case studies with qualitative research. Yin describes a variety of case-study designs as quasi-experiments. In doing so, he is consistent with how Cook and Campbell (1979) describe case studies.

Part Three

Modes of Observation

Having covered the basics of structuring research, from general issues to research design, let's dive into the various observational techniques available for criminal justice research.

We begin with an overview of the three basic ways criminal justice researchers collect data for measurement. Chapter 8 then examines how social scientists go about selecting people or things for observation. Our discussion of sampling addresses the fundamental scientific issue of generalizability. As we'll see, it is possible for us to select a few people or things for observation and then apply what we observe to a much larger group of people or things than we actually observed. It is possible, for example, to ask 1000 people how they feel about "three strikes and you're out" laws and then accurately predict how tens of millions of people feel about it.

Chapter 9 describes survey research and other techniques for collecting data by asking people questions. We'll cover different ways of asking questions and discuss the various uses of surveys and related techniques in criminal justice research.

Chapter 10, on field research, examines what is perhaps the most natural form of data collection: the direct observation of phenomena in natural settings. As we will see, observations can be highly structured and systematic (such as counting pedestrians who walk by some specified point) or less structured and more flexible.

Chapter 11 discusses ways to take advantage of some of the data available all around us. Researchers often examine data collected by criminal justice and other public agencies. Content analysis is a method of collecting data through carefully specifying and counting communications such as news stories, court opinions, or even recorded visual images. Criminal justice researchers may also conduct secondary analysis of data collected by others.

Chapter 8

Overview of Data Collection and Sampling

Three main ways of collecting data are available for criminal justice researchers. Fundamental to each way of collecting data is sampling. Sampling makes it possible to select a few hundred or thousand people for study and discover things that apply to many more people who are not studied.

Introduction

How we collect representative data is fundamental to criminal justice research.

Much of the value of research depends on how data are collected. This chapter introduces some general considerations in all types of data collection and discusses the logic and fundamental principles of sampling.

As with most aspects of designing and executing criminal justice research, the choices we make about data collection and sampling depend on our particular research purpose. And, as we saw in Chapter 5, data collection is closely linked to measurement choices, which, in turn, depend on how we define particular concepts.

In reality, however, researchers often must make compromises. For example, if you are interested in whether mandatory jail sentences reduce highway deaths due to drunk driving, collecting blood samples from all drivers in fatal automobile accidents will be an ideal way to produce a measure of drunk driving. However, because police in many states do not routinely collect blood samples, you might have to develop an alternative measure that would require you to collect data in some other way. In this case, specifying measures of drunk driving and traffic deaths are relatively straightforward; the difficulty arises in actually collecting the data.

In collecting data, criminal justice researchers have a whole world of potential observations, yet nobody can observe everything. A critical part of criminal justice research, then, is deciding what will be observed and what won't. If you want to study drug users, for example, which drug users should you study?

Sampling is the process of selecting observations. Sampling is ordinarily used to select observations for one of two related reasons. First, it is often not possible to collect information from all persons or other units we wish to study. We may wish to know what proportion of all persons arrested in U.S. cities have recently used drugs, but collecting all that data would be virtually impossible. Thus, we have to look at a sample of observations.

The second reason for sampling is that it is often not necessary to collect data from all persons or other units. Probability sampling techniques enable us to make relatively few observations and then generalize from those observations to a much wider population. For example, if we are interested in what proportion of high school students have used marijuana, collecting data from a probability sample of a few thousand students will serve just as well as trying to study every high school student in the country.

Although probability sampling is central to criminal justice research, a variety of nonprobability sampling techniques are frequently used. Though not based on random selection, these methods have their own logic and can provide useful samples for criminal justice inquiry. In this chapter, we examine both the advantages and the shortcomings of such methods, and we discuss where they fit in the larger picture of sampling and collecting data.

Three Sources of Data

Each of the three ways of collecting data presents issues for researchers to consider.

Our examination of different ways to measure crime in Chapter 6 illustrated three general approaches. We can measure crime by (1) asking people questions about victimization or about offenses they have committed, (2) observing actual behavior, or (3) using existing data. These approaches to measuring crime illustrate the three basic ways of collecting data for criminal justice research: (1) asking questions, (2) making observations, and (3) examining written records.

Chapters 9–11 examine each of these techniques in turn. To lay the foundation for that discussion, let's take a broad view of different ways to collect data.

Asking Questions

In criminal justice and other types of social science research, when we collect data by asking people questions, we often use the survey method. The National Crime Victimization Survey (NCVS) and the Monitoring the Future (MTF) survey are examples. A formal questionnaire that embodies operationalizations of concepts is a key element in these and other surveys.

There are also other ways of making observations by asking people questions that we may not normally associate with survey methods. In many criminal justice research projects, investigators interview a small number of specialized research subjects—members of a state parole board, for example. Sometimes, small numbers of people are interviewed together, as a **focus group.** Chapter 9 examines these and other ways of collecting data by asking people questions.

Surveys and other questioning techniques are very common methods of data collection. In asking questions, researchers must always devote attention to the measurement quality issues of validity and reliability. This is especially true because interviews often produce indirect measures that substitute for other ways of making observations.

Making Direct Observations

Direct observation encompasses a broad range of methods for gathering data—from counting the number of participants who attend a community crime prevention meeting to administering urinalysis tests for drug use. The defining characteristic of direct observation is obtaining measurements by observing behavior, traces of behavior, or physical objects without interacting with research subjects. When you ask people questions, either in a face-to-face interview or on a self-administered questionnaire, you interact with them. In contrast, direct observation does not involve verbal interaction. For example, you could measure cocaine use among a group of probationers by having them complete a questionnaire that asked them whether they had used cocaine in the past 48 hours, or you could administer a urinalysis test for cocaine use.

It might seem that direct observation of cocaine use through urinalysis would be superior to asking people whether they had used cocaine. Practical issues often prevent the use of such methods, however. Consider, for example, the ethical issues that might be involved in conducting urinalysis tests on a national sample of high school seniors.

Forms of direct observation other than conducting laboratory tests of drug use present other types of problems. Suppose you are interested in community crime prevention groups. You might attend a group meeting and observe not only how many people attend but also what types of concerns are expressed and how attendees feel about some particular issue—say, neighborhood watch—discussed at the meeting. Although you do not ask people about their views of neighborhood watch, your observations require you to make judgments about particular comments. Were they positive, negative, or mixed? Did they raise questions about some particular aspect of neighborhood watch? Simply observing is not enough in this example. We would have to make additional judgments about what takes place at the meeting.

Chapter 10 examines direct observation in detail. The chapter is titled "Field Research" to reflect that observations are normally made in more natural settings, outside the laboratory.

Examining Written Records

Many measurements are made by consulting written documents or other types of records. The concept of criminal history, for example, may be measured by consulting records maintained by police, juvenile authorities, or criminal courts. Rather than directly observing criminal behavior or asking subjects about arrests or convictions, researchers commonly examine records maintained by public agencies as sources for measures of something like criminal history.

As with other methods of collecting data, written records are used in a variety of ways, corresponding roughly to different types of written records. Criminal justice researchers frequently make use of information routinely collected by government agencies and made available to the general public. Uniform Crime Reports (UCR), published by the FBI, and reports from the decennial census of the U.S. population are examples. Such written records are compiled by the FBI and the Census Bureau for the specific purpose of sharing information with researchers, government officials, and the general public.

Virtually all public agencies maintain other types of records for their own use that are not normally released to the general public but that may be accessible to researchers. Examples include records of juvenile offenses, budget documents, information on inmate populations in correctional institutions, the number of monthly contacts between probation officers and clients, and the number of times police officers stop motorists for traffic violations.

A key point to recognize about written records is that someone originally gathered the data by making direct observations or by asking people questions. Consequently, if we are to use data from written records in our research, we need to understand how those data were originally collected. Chapter 11 expands on this crucial point and examines the various ways written records can serve as sources of data in criminal justice research.

Using Multiple Data Sources

As we design a research or evaluation project, we have to make choices about measurement and data collection together. Such choices are

PUTTING IT ALL TOGETHER

USING THREE TYPES OF DATA IN NEW YORK CITY

Written records

In studying changes in crime in New York City, Rutgers University researchers were obviously interested in data from police files and other written records. New York's UCR figures tell only a small part of the story. More important are detailed data on crime and arrests collected as part of the city's Compstat process. George Kelling and Catherine Coles (1996:147) point to Compstat's

value in "unpacking" crime data—providing street-level detail that helps in strategy formulation. Compstat and related data are not routinely available to the public, but the NYPD granted special access to the Rutgers University researchers. For example, the Rutgers team analyzed weekly data on crime reports and arrests, both citywide and within each of the city's 76 precincts.

Direct observation

Speaking of Compstat, police and public officials from all over the world have visited New York to observe how the department's command staff use crime data to hold the city's precinct commanders accountable for crime in their areas

---

ultimately linked to our purposes for conducting research, subject to constraints on what is possible and ethical. Sometimes, multiple measures of some concept need to be incorporated into a single research design. By the same token, criminal justice research frequently uses multiple sources of data collected through different methods of observation, as described in the box titled "Using Three Types of Data in New York City."

Let's consider an example of a case in which different ways of collecting data might be used. Chapter 5 discussed a widely cited article in which James Q. Wilson and George Kelling (1982) argue that broken windows, graffiti, abandoned buildings, junk cars, and the like are symbols of urban decay that people associate with crime problems. Other researchers have referred to such urban problems as "incivilities," which also include signs of social disorder like the presence of homeless persons, drunks, or teenage gangs on city streets (Skogan, 1990). As you may remember, incivilities can be the source of two related problems: (1) They may facilitate crime directly, or (2) they may contribute to the fear of crime.

How could we measure and collect data on incivilities? As you might realize after a bit of thought, incivilities can be assessed using each of the three ways of collecting data. A survey could show whether urban residents believe incivilities are present in their neighborhoods or perceive them to be problems. Direct observation of neighborhood conditions would reveal the presence of broken windows, graffiti, and people loitering in the street. We might also develop measures that rate the conditions of buildings in a neighborhood, ranging from good to fair to poor, or some similar scale. Or, if litter is viewed as an incivility or a sign that people don't care about neighborhood conditions, direct observation could produce a litter index by counting discarded wine bottles, burger wrappers, and the like. Written records could also be sources of data for incivility measures. Records of arrests for loitering, disturbing the peace, or public indecency are possible candidates. Or housing department records could be consulted to develop a measure of abandoned or substandard buildings. We could check a New York City Web site to find statistics on "Acceptably clean sidewalks," defined

(Silverman, 1999). If we were interested in studying how changes in police strategy contributed to declines in New York's crime, we would probably want to observe Compstat meetings. We could also learn about crime and policing in New York by observing patrol officers and other police on duty. Riding with police on patrol has become a common and important data collection method for researchers who study law enforcement. Research staff from Rutgers regularly attended citywide and lower-level Compstat meetings and observed samples of New York City police on patrol.

Asking questions

While riding with police, we could also interview them. Police ride-alongs make it possible for researchers to informally interview police, as they spend several hours together in a patrol car. This is another element of "squad car anthropology"—asking questions. Our study of police strategy development would probably also lead us to interview police executives and commanders. Asking questions would help us learn what sorts of actions were implemented, in which areas and at what times. Finally, we should consider interviewing residents of different areas in New York. Reflecting our interest in changes in crime rates, we would probably ask about victimization, satisfaction with police, and general concerns about crime. Interviews with patrol officers and those assigned to special units addressed each of these issues and became an important source of data for Rutgers researchers.

as follows: "Percent of sample blocks in the community rated acceptably clean by Mayor's Office field inspectors based on a seven-point picture-based rating scale." (Office of the May-or, 2003).

The box "Multiple Measures in Home Detention" provides another example of how information obtained through each of the three methods of data collection was used to address research questions.

General Issues in Data Collection

Decisions about data collection must take into account a few general issues.

Apart from concerns specific to each data collection technique, we must address some general issues in deciding what data collection approach is best for a specific research application. These include the familiar concepts of reliability and validity of measures. Researchers also need to consider whether measures are obtrusive or unobtrusive. Above all, because measures and data collection plans are never perfect, criminal justice researchers need to be careful and creative.

Measurement Validity and Reliability

As you know, in making plans to collect data, researchers must be attentive to the validity and reliability of their measures. When researchers begin to think more specifically about actually making measurements and when they actually begin to collect data, they often think of validity and reliability questions that might have been overlooked in the design stage. For example, in their study of electronically monitored home detention (ELMO), Terry Baumer and Robert Mendelsohn (1990) initially thought that measuring successful computer-generated phone contacts with people assigned to ELMO would be straightforward; the computer would automatically keep track of calls and their outcomes. This should produce a valid and reliable measure of computer contact; the researchers would simply copy data from computer disks.

After beginning their research, however, Baumer and Mendelsohn encountered three types of problems in using the computer contact data. First was the problem of translating the manufacturer's computer codes into symbols the researchers could understand. This

MULTIPLE MEASURES IN HOME DETENTION

Terry Baumer and Robert Mendelsohn (1990) conducted an experimental evaluation of electronic monitoring (ELMO) as a supplement to home detention. People convicted of misdemeanors or minor nonviolent felonies were randomly assigned to home detention with ELMO (the experimental group) or home detention with manual monitoring (the control group). Subjects in the control group were monitored through phone calls and personal visits to homes and workplaces by staff in the implementing agency, a county community corrections department.

ELMO is intended to enhance the supervision of persons sentenced to home detention while conserving agency staff resources. ELMO subjects were fitted with electronic devices worn on a wrist or ankle; a base unit was attached to their home telephone. Several times per day (and night), a centrally located computer dialed the home of each ELMO subject, announcing that the "On Guard" system was calling and instructing whoever answered the phone to place the electronic anklet or wristlet in the base unit. When done correctly, this completed an electronic circuit and the computer recorded a successful telephone contact.

The evaluation sought to determine whether ELMO reduced misconduct by people while they were on home detention, as well as subsequent arrests up to 1 year after they completed their home detention sentence. In addition, Baumer and Mendelsohn were interested in the program's day-to-day operation in a community corrections agency and in the ways ELMO affected the lives of those who wore the bracelets. More specifically, their research addressed these questions:

1. How many people in the experimental and control groups were re-arrested within one year of their release?
2. Were ELMO subjects more or less frequently cited for misbehavior than subjects on home detention with manual monitoring?
3. Did the implementing agency understand the ELMO technology? Was the ELMO equipment readily integrated into routine agency operations, or did it disrupt normal agency activities?
4. For the experimental group, how did ELMO affect their daily lives? Was wearing the bracelet inconvenient, embarrassing, or uncomfortable? Was being subject to a call at any time of the day or night stressful or annoying?

problem was eventually solved, but only after laborious translation of computer codes.

Second, attempting to contact someone on home detention could be unsuccessful in a surprising variety of ways. Of course, if no one answered the phone after several rings, that was an unsuccessful contact attempt. If the phone was answered but no contact was made between the base unit and the wristlet or anklet, the computer recorded an "unsuccessful." Getting a busy signal, an answering machine, or a voice mail system also resulted in an "unsuccessful."

The third problem was most interesting and troublesome. People assigned to ELMO and manual home detention could legitimately be away from home while working at their job. Normally, the computer would be programmed not to call people during their scheduled working hours. Schedules frequently changed, however, sometimes on short notice. Baumer and Mendelsohn found that ELMO subjects spent more time on the job, often seeking overtime, simply to get out of the house. Problems emerged because community corrections staff were not always able to reprogram the computer's calling schedule to accommodate work schedule changes. Furthermore, when the computer got one unsuccessful call outcome, it was programmed to accelerate the number of repeat calls—something like an increasingly frantic attempt to make contact. This, of course, had the effect of multiplying the number of unsuccessful calls, even if the person to whom the computer was "reaching out" was legitimately absent from home.

In this example, what appeared at first to be a valid measure, reliably recorded by a computer, was, in fact, far from perfect and required

To address these questions, Baumer and Mendelsohn collected data by consulting written records, asking questions, and making direct observations. Police arrest records were used to assess recidivism by persons in the treatment and control groups. To answer the second question, researchers examined records of misconduct that were maintained by the implementing agency. ELMO computer technology afforded another source of information about misconduct, one that was also used by the implementing agency. Results from each computer-generated call to ELMO subjects were automatically recorded, producing a form of direct observation.

Baumer and Mendelsohn conducted extensive observations of day-to-day operations at the community corrections department. From these observations, they concluded that the ELMO technology did initially disrupt other routine tasks. But after some initial difficulties, a staff member integrated the computer-generated data into other information on subject performance that was regularly consulted by agency staff and administrators.

All experimental and control subjects were interviewed before beginning home detention and after completing their sentence. The interview schedule included several questions about personal and family reactions to being constantly subject to a phone call and to having to wear the ELMO wristlet or anklet.

In one sense, the reactions of persons sentenced to ELMO-enhanced home detention could be obtained only by asking questions about their experience. However, Baumer and Mendelsohn took this one step further through participant observation: Each researcher "sentenced" himself to ELMO for 2 weeks, alternating the wristlet and anklet devices. This form of direct observation enabled the investigators to verify subject claims about the punitive aspects of home detention and provided rich detail about discomfort, inconvenience, and annoyance. The researchers, and their spouses, were awakened by 2:00 A.M. greetings from the tireless and tiresome "On Guard" system. Showering was difficult and stressful with one ear listening for the phone. These two male researchers devoted some additional thought to selecting each day's wardrobe; they also realized that the anklet-mounted device would present challenges to women who wore pantyhose or to persons of either gender partial to boots.

careful interpretation. So, in making decisions about measurement and data collection, we must be prepared to make some adjustments in case we encounter unexpected difficulty or ambiguity. After we begin to make actual observations, deficiencies may become evident in what initially appeared to be a valid measure. More commonly, the data collection process will reveal potential reliability problems that are difficult to anticipate in the design stages of a research project. The chapters that follow will describe how to identify and deal with reliability problems in each mode of data collection.

Being attentive to measurement quality is not merely a pro forma exercise that is easily taken care of in a research office. Unless they are using measures and data-collecting techniques that have been widely adopted and accepted by others, researchers are well advised to continually evaluate measurement and data collection procedures.

Obtrusive and Unobtrusive Measures

Social scientists distinguish between obtrusive and unobtrusive measurement. In obtrusive or reactive measurement, research subjects are aware that they are being studied. Unobtrusive measurement does not involve direct interaction between researchers and subjects, and subjects are not aware that they are being studied. For example, asking people whether they have ever stolen some article from a shop is obtrusive; covertly observing people in a shop and then counting how many people steal something is unobtrusive.

Researchers often prefer unobtrusive measures because they can reduce or eliminate the possibility of threats to validity due to testing bias. By not interacting directly with subjects, researchers can obtain measures that are uncontaminated by subjects' reactions to the measurement process.

Exactly what kinds of measurement are obtrusive and unobtrusive is not always a straightforward question. Some textbooks obscure the distinguishing characteristic—Are subjects aware they are being measured?—by stating that direct observation and written records are unobtrusive measures. In many situations, this is true, but not always. Let's consider a hypothetical example.

Assume you are interested in whether restricting the sale of paint in aerosol cans will reduce the incidence of graffiti. That's certainly a reasonable expectation, and a city ordinance prohibiting the sale of spray paint to persons under 18 years of age might be a reasonable approach to trying to reduce graffiti. You might test your hypothesis with a quasi-experimental design in which you obtain pretest and posttest measures before and after the ordinance goes into effect.

Now consider some possible unobtrusive measures of the dependent variable, graffiti. An obvious one is direct observation. You might observe buildings, fences, and other structures or surfaces, counting the number that exhibited graffiti or perhaps measuring the total surface area covered by paint. However, this will work only if you actually make pretest observations before the law goes into effect. If you decide to test your hypothesis some time after the law goes into effect, you obviously cannot make pretest observations.

An alternative measure is to consult police records of arrests for vandalism. You might first check all vandalism arrests before and after the law became effective and then screen the arrests for cases involving graffiti. A decrease might be attributable to the ordinance banning spray paint sales to minors, subject to a careful assessment of possible threats to the validity of that inference.

But are police records of arrests for vandalism really an unobtrusive measure? If you go to the police station to get copies of arrest records, you will not be interacting with subjects, and the subjects themselves—people arrested for vandalism—will not be aware of their role in your research. But such subjects are aware of their role as persons arrested for vandalism, and they do interact with police officers. Although your secondary measurement—getting copies from the police—is clearly unobtrusive, the primary measurement—arrest by police—is anything but unobtrusive. Subjects may not be aware of their participation in your research, but they are certainly aware of their participation in data collection by the arresting officers.

The point here is similar to one mentioned earlier in this chapter: A researcher may collect data from written records, but some previous measurement process actually produced the written records. The idea that written records, or secondary sources of data, are unobtrusive measures can be misleading. The key issue is how the written records were originally produced. To what extent were research subjects aware of the measurement process when measures were originally collected?

Subjects awareness of being measured is an example of testing as a threat to validity, discussed in Chapter 7. Rather than distinguishing between obtrusive and unobtrusive measurement, it is more useful to focus on reducing bias or threats to validity in the measurement process generally. If we suspect that interactive data collection such as a survey will produce biased measures, we should try to develop some noninteractive measures or other procedures that will reduce the potential bias.

Be Careful, but Be Creative

These are our final introductory words of wisdom before we move to the topic of sampling. In the chapters that follow, we highlight the importance of being cautious in formulating questionnaire items, making direct observations, or using data that were originally collected by someone else. Being attentive to questions of validity and reliability is a critical first step in careful measurement and data collection. In particular, researchers who use written records should be diligent in learning how those records were produced.

Being careful is important, but so is being creative. Because measurement is so important but often so difficult in criminal justice research, it is frequently necessary to devise creative substitutes for direct measures. Chapters 9–11 present several examples of creative approaches to measurement and data collection.

The Logic of Probability Sampling

Probability sampling helps researchers generalize from observed cases to unobserved ones.

In selecting a group of subjects for study, social science researchers often use some type of sampling. Sampling in general refers to selecting part of a population. In selecting samples, we want to do two related things. First, we select samples to represent some larger population of people or other things. If we are interested in attitudes about a community correctional facility, for example, we might draw a sample of neighborhood residents, ask them some questions, and use their responses to represent the attitudes of all neighborhood residents. Or, in studying cases in a criminal court, we may not be able to examine all cases, so we select a sample to represent that population of all cases processed through some court.

Second, we may want to generalize from a sample to an unobserved population the sample is intended to represent. If we interview a sample of community residents, we may want to generalize our findings to all community residents—those we interviewed and those we did not. We might similarly expect that our sample of criminal court cases can be generalized to the population of all criminal court cases.

A special type of sampling that enables us to generalize to a larger population is known as **probability sampling,** a method of selection in which each member of a population has a known chance or probability of being selected. Knowing the probability that any individual member of a population could be selected makes it possible for us to make predictions that our sample accurately represents the larger population.

If all members of a population are identical in all respects—demographic characteristics, attitudes, experiences, behaviors, and so on—there is no need for careful sampling procedures. Any sample will be sufficient. In this extreme case of homogeneity, in fact, a single case will be sufficient as a sample to study characteristics of the whole population.

In reality, of course, the human beings who make up any real population are heterogeneous, varying in many ways. Figure 8.1 offers a simplified illustration of a heterogeneous population: The 100 members of this small population differ by gender and race. We'll use this hypothetical micropopulation to illustrate various aspects of sampling.

A sample of individuals from a population, if it is to provide useful descriptions of the total population, must contain essentially the same variations that exist in the population. This is not as simple as it might seem. Let's look at some of the possible biases in selection or ways researchers might go astray. Then we will see how probability sampling provides an efficient method for selecting a sample that should adequately reflect variations that exist in the population.

Conscious and Unconscious Sampling Bias

At first glance, it may seem as if sampling is a rather straightforward matter. To select a sample of 100 lawyers, a researcher might simply go to a courthouse and interview the first 100 lawyers who walk through the door. This kind of sampling method is often used by untrained researchers, but it is subject to serious biases. In connection with sampling, *bias* simply means that those selected are not "typical" or

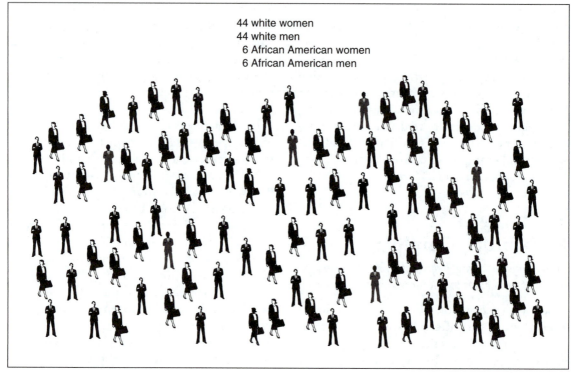

44 white women
44 white men
6 African American women
6 African American men

Figure 8.1   A Population of 100 Folks

"representative" of the larger populations they have been chosen from. This kind of bias is virtually inevitable when a researcher picks subjects casually.

Figure 8.2 illustrates what can happen when we simply select people who are convenient for study. Although women make up only 50 percent of our micropopulation, those closest to the researcher (people in the upper right-hand corner of Figure 8.2) happen to be 70 percent women. Although the population is 12 percent African American, none were selected into this sample of people who happened to be conveniently situated near the researcher.

Moving beyond the risks inherent in simply studying people who are convenient, we need to consider other potential problems as well. To begin, our own personal leanings or biases may affect the sample selected in this manner; hence, the sample will not truly represent the population of lawyers. Suppose a researcher is a little

intimidated by lawyers who look particularly prosperous, believing that they might ridicule his research effort. He might consciously or unconsciously avoid interviewing them. Or he might believe that the attitudes of "establishment" lawyers are irrelevant to his research purposes and avoid interviewing them.

Even if the researcher seeks to interview a "balanced" group of lawyers, he won't know the exact proportions of different types of lawyers who make up such a balance and won't always be able to identify the different types merely by watching them walk by.

The researcher might make a conscious effort to interview, say, every 10th lawyer who enters the courthouse, but he still cannot be sure of a representative sample because different types of lawyers visit the courthouse with different frequencies, and some never go to the courthouse at all. Thus, the resulting sample will overrepresent lawyers who visit the courthouse more often.

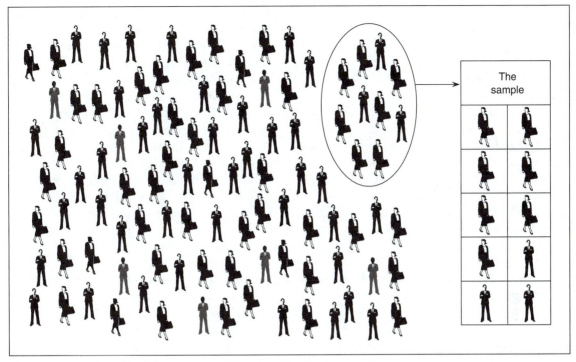

Figure 8.2 A Sample of Convenience: Easy, but Not Representative

Similarly, "public opinion call-in polls"—in which radio stations or newspapers ask people to call specified telephone numbers to register their opinions—cannot be trusted to represent the general population. At the very least, not everyone in the population is even aware of the poll. Those who are aware of it have some things in common simply because they listen to the same radio station or read the same newspaper. As market researchers understand very well, a classical music station has a different audience than a hard rock station. Adding even more bias to the sample, those who are motivated to take part in the poll are probably different from others who are not so motivated.

A similar problem invalidates polls by magazines and newspapers that print coupons for readers to complete and mail in. Even among those who are aware of such polls, not all will express an opinion, especially if doing so will cost them a stamp, an envelope, or a telephone charge.

The possibilities for inadvertent sampling bias are endless and not always obvious. Fortunately, some techniques can help us avoid bias.

Representativeness and Probability of Selection

Although the term *representativeness* has no precise, scientific meaning, it carries a common-sense meaning that makes it useful in the discussion of sampling. As we'll use the term here, a sample is *representative* of the population from which it is selected if the aggregate characteristics of the sample closely approximate those same aggregate characteristics in the population. If the population, for example, contains 50 percent women, a representative sample will also contain "close to" 50 percent women. Later in this chapter, we'll discuss "how close" in detail. Notice that samples need not be representative in all respects; representativeness is limited to those characteristics that are relevant to the substantive interests of the study.

A basic principle of probability sampling is that a sample will be representative of the population from which it is selected if all members of the population have an equal chance of being selected in the sample. Samples that have this quality are often labeled **equal probability of selection method (EPSEM)** samples. This principle forms the basis of probability sampling.

Even carefully selected EPSEM samples are seldom, if ever, perfectly representative of the populations from which they are drawn. Nevertheless, probability sampling offers two special advantages.

First, probability samples, though never perfectly representative, are typically more representative than other types of samples because they avoid the biases discussed in the preceding section. In practice, there is a greater likelihood that a probability sample will be representative of the population from which it is drawn than that a nonprobability sample will be.

Second, and more importantly, probability theory permits us to estimate the accuracy or representativeness of the sample. Conceivably, an uninformed researcher might, through wholly haphazard means, select a sample that nearly perfectly represents the larger population. The odds are against doing so, however, and we cannot estimate the likelihood that a haphazard sample will achieve representativeness. The probability sample, in contrast, can provide an accurate estimate of success or failure.

Probability Theory and Sampling Distribution

Probability theory permits inferences about how sampled data are distributed around the value found in a larger population.

With a basic understanding of the logic of probability sampling in hand, we can examine in more detail how probability sampling works in practice. We will then be able to devise specific sampling techniques and assess the results of those techniques. To do so, we first need to define four important terms.

A **sample element** is that unit about which information is collected and that provides the basis of analysis. Typically, in survey research, elements are people or certain types of people. However, other kinds of units can be the elements for criminal justice research—correctional facilities, gangs, police beats, or court cases, for example. Elements and units of analysis are often the same in a given study, although the former refers to sample selection and the latter to data analysis.

A **population** is the theoretically specified grouping of study elements. Whereas the vague "delinquents" might be the target for a study, the delineation of the population includes the definition of the element "delinquents" (for example, being charged with a delinquent offense) and the time referent for the study (delinquents as of when?). Translating the abstract "adult drug addicts" into a workable population requires specifying the age that defines "adult" and the level of drug use that constitutes an "addict." Specifying "college student" includes a consideration of full- and part-time students, degree and nondegree candidates, undergraduate and graduate students, and so on.

A **population parameter** is the summary description of a given variable in a population. The average income of all families in a city and the age distribution of the city's population are parameters. An important portion of criminal justice research involves estimating population parameters on the basis of sample observations.

The summary description of a given variable in the sample is called a **sample statistic.** Sample statistics are used to make estimates of population parameters. Thus, the average income computed from a sample and the age distribution of that sample are statistics, and those statistics are used to estimate income and age parameters in a population.

Figure 8.3   A Population of 10 People with $0–9

The ultimate purpose of sampling is to select a set of elements from a population in such a way that descriptions of those elements (sample statistics) accurately portray the parameters of the total population from which the elements are selected. Probability sampling enhances the likelihood of accomplishing this aim and also provides methods for estimating the degree of probable success.

The key to this process is random selection. In random selection, each element has an equal chance of being selected independent of any other event in the selection process. Flipping a coin is the most frequently cited example: The "selection" of a head or a tail is independent of previous selections of heads or tails.

There are two reasons for using random selection methods. First, this procedure serves as a check on conscious or unconscious bias on the part of the researcher. The researcher who selects cases on an intuitive basis might choose cases that will support his or her research expectations or hypotheses. Random selection erases this danger. Second, and more importantly, random selection offers access to the body of probability theory, which provides the basis for estimates of population parameters and estimates of error.

The Sampling Distribution of 10 Cases

To see how this works, let's first consider a simple example of sampling and then move to a more elaborate one.* Our ultimate objective here is to understand the **sampling distribution,** defined as the range of sample statistics we will obtain if we select many samples.

Suppose there are 10 people in a group, and each has a certain amount of money in his or her pocket. To simplify, let's assume that one person has no money, another has $1, another has $2, and so forth up to the person who has $9. Figure 8.3 illustrates this population of 10 people.

Our task is to determine the average amount of money one person has—specifically, the

---

* We thank Hanan Selvin for suggesting this way of introducing probability sampling.

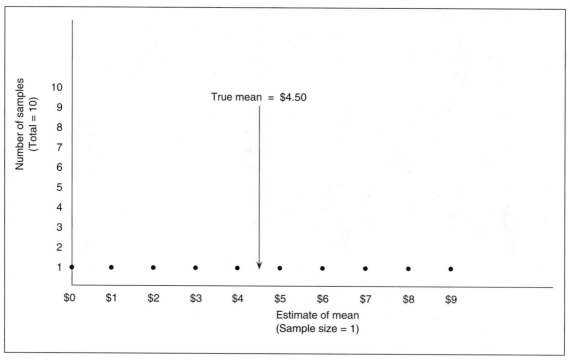

Figure 8.4 The Sampling Distribution of Samples of 1

mean number of dollars. If you simply add up the money shown in Figure 8.3, the total is $45, so the mean is $4.50 (45 ÷ 10). Our purpose in the rest of this example is to estimate that mean without actually observing all 10 individuals. We'll do that by selecting random samples from the population and using the means of those samples to estimate the mean for the whole population.

To start, suppose we select—at random—a sample of only 1 person from the 10. Depending on which person we select, we will estimate the group's mean as anywhere from $0 to $9. Figure 8.4 shows a display of those 10 possible samples. The 10 dots shown on the graph represent the 10 "sample" means we will get as estimates of the population. The range of the dots on the graph is the sampling distribution—it shows how all of our possible samples of 1 are distributed. Obviously, it is not a good idea to select a sample of only 1 because we stand a

good chance of missing the true mean of $4.50 by quite a bit.

What if we take samples of 2 each? As you can see from Figure 8.5, increasing the sample size improves our estimations. Once again, each dot represents a possible sample. There are 45 possible samples of two elements: $0/$1, $0/$2, . . . , $7/$8, $8/$9. Moreover, some of these samples produce the same means. For example, $0/$6, $1/$5, and $2/$4 all produce means of $3. In Figure 8.5, the three dots shown above the $3 mean represent those 3 samples.

Notice that the means we get from the 45 samples are not evenly distributed. Rather, they are somewhat clustered around the true value of $4.50. Only 2 samples deviate by as much as $4 from the true value ($0/$1 and $8/$9), whereas 5 of the samples give the true estimate of $4.50, and another 8 samples miss the mark by only $.50 (plus or minus).

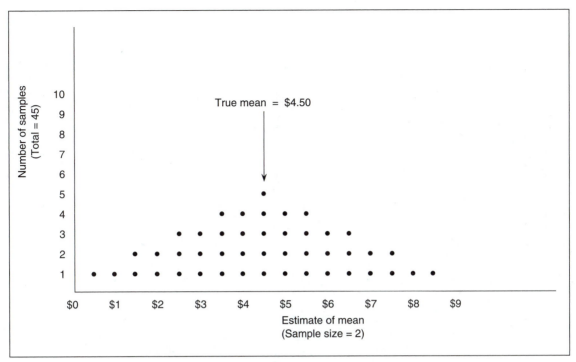

Figure 8.5 The Sampling Distribution of Samples of 2

Now suppose we select even larger samples. What will that do to our estimates of the mean? Figure 8.6 presents the sampling distributions of samples of 3, 4, 5, and 6. The progression of the sampling distributions is clear. Every increase in sample size improves the distribution of estimates of the mean in two related ways. First, in the distribution for samples of 5, for example, no sample means are at the extreme ends of the distribution. Why? Because it is not possible to select five elements from our population and obtain an average of less than $2 or greater than $7. The second way sampling distributions improve with larger samples is that sample means cluster more and more around the true population mean of $4.50. Figure 8.6 clearly shows this tendency.

The limiting case in this procedure, of course, is to select a sample of 10. Then there is only one possible sample (everyone), and it gives the true mean of $4.50.

From Sampling Distribution to Parameter Estimate

Let's turn now to a more realistic sampling situation and see how the notion of sampling distribution applies. Assume that we wish to study the population of Placid Coast, California, to assess the levels of approval or disapproval of a proposed law to ban possession of handguns within the city limits.

Our target population is all adult residents. In order to draw an actual sample, we need some sort of list of elements in our population; such a list is called a **sampling frame.** Assume our sampling frame is a voter registration list of, say, 20,000 registered voters in Placid Coast. The elements are the individual registered voters.

The variable under consideration is attitudes toward the proposed law: approve and disapprove. Measured in this way, attitude toward the law is a binomial variable; it can have

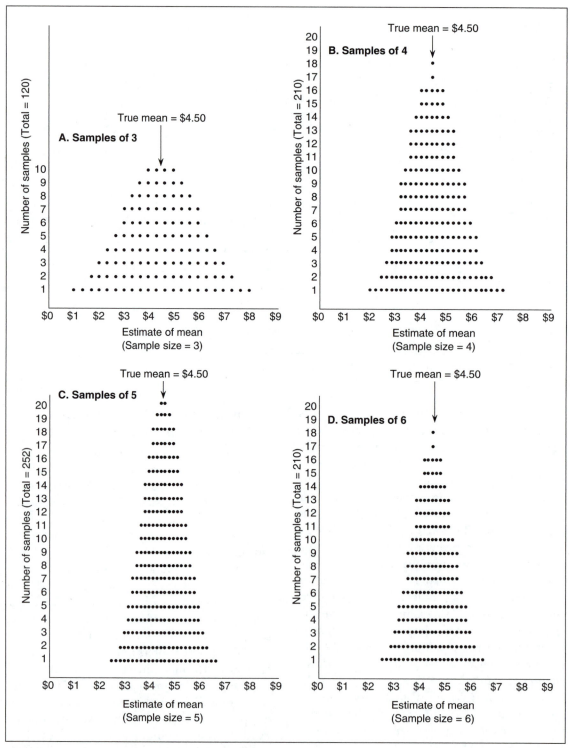

Figure 8.6   The Sampling Distribution of Samples of 3, 4, 5, and 6

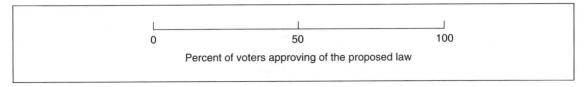

Figure 8.7   The Range of Possible Sample Study Results

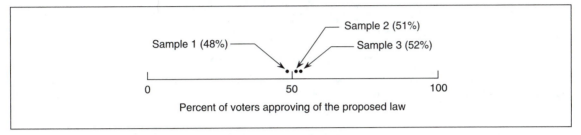

Figure 8.8   Results Produced by Three Hypothetical Samples

only two values. We'll select a random sample of, say, 100 persons for the purpose of estimating the population parameter for approval of the proposed law.

Figure 8.7 presents all the possible values of this parameter in the population—from 0 percent approval to 100 percent approval. The midpoint of the line—50 percent—represents half the voters approving of the handgun ban and the other half disapproving.

To choose our sample, we assign each person on the voter registration list a number and use a computer program to generate 100 random numbers. Then we interview the 100 people whose numbers have been selected and ask for their attitudes toward the handgun ban: whether they approve or disapprove. Suppose this operation gives us 48 people who approve of the law and 52 who disapprove. We present this statistic by placing a dot at the point representing 48 percent, as shown in Figure 8.8.

Now suppose we select another sample of 100 people in exactly the same fashion and measure their approval or disapproval of the proposed law. Perhaps 51 people in the second sample approve of the law. We place another dot in the appropriate place on the line in Fig-

ure 8.8. Repeating this process once more, we may discover that 52 people in the third sample approve of the handgun ban; we add a third dot to Figure 8.8.

Figure 8.8 now presents the three different sample statistics that represent the percentages of people in each of the three random samples who approved of the proposed law. Each of the random samples, then, gives us an estimate of the percentage of people in the total population of registered voters who approve of the handgun law. Unfortunately, we now have three separate estimates.

To rescue ourselves from this dilemma, let's draw more and more samples of 100 registered voters each, question each of the samples concerning their approval or disapproval, and plot the new sample statistics on our summary graph. In drawing many such samples, we discover that some of the new samples provide duplicate estimates, as in our earlier illustration with 10 cases. Figure 8.9 shows the sampling distribution of hundreds of samples. This is often referred to as a normal or bell-shaped curve.

Notice that by increasing the number of samples selected and interviewed we have also increased the range of estimates provided by

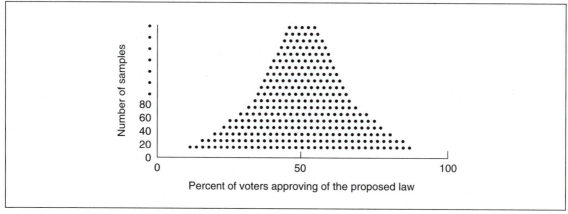

Figure 8.9   The Sampling Distribution

the sampling operation. In one sense, we have increased our dilemma in attempting to find the parameter in the population. Fortunately, probability theory provides certain important rules about the sampling distribution shown in Figure 8.9.

Estimating Sampling Error

Probability theory can help resolve our dilemma with some basic statistical concepts. First, if many independent random samples are selected from a population, then the sample statistics provided by those samples will be distributed around the population parameter in a known way. Thus, although Figure 8.9 shows a wide range of estimates, more of them are in the vicinity of 50 percent than elsewhere in the graph. Probability theory tells us, then, that the true value is in the vicinity of 50 percent.

Second, probability theory gives us a formula for estimating how closely the sample statistics are clustered around the true value:

$$s = \sqrt{\frac{P \times Q}{n}}$$

where s is the **standard error**—defined as a measure of sampling error—n is the number of cases in each sample, and P and Q are the population parameters for the binomial. If 60 percent of registered voters approve of the ban on handguns and 40 percent disapprove, then P

and Q are 60 percent and 40 percent, or .6 and .4, respectively.

To see how probability theory makes it possible for us to estimate sampling error, suppose that in reality 50 percent of the people approve of the proposed law and 50 percent disapprove. These are the population parameters we are trying to estimate with our samples. Recall that we have been selecting samples of 100 cases each. When these numbers are plugged into the formula, we get

$$s = \sqrt{\frac{.5 \times .5}{100}} = .05$$

The standard error equals .05, or 5 percent.

In probability theory, the standard error is a valuable piece of information because it indicates how closely the sample estimates will be distributed around the population parameter. In other words, the standard error tells us how sample statistics will be dispersed or clustered around a population parameter. If you are familiar with the standard deviation in statistics (a topic we cover in Chapter 13), you may recognize that the standard error in this case is the standard deviation of the sampling distribution.

Specifically, probability theory indicates that certain proportions of the sample estimates will fall within specified increments—each equal to one standard error—from the population parameter. Approximately 34 percent (.3413) of the sample estimates will fall within one standard error increment above the population parameter, and another 34 percent will fall within one standard error increment below the parameter. In our example, the standard error increment is 5 percent, so we know that 34 percent of our samples will give estimates of approval between 50 percent (the parameter) and 55 percent (one standard error above); another 34 percent of the samples will give estimates between 50 percent and 45 percent (one standard error below the parameter). Taken together, then, we know that roughly two-thirds (68 percent) of the samples will give estimates between 45 and 55 percent, which is within 5 percent of the parameter.

The standard error is also a function of the sample size—an inverse function. This means that as the sample size increases the standard error decreases. And as the sample size increases, the several samples will be clustered nearer to the true value (Figures 8.5 and 8.6 illustrate this graphically). Another rule of thumb is evident in the formula for the standard error: Because of the square root operation, the standard error is reduced by half if the sample size is quadrupled. In our example, samples of 100 produce a standard error of 5 percent; to reduce the standard error to 2.5 percent, we would have to increase the sample size to 400.

All of this information is provided by established probability theory in reference to the selection of large numbers of random samples. If the population parameter is known and many random samples are selected, probability theory allows us to predict how many of the samples will fall within specified intervals from the parameter.

Of course, this discussion illustrates only the *logic* of probability sampling. It does not describe the way research is actually conducted. Usually, we do not know the parameter; we conduct a sample survey precisely because we want to estimate that value. Moreover, we don't actually select large numbers of samples; we select only one sample. What probability theory does is provide the basis for making inferences about the typical research situation. Knowing what it

would be like to select thousands of samples allows us to make assumptions about the one sample we do select and study.

Confidence Levels and Confidence Intervals

Probability theory specifies that 68 percent of that fictitious large number of samples will produce estimates that fall within one standard error of the parameter. As researchers, we can turn the logic around and infer that any single random sample has a 68 percent chance of falling within that range. In this regard, we speak of **confidence levels:** We are 68 percent confident that our sample estimate is within one standard error of the parameter. Or we may say that we are 95 percent confident that the sample statistic is within two standard errors of the parameter, and so forth. Quite reasonably, our confidence level increases as the margin for error is extended. We are virtually positive (99.9 percent) that our statistic is within three standard errors of the true value.

Although we may be confident (at some level) of being within a certain range of the parameter, we seldom know what the parameter is. To resolve this dilemma, we substitute our sample estimate for the parameter in the formula; lacking the true value, we substitute the best available guess.

The result of these inferences and estimations is that we are able to estimate a population parameter and also the expected degree of error on the basis of one sample drawn from a population. We begin with this question: What percentage of the registered voters in Placid Coast approve of the proposed handgun ban? We select a random sample of 100 registered voters and interview them. We might then report that our best estimate is that 50 percent of registered voters approve of the gun ban and that we are 95 percent confident that between 40 and 60 percent (plus or minus two standard errors) approve. The range from 40 to 60 percent is called the **confidence interval.** At the 68 percent confidence level, the confidence interval is 45–55 percent.

The logic of confidence levels and confidence intervals also provides the basis for determining the appropriate sample size for a study. Once we decide on the sampling error we can tolerate, we can calculate the number of cases needed in our sample.

Random Sampling and Probability Theory Summed Up

This, then, is the basic logic of probability sampling. Random selection permits the researcher to link findings from a sample to the body of probability theory in order to estimate the accuracy of those findings. All statements of accuracy in sampling must specify both a confidence level and a confidence interval. Researchers may report that they are *x* percent confident that the population parameter is between two specific values.

This discussion has considered only one type of statistic: the percentages produced by a binomial variable. The same logic, however, applies to the examination of other statistics, such as mean income. Because those computations are somewhat more complicated, we chose to consider only binomials in this introduction.

Be aware that the survey uses of probability theory as we have been discussing them are not wholly justified technically. The theory of sampling distribution makes assumptions that almost never apply in actual survey conditions. For example, finding the number of samples contained within specified increments of standard errors assumes an infinitely large population and an infinite number of samples, among other things. Moreover, the inferential jump from the distribution of several samples to the probable characteristics of one sample is more complex than our simplified discussion suggests.

These cautions are important because researchers often overestimate the precision of estimates produced by use of probability theory in criminal justice and other social scientific research. Variations in sampling techniques and nonsampling factors may further reduce the legitimacy of such estimates. Nevertheless, the calculations discussed in this section can be ex-

tremely valuable to us in understanding and evaluating our data. Although the calculations do not provide as precise estimates as some researchers might assume, they can be quite valid for practical purposes. They are unquestionably more valid than less rigorously derived estimates based on less rigorous sampling methods.

Most importantly, we should be familiar with the basic logic underlying the calculations. If we are so informed, we will be able to react sensibly to our own data and to those reported by others.

Populations and Sampling Frames

The correspondence between a target population and sampling frames affects the generalizability of samples.

Although as researchers and as consumers of research we need to understand the theoretical foundations of sampling, it is no less important to appreciate the less-than-perfect conditions that exist in the field. One aspect of field conditions that requires a compromise in terms of theoretical conditions and assumptions is the relationship between populations and sampling frames.

A sampling frame is the list or quasi-list of elements from which a probability sample is selected. We say "quasi-list" because, even though an actual list might not exist, we can draw samples as if there were a list. Properly drawn samples provide information appropriate for describing the population of elements that compose the sampling frame — nothing more. This point is important in view of the common tendency for researchers to select samples from a particular sampling frame and then make assertions about a population that is similar, but not identical, to the study population defined by the sampling frame.

For example, if we want to study the attitudes of corrections administrators toward determinant sentencing policies, we might select a sample by consulting the membership roster of the American Correctional Association. In this case, the membership roster is our sampling frame, and corrections administrators are the population we wish to describe. However, unless all corrections administrators are members of the American Correctional Association and all members are listed in the roster, it would be incorrect to generalize results to all corrections administrators.

Studies of organizations are often the simplest from a sampling standpoint because organizations typically have membership lists. In such cases, the list of members may be an acceptable sampling frame. If a random sample is selected from a membership list, then the data collected from that sample may be taken as representative of all members—if all members are included in the list. It is, however, imperative that researchers learn how complete or incomplete such lists might be and limit their generalizations to listed sample elements rather than to an entire population.

Other lists of individuals may be especially relevant to the research needs of a particular study. Lists of licensed drivers, automobile owners, welfare recipients, taxpayers, holders of weapons permits, and licensed professionals are just a few examples. Although it may be difficult to gain access to some of these lists, they provide excellent sampling frames for specialized research purposes.

Telephone directories are frequently used for "quick and dirty" public opinion polls. Undeniably, they are easy and inexpensive to use, and that is no doubt the reason for their popularity. Still, they have several limitations. A given directory will not include new subscribers or those who have requested unlisted numbers. Sampling is further complicated by the inclusion of nonresidential listings in directories. Moreover, telephone directories are all too often taken to be a listing of a city's population, which is simply not the case. Lower-income people are less likely to have telephones, and higher-income people may have more than one line. A growing number of households are served only by wireless phone service and so are not listed in directories. Telephone companies may not publish listings for temporary residents such as students. And persons who live in institutions or group quarters—dormitories, nursing homes, rooming houses, and the like—are not listed in phone directories.

Street directories and tax maps are often used for easy samples of households, but they may also suffer from incompleteness and possible bias. For example, in strictly zoned urban regions, illegal housing units are unlikely to appear on official records. As a result, such units have no chance for selection, and sample findings will not be representative of those units, which are often substandard and overcrowded.

In a more general sense, it's worth viewing sampling frames as operational definitions of a study population. Just as operational definitions of variables describe how abstract concepts will be measured, sampling frames serve as a real-world version of an abstract study population. For example, we may want to study how criminologists deal with ethical issues in their research. We don't know how many criminologists exist out there, but we can develop a general idea about the population of criminologists. We could also operationalize the concept by using the membership directory for the American Society of Criminology—that list is our operational definition of "criminologist."

Types of Sampling Designs

Different types of sampling designs can be used alone or in combination for different research purposes.

The illustrations we have considered so far have been based on simple random sampling. However, researchers have a number of options in choosing their sampling method, each with its own advantages and disadvantages.

Simple Random Sampling

Simple random sampling forms the basis of probability theory and the statistical tools we use to estimate population parameters, standard error, and confidence intervals. More accurately, such statistics assume unbiased sampling, and simple random sampling is the foundation of unbiased sampling.

Once a sampling frame has been established in keeping with the guidelines we presented, to use simple random sampling the researcher assigns a single number to each element in the list, not skipping any number in the process. A table of random numbers, or a computer program for generating them, is then used to select elements for the sample.

If the sampling frame is a computerized database or some other form of machine-readable data, a simple random sample can be selected automatically by computer. In effect, the computer program numbers the elements in the sampling frame, generates its own series of random numbers, and prints out the list of elements selected.

Systematic Sampling

Simple random sampling is seldom used in practice, primarily because it is not usually the most efficient method, and it can be tedious if done manually. It typically requires a list of elements. And when such a list is available, researchers usually use **systematic sampling** rather than simple random sampling.

In systematic sampling, the researcher chooses all elements in the list for inclusion in the sample. If a list contains 10,000 elements and we want a sample of 1000, we select every 10th element for our sample. To ensure against any possible human bias, we should select the first element at random. Thus, to systematically select 1000 from a list of 10,000 elements, we begin by selecting a random number between 1 and 10. The element having that number, plus every 10th element following it, is included in the sample. This method technically is referred to as a systematic sample with a random start.

In practice, systematic sampling is virtually identical to simple random sampling. If the list of elements is indeed randomized before sampling, one might argue that a systematic sample drawn from that list is, in fact, a simple random sample.

Systematic sampling has one danger. A periodic arrangement of elements in the list can make systematic sampling unwise; this arrangement is usually called "periodicity." If the list of elements is arranged in a cyclical pattern that coincides with the sampling interval, a biased sample may be drawn. Suppose we select a sample of apartments in an apartment building. If the sample is drawn from a list of apartments arranged in numerical order (for example, 101, 102, 103, 104, 201, 202, and so on), there is a danger of the sampling interval coinciding with the number of apartments on a floor or some multiple of it. Then the samples might include only northwest-corner apartments or only apartments near the elevator. If these types of apartments have some other particular characteristic in common (for example, higher rent), the sample will be biased. The same potential danger would apply in a systematic sample of houses in a subdivision arranged with the same number of houses on a block.

In considering a systematic sample from a list, then, we need to carefully examine the nature of that list. If the elements are arranged in any particular order, we have to figure out whether that order will bias the sample to be selected and take steps to counteract any possible bias.

In summary, systematic sampling is usually superior to simple random sampling, in terms of convenience if nothing else. Problems in the ordering of elements in the sampling frame can usually be remedied quite easily.

Stratified Sampling

We have discussed two methods of selecting a sample from a list: random and systematic. **Stratification** is not an alternative to these methods, but it represents a possible modification in their use. Simple random sampling and systematic sampling both ensure a degree of representativeness and permit an estimate of the sampling error present. Stratified sampling is a method for obtaining a greater degree of representativeness—decreasing the probable sampling error. To understand why that is the case, we must return briefly to the basic theory of sampling distribution.

Recall that sampling error is reduced by two factors in the sample design: (1) A large sample produces a smaller sampling error than a small sample does, and (2) a homogeneous population produces samples with smaller sampling errors than a heterogeneous population does. If 99 percent of the population agrees with a certain statement, it is extremely unlikely that any probability sample will greatly misrepresent the extent of agreement. If the population is split 50–50 on the statement, then the sampling error will be much greater.

Stratified sampling is based on this second factor in sampling theory. Rather than selecting our sample from the total population at large, we select appropriate numbers of elements from homogeneous subsets of that population. To get a stratified sample of university students, for example, we first organize our population by college class and then draw appropriate numbers of freshmen, sophomores, juniors, and seniors. In a nonstratified sample, representation by class is subject to the same sampling error as other variables. In a sample stratified by class, the sampling error on this variable is reduced to zero.

Even more complex stratification methods are possible. In addition to stratifying by class, we might also stratify by gender, grade-point average, and so forth. In this fashion, we could ensure that our sample contains the proper numbers of freshman men with a 4.0 average, freshman women with a 4.0 average, and so forth.

The ultimate function of stratification, then, is to organize the population into homogeneous subsets (with heterogeneity between subsets) and to select the appropriate number of elements from each. To the extent that the subsets are homogeneous on the stratification variables, they may be homogeneous on other variables as well. Because age is usually related to college class, a sample stratified by class will be more representative in terms of age as well.

The choice of stratification variables typically depends on what variables are available.

Gender can often be determined in a list of names. Many local government sources of information on housing units are arranged geographically. Age, race, education, occupation, and other variables are often included on lists of persons who have had contact with criminal justice officials.

In selecting stratification variables, however, we should be concerned primarily with those that are presumably related to the variables we want to represent accurately. Because gender is related to many variables and is often available for stratification, it is frequently used. Age and race are related to many variables of interest in criminal justice research. Income is also related to many variables, but it is often not available for stratification. Geographic location within a city, state, or nation is related to many things. Within a city, stratification by geographic location usually increases representativeness in social class and ethnicity.

Stratified sampling ensures the proper representation of the stratification variables to enhance representation of other variables related to them. Taken as a whole, then, a stratified sample is likely to be more representative on a number of variables than a simple random sample is.

Disproportionate Stratified Sampling

Another use of stratification is to purposively produce samples that are not representative of a population on some variable, referred to as **disproportionate stratified sampling.** Because the purpose of sampling, as we have been discussing, is to represent a larger population, you may wonder why anyone would want to intentionally produce a sample that was *not* representative.

To understand the logic of disproportionate stratification, consider again the role of population homogeneity in determining sample size. If members of a population vary widely on some variable of interest, then larger samples must be drawn to adequately represent that population. Similarly, if only a small number of people in a population exhibit some attribute or characteristic of interest, then a large sample must be drawn to produce adequate numbers of elements that exhibit the uncommon condition. Disproportionate stratification is a way of obtaining sufficient numbers of these "rare" cases by selecting a number disproportionate to their representation in the population.

The best example of disproportionate sampling in criminal justice is a national crime survey in which one goal is to obtain some minimum number of crime victims in a sample. Because crime victimization for certain offenses—such as robbery or aggravated assault—is relatively rare on a national scale, persons who live in large urban areas, where serious crime is more common, are disproportionately sampled.

The British Crime Survey (BCS) is a nationwide survey of people ages 16 and over in England and Wales. Conducted approximately every other year since 1982, the BCS selectively oversamples people or areas to yield larger numbers of designated subjects than would result from proportionate random samples drawn from the population of England and Wales. In recent years, the BCS has included special questions to better understand contacts between ethnic minorities and police. In the 2000 BCS, ethnic minorities were disproportionately oversampled to produce a large enough number of ethnic minority respondents for later analysis.

Multistage Cluster Sampling

The preceding sections have described reasonably simple procedures for sampling from lists of elements. Unfortunately, however, many interesting research problems require the selection of samples from populations that cannot easily be listed for sampling purposes; that is, sampling frames are not readily available. Examples are the population of a city, state, or nation, and all police officers in the United States. In such cases, the sample design must be much more complex. Such a design typically involves the initial sampling of groups of elements—

clusters—followed by the selection of elements within each of the selected clusters. This procedure is called multistage **cluster sampling.**

Cluster sampling may be used when it is either impossible or impractical to compile an exhaustive list of the elements that compose the target population, such as all law enforcement officers in the United States. Often, however, population elements are already grouped into subpopulations, and a list of those subpopulations either exists or can be created.

Population elements, or aggregations of those elements, are referred to as **sampling units.** In the simplest forms of sampling, elements and units are the same thing—usually, people. But in cases in which a listing of elements is not available, we can often use some other unit that includes a grouping of elements.

Because U.S. law enforcement officers are employed by individual cities, counties, or states, it is possible to create lists of those political units. For cluster sampling, then, we could sample the list of cities, counties, and states in some manner as discussed previously (for example, a systematic sample stratified by population). Next, we could obtain lists of law enforcement officers from agencies in each of the selected jurisdictions. We could then sample each of the lists to provide samples of police officers for study.

Another typical situation concerns sampling among population areas such as a city. Although there is no single list of a city's population, citizens reside on discrete city blocks or census blocks. It is possible, therefore, to select a sample of blocks initially, create a list of persons who live on each of the selected blocks, and then sample persons from that list. In this case, blocks are treated as the primary sampling unit.

In a more complex design, we might sample blocks, list the households on each selected block, sample the households, list the persons who reside in each household, and, finally, sample persons within each selected household. This multistage sample design will lead to the ultimate selection of a sample of individuals without requiring the initial listing of all individuals in the city's population.

Multistage cluster sampling, then, involves the repetition of two basic steps: listing and sampling. The list of primary sampling units (city blocks) is compiled and perhaps stratified for sampling. Next, a sample of those units is selected. The list of secondary sampling units is then sampled, and the process continues.

Cluster sampling is highly recommended for its efficiency, but the price of that efficiency is a less accurate sample. A simple random sample drawn from a population list is subject to a single sampling error, but a two-stage cluster sample is subject to two sampling errors. First, the initial sample of clusters represents the population of clusters only within a range of sampling error. Second, the sample of elements selected within a given cluster represents all the elements in that cluster only within a range of sampling error. Thus, for example, we run a certain risk of selecting a sample of disproportionately wealthy city blocks, plus a sample of disproportionately wealthy households within those blocks. The best solution to this problem involves the number of clusters selected initially and the number of elements selected within each cluster.

Recall that sampling error is reduced by two factors: (1) an increase in the sample size and (2) increased homogeneity of the elements being sampled. These factors operate at each level of a multistage sample design. A sample of clusters will best represent all clusters if a large number are selected and if all clusters are very much alike. A sample of elements will best represent all elements in a given cluster if a large number are selected from the cluster and if all the elements in the cluster are very much alike.

A good general guideline for cluster design is to maximize the number of clusters selected while decreasing the number of elements within each cluster. But this scientific guideline must be balanced against an administrative constraint. The efficiency of cluster sampling is based on the ability to minimize the list of population elements. By initially selecting clusters, we need only list the elements that make up the selected clusters, not all elements in the entire population. Increasing the number of clusters, however, reduces this efficiency in cluster sampling. A small number of clusters may be listed more quickly and more cheaply than a large number. Remember that all the elements in a selected cluster must be listed even if only a few are to be chosen in the sample.

The final sample design will reflect these two constraints. In effect, we will probably select as many clusters as we can afford. So as not to leave this issue too open-ended, here is a rule of thumb: Population researchers conventionally aim for the selection of 5 households per census block. If a total of 2000 households are to be interviewed, researchers select 400 blocks with 5 household interviews on each. Figure 8.10 presents a graphic overview of this process.

As we turn to more detailed procedures in cluster sampling, keep in mind that this method almost inevitably involves a loss of accuracy. First, as noted earlier, a multistage sample design is subject to a sampling error at each stage. Because the sample size is necessarily smaller at each stage than the total sample size, the sampling error at each stage will be greater than would be the case for a single-stage random sample of elements. Second, sampling error is estimated on the basis of observed variance among the sample elements. When those elements are drawn from relatively homogeneous clusters, the estimated sampling error will be too optimistic and so must be corrected in light of the cluster sample design.

Multistage Cluster Sampling with Stratification

Thus far, we have looked at cluster sampling as though a simple random sample were selected at each stage of the design. In fact, we can use stratification techniques to refine and improve the sample being selected. The basic options available are essentially the same as those possible in single-stage sampling from a list. In

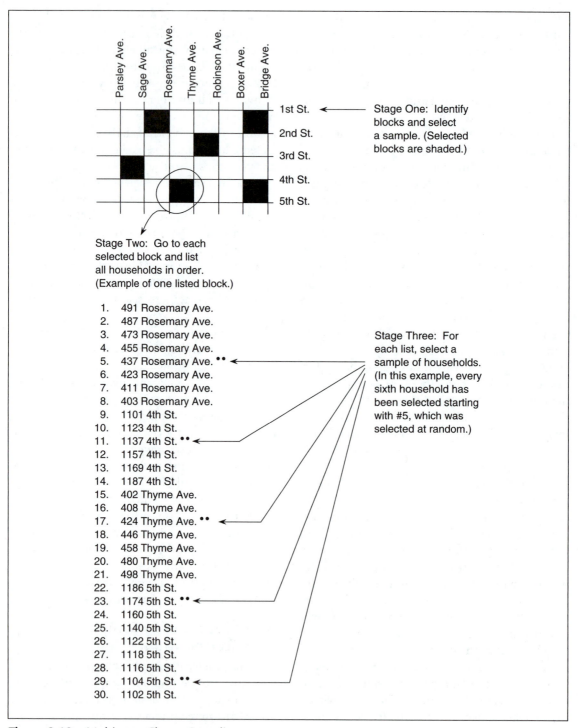

Figure 8.10   Multistage Cluster Sampling

selecting a national sample of law enforcement officers, for example, we might initially stratify our list of agencies by type (state, county, municipal), geographic region, size, and rural or urban location.

Once the primary sampling units (law enforcement agencies) have been grouped according to the relevant, available stratification variables, either simple random or systematic sampling techniques can be used to select the sample. We might select a specified number of units from each group or stratum, or we might arrange the stratified clusters in a continuous list and systematically sample that list.

To the extent that clusters are combined into homogeneous strata, the sampling error at this stage will be reduced. The primary goal of stratification, as before, is homogeneity.

In principle, stratification can take place at each level of sampling. The elements listed within a selected cluster might be stratified before the next stage of sampling. Typically, however, that is not done because we strive for relative homogeneity within clusters. If clusters are sufficiently similar, it is not necessary to stratify again.

Illustration: Two National Crime Surveys

Two national crime surveys show different ways of designing samples to achieve desired results.

Our discussion of sampling designs suggests that researchers can combine many different techniques of sampling and their various components in different ways to suit various needs. In fact, the different components of sampling can be tailored to specific purposes in much the same way that research design principles can be modified to suit various needs. Because sample frames suitable for simple random sampling are often unavailable, researchers use multistage cluster sampling to move from aggregate sample units to actual sample elements. We can add stratification to ensure that samples are representative of important variables. And we can design samples to produce elements that are proportionate or disproportionate to the population.

Two national crime surveys illustrate how these various building blocks may be combined in complex ways: (1) the National Crime Victimization Survey (NCVS), conducted by the Census Bureau, and (2) the British Crime Survey (BCS). Each is a multistage cluster sample, but the two surveys use different strategies to produce sufficient numbers of cases that exhibit one important attribute of interest—victimization. Our summary description is adapted from Callie Rennison (2002) for the NCVS and from Chris Kershaw and associates (2000) for the BCS.

The National Crime Victimization Survey

Although various parts of the NCVS have been modified since the surveys were begun in 1972, the basic sampling strategies have remained relatively constant. The most significant changes have been fluctuations in sample size and a shift to telephone interviewing, with samples of telephone number listings eventually leading to households.

The NCVS seeks to represent the nationwide population of persons ages 12 and over who are living in households. We noted in Chapter 6 that the phrase "living in households" is significant; this is especially true in our current discussion of sampling. NCVS procedures are not designed to sample homeless persons or people who live in institutional settings such as military group housing, temporary housing, or correctional facilities. Also, because the sample targets persons who live in households, it cannot provide estimates of crimes in which a commercial establishment or business is the victim.

Because there is no national list of households in the United States, multistage sampling must be used to proceed from larger units to households and their residents. The national sampling frame used in the first stage defines primary sampling units (PSUs) as large metropolitan areas, nonmetropolitan counties, or groups of contiguous counties (to represent rural areas).

The largest 93 PSUs are specified as "self-representing" and are automatically included in the first stage of sampling. The remaining PSUs are stratified by size, population density, reported crimes, and other variables. An additional 110 non-self-representing PSUs are then selected with a probability proportionate to the population of the PSU. Thus, for example, if one stratum includes Bugtussle, Texas (population 7000), Punkinseed, Indiana (5000), and Rancid, California (3000), the probability that each PSU will be selected is: 7 in 15 for Bugtussle, 5 in 15 for Punkinseed, and 3 in 15 for Rancid.

The second stage of sampling involves designating four different sampling frames within each PSU. Each of these frames is used to select different types of subsequent units. First, the housing unit frame lists addresses of housing units from census records. Second, a group quarters frame lists group quarters such as dormitories and rooming houses from census records. Third, a building permit frame lists newly constructed housing units from local government sources. Finally, an area frame lists census blocks (physical geographic units), from which independent address lists are generated and sampled. Notice that these four frames are necessary because comprehensive, up-to-date lists of residential addresses are not available in this country.

For the 2001 NCVS, these procedures yielded a sample of approximately 44,000 housing units. Completed interviews were obtained from about 80,000 individuals living in households.

The sample design for the NCVS is an excellent illustration of the relationship between sample size and variation in the target population. Because serious crime is a relatively rare event when averaged across the entire U.S. population, very large samples must be drawn. And because no single list of the target population exists, samples are drawn in several stages. The NCVS is an extremely complex survey that uses equally complex sampling methods.

For further information, consult NCVS documentation maintained by the Bureau of Justice Statistics (http://www.ojp.usdoj.gov/bjs/cvictgen.htm). Also see the "National Crime Victimization Survey Resource Guide," maintained at the National Archive of Criminal Justice Data (http://www.icpsr.umich.edu/nacjd/ncvs).

The British Crime Survey

Whereas NCVS respondents are interviewed every 6 months to provide annual estimates of victimization, as of 2000, the BCS had been conducted eight times—approximately every 2 years since 1982. In part, this reflects the intent of the BCS to support research and policy development in addition to estimating crime. We have seen that NCVS sampling procedures begin with demographic units and work down to selection of housing units. BCS sampling is simplified by the existence of a national list of something close to addresses. The Postcode Address File (PAF) lists postal delivery points nationwide and is further subdivided to distinguish "small users," those addresses receiving less than 50 items per day. Even though 50 pieces of mail might still seem like quite a bit, this classification makes it easier to distinguish household addresses from commercial ones.

Postcode sectors, roughly corresponding to U.S. five-digit zip codes, are easily defined clusters of addresses from the PAF. Samples of addresses are then selected from within these sectors. In most cases, 32 addresses are selected from within the postcode. In addition, BCS researchers devised a "booster sample" of ethnic minorities to facilitate detailed analysis of victimization reported by black and Asian respondents. This was accomplished by sampling 75 addresses from postcode sectors where 19 percent or more of households were identified as having ethnic minority heads of households from the English equivalent of census data.

One final sampling dimension reflects the regional organization of police in England and Wales into 43 police areas. The BCS was further stratified to produce at least 300 interviews in each police area to support analysis within those areas.

Once individual households are selected, one person age 16 or over is randomly chosen to provide information for all household members. Sampling procedures initially produced about 28,900 addresses for the year 2000 BCS. About 9 percent of these were eliminated because they were vacant, had been demolished, or contained a business, not a private household. Of the remaining 26,300 addresses, interviews were completed with 19,411 individuals for a response rate of about 74 percent.

Although sampling designs for both the BCS and the NCVS are more complex than we have represented in this discussion, the important point is how multistage cluster sampling is used in each. Notice two principal differences between the samples. First, the NCVS uses proportionate sampling to select a large number of respondents who may then represent the relatively rare attribute of victimization. The BCS samples a disproportionate number of minority residents, who are more likely to be victims of crime. Second, sampling procedures for the BCS are somewhat simpler than those for the NCVS, largely due to the existence of a suitable sampling frame at the national level. Stratification and later-stage sampling is conducted to more efficiently represent each police area and to oversample minority respondents.

Probability Sampling in Review

Depending on the field situation, probability sampling can be very simple or extremely complex, time consuming, and expensive. Whatever the situation, however, it is usually the preferred method for selecting study elements. It's worth restating the two main reasons for this.

First, probability sampling avoids conscious or unconscious biases in element selection on the part of the researcher. If all elements in the population have an equal (or unequal and subsequently weighted) chance of selection, there is an excellent chance that the sample so selected will closely represent the population of all elements.

Second, probability sampling permits estimates of sampling error. Although no probability sample will be perfectly representative in all respects, controlled selection methods permit the researcher to estimate the degree of expected error.

Despite these advantages, it is sometimes impossible to use standard probability sampling methods. Sometimes, it isn't even appropriate to do so. In those cases, researchers turn to nonprobability sampling.

Nonprobability Sampling

In many research applications, nonprobability samples are necessary or advantageous.

You can no doubt envision situations in which it would be either impossible or unfeasible to select the kinds of probability samples we have described. Suppose we want to study auto thieves. There is no list of all auto thieves, nor are we likely to be able to create anything other than a partial and highly selective list. Moreover, probability sampling is sometimes inappropriate even if it is possible. In many such situations, **nonprobability sampling** procedures are called for. Recall that probability samples are defined as those in which the probability that any given sampling element will be selected is known. Conversely, in nonprobability sampling, the likelihood that any given element will be selected is not known.

We'll examine four types of nonprobability samples in this section: (1) purposive or judgmental sampling, (2) quota sampling, (3) the reliance on available subjects, and (4) snowball sampling.

Purposive or Judgmental Sampling

Occasionally, it may be appropriate to select a sample on the basis of our own knowledge of the population, its elements, and the nature of

PUTTING IT ALL TOGETHER

SAMPLING NEW YORK CITY POLICE PRECINCTS

New York is by far the nation's largest city, and even though crime has declined since the early 1990s, New York police still deal with large numbers of crimes each year. We could analyze all police records of robbery, assault, homicide, and other violent crimes without much difficulty. We could even statistically handle the much larger

number of property crimes New York police respond to each year.

But if we wanted to look more closely at New York's crime data, we would almost certainly want to draw samples of something to make our task more manageable. In fact, we could combine a broad analysis of all crime reports in New York over a 10-year period with a deep analysis of some subset of crime information. This means we would conduct statistical analysis of all crime reports and do some more detailed field research (Chapter 10) on a sample of areas, or dates, or crime reports, or something else.

our research aims—in short, based on our judgment and the purpose of the study. Such a sample is called a **purposive sample.**

We may wish to study a small subset of a larger population in which many members of the subset are easily identified but the enumeration of all of them would be nearly impossible. For example, we might want to study members of community crime prevention groups; many members are easily visible, but it is not feasible to define and sample all members of community crime prevention organizations. In studying a sample of the most visible members, however, we may collect data sufficient for our purposes.

Criminal justice research often compares practices in different jurisdictions—cities or states, for example. In such cases, study elements may be selected because they exhibit some particular attribute. For instance, Cassia Spohn and Julie Horney (1991) were interested in how differences among states in rape shield laws affected the use of evidence in sexual assault cases. Strong rape shield laws restricted the use of evidence or testimony about a rape victim's sexual behavior, whereas weak laws routinely permitted such testimony. Spohn and Horney selected a purposive sample of six states

for analysis based on the strength of their rape shield laws. Similarly, Michael Leiber and Jayne Stairs (1999) were interested in how economic inequality combined with race to affect sentencing practices in Iowa juvenile courts. After controlling for economic status, they found that African American defendants received more restrictive sentences than white defendants. Leiber and Stairs selected three jurisdictions purposively, to obtain sample elements with adequate racial diversity in the state of Iowa. The researchers then selected over 5000 juvenile cases processed in those three courts.

Researchers may also use purposive or judgmental sampling to represent patterns of complex variation. In their study of fear of crime, Wesley Skogan and Michael Maxfield (1981) analyzed survey data from several neighborhoods in three cities. Within each city, they selected three types of neighborhoods: (1) stable, working-class; (2) low-income, high-transition; and (3) middle-class with a high proportion of owner-occupied homes. Within each neighborhood, they drew probability samples of residents for telephone interviews. By combining purposive and probability sampling techniques, Skogan and Maxfield obtained homogeneous samples within neighborhoods and also repre-

One approach, taken by researchers at Rutgers University, was to combine statistical analysis of citywide crime data with more detailed studies of individual police precincts. New York police are distributed in 76 precincts across five boroughs citywide. Rutgers researchers purposively selected six precincts for in-depth study. The six precincts were specifically chosen to represent a range of variation throughout a very heterogeneous city. Manhattan and Brooklyn are the city's two largest boroughs in terms of people and crime reports. Two precincts were selected from each borough; each was purposively selected to represent different types of neighborhoods. One precinct each was chosen for Queens and the Bronx. Crime

problems in Staten Island, the fifth New York borough, have historically been much different than in the other four boroughs, so Staten Island was not represented.

Even though a probability sample could have been drawn, researchers worked with police officials to select these six precincts to represent specific characteristics. Michael Quinn Patton (1990:174–75) refers to this as "critical case sampling," in which cases are selected because they exhibit certain key patterns of variation.

Given what you now know about sampling, what are some advantages and disadvantages of choosing these six precincts as described? Can you suggest alternative sampling methods?

sented the considerable heterogeneity across neighborhoods.

One of the best-known social science applications of judgmental sampling is the selection of voting precincts for exit polls on election days. On the basis of previous voting results in a given area (city, state, nation), TV networks select voting precincts that, in combination, produce results similar to those of the entire area. The theory is that the selected precincts represent a cross section of the entire electorate. Each time an election is held, analysts evaluate the adequacy of selected precincts and make revisions, additions, or deletions. The goal is to update the group of precincts to ensure that it provides a good representation of all precincts.

Pretesting a questionnaire is another situation in which purposive sampling is common. If, for example, we plan to study people's attitudes about court-ordered restitution for crime victims, we might want to test the questionnaire on a sample of crime victims. Instead of selecting a probability sample of the general population, we might select some number of known crime victims, perhaps from court records. The box titled "Sampling New York City Police Precincts" explains how researchers have used

purposive sampling to analyze crime data in New York.

Quota Sampling

Like probability sampling, **quota sampling** addresses the issue of representativeness, although the two methods approach the issue quite differently. Quota sampling begins with a matrix or table describing the characteristics of the target population we wish to represent. To do this, we need to know, for example, what proportion of the population is male or female and what proportions fall into various age categories, education levels, ethnic groups, and so forth. In establishing a national quota sample, we need to know what proportion of the national population is, say, urban, eastern, male, under 25, white, working-class, and all the combinations of these attributes.

Once we have created such a matrix and assigned a relative proportion to each cell in the matrix, we can collect data from people who have all the characteristics of a given cell. We then assign all the persons in a given cell a weight appropriate to their portion of the total population. When all the sample elements are weighted in this way, the overall data should provide a reasonable representation of the total population.

Although quota sampling may resemble probability sampling, it has two inherent problems. First, the quota frame (the proportions that different cells represent) must be accurate, and it is often difficult to get up-to-date information for this purpose. A quota sample of auto thieves or teenage vandals would obviously suffer from this difficulty. Second, biases may exist in the selection of sample elements within a given cell—even though its proportion of the population is accurately estimated. An interviewer, instructed to interview five persons who meet a given complex set of characteristics, may still avoid people who live at the top of seven-story walk-ups, have particularly run-down homes, or own vicious dogs.

Quota and purposive sampling may be combined to produce samples that are intuitively, if not statistically, representative. For example, Kate Painter and David Farrington (1998) designed a survey to study marital and partner violence. They wished to represent several variables: marital status, age, an occupational measure of social status, and each of 10 standard regions in the United Kingdom. A probability sample was rejected because the authors wished to get adequate numbers of respondents in each of several categories, and some of the categories were thought to be relatively uncommon. Instead, the authors selected quota samples of 100 women in each of 10 regions and sought equal numbers of respondents in each of five occupational status categories.

Reliance on Available Subjects

Relying on available subjects—that is, stopping people at a street corner or some other location—is sometimes called "convenience sampling." University researchers frequently conduct surveys among the students enrolled in large lecture classes. The ease and economy of such a method explain its popularity; however, it seldom produces data of any general value. It may be useful to pretest a questionnaire, but it

should not be used for a study purportedly describing students as a whole.

Reliance on available subjects can be an appropriate sampling method in some situations. In general, however, it is best justified if the researcher wants to study the characteristics of people who are passing the sampling point at some specified time. For example, in her study of street lighting as a crime prevention strategy, Painter (1996) interviewed samples of pedestrians as they walked through specified areas of London just before and 6 weeks after improvements were made in lighting conditions. Painter clearly understood the scope and limits of this sampling technique. Her findings are described as applying to people who actually use area streets after dark, while recognizing that this population may be quite different from the population of area residents. Interviewing a sample of available evening pedestrians is an appropriate sampling technique for generalizing to the population of evening pedestrians, and the population of pedestrians will not be the same as the population of residents.

In a more general sense, samples like Painter's select elements of a *process*—the process that generates evening pedestrians—rather than elements of a *population*. If we can safely assume that no systematic pattern generates elements of a process, then a sample of available elements as they happen to pass by can be considered to be representative. The technical term for this is a *Poisson process*. So, for example, if you are interested in studying crimes reported to police, then a sample of, say, every seventh crime report over a 2-month period will be representative of the general population of crime reports over that 2-month period.

Baumer and Rosenbaum (1982) provide another good example of the appropriate use of samples of available subjects. They were interested in two general questions about shoplifting: (1) What proportion of shoppers in a store steal something? and (2) How effective is store security in detecting shoplifters? Their approach was to observe a sample of people from the time they entered a large department store until the time they left. Assuming that persons who enter a store represent a Poisson process, Baumer and Rosenbaum could generalize from their sample—observing every 20th person to enter—to the larger population of shoppers at that store. We will return to this study in more detail in Chapter 10, on field research, because Baumer and Rosenbaum used clever techniques to actually conduct their observations.

Finally, Marcus Felson and associates (1996) report on efforts to reduce crime and disorder in New York's Port Authority bus terminal, a place they claim is the world's busiest bus station. Among the most important objectives were to reduce perceptions of crime problems and to improve how travelers felt about the Port Authority terminal. These are research questions appropriate to some sort of survey. Because more than 170,000 passengers pass through the bus station on an average spring day, there should be no difficulty obtaining a sufficiently large sample of users. The problem was how to select a sample. Felson and associates point out that stopping passengers on their way to or from a bus was out of the question. Most passengers are commuters whose journey to and from work is timed to the minute, with none to spare for interviewers' questions. Here's how Felson and associates describe the solution and the sampling strategy it embodied (1996:90–91):

> Response rates would have been low if the Port Authority had tried to interview rushing customers or to hand out questionnaires to be returned later. Their solution was ingenious. The Port Authority drew a sample of outgoing buses . . . and placed representatives aboard. After the bus had departed, he or she would hand out a questionnaire to be completed during the trip

> . . . [and] collect these questionnaires as each customer arrived at the destination. This procedure produced a very high response rate and high completion rate for each item.

Snowball Sampling

Another type of nonprobability sampling that closely resembles the available-subjects approach is called snowball sampling. Commonly used in field observation studies or specialized interviewing, **snowball sampling** begins by identifying a single subject or small number of subjects and then ask the subject(s) to identify others like him or her who might be willing to participate in a study.

Criminal justice research on active criminals or deviants frequently uses snowball sampling techniques. The researcher often makes an initial contact by consulting criminal justice agency records to identify, say, someone convicted of auto theft and placed on probation. That person is interviewed and asked to suggest other auto thieves whom researchers could contact. Stephen Baron and Timothy Hartnagel (1998) studied violence among homeless youths in Edmonton, Canada, identifying their sample through snowball techniques. Similarly, snowball sampling is often used to study drug users and dealers. Leon Pettiway (1995) describes crack cocaine markets in Philadelphia through the eyes of his snowball sample. Bruce Jacobs and Jody Miller (1998) accumulated a sample of 25 female crack dealers in St. Louis to study specific techniques to avoid arrest.

Contacting an initial subject or informant who will then refer the researcher to other subjects can be especially difficult in studies of active offenders. As in most aspects of criminal justice research, the various approaches to initiating contacts for snowball sampling have advantages and disadvantages. Beginning with subjects who have a previous arrest or conviction is usually the easiest method for researchers, but it suffers from potential bias by depending on offenders who are known to police or other officials (McCall, 1978).

Because snowball samples are used most commonly in field research, we'll return to this method of selecting subjects in Chapter 10 on field methods and observation. In the meantime, recent studies by researchers at the University of Missouri–St. Louis offer good examples of snowball samples of offenders that are not dependent on contacts with criminal justice officials. Beginning with a street-savvy ex-offender, these researchers identified samples of burglars (Wright and Decker, 1994), members of youth gangs (Decker and Van Winkle, 1996), and armed robbers (Wright and Decker, 1997). It's especially difficult to identify active offenders as research subjects, but these examples illustrate notably clever uses of snowball sampling techniques.

Nonprobability Sampling in Review

Snowball samples are essentially variations on purposive samples (we want to sample juvenile gang members) and on samples of available subjects (sample elements identify other sample elements that are available to us). Each of these is a nonprobability sampling technique. And, like other types of nonprobability samples, snowball samples are most appropriate when it is impossible to determine the probability that any given element will be selected in a sample. Furthermore, snowball sampling and related techniques may be necessary when the target population is difficult to locate or even identify. Approaching pedestrians who happen to pass by, for example, is not an efficient way to select a sample of prostitutes or juvenile gang members. In contrast, approaching pedestrians is an appropriate sampling method for studying pedestrians, while drawing a probability sample of urban residents to identify people who walk in specific areas of the city would be costly and inefficient.

Like other elements of criminal justice research, sampling plans must be adapted to specific research applications. When it's important to make estimates of the accuracy of our samples, and when suitable sampling frames are possible, we use probability sampling techniques. When no reasonable sampling frame is available, and we cannot draw a probability sample, we cannot make estimates about sample accuracy. Fortunately, in such situations, we can make use of a variety of approaches for drawing nonprobability samples.

✪ *Main Points*

- Asking questions, making observations, and examining written records are three ways to collect criminal justice data. Each source of data is widely used in criminal justice research; each has its own advantages and disadvantages. Sometimes, researchers use multiple methods of data collection in combination.
- Regardless of which data collection methods are used, researchers must carefully consider measurement reliability and validity and the extent to which subjects are aware of the data collection process. Criminal justice researchers should routinely be careful and creative in data collection.
- The logic of probability sampling forms the foundation for representing large populations with small subsets of those populations.
- The chief criterion of a sample's quality is the degree to which it is representative—the extent to which the characteristics of the sample are the same as those of the population from which it was selected.
- The most carefully selected sample is almost never a perfect representation of the population from which it was selected. Some degree of sampling error always exists.
- Probability sampling methods provide one excellent way of selecting samples that will be quite representative. They make it possible to estimate the amount of sampling error that should be expected in a given sample.
- The chief principle of probability sampling is that every member of the total population must have some known nonzero probability of being selected into the sample.

- Our ability to estimate population parameters with sample statistics is rooted in the sampling distribution and probability theory. If we draw a large number of samples of a given size, sample statistics will cluster around the true population parameter. As sample size increases, the cluster becomes tighter.
- A variety of sampling designs can be used and combined to suit different populations and research purposes. Each type of sampling has its own advantages and disadvantages.
- Simple random sampling is logically the most fundamental technique in probability sampling although it is seldom used in practice.
- Systematic sampling involves using a sampling frame to select units that appear at some specified interval—for example, every 8th, or 15th, or 1023rd unit. This method is functionally equivalent to simple random sampling.
- Stratification improves the representativeness of a sample by reducing the sampling error.
- Disproportionate stratified sampling is especially useful when we want to select adequate numbers of certain types of subjects who are relatively rare in the population we are studying.
- Multistage cluster sampling is frequently used when there is no list of all the members of a population.
- The NCVS and the BCS are national crime surveys based on multistage cluster samples. Sampling methods for each survey illustrate different approaches to representing relatively rare events.
- Nonprobability sampling methods are less statistically representative and less reliable than probability sampling methods. However, they are often easier and cheaper to use.
- Purposive sampling is used when researchers wish to select specific elements of a population. This may be because the elements are believed to be representative, extreme cases or because they represent the range of variation expected in a population.
- In quota sampling, researchers begin with a detailed description of the characteristics of the total population and then select sample members in a way that includes the different composite profiles that exist in the population.
- In cases in which it's not possible to draw nonprobability samples through other means, researchers often rely on available subjects. Professors sometimes do this—students in their classes are available subjects.
- Snowball samples accumulate subjects through chains of referrals and are most commonly used in field research.

✪ Key Terms

Cluster sample	Probability sample
Confidence interval	Purposive sample
Confidence level	Quota sample
Disproportionate stratified sampling	Sample element
	Sample statistic
Equal probability of selection method (EPSEM)	Sampling distribution
	Sampling frame
	Sampling units
Focus group	Simple random sample
Nonprobability sample	Snowball sampling
	Standard error
Population	Stratification
Population parameter	Systematic sampling

✪ Review Questions and Exercises

1. Review the summary of the National Institute of Justice Arrestee Drug Abuse Monitoring (ADAM) program in Chapter 6. Specify the target population, study population, sampling frame, and elements used in the ADAM program. Describe what type of sample ADAM uses, and discuss the advantages and disadvantages of ADAM sampling procedures.

2. Discuss possible study populations, elements, sampling units, and sampling frames for drawing a sample to represent the populations listed here. You may wish to limit your discussion to populations in a specific state or other jurisdiction.
   a. Municipal police officers
   b. Felony court judges
   c. Auto thieves
   d. Licensed automobile drivers
   e. State police superintendents
   f. Persons incarcerated in county jails

3. Assume you are interested in traffic safety around your campus—specifically, in speeding on one of the main streets that borders your campus. Describe how you might collect data on speeding by asking questions, making observations, or examining written records. What

study population will be represented by data collected in each manner?

✪ Internet Exercises

To ensure that you always have access to live, correct Web links for the Web sites referenced in the following exercises, we provide the necessary links on the companion Web site for *Research Methods for Criminal Justice and Criminology* at http://cj.wadsworth. com/maxfield_babbie/research_methods4e. Once at the companion Web site, select this specific chapter, click on "Chapter Resources," then click on "Web Links."

1. The National Archive of Criminal Justice Data (NACJD) contains criminal justice data from numerous sources. Each data set has extensive documentation listing the source of the data, the sampling frame, the sample, and so on. Visit the NACJD Web site and select the "access data" option. Then click on "browse by subject" and select an area that interests you. Scroll down the list of studies and click on "description" for at least two. After reading the description, list the following: the population (universe), the sampling frame, the study population, the observation unit, and the sampling method that was used to gather the sample. Try to choose studies completed since 1985.

2. The U.S. Census involves taking an actual count of all individuals residing within the United States. Prior to the 2000 census, there was much discussion of the pros and cons of sampling rather than counting to obtain estimates of the true population of the country. Use your favorite search engine, and enter the terms *sampling* AND *census* to bring up multiple sites that discuss this issue. Explore some of these sites, and summarize what you find regarding the pros and cons of sampling in the 2000 census. List the Web addresses of each site you use in your discussion.

✪ InfoTrac College Edition

Using one of the nonprobability sampling methods described in this chapter as a keyword, find and read an article that describes its use in a criminal justice study. Explain why the author(s) chose to use a nonprobability sampling method to study this topic.

✪ The NEW Companion Web Site for Research Methods for Criminal Justice and Criminology, *Fourth Edition*

http://cj.wadsworth.com/maxfield_babbie/research_methods4e

Supplement your review of this chapter by going to the new companion Web site to take one of the Tutorial Quizzes, use the flash cards to master key terms, and check out the many other study aids you'll find there. You'll also find special features such as quantitative and qualitative data analysis primers to help you with a special project or do some research on your own.

✪ Additional Readings

General Accounting Office, *Using Statistical Sampling* (Washington, DC: U.S. General Accounting Office, 1992). One of a series of handbooks on evaluation methods, this is a rich source of practical information on how to draw probability samples. You will also find suggestions on how to work around various difficulties in actually selecting samples, as well as illustrations of sampling people and other types of elements.

Kish, Leslie, *Survey Sampling* (New York: Wiley, 1965). Unquestionably the definitive work on sampling in social research. Kish's coverage ranges from the simplest matters to the most complex and mathematical. He is both highly theoretical and downright practical. Easily readable and difficult passages intermingle as Kish dissects everything you could want or need to know about each aspect of sampling.

Patton, Michael Quinn, *Qualitative Research and Evaluation Methods,* 3rd ed. (Thousand Oaks, CA: Sage, 2001). Though its focus is evaluation, this book presents one of the best discussions of nonprobability sampling available. Patton covers a wide range of variations on purposive sampling.

Weisel, Deborah, *Conducting Community Surveys: A Practical Guide for Law Enforcement Agencies* (Washington, DC: U.S. Department of Justice, Office of Justice Programs, Bureau of Justice Statistics, 1999). This short handbook offers good, basic advice on drawing samples for community-level victimization surveys. The information on estimating sample size is especially good.

Chapter 9

Survey Research and Other Ways of Asking Questions

We'll examine how mail, interview, and telephone surveys can be used in criminal justice research. We'll also consider other ways of collecting data by asking people questions.

(continued)

Introduction

Asking people questions is the most common data-collection method in social science.

Gathering data by asking questions is a very old research technique. We find this passage in the Old Testament:

> After the plague the Lord said to Moses and to Eleazar the son of Aaron, the priest, "Take a census of all the congregation of the people of Israel, from 20 years old and upward." (Numbers 26:1–2)

Ancient Egyptian rulers conducted censuses for the purpose of administering their kingdoms. And Jesus was born away from home because

Joseph and Mary were journeying to Joseph's ancestral home for a Roman census.

A little-known survey was attempted among French workers in 1880. A German political sociologist mailed some 25,000 questionnaires to workers to determine the extent of their exploitation by employers. The rather lengthy questionnaire included items such as these:

> Does your employer or his representative resort to trickery in order to defraud you of a part of your earnings? If you are paid piece rates, is the quality of the article made a pretext for fraudulent deductions from your wages?

The survey researcher in this case was not George Gallup but Karl Marx (1880:208). Although 25,000 questionnaires were mailed out, there is no record of any being returned. And you need not know much about survey methods to recognize the loaded questions posed by Marx.

Survey research is perhaps the most frequently used mode of observation in sociology and political science, and surveys are often used in criminal justice research as well. You have no doubt been a respondent in a survey, and you may have conducted surveys yourself.

We begin this chapter by discussing the criminal justice topics that are most appropriate for survey methods. Next, we cover the basic principles of how to ask people questions for research purposes, including some of the details of questionnaire construction. We describe the three basic ways of administering questionnaires—self-administration, face-to-face interviews, and telephone interviews—and summarize the strengths and weaknesses of each method. After discussing more specialized interviewing techniques, such as focus groups, we conclude the chapter with some advice on the benefits and pitfalls of conducting your own surveys.

Topics Appropriate to Survey Research

Surveys have a wide variety of uses in basic and applied criminal justice research.

Surveys may be used for descriptive, explanatory, exploratory, and applied research. They are best suited for studies that have individual people as the units of analysis. They are often used for other units of analysis as well, such as households or organizations. Even in these cases, however, one or more individual people act as respondents or informants.

For example, researchers sometimes use victimization incidents as units of analysis in examining data from crime surveys. The fact that some people may be victimized more than once and others not at all means that victimization incidents are not the same units as individuals.

However, a survey questionnaire must still be administered to people who provide information about victimization incidents. In a similar fashion, the National Jail Census, conducted every 5 or so years by the Census Bureau, collects information about local detention facilities. Jails are the units of analysis, but information about each jail is provided by individuals. Quite a lot of research on police practices was conducted following passage of the 1994 Crime Bill, and in most cases, law enforcement agencies were units of analysis; individual people, however, provided information for the surveys of police departments.

We now consider some broad categories of research applications in which survey methods are especially appropriate.

Counting Crime

Chapter 6 covered this use of surveys in detail. Asking people about victimizations is a measure of crime that adjusts for some of the problems found in data collected by police. Of course, survey measures have their own shortcomings. Most of these difficulties, such as recall error and reluctance to discuss victimization with interviewers, are inherent in survey methods. Nevertheless, due to continued efforts to reduce such problems, victim surveys have become important sources of data about the volume of crime in the United States and in other countries.

Self-Reports

Surveys that ask people about crimes they may have committed were also discussed in Chapter 6. Robert O'Brien (1985:65) describes self-report surveys as "the dominant method in criminology for studying the etiology of crime." For research that seeks to explore or explain why people commit criminal, delinquent, or deviant acts, asking questions is the best method available.

Within the general category of self-report surveys, two different applications are distinguished by their target population and sampling methods. Studies of offenders select samples of respondents known to have committed crimes, often prisoners. Typically, the focus is on the *frequency* of offending—how many crimes of various types are committed by active offenders over a period of time. A study of incarcerated felons by Jan and Marcia Chaiken (1982) is among the best-known self-report surveys of offenders. John Ball and associates (Ball, Rosen, Flueck, and Nurco, 1982) studied a sample of heroin addicts, documenting the crimes they committed over several years.

The other type of self-report survey focuses on the *prevalence* of offending—how many people commit crimes, in contrast to how many crimes are committed by a target population of offenders. Such surveys typically use samples that represent a broader population, such as U.S. households, adult males, or high school seniors. The National Youth Survey (NYS), sponsored by the National Institute for Mental Health and the Office of Juvenile Justice and Delinquency Prevention, was conducted eight times from 1976 through 1989. The NYS is a panel study (described in Chapter 4) that began with a national probability sample of children who were then ages 11–17. Since the survey's first wave, data from the NYS have been used to make estimates of the prevalence of criminal and delinquent acts. Delbert Elliott and associates (Elliott, Huizinga, and Menard, 1989) present comprehensive results from the NYS, and Finn-Age Esbensen and Delbert Elliott (1994) describe patterns of drug use over eight waves of the survey. Other examples of self-report surveys were described in Chapter 6.

General-population surveys and surveys of offenders tend to present different types of difficulties in connection with the validity and reliability of self-reports. Recall error and the reporting of fabricated offenses may be problems in a survey of high-rate offenders (Horney and Marshall, 1992), while respondents in general-population self-report surveys may be reluctant to disclose illegal behavior. When we discuss questionnaire construction later in this chap-

ter, we will present examples and suggestions for creating self-report items.

Perceptions and Attitudes

Another application of surveys in criminal justice is to learn how people feel about crime and criminal justice policy. Public views about sentencing policies, gun control, police performance, and drug abuse are often solicited in opinion polls. Begun in 1972, the General Social Survey is an ongoing survey of social indicators in the United States. Questions about fear of crime and other perceptions of crime problems are regularly included. Since the mid-1970s, a growing number of explanatory studies have been conducted on public perceptions of crime and crime problems. A large body of research on fear of crime has grown, in part, from the realization that fear and its behavioral consequences are much more widespread among the population than is actual criminal victimization (Hale, 1996).

Policy Proposals

The intractability of crime prompts a continuous search for policy responses, and many of these responses require the participation of, or at least approval by, the general public. Surveys are well suited to gauge public reaction to proposals like community policing or neighborhood watch. For instance, the 1984 British Crime Survey (BCS) included a series of items describing neighborhood watch programs and asked respondents whether they would be willing to participate in such a program in their community. Although most people expressed general support, only about a third of respondents indicated that they would be willing to join a neighborhood watch organization. As a result, officials in the British Home Office began to rethink the viability of neighborhood watch programs (Hough and Mayhew, 1985: 48–49).

Community policing links police and neighborhood residents in a joint effort to address urban crime problems. One crucial element of community policing is that police officers learn more about crime and public order problems that most concern people. Rather than simply reacting to citizen crime reports, police are expected to become more proactive in identifying neighborhood problems that contribute to crime. Neighborhood surveys, conducted for or by police, can be helpful in sorting out the types of problems that trouble residents. Recognizing this, the Bureau of Justice Statistics (BJS) and the Office of Community Oriented Policing Services (COPS) have created a guide to conducting community surveys to assess victimization, citizen perceptions of police, and related issues (Weisel, 1999).

Targeted Victim Surveys

Victim surveys that target individual cities or neighborhoods are important tools for evaluating policy innovations. Many criminal justice programs seek to prevent or reduce crime in some specific area, but crimes reported to police cannot be used to evaluate many types of programs.

To see why this is so, consider a hypothetical community policing program that encourages neighborhood residents to report all suspected crimes to the police. We saw in Chapter 6 that many minor incidents are not reported because victims believe that police will not want to be bothered. But if a new program stresses that police actually *want* to be bothered, the proportion of crimes reported may increase, resulting in what appears to be an increase in crime.

The solution is to conduct targeted victim surveys before and after introducing some policy change. Such victim surveys are especially appropriate for evaluating any policy that may increase crime reporting as a side effect.

Consider also that large-scale surveys such as the National Crime Victimization Survey (NCVS) cannot be used to evaluate local crime prevention programs. This is because, as we have seen, the NCVS is designed to represent the national population of persons who live in households. Although NCVS data for the 11

largest states can be analyzed separately (Maltz, 1998), the NCVS is not representative of any particular local jurisdiction. It is not possible to identify the specific location of victimizations from NCVS data.

The community victim surveys designed by the BJS and the COPS Office help with each of these needs. Local surveys can be launched specifically to evaluate local crime prevention efforts. Or innovative programs can be timed to correspond to regular cycles of local surveys. In each case, the BJS/COPS (Weisel, 1999) guide presents advice on drawing samples to represent local jurisdictions.

Another type of targeted victim survey is one that focuses on particular types of incidents that might target more narrowly defined population segments. A good example is the National Violence Against Women Survey, a joint effort of the National Institute of Justice and a violence prevention bureau in the National Institutes of Health (Tjaden and Thoennes, 2000). Screening questions present explicit descriptions of sexual and other violence with the specific purpose of providing better information about these incidents that have proved difficult to measure through general-purpose crime surveys.

Other Evaluation Uses

Other types of surveys may be appropriate for applied studies. A good illustration of this is a continuing series of neighborhood surveys to evaluate community policing in Chicago. Here's an example of how the researchers link their information needs to surveys (Chicago Community Policing Evaluation Consortium, 1999:12):

> Because so much of the program involves citizen participation, the Chicago Alternative Policing Strategy evaluation focuses extensively on its visibility in the community and factors that are associated with actual involvement in its activities. In order to assess the visibility of the city's

programs, a survey of Chicago residents was conducted between April and September 1998.

In general, surveys can be used to evaluate policy that seeks to change attitudes, beliefs, or perceptions. For example, consider a program designed to promote victim and witness cooperation in criminal court by reducing case processing time. At first, we might consider direct measures of case processing time as indicators of program success. If the program goal is to increase cooperation, however, a survey that asks how victims and witnesses *perceive* case processing time will be more appropriate.

General-Purpose Crime Surveys

As the name implies, these surveys are designed for more than one of the purposes we have mentioned. Since its inception in 1982, the BCS has included special batteries of questions about various topics: fear of crime (1984), contacts with the police (1988, 1996, 2000), self-reported drug use (1994), security measures used to protect households and vehicles (1996), and attitudes toward criminal sentencing (2000).

The NCVS has traditionally focused on counting crime. In recent years, however, efforts have been devoted to incrementally redesigning the survey to broaden its scope (Bachman and Taylor, 1994; Lynch, 1990). Beginning in 1996, the NCVS added a series of questions on police–public contacts other than those in connection with victimization. The most interesting type of such contact is a traffic stop — survey respondents describe their experiences with police in connection with traffic violations. Using the NCVS as a research platform in this way has produced a new source of data with which to assess the scope of race-based disparities in police–public contacts. See Langan and associates (Langan, Greenfield, Smith, Durose, and Levin, 2001) and Schmitt and associates (Schmitt, Langan, and Durose, 2002) for examples of tabulations from this feature of the NCVS.

Guidelines for Asking Questions

How questions are asked is the single most important feature of survey research.

A defining feature of survey methods is that research concepts are operationalized by asking people questions. Several general guidelines can assist in framing and asking questions that serve as excellent operationalizations of variables. It is important also to be aware of pitfalls that can result in useless and even misleading information. We'll begin with some of the options available for creating questionnaires.

Open-Ended and Closed-Ended Questions

In asking questions, researchers have two basic options, and each can accommodate certain variations. The first is **open-ended questions,** in which the respondent is asked to provide his or her own answers. For example, the respondent may be asked, "What do you feel is the most important crime problem facing the police in your city today?" and be provided with a space to write in the answer (or be asked to report it orally to an interviewer). The other option is **closed-ended questions,** in which the respondent is asked to select an answer from among a list provided by the researcher.

Closed-ended questions are especially useful because they provide more uniform responses and are more easily processed. They often can be transferred directly into a data file. Open-ended responses, in contrast, must be coded before they can be processed for analysis. This coding process often requires that the researcher interpret the meaning of responses, which opens up the possibility of misunderstanding and researcher bias. Also, some respondents may give answers that are essentially irrelevant to the researcher's intent.

The chief shortcoming of closed-ended questions lies in the researcher's structuring of responses. When the relevant answers to a given question are relatively clear, there should be no problem. In some cases, however, the researcher's list of responses may fail to include some important answers. When we ask about "the most important crime problem facing the police in your city today," for example, our checklist might omit certain crime problems that respondents consider important.

In constructing closed-ended questions, we are best guided by two of the requirements for operationalizing variables stated in Chapter 5. First, the response categories provided should be exhaustive: They should include all the possible responses that might be expected. Often, researchers ensure this by adding a category labeled something like "Other (Please specify: _____)." Second, the answer categories must be mutually exclusive: The respondent should not feel compelled to select more than one. In some cases, researchers solicit multiple answers, but doing so can create difficulties in subsequent data processing and analysis. To ensure that categories are mutually exclusive, we should carefully consider each combination of categories, asking whether a person could reasonably choose more than one answer. In addition, it is useful to add an instruction that respondents should select the one best answer. However, this is still not a satisfactory substitute for a carefully constructed set of responses.

Questions and Statements

The term **questionnaire** suggests a collection of questions, but a typical questionnaire probably has as many statements as questions. This is because researchers often are interested in determining the extent to which respondents hold a particular attitude or perspective. Researchers try to summarize the attitude in a fairly brief statement; then they present that statement and ask respondents whether they agree or disagree with it. Rensis Likert formalized this procedure through the creation of the Likert scale, a format in which respondents are asked whether they strongly agree, agree, disagree, or strongly disagree, or perhaps strongly approve, approve, and so forth.

Both questions and statements may be used profitably. Using both in a questionnaire adds flexibility in the design of items and can make the questionnaire more interesting as well.

Make Items Clear

It should go without saying that questionnaire items must be clear and unambiguous, but the broad proliferation of unclear and ambiguous questions in surveys makes the point worth stressing here. Researchers commonly become so deeply involved in the topic that opinions and perspectives that are clear to them will not be at all clear to respondents, many of whom have given little or no thought to the topic. Or researchers may have only a superficial understanding of the topic and so may fail to specify the intent of a question sufficiently. The question "What do you think about the governor's decision concerning prison furloughs?" may evoke in the respondent a counterquestion or two: "Which governor's decision?" "What are prison furloughs?" Questionnaire items should be precise so that the respondent knows exactly what the researcher wants an answer to.

Frequently, researchers ask respondents for a single answer to a combination question. Such "double-barreled" questions seem to occur most often when the researcher has personally identified with a complex question. For example, the researcher might ask respondents to agree or disagree with the statement "The Department of Corrections should stop releasing inmates for weekend furloughs and concentrate on rehabilitating criminals." Although many people will unequivocally agree with the statement and others will unequivocally disagree, still others will be unable to answer. Some might want to terminate the furlough program and punish — not rehabilitate — prisoners. Others might want to expand rehabilitation efforts while maintaining weekend furloughs; they can neither agree nor disagree without misleading the researcher.

Short Items Are Best

In the interest of being unambiguous and precise and pointing to the relevance of an issue, researchers often create long, complicated items. That should be avoided. In the case of questionnaires respondents complete themselves, they are often unwilling to study an item in order to understand it. The respondent should be able to read an item quickly, understand its intent, and select or provide an answer without difficulty. In general, it's safe to assume that respondents will read items quickly and give quick answers; therefore, short, clear items that will not be misinterpreted under those conditions are best. Questions read to respondents in person or over the phone should be similarly brief.

Avoid Negative Items

A negation in a questionnaire item paves the way for easy misinterpretation. Asked to agree or disagree with the statement "Drugs such as marijuana should not be legalized," many respondents will overlook the word not and answer on that basis. Thus, some will agree with the statement when they are in favor of legalizing marijuana, and others will agree when they oppose it. And we may never know which is which.

Biased Items and Terms

Recall from the earlier discussion of conceptualization and operationalization that there are no ultimately true meanings for any of the concepts we typically study in social science. This same general principle applies to the responses we get from persons in a survey.

The meaning of a given response to a question depends in large part on the wording of the question. That is true of every question and answer. Some questions seem to encourage particular responses more than do other questions. Questions that encourage respondents to answer in a particular way are *biased*. Most researchers recognize the likely effect of a question such as "Do you support the president's

initiatives to promote the safety and security of all Americans?" and no reputable researcher would use such an item. The biasing effect of items and terms is far subtler than this example suggests, however.

The mere identification of an attitude or position with a prestigious (or unpopular) person or agency can bias responses. For example, an item that starts with "Do you agree or disagree with the recent Supreme Court decision that..." might have this effect. We are not suggesting that such wording will necessarily produce consensus or even a majority in support of the position identified with the prestigious person or agency. Rather, support will likely be greater than what would have been obtained without such identification.

Sometimes, the impact of different forms of question wording is relatively subtle. For example, Kenneth Rasinski (1989) analyzed the results of several General Social Survey studies of attitudes toward government spending. He found that the way programs were identified had an impact on the amount of public support they received. Here are some comparisons:

More Support	Less Support
"Assistance to the poor"	"Welfare"
"Halting the rising crime rate"	"Law enforcement"
"Dealing with drug addiction"	"Drug rehabilitation"

In 1986, for example, 63 percent of respondents said too little money was being spent on "assistance to the poor," while in a matched survey that year, only 23 percent said we were spending too little on "welfare."

The main guidance we offer for avoiding bias is that researchers imagine how they would feel giving each of the answers they offer to respondents. If they would feel embarrassed, perverted, inhumane, stupid, irresponsible, or anything like that, then they should give some serious thought to whether others will be willing to give those answers. Researchers must carefully examine the purpose of their inquiry and construct items that will be most useful to it.

We also need to be generally wary of what researchers call the "social desirability" of questions and answers. Whenever we ask people for information, they answer through a filter of what will make them look good. That is especially true if they are being interviewed in a face-to-face situation.

Designing Self-Report Items

Social desirability is one of the problems that plagues self-report crime questions in general-population surveys. Adhering to the ethical principles of confidentiality and anonymity, as well as convincing respondents that we are doing so, is one way of getting more truthful responses to self-report items. Other techniques can help us avoid or reduce problems with self-report items.

One method, used in earlier versions of the BCS, is to introduce a group of self-report items with a disclaimer and to sanitize the presentation of offenses. The self-report section of the 1984 BCS began with this introduction:

> There are lots of things which are actually crimes, but which are done by lots of people, and which many people do not think of as crimes. On this card [printed card handed to respondents] are a list of eight of them. For each one can you tell me how many people you think do it—most people, a lot of people, or no one.

Respondents then read a card, shown in Figure 9.1, that presented descriptions of various offenses. Interviewers first asked respondents how many people they thought ever did X, where X corresponded to the letter for an offense shown in Figure 9.1. Next, respondents were asked whether they had ever done X. Interviewers then moved on down the list of letters for each offense on the card.

This procedure incorporates three techniques to guard against the socially desirable response of not admitting to having committed

---

A. Taken office supplies from work (such as stationery, envelopes, and pens) when not supposed to.

B. Taken things other than office supplies from work (such as tools, money, or other goods) when not supposed to.

C. Fiddled expenses [*fiddled* is the Queen's English equivalent of *fudged*].

D. Deliberately traveled [on a train] without a ticket or paid too low a fare.

E. Failed to declare something at customs on which duty was payable.

F. Cheated on tax.

G. Used cannabis (hashish, marijuana, ganga, grass).

H. Regularly driven a car when they know they have drunk enough to be well above the legal limit.

Figure 9.1 Showcard for Self-Report Items, 1984 British Crime Survey

Source: Adapted from the 1984 British Crime Survey (NOP Market Research Limited, 1985).

---

a crime. First, the disclaimer seeks to reassure respondents that "many people" do not really think of various acts as crimes. Second, respondents are asked how many people they think commit each offense before being asked whether they have done so themselves. This takes advantage of a common human justification for engaging in certain kinds of behavior—other people do it. Third, asking whether they "have ever done X" is less confrontational than asking whether they "have ever cheated on an expense account." Again, the foibles of human behavior are at work here, in much the same way that people use euphemisms such as "rest room" and "sleep together" for "toilet" and "have sexual intercourse." It is, of course, not realistic to expect that such ploys will reassure all respondents. Furthermore, disclaimers about serious offenses such as rape or bank robbery would be ludicrous. But such techniques illustrate how thoughtful wording and introductions can be incorporated into sensitive questions.

Self-report surveys of known offenders encounter different problems. Incarcerated persons may be reluctant to admit committing crimes because of the legal consequences. High-rate offenders may have difficulty distinguishing among a number of different crimes or remembering even approximate dates. As discussed in Chapter 3, promises of immunity from prosecution for offenses revealed in certain forms of sponsored research can allay the fears of many active offenders. Sorting out dates and details of individual crimes among high-rate offenders requires different strategies.

One technique that is useful in surveys of active offenders is to interview subjects several times at regular intervals. For example, Lisa Maher (1997) interviewed her sample of heroin- or cocaine-addicted women repeatedly (sometimes daily) over the course of 3 years. Each subject was asked about her background, intimate relationships with men, income-generating activities, and drug use habits. Having regular interviews helped respondents recall offending.

A similar approach was used by Julie Horney and Ineke Haen Marshall (1992), who questioned methods used by RAND Corporation researchers to obtain self-report data from prisoners. In the RAND study (Chaiken and Chaiken, 1982), high-rate offenders were asked to estimate their usual level of criminal activity, a procedure that Horney and Marshall believed might produce inflated estimates of crimes committed. Their solution was to present inmates with a "crime calendar" on which they recorded month-by-month lists of offenses. In an experimental comparison of the crime calendar approach with the RAND method, Horney and Marshall found no differences in the numbers of crimes recalled by subjects. It is likely, however, that the monthly diary format helped subjects more accurately recall the numbers and characteristics of crimes they had committed.

Obtaining valid and reliable results from self-report items is challenging, but self-report survey techniques are important tools for addressing certain types of criminal justice research questions. Because of this, researchers are con-

stantly striving to improve self-report items. See the collection of essays by Joseph Gfroerer and associates (Gfroerer, Eyerman, and Chromy, 2002) for a detailed discussion of issues involved in measuring self-reported drug use through the National Household Survey on Drug Abuse. A National Research Council report (2001) discusses self-report survey measures more generally.

Computer technology has made it possible to significantly improve self-reported items. We present examples later in the chapter when we focus on different modes of survey administration.

Questionnaire Construction

After settling on question content, researchers must consider the format and organization of all items in a questionnaire.

Because questionnaires are the fundamental instruments of survey research, we now turn our attention to some of the established techniques for constructing them. The following sections are best considered as a continuation of our theoretical discussions in Chapter 5 of conceptualization and measurement.

Of course, how a questionnaire is constructed depends on how the questionnaire will be administered to respondents. Later in this chapter, we will consider the three modes of administration: (1) self-administered, (2) in-person interview, and (3) telephone interview. For now, we simply point out that a rough continuum of questionnaire complexity is associated with the three modes of administration. In general, questionnaires administered through in-person interviews are the most complex. Self-administered questionnaires tend to be the least complex and must be more carefully formatted than questionnaires administered by trained interviewers, either in person or by telephone.

General Questionnaire Format

The format of a questionnaire is just as important as the nature and wording of the questions. An improperly laid-out questionnaire can cause respondents to miss questions, confuse them about the nature of the data desired, and, in the extreme, lead them to throw the questionnaire away.

As a general rule, the questionnaire should be uncluttered. Inexperienced researchers tend to fear that their questionnaire will look too long, so they squeeze several questions onto a single line, abbreviate questions, and try to use as few pages as possible. Such efforts are ill-advised and even counterproductive. Putting more than one question on a line will cause some respondents to miss the second question altogether. Some respondents will misinterpret abbreviated questions. And, more generally, respondents who have spent considerable time on the first page of what seemed a short questionnaire will be more demoralized than respondents who quickly completed the first several pages of what initially seemed a long form. Moreover, the latter will have made fewer errors and will not have been forced to reread confusing, abbreviated questions. Nor will they have been forced to write a long answer in a tiny space.

The desirability of spreading questions out in the questionnaire cannot be overemphasized. Squeezed-together questionnaires are disastrous, whether they are to be completed by the respondents themselves or administered by trained interviewers. And the processing of such questionnaires, with feeble check marks and tiny words scrawled in blanks, can be another nightmare.

Contingency Questions

Quite often in questionnaires, certain questions are clearly relevant to only some of the respondents and irrelevant to others. A victim survey, for example, presents batteries of questions about victimization incidents that are meaningful only to crime victims.

Frequently, this situation—realizing that the topic is relevant only to some respondents—arises when we wish to ask a series of questions about a certain topic. We may want to ask whether respondents belong to a particular organization and, if so, how often they attend meetings, whether they have held office in the organization, and so forth. Or we might want to ask whether respondents have heard anything about a certain policy proposal, such as opening a youth shelter in the neighborhood, and then investigate the attitudes of those who have heard of it.

The subsequent questions in series such as these are called "contingency questions"; whether they are to be asked and answered is *contingent* on the response to the first question in the series. The proper use of contingency questions can make it easier for respondents to complete the questionnaire because they do not have to answer questions that are irrelevant to them.

Contingency questions can be presented in several formats. The one shown in Figure 9.2 is probably the clearest and most effective. Note that the questions shown in the figure could have been dealt with in a single question: "How many times, if any, have you smoked marijuana?" The response categories then would be: "Never," "Once," "2 to 5 times," and so forth. This single question would apply to all respondents, and each would find an appropriate answer category. Such a question, however, might put pressure on some respondents to report having smoked marijuana, because the main question asks how many times they have smoked it. The contingency question format illustrated in Figure 9.2 reduces the subtle pressure on respondents to report having smoked marijuana. This discussion shows how seemingly theoretical issues of validity and reliability are involved in so mundane a matter as how to format questions on a piece of paper.

Used properly, even complex sets of contingency questions can be constructed without confusing respondents. Sometimes, a set of contingency questions is long enough to extend over several pages.

Victim surveys typically include many contingency questions. Figure 9.3 presents a few questions from the NCVS questionnaire used in 2001. All respondents are asked a series of

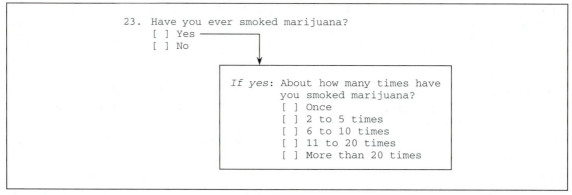

Figure 9.2   Contingency Question Format

screening questions to reveal possible victimizations. Persons who answer yes to any of the screening questions then complete a crime incident report that presents a large number of items designed to measure details of the victimization incident.

As Figure 9.3 shows, the crime incident report itself also contains contingency questions. You might notice that even this brief adaptation from the NCVS screening and crime incident report questionnaires is rather complex. NCVS questionnaires are administered primarily through computer-assisted telephone interviews in which the flow of contingency questions is more or less automated. It would be difficult to construct a self-administered victimization questionnaire with such complicated contingency questions.

Matrix Questions

Often, researchers want to ask several questions that have the same set of answer categories. This happens whenever the Likert response categories are used. Then it is often possible to construct a matrix of items and answers, as illustrated in Figure 9.4.

This format has three advantages. First, it uses space efficiently. Second, respondents probably find it easier to complete a set of questions presented in this fashion. In addition, this format may increase the comparability of responses given to different questions for the re-

spondent, as well as for the researcher. Because respondents can quickly review their answers to earlier items in the set, they might choose between, say, "strongly agree" and "agree" on a given statement by comparing their strength of agreement with their earlier responses in the set.

Some dangers are inherent in using this format as well. Its advantages may promote structuring an item so that the responses fit into the matrix format when a different, more idiosyncratic, set of responses might be more appropriate. Also, the matrix question format can generate a response set among some respondents. This means that respondents may develop a pattern of, say, agreeing with all the statements, without really thinking about what the statements mean. That is especially likely if the set of statements begins with several that indicate a particular orientation (for example, a conservative political perspective) and then offers only a few subsequent ones that represent the opposite orientation. Respondents might assume that all the statements represent the same orientation and, reading quickly, misread some of them, thereby giving the wrong answers. This problem can be reduced somewhat by alternating statements that represent different orientations and by making all statements short and clear.

A more difficult problem is when responses are generated through respondent boredom or fatigue. This can be avoided by keeping matrix

Screening Question:

36a.   I'm going to read you some examples that will give you an idea of the kinds of crimes this study covers. As I go through them, tell me if any of these happened to you in the last 6 months, that is, since [date].

Was something belonging to YOU stolen, such as-

(a)   Things that you carry, like luggage, a wallet, purse, briefcase, book-
(b)   Clothing, jewelry or calculator-
(c)   Bicycle or sports equipment-
(d)   Things in your home—like a TV, stereo, or tools-
(e)   Things outside your home, such as a garden hose or lawn furniture-
(f)   Things belonging to children in the household-
(g)   Things from a vehicle, such as a package, groceries, camera, or tapes-
OR
(h)   Did anyone ATTEMPT to steal anything belonging to you?

Crime Incident Report:

20a.   Were you or any other member of this household present when this incident occurred?

___ Yes [ask item 20b]

___ No [skip to 56, page 8]

20b.   Which household members were present

___ Respondent only [ask item 21]

___ Respondent and other household member(s) [ask item 21]

___ Only other household member(s) [skip to 59, page 8]

21.   Did you personally see an offender?

___ Yes

___ No

. . . .

56.   Do you know or have you learned anything about the offender(s)—for instance, whether there was one or more than one offender involved, whether it was someone young or old, or male or female?

___ Yes [ask 57]

___ No [skip to 88, page 11]

Figure 9.3   NCVS Screening Questions and Crime Incident Report

Source: Adapted from National Crime Victimization Survey, NCVS-1 Basic Screen Questionnaire, 5/10/2001 version, http://www.ojp.usdoj.gov/bjs/pub/pdf/ncvs1.pdf, accessed May 7, 2003; National Crime Victimization Survey, NCVS-2 Crime Incident Report, 10/3/2001 version, http://www.ojp.usdoj.gov/bjs/pub/pdf/ncvs2.pdf, accessed May 7, 2003.

17.   Beside each of the statements presented below, please indicate whether you Strongly Agree (SA), Agree (A), Disagree (D), Strongly Disagree (SD), or are Undecided (U).

	SA	A	D	SD	U
a. What this country needs is more law and order	[ ]	[ ]	[ ]	[ ]	[ ]
b. Police in America should not carry guns	[ ]	[ ]	[ ]	[ ]	[ ]
c. Repeat drug dealers should receive life sentences	[ ]	[ ]	[ ]	[ ]	[ ]

Figure 9.4   Matrix Question Format

questions and the entire questionnaire as short as possible. Later in this chapter, in the section on comparing different methods of questionnaire administration, we will describe a useful technique for avoiding response sets generated by respondent fatigue.

Ordering Questions in a Questionnaire

The order in which questions are asked can also affect the answers given. The content of one question can affect the answers given to later ones. For example, if several questions ask about the dangers of illegal drug use and then a question asks respondents to volunteer (open-ended) what they believe to be the most serious crime problems in U.S. cities, drug use will receive more mentions than would otherwise be the case. In this situation, it is preferable to ask the open-ended question first.

If respondents are asked to rate the overall effectiveness of corrections policy, they will answer subsequent questions about specific aspects of correctional institutions in a way that is consistent with their initial assessment. The converse is true as well: If respondents are first asked specific questions about prisons and other correctional facilities, their subsequent overall assessment will be influenced by the earlier question.

The best solution is sensitivity to the problem. Although we cannot avoid the effect of question order, we should attempt to estimate what that effect will be. Then we will be able to interpret results in a meaningful fashion. If the order of questions seems an especially important issue in a given study, we could construct several versions of the questionnaire that contain the different possible orderings of questions. We could then determine the effects of ordering. At the very least, different versions of the questionnaire should be pretested.

The desired ordering of questions differs somewhat between self-administered questionnaires and interviews. In the former, it is usually best to begin the questionnaire with the most interesting questions. Potential respondents who glance casually at the first few questions should want to answer them. Perhaps the questions involve opinions that they are aching to express. At the same time, however, the initial questions should be neither threatening nor sensitive. It might be a bad idea to begin with questions about sexual behavior or drug use. Requests for duller demographic data (age, gender, and the like) should generally be placed at the end of a self-administered questionnaire. Placing these questions at the beginning, as many inexperienced researchers are tempted to do, gives the questionnaire the initial appearance of a routine form, and the person who receives it may not be motivated to complete it.

Just the opposite is generally true for in-person interview and telephone surveys. When the potential respondent's door first opens, the interviewer must begin to establish rapport quickly. After a short introduction to the study, the interviewer can best begin by enumerating the members of the household, obtaining demographic data about each. Such questions are easily answered and generally nonthreatening. Once the initial rapport has been established, the interviewer can move into more sensitive areas. An interview that begins with the question "Do you ever worry about strangers appearing at your doorstep?" will probably end rather quickly.

Finally, it's common for less experienced researchers to assume that questionnaires must be newly constructed for each application. In contrast, it's almost always possible—and usually preferable—to use an existing questionnaire as a point of departure. See the box "Don't Start from Scratch!" for more on this.

Self-Administered Questionnaires

Self-administered questionnaires are generally the least expensive and easiest to complete.

Although the mail survey is the typical method used in self-administered studies, several other methods are also possible. In some cases, it may be appropriate to administer the question-

DON'T START FROM SCRATCH!

It's always easier to modify an existing questionnaire for a particular research application than it is to start from scratch. It's also difficult to imagine asking questions that nobody has asked before. Here are examples of Web sites that present complete questionnaires or batteries of questionnaire items.

- Bureau of Justice Statistics (BJS). In addition to administering the NCVS, the BJS collects information from a variety of justice organizations. Copies of recent questionnaires for all BJS-sponsored surveys are available at: http://www.ojp.usdoj.gov/bjs/quest.htm
- California Healthy Kids Survey. This set of questionnaires is useful for assessing behavior routines. Most include items on alcohol, tobacco, and other drug use; fighting; and other behaviors of potential interest for school-based interventions. English and Spanish versions are available for elementary, middle, and high school: http://www.wested.org/hks/

- Centers for Disease Control (CDC). Various centers within the CDC regularly collect a variety of health-related data through questionnaires and other data collection systems. Copies of instruments are available at: http://www.cdc.gov/nchs/express.htm
- The Measurement Group. This provides links to questionnaires designed for use in public health studies, but many of these include items of potential interest to treatment-related initiatives: http:www.themeasurementgroup.com/evalbttn.htm
- Community Development–Data Information and Analysis Laboratory (CD-DIAL). This Iowa State University center conducts surveys on a variety of topics. Examples of questionnaires are provided here for potential use by community organizations and others. Available at: http://dbs.extension.iastate.edu/cd-dial/surveys.asp

Source: Adapted from Maxfield (2001).

---

naire to a group of respondents gathered at the same place at the same time, such as police officers at roll call or prison inmates at some specially arranged assembly. Or probationers might complete a questionnaire when they report for a meeting with their probation supervisor. The Monitoring the Future survey (see Chapter 6) has high school seniors complete self-administered questionnaires in class.

Some experimentation has been conducted on the home delivery of questionnaires. A research worker delivers the questionnaire to the home of sample respondents and explains the study. Then the questionnaire is left for the respondent to complete, and the researcher picks it up later.

Home delivery and the mail can be used in combination as well. Questionnaires can be mailed to families, and then research workers may visit the homes to pick up the questionnaires and check them for completeness. In the opposite approach, survey packets are hand delivered by research workers with a request that the respondents mail the completed questionnaires to the research office. In general, when a research worker delivers the questionnaire, picks it up, or both, the completion rate is higher than for straightforward mail surveys.

Most recently, the explosive growth of the Internet has made it possible to have respondents complete self-administered questionnaires online. Before discussing more recent developments, let us turn our attention to the fundamentals of mail surveys, still the most typical form of self-administration used by researchers.

Mail Distribution and Return

The basic method for collecting data through the mail is transmittal of a questionnaire accompanied by a letter of explanation and a self-addressed, stamped envelope for returning the questionnaire. You have probably received a few in your lifetime. As a respondent, you are expected to complete the questionnaire, put it in the envelope, and mail it back. If, by any chance, you have received such a questionnaire and failed to return it, it would be a valuable exercise for you to recall your reasons for not returning it—and keep those in mind any time you plan to send questionnaires to others.

One big reason people do not return questionnaires is that it seems like too much trouble. To overcome this problem, researchers have developed ways to make the return of questionnaires easier. One method involves a self-mailing questionnaire that requires no return envelope. The questionnaire is designed so that when it is folded in a particular fashion, the return address appears on the outside. That way, the respondent doesn't have to worry about losing the envelope.

One factor to consider in the actual mailing of questionnaires is timing. In most cases, the holiday months of November, December, and January should be avoided. Overall mail volume is greatest during those periods, which can substantially slow down the process of both distribution and return of questionnaires. And because a greater volume of mail is flowing through post offices, people receive more mail of all types. If a questionnaire arrives in the company of glossy gift catalogs, holiday greetings, bills, and assorted junk mail, respondents will be more likely to discard the survey packet.

Warning Mailings and Cover Letters

The U.S. population, especially that proportion residing in urban areas, is becoming increasingly mobile. This mobility, together with the fact that sampling frames used to obtain addresses may be dated, has prompted researchers to use warning mailings for the purpose of verifying, or "cleaning," addresses. Certain types of warning mailings can also be effective in increasing response rates.

Warning mailings work like this: After researchers generate a sample, they send a postcard to each selected respondent, with the notation "Address correction requested" printed on the postcard. If the addressee has moved and left a forwarding address, the actual questionnaire is sent to the new address. In cases in which someone has moved and not left a forwarding address, or more than a year has elapsed and the post office no longer has information about a new address, the postcard is returned marked something like "Addressee unknown."

Selected persons who still reside at the original listed address are "warned" in suitable language to expect a questionnaire in the mail. In such cases, postcards should briefly describe the purpose of the survey for which the respondent has been selected.

Warning letters can be more effective than postcards in increasing response rates, and they can also serve the purpose of cleaning addresses. Letters printed on letterhead stationery can present a longer description of the survey's purpose and a more reasoned explanation of why it is important for everyone to respond.

Cover letters accompanying the actual questionnaire offer a similar opportunity to increase response rates. Two features of cover letters warrant some attention. First, the content of the letter is obviously important. The message should communicate why a survey is being conducted, how and why the respondent was selected, and why it is important for the respondent to complete the questionnaire. In line with our discussion of the protection of human subjects in Chapter 3, the cover letter should also assure respondents that their answers will be confidential.

Second, the cover letter should identify the institutional affiliation or sponsorship of the survey. The two alternatives are (1) some institution that the respondent respects or can identify with or (2) a neutral but impressive-sounding affiliation. For example, if we are conducting a mail survey of police chiefs, printing our cover letter on International Association of Chiefs of Police (IACP) stationery and having the letter signed by an official in the IACP might increase the response rate. Of course, we cannot adopt such a procedure unless the survey actually is endorsed by the IACP.

By the same token, it is important to avoid controversial affiliations or those inappropriate for the target population. The National Organization for Reform of Marijuana Laws, for instance, is not suitable for most target populations. A university affiliation is appropriate in many cases, unless the university is on bad terms with the target population.

Follow-Up Mailings

Follow-up mailings may be administered in a number of ways. In the simplest, nonrespondents are sent a letter of additional encouragement to participate. A better method, however, is to send a new copy of the survey questionnaire with the follow-up letter. If potential respondents have not returned their questionnaires after 2 or 3 weeks, the questionnaires probably have been lost or misplaced.

The methodological literature on follow-up mailings strongly suggests that they are effective in increasing return rates in mail surveys. In general, the longer a potential respondent delays replying, the less likely he or she is to do so at all. Properly timed follow-up mailings provide additional stimuli to respond.

The effects of follow-up mailings may be seen by monitoring the number of questionnaires received over time. Initial mailings will be followed by a rise in and subsequent subsiding of returns, and follow-up mailings will spur a resurgence of returns. In practice, three mailings (an original and two follow-ups) are the most effective.

Acceptable Response Rates

A question frequently asked about mail surveys concerns the percentage return rate that should be achieved. Note that the body of inferential statistics used in connection with survey analysis assumes that *all* members of the initial sample complete and return their questionnaires. Because this almost never happens, response bias becomes a concern. Researchers must test (and hope for) the possibility that respondents look essentially like a random sample of the initial sample and thus a somewhat smaller random sample of the total population. For example, if the gender of all people in the sample is known, a researcher can compare the percentages of males and females indicated on returned questionnaires with the percentages for the entire sample.

Nevertheless, overall response rate is one guide to the representativeness of the sample respondents. If the response rate is high, then there is less chance of significant response bias than if the rate is low. But what is a high response rate?

A quick review of the survey literature uncovers a wide range of response rates. Each may be accompanied by a statement like "This is regarded as a relatively high response rate for a survey of this type." (A U.S. senator made this statement about a poll of constituents that achieved a 4 percent return rate!) Even so, it's possible to state some rules of thumb about return rates. A response rate of at least 50 percent is adequate for analysis and reporting. A response of at least 60 percent is good. And a response rate of 70 percent is very good.

Bear in mind, however, that these are only rough guides; they have no statistical basis, and a demonstrated lack of response bias is far more important than a high response rate. Response rates tend to be higher for surveys that target a narrowly defined population, while general-population surveys yield lower response rates.

As you can imagine, one of the more persistent discussions among survey researchers concerns ways to increase response rates. Ingenious techniques have been developed to address this problem. Some researchers have experimented with novel formats. Others have tried paying respondents to participate. The problem with paying, of course, is that it's expensive to make meaningful payments to hundreds or thousands of respondents.

Don Dillman (1999) has undertaken an extensive review of the various techniques survey researchers use to increase return rates on mail surveys, and he evaluates the impact of each. More importantly, Dillman stresses the necessity of paying attention to all aspects of the study—what he calls the "total design method"—rather than one or two special gimmicks.

Computer-Based Self-Administration

Advances in computer and telecommunications technology over the past several decades have produced additional options for distributing and collecting self-administered questionnaires. Jeffrey Walker (1994) describes variations on conducting surveys by fax machine. Questionnaires are faxed to respondents, who are asked to fax their answers back. Of course, such surveys can only represent that part of the population that has fax machines. Walker reports that fax surveys don't achieve as high a response rate as do face-to-face interviews, but, because of the perceived urgency, they do produce higher response rates than do mail or telephone surveys. In one test case, all those who had ignored a mail questionnaire were sent a fax follow-up, and 83 percent responded.

As the Internet and Web have permeated work and leisure activities, different types of computer-assisted self-administered surveys have become more common. David Shannon and associates (Shannon, Johnson, Scarcy, and Lott, 2002) describe three general types of electronic surveys. The first is a disk-based survey. Respondents load a questionnaire from a disk or CD into their own computer, key in responses to survey items, and then either mail the disk back to researchers or transmit the information electronically. As the earliest form of electronic survey, the disk-based survey is a relic of stand-alone personal computers. Disk-based surveys are now virtually obsolete as personal computers are now routinely connected to the Web in one way or another.

The second type, e-mail surveys, has a few variations. Researchers can include a few simple questions in an e-mail message and ask respondents to reply by e-mail. More elaborate versions can embed complex questionnaires in e-mail messages. Respondents might be asked to open an attached file that contains a questionnaire, or they might be directed to another Web page that contains a formatted questionnaire. That brings us to the third type of electronic survey described by Shannon and associates—a questionnaire posted on a Web page.

The advantages of this method are obvious. Responses are automatically recorded in computer files, saving time and money. Web page design tools make it possible to create attractive questionnaires that include contingency questions, matrixes, and other complex tools for presenting items to respondents. Dillman, long recognized for his total design approach to conducting mail surveys, has written a comprehensive guide to conducting mail, Web-based, and other self-administered surveys.

All electronic versions of self-administered questionnaires face a couple of problems. The first concerns representativeness: Will the people who can be surveyed online be representative of meaningful populations, such as all U.S. adults, all registered voters, or all residents of particular urban neighborhoods? This criticism has also been raised with regard to surveys via fax and, in the mid-20th century, with regard to telephone surveys. Put in terms that should be familiar from the previous chapter, how closely do available sampling frames for electronic surveys match possible target populations? If, for example, our target population is university students, how can we obtain a list of e-mail addresses or other identifiers that will enable us to survey a representative sample? It's easy to think of other target populations of interest to criminal justice researchers that might be difficult to reach via e-mail or Web-based questionnaires.

The second problem is an unfortunate consequence of the rapid growth of e-mail and related technologies. Just as junk mail clutters our physical mailboxes with all sorts of advertising, junk e-mail ("spam") pops up all too often in our virtual mailboxes. The proliferation of junk e-mail has led to the development of antispam filters that screen out unwanted correspondence. Unfortunately, such programs also can screen out unfamiliar but well-meaning mail such as e-mail questionnaires. We will see later in this chapter how similar problems with telemarketing have made it increasingly difficult to conduct surveys by telephone.

We should keep one basic principle in mind when considering whether a self-administered questionnaire can be distributed electronically: Web-based surveys depend on access to the Web, which, of course, implies having a computer. Although the use of computers and the Web continues to increase rapidly, access to this technology still is unequally distributed across socioeconomic classes and other dimensions of interest to criminal justice researchers.

Here's a useful illustration of that point: In writing their article on electronic self-administered surveys, Shannon and associates distributed questionnaires to a sample of members of the American Educational Research Association. Respondents were presented with a variety of Likert scale items that measured their beliefs and attitudes about electronic surveys. How did Shannon and associates distribute their questionnaires? They sent them by regular mail, and respondents were asked to return the completed questionnaires by regular mail.

In-Person Interview Surveys

Face-to-face interviews are best for complex questionnaires and other specialized needs.

The in-person interview is an alternative method of collecting survey data. Rather than asking respondents to read questionnaires and enter their own answers, researchers send interviewers to ask the questions orally and record respondents' answers. Most interview surveys require more than one interviewer, although a researcher might undertake a small-scale interview survey by him- or herself.

The Role of the Interviewer

Not surprisingly, in-person interview surveys typically attain higher response rates than mail surveys. Respondents seem more reluctant to turn down an interviewer who is standing on their doorstep than to throw away a mail questionnaire. A properly designed and executed interview survey ought to achieve a completion rate of at least 80–85 percent.

The presence of an interviewer generally decreases the number of "don't knows" and "no answers." If minimizing such responses is important to the study, the interviewer can be instructed to probe for answers ("If you had to pick one of the answers, which do you think would come closest to your feelings?").

The interviewer can also help respondents with confusing questionnaire items. If the respondent clearly misunderstands the intent of a question, the interviewer can clarify matters and thereby obtain a relevant response. Such clarifications must be strictly controlled, however, through formal specifications.

Finally, the interviewer can observe as well as ask questions. For example, the interviewer can make observations about the quality of the dwelling, the presence of various possessions, the respondent's ability to speak English, the respondent's general reactions to the study, and so forth. Interviewers for the BCS and for a 1983 supplement to the NCVS made detailed observations of the physical conditions surrounding each respondent's home. Later analysis compared interviewer ratings of such things as litter and graffiti with respondent perceptions of the same problems (Maxfield, 1987b).

Survey research is, of necessity, based on an unrealistic stimulus–response theory of cognition and behavior. That is, it is based on the assumption that a questionnaire item will mean the same thing to every respondent, and every given response must mean the same thing when given by different respondents. Although this is an impossible goal, survey questions are drafted to approximate the ideal as closely as possible. The interviewer also plays a role in this ideal situation. The interviewer's presence should not affect a respondent's perception of a question or the answer given. The interviewer, then, should be a neutral medium through which questions and answers are transmitted. If this goal is met, different interviewers will obtain the same responses from a given respondent, an example of reliability in measurement (see Chapter 5).

General Rules for Interviewing

The way interviews ought to be conducted will vary somewhat by the survey population and survey content. Nevertheless, some general guidelines apply to most interviewing situations, including sample surveys and more specialized interviewing.

Appearance and Demeanor   As a general rule, the interviewer should dress in a fashion similar to that of the people he or she will be interviewing. An interviewer wearing business attire will probably have difficulty getting cooperation and good responses from poorer respondents. And a poorly dressed interviewer will have similar difficulties with richer respondents.

To the extent that the interviewer's dress and grooming differ from that of the respondents, it should be in the direction of cleanliness, neatness, and modesty. Although middle-class standards of dress and grooming are not accepted by all sectors of American society, they remain the norm and are likely to be acceptable to the largest number of respondents.

The importance of considering the target population cannot be overemphasized. "Establishment" attire should be the norm when interviewing most criminal justice officials. However, the middle-class norm in clothing may foster suspicion among street people or incarcerated individuals.

In demeanor, interviewers should be pleasant if nothing else. Because they will be prying into the respondent's personal life and thoughts,

they must communicate a genuine interest in getting to know the respondent without appearing to spy. They must be relaxed and friendly without being too casual or clinging. Good interviewers also have the ability to quickly determine the kind of person the respondent feels most comfortable with or most enjoys talking to, and they adapt accordingly.

Familiarity with the Questionnaire   The interviewer must be able to read the questionnaire items to respondents without stumbling over words and phrases. A good model for interviewers is the actor reading lines in a play or film. The interviewer must read the questions as though they are part of a natural conversation, but that "conversation" must precisely follow the language set down in the question.

By the same token, the interviewer must be familiar with the specifications for administering the questionnaire. Inevitably, some questions will not exactly fit a given respondent's situation, and the interviewer must determine how those questions should be interpreted in that situation. The specifications provided to the interviewer should include adequate guidelines in such cases, but the interviewer must know the organization and contents of the specifications well enough to refer to them efficiently.

Probing for Responses   Probes are frequently required to elicit responses to open-ended questions. For example, to a question about neighborhood crime problems, the respondent might simply reply, "Pretty bad." The interviewer could obtain an elaboration on this response through a variety of probes. Sometimes, the best probe is silence; if the interviewer sits quietly with pencil poised, the respondent will probably fill the pause with additional comments. Appropriate verbal probes are "How is that?" and "In what ways?" Perhaps the most generally useful probe is "Anything else?"

In every case, however, it is imperative that the probe be completely neutral. The probe must not in any way affect the nature of the subsequent response. If we anticipate that a given question may require probing for appropriate responses, we should write one or more useful probes next to the item in the questionnaire. This practice has two important advantages. First, it allows for more time to devise the best, most neutral probes. Second, it ensures that all interviewers will use the same probes as needed. Thus, even if the probe is not perfectly neutral, the same stimulus is presented to all respondents. This is the same logical guideline as for question wording. Although a question should not be loaded or biased, it is essential that every respondent be presented with the same question, even if a biased one.

Coordination and Control

Whenever more than one interviewer will administer a survey, it is essential that the efforts be carefully coordinated and controlled. Two ways to ensure this control are by (1) training interviewers and (2) supervising them after they begin work.

Whether the researchers will be administering a survey themselves or paying a professional firm to do it for them, they should be attentive to the importance of training interviewers. The interviewers usually should know what the study is all about. Even though the interviewers may be involved only in the data collection phase of the project, they should understand what will be done with the information they gather and what purpose will be served.

There may be some exceptions to this, however. For example, in their follow-up study of child abuse victims and controls, Cathy Spatz Widom and associates (Widom, Weiler, and Cotler, 1999) did not inform the professional interviewers who gathered data that their interest was in the long-term effects of child abuse. This safeguard was used to avoid even the slightest chance that interviewers' knowledge of the study focus would affect how they conducted interviews.

Obviously, training should ensure that interviewers understand the questionnaire. Interviewers should also be clear on procedures to select respondents from among household members. And interviewers should recognize circumstances in which substitute sample elements may be used in place of addresses that no longer exist, families who have moved, or persons who simply refuse to be interviewed.

Training should include practice sessions in which interviewers administer the questionnaire to one another. The final stage of the training should involve some "real" interviews conducted under conditions like those in the actual survey.

While interviews are being conducted, it is a good idea to review questionnaires as they are completed. This may reveal questions or groups of questions that respondents do not understand. Alternatively, reviewing completed questionnaires can signal that an interviewer is encountering difficulties.

Computer-Assisted In-Person Interviews

Just as e-mail and Web-based surveys apply new technology to the gathering of survey data through self-administration, laptop and hand-held computers are increasingly being used to conduct in-person interviews. Different forms of **computer-assisted interviewing** (CAI) offer major advantages in the collection of survey data. At the same time, CAI has certain disadvantages that must be considered. We'll begin by describing an example of how this technology was adopted in the BCS, one of the earliest uses of CAI in a general-purpose crime survey.

CAI in the British Crime Survey Previous waves of the BCS, a face-to-face interview survey, asked respondents to complete a self-administered questionnaire about drug use, printed as a small booklet that was prominently marked "Confidential." Beginning with the 1994 survey, respondents answered self-report questions on laptop computers. The BCS includes two related versions of CAI. In computer-assisted personal interviewing (CAPI), interviewers read questions from computer screens and then key in respondents' answers. For self-report items, interviewers hand the computers to subjects, who then key in the responses themselves. This approach is known as computer-assisted self-interviewing (CASI). In addition, CASI as used in the BCS is supplemented with audio instructions—respondents listen to interview prompts on headphones connected to the computer. After subjects key in their responses to self-report items, the answers are scrambled so the interviewer cannot access them. Notice how this feature of CASI enhances the researcher's ethical obligation to keep responses confidential.

Malcolm Ramsay and Andrew Percy (1996) report that CASI has at least two benefits. First, respondents seem to sense a greater degree of confidentiality when they respond to questions on a computer screen as opposed to questions on a written form. Second, the laptop computers are something of a novelty that stimulate respondents' interest; this is especially true for younger respondents.

Examining results from the BCS reveals that CASI techniques produced higher estimates of illegal drug use than those revealed in previous surveys. Table 9.1 compares self-reported drug use from the 1998 BCS (Ramsey and Partridge, 1999) with results from the 1992 BCS (Mott and Mirrlees-Black, 1995), in which respondents answered questions in printed booklets. We present results for only three drugs here, together with tabulations about the use of any drug. For each drug, the survey measured lifetime use ("Ever used?") and use in the past 12 months. Notice that rates of self-reported use were substantially higher in 1998 than in 1992, with the exception of "semeron" use, reported by very few respondents in 1992 and none in 1998. If you've never heard of semeron, you're not alone. It's a fictitious drug, included in the list of real drugs to detect untruthful or exaggerated responses. If someone confessed to using semeron, his or her responses to other self-reported items

Table 9.1   Self-Reported Drug Use, 1992 and 1998 British Crime Survey

	Percentage of Respondents Ages 16–29 Who Report Use	
	1992	1998
Marijuana or cannabis		
Ever used?	24	42
Used in previous 12 months?	12	23
Amphetamines		
Ever used?	9	20
Used in previous 12 months?	4	8
Semeron		
Ever used?	0.3	0.0
Used in previous 12 months?	0.1	0.0
Any drug		
Ever used?	28	49
Used in previous 12 months?	14	25

Source: 1992 data adapted from Mott and Mirrlees-Black (1995:41–42); 1998 data adapted from Ramsay and Partridge (1999:68–71).

would be suspect. Notice in Table 9.1 that CASI use in 1998 reduced the number of respondents who admitted using a drug that doesn't exist.

CASI has also been used in the BCS since 1996 to measure domestic violence committed by partners and ex-partners of males and females ages 16–59. Catriona Mirrlees-Black (1999) reports that CASI techniques reveal higher estimates of domestic violence victimization among both females and males.

Advantages and Disadvantages   Different types of CAI offer a number of advantages for in-person interviews. The BCS and other surveys that include self-report items indicate that CAI is more "productive" in that self-reports of drug use and other offending tend to be higher. In 1999, the National Household Survey on Drug Abuse shifted completely to CAI (Wright, Barker, Gfoerer, and Piper, 2002). Other advantages include the following:

- Responses can be quickly keyed in and automatically reformatted into data files for analysis.
- Complex sequences of contingency questions can be automated. Instead of printing many examples of "If answer is yes, go to question 43a; if no . . . ," computer-based questionnaires automatically jump to the next appropriate question contingent on responses to earlier ones.
- CAI offers a way to break up the monotony of a long interview by shifting from verbal interviewer prompts to self-interviewing, with or without an audio supplement.
- Questionnaires for self-interviewing can be programmed in different languages, readily switching to the language appropriate for a particular respondent.
- Audio-supplemented CASI produces a standardized interview, avoiding any bias that might emerge from interviewer effects.
- Audio supplements, in different languages, facilitate self-interviews of respondents who cannot read.

At the same time, CAI has certain disadvantages that preclude its use in many survey applications:

- Although computers become more of a bargain each day, doing a large-scale in-person interview survey requires providing computers for each interviewer. Costs can quickly add up. CAI also requires specialized software to format and present on-screen questionnaires.
- Although CAI reduces costs in data processing, it requires more up-front investment in programming questionnaires, skip sequences, and the like.
- Automated skip sequences for contingency questions are great, but if something goes wrong with the programmed questionnaire, all sorts of subsequent problems are possible. As Emma Forster and Alison McCleery (1999) point out, such question-routing

mistakes might mean whole portions of a questionnaire are skipped. Whereas occasional random errors are possible with pen-and-paper interviews, large-scale systematic error can happen with CAI technology.

- Proofreading printed questionnaires is straightforward, but it can be difficult to audit a computerized questionnaire. Doing so might require special technical skills.
- It can be difficult to print and archive a complex questionnaire used in CAI. This was a problem with early applications of CAI technology, but improvements in software are helping to solve it.
- Batteries of laptops run down, and computers and software are more vulnerable to malfunctions and random weirdness than are stacks of printed questionnaires.

In sum, CAI can be costly and requires some specialized skills. As a result, these and related technologies are best suited for use by professional survey researchers or research centers that regularly conduct large-scale in-person interviews. We will return to this issue in the concluding section of this chapter.

Telephone Surveys

Telephone surveys are fastest and relatively low cost.

Telephone surveys have many advantages that make them a popular method. Probably the greatest advantages involve money and time. In a face-to-face household interview, a researcher may drive several miles to a respondent's home, find no one there, return to the research office, and drive back the next day—possibly finding no one there again. It's cheaper and quicker to "let your fingers do the walking."

Interviewing by telephone, researchers can dress any way they please, and it will have no effect on the answers respondents give. And respondents may be more honest in giving socially disapproved answers if they don't have to look the questioner in the eye. Similarly, it may be possible to probe into more sensitive areas, although that is not necessarily the case. People are, to some extent, more suspicious when they can't see the person asking them questions—perhaps a consequence of telemarketing and salespeople conducting bogus surveys prior to making sales pitches.

Telephone surveys can give a researcher greater control over data collection if several interviewers are engaged in the project. If all the interviewers are calling from the research office, they can get clarification from the supervisor whenever problems occur, as they inevitably do. Alone in the field, an interviewer may have to wing it between weekly visits with the interviewing supervisor.

A related advantage is rooted in the growing diversity of U.S. cities. Because many major cities have growing immigrant populations, interviews may need to be conducted in different languages. Telephone interviews are usually conducted from a central site, so that one or more multilingual interviewers can be quickly summoned if an English-speaking interviewer makes contact with, say, a Spanish-speaking respondent. In-person interview surveys present much more difficult logistical problems in handling multiple languages. And mail surveys require printing and distributing questionnaires in different languages.

Another important factor in the increasing use of telephone surveys is personal safety. Dillman (1978:4) described perceptions of risk in in-person interviews:

> Interviewers must be able to operate comfortably in a climate in which strangers are viewed with distrust and must successfully counter respondents' objections to being interviewed. Increasingly, interviewers must be willing to work at night to contact residents in many households. In some cases, this necessitates providing protection for interviewers working in areas of a city in which a definite threat to the safety of individuals exists.

Concerns for safety, therefore, can work two ways to hamper face-to-face interviews. First, potential respondents may refuse to be interviewed because they fear the stranger-interviewer. Second, the interviewers themselves may be in danger. Telephone surveys eliminate risks to interviewers and reduce the concerns of respondents who may be uneasy about opening their doors to strangers.

Telephone interviewing has its problems, however. Telephone surveys are limited by definition to people who own telephones. Years ago, this method produced a substantial social-class bias by excluding poor people. Over time, however, the telephone has become a standard fixture in almost all American homes. The U.S. Census Bureau estimates that 94 percent of all households now have telephones, so the earlier class bias has been substantially reduced (U.S. Bureau of the Census, 2002:Table 1103). The NCVS, traditionally an in-person interview, has increased its use of telephone interviews as part of the crime survey's redesign.

At the same time, phone surveys are much less suitable for individuals not living in households. Homeless people are obvious examples; those who live in institutions are also difficult to reach out and touch via telephone. Patricia Tjaden and Nancy Thoennes (2000) cite single-adult households and people living in rural or inner-city areas as targets least likely to have telephone coverage.

A related sampling problem involves unlisted numbers. If the survey sample is selected from the pages of a local telephone directory, it totally omits all those people who have requested that their numbers not be published. Also, as we mentioned in Chapter 8, recent movers and transient residents are not well represented in published telephone directories. This potential bias has been eliminated through random-digit dialing (RDD), a technique that has advanced telephone sampling substantially.

RDD samples use computer algorithms to generate lists of random telephone numbers—usually, the last four digits. This procedure gets around the sampling problem of unlisted telephone numbers but may substitute an administrative problem. Randomly generating phone numbers produces numbers that are not in operation or that serve a business establishment or pay phone. In most cases, businesses and pay phones are not included in the target population; dialing these numbers and learning that they're "out of scope" will take time away from producing completed interviews with the target population.

Weisel (1999) offers an excellent description of RDD samples for use in community crime surveys. Among the increasingly important issues in RDD samples is the growing number of telephone numbers in use for cell phones, pagers, and home access to the Internet. This means that the rate of ineligible telephone numbers generated through RDD is increasing. Weisel's rule of thumb is that ineligible numbers account for an estimated 60 percent of phone numbers produced by typical RDD procedures. Thus, if RDD is used, researchers should plan on making five calls to reach two households.

The ease with which people can hang up is, of course, another shortcoming of telephone surveys. Once a researcher is inside someone's home for an interview, that person is unlikely to order the researcher out of the house in mid-interview. It's much easier to terminate a telephone interview abruptly, saying something like "Whoops! Someone's at the door. Gotta go" or simply hanging up.

Another, more difficult, challenge with telephone surveys involves the explosion of telemarketing. The volume of junk phone calls now rivals that of junk mail, and salespeople often begin their pitch by describing a "survey." The viability of legitimate surveys is now hampered by the proliferation of bogus surveys, which are actually sales campaigns disguised as research. As if that weren't bad enough, telemarketing has become so annoying that many people simply hang up whenever they hear a strange voice announcing some institutional affiliation.

Partly as a consequence, residential phone customers seek to exercise greater control over incoming calls through caller identification, phone number blocking, and other new services. Such devices enable phone users to screen calls before picking up the receiver, making it more difficult for legitimate survey researchers to make contact.

Following action in several states, the Federal Trade Commission approved new regulations restricting telemarketing by enabling individuals to place their phone numbers on a national do-not-call registry ("Telemarketing Sales Rule," 2003). The rule went into effect in October 2003 after withstanding vigorous legal challenges by the telemarketing industry. The impact of this regulation remains to be seen, but it has the potential to make life easier for legitimate telephone survey researchers.

Computer-Assisted Telephone Interviewing

Much of the growth in telemarketing has been fueled by advances in computer and telecommunications technology. Computers generate and dial phone numbers (in some cases, computers even control recorded sales pitches); operators enter customer and order information in forms displayed on computer screens. Beginning in the 1980s, much of the same technology came to be widely used in telephone surveys, referred to as computer-assisted telephone interviewing (CATI). Here's how it works.

Interviewers wearing telephone headsets sit at computer workstations. Computer programs dial sampled phone numbers, which can be either generated through RDD or extracted from a database of phone numbers compiled from some source. As soon as phone contact is made, the computer screen displays an introduction ("Hello, my name is . . . calling from the Survey Research Center at Ivory Tower University") and the first question to be asked, often a query about the number of residents who live in the household. As interviewers key in answers to each question, the computer program displays a new screen that presents the next question, until the end of the interview is reached.

CATI systems offer several advantages over procedures in which an interviewer works through a printed interview schedule. Speed is one obvious plus. Forms on computer screens can be filled in more quickly than can paper forms. Typing answers to open-ended questions is much faster than writing them by hand. And CATI software immediately formats responses into a data file as they are keyed in, which eliminates the step of manually transferring answers from paper to computer.

Perhaps you've occasionally marveled at newspaper stories that report the results of a nationwide opinion poll the day after some major speech or event. The speed of CATI technology, coupled with RDD, makes these instant poll reports possible.

Accuracy is also enhanced by CATI systems in several ways. First, CATI programs can be designed to accept only valid responses to a given questionnaire item. For example, if valid responses to respondent "gender" are *f* for female and *m* for male, the computer will accept only those two letters, emitting a disagreeable noise and refusing to proceed if something else is keyed in. Second, the software can be programmed to automate contingency questions and skip sequences, thus ensuring that the interviewer skips over inappropriate items and rapidly gets to the next appropriate question. This can be especially handy in a victim survey, in which affirmative answers to screening questions automatically bring up detailed questions about each crime incident.

Comparison of the Three Methods

Cost, speed, and question content are issues to consider in selecting a survey method.

We've now examined three ways of collecting survey data: self-administered questionnaires, in-person interviews, and telephone surveys. We

have also considered some recent advances in each mode of administration. Although we've touched on some of the relative advantages and disadvantages of each, let's take a minute to compare them more directly.

Self-administered questionnaires are generally cheaper to use than interview surveys. Moreover, for self-administered e-mail or Web-based surveys, it costs no more to conduct a national survey than a local one. Obviously, the cost difference between a local and a national in-person interview survey is considerable. Telephone surveys are somewhere in between. Although national surveys can inflate costs somewhat through long-distance telephone charges, flat-rate long-distance service can be negotiated. Mail surveys typically require a small staff. One person can conduct a reasonable mail survey, although it is important not to underestimate the work involved.

Up to a point, cost and speed are inversely related. In-person interview surveys can be completed very quickly if a large pool of interviewers is available and funding is adequate to pay them. In contrast, if a small number of people are conducting a larger number of face-to-face interviews, costs are generally lower, but the survey takes much longer to complete. Telephone surveys that use CATI technology are easily the fastest.

Self-administered surveys may be more appropriate to use with especially sensitive issues if the surveys offer complete anonymity. Respondents are sometimes reluctant to report controversial or deviant attitudes or behaviors in interviews, but they may be willing to respond to an anonymous self-administered questionnaire. However, the successful use of computers for self-report items in the BCS and the National Household Survey on Drug Abuse suggests that interacting with a machine can promote more candid responses.

Interview surveys have many advantages, too. For example, in-person or telephone surveys are more appropriate when respondent literacy may be a problem. Interview surveys also result in fewer incomplete questionnaires.

Although respondents may skip questions in a self-administered questionnaire, interviewers are trained not to do so. CAI offers a further check on this in telephone and in-person surveys.

Although self-administered questionnaires may be more effective in dealing with sensitive issues, interview surveys are definitely more effective in dealing with complicated ones. Interviewers can explain complex questions to respondents and use visual aids that are not possible in mail or phone surveys.

The 1984 BCS contained a good example of such techniques that did not depend on computer technology. The survey included a series of questions about attitudes toward neighborhood watch programs. Pretests of certain questionnaire items revealed that many people were unfamiliar with neighborhood watch. In conducting the actual survey, interviewers handed respondents a card that presented a brief description of neighborhood watch. Respondents were asked a battery of questions about their opinions of such programs after they had read the card.

In general, this may be called an "information–opinion" technique, in which each respondent is first exposed to a standard description of some object and is then asked to give an opinion about the object. This technique cannot be used effectively in self-administered questionnaires because respondents might skip over a lengthy written description and begin to answer questions right away.

In-person interviews, especially with computer technology, can also help reduce response sets. Respondents (like students?) eventually become bored listening to a lengthy series of similar types of questions. It's easier to maintain individuals' interest by changing the kind of stimulation they are exposed to. A mix of questions verbalized by a person, presented on a computer screen, and heard privately through earphones is more interesting for respondents and reduces fatigue.

As mentioned earlier, interviewers who question respondents face to face are also able to

make important observations aside from responses to questions asked in the interview. In a household interview, they may summarize characteristics of the neighborhood, the dwelling unit, and so forth. They may also note characteristics of the respondents or the quality of their interaction with the respondents—whether the respondent had difficulty communicating, was hostile, seemed to be lying, and so on. Finally, when the safety of interviewers is an issue, a mail or phone survey may be the best option.

Ultimately, researchers must weigh all these advantages and disadvantages of the three methods against research needs and available resources.

Strengths and Weaknesses of Survey Research

Surveys tend to be high on reliability and generalizability, but validity can often be a weak point.

Like other modes of collecting data in criminal justice research, surveys have strengths and weaknesses. It is important to consider these in deciding whether the survey format is appropriate for a specific research purpose.

Surveys are particularly useful in describing the characteristics of a large population. The NCVS has become an important tool for researchers and public officials because of its ability to describe levels of crime. A carefully selected probability sample, in combination with a standardized questionnaire, allows researchers to make refined descriptive statements about a neighborhood, a city, a nation, or some other large population.

Standardized questionnaires have an important advantage in regard to measurement. Earlier chapters discussed the ambiguous nature of concepts: They ultimately have no real meanings. One person's view about, say, crime seriousness or punishment severity is quite different from another's. Although we must be able to define concepts in ways that are most relevant to research goals, it's not always easy to apply the same definitions uniformly to all subjects. Nevertheless, the survey researcher is bound to the requirement of having to ask exactly the same questions of all subjects and having to impute the same intent to all respondents giving a particular response.

At the same time, survey research has its weaknesses. First, the requirement for standardization might mean that we are trying to fit round pegs into square holes. Standardized questionnaire items often represent the least common denominator in assessing people's attitudes, orientations, circumstances, and experiences. By designing questions that are at least *minimally* appropriate to all respondents, we may miss what is *most* appropriate to many respondents. In this sense, surveys often appear superficial in their coverage of complex topics.

Similarly, survey research cannot readily deal with the specific contexts of social life. Although questionnaires may provide information in this area, the survey researcher seldom develops a feel for the total life situation in which respondents are thinking and acting. This is in contrast to the experiences of the participant observer (Chapter 10). Many researchers are dissatisfied with standard survey questions about important criminal justice concepts such as fear of crime, routine behavior, and crime prevention. NCVS procedures for counting series victimizations remain inadequate even after 30 years experience with the survey.

Although surveys are flexible in the sense mentioned earlier, they cannot be changed once interviewing has begun. Studies that involve direct observation can be modified as field conditions warrant, but surveys typically require that an initial study design remain unchanged throughout.

Using surveys to study crime and criminal justice policy presents special challenges. The target population frequently includes lower-income, transient persons who are difficult to contact through customary sampling methods. For example, homeless persons are excluded from any survey that samples households, but people who live on the street no doubt figure prominently as victims and offenders. Maxfield (1999) describes how new data from the National Incident-Based Reporting System suggest that a number of "nonhousehold-associated" persons are systematically undercounted by sampling procedures used in the NCVS. Crime surveys such as the NCVS and the BCS have been deficient in getting information about crimes of violence when the victim and offender have some prior relationship. This is particularly true for domestic violence.

Underreporting of domestic violence appears to be due, in part, to the very general nature of large-scale crime surveys. Catriona Mirrlees-Black (1995:8) of the British Home Office summarizes the trade-offs of using survey techniques to learn about domestic violence:

> Measuring domestic violence is difficult territory. The advantage of the BCS is that it is based on a large nationally representative sample, has a relatively high response rate, and collects information on enough incidents to provide reliable details of their nature. One disadvantage is that domestic violence is measured in the context of a crime survey, and some women may not see what happened to them as "crime," or be reluctant to do so. Also, there is little time to approach the topic "gently." A specially designed questionnaire with carefully selected interviewers may well have the edge here.

In recent years, both the NCVS and the BCS have been revised to produce better measures of domestic and intimate violence. Estimates of domestic violence increased in the 1996 wave of the BCS, and researchers think that the increase reflects a greater willingness by respondents to discuss domestic violence with interviewers (Mirrlees-Black, Mayhew, and Percy, 1996). Most recently, the use of computer-assisted self-interviewing in the BCS has produced higher estimates of victimization prevalence among women, as well as the first measurable rates of domestic violence victimization for males (Mirrlees-Black, 1999).

We have mentioned that national crime surveys cannot be used to estimate the frequency of victimization in local areas like individual cities. For this reason, the Census Bureau conducted a series of victim surveys in cities in the 1970s. City crime surveys suffer problems of their own, however. Because sampling procedures are almost always based on some sample frame of city residents, city-specific surveys are not able to measure crimes that involve nonresident victims. For example, an RDD survey of Key West, Florida, residents could not possibly count the robbery of a visitor who came down from Cincinnati. This problem still exists in the resurrection of city surveys by the BJS and the COPS office (Smith, Steadman, Minton, and Townsend, 1999). City-level surveys are based on samples of residents and so cannot measure incidents that affect nonresident victims.

Survey research is generally weaker on validity and stronger on reliability. In comparison with field research, for instance, the artificiality of the survey format puts a strain on validity. As an illustration, most researchers agree that fear of crime is not well measured by the standard question "How safe do you feel, or would you feel, out alone in your neighborhood at night?" Survey responses to that question are, at best, approximate indicators of what we have in mind when we conceptualize fear of crime.

Reliability is a different matter. By presenting all subjects with a standardized stimulus, survey research goes a long way toward eliminating unreliability in observations made by the researcher.

However, even this statement is subject to qualification. Critics of survey methods argue that questionnaires for standard crime surveys and many specialized studies embody a narrow, legalistic conception of crime that cannot reflect the perceptions and experiences of minorities and women. Survey questions typically are based on male views and do not adequately tap

victimization or fear of crime among women (Straus, 1999; Tjaden and Thoennes, 2000). Concern that survey questions might mean different things to different respondents raises important questions about reliability and about the generalizability of survey results across subgroups of a population.

As with all methods of observation, a full awareness of the inherent or probable weaknesses of survey research may partially resolve them. Ultimately, though, we are on the safest ground when we can use several different research methods to study a given topic.

Other Ways of Asking Questions

Specialized interviews and focus groups are alternative ways of gathering question-based data.

Sample surveys are perhaps the best-known application of asking questions as a data-gathering strategy for criminal justice research. Often, however, more specialized interviewing techniques are appropriate.

Specialized Interviewing

No precise definition of the term *survey* enables us to distinguish a survey from other types of interview situations. As a rule of thumb, a sample survey (even one that uses nonprobability sampling methods) is an interview-based technique for generalizing to a larger population. In contrast, specialized interviewing focuses on the views and opinions of only those individuals who are interviewed.

Let's say we are interested in how mental health professionals view different drug treatment programs for prison inmates. One approach is to conduct a sample survey of psychologists who work in state correctional facilities in which each sampled psychologist completes a structured questionnaire concerning drug treatment programs. This approach will enable us to generalize to the population of state prison psychologists.

Another approach is to study one or two correctional institutions (or some small number) intensively. We might interview a psychologist in each institution and present questions about various approaches to drug treatment therapy. In all likelihood, we will use, not a highly structured questionnaire, but rather a list of questions or topics we wish to discuss with each subject. And we will treat the interview as more of a directed conversation than a formal interview. Of course, we cannot generalize from interviews with one or two prison psychologists to any larger population. However, we will gain an understanding (and probably a more detailed one) of how staff psychologists in specific institutions feel about different drug treatment programs.

Specialized interviewing asks questions of a small number of subjects, typically using an interview schedule that is much less structured than that in sample surveys. Michael Quinn Patton (2001) distinguishes two variations of specialized interviews. The less structured alternative is to prepare a general interview guide that includes the issues, topics, or questions the researcher wishes to cover. Issues and items are not presented to respondents in any standardized order. The interview guide is more like a checklist than an interview schedule, ensuring that planned topics are addressed at some point in the interview. The standardized open-ended interview, in contrast, is more structured, using specific questions arranged in a particular order. The researcher presents each respondent with the same questions in the same sequence (subject to any contingency questions). The questions are open-ended, but their format and presentation are standardized.

To underscore the flexibility of specialized interviewing, Patton describes how the two approaches can be used in combination (2001: 347):

> A conversational strategy can be used within an interview guide approach, or you can combine a guide approach.... This combined strategy offers the interviewer flexibility in probing and in determining when it is appropriate to explore certain subjects in greater depth, or even to pose questions about new areas of inquiry that were not originally anticipated in the interview instrument's development.

Open-ended questions are ordinarily used because they capture rich detail better. The primary disadvantage of open-ended questions—having to categorize responses—is not a problem in specialized interviewing because of the small numbers of subjects and because researchers are more interested in describing than in generalizing.

Specialized interviewing can be incorporated into any research project as a supplementary source of information. If, for example, we are interested in the effects of determinant sentencing on prison populations, we can analyze data from the Census of State Adult Correctional Facilities, conducted by the BJS. We might also interview a small number of corrections administrators, perhaps asking them to react to our data analysis. Evaluation studies and other applied research projects frequently use specialized interviewing techniques, alone or in combination with other sources of data.

Focus Groups

Like sample surveys, focus group techniques were refined by market research firms in the years following World War II. As the name implies, market research explores questions about the potential for sales of consumer products. Because a firm may spend millions of dollars developing, advertising, and distributing some new item, market research is an important tool to test consumer reactions before large sums of money are invested in a product.

Surveys have two disadvantages in market research. First, a nationwide or large-scale probability survey can be expensive. Second, it may be difficult to present advertising messages or other product images in a survey format. Focus groups have proved to be more suitable for many market research applications. In recent years, focus groups have commonly been used as substitutes for surveys in criminal justice and other social science research.

In a focus group, 8–15 people are brought together in a room to engage in a guided group discussion of some topic. Although focus groups cannot be used to make statistical estimates about a population, members are nevertheless selected to represent a target population. Richard Krueger and Mary Anne Casey (2000) and D. W. Stewart and P. N. Shamdasani (1990) describe focus groups, their applications, and their advantages and disadvantages in detail.

For example, the location of community correctional facilities such as work-release centers and halfway houses often prompts a classic "Not in my backyard!" (NIMBY) response from people who live in neighborhoods where proposed facilities will be built. Recognizing this, a mayor who wants to find a suitable site without annoying neighborhood residents (voters) is well advised to convene a focus group that includes people who live in areas near possible facility locations. A focus group can test the "market acceptability" of a work-release center, which might include the best way to package and sell the product. Such an exercise might reveal that an appeal to altruism ("We all have to make sacrifices in the fight against crime") is much less effective in gaining support than an alternative sales pitch that stresses potential economic benefits ("This new facility will provide jobs for neighborhood residents").

Generalizations from focus groups to target populations cannot be precise; however, a study by V. M. Ward and associates (Ward, Bertrand, and Brown, 1991) found that focus group and survey results can be quite consistent under certain conditions. They conclude that focus groups are most useful in two cases: (1) when precise generalization to a larger population is not necessary, and (2) when focus group participants and the larger population they are intended to represent are relatively homogeneous. So, for example, a focus group is not appropriate to predict how all city residents will react to a ban on handgun ownership. But a focus group of registered handgun owners could help evaluate a proposed city campaign to buy back handguns.

Focus groups may also be used in combination with survey research in one of two ways. First, a focus group can be valuable in questionnaire development. When researchers are uncertain how to present items to respondents, a focus group discussion about the topic can generate possible item formats. For instance, James Nolan and Yoshio Akiyama (1999) studied police routines for making records of hate crimes. In a general sense, they knew what concepts they wanted to measure but were unsure how to operationalize them. They convened five focus groups in different cities, including police administrators, midlevel managers, patrol officers, and civilian employees, to learn about different perspectives on hate crime recording. Analyzing focus group results, Nolan and Akiyama prepared a self-administered questionnaire that was sent to a large number of individuals in four police departments.

Second, after a survey has been completed and preliminary results tabulated, focus groups may be used to guide the interpretation of some results. After a citywide survey in which we find, for example, that recent immigrants from Southeast Asian countries are least supportive of community policing, we might conduct a focus group of Asian residents to delve more deeply into their concerns.

Focus groups are flexible and can be adapted to many uses in basic and applied research. Keep in mind, however, two key elements expressed in the name of this data collection technique. *Focus* means that researchers present specific questions or issues for directed discussion. Having a free-for-all discussion about hate crime, for example, would not have yielded much useful insight for Nolan and Akiyama to develop a survey instrument. *Group* calls our attention to

PUTTING IT ALL TOGETHER

ASKING QUESTIONS IN NEW YORK CITY

"Can the decline in New York City crime be attributed to police action?" That's not the kind of question that lends itself to survey research. "Do people believe police action is responsible for reduced crime?" *is* appropriate for survey research, but this is not the type of question Rutgers researchers addressed. A victim survey might indirectly be useful if it was suspected that the decline in police-recorded crime was due to sloppy or fraudulent record-keeping. However, it is almost inconceivable that record-keeping changes could produce major drops in all crime categories over a 10-year period.

Survey research *would* be appropriate if research questions centered on citizen perceptions of police behavior, an issue increasingly important to New Yorkers following highly publicized incidents of brutal assaults by officers and police shootings of innocent citizens. And surveys would be useful in asking a large number of police officers about their views on how police action reduces crime. But neither of those sets of research questions addresses the purpose of this project.

---

potential participants in the focused discussions. Like market researchers, we should select participants from a specific target population that relates to our research questions. If we're interested in how residents of a specific neighborhood will feel about opening a work-release center, we should select group participants who live in the target neighborhood or one very much like it.

Should You Do It Yourself?

Anyone can do a mail or simple telephone survey, but many times it's better to use professional survey researchers.

The final issue we address in this chapter is who should conduct surveys. Drawing a sample, constructing a questionnaire, and either conducting interviews or distributing self-administered instruments are not especially difficult. Equipped with the basic principles we have discussed so far in this book, you could complete a modest in-person or telephone survey yourself. Mail surveys of large numbers of subjects are entirely possible, especially with present-day computer capabilities.

At the same time, the different tasks involved in completing a survey require a lot of work and attention to detail. We have presented many tips for constructing questionnaires, but our guidelines barely scratch the surface. Many books describe survey techniques in more detail, and a growing number focus specifically on telephone or mail techniques (see the list of Additional Readings at the end of this chapter). In many respects, however, designing and executing a survey of even modest size can be challenging.

Consider the start-up costs involved in in-person or telephone interview surveys of any size. Finding, training, and paying interviewers are time consuming and potentially costly and require some degree of expertise. The price of computer equipment continues downward, but a CATI setup or supply of laptops and associated software for interviewers still represents a substantial investment that cannot easily be justified for a single survey.

If interview surveys are beyond a researcher's means, he or she might fall back on a mail or Web-based survey. Few capital costs are involved; most expenses are in consumables such

Researchers at Rutgers University used specialized interviews. In most cases, however, these interviews took place in field settings and were conducted in connection with field observations.

What about focus groups? Researchers discussed this as a relatively efficient way of interviewing a number of officers about how their actions had changed in recent years. Interviewing groups of officers in the six intensive-study New York precincts about specific tactics they employed was also considered. But this approach was not pursued for three reasons.

First, it takes time to prepare for, conduct, and then write up notes from focus groups. The research was conducted by a very small staff, and they were thinly spread over a large area, spanning four of New York's boroughs. In planning the project, researchers did not anticipate how much time it would take to travel around. It would have been possible to have a market research firm conduct the focus groups, but the project budget was modest and did not include outside professional help. Faced with the choice of conducting quick-and-dirty focus groups or not doing so, researchers opted for the latter; so cost was the second reason.

Finally, focus groups work best when participants are strangers. People who know each other often assume something of a performance mode in focus group discussions. Individuals try to impress each other; simmering disputes among acquaintances sometimes surface. The possibility of this happening with groups of New York City police officers was the third reason researchers decided not to conduct focus group interviews.

as envelopes, stamps, and stationery. One or two persons can orchestrate a mail survey reasonably well at minimal expense. Perhaps a consultant could be hired to design a Web-based survey at modest cost. But consider two issues.

First, the business of completing a survey involves a great deal of tedious work. In mail surveys, for example, questionnaires and cover letters must be printed, folded or stuffed into envelopes, stamped, and delivered (finally!) to the post office. None of this is much fun. The enjoyment starts when completed questionnaires start to trickle in. It's rewarding to begin the actual empirical research, and the excitement may get the researcher past the next stretch of tedium: going from paper questionnaires to actual data. So it's possible for one individual to do a mail survey, but the researcher must be prepared for lots of work; even then, it will be more work than expected. Web-based surveys have their own trade-offs. Economizing on up-front programming costs entails the risk of being swamped by unusable electronic questionnaires.

The second issue is more difficult to deal with and is often overlooked by researchers. We have examined at some length the advantages and disadvantages of the three methods of questionnaire administration. Some methods are more or less appropriate than others for different kinds of research questions. If a telephone or an in-person interview survey is best for the particular research needs, conducting a mail or Web-based survey will be a compromise, perhaps an unacceptable one. But the researcher's excitement at actually beginning the research may lead him or her to overlook or minimize problems with doing a mail survey on the cheap, in much the same way that researchers often are not in a position to recognize ethical problems with their own work, as we saw in Chapter 3. Doing a mail survey because it's all you can afford does not necessarily make the mail survey worth doing.

The alternative to doing it yourself is to contract with a professional survey research firm or a company that routinely conducts surveys. Most universities have a survey research center or institute, often affiliated with a sociology or political science department. Such institutes are usually available to conduct surveys for government organizations as well as university researchers, and they can often do so very economically. Private research firms are another possibility. Most have the capability to conduct all types of surveys as well as focus groups.

Using a professional survey firm or institute has several advantages. Chapter 8 described the basic principles of sampling, but actually drawing a probability sample can be complex. Even the BJS/COPS do-it-yourself guidebook for community crime surveys (Weisel, 1999) counsels police departments and others to consult with experts in drawing RDD samples. Professional firms regularly use sampling frames that can represent city, state, and national samples, or whatever combination is appropriate.

We have emphasized the importance of measurement throughout this book. Researchers should develop conceptual and operational definitions and be attentive to all phases of the measurement process. However, constructing an actual questionnaire requires attention to details that may not always be obvious to researchers. Survey firms are experienced in preparing standard demographic items, batteries of matrix questions, and complex contingency questions with appropriate skip sequences.

Although it is often best for researchers to discuss specific concepts and even to draft questions, professional firms offer the considerable benefit of experience in pulling it all together. This is not to say that a researcher should simply propose some ideas for questions and then leave the details to the pros. Working together with a survey institute or market research firm to propose questionnaire items, review draft instruments, evaluate pretests, and make final modifications is usually the best approach.

Perhaps the chief benefit of contracting for a survey is that professional firms have a pool of trained interviewers or the equipment to conduct computer-assisted telephone interviews. Survey research centers and other professional organizations have the latest specialized equipment, software, and know-how to take advantage of advances in all forms of CAI. Further-

more, such companies can more readily handle such administrative details as training interviewers, arranging travel for in-person surveys, coordinating mail surveys, and providing general supervision. This frees researchers from much of the tedium of survey research, enabling them to focus on more substantive issues.

Researchers must ultimately decide whether to conduct a survey themselves or contract with a professional firm. And the decision is best made after carefully considering the pros and cons of each approach. Too often, university faculty assume that students can get the job done while overlooking the important issues of how to maintain quality control and whether a survey is a worthwhile investment of students' time. Similarly, criminal justice practitioners may believe that agency staff can handle a mail survey or conduct phone interviews from the office. Again, compromises in the quality of results, together with the opportunity costs of diverting staff from other tasks, must be considered. The do-it-yourself strategy may seem cheaper in the short run, but it often becomes a false economy when attention turns to data analysis and interpretation.

We'll close this section with an apocryphal story about a consultant's business card; the card reads: "Fast! Low cost! High quality! Pick any two." It's best to make an informed choice that best suits your needs.

✪ *Main Points*

- Survey research, a popular social research method, involves the administration of questionnaires to a sample of respondents selected from some population.
- Survey research is especially appropriate for descriptive or exploratory studies of large populations, but surveys have many other uses in criminal justice research.
- Surveys are the method of choice for obtaining self-reported offending data. Continuing efforts to improve self-report surveys include using confidential computer-assisted personal interviews.

- Questions may be open-ended or closed-ended. Each technique for formulating questions has advantages and disadvantages.
- Short items in a questionnaire are usually better than long ones.
- Bias in questionnaire items encourages respondents to answer in a particular way or to support a particular point of view. It should be avoided.
- Questionnaires may be administered in three basically different ways: self-administered questionnaires, face-to-face interviews, and telephone interviews. Each mode of administration can be varied in a number of ways.
- Computers can be used to enhance each type of survey. Computer-assisted surveys have many advantages, but they often require special skills and equipment.
- It is generally advisable to plan follow-up mailings for self-administered questionnaires, sending new questionnaires to respondents who fail to respond to the initial appeal.
- The essential characteristic of interviewers is that they be neutral; their presence in the data collection process must not have any effect on the responses given to questionnaire items.
- Surveys conducted over the telephone are fast and flexible.
- Each method of survey administration has a variety of advantages and disadvantages.
- Survey research has the weaknesses of being somewhat artificial and potentially superficial. It is difficult to gain a full sense of social processes in their natural settings through the use of surveys.
- Specialized interviews with a small number of people and focus groups are additional ways of collecting data by asking questions.
- Although the particular tasks required to complete a survey are not especially difficult, researchers must carefully consider whether to conduct surveys themselves or contract with a professional organization.

✪ Key Terms

Closed-ended questions	Open-ended
Computer-assisted	questions
interviewing	Questionnaire

✪ Review Questions and Exercises

1. Find a questionnaire on the Internet. Bring the questionnaire to class and critique it. Critique other aspects of the survey design as well.
2. For each of the open-ended questions listed, construct a closed-ended question that could be used in a questionnaire.
   a. What was your family's total income last year?
   b. How do you feel about shock incarceration, or "boot camp" programs?
   c. How do people in your neighborhood feel about the police?
   d. What do you feel is the biggest problem facing this community?
   e. How do you protect your home from burglary?
3. Prepare a brief questionnaire to study perceptions of crime near your college or university. Include questions asking respondents to describe a nearby area where they either are afraid to go after dark or think crime is a problem. Then use your questionnaire to interview at least 10 students.
4. A recent evaluation of a federal program to support community policing included sending questionnaires to a sample of about 1200 police chiefs. Each questionnaire included a number of items asking about specific features of community policing and whether they were being used in the department. Almost all the police chiefs had someone else complete the questionnaire. What's the unit of analysis in this survey? What problems might result from having an individual complete such a questionnaire?

✪ Internet Exercises

To ensure that you always have access to live, correct Web links for the Web sites referenced in the following exercises, we provide the necessary links on the companion Web site for *Research Methods for Criminal Justice and Criminology* at http://cj.wadsworth.com/maxfield_babbie/research_methods4e. Once at the companion Web site, select this specific chapter, click on "Chapter Resources," then click on "Web Links."

1. Visit the Cornell University Web-Based Survey Tools Web site, and write a brief summary of

resources that are available to develop Web-based surveys.

2. Visit the Social Research Update Web site. Review and summarize articles on two issues that deal with survey research or other forms of interviewing.

3. Using your favorite search engine, type in the phrase "web-based survey." You'll find a large number of commercial sites. Visit one and briefly summarize what services are available.

4. For an example of what sorts of things interviewers need to consider in complex national surveys, see the *Field Interviewer Manual* at the 2002 National Survey on Drug Abuse and Health Web site.

✪ *InfoTrac College Edition*

Use the keyword *telephone survey* to locate a criminal justice or criminology article that uses this method to collect data. Why did the author(s) use this method to collect data instead of an in-person interview or self-administered questionnaire? What response rate was obtained? What procedures were used to enhance the response rate?

✪ *The NEW Companion Web Site for* **Research Methods for Criminal Justice and Criminology,** *Fourth Edition*

http://cj.wadsworth.com/maxfield_babbie/research_methods4e

Supplement your review of this chapter by going to the new companion Web site to take one of the Tutorial Quizzes, use the flash cards to master key terms, and check out the many other study aids you'll find there. You'll also find special features such as quantitative and qualitative data analysis primers to help you with a special project or do some research on your own.

✪ *Additional Readings*

Babbie, Earl, *Survey Research Methods* (Belmont, CA: Wadsworth, 1990). A comprehensive overview of survey methods, this textbook covers many aspects of survey techniques that are omitted here.

Dillman, Don A., *Mail and Internet Surveys: The Tailored Design Method,* 2nd ed. (New York: Wiley, 1999). This update of a classic reference on self-administered surveys includes a variety of Web-based techniques. Dillman makes many good suggestions for improving response rates.

General Accounting Office, *Using Structured Interviewing Techniques* (Washington, DC: General Accounting Office, 1991). This is another useful handbook in the GAO series on evaluation methods. In contrast to Patton (below), the GAO emphasizes getting comparable information from respondents through structured interviews. This is very useful step-by-step guide.

Krueger, Richard A., and Casey, Mary Anne, *Focus Groups: A Practical Guide for Applied Research,* 3rd ed. (Thousand Oaks, CA: Sage, 2000). A clear and comprehensive introduction to focus groups, this book really lives up to its title, describing basic principles of focus groups and giving numerous practical tips.

Patton, Michael Quinn, *Qualitative Research and Evaluation Methods,* 3rd ed. (Thousand Oaks, CA: Sage, 2001). This is a thorough discussion of specialized interviewing. Patton's advice will also be useful in constructing questionnaires for surveys in general.

Weisel, Deborah, *Conducting Community Surveys: A Practical Guide for Law Enforcement Agencies* (Washington, DC: U.S. Department of Justice, Office of Justice Programs, Bureau of Justice Statistics, and Office of Community Oriented Police Services, 1999). Another practical guide, this brief publication is prepared for use by public officials, not researchers. As such, it's a very good description of the nuts and bolts of doing telephone surveys.

Chapter 10

Field Research

The techniques described in this chapter focus on observing life in its natural habitat—going where the action is and watching. We'll consider how to prepare for the field, how to observe, how to make records of what is observed, and how to recognize the relative strengths and weaknesses of field research.

(continued)

Introduction

Field research is often associated with qualitative techniques, though many other applications are possible.

We turn now to what may seem like the most obvious method of making observations: field research. If researchers want to know about something, why not simply go where it's happening and watch it happen?

Field research encompasses two different methods of obtaining data: (1) making direct observation and (2) asking questions. This chapter concentrates primarily on observation, although we will briefly describe techniques for specialized interviewing in field studies.

Most of the observation methods discussed in this book are designed to produce data appropriate for *quantitative* (statistical) analysis. Surveys provide data to calculate things like the percentage of crime victims in a population or the mean value of property lost in burglaries. Field research may yield *qualitative* data—observations not easily reduced to numbers—in addition to quantitative data. For example, a field researcher who is studying burglars may note how many times subjects have been arrested (quantitative), as well as whether individual burglars tend to select certain types of targets (qualitative).

Qualitative field research is often a theory- or hypothesis-generating activity as well. In many types of field studies, researchers do not have precisely defined hypotheses to be tested. Field observation may be used to make sense

out of an ongoing process that cannot be predicted in advance. This process involves making initial observations, developing tentative general conclusions that suggest further observations, making those observations, revising the prior conclusions, and so forth.

For example, Ross Homel and associates (Homel, Tomsen, and Thommeny, 1992) conducted a field study of violence in bars in Sydney, Australia, and found that certain situations tended to trigger violent incidents. A subsequent study tested a series of hypotheses about the links between certain situations and violence (Homel and Clark, 1994). Barney Glaser and Anselm Strauss (1967) referred to this process as "grounded theory." Rather than following the deductive approach to theory building described in Chapter 2, grounded theory is based on (or grounded in) experience, usually through observations made in the field.

Field studies in criminal justice may also produce quantitative data that can be used to test hypotheses or evaluate policy innovations. Typically, qualitative exploratory observations help define the nature of some crime problem and suggest possible policy responses. Following the policy response, further observations are made to assess the policy's impact. For example, we briefly described the situational crime prevention approach in Chapter 2. The first and last of the five steps in a situational crime prevention project illustrate the dual uses of observation for problem definition and hypothesis testing (Clarke, 1997b:5):

1. Collect data about the nature and dimensions of the specific crime problem.
5. Monitor results and disseminate experience.

By now, especially if you have experience as a criminal justice professional, you may be thinking that field research is not much different from what police officers and many other people do every day—make observations in the field and ask people questions. Police may also collect data about particular crime problems, take action, and monitor results. So what's new here?

Compared with criminal justice professionals, researchers tend to be more concerned with making generalizations and then using systematic field research techniques to support those generalizations. For example, consider the different goals and approaches used by two people who might observe shoplifters: a retail store security guard and a criminal justice researcher. The security guard wishes to capture a thief and prevent the loss of shop merchandise. Toward those ends, he or she adapts surveillance techniques to the behavior of a particular suspected shoplifter. The researcher's interests are different; perhaps she or he estimates the frequency of shoplifting, describes characteristics of shoplifters, or evaluates some specific measure to prevent shoplifting. In all likelihood, researchers use more standardized methods of observation aimed toward a generalized understanding.

In a sense, we all do field research whenever we observe or participate in social behavior and try to understand it, whether at a corner tavern, in a doctor's waiting room, or on an airplane. When we report our observations to others, we are reporting our field research efforts.

This chapter examines field research methods in some detail, providing a logical overview and suggesting some specific skills and techniques that make scientific field research more useful than the casual observation we all engage in. As we cover the various applications and techniques of field research, it's useful to recall the distinction we made, way back in Chapter 1, between ordinary human inquiry and social scientific research. Field methods illustrate how the common techniques of observation that we all use in ordinary inquiry can be deployed in systematic ways.

Topics Appropriate to Field Research

When conditions or behavior must be studied in natural settings, field research is usually the best approach.

One of the key strengths of field research is the comprehensive perspective it gives the researcher. This aspect of field research enhances its validity. By going directly to the phenomenon under study and observing it as completely as possible, we can develop a deeper and fuller understanding of it. This mode of observation, then, is especially (though not exclusively) appropriate to research topics that appear to defy simple quantification. The field researcher may recognize nuances of attitude, behavior, and setting that escape researchers using other methods.

For example, Clifford Shearing and Phillip Stenning (1992:251) describe how Disney World employs subtle but pervasive mechanisms of informal social control that are largely invisible to millions of theme park visitors. It is difficult to imagine any technique other than direct observation that could produce these insights:

> Control strategies are embedded in both environmental features and structural relations. In both cases control structures and activities have other functions which are highlighted so that the control function is overshadowed. For example, virtually every pool, fountain, and flower garden serves both as an aesthetic object and to direct visitors away from, or towards, particular locations. Similarly, every Disney employee,

while visibly and primarily engaged in other functions, is also engaged in the maintenance of order.

Many of the different uses of field observation in criminal justice research are nicely summarized by George McCall. Comparing the three principal ways of collecting data—observing, asking questions, and consulting written records—McCall (1978:8–9) stated that observation is most appropriate for obtaining information about physical or social settings, behaviors, and events.

Observation is not the only way of getting data about settings, behaviors, and events. Information about the number of households on a block (setting) may be found in a city clerk's office; crime surveys routinely ask about victimization (events) and whether crimes were reported to police (behavior). However, in many circumstances, field observation is the preferred method.

Field research is especially appropriate for topics that can best be understood within their natural settings. Surveys may be able to measure behaviors and attitudes in somewhat artificial settings, but not all behavior is best measured this way. For example, field research is a superior method for studying how street-level drug dealers interpret behavioral and situational cues to distinguish potential customers, normal street traffic, and undercover police officers. It would be difficult to study these skills through a survey.

Field research on actual crimes involves obtaining information about events. McCall (1978) pointed out that observational studies of vice—such as prostitution and drug use—are much more common than observational studies of other crimes, largely because these behaviors depend at least in part on being visible and attracting customers. One notable exception is research on shoplifting. A classic study by Terry Baumer and Dennis Rosenbaum (1982) had two goals: (1) to estimate the incidence of shoplifting in a large department store and (2) to assess the effectiveness of different store security measures. Each objective required devising some measure of shoplifting, which Baumer and Rosenbaum obtained through direct observation. Samples of persons were followed by research staff from the time they entered the store until they left. Observers, posing as fellow shoppers, watched for any theft by the person they had been assigned to follow. We'll have more to say about this study later in the chapter.

Many aspects of physical settings are probably best studied through direct observation. The prevalence and patterns of gang graffiti in public places could not be reliably measured through surveys, unless the goal was to measure perceptions of graffiti. The work of Oscar Newman (1972, 1996), Ray Jeffery (1977), and Patricia and Paul Brantingham (1991) on the relationship between crime and environmental design depends crucially on field observation of settings. If opportunities for crime vary by physical setting, then observation of the physical characteristics of a setting is required.

An evaluation of street lighting as a crime prevention tool in two areas of London illustrates how observation can be used to measure both physical settings and behavior. Kate Painter (1991, 1996) was interested in the relationships between street lighting, certain crime rates (measured by victim surveys), fear of crime, and nighttime mobility. Improvements in street lighting were made in selected streets; surveys of pedestrians and households in the affected areas were conducted before and after the lighting improvements. Survey questions included items about victimization, perceptions of crime problems and lighting quality, and reports about routine nighttime behavior in areas affected by the lighting.

Although the pretest and posttest survey items could have been used to assess changes in attitudes and behavior associated with improved lighting, field observations provided better measures of behavior. Painter conducted systematic counts of pedestrians in areas both before and after street lighting was enhanced.

Observations like this are better measures of such behavior than are survey items because people often have difficulty recalling actions such as how often they walk through some area after dark.

Painter's research also included provisions to observe physical settings. First, light levels (measured in lux units) were assessed in the experimental areas before and after changes in streetlighting equipment (1991:176). Second, interviewers who conducted household interviews made observations of physical settings in the areas around sampled households.

The Various Roles of the Observer

Field observer roles range from full participation to fully detached observation.

The term *field research* is broader and more inclusive than the common term *participant observation*. Field researchers need not always participate in what they are studying, although they usually will study it directly at the scene of the action. As Catherine Marshall and Gretchen Rossman (1995:60) point out:

> The researcher may plan a role that entails varying degrees of "participantness"—that is, the degree of actual participation in daily life. At one extreme is the full participant, who goes about ordinary life in a role or set of roles constructed in the setting. At the other extreme is the complete observer, who engages not at all in social interaction and may even shun involvement in the world being studied. And, of course, all possible complementary mixes along the continuum are available to the researcher.

The full participant, in this sense, may be a genuine participant in what he or she is studying (for example, a participant in a demonstration against capital punishment)—or at least pretend to be a genuine participant. In any event, if you are acting as a full participant, you let people see you only as a participant, not as a researcher.

That raises an ethical question: Is it ethical to deceive the people we are studying in the hope that they will confide in us as they would not confide in an identified researcher? Do the interests of science—the scientific values of the research—offset any ethical concerns?

Related to this ethical consideration is a scientific one. No researcher deceives his or her subjects solely for the purpose of deception. Rather, it is done in the belief that the data will be more valid and reliable, that the subjects will be more natural and honest if they do not know the researcher is doing a research project. If the people being studied know they are being studied, they might reject the researcher or modify their speech and behavior to appear more respectable than they otherwise would. In either case, the process being observed might radically change.

On the other side of the coin, if we assume the role of complete participant, we may affect what we are studying. To play the role of participant, we must *participate*, yet our participation may affect the social process we are studying. Additional problems may emerge in any participant observation study of active criminals. Legal and physical risks, mentioned in Chapter 3, present obstacles to the complete participant in field research among active offenders or delinquents.

Finally, complete participation in field studies of criminal justice institutions is seldom possible. Although it is common for police officers to become criminal justice researchers, practical constraints on the official duties of police present major obstacles to simultaneously acting as researcher and police officer. Similarly, the responsibilities of judges, prosecutors, probation officers, and corrections workers are not normally compatible with collecting data for research.

Because of these considerations—ethical, scientific, practical, and safety—field researchers most often choose a different role. The role *participant-as-observer* participates with the group under study but makes it clear that he or she is also undertaking research. If someone has been convicted of some offense and been placed on probation, for example, that might present an opportunity to launch a study of probation officers.

McCall (1978) suggested that field researchers who study active offenders may comfortably occupy positions around the periphery of criminal activity. Acting as a participant in certain types of leisure activities, such as frequenting selected bars or dance clubs, may be appropriate roles. This approach was used by Dina Perrone in her research on drug use in New York dance clubs (see Chapter 3). Furthermore, McCall described how making one's role as a researcher known to criminals and becoming known as a "right square" is more acceptable to subjects than an unsuccessful attempt to masquerade as a colleague. There are dangers in this role also, however. The people being studied may shift their attention to the research project, and the process being observed may no longer be typical. Conversely, a researcher may come to identify too much with the interests and viewpoints of the participants. This is referred to as "going native" and results in a loss of detachment necessary for social science.

The *observer-as-participant* identifies him or herself as a researcher and interacts with the participants in the course of their routine activities but makes no pretense of actually being a participant. Many observational studies of police patrol are examples of this approach. Researchers typically accompany police officers on patrol, observing routine activities and interactions between police and citizens. Spending several hours in the company of a police officer also affords opportunities for unstructured interviewing.

Although the researcher's role in the eyes of police is exclusively observational, people with whom police come into contact may assume that an observer is actually a plainclothes officer. As a consequence, observation of citizens in their encounters with police tends to be less contaminated by the presence of a researcher than is observation of police themselves.

McCall (1978:88) noted that going native is a common tendency among field workers, especially in observational studies of police. For example, observers may become more sympathetic toward officers' behavior and toward the views police express about the people they encounter. Observers may even actively assist officers on patrol. In either case, going native is often the product of the researcher's efforts to be accepted by police and the natural tendency of police to justify their actions to observers.

The *complete observer,* at the other extreme, observes some location or process without becoming a part of it in any way. The subjects of study might not even realize they are being studied because of the researcher's unobtrusiveness. An individual making observations while sitting in a courtroom is an example. Although the complete observer is less likely to affect what is being studied and less likely to go native than the complete participant, he or she may also be less able to develop a full appreciation of what is being studied. A courtroom observer, for example, witnesses only the public acts that take place in the courtroom, not private conferences between judges and attorneys.

McCall (1978:45) pointed out an interesting and often unnoticed trade-off between the role observers adopt and their ability to learn from what they see. If their role is covert (complete participation) or detached (complete observation), they are less able to ask questions to clarify what they we observe. As complete participants, they take pains to conceal their observations and must exercise care in querying subjects. Similarly, complete observation means that it is generally not possible to interact with the persons or things being observed.

Researchers have to think carefully about the trade-off. If it is most important that subjects not be affected by their role as observer, then complete participation or observation is preferred. If being able to ask questions about what they observe is important, then some role that combines participation and observation is better.

More generally, the appropriate role for observers hinges on what they want to learn and how their inquiry is affected by opportunities and constraints. Different situations require different roles for researchers. Unfortunately, there are no clear guidelines for making this choice; field researchers rely on their understanding of the situation, their judgment, and their experience. In making a decision, researchers must be guided by both methodological and ethical considerations. Because these often conflict, deciding on the appropriate role may be difficult. Often, researchers find that their role limits the scope of their study.

Asking Questions

Field researchers frequently supplement observations by interviewing subjects.

Field research often involves going where the action is and simply watching and listening. Researchers can learn a lot merely by being attentive to what's going on. Field research can also involve more active inquiry. Sometimes, it's appropriate to ask people questions and record their answers. Richard Wright and Trevor Bennett (1990) describe observing and interviewing as two complementary ways to study offenders.

We examined interviewing in Chapter 9 on survey research. The interviewing normally done in connection with field observation falls into the category of specialized interviewing.

Field research interviews are usually much less structured than survey interviews. At one extreme, an unstructured interview is essentially a conversation in which the interviewer establishes a general direction for the conversation and pursues specific topics raised by the respondent. Ideally, the respondent does most of the talking. Michael Patton (2001) refers to this type as an "informal conversational interview," which is especially well suited to in-depth probing.

Unstructured interviews are most appropriate when researchers have little knowledge about a topic and when it's reasonable for them to have a casual conversation with a subject. This is a good strategy for interviewing active criminals. Unstructured interviews are also appropriate when researchers and subjects are together for an extended time, such as a researcher accompanying police on patrol.

In other field research situations, interviews will be somewhat more structured. The conversational approach may be difficult to use with officials in criminal justice or other agencies, who will respond best (at least initially) to a specific set of open-ended questions. This is because it is usually necessary to arrange appointments to conduct field research interviews with judges, prosecutors, bail commissioners, and other officials. Having arranged such an appointment, it would be awkward to initiate a casual conversation in hopes of eliciting the desired information.

At the same time, one of the special strengths of field research is its flexibility in the field. Even during structured interviews with public officials, the answers evoked by initial questions should shape subsequent ones. It isn't enough merely to ask preestablished questions and record the answers. The researcher needs to ask a question, hear the answer, interpret its meaning relative to the general inquiry, and then frame another question either to explore the earlier answer in more depth or to redirect the respondent's attention to an area more relevant to the inquiry. In short, the researcher needs to be able to listen, think, and talk almost simultaneously.

For example, Michael Maxfield and W. Carsten Andresen (2002) studied the use of video recording equipment to document traffic stops by a police organization in the northeastern United States. Very little published research existed on either the use of video equipment by police or even the ways in which they go about doing traffic enforcement. Part of the research involved semistructured field interviews with

1. What do you feel are the main uses of the mobile video system (MVS) for supervisors? [probe contingent on responses]

2. Please describe how you use tapes from the MVS system to periodically review officer performance. [probes]

   - Compare tapes with incident reports.

   - Review tapes from certain types of incidents. [probe: Please describe types and why these types.]

   - Keep an eye on individual officers. [probe: Please describe what might prompt you to select individual officer. I do not want you to name individuals. Instead, can you describe the reasons why you might want to keep an eye on specific individuals?]

3. For routine review, how do you decide which tapes to select for review?

   - Does it vary by shift?

   - Do you try to review a certain number of incidents?

   - Or do you scan through tapes sort of at random?

4. Think back to when the system first became operational in cars at this station. What were some questions, concerns, or problems that concerned officers at the beginning?

5. How do officers under your command feel about the system now?

6. What, if any, technical problems seem to come up regularly? Occasionally?

7. Have you encountered any problems, or do you have any concerns about the MVS? [probe: operational issues; tape custody issues; other]

8. Please describe any specific ways you think the system can or should be improved.

9. If you want to find the tape for an individual officer on a specific day, and for a specific incident, would you say that's pretty easy, not difficult, or somewhat difficult? Do you have any suggestions for changing the way tapes are filed and controlled?

10. I would like to now view some sample tapes. Can we now go to the tape cabinet and find a tape for [select date from list]?

Figure 10.1   Interview Guide for Field Study of Police Supervisors

Source: Adapted from Maxfield and Andresen (2002).

police commanders, supervisors, and officers. Figure 10.1 shows the interview guide Maxfield and Andresen used with supervisors. This guide was just that—a guide. Some supervisors were friendly and wanted to talk, so the interview became more of a conversation that eventually yielded answers to the queries in the guide. Others were wary, probably because the agency had been subject to criticism over alleged discriminatory enforcement. Interviews with such supervisors were brief, and they followed the guide very closely.

The discussion of probes in Chapter 9 offers useful guidelines for getting more in-depth answers without biasing later answers. Researchers must learn the skill of being a good listener, of being more interested than interesting. They learn to say things like "How is that?" "In what ways?" "How do you mean that?" and "What would be an example of that?" They learn to look and listen expectantly and to let the person they are interviewing break the silence.

At its best, a field research interview is much like normal conversation. Because of this, it is essential to keep reminding ourselves that we are *not* having a normal conversation. In normal conversations, each of us wants to come across as an interesting, worthwhile person. Often, we don't really hear each other because we're too busy thinking of what we'll say next. As an interviewer, the desire to appear interesting is counterproductive to the task. We need to make the other person seem interesting by being interested ourselves. By the way, if you do this, people will actually regard you as a great conversationalist.

Like other aspects of field research, interviewing improves with practice. Fortunately, it is something you can practice any time you want. Practice on your friends.

Gaining Access to Subjects

Arranging access to subjects in formal organizations or those in subcultures begins with an initial contact.

Suppose you decide to undertake field research on a community corrections agency in a large city. Let's assume that you do not know a great deal about the agency and that you will identify yourself as a researcher to staff and other people you encounter. Your research interests are primarily descriptive: You want to observe the routine operations of the agency in the office and elsewhere. In addition, you want to interview agency staff and persons who are serving community corrections sentences. This section will discuss some of the ways you might prepare before you conduct your interviews and direct observations.

As usual, you are well advised to begin with a search of the relevant literature, filling in your knowledge of the subject and learning what others have said about it.

Gaining Access to Formal Organizations

Any research on a criminal justice institution, or on persons who work either in or under the supervision of an institution, normally requires a formal request and approval. One of the first steps in preparing for the field, then, is to arrange access to the community corrections agency.

Obtaining initial approval can be confusing and frustrating. Many criminal justice agencies in large cities have a complex organization, combining a formal hierarchy with a bewildering variety of informal organizational cultures. For example, criminal courts are highly structured organizations in which a presiding judge may oversee court assignments and case scheduling for judges and many support personnel. At the same time, courts are chaotic organizations in which three constellations of professionals—prosecutors, defense attorneys, and judges—episodically interact to process large numbers of cases.

To further complicate field research in criminal justice agencies, the obvious strategy of gaining approval from a single executive—such as a corrections commissioner or police chief—does not guarantee that operations staff at lower levels will cooperate. Researchers are often required to negotiate access at multiple levels. For example, Maxfield is engaged in an ongoing project to study auto theft in New Jersey. Over the course of 18 months or so, he has worked with police chiefs, county prosecutors, executives from insurance agencies, and members of other organizations throughout the state. However, seeking to interview a staff person in a diversionary program for juvenile auto thieves in one New Jersey county, Maxfield was referred to a judge, who then sought approval from the county's chief judge, who subsequently forwarded the request to a state agency that oversees New Jersey courts. The process continues.

Continuing with the example of your research on community corrections, the best strategy in gaining access to virtually any other formal criminal justice organization is to use a four-step procedure: sponsor, letter, phone call, and meeting. Our discussion of these steps assumes that you will begin your field research by interviewing the agency executive director and gaining that person's approval for subsequent interviews and observations.

Sponsor The first step is to find a sponsor—a person who is personally known to and respected by the executive director. Ideally, a sponsor will be able to advise you on a person to contact, that person's formal position in the organization, and her or his informal status, including her or his relationships with other key officials. Such advice can be important in helping you initiate contact with the right person while avoiding people who have bad reputations.

For example, you may initially think that a particular judge who is often mentioned in newspaper stories about community corrections

Jane Adams
Executive Director
Chaos County Community Corrections
Anxiety Falls, Colorado   1 May 2004

Dear Ms. Adams:

My colleague, Professor Marcus Nelson, suggested I contact you for assistance in my research on community corrections. I will be conducting a study of community corrections programs and wish to include the Chaos County agency in my research.

Briefly, I am interested in learning more about the different types of sentences that judges impose in jurisdictions with community corrections agencies. As you know, Colorado's community corrections statute grants considerable discretion to individual counties in arranging locally administered corrections programs. Because of this, it is generally believed that a wide variety of corrections programs and sentences have been developed throughout the state. My research seeks to learn more about these programs as a first step toward developing recommendations that may guide the development of programs in other states. I also wish to learn more about the routine administration of a community corrections program such as yours.

I would like to meet with you to discuss what programs Chaos County has developed, including current programs and those that were considered but not implemented. In addition, any information about different types of community corrections sentences that Chaos County judges impose would be very useful. Finally, I would appreciate your suggestions on further sources of information about community corrections programs in Chaos County and other areas.

I will call your office at about 10:00 a.m. on Monday, May 8, to arrange a meeting. If that time will not be convenient, or if you have any questions about my research, please contact me at the number below.

Thanks in advance for your help.

Sincerely,

Alfred Nobel
Research Assistant
Institute for Advanced Studies
(201) 555-1212

Figure 10.2   Sample Letter for Sponsor

would be a useful source of information. However, your sponsor might advise you that the judge is not held in high regard by prosecutors and community corrections staff. Your association with this judge would generate suspicion on the part of other officials whom you might eventually want to contact and may frustrate your attempts to obtain information.

By the way, finding the right sponsor is often the most important step in gaining access. It may, in fact, require a couple of extra steps, because you might first need to ask a professor whether she or he knows someone. You could then contact that person (with the spon-

sorship of your professor) and ask for further assistance.

For purposes of illustration, we will assume that your professor is knowledgeable, well connected, and happy to act as your sponsor. Your professor confirms your view that it is best to begin with the executive director of community corrections.

Letter   Next, write a letter to the executive director. Your letter should have three parts: introduction, brief statement of your research purpose, and action request. See Figure 10.2 for an example. The introduction begins by naming your sponsor, thus immediately establishing your mutual acquaintance. This is a key part of the process; if you do not name a sponsor, or if you name the wrong sponsor, you might get no further.

Next, you describe your research purpose succinctly. This is not the place to give a detailed description as you would in a proposal. If possible, keep the description to one or two paragraphs, as in Figure 10.2. If a longer description is necessary to explain what you will be doing, you should still include only a brief description in your introductory letter, referring the reader to a separate attachment in which you summarize your research.

The action request describes what immediate role you are asking the contact person to play in your research. You may simply be requesting an interview, or you may want the person to help you gain access to other officials. Notice how the sample in Figure 10.2 mentions both an interview and "suggestions on further sources of information about community corrections." In any case, you will usually want to arrange to meet or at least talk with the contact person. That leads to the third step.

Phone Call   You probably already know that it can be difficult to arrange meetings with public officials (and often professors) or even to reach people by telephone. You can simplify this task by concluding your letter with a proposal for this step: arranging a phone call. The example in Figure 10.2 specifies a date and approximate time when you will call. To be safe, specify a date about a week from the date of your letter. Notice also the request that the executive director call you if some other time will be more convenient.

When you make the call, the executive director will have some idea of who you are and what you want. She will also have had the opportunity to contact your sponsor if she wants to verify any information in your introductory letter.

The actual phone call should go smoothly. Even if you are not able to talk with the executive director personally, you will probably be able to talk to an assistant and make an appointment for a meeting (the next step). Again, this will be possible because your letter described what you eventually want—a meeting with the executive director—and established your legitimacy by naming a sponsor.

Meeting   The final step is meeting with or interviewing the contact person. Because you have used the letter–phone call–meeting procedure, the contact person may have already taken preliminary steps to help you. For example, because the letter in Figure 10.2 indicates that you wish to interview the executive director about different types of community corrections sentences, she may have assembled some procedures manuals or reports in preparation for your meeting.

This procedure generally works well in gaining initial access to public officials or other people who work in formal organizations. Once initial access is gained, it is up to the researcher to use interviewing skills and other techniques to elicit the desired information. This is not as difficult as it might seem to novice (or apprentice) researchers for a couple of reasons.

First, most people are at least a bit flattered that their work, ideas, and knowledge are of interest to a researcher. And researchers can take advantage of this with the right words of encouragement. Second, criminal justice professionals are often happy to talk about their work with a knowledgeable outsider. Police, probation officers, and corrections workers usually encounter only their colleagues and their clients on the job. Interactions with colleagues become routinized and suffused with office politics, and interactions with clients are common sources of stress for them. Talking with an interested and knowledgeable researcher is often seen as a pleasant diversion.

By the same token, Richard Wright and Scott Decker (1994) report that most members of their sample of active burglars were both happy and flattered to discuss the craft of burglary. Because they were engaged in illegal activities, burglars had to be more circumspect about sharing their experiences, unlike the way many people talk about events at work. As a result, burglars enjoyed the chance to describe their work to interested researchers who both promised confidentiality and treated them "as having expert knowledge normally unavailable to outsiders" (1994:26).

Gaining Access to Subcultures

Research by Wright and Decker illustrates how gaining access to subcultures in criminal justice—active criminals, deviants, juvenile gangs, and inmates—requires tactics that differ in some respects from those used to meet with public officials. Letters, phone calls, and formal meetings are usually not appropriate for initiating field research among active offenders. However, the basic principle of using a sponsor to gain initial access operates in much the same way, although the word *informant* is normally used to refer to someone who helps make contact with subcultures.

Informants may be people whose job involves working with criminals—for example, police, juvenile caseworkers, probation officers, attorneys, and counselors at drug clinics. Lawyers who specialize in criminal defense work can be especially useful sources of information about potential subjects. Francis Gant and Peter Grabosky (2001) contacted a private investigator to help locate car thieves and people working in auto-related businesses who were reputed to deal in stolen parts.

As McCall (1978:31) noted, obtaining initial access to criminals is not usually difficult, but chains of referrals may be necessary:

> If a researcher wants to make contact with, say, a bootlegger, he thinks of a person he knows who is closest to the social structure of bootlegging. Perhaps that person will be a police officer, a judge, a liquor store owner, a crime reporter, or a recently arrived Southern migrant. If he doesn't personally know a judge or a crime reporter, he surely knows someone (his own lawyer . . .) who does and who would be willing to introduce him. By means of a very short chain

of such referrals, the researcher can obtain an introduction to virtually any type of criminal.

For example, in their study of New York heroin users, Bruce Johnson and associates (1985:16, 195–97) initially recruited former addicts they contacted through methadone treatment centers. These persons, employed as research fieldworkers, used their network of social contacts in two Harlem neighborhoods to identify active heroin users who would serve as research subjects. And the first group of research subjects identified additional heroin users and criminals, who themselves became subjects.

Wright and Decker (1994) were fortunate to encounter a former offender who was well connected with active criminals. Playing the role of sponsor, the ex-offender helped researchers in two related ways. First, he referred them to other people, who, in turn, found active burglars willing to participate in the study. Second, he was well known and respected among burglars, and his sponsorship of the researchers made it possible for them to study a group of naturally suspicious subjects.

A different approach for gaining access to subcultures is to hang around places where criminals hang out. Wright and Decker rejected that strategy as a time-consuming and uncertain way to find burglars, in part because they were not sure where burglars hung out. In contrast, Bruce Jacobs (1996) initiated contact with street-level drug dealers by hanging around and being noticed in locations known for crack availability. Consider how this tactic might make sense for finding drug dealers, whose illegal work requires customers. In contrast, the offense of burglary is more secretive, and it's more difficult to imagine how one would find an area known for the presence of burglars.

Whatever techniques are used to identify subjects among subcultures, it is generally not possible to produce a probability sample, and so the sample cannot be assumed to represent some larger population within specified confidence intervals. It is also important to think

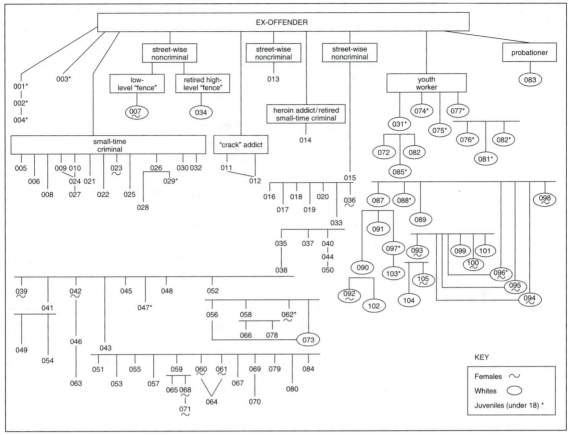

Figure 10.3 "Snowball" Referral Chart

Source: Reprinted from Richard T. Wright and Scott H. Decker, *Burglars on the Job: Streetlife and Residential Break-Ins* (Boston: Northeastern University Press, 1994), p. 19. Reprinted by permission of Northeastern University Press.

about potential selection biases in whatever procedures are used to recruit subjects. Although we can't make probability statements about samples of active offenders, such samples may be representative of a subculture target population.

Selecting Cases for Observation

This brings us to the more general question of how to select cases for observation in field research. The techniques used by Wright and Decker, as well as by many other researchers who have studied active criminals, combine the use of informants and what is called **snowball sampling.** As we mentioned in Chapter 8, with snowball sampling, initial research subjects (or

informants) identify other persons who might also become subjects, who, in turn, suggest more potential subjects, and so on. In this way, a group of subjects is accumulated through a series of referrals.

Wright and Decker's (1994) study provides a good example. The ex-offender contacted a few active burglars and a few "street-wise noncriminals," who, in turn, referred researchers to additional subjects, and so on. This process is illustrated in Figure 10.3, which shows the chain of referrals that accumulated a snowball sample of 105 individuals.

Starting at the top of Figure 10.3, the ex-offender put researchers in contact with two subjects directly (001 and 003), a small-time criminal, three street-wise noncriminals, a crack addict, a youth worker, and someone serving probation. Continuing downward, the small-time criminal was especially helpful, identifying 12 subjects who participated in the study (005, 006, 008, 009, 010, 021, 022, 023, 025, 026, 030, 032). Notice how the snowball effect continues, with subject 026 identifying subjects 028 and 029. Notice also that some subjects were themselves "nominated" by more than one source. In the middle of the bottom row in Figure 10.3, for example, subject 064 was mentioned by subjects 060 and 061.

There are, of course, other ways of selecting subjects for observation. Chapter 8 discussed the more conventional techniques involved in probability sampling and the accompanying logic. Although the general principles of representativeness should be remembered in field research, controlled sampling techniques are often not possible.

As an illustration, consider the potential selection biases involved in a field study of deviants. Let's say we want to study a small number of drug dealers. We have a friend who works in the probation department of a large city who is willing to introduce us to people convicted of drug dealing and sentenced to probation. What selection problems might result from studying subjects identified in this way? How might our subjects not be representative of the general population of drug dealers? If we work our way backward from the chain of events that begins with a crime and ends with a criminal sentence, the answers should become clear.

First, drug dealers sentenced to probation may be first-time offenders or persons convicted of dealing small amounts of "softer" drugs. Repeat offenders and "kingpin" cocaine dealers will not be in this group. Second, it is possible that people initially charged with drug dealing were convicted of simple possession through a plea bargain; because of our focus on people *convicted* of dealing, our selection procedure will miss this group as well. Finally, by selecting dealers who have been arrested and convicted,

we may be gaining access only to those less skilled dealers who got caught. More skilled or experienced dealers may be less likely to be arrested in the first place; they may be different in important ways from the dealers we wish to study. Also, if dealers in street drug markets are more likely to be arrested than dealers who work through social networks of friends and acquaintances, a sample based on arrested dealers could be biased in more subtle ways.

To see why this raises an important issue in selecting cases for field research, let's return again to the sample of burglars studied by Wright and Decker. Notice that their snowball sample began with an ex-offender and that they sought out active burglars. An alternative approach would be to select a probability or other sample of convicted burglars, perhaps in prison or on probation. But Wright and Decker rejected this strategy for sampling because of the possibility that they would overlook burglars who had not been caught. After accumulating their sample, the researchers were in a position to test this assumption by examining arrest records for their subjects. Only about one-fourth of the active burglars had ever been convicted of burglary; an additional one-third had been arrested for burglary but not convicted. More than 40 percent had no burglary arrests, and 8 percent had never been arrested for any offense (1994:12).

Putting all this together, Wright and Decker concluded that about *three-fourths* of their subjects would not have been eligible for inclusion if the researchers had based their sample on persons convicted of burglary. Thus, little overlap exists between the population of active burglars and the population of convicted burglars.

Purposive Sampling in Field Research

Sampling in field research tends to be more complicated than in other kinds of research. In many types of field studies, researchers attempt to observe everything within their field of study; thus, in a sense, they do not sample at all. In reality, of course, it is impossible to observe every-thing. To the extent that field researchers ob-serve only a portion of what happens, then, what they do observe is a de facto sample of all the possible observations that might have been made. We can seldom select a controlled sample of such observations. But we can keep in mind the general principles of representativeness and interpret our observations accordingly.

The ability to systematically sample cases for observation depends on the degree of structure and predictability of the phenomenon being ob-served. This is more of a general guideline than a hard-and-fast rule. For example, the actions of youth gangs, burglars, and auto thieves are less structured and predictable than those of police officers. It is possible to select a probability sample of police officers for observation because the behavior of police officers in a given city is structured and predictable in many dimensions. Because the population of active criminals is unknown, however, it is not possible to select a probability sample for observation.

This example should call to mind our dis-cussion of sampling frames in Chapter 8. A roster of police officers and their assignments to patrol sectors and shifts could serve as a sampling frame for selecting subjects to ob-serve. No such roster of gang members, bur-glars, and auto thieves is available. Criminal his-tory records could serve as a sampling frame for selecting persons with previous arrests or con-victions, subject to the problems of selectivity we have mentioned.

Now consider the case in which a sampling frame is less important than the regularity of a process. The regular, predictable passage of people on city sidewalks makes it possible to sys-tematically select a sample of cases for observa-tion. There is no sampling frame of pedestrians, but studies such as Painter's research (1991) on the effects of street lighting can depend on the reliable flow of passersby who may be observed.

In an observational study such as Painter's, we might also make observations at a number of different locations on different streets. We

Table 10.1   Sampling Dimensions in Field Research

Sampling Dimension	Variation in
Population	Behavior and characteristics
Space	Behavior Physical characteristics of locations
Time, micro	Behavior by time of day, day of week Lighting by time of day Business, store, entertainment activities by time of day, day of week
Time, macro	Behavior by season, holiday Entertainment by season, holiday
Weather	Behavior by weather

could pick the sample of locations through standard probability methods, or, more likely, we could use a rough quota system, observing wide streets and narrow ones, busy streets and quiet ones, or samples from different times of day. In a study of pedestrian traffic, we might also observe people in different types of urban neighborhoods—comparing residential and commercial areas, for example.

Table 10.1 summarizes different sampling dimensions that might be considered in plan-ning field research. The behavior of people, to-gether with the characteristics of people and places, can vary by population group, location, time, and weather. We have already touched on the first two in this chapter; now we will briefly discuss how sampling plans might consider time and weather dimensions.

People tend to engage in more out-of-door activities in fair weather than in wet or snowy conditions. In northern cities, people are out-side more when the weather is warm. Any study of outdoor activity should therefore consider the potential effects of variation in the weather. For example, in Painter's study of pedestrian traffic before and after improvements in street lighting, it was important to consider weather conditions during the times observations were made.

Behavior also varies by time, presented as micro- and macrodimensions in Table 10.1. City streets in a central business district are busiest during working hours, while more people are in residential areas at other times. And, of course, people do different things on weekends than during the work week. Seasonal variation, the macro time dimension, may also be important in criminal justice research. Daylight is longer in summer months, which affects the amount of time people spend outdoors. Shopping peaks from Thanksgiving to Christmas, increasing the number of shoppers, who along with their automobiles may become targets for thieves. A study of assault in Dallas by Keith Harries and associates (Harries, Stadler, and Zdorkowski, 1984) found variation in assault rates by time of year and day of the week, with assaults tending to peak in summer months and on weekends. Marcus Felson and associates (1996) describe variations in the rhythms of activity at New York's Port Authority bus terminal. Time of day, day of week, season, and weather affect the facility's use by bus passengers, transients, and a variety of offenders.

In practice, controlled probability sampling is seldom used in field research. Different types of purposive samples are much more common. Patton (2001:230) describes a broad range of approaches to purposive sampling and offers a useful comparison of probability and purposive samples:

> The logic and power of probability sampling derive from statistical probability theory. A random and statistically representative sample permits confident generalization from a sample to a larger population. ... The logic and power of purposeful sampling lies in selecting *information-rich cases* for study in depth. (emphasis in original)

Nonetheless, if researchers understand the principles and logic of more formal sampling methods, they are likely to produce more effective purposive sampling in field research.

In field research, it is important to bear in mind questions that correspond to two stages of sampling. First, to what extent are the total situations available for observation representative of the more general class of phenomena we wish to describe and explain? For example, are the three juvenile gangs being observed representative of all gangs? Second, are actual observations within those total situations representative of all the possible observations? For example, have we observed a representative sample of the members of the three gangs? Have we observed a representative sample of the interactions that took place? Even when controlled probability sampling methods are impossible or inappropriate, the logical link between representativeness and generalizability still holds. Careful purposive sampling can produce observations that represent the phenomena of interest. However, we cannot make probabilistic statements of representativeness like those examined in Chapter 8.

Recording Observations

Many different methods are available for collecting and recording field observations.

Just as there is great variety in the types of field studies we might conduct, we have many options for making records of field observations. In conducting field interviews, for example, researchers almost certainly write notes of some kind, but they might also tape-record interviews. Videotaping may be useful in field interviews to capture visual images of dress and body language. Photographs or videotapes can be used to make records of visual images such as a block of apartment buildings before and after some physical design change or to serve as a pretest for an experimental neighborhood cleanup campaign. This technique was used by Robert Sampson and Stephen Raudenbush (1999) in connection with probability samples of city blocks in Chicago. Videotapes were made of sampled blocks, and the recordings were then viewed to assess physical and social conditions in those areas.

We can think of a continuum of methods for recording observations. At one extreme is traditional field observation and note taking with pen and paper, such as we might use in field interviews. The opposite extreme includes various types of automated and remote measurement, such as videotapes, devices that count automobile traffic, or computer tabulations of mass transit users. In between is a host of methods that have many potential applications in criminal justice research.

Of course, the methods selected for recording observations are directly related to issues of measurement—especially how key concepts are operationalized. Thinking back to our discussion of measurement in Chapter 5, you should recognize why this is so. If, for example, we are interested in policies to increase nighttime pedestrian traffic in some city, we might want to know why people do or do not go out at night and how many people stroll around different neighborhoods. Interviews—perhaps in connection with a survey—can determine people's reasons for going out or not, while video recordings of passersby can provide simple counts. By the same token, a traffic-counting device can produce information about the number of automobiles that pass a particular point on the road, but it cannot measure what the blood alcohol levels of drivers are, whether riders are wearing seat belts, or how fast a vehicle is traveling.

Automated devices to record observations have many potential uses. In Chapter 8, we mentioned research on electronic monitoring (ELMO) technology that records the physical location of individuals. In addition to the ELMO telephone technology—studied by Terry Baumer and associates (Baumer, Maxfield, and Mendelsohn, 1993)—other useful technological aids include devices for videotaping offenders in their home, devices that allow voice pattern recognition, and global satellite tracking devices similar to those attached to animals whose movements are of interest to zoologists.

Cameras and Tape Recorders

Video cameras may be used in public places to record relatively simple phenomena, such as the passage of people or automobiles, or more complex social processes. For several years, London police have monitored traffic conditions at dozens of key intersections using video cameras mounted on building rooftops. Increasingly, police departments in U.S. cities have installed video surveillance cameras in selected locations. Ronald Clarke (1996) studied speeding in Illinois, drawing on observations automatically recorded by cameras placed at several locations throughout the state.

In an effort to develop ways to control aggressive panhandling in New York, George Kelling made videotapes of "squeegee people," who wipe the windshields of motorists stopped at intersections and then demand payment for their services. Kelling taped naturally occurring interactions between squeegee people and motorists, and he also staged contacts that involved plainclothes police in unmarked cars. The video recordings made it possible to study the specific tactics used by squeegee people to intimidate motorists and the motorists' reaction to unwanted windshield service (Kelling and Coles, 1996:141–43).

Still photographs may be appropriate to record some types of observations, such as graffiti or litter. Photos have the added benefit of preserving visual images that can later be viewed and coded by more than one person, thus facilitating interrater reliability checks. For example, if we are interested in studying pedestrian traffic on city streets, we might gather data about what types of people we see and how many there are. As the number and complexity of our observations increase, it becomes more difficult to reliably record how many males and females we see, how many adults and juveniles, and so on. Taking photographs of sampled areas will enable us to be more confident in our measurements and will also make it possible for another person to check on our interpretation of the photographs.

This approach was used by James Lange and associates (Lange, Blackman, and Johnson, 2001) in their study of speeding on the New Jersey Turnpike. The researchers deployed radar devices and digital cameras to measure the speed of vehicles and to take photos of drivers. Equipment was housed in an unmarked van parked at sample locations on the turnpike. The race of drivers was later coded by teams of researchers who studied the digital images. Agreement by at least two of three coders was required to accept the photos for further analysis.

In addition to their use in interviews, audiotape recorders are useful for dictating observations. For example, a researcher interested in patterns of activity on urban streets can dictate observations while riding through selected areas in an automobile. It is possible to dictate observations in an unstructured manner, describing each street scene as it unfolds. Or a tape recorder can be used more like an audio checklist, with observers noting specified items seen in preselected areas.

Field Notes

Even tape recorders and cameras cannot capture all the relevant aspects of social processes. Most field researchers make some records of observations as written notes, perhaps in a field journal. Field notes should include both empirical observations and interpretations of them. They should record what we "know" we have observed and what we "think" we have observed. It is important, however, that these different kinds of notes be identified for what they are. For example, we might note that person X approached and handed something to person Y— a known drug dealer—that we think this was a drug transaction, and that we think person X was a new customer.

We can anticipate some of the most important observations before we begin the study; others will become apparent as our observations progress. Our note taking will be easier if we prepare standardized recording forms in advance. In a study of nighttime pedestrian traffic, for example, we might anticipate the characteristics of pedestrians who are most likely to be useful for analysis—age, gender, ethnicity, and so forth—and prepare a form on which the actual observations can easily be

recorded. Or we might develop a symbolic shorthand in advance to speed up recording. In studying participation at a meeting of a community crime prevention group, we might want to construct a numbered grid of the different sections of the meeting room; then we could record the locations of participants easily, quickly, and accurately.

None of this advance preparation should limit recording of unanticipated events and aspects of the situation. Quite the contrary: The speedy handling of anticipated observations gives the researcher more freedom to observe the unanticipated.

Every student is familiar with the process of taking notes. Good note taking in field research requires more careful and deliberate attention and involves some specific skills. Three guidelines are particularly important.

First, don't trust your memory any more than you have to; it's untrustworthy. Even if you pride yourself on having a photographic memory, it's a good idea to take notes, either during the observation or as soon afterward as possible. If you are taking notes during the observation, do it unobtrusively because people are likely to behave differently if they see you writing down everything they say or do.

Second, it's usually a good idea to take notes in stages. In the first stage, you may need to take sketchy notes (words and phrases) to keep abreast of what's happening. Then remove yourself and rewrite your notes in more detail. If you do this soon after the events you've observed, the sketchy notes will help you recall most of the details. The longer you delay, the less likely you are to recall things accurately and fully. James Roberts (2002), in his study of aggression in New Jersey nightclubs, was reluctant to take any notes while inside clubs, so he retired to his car to make sketchy notes about observations, then wrote them up in more detail later.

Third, you will inevitably wonder how much you should record. Is it really worth the effort to write out all the details you can recall right after the observation session? The basic answer is yes.

In field research, you can't really be sure what's important and unimportant until you've had a chance to review and analyze a great volume of information, so you should record even things that don't seem important at the time. They may turn out to be significant after all. In addition, the act of recording the details of something "unimportant" may jog your memory on something that is important.

Structured Observations

Field notes may be recorded on highly structured forms in which observers mark items in much the same way a survey interviewer marks a closed-ended questionnaire. For example, Steve Mastrofski and associates (1998:11) describe how police performance can be recorded on field observation questionnaires:

> Unlike ethnographic research, which relies heavily on the field researcher to make choices about what to observe and how to interpret it, the observer using [structured observation] is guided by . . . instruments designed by presumably experienced and knowledgeable police researchers.

Training for such efforts is extensive and time consuming. But Mastrofski and associates compared structured observation to closed-ended questions on a questionnaire. If researchers can anticipate in advance that observers will encounter a limited number of situations in the field, those situations can be recorded on structured observation forms. And, like closed-ended survey questions, structured observations have higher reliability.

In a long-term study, Ralph Taylor (1999) developed forms to code a range of physical characteristics in a sample of Baltimore neighborhoods. Observers recorded information on closed-ended items about housing layout, street length and width, traffic volume, type of nonresidential land use, graffiti, persons hanging out, and so forth. Observations were completed in the same neighborhoods in 1981 and 1994.

Because structured field observation forms often resemble survey questionnaires, the use of such forms has the benefit of enabling researchers to generate numeric measures of conditions observed in the field. The Bureau of Justice Assistance (1993:43) has produced a handbook containing guidelines for conducting structured field observations, called **environmental surveys.** The name is significant because observers record information about the conditions of a specified environment:

> [Environmental] surveys seek to assess, as systematically and objectively as possible, the overall physical environment of an area. That physical environment comprises the buildings, parks, streets, transportation facilities, and overall landscaping of an area as well as the functions and conditions of those entities.

Environmental surveys have come to be an important component of problem-oriented policing and situational crime prevention. For example, Figure 10-.4 is adapted from an environmental survey form used by the Philadelphia Police Department in drug enforcement initiatives. Environmental surveys are conducted to plan police strategy in drug enforcement in small areas and to assess changes in conditions following targeted enforcement. Notice that the form can be used to record both information about physical conditions (street width, traffic volume, streetlights) and counts of people and their activities.

Like interview surveys, environmental surveys require that observers be carefully trained in what to observe and how to interpret it. For example, the instructions that accompany the environmental survey excerpted in Figure 10.4 include guidance on coding abandoned automobiles:

> Count as abandoned if it appears nondrivable (i.e., has shattered windows, dismantled body parts, missing tires, missing license plates). Consider it abandoned if it

Date:_____ Day of week:_____ Time:_____

Observer:_____

Street name:_____

Cross streets:_____

1. Street width
   Number of drivable lanes   ____
   Number of parking lanes   ____
   Median present? (yes = 1, no = 2)   ____

2. Volume of traffic flow: (check one)
   a. very light   ____
   b. light   ____
   c. moderate   ____
   d. heavy   ____
   e. very heavy   ____

3. Number of street lights   ____

4. Number of broken street lights   ____

5. Number of abandoned automobiles   ____

6. List all the people on the block and their activities:

Males	Hanging out	Playing	Working	Walking	Other
Young (up to age 12)	____	____	____	____	____
Teens (13–19)	____	____	____	____	____
Adult (20–60)	____	____	____	____	____
Seniors (61+)	____	____	____	____	____
Females					
Young (up to age 12)	____	____	____	____	____
Teens (13–19)	____	____	____	____	____
Adult (20–60)	____	____	____	____	____
Seniors (61+)	____	____	____	____	____

Figure 10.4   Example of Environmental Survey

Source: Adapted from Bureau of Justice Assistance (1993:Appendix B).

appears that it has not been driven for some time and that it is not going to be for some time to come.

Other instructions provide details on how to count drivable lanes, what sorts of activities constitute "playing" and "working," how to estimate the ages of people observed, and so on.

Linking Field Observations and Other Data

Criminal justice research sometimes combines field research with surveys or data from official records.

Although criminal justice research may utilize field methods or sample surveys exclusively, a given project will often collect data from several sources. This is consistent with general advice about using appropriate measures and data collection methods. Simply saying "I am going to conduct an observational study of youth gangs" restricts the research focus at the outset to the kinds of information that can be gathered through observation. Such a study may be useful and interesting, but a researcher is better advised to consider what data collection methods are necessary in any particular study.

For example, in their Baltimore study, Ralph Taylor and associates (Taylor, Shumaker, and Gottfredson, 1985) were interested in the effects of neighborhood physical characteristics on residents' perceptions of crime problems. Collecting data on physical characteristics required field observation, but sample surveys were necessary for gathering data on perceptions. So Taylor and colleagues conducted a survey of households in the neighborhoods where observations were made. Finally, they compared census data and crime reports from Baltimore police records with information from observations and household surveys.

These three sources of data provided different types of measures that, in combination, yielded a great deal of information about neighborhoods and neighborhood residents in the study sites. Surveys measured respondents' perceptions and beliefs about crime and other problems. Police records represented crimes reported to police by area residents. Field observations yielded data on physical characteristics and conditions of neighborhoods as rated by outside observers. Census data made it possible to control for the effects of socioeconomic status variables such as income, employment status, and housing tenure.

Finally, Taylor (1999) conducted follow-up field observations and interviews in 1994— 13 years after initial data collection. He found that physical conditions had declined since the first series of observations in 1981 but that residents in selected neighborhoods did not *perceive* that conditions were worse. Thus, Taylor was able to compare changes in conditions observed by researchers in the field to what survey re-

spondents reported to interviewers. The different methods of data collection yielded different results because they measured different dimensions of neighborhoods—field observations measured conditions, while surveys measured perceptions.

A long-term research project on community policing in Chicago similarly draws on data from surveys, field observation, and police records (Chicago Community Policing Evaluation Consortium, 2003). As just one example, researchers studied what sorts of activities and discussions emerged at community meetings in 130 of the city's 270 police beats that covered residential areas. Observers attended meetings, making detailed notes and completing structured observation forms. One section of the form, shown in Figure 10.5, instructed observers to make notes of specific types of neighborhood problems that were discussed at the meeting (Bennis, Skogan, and Steiner, 2003). Here is an excerpt from the narrative notes that supplemented this section of the form:

> They . . . had very serious concerns in regard to a dilapidated building in their block that was being used for drug sales. The drug seller's people were also squatting in the basement of the building. The main concern was that the four adults who were squatting also had three children under the age of four with them. (Chicago Community Policing Evaluation Consortium, 2003:37)

In addition, observers distributed questionnaires to community residents and police officers attending each meeting. Items asked how often people attended beat meetings, what sorts of other civic activities they pursued, and whether they thought various other issues were problems in their neighborhood. As an example, the combination of field observation data and survey questionnaires enabled researchers to assess the degree of general social activism among those who attended beat meetings.

Field research can also be conducted after a survey. For example, a survey intended to

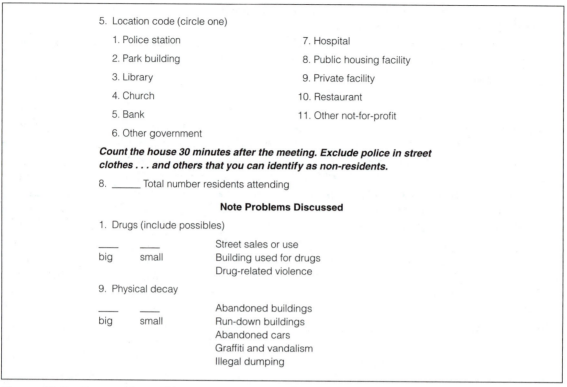

5. Location code (circle one)

1. Police station
2. Park building
3. Library
4. Church
5. Bank
6. Other government

7. Hospital
8. Public housing facility
9. Private facility
10. Restaurant
11. Other not-for-profit

Count the house 30 minutes after the meeting. Exclude police in street clothes . . . and others that you can identify as non-residents.

8. _____ Total number residents attending

Note Problems Discussed

1. Drugs (include possibles)

____   ____
big   small

Street sales or use
Building used for drugs
Drug-related violence

9. Physical decay

____   ____
big   small

Abandoned buildings
Run-down buildings
Abandoned cars
Graffiti and vandalism
Illegal dumping

Figure 10.5   Excerpts from Chicago Beat Meeting Observation Form
Source: Adapted from Bennis, Skogan, and Steiner (2003: Appendix 1).

measure fear of crime and related concepts might ask respondents to specify any area near their residence that they believe is particularly dangerous. Follow-up field visits to the named areas could then be conducted, during which observers record information about physical characteristics, land use, numbers of people present, and so forth.

The box titled "Conducting a Safety Audit" describes how structured field observations were combined with a focus group discussion to assess the scope of environmental design changes in Toronto, Canada.

The flexibility of field methods is one reason observation and field interviews can readily be incorporated into many research projects. And field observation often provides a much richer understanding of a phenomenon that is imperfectly revealed through a survey questionnaire.

In Chapter 8, we mentioned how Terry Baumer and Robert Mendelsohn (1990) supplemented interviews with persons sentenced to electronic monitoring by actually wearing the devices themselves for several days. Their participant observation enabled them to experience punitive features of home detention that would have been difficult to appreciate any other way.

Illustrations of Field Research

Examples illustrate different applications of field research to study shoplifting, traffic, and violence in bars.

Before concluding this chapter on field research, let's examine some illustrations of the method in action. These descriptions will provide a clearer sense of how researchers use field observations and interviews in criminal justice research.

Shoplifting

We have briefly mentioned the research on shop-lifting by Baumer and Rosenbaum (1982). A fuller discussion of this unusual study illustrates much of the potential of field research, some problems that may be encountered, and the clever approaches to these problems adopted by Baumer and Rosenbaum.

This study was undertaken with two objectives: (1) to estimate the prevalence of shoplifting and (2) to assess the effectiveness of store security in identifying shoplifters. As we noted earlier, it is difficult to obtain reliable counts of offenses such as shoplifting and so-called victimless crimes. Shoplifting is usually counted only when an offense is witnessed by police or store security personnel. Store inventory records could be used to estimate losses by customer theft, but as Baumer and Rosenbaum note, this obscures the difference between shoplifting by customers and employee theft. The approach they adopted was direct observation.

McCall (1978:20) described three difficulties in observational studies of crime. First, most offenses are relatively rare and unpredictable; an observer might spend weeks or months in the field without witnessing a single burglary, for example. Second, unless they are carefully concealed, field observers, by their very presence, are likely to deter criminals anxious to keep their actions from public view. Finally, there is some danger to field workers who attentively observe crimes in progress while taking careful field notes.

Baumer and Rosenbaum reasoned that shoplifting is largely immune from these problems. First, because shoplifting by definition takes place in only certain specific locations, observers can focus their attention there. Baumer and Rosenbaum selected a large department store in downtown Chicago as the site of their research. The second and third problems mentioned by McCall are also largely absent because shoplifters commit their offenses in the presence of other shoppers; the crime is one of stealth, not confrontation. Field workers could readily adopt the participant observation role of shopper with no more fear for their own safety than that experienced by other shoppers.

Field observers could therefore be used in much the same way undercover retail security workers are deployed in many stores: Pose as a shopper and watch for thefts by other shoppers. When a theft is witnessed, that's shoplifting.

What about selecting subjects for observation? And how can simple counts of observed thefts be used to estimate the prevalence of shoplifting? "Shoplifting prevalence" was defined as the number of shoppers who stole something during their visit to the store divided by the total number of shoppers. This meant that it was necessary to obtain counts of shoppers as well as shoplifters. Because shopping is a predictable activity (if it were not, there would be no shops!), it is possible to use systematic sampling methods to select people to observe.

Baumer and Rosenbaum chose a variety of days and times to conduct observations. During these times, observers and field supervisors were stationed at each entrance to the department store. Field supervisors counted everyone who entered the store and assigned observers to follow selected individuals from the time they entered until they left. Subjects were selected by systematic sampling in which, say, every 20th person who entered during the observation period was followed by a field observer. Dividing the number of thefts witnessed by the number of shoppers observed yielded an estimate of shoplifting prevalence. For instance, if observers were assigned to follow 500 people, and they witnessed thefts by 20 of them, the prevalence of shoplifting was 4 percent.

Counts of observed thefts also provided one way to assess store security. Comparing the number of thefts witnessed by participant observers to the number detected by store security staff was one obvious way to evaluate store

CONDUCTING A SAFETY AUDIT

by Gisela Bichler-Robertson
California State University at San Bernadino

A safety audit involves a careful inventory of specific environmental and situational factors that may contribute to feelings of discomfort, fear of victimization, or crime itself. The goal of a safety audit is to devise recommendations that will improve a specific area by reducing fear and crime.

Safety audits combine features of focus groups and structured field observations. To begin, the researcher assembles a small group of individuals (10 or fewer) considered to be vulnerable. Examples include: senior citizens, physically challenged individuals, young women who travel alone, students, youth, and parents with young children. Assembling diverse groups helps to identify a greater variety of environmental and situational factors for the particular area.

After explaining safety audit procedures, an audit leader then takes the group on a tour of the audit site. Since perceptions differ by time of day, at least two audits are conducted for each site—one during daylight and one after dark.

When touring audit sites, individuals do not speak to one another. The audit leader instructs group members to imagine that they are walking through the area alone. Each person is equipped with a structured form for documenting their observations and perceptions. Forms vary, depending on the group and site. In general, however, safety audit participants are instructed to document the following items:

1. Before walking through the area, briefly describe the type of space you are reviewing (e.g., a parking deck, park, shopping district). Record the number of entrances, general volume of users, design of structures, materials used in design, and type of lighting.
2. Complete the following while walking through the area.

General feelings of safety:
- Identify the places in which you feel unsafe and uncomfortable.
- What is it about each place that makes you feel this way?
- Identify the places in which you feel safe.
- What is it about each place that makes you feel this way?

General visibility:
- Can you see very far in front of you?
- Can you see behind you?
- Are there any structures or vegetation that restrict your sightlines?
- How dense are the trees/bushes?
- Are there any hiding spots or entrapment zones?
- Is the lighting adequate? Can you see the face of someone 15 meters in front of you?
- Are the paths/hallways open or are they very narrow?
- Are there any sharp corners (90° angles)?

security. Baumer and Rosenbaum devised another method, however, one that solved a potential problem with their approach to counting shoplifting. The problem may have already occurred to you.

If you were an observer in this research, how confident would you be in your ability to detect shoplifting? Stated somewhat differently, how reliable would your observations be? Retail thieves are at least somewhat careful to conceal their crime. As a participant observer, you would have to balance your diligence in watching people to whom you were assigned (observation) with care to not appear too interested in what your fellow shoppers were doing (participation).

Baumer and Rosenbaum used an ingenious adaptation of double-blind experimental methods—discussed in Chapter 7—to assess the reliability of field observers. Unknown to field observers, other research staff were employed as confederate shoplifters. Their job was to enter the store and steal something. Field supervisors, knowing when confederates would be entering

Perceived control over the space:

- Could you see danger approaching with enough time to choose an alternative route?
- Are you visible to others on the street or in other buildings?
- Can you see any evidence of a security system?

Presence of others:

- Does the area seem to be deserted?
- Are there many women around?
- Are you alone in the presence of men?
- What do the other people seem to be doing?
- Are there any undesirables—vagrants (homeless or beggars), drunks, etc.?
- Do you see people who you know?
- Are there any police or security officers present?

General safety:

- Do you have access to a phone or other way of summoning help?
- What is your general perception of criminal behavior?
- Are there any places where you feel you could be attacked or confronted in an uncomfortable way?

Past experience in this space:

- Have you been harassed in this space?
- Have you heard of anyone who had a bad experience in this place (any legends or real experiences)?

- Is it likely that you may be harassed here (e.g., drunk young men coming out of the pub)?
- Have you noticed any social incivilities (minor deviant behavior—i.e., public drinking, vandalism, roughhousing, or skateboarding)?
- Is there much in the way of physical incivilities (broken windows, litter, broken bottles, vandalism)?

Following the site visit, the group finds a secure setting for a focused discussion of the various elements they identified. Harvesting observations about good and bad spaces helps to develop recommendations for physical improvement. Group members may also share perceptions and ideas about personal safety. This process should begin with a brain-storming discussion and finish with identifying the key issues of concern and most reasonable recommendations for addressing those issues.

This method of structured observation has proven to be invaluable. Much of the public space in Toronto including university campuses, public parks, transportation centers, and garages have been improved through such endeavors.

Source: Adapted from materials developed by the Metro Action Committee on Public Violence Against Women and Children (METRAC) (Toronto, Canada: METRAC, 1987). Used by permission.

---

the store, periodically instructed observers to follow one of these persons. Confederates committed known thefts and made it possible to determine whether observers were able to detect the incident.

In this way, the researchers could measure the reliability of field observations. If an observer detected 85 percent of the known thefts, that observer's count of shoplifting by real shoppers could be considered 85 percent accurate. Reliability figures were used to adjust estimates of shoplifting prevalence. For example, if

the prevalence estimate for all observers was 4 percent and all observers were 85 percent reliable, then the adjusted prevalence rate was 4.7 percent (0.04/0.85).

One of the lessons from this study is that simple observation is often not so simple. This is especially true when researchers are trying to observe people doing something they wish to conceal from observers. Our next example offers similar guidance in planning observations of people who are doing something required by law.

How Many People Wear Seat Belts?

Although nations in Europe and other parts of the world have required drivers to use seat belts for many years, laws mandating seat belt use were rare in the United States until the 1980s. Problems in enforcing such laws, as well as general resistance to regulation, are among the reasons these laws were late in coming. These concerns promoted interest in the degree of compliance with mandated seat belt use.

Indiana University's Transportation Research Center (TRC) conducted pilot studies in Indiana to develop methods of observing seat belt use. One of several research reports issued by TRC (Cornwell, Doherty, Mitter, and Drayer, 1989) illustrates sampling issues in field observations and offers a good example of why reliability is so important in field research.

The first decision faced by TRC researchers was how to conduct the observations. They opted for stationary observers posted at roadsides rather than mobile observers riding around in cars. The primary reason for this choice was the need to calculate the rates of seat belt use, expressed as the number of people seen to be wearing belts divided by the number of cars observed. Keeping track of the number of vehicles observed is easier when they can be counted as they pass by some stationary point. Trying to count cars in view while riding in a car yourself is more difficult.

Where to place stationary observers was the next decision. Cornwell and associates describe how detecting seat belt use in moving vehicles is difficult. For this reason, most observers were stationed at controlled intersections—those with a stop sign or traffic light. Because interstate highways do not have intersections, other observers were posted at entrance ramps where cars were traveling more slowly.

Because it is impossible to know the number of autos in operation throughout Indiana at any given time, TRC researchers could not select a probability sample of vehicles to observe. Instead, they used systematic procedures to sample observations on three dimensions that might be associated with seat belt use: time of day, roadway type, and observation site. In addition to considerations about site type, Cornwell and colleagues wished to stratify sites by density of auto ownership. Finding that this was highly correlated with population, they divided Indiana counties into three strata based on population and selected sites within each stratum. Small counties were oversampled to ensure that different geographic areas of the state were represented.

Roadway type included interstate highways, U.S. and state roads, and local streets. Observations were made for each day of the week and at different times of day to represent the various trip purposes. For example, weekday observations at 6:30–7:30 A.M. represented blue-collar home-to-work trips, later morning times were for white-collar commuters, and midday hours represented lunch breaks.

Standing by the roadside and trying to determine whether drivers and front-seat passengers are wearing safety belts was easier than observing shoplifters but still presented some difficulties. Cornwell and associates describe training procedures and steps they took to maximize the accuracy of observations. All observers completed a training period in which they worked under the supervision of an experienced fieldworker. If you had been a neophyte observer for the seat belt study, here are some of the things you would have been told about your role.

"First, you realize, of course, that we are complete observers, not participant observers. We don't try to conceal ourselves because we would not be able to see the cars very well if we hid behind signs or something. Sure, drivers can see us standing here with our clipboards, and they may wonder what we're doing. We've posted a sign that says, 'Traffic Safety Research in Progress,' but there's no way they can know that we're checking seat belt use. So try to relax and don't feel self-conscious about standing on the side of the road in your orange vest watching cars.

"Second, remember that you should check only passenger cars and station wagons. Trucks, buses, recreational vehicles, and taxicabs are not covered by the law. Also, this is Indiana, not California, so you won't see too many older cars that don't have shoulder belts. Even if you do, don't try to observe them because they aren't covered by the law either. And remember, we're interested only in front-seat occupants; ignore the back seat.

"Most importantly, record only safety belts that you can see. If you see a belt in use, great; mark a *Y* for yes on the coding form. If you see a belt that is NOT in use, mark *N* for no. But if you can't see that someone is wearing a belt and you can't actually see a safety belt that the person is not wearing, mark a *U* for uncertain. I know you're a good observer; we're all good observers. But sometimes cars go by so fast that you can't see whether a person is wearing a belt. It happens to all of us. Just be sure you mark *U* when you're uncertain.

"Now, I have been doing this for about 6 months and I've learned some things that they didn't tell me when I started. We have run into some problems that nobody thought about when they first designed this study. For example, you're lucky to be starting in May, when the weather is good and the sun is up. In wintertime, people are wearing heavy coats, and it's much harder to tell whether they are wearing their safety belt. On cold mornings, the windows on cars can be fogged up, making it hard to see inside. Also, when I started working the 6:30–7:30 A.M. shift in January, it was still dark and we couldn't see anything. We had to revise the time-of-day sampling plan because of that.

"From our site here, we have four lanes of roadway to observe. Concentrate on the traffic lanes closest to us. You will be able to see the cars in those lanes better than you can see those in the far lanes. When traffic is stopped at the light it's not too bad, but when cars are moving you won't be able to observe everybody. Just remember, it's better to observe a smaller number of cars where you can confidently code *Y* or *N* than it is to try to see more cars but have to mark *U* because you can't be sure. There is no reason to expect that drivers in the far lanes will be any different than those in the near lanes. Code cars in all lanes when possible, but when in doubt focus on those closest to you."

The National Highway Traffic Safety Administration (NHTSA) now conducts observation studies of safety belt use in most states. Donna Glassbrenner (2003) presents an example of annual tabulations. For further details on how these observations were conducted, see her technical report (Glassbrenner, 2002), which also describes how observation procedures have evolved over the years.

"Driving While Black"

Racial profiling of drivers on the nation's highways and of pedestrians in large cities emerged as a critical issue in the mid-1990s. From a personal and policy perspective, racial profiling refers to disproportionate traffic stops or foot stops of racial minorities. A research perspective might ask, "What is disproportionate?" and raise questions of how one measures traffic and foot stops of minorities disproportionate to their numbers on highways or sidewalks.

Some research, such as that of David Harris (1997), compares the race of drivers stopped with the racial makeup of a state's population or the racial makeup of registered drivers in a state. But this method has several drawbacks. Drivers stopped in a given state can be nonresident travelers. Traffic stops tend to be more common on interstate highways, and the race of drivers on those highways may differ from that of state residents. Most researchers now recognize that comparing the race of drivers with race distributions for a resident population is misleading at best (General Accounting Office, 2000).

John Lamberth (1996) employed observational methods to assess whether African American drivers were disproportionately stopped on the New Jersey Turnpike, a link in the East Coast interstate system where racial profiling has long been perceived as a problem. Sampling times and dates, Lamberth took advantage of the fact that the turnpike is a toll road by placing stationary observers at toll booths. As cars entered the highway, it was relatively easy to record the race of drivers.

This provided an estimate of *drivers,* but traffic stops must be justified by a moving violation or a visible equipment problem such as broken lights. What was needed was an estimate of the number of cars eligible to be stopped—the number of cars committing some violation—and the race of drivers for those cars. Lamberth adopted mobile observation procedures to estimate part of the traffic offender population. Teams of researchers drove sampled sections of the turnpike, traveling at a constant speed 5 miles per hour over the speed limit. Observers then counted cars passing the research vehicle and recorded the race of drivers, thus providing an estimate of drivers who were speeding.

Tabulating results, Lamberth found that African Americans were drivers of 13.5 percent of vehicles on the turnpike and 15 percent of vehicles observed to be speeding. Consulting records, Lamberth found that 35 percent of drivers stopped by police were black and that 73 percent of those arrested after the stop were black.

Note that Lamberth's observations counted only the race of people speeding; cars may have been stopped for a variety of other violations. Recognizing this, a later study by Lange and associates (2001) used systematic observation to measure high-end speeding—drivers exceeding the speed limit by 15 or more miles per hour. Researchers assumed that virtually all drivers exceeding posted speed limits by that much

would be stopped by state police. As we mentioned earlier in this chapter, a van containing radar detection equipment was linked to cameras that recorded the speed of vehicles and digital images of drivers. Lange and associates sought to measure not just the population of drivers, but drivers *eligible to be stopped.* Observation, in this cases aided by sophisticated (and expensive) equipment, is the best way to make those measures.

Bars and Violence

Researchers in the first three examples conducted systematic observations for specific purposes and produced quantitative estimates of shoplifting prevalence, seat belt use, and driving, respectively. Field research is commonly used in more qualitative studies as well, in which precise quantitative estimates are neither available nor needed. A fascinating study of violence in Australian bars by Ross Homel and associates (Homel, Tomsen, and Thommeny, 1992) provides an example.

Anyone with any sort of experience in or knowledge about crime will be at least casually familiar with the relationship between drinking and violence. Psychologists and medical researchers have found a physiological disinhibiting effect of alcohol that can lead to aggression and subsequent violence. In a large proportion of homicides, either the victim or the offender (or both) had been drinking. Barroom brawls are known to most people by reputation if not by experience.

Homel and associates set out to learn how various situational factors related to public drinking might promote or inhibit violence in Australian bars and nightclubs. Think for a moment about how you might approach their research question: "whether alcohol consumption itself contributes in some way to the likelihood of violence, or whether aspects of the drinkers or of the drinking settings are the critical factors" (1992:681). Examining police records might reveal that assault reports are more likely to come from bars than from, say, public libraries. Or a survey might find that self-reported bar patrons were more likely to have witnessed or participated in violence than respondents who did not frequent bars or nightclubs. But neither of these approaches will yield measures of the setting or situational factors that might provoke violence. Field research can produce direct observation of barroom settings and is well suited to addressing the question framed by Homel and associates.

Researchers began by selecting 4 "high-risk" and 2 "low-risk" sites based on Sydney police records and preliminary scouting visits. These 6 sites were visited five or more times, and an additional 16 sites were visited once in the course of scouting.

Visits to bars were conducted by pairs of observers who stayed 2–6 hours at each site. Their role is best described as complete participant because they were permitted one alcoholic drink per hour and otherwise played the role of bar patron. Observers made no notes while onsite. As soon as possible after leaving a bar, they wrote up separate narrative accounts. Later, at group meetings of observers and research staff, the narrative accounts were discussed and any discrepancies resolved. Narratives were later coded by research staff to identify categories of situations, people, and activities that seemed to be associated with the likelihood of violence. These eventually included physical and social atmosphere, drinking patterns, characteristics of patrons, and characteristics of staff.

The researchers began their study by assuming that some thing or things distinguished bars in which violence was common from those in which it was less common. After beginning their field work, however, Homel and associates (1992:684) realized that circumstances and situations were the more important factors:

> During field research it soon became apparent that the violent premises are for most of the time not violent. Violent occasions in these places seemed to have characteristics that clearly marked them out from nonviolent times. . . . This unexpectedly helped us refine our ideas about

the relevant situational variables, and to some extent reduced the importance of comparisons with the premises selected as controls.

In other words, the research question was partly restated. What began as a study to determine *why* some bars in Sydney were violent was revised to determine *what situations* seemed to contribute violence.

This illustrates one of the strengths of field research—the ability to make adjustments while in the field. You may recognize this as an example of inductive reasoning. Learning that even violent clubs were peaceful most of the time, Homel and associates were able to focus observers' attention on looking for more specific features of the bar environment and staff and patron characteristics. Such adjustments "on the fly" would be difficult, if not impossible, if you were doing a survey.

Altogether, field observers made 55 visits to 23 sites, for a total of about 300 hours of field observation. During these visits, observers witnessed 32 incidents of physical violence. Examining detailed field notes, researchers attributed violent incidents to a variety of interrelated factors.

With respect to patrons, violence was most likely to break out in bars frequented by young, working-class males. However, these personal characteristics were deemed less important than the flow of people in and out of bars. Violent incidents were often triggered when groups of males entered a club and encountered other groups of males they did not know.

Physical features mattered little unless they contributed to crowding or other adverse characteristics of the social atmosphere. Chief among social features associated with violence were discomfort and boredom. A crowded, uncomfortable bar with no entertainment spelled trouble.

Drinking patterns made a difference; violent incidents were most common when bar patrons were very drunk. More importantly, certain management practices seemed to produce more

PUTTING IT ALL TOGETHER

FIELD RESEARCH IN NEW YORK CITY

Field observation was a central part of research on how changes in policing affected crime in New York. Rutgers Researchers observed police activities in formal settings such as Compstat meetings and other planned sessions in which officers and commanders discussed crime problems and police action. To study the implementation of these actions, researchers accompanied uniformed officers and special units on the streets of New York. In all cases, researchers acted as complete observers.

Access to the NYPD

As might be expected, it was necessary to negotiate access for field observations and other tasks we have mentioned in this running example. This process was more complicated and formal in New York than for other police departments Rutgers researchers have studied.

One professor at Rutgers had a long history of working with the NYPD, so all initial contacts and discussions were channeled through that individual. After a series of telephone calls, meetings, and serendipitous conversations over the course of a year, researchers were invited to submit a proposal for their study. The research proposal was approved, and access was negotiated to obtain department records and make observations. The latter required several meetings to inform police commanders and officers about the study and to obtain their consent to participate. One meeting in particular brought together Rutgers researchers, commanders of the six case-study precincts, the chief of department (the top uniformed commander in the city), and two deputy commissioners. Then researchers visited each of the six precincts to explain the study to officers and supervisors.

Observing Formal Meetings

Compstat meetings had quickly become well known around the world, with each week's meeting attended by a number of visitors. Since the September 11, 2001, attacks, Compstat meetings have been closed to the general public. While observed by Rutgers researchers, however, Compstat meetings resembled public events like court trials and city council sessions. This made it easy for researchers to maintain a complete observer role, sitting in the designated visitor section and openly taking copious notes.

Researchers also attended meetings at the precinct and borough level. Each of the six case-study precincts is part of a police borough—a command area that includes many precincts. Precinct meetings are less formal than Compstat meetings. This is where precinct commanders, in anticipation of appearing at Compstat sessions, review crime data and plan responses. Borough-level meetings lie between precinct and Compstat meetings. Visitors are quite rare at these lower-level meetings, so the researcher's presence was more conspicuous. But having negotiated access to all levels of the NYPD, researchers openly took notes and sometimes asked questions to clarify what was observed at these meetings.

On the Street

While observing the top brass at their world-famous Compstat meetings was interesting, accompanying New York police on patrol was often fascinating. Researchers studied very different areas of the city, from a Brooklyn precinct with high levels of violence and drug crimes to one of the trendiest nightclub districts in Manhattan. Each area presented a different face of the city.

The researcher's role was still one of complete observer, but subtle differences existed. First, accompanying police in their cars or on foot patrol is much more obtrusive than trying to act like a piece of furniture in a formal meeting. Researchers made special efforts to put officers at ease but always kept in mind that research subjects act at least somewhat differently in the presence of observers. The second subtle difference involved the fact that observers often appear to be participants to the citizens who come into contact with police. This meant that the behavior of citizens was much less likely to be affected by the researcher's presence.

Because police observed in the field knew about the observer's role, it would appear that detailed field notes could be openly taken. This was partly true, as it was not necessary to conceal anything. However, researchers were careful not to make lengthy notes in the presence of police. The belief was that police would be more self-conscious if they felt that all their actions and remarks were being recorded in detail. At the same time, taking notes can subtly enhance rapport with subjects, in that writing down what someone says signals respect for that person's wisdom or experience. Finding the right balance is sometimes tricky.

Ride-Along Observations

Precinct: _____ Tour: _____ Date: _____ Unit: _____ # Officers: _____

Unit's general directive: _____

_____

Unit's deployment: _____

Summarize initial discussion (if any): _____

_____

Today's specific focus (if any): _____

_____

How else is unit aware of today's efforts? _____

_____

Are today's efforts addressing a specific spike, trend, pattern, etc.? _____

_____

Is today's focus part of a larger initiative? _____

_____

Describe communication with other units: _____

_____

Activities. Record time and describe events: _____

_____

_____

_____

_____

_____

_____

A semistructured form, shown here, was created to record observations. As mentioned in Chapter 5, defining measures for police activity was difficult. In general, open-ended survey questions and semistructured or unstructured field notes are more appropriate when researchers are less certain about the kinds of responses or events they will encounter. That was certainly the case for police activity. The semistructured form included space for recording the time when activities began and ended and descriptions of what the activities involved. This information was transcribed to computer files and coded to reflect the inductive generation of activity categories. This is common practice with field observations and open-ended interview questions and represents something of a content analysis, one of our topics in Chapter 11.

drunk patrons. Fewer customers were drunk in bars that had either a restaurant or a snack table. Bars with high cover charges and cheap drinks produced a high density of drunk patrons and violence. The economics of this situation are clear: If you must pay to enter a bar that serves cheap drinks, you'll get more for your money by drinking a lot.

The final ingredient found to contribute to violence was aggressive bouncers. "Many bouncers seem poorly trained, obsessed with their own machismo (relating badly to groups of male strangers), and some of them appear to regard their employment as a license to assault people" (1992:688). Rather than reducing violence by rejecting unruly patrons, bouncers sometimes escalated violence by starting fights.

Field observation was necessary to identify what situations produce violence in bars. No other way of collecting data could have yielded the rich and detailed information that enabled Homel and associates (1992:688) to diagnose the complex relationships that produce violence in bars:

> Violent incidents in public drinking locations do not occur simply because of the presence of young or rough patrons or because of rock bands, or any other single variable. Violent occasions are characterized by subtle interactions of several variables. Chief among these are groups of male strangers, low comfort, high boredom, high drunkenness, as well as aggressive and unreasonable bouncers and floorstaff. (1992:688)

Strengths and Weaknesses of Field Research

Validity is usually a strength of field research, but reliability and generalizability are sometimes weaknesses.

As we have seen, field research is especially effective for studying the subtle nuances of behavior and for examining processes over time. For these reasons, the chief strength of this method is the depth of understanding it permits.

Conducting field studies of behavior is often more appropriate than trying to measure behavior through surveys. Counts of seat belt use or theft by shoppers obtained through observation are not subject to the effects of social desirability that we might expect in survey questions about those behaviors.

Flexibility is another advantage of field research. Researchers can modify their research design at any time. Moreover, they are always prepared to engage in qualitative field research if the occasion arises, whereas launching a survey requires considerable advance work.

Field research can be relatively inexpensive. Other research methods may require costly equipment or a large research staff, but field research often can be undertaken by one researcher with a notebook and a pen. This is not to say that field research is never expensive. The shoplifting research, seat belt study, and race profiling investigation required many trained observers. Expensive recording equipment may be needed, or the researcher may wish to travel to Australia to replicate the study by Homel and associates.

Field research has its weaknesses, too. First, qualitative studies seldom yield precise descriptive statements about a large population. Observing casual discussions among corrections officers in a cafeteria, for example, does not yield trustworthy estimates about prison conditions. Nevertheless, it could provide important insights into some of the problems facing staff and inmates in a specific institution.

Second, field observation can produce systematic counts of behaviors and reasonable estimates for a large population of behaviors beyond those actually observed. However, because it is difficult to know the total population of given phenomena—shoppers or drivers, for example—precise probability samples cannot normally be drawn. In designing a quantitative field study or assessing the representativeness of some other study, researchers must think carefully about the density and predictability of what will be observed. Then they must decide whether sampling procedures are likely to tap representative instances of cases they will observe.

More generally, the advantages and disadvantages of different types of field studies can be considered in terms of their validity, reliability, and generalizability. As we have seen, validity and reliability are both qualities of measurements. *Validity* concerns whether measurements actually measure what they are supposed to, not something else. *Reliability* is a matter of dependability: If researchers make the same measurement again and again, will they get the same result? Note that some examples we described in this chapter included special steps to improve reliability. Finally, *generalizability* refers to whether specific research findings apply to people, places, and things not actually observed. Let's see how field research stacks up in these respects.

Validity

Survey measurements are sometimes criticized as superficial and weak on validity. Observational studies have the potential to yield measures that are more valid. With respect to qualitative field research, "being there" is a powerful technique for gaining insights into the nature of human affairs.

Recall our discussion in Chapter 9 of some of the limitations of using survey methods to study domestic violence. An alternative is a field study in which the researcher interacts at length with victims of domestic violence. The relative strengths of each approach are nicely illustrated in a pair of articles that examine domestic violence in England. Chapter 9 quoted from Catriona Mirrlees-Black's (1995) article on domestic violence as measured in the British Crime Survey. John Hood-Williams and Tracey Bush (1995) provide a different perspective through their study published in the same issue of the *Home Office Research Bulletin*.

Tracey Bush lived in a London public housing project (termed "housing estate" in England) for about 5 years. This enabled her to study domestic violence in a natural setting: "The views of men and women on the estate about relationships and domestic violence have been gathered through the researcher's network of friends, neighbours, acquaintances, and contacts" (Hood-Williams and Bush, 1995:11). Through long and patient field work, Bush learned that women sometimes "normalize" low levels of violence, seeing it as an unfortunate but unavoidable consequence of their relationship with a male partner. When violence escalates, victims may blame themselves. Victims may also remain in an abusive relationship in hopes that things will get better: "She reported that she wanted the companionship and respect that she had received at the beginning of the relationship. It was the earlier, nonviolent man, whom she had met and fallen in love with, that she wanted back" (1995:13).

Mirrlees-Black (1995) notes that measuring domestic violence is "difficult territory" in part because women may not recognize assault by a partner as a crime. Field research such as that by Hood-Williams and Bush offers an example of this phenomenon and helps us understand why it exists.

Validity is a particular strength of field research. Quantitative measurements based on surveys or on simple counts of some phenomenon often give an incomplete picture of the fundamental concept of interest. Survey responses to questions about domestic violence victimization, however carefully phrased, are limited in their ability to count incidents that victims don't recognize as crimes. More importantly, survey methods cannot yield the rich understanding of domestic violence and its context that Tracey Bush discovered in her 5 years of field research.

In field research, validity often refers to whether the intended meaning of the things observed or people interviewed has been accurately captured. In the case of interviews, Joseph Maxwell (1996) suggests getting feedback on the measures from the people being studied. For example, Wright and Decker (1994) conducted lengthy semistructured interviews with their sample of burglars. The researchers recognized that their limited understanding of the social context of burglary may have produced some errors in interpreting what they learned from subjects. To guard against this, Wright and Decker had some of their subjects review what they thought they had learned:

> As the writing proceeded, we read various parts of the manuscript to selected members of our sample. This allowed us to check our interpretations against those of insiders and to enlist their help in reformulating passages they regarded as misleading or inaccurate. . . . The result of using this procedure, we believe, is a book that faithfully conveys the offender's perspective on the process of committing residential burglaries. (1994:33–34)

This approach is possible only if subjects are aware of the researcher's role as a researcher. In that case, having informants review draft field notes or interview transcripts can be an excellent strategy for improving validity.

Reliability

Qualitative field research can have a potential problem with reliability. Suppose you characterize your best friend's political orientations based on everything you know about him or her. There's certainly no question that your assessment of that person's politics is at least somewhat idiosyncratic. The measurement you arrive at will appear to have considerable validity. We can't be sure, however, that someone else will characterize your friend's politics the same way you do, even with the same amount of observation.

Field research measurements—even in-depth ones—are also often very personal. If, for example, you wished to conduct a field study of bars and honky-tonks near your campus, you might judge levels of disorder on a Friday night to be low or moderate. In contrast, older adults might observe the same levels of noise and commotion and rate levels of disorder as intolerably high. How we interpret the phenomena we observe depends very much on our own experiences and preferences.

The reliability of quantitative field studies can be enhanced by careful attention to the details of observation. We have seen examples of this in studies of shoplifting and seat belt use. Environmental surveys can likewise promote reliable observations by including detailed instructions on how to classify what is observed. Reliability can be strengthened by reviewing the products of field observations. Homel and associates sought to increase the reliability of observers' narrative descriptions by having group discussions about discrepancies in reports by different observers.

In a more general sense, reliability will increase as the degree of interpretation required in making actual observations decreases. Participant observation or unstructured interviews may require a considerable degree of interpretation on the part of the observer, and most of us draw on our own experiences and backgrounds in interpreting what we observe. At another extreme, electronic devices and machines can produce very reliable counts of persons who enter a store or of cars that pass some particular point. Somewhere in the middle are field workers who observe shoplifters, motorists, or pedestrians and tabulate some specific behavior.

Generalizability

One of the chief goals of social science is generalization. We study particular situations and events to learn about life in general. Usually, nobody is interested in the specific subjects observed by the researcher. Who cares, after all, about the 18 people who told NCVS interviewers about their stolen bicycles? We are interested only if their victimization experiences can be generalized to all U.S. households.

Generalizability can be a problem for qualitative field research. It crops up in two forms. First, the personal nature of the observations and measurements made by the researcher can produce results that will not necessarily be replicated by another independent researcher. If the observation depends in part on the individual observers, it is more valuable as a source of particular insight than as a general truth. You may recognize the similarity between this and the more general issue of reliability.

Second, because field researchers get a full and in-depth view of their subject matter, they can reach an unusually comprehensive understanding. By its very comprehensiveness, however, this understanding is less generalizable than results based on rigorous sampling and standardized measurements.

For example, Maxfield is conducting observational research with the New Jersey State Police. This has taken several forms, but one recent experience involved learning about radar speed enforcement on a 50-mile segment of the New Jersey Turnpike. Maxfield accompanied troopers on a thorough tour of this segment, identifying where radar units were routinely stationed (termed "fishing holes" by troopers). In his field work, he also examined physical characteristics of the roadway; patterns of in- and out-of-state travel; and areas where entrance ramps, slight upward grades, and other features affected vehicle speed. Finally, he gained extensive information on priorities and patterns in speed enforcement—learning what affects troopers' decisions to stop certain vehicles.

As a result, Maxfield has detailed knowledge about that 50-mile segment of the New Jersey Turnpike. How generalizable is that knowledge? In one sense, learning about "fishing holes" in very specific terms can help identify such sites on other roads. And learning how slight upward grades can slow traffic in one situation may help us understand traffic on other upward grades. But a detailed, idiosyncratic understanding of 50 miles of highway is just that—idiosyncratic. Knowing all there is to know about a straight, largely level stretch of limited-access toll road with few exits is not generalizable to other roadways—winding roads in mountainous areas, with many exits, for example.

Even quantitative field studies may be weak on generalizability. Baumer and Rosenbaum's (1982) estimates of shoplifting prevalence were based on observations in a single large department store in downtown Chicago. The situation is likely to be different in smaller specialty shops, newer department stores in suburban malls, or other downtown stores in other cities. Similarly, conclusions about seat belt use in Indiana may not apply in New York or Idaho. At the time, Indiana's law called for a $25 fine for not wearing a seat belt and could be invoked only if a driver was stopped for some other reason. Compliance may be different in states that have stiffer penalties and where police are permitted to stop drivers for not wearing seat belts.

At the same time, some field studies are less rooted in the local context of the subject under study. Wright and Decker (1994) studied burglars in St. Louis, and it's certainly reasonable to wonder whether their findings apply to residential burglars in St. Petersburg, Florida. The actions and routines of burglars might be affected by local police strategies, differences in the age or style of dwelling units, or even the type and amount of vegetation screening buildings from the street. However, Wright and Decker draw general conclusions about how burglars search for targets, what features of dwellings signal vulnerability, how opportunistic knowledge can trigger an offense, and what strategies exist for fencing stolen goods. It's likely that their findings about the technology and incentives that affect St. Louis burglars apply generally to residential burglars in other cities.

In reviewing reports of field research projects, it's important to determine where and to what extent the researcher is generalizing beyond her or his specific observations to other settings. Such generalizations may be in order, but it is necessary to judge that. Nothing in this research method guarantees it.

As we've seen, field research is a potentially powerful tool for criminal justice research, one that provides a useful balance to surveys.

✪ *Main Points*

- Field research is a data collection method that involves the direct observation of phenomena in their natural settings.
- Field observation is usually the preferred data collection method for obtaining information

about physical or social settings, behavior, and events.

- Field research in criminal justice may produce either qualitative or quantitative data. Grounded theory is typically built from qualitative field observations. Or observations that can be quantified may produce measures for hypothesis testing.

- Observations made through field research can often be integrated with data collected from other sources. In this way, field observations can help researchers interpret other data.

- Asking questions through a form of specialized interviewing is often integrated with field observation.

- Field researchers may or may not identify themselves as researchers to the people they are observing. Being identified as a researcher may have some effect on what is observed.

- Preparing for the field involves negotiating or arranging access to subjects. Specific strategies depend on whether formal organizations, subcultures, or something in between are being studied.

- Controlled probability sampling techniques are not usually possible in field research.

- Snowball sampling is a method for acquiring an ever-increasing number of sample observations. One participant is asked to recommend others for interviewing, and each of these other participants is asked for more recommendations.

- If field observations will be made on a phenomenon that occurs with some degree of regularity, purposive sampling techniques can be used to select cases for observation.

- Alternatives for recording field observations range from video, audio, and other equipment to unstructured field notes. In between are observations recorded on structured forms; environmental surveys are examples.

- Field notes should be planned in advance to the greatest extent possible. However, note taking should be flexible enough to make records of unexpected observations.

- Compared with surveys, field research measurements generally have more validity but less reliability, and field research results cannot be generalized as safely as those based on rigorous sampling and standardized questionnaires.

✪ Key Terms

Environmental survey	Snowball sampling

✪ Review Questions and Exercises

1. Think of some group or activity you participate in or are familiar with. In two or three paragraphs, describe how an outsider might effectively go about studying that group or activity. What should he or she read, what contacts should be made, and so on?

2. Review the box titled "Conducting a Safety Audit" by Gisela Bichler-Robertson. Try conducting a safety audit on your campus or in an area near your campus.

3. Many police departments encourage citizen ride-alongs as a component of community policing. If this is the case for a police or sheriff's department near you, take advantage of this excellent opportunity to test your observation and unstructured interviewing skills.

4. This question is linked to Exercise 3 in Chapter 9. After tabulating responses to your questions about nearby areas where respondents feel unsafe or believe crime to be a problem, plan and conduct field observations in those areas. First, visit one or more areas and make detailed field notes about the area's characteristics, thinking especially about how those characteristics might be associated with perceptions of crime problems. Second, use your notes and observations to develop a form for making structured field observations. Third, visit more areas cited by your respondents and use your form to record area characteristics.

✪ Internet Exercises

To ensure that you always have access to live, correct Web links for the Web sites referenced in the following exercises, we provide the necessary links on the companion Web site for *Research Methods for Criminal Justice and Criminology* at http://cj.wadsworth.com/maxfield_babbie/research_methods4e. Once at the companion Web site, select this specific chapter, click on "Chapter Resources," then click on "Web Links."

1. Visit either the Bill Trochim's Center for Social Research Methods or the University of Surrey Social Research Update Web site, and study the topics listed. Keeping in mind that field research can assume many forms, follow at least three links that provide additional information about collecting data by observation in the field. Write a brief summary of each link visited.

2. Since 1992, researchers have combined observation and surveys to study community policing in Chicago. Many published reports and working papers are available to illustrate how these methods are used. Visit the Institute for Policy Research Community Policing Evaluation Web site and review one working paper that either uses or describes observation methods. Find a working paper that includes copies of observation forms.

○ *InfoTrac College Edition*

Field research can be used to investigate many topics. Use the term *field research* as a keyword to begin your search for articles that have used this approach. Skimming the results of your search, how many different major topic areas appear to have used this approach (medicine, sociology, anthropology, and so on)? After this initial look, you might want to narrow your search by adding terms such as crime (*field research* AND *crime*) in order to locate an article that is more relevant to your area of study. Be prepared to describe this process and your results.

○ *The NEW Companion Web Site for* **Research Methods for Criminal Justice and Criminology,** *Fourth Edition*

http://cj.wadsworth.com/maxfield_babbie/
research_methods4e

Supplement your review of this chapter by going to the new companion Web site to take one of the Tutorial Quizzes, use the flash cards to master key terms, and check out the many other study aids you'll find there. You'll also find special features such as quantitative and qualitative data analysis primers to help you with a special project or do some research on your own.

○ *Additional Readings*

Bureau of Justice Assistance, *A Police Guide to Surveying Citizens and Their Environment* (Washington, DC: U.S. Department of Justice, Office of Justice Programs, Bureau of Justice Assistance, 1993). Intended for use in community policing initiatives, this publication is a useful source of ideas about conducting structured observations. Appendixes include detailed examples of environmental surveys. You can also download this publication in text form (no drawings) from the Web (http://www.ncjrs.org/txtfiles/polc.txt).

Felson, Marcus, *Crime and Everyday Life,* 3rd ed. (Thousand Oaks, CA: Sage, 2002). We mentioned this book as an example of criminal justice theory in Chapter 2. Many of Felson's explanations of how everyday life is linked to crime describe physical features of cities and other land use patterns. This entertaining book suggests many opportunities for conducting field research.

Miller, Joel, *Profiling Populations Available for Stops and Searches* (London: Home Office Policing and Reducing Crime Unit, 2000). Race-biased policing has been a concern in England for many years. This report presents a thorough description of observation to produce baseline measures of populations eligible to be stopped by police. Similar efforts have been underway in many U.S. states and cities, but published reports of such studies had not been released as of spring 2003. (http://www.homeoffice.gov.uk/rds/policerspubs1.html, click on #131).

Patton, Michael Quinn, *Qualitative Research and Evaluation Methods,* 3rd ed. (Thousand Oaks, CA: Sage, 2001). We mentioned this book in Chapter 9 as a good source of guidance on questionnaire construction. Likewise, Patton offers in-depth information on observation techniques, along with tips on conducting unstructured and semistructured field interviews. Finally, Patton describes a variety of purposive sampling techniques for qualitative interviewing and field research.

Smith, Steven K., and DeFrances, Carolyn C., *Assessing Measurement Techniques for Identifying Race, Ethnicity, and Gender: Observation-Based Data Collection in Airports and at Immigration Checkpoints* (Washington, DC: Bureau of Justice Statistics, 2003). Racial profiling and the September 11, 2001, attacks on New York and Washington prompted researchers and public officials to consider observational studies of drivers and others. This report by the Bureau of Justice Statistics describes experiments to test observation methods.

Chapter 11

Agency Records, Content Analysis, and Secondary Data

We'll examine three sources of existing data: agency records, content analysis, and data collected by other researchers. Data from these sources have many applications in criminal justice research.

Introduction

Agency records, secondary data, and content analysis do not require direct interaction with research subjects.

Except for the complete observer in field research, the modes of observation discussed so far require the researcher to intrude to some degree into whatever he or she is studying. This is most obvious with survey research. Even the field researcher, as we've seen, can change things in the process of studying them.

Other ways of collecting data do not involve intrusion by observers. In this chapter, we'll consider three different approaches to using information that has been collected by others, often as a routine practice.

First, a great deal of criminal justice research uses data collected by state and local agencies such as police, criminal courts, probation offices, juvenile authorities, and corrections departments. Federal organizations such as the FBI, the Bureau of Justice Statistics, the Federal Bureau of Prisons, and the National Institute of Corrections compile information about crime problems and criminal justice institutions. In addition, nongovernment organizations such as the National Center for State Courts and the American Prosecutors' Research Institute collect data from members.

Government agencies gather a vast amount of crime and criminal justice data, probably rivaled only by efforts to produce economic and public health indicators. We refer to such information as "data from agency records." In this chapter, we will describe different types of such data that are available for criminal justice research, together with the promise and potential pitfalls of using information from agency records.

Second, in content analysis, researchers examine a class of social artifacts—written documents or other types of messages. Suppose, for example, you want to contrast the importance of criminal justice policy and health care policy for Americans in 1992 and 2004. One option is to examine public opinion polls from these years. Another method is to analyze articles from newspapers published in each year. The latter is an example of content analysis: the analysis of communications.

Finally, information collected by others is frequently used in criminal justice research, which in this case involves **secondary analysis** of existing data. Investigators who conduct research funded by federal agencies such as the National Institute of Justice are usually obliged to release their data for public use. Thus, for example, if you are interested in establishing a system for using bail guidelines to make pretrial release decisions, you might analyze data collected by John Goldkamp and Doris Weiland (1993) in their research on judicial decision guidelines for bail. This chapter briefly describes some sources of secondary data, which are covered more fully in Appendix D on the companion Web site.

Before we begin to explore each of these sources of data in detail, recall our caution in Chapter 8 about obtrusive and unobtrusive measurement. When you go to the library to consult published statistics about persons under correctional supervision or to conduct secondary analysis of a prison inmate survey directed by the RAND Corporation, you are not interacting with research subjects. Do not, however, be too quick to describe such measurement as unobtrusive. Inmates interviewed by RAND researchers were certainly aware of their role in providing information for research, even if they had no idea that you would later examine the data. You may gather jail census figures from a published report, but those data were originally obtained from a survey questionnaire completed by one or more persons directly involved in the measurement process.

In a general sense, then, most data you obtain from agency records or research projects conducted by others are secondary data. Someone else gathered the original data, usually for purposes that differ from yours.

Topics Appropriate for Agency Records and Content Analysis

Agency records support a wide variety of research applications.

Data from agency records or archives may have originally been gathered in any number of ways, from sample surveys to direct observation. Because of this, such data may, in principle, be appropriate for just about any criminal justice research topic.

Published statistics and agency records are most commonly used in descriptive or exploratory studies. This is consistent with the fact that many of the criminal justice data published by government agencies are intended to describe something. For instance, the Bureau of Justice Statistics (BJS) publishes annual figures on prison populations. If we are interested in describing differences in prison populations between states or changes in prison populations from 1990 through 2002, a good place to begin is with the annual data published by BJS. Simi-

larly, published figures on crimes reported to police, criminal victimization, felony court caseloads, drug use by high school seniors, and a host of other measures are available over time — for 25 years or longer in many cases.

Agency records may also be used in explanatory studies. Nancy Sinauer and colleagues (1999) examined medical examiner records for over 1000 female homicide victims in North Carolina to understand the relationship between female homicide and residence in urban versus rural counties. They found that counties on the outskirts of cities had higher female homicide rates than either urban or rural counties.

Agency records are frequently used in applied studies as well. Evaluations of new policies that seek to reduce recidivism might draw on arrest or conviction data for measures of recidivism. A study of arrest as a presumptive response to domestic violence traced arrest records for experimental and control subjects (Sherman, 1992). In another study, Lawrence Winner and associates (Winner, Lanza-Kaduce, Bishop, and Frazier, 1997) compared re-arrest records for juveniles transferred to the adult court system with those who had been kept in the juvenile system. Sometimes, records obtained from private firms can be used in applied studies; Gisela Bichler and Ronald Clarke (1996) examined records of international telephone calls in their evaluation of efforts to reduce telephone fraud in New York City.

In a different type of applied study, Pamela Lattimore and Joanna Baker (1992) combined data on prison releases and capacities, reincarcerations, and general-population forecasts to develop a mathematical model that predicts future prison populations in North Carolina. This is an example of forecasting, in which past relationships among arrest rates and prison sentences for different age groups are compared with estimates of future population by age group. Assuming that past associations between age, arrest, and prison sentence will remain constant in future years, demographic models of future population can be used to predict future admissions to prison.

Topics appropriate to research using content analysis center on the important links between communication, perceptions of crime problems, individual behavior, and criminal justice policy. The prevalence of violence on fictional television dramas has long been a concern of researchers and public officials (Gerbner and Gross, 1980). Wesley Skogan and Michael Maxfield (1981) studied the link between mass media news stories about crime and people's perceptions. Numerous attempts have been made to explore relationships between exposure to pornography and sexual assault (see, for example, Donnerstein, Linz, and Penrod, 1987; Pollard, 1995). Mass media also play an important role in affecting policy action by public officials. Many studies have examined the influence of media agenda setting for criminal justice policy (see, for example, Chermak and Weiss, 1997; Fishman, 1980).

Research data collected by other investigators, through surveys or field observation, may be used for a broad variety of later studies. National Crime Victimization Survey (NCVS) data have been used by a large number of researchers in countless descriptive and explanatory studies since the 1970s. In a notably ambitious use of secondary data, Robert Sampson and John Laub (1993) recovered life history data on 500 delinquents and 500 nondelinquents originally collected by Sheldon and Eleanor Glueck in the 1940s. Taking advantage of theoretical and empirical advances in criminological research over the ensuing 40 years, Sampson and Laub produced a major contribution to knowledge of criminal career development in childhood.

Existing data may also be considered as a supplemental source of data. For example, a researcher planning to survey correctional facility administrators about their views on the need for drug treatment programs will do well to examine existing data on the number of drug users sentenced to prison terms. Or, if we are evaluating an experimental morale-building program in a probation services department, statistics on absenteeism will be useful in connection with the data our own research will generate.

This is not to say that agency records and secondary data can always provide answers to research questions. If this were true, much of this book would be unnecessary. The key to distinguishing appropriate and inappropriate uses of agency records, content analysis, and secondary data is understanding how these written records are produced. We cannot emphasize this point too strongly. Much of this chapter will underscore the importance of learning where data come from and how they are gathered.

Types of Agency Records

Researchers use a variety of published statistics and nonpublic agency records.

Information collected by or for public agencies usually falls into one of three general categories: (1) published statistics, (2) nonpublic agency records routinely collected for internal use, and (3) new data collected by agency staff for specific research purposes. Each category varies in the extent to which data are readily available to the researcher and in the researcher's degree of control over the data collection process.

Published Statistics

Most government organizations routinely collect and publish compilations of data. Examples are the Census Bureau, the FBI, the Administrative Office of U.S. Courts, the Federal Bureau of Prisons, and the BJS. Two of these organizations merit special mention. First, the Census Bureau conducts enumerations and sample surveys for several other federal organizations. Notable examples are the NCVS, Census of Children in Custody, Survey of Inmates in Local Jails, Correctional Populations in the United States, and Survey of Justice Expenditure and Employment.

Second, the BJS compiles data from several sources and publishes annual and special

Table 11.1   Victimization Rates by Type of Crime, Form of Tenure, and Race of Head of Household, 2001 (rates per 1000 households)

	Household Crimes			
	Burglary	Motor Vehicle Theft	Theft	Total Number of Households
Race of Head of Household				
White	26.6	8.2	130.3	91,732,200
Black	42.8	16.1	120.6	13,827,190
Home Ownership				
Owned	23.8	7.3	115.2	73,957,330
Rented	38.8	13.1	157.8	35,611,120

Source: Adapted from Rennison (2002: Table 7)

reports on most data series. For example, *Criminal Victimization in the United States* reports summary data from the NCVS each year. Table 11.1 presents a sample breakdown of victimization rates by race and home ownership from the report for 2001. The BJS also issues reports on people under correctional supervision. These are based on sample surveys and enumerations of jail, prison, and juvenile facility populations. Sample tabulations of females serving sentences in state and federal prison in 1997 and 1998 are shown in Table 11.2. And the series *Federal Criminal Case Processing* reports detailed data on federal court activity.

The most comprehensive BJS publication on criminal justice data is the annual *Sourcebook of Criminal Justice Statistics.* Since 1972, this report has summarized hundreds of criminal justice data series, ranging from public perceptions about crime, to characteristics of criminal justice agencies, to tables on how states execute capital offenders. Data from private sources such as the Gallup Poll are included with statistics collected by government agencies. Most importantly, each year's *Sourcebook* concludes with notes on data sources, appendixes summarizing data collection procedures for major series, and addresses of organizations that either collect or archive original data.

Compilations of published data on crime and criminal justice are readily available from many sources. For example, the *Sourcebook* is available on the Web (http://www.albany.edu/sourcebook). Appendix D on the companion Web site presents a more comprehensive list, together with some guidelines on how to get more information from the BJS and other major sources. At this point, however, we want to suggest some possible uses, and limits, of what Herbert Jacob (1984:9) refers to as being "like the apple in the Garden of Eden: tempting but full of danger . . . [for] the unwary researcher."

Referring to Tables 11.1 and 11.2, you may recognize that published data from series such as the NCVS or *Correctional Populations in the United States* are summary data, as discussed in Chapters 4 and 6. This means that data are presented in highly aggregated form and cannot be used to analyze the individuals from or about whom information was originally collected. For example, Table 11.2 shows that in 1998, 3502 women were serving sentences of one year or more in state and federal correctional institutions in New York. By comparing that figure with figures from other states, we can make some descriptive statements about prison populations in different states. We can also consult earlier editions of *Correctional Populations* to examine trends in prison populations over time or to compare rates of growth from state to state.

Summary data cannot, however, be used to reveal anything about individual correctional facilities, let alone facility inmates. Individual-

Table 11.2   Female Prisoners Under Jurisdiction of State and Federal Correctional Authorities, 1997–98

	Total 1998	Percent Change 1997–98	Sentence 1 Year or More	
			Total 1998	Percent Change 1997–98
Northeast	9,281	3.5	8,151	3.1
Connecticut	1,357	−3.1	729	−8.0
Maine	103	66.1	96	65.5
Massachusetts	746	1.8	427	−3.2
New Hampshire	116	6.4	116	6.4
New Jersey	1,653	17.7	1,653	17.7
New York	3,502	−1.9	3,502	−1.9
Pennsylvania	1,517	6.5	1,515	6.5
Rhode Island	235	10.3	91	21.3
Vermont	52	−1.9	22	−35.5
Midwest	13,710	7.4	13,620	7.6
South	33,262	5.1	31,837	4.9
West	18,688	6.8	17,578	7.6

Source: Adapted from Bureau of Justice Statistics (2002: Table 5.3)

level data about inmates and institutions are available from the Census Bureau in electronic form, but published tabulations present only summaries.

This is not to say that published data are useless to criminal justice researchers. Highly aggregated summary data from published statistical series are frequently used in descriptive, explanatory, and applied studies. For example, Eric Baumer and colleagues (Baumer, Lauritsen, Rosenfeld, and Wright, 1998) examined UCR, DAWN, and DUF data for 142 U.S. cities from 1984 to 1992. Interested in the relationship between crack cocaine use and robbery, burglary, and homicide rates, the researchers found that high levels of crack cocaine use in the population were found in cities that also had high rates of robbery. In contrast, burglary rates were lower in cities with high levels of crack cocaine use. In another study, Alfred Blumstein and associates (Blumstein, Cohen, and Rosenfeld, 1991) compared published UCR and NCVS data for burglary and robbery and concluded that the different measures of crime covaried relatively consistently from 1973 through 1985.

Ted Robert Gurr (1989) used published statistics on violent crime dating back to 13th-century England to examine how social and political events affected patterns of homicide through 1984. A long-term decline in homicide rates has been punctuated by spikes during periods of social dislocation, when

significant segments of a population have been separated from the regulating institutions that instill and reinforce the basic Western injunctions against interpersonal violence. They may be migrants, demobilized veterans, a growing population of resentful young people for whom there is no social or economic niche, or badly educated young black men trapped in the decaying ghettos of an affluent society. (1989: 48–49)

Published data can therefore address questions about highly aggregated patterns or trends—drug use and crime, the covariation in two estimates of crime, or epochal change in fatal violence. Published data also have the distinct advantage of being readily available; a Web search or a trip to the library can quickly place several data series at your disposal. You can obtain copies of most publications by the BJS and other Justice Department offices on the Internet; most documents published since about 1994 are available electronically. Some formerly printed data reports are now available only in electronic format.

Electronic formats have many advantages. Data fields may be read directly into statistical or graphics computer programs for analysis. Many basic crime data can be downloaded from the BJS Web site in spreadsheet formats or read directly into presentation software. More importantly, complete data series are available in electronic formats. Although printed reports of the NCVS limit you to summary tabulations such as those in Table 11.1, electronic and optical media include the original survey data from 80,000 or more respondents.

Of course, before using either original data or tabulations from published sources, researchers must consider the issues of validity and reliability and the more general question of how well these data meet specific research purposes. It would make little sense to use only FBI data on homicides in a descriptive study of domestic violence because murder records measure only incidents of fatal violence. Or data from an annual prison census would not be appropriate for research on changes in sentences to community corrections programs.

Nonpublic Agency Records

Despite the large volume of published statistics in criminal justice, those data represent only the tip of the proverbial iceberg. The FBI publishes the summary UCR, but each of the nation's several thousand law enforcement agencies produces an incredible volume of data not routinely released for public distribution. The BJS publication *Correctional Populations in the United States* presents statistics on prison inmates collected from annual surveys of correctional facilities, but any given facility also maintains detailed case files on individual inmates. The volume *Court Caseload Statistics,* published by the

National Center for State Courts, contains summary data on cases filed and disposed in state courts, but any courthouse in any large city houses paper or computer files on thousands of individual defendants. Finally, reports on the annual survey of expenditures and employment in criminal justice are sources of summary data on budgets and personnel, but every agency also maintains its own detailed records of expenditures and human resources.

Although we have labeled this data source "nonpublic agency records," most criminal justice organizations will make such data available to criminal justice researchers. But obtaining agency records is not as simple as strolling into a library and asking for a BJS publication, or clicking a download button on the Census Bureau's Web page. Obtaining access to nonpublic records involves many of the same steps we outlined in Chapter 10 for gaining entry for field research.

At the outset, we want to emphasize that the potential promise of agency records is not without cost. Jacob's caution about the hidden perils to unwary researchers who uncritically accept published data applies to nonpublic agency records as well. On the one hand, we could devote an entire book to describing the potential applications of agency records in criminal justice research, together with advice on how to use and interpret such data. On the other hand, we can summarize that unwritten book with one piece of advice: Understand how agency records are produced. Restated slightly, researchers can find the road to happiness in using agency records by following the paper trail.

By way of illustrating this humble maxim, we present two types of examples. First, we describe two studies in which nonpublic agency records were used to reveal important findings about the etiology of crime and its spatial distribution. Second, we briefly review two studies in which the authors recognized validity and reliability problems but still were able to draw conclusions about the behavior of criminal justice organizations. At the end of this section, we summarize the promise of agency records for research and note cautions that must be exercised if such records are to be used effectively.

Child Abuse, Delinquency, and Adult Arrests

In earlier chapters, we described Cathy Spatz Widom's research on child abuse as an example of a quasi-experimental design. For present purposes, her research illustrates the use of several different types of agency records.

Widom (1989b) identified cases of child abuse and neglect by consulting records from juvenile and adult criminal courts in a large midwestern city. Unlike adult courts, juvenile court proceedings are not open to the public, and juvenile records may not be released. However, after obtaining institutional review board approval, Widom was granted access to these files for research purposes by court authorities. From juvenile court records, she selected 774 cases of neglect, physical abuse, or sexual abuse. Cases of extreme abuse were processed in adult criminal court, where charges were filed against the offender. Criminal court records yielded an additional 134 cases.

As described in Chapter 7, Widom constructed a comparison group of nonabused children through individual matching. Comparison subjects were found from two different sources of agency records. First, abused children who were ages 6–11 at the time of the abuse were matched to comparison subjects by consulting public school records. An abused child was matched with a comparison child of the same sex, race, and age (within 6 months) who attended the same school. Second, children who were younger than 6 years old at the time of abuse were matched on similar criteria by consulting birth records and selecting a comparison subject born in the same hospital.

These two types of public records and matching criteria—attending the same public school and being born in the same hospital—were used in an attempt to control for socioeconomic status. Although such criteria may be viewed with skepticism today, Widom (1989b:

360) points out that during this time period (1967–1971), school busing was not used in the area where her study was conducted, and "elementary schools represented very homogeneous neighborhoods." Similarly, in the late 1960s, hospitals tended to serve local communities, unlike contemporary medical-industrial complexes that advertise their services far and wide. Widom assumed that children born in the same hospital were more likely to be from similar socioeconomic backgrounds than children born in different hospitals. Though far from perfect, school and birth records enabled Widom to construct approximate matches on socioeconomic status, which illustrates our earlier advice to be creative while being careful.

Widom's research purpose was explanatory—to examine the link between early child abuse and later delinquency or adult criminal behavior. These two dependent variables were measured by consulting additional agency records for information on arrests of abused subjects and comparison subjects for the years 1971 through 1986. Juvenile court files yielded information on delinquency. Adult arrests were measured from criminal history files maintained by local, state, and national law enforcement agencies. In an effort to locate as many subjects as possible, Widom searched state Bureau of Motor Vehicles files for current addresses and Social Security numbers. Finally, "marriage license bureau records were searched to find married names for the females" (1989b:361).

Findings revealed modest but statistically significant differences between abused and comparison subjects. As a group, abused subjects were more likely to have records of delinquency or adult arrests (Maxfield and Widom, 1996). However, Widom (1992) also found differences in these dependent variables by race and gender.

Now let's consider two potential validity and reliability issues that might be raised by Widom's use of nonpublic agency records. First, data from juvenile and adult criminal courts reveal only cases of abuse that come to the attention of public officials. Unreported and unsubstantiated cases of abuse or neglect are excluded, and this raises a question about the validity of Widom's measure of the independent variable. Second, dependent variable measures are similarly flawed because juvenile and adult arrests do not reflect all delinquent or criminal behavior.

Recognizing these problems, Widom is careful to point out that her measure of abuse probably reflects only the most severe cases, those that were brought to the attention of public officials. She also notes that cases in her study were processed before officials and the general public had become more aware of the problem of child abuse. Widom (1989b:365–66) understood the limits of official records and qualified her conclusions accordingly: "These findings, then, are not generalizable to unreported cases of abuse or neglect. Ours are also the cases in which agencies have intervened, and in which there is little doubt of abuse or neglect. Thus, these findings are confounded with the processing factor."

Crime "Hot Spots"   Law enforcement officials and criminal justice researchers have long been interested in the spatial concentration of crime. A growing number of police departments employ crime analysts to identify "hot spots"— geographic areas and times of day that signal concentrations of various types of crime (Boba, 2003). Additionally, researchers have recognized that some individual people (and places) are repeatedly victimized and that these repeat victims play a major role in producing hot spots (Pease and Laycock, 1996).

Research and policy interest in hot spots and repeat victimization can be traced to an influential article by Lawrence Sherman and associates (Sherman, Gartin, and Buerger, 1989). Their analysis used a long-neglected measure produced in great volume by police departments. Calls for service (CFS) represent the initial reports of crime and other problems to police departments. Most large police departments record basic information about CFS—location,

time, nature of complaint—on audiotapes. Telephone operators respond to most CFS by dispatching a patrol car, a process that is automatically recorded on a computer. This produces a source of data on incidents brought to the attention of police.

Truly astonishing numbers of crime victims, witnesses, or people with some sort of noncrime problem telephone police departments each year. Sherman and associates (1989:36) analyzed more than 300,000 such calls to the Minneapolis Police Department in 1986, proposing that "calls to the police provide the most extensive and faithful account of what the public tells the police about crime, with the specific errors and biases that that entails." As we pointed out in Chapter 6, UCR and similar data on recorded crime are subject to validity and reliability problems that reflect decisions by police and complainants. CFS are recorded (automatically) before most such decisions are made and so are less subject to screening by police or the public. An additional advantage, and one crucial for Sherman's research on the "criminology of place," is that CFS data provide microlevel information on where incidents occur.

Because Sherman and colleagues (1989:37) were interested in the concentration of calls in certain locations, they required some measure of the number of distinct locations in Minneapolis. Consulting records from the city tax assessor's office, the Administrative Engineering Service, and the Traffic Engineering Office, researchers concluded that it was not possible to obtain a precise count of locations. A denominator of places for computing CFS rates was estimated at 115,000, which included 109,000 street addresses and 6000 intersections.

In a slight digression, we point out that this approximation illustrates another point made by Jacob (1984:39). Given the many sources of potential error in published statistics and agency records, researchers who use such data should report rounded figures and thereby avoid the illusion of exaggerated accuracy that precise numbers imply. For example, there is no way of knowing whether Minneapolis has 107,037 or 111,252 street addresses because of varying definitions used by different agencies. It is therefore safer to state "about 109,000 street addresses" than to report either a specific estimate or a "precise" average of the two estimates (109,144.5), which falsely inflates the accuracy of data.

Addressing first the general question of concentration, Sherman and colleagues (1989:38) found that about 50 percent of calls for service occurred in just 3 percent of Minneapolis locations. Looking more closely at types of incidents sheds light on the links between type of offense and type of place. For example, hot spots such as discount department stores and large parking lots produced large numbers of shoplifting reports and calls from motorists locked out of their cars. One hotel stood out with a large number of calls for burglary and violent crime but turned out to be more of a "cool spot" when standardized by the hotel's average daily population of more than 3000 guests and employees. In contrast, the approximate robbery rate for a single bar that had an estimated daily population of about 300 was 83 per 1000 persons at risk.

With these interesting descriptive analyses in hand, Sherman and associates (1989:47–48) next addressed the question of crime displacement, arguing that the potential for displacement varies by type of incident. Predatory crimes such as robbery and burglary are at least partly dependent on an opportunity structure that can be modified. Citing measures for reducing convenience store robberies, the researchers proposed that features of such places—physical design and staffing patterns—can deter motivated offenders. In contrast, incidents such as interpersonal violence and vice are less place-dependent. Domestic violence can occur any place two people live. Prostitution or drug sales depend on market attractions between seller and buyer. Parties to the transaction are mobile and can easily relocate to a place where surveillance or other inhibiting factors

are absent. Thus, there is a greater potential for displacement of crimes linked to intimate or market relationships, while prevention may be possible for incidents that are more dependent on characteristics of place.

This example is different from Widom's study in many respects; however, the researchers all recognized the potential promise and shortcomings of data from agency records—in each case, they were careful and creative. Despite the advantages of using CFS data, Sherman and associates describe three possible problems: the potential for duplicate records of the same incident; false reports, equivalent to false fire alarms; and misleading hot spots such as hospitals and police stations that produce secondary crime reports. After taking these problems into consideration, Sherman and colleagues (1989) concluded that the advantages of CFS data outweigh the disadvantages. Readers can form their own conclusions, aided by the careful description of the paper trail—how CFS data are produced—provided by Sherman and colleagues.

Agency Records as Measures of Decision Making Two studies mentioned in earlier chapters illustrate how flaws in agency record-keeping practices can be used to infer something about agency behavior. In Chapters 5 and 7, we mentioned research by Richard McCleary and associates (McCleary, Nienstedt, and Erven, 1982) as an illustration of measurement problems and the ways in which those problems threaten certain quasi-experimental designs. Recall that McCleary and associates discovered that an apparent reduction in burglary rates was, in fact, due to changes in record-keeping practices. Assigning officers from a special unit to investigate burglaries revealed that earlier investigative procedures sometimes resulted in double counts of a single incident; the special unit also reduced misclassification of larcenies as burglaries.

McCleary and colleagues became suspicious of police records when they detected an immediate decline in burglary rates following the introduction of the special unit, a pattern that was not reasonable given the technology of burglary. Following the paper trail, they were able to discover how changes in procedures affected these measures. In the same article, they describe additional examples—how replacement of a police chief and changes in patrol dispatch procedures produced apparent increases in crime and calls for service. However, after carefully investigating how these records were produced, they were able to link changes in the indicators to changes in agency behavior rather than changes in the frequency of crime.

Terry Baumer and associates (Baumer, Maxfield, and Mendelsohn, 1993) discovered a similar phenomenon when they detected inconsistencies between court records of juvenile probation violations and other indicators of probation client behavior. (See the box titled "Home Detention" in Chapter 1.) After locating virtually no instances of probation violations in agency records, Baumer and associates found that arrest histories and data from electronic monitoring showed evidence of infractions. This led them to follow the paper trail through juvenile court, where they learned that juvenile probation staff were only minimally supervising their clients. Becoming more suspicious, the authors uncovered other inconsistencies in program implementation by juvenile court staff. So, data intended to monitor the behavior of juvenile probationers instead showed that probation staff were not doing their jobs.

These two examples point to an important lesson in the use of agency records for criminal justice research: *Expect the expected.* If unexpected findings or patterns emerge, review data collection procedures once again before accepting the unexpected. In these two examples, researchers suspected record-keeping problems when data analysis produced results that were sharply discrepant with their expectations. Changing the way burglaries are investigated is unlikely to produce a pronounced, immediate decline in burglary. And it is implausible that an experimental program for juvenile offenders will be 99 percent successful. Such clues prompted researchers to inquire further how such suspicious indicators were produced.

New Data Collected by Agency Staff

Thus far, we have concentrated on the research uses of information routinely collected by or for public agencies. Such data are readily available, but researchers have little control over the actual data collection process. Furthermore, agency procedures and definitions may not correspond with the needs of researchers.

It is sometimes possible to use a hybrid source of data in which criminal justice agency staff collect information for specific research purposes. We refer to this as a "hybrid" source because it combines the collection of new data—through observation or interviews—with day-to-day criminal justice agency activities. Virtually all criminal justice organizations routinely document their actions, from investigating crime reports to housing convicted felons. By slightly modifying forms normally used for recording information, researchers may be able to have agency staff collect original data for them.

For example, let's say we are interested in the general question of how many crimes reported to police involve nonresident victims. Reading about violent crime against international tourists in south Florida, we wonder how common such incidents are and decide to systematically investigate the problem. It doesn't take us long to learn that no published data are available on the resident or nonresident status of Dade County crime victims. We next try the Miami and Miami-Dade Police Departments, suspecting that such information might be recorded on crime report forms. No luck here, either. Incident report forms include victim name and address, but we are told that police routinely record the local address for tourists, typically a hotel, motel, or guest house. Staff in the police crime records office inform us that officers sometimes write down something like "tourist, resident of Montreal" in the comments section of the crime report form, but they are neither required nor asked to do this.

Assuming we can gain approval to conduct our study from police and other relevant parties, we may be able to supplement the standard police report form. Adding an entry such as the following will do the trick:

Is complainant a resident of Dade County?

_____ yes _____ no

If "no," record permanent address here:

_____

A seemingly simple modification of crime report forms may not happen quite so easily. Approval from the department is, of course, one of the first requirements. And recall our discussion in Chapter 10 on the need to gain approval for research from criminal justice agency staff at all levels. Individual officers who complete crime report forms must be made aware of the change and told why the new item was added. We might distribute a memorandum that explains the reasons for adopting a new crime report form. It might also be a good idea to have supervisors describe the new form at roll call before each shift of officers heads out on patrol. Finally, we could review samples of the new forms over the first few days they are used to determine the extent to which officers are completing the new item.

Incorporating new data collection procedures into agency routine has two major advantages. First, and most obvious, having agency staff collect data for us is much less costly than fielding a team of research assistants. It is difficult to imagine how original data on the resident status of Dade County victims could be collected in any other way.

Second, we have more control over the measurement process than we would by relying on agency definitions. Some Dade County officers might note information on victim residence, but most probably would not. Adding a specific question enhances the reliability of data collection. We might consider using an existing crime report item for "victim address," but the ten-dency of officers to record local addresses for tourists would undermine measurement validity. A specific "resident/nonresident" item is a more valid indicator.

The box by Marie Mele, titled "Improving Police Records of Domestic Violence," gives an example of this approach to gathering new data from agency records. You should recognize the importance of collaboration in this example. Less obvious, but equally important, is a lesson we will return to later in this chapter: Agency records are not usually intended for research purposes and, as a consequence, are not always well suited to researchers' needs. Sometimes, as was the case for Marie Mele, some subtle tweaking can transform unusable mounds of paper files into computer-based record systems. In any event, researchers are well advised to be careful, not assuming that existing data will meet their needs, but to also be creative in seeking ways to improve the quality of agency data.

This approach to data collection has many potential applications. Probation officers or other court staff in many jurisdictions complete some type of presentence investigation on convicted offenders. A researcher might be able to supplement standard interview forms with additional items appropriate for some specific research interest. In their experimental study of intensive probation, Joan Petersilia and Susan Turner (1991) obtained the cooperation of probation staff to complete three data collection forms on each research subject. Intake forms yielded demographic and criminal history information. Review forms completed after 6 and 12 months documented the nature and types of services that probation staff delivered to experimental and control subjects (1991:621). Additional agency records provided data on probationer performance, but the supplementary data were needed to measure implementation of the intensive probation program.

The National Institute of Justice (NIJ) (1999a) integrated new data collection into routine arrest procedures with its Arrestee Drug Abuse Monitoring (ADAM) system. As we saw

IMPROVING POLICE RECORDS OF DOMESTIC VIOLENCE

By Marie Mele
LaSalle University

An interest in domestic violence led me to learn more about repeat victimization. Research conducted in England has indicated that repeated domestic violence involving the same victim and offender is quite common (Hanmer, Griffiths, and Jerwood, 1999; Farrell, Edmunds, Hibbs, and Laycock, 2000). For example, combining data from four British Crime Surveys, Pease (1998:3) reports that about 1 percent of respondents had four or more personal victimizations and that these victims accounted for 59 percent of all personal victimization incidents disclosed to BCS interviewers. Other studies in England have shown that many other types of offenses are disproportionately concentrated among small groups of victims. Identifying repeat victims and directing prevention and enforcement resources to them has the potential to produce a large decrease in crime rates.

My interest centered on determining the distributions of incidents, victims, and offenders in cases of domestic violence reported to police in a large city in the northeastern United States. Partly this was exploratory research, but I also wished to make policy recommendations to reduce repeat victimization. Working with Michael Maxfield, my initial inquiries found that, although data on assaults and other offenses were available in paper files, it was not possible to efficiently count the number of repeat incidents for victims and offenders. However, seeing the potential value of gathering more systematic information on repeat offenders and victims, senior department staff collaborated with Maxfield and me to produce a database that reorganized existing data on domestic violence incidents. A pilot data system was developed in November 2001. Plans called for the database to be maintained by the department's domestic violence and sexual assault unit (DVSAU); staff would begin entering new incidents in January 2002. In the meantime, I proposed to test the database and its entry procedures by personally entering incidents from August through December 2001. After ironing out a few kinks, the final system was established, and I continued entering new incident reports for a period of time.

in Chapter 6, samples of persons arrested in each participating city are selected four times each year and asked to voluntarily submit a urine sample for anonymous testing. Results are tabulated to estimate the prevalence of drug use among people arrested for different types of offenses. Thus, research data are collected in connection with samples of arrested persons.

The NIJ has tried to incrementally expand the use of ADAM as a "research platform," as illustrated in a study by Scott Decker and associates (Decker, Pennell, and Caldwell, 1997). Chapter 6 described how arrestees selected for ADAM participation are interviewed in addition to contributing a urine sample. Since ADAM was implemented in 1987 (though it was called "Drug Abuse Forecasting" until 1998), these interviews have provided an ongoing

source of information about the characteristics of arrestees who test positive for drug use. Decker and associates supplemented the interview questionnaire in 11 ADAM sites by asking questions about firearm availability and use. The researchers found no association between drug use and firearm use, but they did discover that gun use was common among juvenile males and especially widespread among admitted gang members. By piggybacking on ADAM in this way, Decker and associates were able to obtain information from more than 7000 subjects at very low cost, which illustrates the principal strength of enlisting agency staff in data collection efforts.

At the same time, having agencies collect original research data has some disadvantages. An obvious one is the need to obtain the coop-

This is an admittedly brief description of a process that unfolded over several months. The process began as an attempt to obtain what we thought were existing data. Finding that suitable data were not available, Maxfield had sufficient access to the department to begin discussions of how to supplement existing record-keeping practices to tabulate repeat victimization. Many public agencies will accommodate researchers if such accommodation does not unduly burden the agency. Collecting new data for researchers *does* qualify as unduly burdensome for most public organizations. The key here was collaboration in a way that helped both the researchers and the host organization.

It's obvious that my research benefited from having the department design and ultimately assume responsibility for tabulating repeat victimization. The department benefited in three ways. First, DVSAU staff recognized how a data file that identified repeat *offenders* and victims could produce information that would aid their investigations of incidents. I emphasize *offenders* here because, all other things being equal, police are more interested in offenders than they are in victims. So the database was designed to track people (offenders) of special interest to police and people (victims) of special interest to my re-

search. Second, recognizing that setting up a new data system is especially difficult in a tradition-bound organization, I was able to ease the transition somewhat by initially entering data myself. One intentional by-product of this was to establish quality-control procedures during a shakedown period. As a criminal justice researcher, I knew that the reliability of data-gathering procedures was important and was able to establish reliable data entry routines for the department.

The DVSAU staff benefited in yet another way that was probably most important of all. This department had incorporated its version of Compstat for about 3 years. Two important components of Compstat are timely data and accountability. Each week, the DVSAU commander was required to present a summary of the unit's activity and was held accountable for the performance of unit staff. Before the database was developed, the DVSAU commander spent several hours compiling data to prepare for each week's Compstat meeting. After the database was operational, preparation time was reduced to minutes. In addition, the DVSAU commander was able to introduce new performance measures—repeat offenders and victims—that came to be valued by the department's chief.

---

eration of organizations and staff. The difficulty of this varies in direct proportion to the intrusiveness of data collection. Cooperation is less likely if some major additional effort is required of agency personnel or if data collection activities disrupt routine operations. The potential benefit to participating agencies is a related point. If a research project or an experimental program is likely to economize agency operations or improve staff performance, as was the case for Marie Mele's research, it will be easier to enlist their assistance.

Researchers have less control over the data collection process when they rely on agency staff. Petersilia (1989:442) points out that agency personnel have competing demands on their time and naturally place a lower priority on data collection than on their primary duties.

If you were a probation officer serving a heavy caseload and were asked to complete detailed 6- and 12-month reports on services provided to individual clients, would you devote more attention to keeping up with your clients or filling out data collection forms?

Units of Analysis and Sampling

Researchers must be especially attentive to the units of agency records, particularly in selecting samples for analysis.

After determining that agency records will be suitable for some particular research purpose, several decisions and tasks remain. We will consider two of them briefly because each is covered in more detail elsewhere in the book: units of analysis and sampling.

Units of Analysis

Archives and agency records may be based on units of analysis that are not suitable for particular research questions. If we are interested in studying individual probationers, for example, we need individual-level data about persons sentenced to probation. Summary data on the number of probationers served each week might not meet our research needs. Or if we wish to examine whether probationers convicted of drug offenses are supervised more closely than those convicted of assault, data on individuals sentenced to probation will have to be aggregated into categories based on convicted offense.

A general rule we mentioned in Chapter 4 bears repeating here: It is possible to move from individual to aggregate units of analysis, but not the other way around. Thus, we could aggregate records on individual probationers into groups that reflected convicted offense, but we could not disaggregate weekly reports to produce information about individuals. In any case, researchers using agency records must be attentive to the match or mismatch between the units of analysis required to address specific research questions and the level of aggregation represented in agency records.

Units of analysis can be especially troublesome in studies of criminal justice processes or studies of people moving through some institutional process. This is because criminal justice agencies use different units of count in keeping records of their activities. Figure 11.1, adapted from a report prepared by officials in a New York criminal justice agency (Poklemba, 1988), lists many of the counting units recorded at various stages of processing.

The units listed in Figure 11.1 can be grouped into two different categories: counts of events and counts of cases (Poklemba, 1988:III3). Counts of events—such as an arrest, indictment, or admission—are more straightforward because they are of short duration. Cases, however, may persist over longer times

Criminal Activity	Apprehension
Incidents	Arrests
Crimes violated	Offenders
Victims	Charges
Offenders	Counts
Court Activity	Corrections
Defendants	Offenders
Filings	Admissions
Charges and counts	Returns
Cases	Discharges
Appearances	
Dispositions	
Sentences	

Figure 11.1 Units of Count in Criminal Justice Data
Source: Adapted from Poklemba (1988:III1–III3).

that are bounded by initiating or terminating events. Cases are directly linked to individual persons, though in complex ways. For example, an indictment event begins a court case that does not terminate until a court disposition event. Or a prison admission event begins an inmate case that ends at prison discharge event. Further complicating matters is the multitude of possible relationships between units of count. For example, a court case can include multiple defendants, each facing multiple counts that can produce multiple dispositions.

The best solution for many research purposes is to define some equivalent to a person—a defendant, for example—as the unit of analysis. This was the approach used by James Eisenstein and Herbert Jacob (1977:175–76) in their study of felony courts:

> Indictments and cases are full of definitional ambiguities that vary from city to city. Some defendants are named in multiple indictments whereas others are not; many defendants are washed out of the process before being indicted but after receiving some punishment. Cases may involve a single defendant or many, and tend to be linked together if there are overlapping defendants or indictments. The concept of "defendants" suffers from none of

these ambiguities. Using defendants as our unit of analysis permits us to discern the number of indictments each defendant faced, the number of court cases in which each was involved, and the ultimate [disposition] each [defendant] faced.

Defining individual people as units can resolve the conceptual problems that emerge from complex relationships between different units of count. Practical difficulties may remain in linking individuals to other units of count, however, or in tracing the movement of individuals from one institution to another.

Sampling

It is often necessary to select subsets of agency records for particular research purposes. Just as we would not need to interview every resident of New York City to learn how they feel about subway crime, it may not be necessary to examine all court cases to understand patterns of case disposition or sentences.

You will be glad to hear that once units of analysis are defined sampling agency records is relatively simple. In most cases, a target population and sample frame may be readily defined. If, for example, we want to study the disposition of felony arrests in New York, our target population might be all cases that reached final disposition in the year 2003. We could then get a list or computer file that contains identifying numbers for all 2003 felony cases and draw a sample using systematic or other sampling procedures described in Chapter 8. We have to be alert for potential biases in the sample frame, however, such as a recurring pattern in the listing of cases.

Reliability and Validity

Understanding the details of how agency records are produced is the best guard against reliability and validity problems.

The key to evaluating the reliability and validity of agency records, as well as the general suitability of those data for a research project, is to understand as completely as possible how the data were originally collected. Doing so can help researchers identify potential new uses of data, as in Sherman and associates' (1989) study of hot spots. They will also be better able to anticipate and detect potential reliability or validity problems in agency records.

Any researcher who considers using agency records will benefit from a careful reading of Jacob's invaluable little guide *Using Published Data: Errors and Remedies* (1984). In addition to warning readers about general problems with reliability and validity, such as those we discussed in Chapter 5, Jacob cautions users of these data to be aware of other potential errors that can be revealed by scrutinizing source notes. Clerical errors, for example, are unavoidable in such large-scale reporting systems as the UCR. These errors may be detected and reported in correction notices appended to later reports.

Users of data series collected over time must be especially attentive to changes in data collection procedures or changes in the operational definitions of key indicators. As you might expect, such changes are more likely to occur in data series that extend over several years. Charles Kindermann and associates (Kindermann, Lynch, and Cantor, 1997) describe how changes in the NCVS, especially the redesign elements introduced in 1992, should be kept in mind for any long-term analysis of NCVS data. In earlier chapters, we described the NCVS redesign that was completed in 1994. If we plan to conduct research on victimization over time, we will have to consider how changes in sample size and design, increased use of telephone interviews, and questionnaire revisions might affect our findings.

Longitudinal researchers must therefore diligently search for modifications of procedures or definitions over time in order to avoid attributing some substantive meaning to a change in a particular measure. Furthermore, as the time interval under investigation increases, so does the potential for change in measurement. Ted Robert Gurr (1989:24) cites a good example:

In the first two decades of the 20th century many American police forces treated the fatalities of the auto age as homicides. The sharp increase in "homicide" rates that followed has led to some dubious conclusions. Careful study of the sources and their historical and institutional context is necessary to identify and screen out the potentially misleading effects of these factors on long-term trends.

This example suggests that cross-sectional researchers must be alert for a slightly different type of potential error. Roger Lane (1997) points out that the tendency to classify fatal accidents as homicides was greater in some cities than in others.

The central point here is that researchers who analyze criminal justice data produced by different cities or states or other jurisdictions must be alert to variations in the definitions and measurement of key variables. Even in cases in which definitions and measurement seem straightforward, they may run into problems. For example, Craig Perkins and Darrell Gilliard (1992:4)—statisticians at the Bureau of Justice Statistics—caution potential users of corrections data:

> Care should be exercised when comparing groups of inmates on sentence length and time served. Differences may be the result of factors not described in the tables, including variations in the criminal histories of each group, variations in the offense composition of each group, and variations among participating jurisdictions in their sentencing and correctional practices.

Fortunately, most published reports on regular data series present basic information on definitions and collection procedures. Many BJS publications include copies of the questionnaires used in surveys and enumerations. Researchers should, however, view summary descriptions in printed reports as no more than a starting point in their search for information on how data were collected. Before analyzing published data in earnest, they should contact the issuing organization to obtain details, perhaps in the form of technical reports.

All criminal justice researchers should read Jacob (1984). For more specific details on published data commonly used in criminal justice research, see the dated but still valuable book *Measuring Crime*, edited by Doris Layton MacKenzie, Phyllis Baunach, and Roy Roberg (1990).

Sources of Reliability and Validity Problems

We conclude this section on agency records by discussing some general characteristics of record keeping by public agencies. Think carefully about each of the features we mention, considering how each might apply to specific types of criminal justice research. It will also be extremely useful for you to think of some examples in addition to those we mention, perhaps discussing them with your instructor or others in your class.

Social Production of Data   Virtually all criminal justice record keeping is a social process. By this we mean that indicators of, say, arrests, juvenile probation violations, court convictions, or rule infractions by prison inmates reflect decisions made by criminal justice officials in addition to the actual behavior of juvenile or adult offenders. As Baumer and associates state: "Researchers must realize that performance measures are *composites* of offenders' behavior, organizational capacity to detect behavior, and decisions about how to respond to offenders' misbehavior" (1993:139; emphasis added). A small number of classic articles illustrate the social production of crime records by police (Black, 1970; Kitsuse and Cicourel, 1963; Seidman and Couzens, 1974). Richard McCleary (1992) describes the social production of data by parole officers. They may fail to record minor infractions to avoid paperwork or, alternatively, may keep careful records of such incidents in an effort to punish troublesome parolees by returning them to prison.

Discretionary actions by criminal justice officials and others affect the production of virtually all agency records. Police neither learn about all crimes nor arrest all offenders who come to their attention. Similarly, prosecutors, probation officers, and corrections staff are selectively attentive to charges filed or to rule violations by probationers and inmates. At a more general level, the degree of attention state legislatures and criminal justice officials devote to various crime problems varies over time. Levels of tolerance of such behaviors as child abuse, drug use, acquaintance rape, and even alcohol consumption have changed over the years.

Agency Data Are Not Designed for Research
In many cases, criminal justice officials collect data because the law requires them to do so. More generally, agencies tend to collect data for their own use, not for the use of researchers. Court disposition records are maintained in part because of legal mandates, and such records are designed for the use of judges, prosecutors, and other officials. Record-keeping procedures reflect internal needs and directives from higher authorities. As a consequence, researchers sometimes find it difficult to adapt agency records for a specific research purpose.

For example, Maxfield once wished to trace court dispositions for arrests made by individual police officers in Louisville, Kentucky. "No problem," he was assured by a deputy prosecutor, "we keep all disposition records on the computer." Following this electronic version of a paper trail to the county data-processing facility, Maxfield discovered that only the previous year's cases were maintained on computer tape. Such tapes were said to be expensive (about $17), and nobody had authorized the data-processing staff to buy new tapes for each year's files. Instead, voluminous computer printouts from the previous year were microfilmed and saved, while the "costly" computer tape was erased for the new year. Maxfield abandoned the

project after realizing that data collection would involve viewing literally hundreds of thousands of microfilmed case files, instead of running a quick-and-easy computer search.

The key point is that our research needs may not be congruent with agency record-keeping practices. Courts or police departments commonly use idiosyncratic definitions or methods of classifying information that make such records difficult to use. Also recognize that our conceptual and operational definitions of key concepts, however thoughtful and precise, will seldom be identical to actual measures maintained by criminal justice agencies.

Even when agencies have advanced record-keeping and data management systems, researchers may still encounter problems. The Chicago Police Department, for example, has developed one of the most advanced systems for collecting and analyzing crime and calls for service data. Richard and Carolyn Block (1995) sought to take advantage of this in an analysis relating the density of taverns and liquor stores to police crime reports from taverns. The researchers wanted to learn whether areas with high concentrations of taverns and liquor stores generated a disproportionate number of crime reports on which police had indicated "tavern or liquor store." Because the Chicago Police Department recorded addresses and type of location, and the city Department of Revenue recorded addresses for liquor license holders, the task seemed straightforward enough: Match the addresses from the two data sources, and analyze the correspondence between crime and liquor establishments.

It wasn't so simple. The Blocks discovered inconsistent recording of addresses in crime reports. Sometimes, police approximated a location by recording the nearest intersection—for example, "Clark and Division." Some large establishments spanned several street addresses, and police recorded one address when the liquor license data had a different address. Other times, police recorded the name of the tavern—for example, "Red Rooster on Wilson

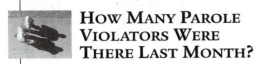

HOW MANY PAROLE VIOLATORS WERE THERE LAST MONTH?

by John J. Poklemba
New York State Division of Criminal Justice
Services

Question: How many parole violators were there last month? Answer: It depends. More accurately, it depends on which agency is asked. Each of the three answers below is right in its own way:

New York State Commission of Correction	611
New York Department of Correctional Services	670
New York Division of Parole	356

The State Commission of Correction (SCOC) maintains daily aggregate information on the local under-custody population. Data are gathered from local sheriffs, using a set of common definitions. The SCOC defines a parole violator as follows: an alleged parole violator being held as a result of allegedly having violated a condition of parole—for example, a new arrest. This makes sense for local jails; a special category is devoted to counting alleged parole violators with new arrests. However, New York City does not distinguish between parole violators with and without new arrests, so the SCOC figure includes violators from upstate New York only.

The Department of Correctional Services (DOCS) is less interested in why people are in jail; their concern centers on the backlog of inmates whom they will soon need to accommodate. Furthermore, as far as DOCS is concerned, the only true parole violator is a technical parole violator. This makes sense for DOCS, because a parole violator convicted of a new crime will enter DOCS as a new admission, who—from an administrative standpoint—will be treated differently than a parolee returned to prison for a technical violation.

The Division of Parole classifies parole violators into one of four categories: (1) those who have violated a condition of parole, (2) those who

Avenue." In sum, police recorded addresses to meet their needs—to locate a tavern or liquor store so that officers could find it—while the Department of Revenue recorded a precise address on a license application. Each address was accurate for each agency's purpose, but addresses did not match in about 40 percent of the cases analyzed by the Blocks.

For another example of how definitional differences can be traced to different agency needs, see the box titled "How Many Parole Violators Were There Last Month?"

Tracking People, Not Patterns   At the operational level, officials in criminal justice organizations are generally more interested in keeping track of individual cases than in examining patterns. Police patrol officers and investigators deal with individual calls for service, arrests, or case files. Prosecutors and judges are most attentive to court dockets and the clearing of individual cases, while corrections officials maintain records on individual inmates. Although each organization produces summary reports on weekly, monthly, or annual activity, officials tend to be much more interested in individual cases. Michael Geerken (1994) makes this point clearly in his discussion of problems researchers are likely to encounter in analyzing police arrest records. Few rap sheet databases are regularly reviewed for accuracy; rather, they simply accumulate arrest records submitted by individual officers. Joel Best (2001) offers additional examples of how small errors in case-by-case record-keeping can accumulate to produce compound errors in summary data.

With continued advances in computer and telecommunications technology, more criminal justice agencies are developing the capability to analyze data in addition to tracing individual cases. Crime analysis by police tracks spatial patterns of recent incidents; prosecutors are at-

have absconded, (3) those who have been arrested for a new crime, and (4) those who have been convicted of a new crime. Once again, this makes sense, because the Division of Parole is responsible for monitoring parolee performance and wishes to distinguish different types of parole violations. The Division also classifies a parole violation as either alleged (yet to be confirmed by a parole board) or actual (the violation has been confirmed and entered into the parolee's file). Further differences in the fluid status of parolees and their violations, together with differences between New York City and other areas, add to the confusion.

Taking the varying perspectives and roles of these three organizations into account, answers to the "How many" question can be made more specific:

SCOC: Last month, there were 611 alleged parole violators who were believed to have violated a condition of their parole by being arrested for a new offense and are being held in upstate New York jails.

DOCS: Last month, there were 670 actual parole violators who were judged to have violated a condition of their parole and are counted among the backlog of persons ready for admission to state correctional facilities.

Parole Division: Last month, 356 parolees from the Division's aggregate population were actually removed from the Division's caseload and were en route to DOCS.

One of the major reasons that agency counts do not match is that agency information systems have been developed to meet internal operational needs. A systemwide perspective is lacking. Questions that depend on data from more than one agency are often impossible to answer with confidence. Recognize also that the availability and quality of state data depend on data from local agencies.

As stated above, the best answer to the question is: It depends.

Source: Adapted from Poklemba (1988:11–13).

tentive to their scorecards; state correctional intake facilities consider prison capacity, security classification, and program availability in deciding where to send new admissions.

As problem-oriented and community approaches to policing become more widely adopted, many law enforcement agencies have improved their record-keeping and crime analysis practices. New York City's reduction in reported crime—our running example—has been attributed to the use of timely, accurate crime data by police managers to plan and evaluate specific anticrime tactics (Bratton, 1999; Kelling and Coles, 1996; Maple, 1999). This illustrates an important general principle about the accuracy of agency-produced data: When agency managers routinely use data to make decisions, they will be more attentive to data quality. The box describing Marie Mele's research offers another example—when domestic violence detectives realized how a database would help them

prepare for Compstat, they endorsed the effort to improve their record-keeping procedures.

However, record-keeping systems used in most cities today are still designed more to track individual cases for individual departments than to produce data for management or research purposes. Individual agencies maintain what are sometimes called "silo databases," a colorful label that refers to stacks of data that are isolated from each other.

This does not mean that computerized criminal history, court disposition, or prison intake records are of little use to researchers. However, researchers must be aware that even state-of-the-art systems may not be readily adaptable for research purposes. The Louisville system described earlier was fine for the needs of court staff who might have to check on some individual past case, but it was virtually unusable for Maxfield's research, which required data about patterns of dispositions.

Error Increases with Volume   The potential for clerical errors increases as the number of clerical entries increases. This seemingly obvious point is nonetheless important to keep in mind when analyzing criminal justice records. Lawrence Sherman and Ellen Cohn (1989:34) describe the "mirror effect" of duplicate CFS records. Handling a large volume of CFS, phone operators in Minneapolis, or any large city for that matter, are not always able to distinguish duplicate reports of the same incident. An updated report about a CFS may be treated as a new incident. In either case, duplicate data result. Richard McCleary and associates (McCleary, Nienstedt, and Erven, 1982) describe a similar problem with burglary reports.

The relationship between volume of data entry and the potential for error can be especially troublesome for studies of relatively rare crimes or incidents. Although murder is rare compared with other crimes, information about individual homicides might be keyed into a computer by the same clerk who inputs data on parking violations. If a murder record is just one case among hundreds of parking tickets and petty thefts awaiting a clerk, there is no guarantee that the rare event will be treated any differently than the everyday ones.

While preparing a briefing for an Indianapolis commission on violence, Maxfield discovered that a single incident in which four people had been murdered in a rural area appeared twice in computerized FBI homicide records. This was traced to the fact that officers from two agencies—sheriff's deputies and state police—investigated the crime, and each agency filed a report with the FBI. But the thousands of murders entered into FBI computer files for that year obscured the fact that duplicate records had been keyed in for one multiple murder in a rural area of Indiana. Colin Loftin (1986) discusses different types of error in murder records. For all their advantages, computers have the capacity to magnify clerical errors with a vengeance.

In concluding our lengthy discussion of agency records, we do not mean to leave you with the impression that data produced by and for criminal justice organizations are fatally flawed. Thousands of studies making appropriate use of such data are produced each year. It is, however, essential that researchers understand potential sources of reliability and validity problems, as well as ways they can be overcome. Public agencies do not normally collect information for research purposes. The data they do collect often reflect discretionary decisions by numerous individuals. And, like any large-scale human activity, making observations on large numbers of people and processes inevitably produces some error.

Content Analysis

Content analysis involves the systematic study of messages.

The Office of Community Oriented Policing Services (COPS) was established by the 1994 Crime Bill to promote community policing by providing funds to local law enforcement agencies. In addition to being concerned about the effectiveness of these efforts, COPS staff wanted to know something about the public image of community policing as presented in local newspapers. Stephen Mastrofski and Richard Ritti (1999) conducted a content analysis of stories about community policing in newspapers serving 26 cities. The researchers found over 7500 stories from 1993 through 1997, with most focusing on a small number of themes: "community, resources, and producing real results for the community. Stories that offer a viewpoint on community policing are nearly always overwhelmingly positive" (1999:10–11).

This is an example of content analysis, the systematic study of messages and the meaning those messages convey. For the COPS office, the study by Mastrofski and Ritti was satisfying—many stories about community policing were published in urban newspapers, and most stories presented positive images.

Content analysis methods may be applied to virtually any form of communication. Among the possible artifacts for study are books, magazines, films, songs, speeches, television programs, letters, laws, and constitutions, as well as any components or collections of these. Suppose you're interested in violence on television. Maybe you suspect that the manufacturers of consumer products for men are more likely to sponsor violent TV shows than are other kinds of sponsors. Content analysis would be the best way of finding out if that's true.

Briefly, here's how you might go about conducting that study. First, you develop operational definitions of the two key variables in your inquiry: men's products and violence. Our later discussion of coding will explore some of the ways you can do that. Ultimately, you need a plan that allows you to watch television, classify sponsors, and rate the degree of violence on particular shows. Next, you have to decide (1) what stations to watch, (2) for what days or period, and (3) at what hours. Then you stock up on snacks and start watching, classifying, and recording. Once you have completed your observations, you can analyze the data you collected and determine whether men's product manufacturers sponsor more blood and gore than other sponsors.

Content analysis, then, is particularly well suited to the study of communications and to answering the classic question of communications research: Who says what, to whom, why, how, and with what effect? As a mode of observation, content analysis requires a considered handling of the *what,* and the analysis of data collected in this mode, as in others, addresses the *why* and *with what effect.*

Units of Analysis and Sampling in Content Analysis

In the study of communications, as in the study of people, it is usually impossible for researchers to directly observe all that interests them. In your study of television violence and sponsorship, you are well advised not to try to watch everything that's broadcast. It's not possible, and your brain will probably short-circuit before you get close to discovering that for yourself. Usually,

then, it's appropriate to sample the units on which content analysis will be conducted.

As we mentioned with respect to agency records in general, determining appropriate units of analysis can be a complicated task. For example, we may wish to compare crime rates of different cities in terms of their size, geographic region, racial composition, and other differences. Even though the characteristics of these cities are partly a function of the behaviors and characteristics of their individual residents, the cities will ultimately be the units of analysis.

The complexity of this issue is often more apparent in content analysis than in other research methods. That is especially the case when the units of observation differ from the units of analysis. A few examples should clarify this distinction.

Suppose we want to find out whether criminal law or civil law makes the most distinctions between juveniles and adults. In this instance, individual laws are both the units of observation and the units of analysis. We might select a sample of a state's criminal and civil laws and then categorize each law by whether it makes a distinction between juveniles and adults. In this fashion, we could determine whether criminal or civil law distinguishes more by age.

Now, let's look at a trickier example: the study of television violence and sponsors. What is the unit of analysis for the research question "Are manufacturers of men's products more likely to sponsor violent shows than are other sponsors?" Is it the TV show? The sponsor? The instance of violence? In the simplest study design, it is none of these.

Although you might structure your inquiry in various ways, the most straightforward design is based on the commercial as the unit of analysis. Here, you use two kinds of observational units: the commercial and the program that gets squeezed in between commercials. You want to observe both units. You classify the commercials by whether they advertise men's products and the programs by their violence. The program classifications are transferred

Sponsor	Men's Product?			Number of Instances of Violence	
	Yes	No	?	Before	After
Grunt aftershave	X			6	4
Reef-buster jet skis	X			6	4
Roperoot cigars	X			4	3
Grunt aftershave	X			3	0
Snowflake toothpaste		X		3	0
Godliness cleanser		X		3	0
Micro-zap computers			X	0	1
Snowflake toothpaste		X		1	0
Micro-zap computers			X	1	0
Precious perfume		X		0	0

Figure 11.2   Example of Recording Sheet for TV Violence

to the commercials that are near them. Figure 11.2 is an example of the kind of record you might keep.

Notice that in the research design illustrated in the figure, all the commercials that appear together are bracketed and get the same scores. Also, the number of violent instances recorded as following one commercial is the same as the number preceding the next commercial. This simple design allows us to classify each commercial by its sponsorship and the degree of violence associated with it. Thus, for example, the first Grunt aftershave commercial is coded as being a men's product and as having 10 instances of violence associated with it. The Precious perfume commercial is coded as not being a men's product and as having no violent instances associated with it.

In Figure 11.2, we have four men's product commercials with, on average, 7.5 violent instances associated with each. The four commercials classified as definitely not men's products have an average of 1.75, and the two that might or might not be considered men's products have an average of 1.0. If this pattern of differences persists across a much larger number of observations, we will probably conclude that manufacturers of men's products are more likely to sponsor TV violence than are other sponsors.

The point of this illustration is to demonstrate how units of analysis figure into data collection and analysis. You need to be clear about your unit of analysis before planning your sampling strategy, but in this case, you can't sample commercials. Unless you have access to the stations' broadcasting logs, you won't know when the commercials are going to run. Moreover, you need to observe the programming as well as the commercials. As a result, you must set up a sampling design that includes everything you need to observe.

In designing the sample, you need to establish the universe to be sampled. In this case, what TV stations will you observe? What will be the period of the study—the number of days? And what hours of each day will you observe? Also, how many commercials do you want to observe and code for analysis? Watch television for a while and find out how many commercials occur each hour; then you can figure out how many hours of observation you'll need.

Now you're ready to design the sample selection. As a practical matter, you wouldn't have to sample among the different stations if you had assistants; each of you could watch a different channel during the same time period. But let's suppose you are working alone. Your final sampling frame, from which a sample will be selected and watched, might look something like this:

Jan. 7, Channel 2, 7–9 P.M.
Jan. 7, Channel 4, 7–9 P.M.
Jan. 7, Channel 9, 7–9 P.M.
Jan. 7, Channel 2, 9–11 P.M.
Jan. 7, Channel 4, 9–11 P.M.
Jan. 7, Channel 9, 9–11 P.M.
Jan. 8, Channel 2, 7–9 P.M.
Jan. 8, Channel 4, 7–9 P.M.
Jan. 8, Channel 9, 7–9 P.M.
Jan. 8, Channel 2, 9–11 P.M.
Jan. 8, Channel 4, 9–11 P.M.
Jan. 8, Channel 9, 9–11 P.M.
Jan. 9, Channel 2, 7–9 P.M.
Jan. 9, Channel 4, 7–9 P.M.

Notice that three decisions have been made for you in the illustration. First, it is assumed that Channels 2, 4, and 9 are the ones appropriate to your study. Second, it is assumed that the 7–11 P.M. prime-time hours are the most relevant and that 2-hour periods will do the job. January 7 was picked out of the hat for a starting date. In practice, of course, these decisions

should be based on your careful consideration of what is appropriate to your particular study.

Once you are clear about your units of analysis and the observations appropriate to those units, and have created a sampling frame like the one illustrated, sampling is simple and straightforward. The alternative procedures available to you are the same ones described in Chapter 8: random, systematic, stratified, and so on.

If you want to analyze crime stories in major metropolitan newspapers, you might begin with a list of cities and then draw a systematic sample from that list. For cities with more than one newspaper, you will have to develop procedures for sampling papers within each city. Or suppose you are interested in studying how popular fiction depicts male and female detectives. Assuming you do not wish to read all published detective stories, you might consider stratifying by author's gender and drawing samples of books by male and female authors. As another example, how might you sample movie videos for an analysis of violent acts by and against police officers? By thinking through these examples, you will gain a better understanding of sampling in general, as well as of the ways sampling methods are used in content analysis.

Coding in Content Analysis

Content analysis is essentially a coding operation, and, of course, coding represents the measurement process in content analysis. Communications—oral, written, or other—are coded or classified according to some conceptual framework. Thus, for example, newspaper editorials might be coded as liberal or conservative. Radio talk shows might be coded as bombastic or not. Novels might be coded as detective fiction or not. Political speeches might be coded as containing unsupported rhetoric about crime or not. Recall that terms such as these are subject to many interpretations, and the researcher must specify definitions clearly.

Coding in content analysis involves the logic of conceptualization and operationalization we considered in Chapter 5. In content analysis, as in other research methods, researchers must refine their conceptual framework and develop specific methods for observing in relation to that framework.

For all research methods, conceptualization and operationalization typically involve the interaction of theoretical concerns and empirical observations. If, for example, you believe some newspaper editorials support liberal crime policies and others support conservative ones, ask yourself why you think so. Read some editorials, asking which ones are liberal and which ones are conservative. Is the political orientation of a particular editorial most clearly indicated by its manifest content or by its overall tone? Is your decision based on the use of certain terms (for example, *moral decay* or *need for rehabilitation*) or on the support or opposition given to a particular issue, such as mandatory prison sentences versus treatment programs for drug users?

As in other decisions relating to measurement, the researcher faces a fundamental choice between depth and specificity of understanding. The survey researcher must decide whether specific closed-ended questions or more general open-ended questions will better suit her or his needs. By the same token, the content analyst has a choice between searching for manifest or for latent content. Coding the **manifest content**—the visible, surface content—of a communication more closely approximates the use of closed-ended items in a survey questionnaire. Alternatively, coding the **latent content** of the communication—its underlying meaning—is an option. In the most general sense, manifest and latent content can be distinguished by the degree of interpretation required in measurement.

Throughout the process of conceptualizing manifest- and latent-content coding procedures, remember that the operational definition of any variable is composed of the attributes included in it. Such attributes, moreover, should be mutually exclusive and exhaustive. A newspaper editorial, for example, should not be described as both liberal and conservative, although we should probably allow for some to be middle-of-the-road. It may be sufficient to code TV programs as being violent or not violent, but it is also possible that some programs could be antiviolence.

No coding scheme should be used in content analysis unless it has been carefully pretested. We must decide what manifest or latent contents of communications will be regarded as indicators of the different attributes that make up our research variables, write down these operational definitions, and use them in the actual coding of several units of observation. If we plan to use more than one coder in the final project, each of them should independently code the same set of observations so that we can determine the extent of agreement. In any event, we'll want to take special note of any difficult cases—observations that were not easily classified using the operational definition. Finally, we should review the overall results of the pretest to ensure that they are appropriate to our analytic concerns. If, for example, all of the pretest newspaper editorials have been coded as liberal, we should certainly reconsider our definition of that attribute.

Before beginning to code newspapers, crime dramas on TV, or detective fiction, we need to make plans to assess the reliability of coding. Fortunately, reliability in content analysis can readily be tested, if not guaranteed, in two related ways. First, interrater reliability can be determined by having two different people code the same message and then computing the proportion of items coded the same. For example, if 20 attributes of newspaper stories about crime are being coded and two coders score 18 attributes identically, their reliability is 90 percent. The second way to assess coding reliability is the test–retest method, in which one person codes the same message twice. Of course, some time should elapse between the two coding operations. Test–retest procedures can be used when only one person is doing the coding; reliability can be computed in the same way as if the interrater method were being used.

Illustrations of Content Analysis

We now turn to examples of content analysis in action. The first illustration uses content analysis to measure and characterize newspaper crime stories. The second describes content analysis of a different sort of message—body language. The third demonstrates how extracting information from police records is a form of content analysis.

Newspaper Stories About Crime   Steven Chermak (1998) conducted a content analysis of crime stories in newspapers from six different cities. Crime stories were the units of analysis; Chermak sampled all crime stories every fifth day in the first 6 months of 1990, for a total of 1557 stories.

Chermak's principal hypothesis was that the content of articles determines how much space they are allotted and how prominently they are placed in the newspaper. Prominence was assessed by how many inches of coverage were devoted to each story, where stories were placed, and how big the headlines were. Information on the type of offense, number of crimes mentioned in the story, weapons usage, location of offense, and offender and victim characteristics was also collected. These are examples of manifest content—news story characteristics that require little or no interpretation and can be reliably coded.

Other features of crime news stories are more difficult to code, largely because they refer to latent content and require more interpretation by coders. For example, in connection with a larger research project on reactions to crime, Margaret Gordon and associates (Gordon, Reis, and Tyler, 1979) conducted a content analysis of crime stories in nine metropolitan newspapers serving three cities. They examined all stories in each newspaper issue from November 1977 through April 1978, coding information from more than 11,000 stories concerning violent crime. Gordon and associates coded extensive details about crime news coverage in each story, including latent content. For example, each story was classified with respect to bias or slant in its overall tone. Instructions to coders for this item read as follows: "The categories for this variable represent a continuum: objective—biasing word or two—somewhat sympathetic—biased, slanted. 'Toward victim' [is] construed to include 'against suspect,' and 'toward suspect' includes 'against victim'" (1979:Appendix E).

As you might expect, it was much more difficult for coders to interpret the bias or slant of a story than it was for them to determine, for example, whether the story was a news article, feature, or editorial. Evaluation of police action also proved difficult to code because a single story could be critical of an individual police officer yet praise police administrators for handling the misbehavior of an individual officer.

Does Body Language Attract Assault?   Now consider another very different example of content analysis in which seemingly complex communication messages were readily reduced to coding categories. Betty Grayson and Morris Stein (1981:68) began a fascinating article by asking, "Are there specific movements or behaviors that identify a potential victim of an assault and which signal . . . this vulnerability to a criminal?" How would you go about answering that question? Notice the implicit reference to body language, not spoken communication. Grayson and Stein used a combination of data collection methods—direct observation, field interviews, and content analysis—to produce behavioral profiles of more and less desirable mugging targets.

First, the researchers used videocameras to record, over a 3-day period, people walking in a high-crime area in New York City. From tapes of a large number of individuals, 60 were grouped into four categories according to gender and approximate age. There were 15 tape segments each for older men, older women, younger men, and younger women (1981:69).

Second, two groups of prisoners who were serving sentences for assault against strangers viewed the tapes and rated each person on a

10-point scale ranging from 1 for "a very easy ripoff" to 10 for "would avoid it, too big a situation, too heavy" (1981:70). Based on these ratings, researchers classified taped persons with lower scores as *victims* and those with higher scores as *nonvictims.*

Grayson and Stein then used a movement classification technique that had been developed for training dancers. Trained dance analysts, unaware of video subjects' victim/nonvictim classification, viewed each tape segment and coded 21 characteristics of body movement for each subject. These included such things as stride length, type of weight shift, foot height, and arm–leg coordination (1981:72).

Finally, researchers compared the ratings produced by dance analysts with the victim/nonvictim classifications by convicted muggers. This step revealed specific body language profiles that distinguished victims from nonvictims. Victims tended to have long or short strides, shifted their weight in two dimensions, lifted their feet when walking, and moved only one side of their body at a time. In contrast, nonvictims used medium stride length, shifted weight in three dimensions (sort of a rolling gait, rather than straight-ahead walking), swung their feet, and exhibited coordinated arm and leg movement in opposite directions (1981:73–74). In summary, "The prime difference between perceived victim and nonvictim groups . . . seems to revolve around a 'wholeness' or consistency of movement. Nonvictims have an organized quality about their body movements. . . . In contrast, the gestural movement of victims seems to communicate inconsistency and dissonance" (1981:74).

Through this form of content analysis, Grayson and Stein were able to classify the seemingly complex latent content of body language into quantifiable manifest-content categories. You may recognize some similarities between this study and what we had to say about observation in Chapter 10. Information was initially recorded through direct observation, and then those observations were analyzed as communication using content analysis. In much the

same way, we might collect data on gang graffiti through field observation and then use content analysis to categorize messages conveyed by the graffiti.

Classifying Gang-Related Homicides   When is a homicide gang-related? Are there different types of gang-related homicides? These two questions guided research by Rosenfeld and associates (Rosenfeld, Bray, and Egley, 1999) to understand how gang membership might facilitate homicide in different ways. To address these questions, the researchers conducted a content analysis of police case files for homicides in St. Louis over a 10-year period.

By now, you should recognize the importance of conceptualization in most criminal justice research. Rosenfeld and associates began by further specifying the ambiguous term *gang-related.* They distinguished *gang-motivated* and *gang-affiliated* homicides. Gang-motivated killings "resulted from gang behavior or relationships, such as an initiation ritual, the 'throwing' of gang signs, or a gang fight" (1999:500). Gang-affiliated homicides involved a gang member as victim or offender, but with no indication of specific gang activity; a gang member killing a nongang person during a robbery is an example. A third category, nongang youth homicide, included all other murders in which no evidence of gang activity was available, and the suspected offender was between ages 10 and 24.

Because St. Louis police did not apply the labels "gang-affiliated" or "gang-motivated," it was necessary for researchers to code each case into one of the three categories using information from case files. This was a form of content analysis—systematically classifying the messages contained in homicide case files. Homicide case files are good examples of police records that are not maintained for research purposes. Recognizing this, Rosenfeld and associates coded the files in a two-stage process, building reliability checks into each stage.

First, one person coded each case as either gang-related or not gang-related. This might seem a step backwards, but it focused researchers' measurement on the separate dimensions of homicide of interest to them by simplifying the coding process. It was relatively easy to determine whether any evidence of gang activity or membership was present; if not, the case was classified as a nongang youth killing and set aside. Cases that had some evidence of gang involvement were retained for the second coding stage. During this stage, a second researcher randomly selected a 10 percent sample of cases and coded them again, without knowing how the first coder had classified the sampled cases. You will recognize this as an example of interrater reliability.

The second coding stage involved the finer and more difficult classification of cases as either gang-motivated or gang-affiliated. Interrater reliability checks were again conducted, this time on a 25 percent sample of cases. More cases were selected because reliability was lower in this stage—the two coders exhibited less agreement on how to classify gang homicides. Cases in which independent coding produced discrepancies were reviewed and discussed by the two coders until they agreed on how the homicide should be classified.

From these very different examples, we expect that you can think of many additional applications of content analysis in criminal justice research. You might wish to consult Ray Surette's (1992) excellent book *Media, Crime, and Justice: Images and Realities* to learn more about the scope of topics for which content analysis can be used. The General Accounting Office (1996) has an excellent guide to content analysis generally.

Secondary Analysis

Data collected by other researchers are often used to address new research questions.

Our final topic encompasses all sources of criminal justice data we have described in this and preceding chapters: content analysis, agency records, field observation, and surveys. We begin with an example of an unusually ambitious

use of secondary data by a prolific criminal justice scholar.

For almost three decades, Wesley Skogan has examined the influence of crime on the lives of urban residents. In most cases, his research has relied on sample surveys to investigate questions about fear of crime (Skogan and Maxfield, 1981), community crime prevention (Skogan, 1988), and the relationships between urban residents and police (Skogan, 1990), among others. He has long recognized the importance of incivilities—symbols of social disorder—as indicators of neighborhood crime problems and as sources of fear for urban residents.

In 1990, Skogan published a comprehensive study of incivilities, drawing on his own research as well as studies by others (Skogan, 1990). However, instead of conducting new surveys to collect original data, Skogan's findings were based on secondary analysis of 40 surveys conducted in six cities from 1977 through 1983. He aggregated responses from about 13,000 individuals and examined questions about the sources of disorder, its impact, and the scope of action by individuals and police.

Secondary analysis of data collected by other researchers has become an increasingly important tool. Like Skogan, numerous criminal justice researchers have reanalyzed data collected by others. Several factors contribute to this, including the high cost of collecting original data through surveys or other means. More important, however, is that data for secondary analysis are readily available, largely due to efforts by the National Institute of Justice (NIJ), the BJS, and the Interuniversity Consortium for Political and Social Research (ICPSR).

Suppose you are interested in the relationship between delinquency, drug use, and school performance among adolescents. The National Youth Survey (NYS), which includes responses from 1725 youths interviewed eight times from 1975 through 1989, might suit your needs nicely. NYS data were originally collected by Delbert Elliott and associates (for example, Elliott, Huizinga, and Ageton, 1985). However, like Janet Lauritsen and associates (Lauritsen,

Sampson, and Laub, 1991), who used the NYS to examine links between delinquency and victimization, you may be able to reanalyze the survey data to address your own research questions.

Or perhaps you wish to learn whether there are differences in the sentencing decisions of black and white judges. Cassia Spohn (1990) addressed this question using data originally collected by Milton Heumann and Colin Loftin (1979), who were interested in the effect of a new Michigan law on plea bargaining. Spohn was able to conduct a secondary analysis of the same data to answer a different research question. Let's examine these examples more closely to see how they illustrate the uses and advantages of secondary analysis.

Original NYS data were collected by Elliott and associates (1985:91) for three related research purposes: (1) to estimate the prevalence and incidence of delinquency and drug use among U.S. adolescents, (2) to assess causal relationships between drug use and delinquency, and (3) to test a comprehensive theory of delinquency. The NYS was designed as a panel survey, in which a nationally representative sample of youths ages 11–17 in 1976 was interviewed once each year from 1976 through 1989. As we described in Chapter 4, this is an example of a longitudinal study, and it is especially well suited to disentangling the time ordering of such behaviors as drug use and delinquency.

Lauritsen and associates (1991) were interested in the time order of somewhat different behaviors—delinquency and victimization—that were not directly addressed by the original researchers. A longitudinal design was equally important in this secondary analysis because Lauritsen and associates sought to determine whether youths experienced violent victimization after committing delinquent acts, or vice versa. Given this research interest, they faced two choices: collect original data by conducting a new panel survey, or reanalyze existing data from a panel survey that included questions on victimization and self-reported delinquency. Because the NYS included questions appropriate for their research purpose, Lauritsen and

colleagues were spared the need and (considerable) expense of conducting a new panel study.

The second example mentioned earlier differs in two ways. First, the research questions addressed by Spohn (1990) and by Heumann and Loftin (1979), who collected the original data, are quite different. Heumann and Loftin studied the impact of a new Michigan law that specified mandatory minimum prison sentences for defendants who used firearms in the course of committing a felony offense. Their primary interest was in reductions in plea bargaining by prosecutors in Michigan's largest county following passage of the firearm statute. Spohn, however, used the same data to address the very different question of whether sentences imposed by black judges systematically differed from those imposed by white judges. Her research interest required data from a site with a sufficient number of black criminal court judges, a condition that was met by Detroit Recorder's Court in Wayne County (Michigan), where Heumann and Loftin had conducted their original research.

You may have already guessed the second difference between our two examples: Research by Spohn used data that had been collected from court records, while Lauritsen and associates conducted secondary analysis of survey data. Spohn could have gathered original information from court records, in Detroit or some other city, but she was able to address her research question by conducting a new analysis of data that had already been collected from court records.

Sources of Secondary Data

As a college student, you probably would not be able to launch an eight-wave panel study of a national sample of adolescents, or even gather records from some 2600 felony cases in Wayne County. You do, however, have access to the same data used in those studies, together with data from thousands of other research projects, through the ICPSR at the University of Michigan. For over 40 years, the ICPSR has served as a central repository of machine-readable data collected by social science researchers. Current holdings include data from thousands of studies conducted by researchers all over the world.

Of particular interest to criminal justice researchers is the National Archive of Criminal Justice Data (NACJD), established by the BJS in cooperation with the ICPSR. Here, you will find the NYS, Heumann and Loftin's sentencing data, and each of the 40 surveys analyzed by Skogan for the book we mentioned earlier. There's more, including surveys on criminal justice topics by national polling firms, the NCVS from 1972 to the present, periodic censuses of juvenile detention and correctional facilities, a study of thefts from commercial trucks in New York City, and data from Marvin Wolfgang's classic study of a Philadelphia birth cohort. Data from the growing National Incident-Based Reporting System (NIBRS) are now available, with an expanding number of participating agencies dating from 1996. Data from selected studies are even available for online data analysis. The possibilities are almost endless and grow each year as new data are added to the archives.

One of the most useful Web sites for aggregate secondary data is maintained by the BJS. Summary tabulations for many published data series are presented as graphs or tables. In addition, it's possible to download summary data in spreadsheet format to easily conduct additional analysis, to display graphs in different forms, and even to prepare transparencies for presentations.

Other sites on the Internet offer a virtually unlimited source of secondary data. You can obtain documentation for most data archived by the ICPSR and the NACJD, as well as health statistics, census data, and other sources limited only by your imagination. See Appendix D on the companion Web site for more information.

Advantages and Disadvantages of Secondary Data

The advantages of secondary analysis are obvious and enormous: It is cheaper and faster than collecting original data, and, depending on who did the original study, you may benefit from the work of topflight professionals and esteemed academics.

Potential disadvantages must be kept in mind, however. The key problem involves the recurrent question of validity. When one researcher collects data for one particular purpose, you have no assurance that those data will be appropriate to your research interests. Typically, you'll find that the original researcher collected data that "come close" to measuring what you are interested in, but you may wish key variables had been operationalized just a little differently. The question, then, is whether secondary data provide valid measures of the variables you want to analyze.

This closely resembles one of the key problems in the use of agency records. Perhaps a particular set of data do not provide a totally satisfactory measure of what interests you, but other sets of data are available. Even if no one set of data provides totally valid measures, you can build up a weight of evidence by analyzing all the possibilities. If each of the imperfect measures points to the same research conclusion, you will have developed considerable support for its accuracy. The use of replication lessens the problem.

In general, secondary data are least useful for evaluation studies. This is the case because evaluations are designed to answer specific questions about specific programs. It is always possible to reanalyze data from evaluation studies, but secondary data cannot be used to evaluate an entirely different program. Thus, for example, a number of researchers have reexamined data collected for a series of domestic violence experiments conducted by Lawrence Sherman and others in several cities (see Sherman, 1992, for a summary). In most cases, these secondary researchers (such as Maxwell, Garner, and Fagan, 2001) wished to verify or reassess findings from the orginal studies. But it is not possible to use those data to answer questions about domestic violence interventions other than arrest or to evaluate arrest policies in new cities where the experiments did not take place.

PUTTING IT ALL TOGETHER

NYPD
AGENCY
RECORDS

Although data from interviews and observations were important in assessing the impact of policing on crime in New York, Rutgers researchers used agency records for much analysis. NYPD produces an astonishing amount of data on crime, arrests, and other measures of police activity, but only a small portion is routinely published. Researchers examined indicators produced primarily for internal department use.

Even though we have pointed out that data collected for agency use often will not meet the needs of researchers, this is less true in New York because the use of data to develop and evaluate police actions is a fundamental part of NYPD's innovations. A great deal of attention is devoted to obtaining detailed indicators and to developing quality control measures that enhance the integrity of police data.

Published Reports

Despite the large volume and variety of data produced by NYPD, relatively little is distributed in the form of published reports. Quite a lot of information has become available on Web sites. For example, go to http://www.nyc.gov, click on "City Agencies" (at the top of your screen), then scroll down to "Citywide Accountability Program." Following this link produces listings of agencies for which offical data are available. The Web page (in June 2003) was introduced with the following:

> The Citywide Accountability Program (CAP) uses the Police Department's "Compstat" program's approach to evaluate performance in defined areas of accountability for all levels of management at city agen-

cies, to achieve the goals and objectives of those agencies. Through the collection of statistical information, constant performance tracking is made possible, enabling prompt and effective operational decision making, for the purpose of providing effective delivery of services at city agencies. View an agency's performance indicators by clicking on its link below.

You will then find a link to weekly Compstat reports for each police precinct in the city. Other cities publish much more extensive records of crime data. For example, San Diego County maintains many different crime maps on its regional Web site. Start at http://www.arjis.org. Then click on "Crime maps" on the left side of the page.

Radio Runs

"Radio runs" is the New York label for calls for service—citizen requests for police assistance, usually received by telephone. We mentioned in this chapter that calls for service are increasingly being used as partial measures of crime. Researchers analyzed weekly changes in radio runs as indicators of crime reported to police. If radio runs show patterns of decline, that's evidence of a decline in crimes brought to the attention of police.

NYPD also uses radio runs as one of its integrity measures, by tabulating the number of "unfounded" radio runs. When police are dispatched to a radio call, they are expected to investigate and prepare a report. If police cannot locate a complainant or any other source of information about the call, they may record it as unfounded. But some researchers have shown how police can effectively reduce their workload by recording radio runs as unfounded, thus not having to complete any paperwork. NYPD commanders monitor this by examining weekly reports of the percentage of radio runs recorded as unfounded.

Gun Seizures

Drops in violent crime, especially gun crimes, in New York were especially dramatic. The strategy of policing that targets lower-level offenses—so called quality-of-life crimes—may be partly responsible. Cracking down on subway fare evasion is one example of targeting lower-level offenses. Fare evasion was most commonly executed by jumping subway turnstiles, a relatively easy feat for any moderately agile person. Reasoning that offenders who intended to rob subway riders or commit other offenses would not be inclined to pay fares, police believed fare evasion was linked to other offenses. So cracking down on fare evasion seemed to make sense.

What was not initially anticipated was the relationship between arresting fare evaders and guns. In the early years of the fare evasion crackdown, it was common to find guns on turnstile jumpers. Interestingly, after a while, the number of guns seized declined, and this decline coincided with reductions in gun violence.

Guns seized from turnstile jumpers, and from other persons arrested for lower-level offenses, served as a measure of interim results of police activity. Like most other people in New York, offenders depend on the subway to get around town. After the crackdown on turnstile jumpers, offenders using the subway are either paying fares like other riders or not carrying their guns.

Complaints Against Police

In 1999 and 2000, widely publicized police shootings of unarmed minority males led many people to question whether New York's dramatic reductions in crime were being achieved at an unacceptable price. Aggressive policing, especially in connection with drug offenses, was said to be accompanied by racial profiling—selective traffic and foot stops of minorities.

In an effort to assess this side effect of changes in New York policing, Rutgers researchers examined data on complaints against the police. If de-clines in crime correspond with increases in complaints about excessive force or uncivil behavior by police, police tactics may be overly aggressive.

You should, however, be able to recognize how complaints against police might be subject to reliability and validity problems. For example, complaints might decline if citizens were so fearful of police that they refused to register complaints. In that case, complaints would be an ambiguous measure.

Different Levels of Data

Researchers examined the indicators described here, and others, at different levels of aggregation. First, city-level totals provide information from all police precincts and for subway crimes and gun seizures throughout the vast mass transit system. Precinct-level analysis is possible with Compstat data and other indicators maintained at different police substations.

Quality Control

NYPD officials point to a variety of data audit provisions as evidence for the integrity of police data. Crime reports submitted by precinct commanders are periodically audited by units in the department's Crime Analysis and Program Planning section. Staff in this section use a variety of strategies in efforts to ferret out systematic manipulation of crime data. In the early months of management changes in NYPD, questionable data from the precincts resulted in a number of command changes.

We have mentioned in this and other chapters of this book how researchers often compare multiple indicators as a way of getting better measures of crime and criminal justice concepts. NYPD data auditors adopt a similar approach. Reviewing unfounded radio runs is one example of integrity monitoring. We suggest that you discuss how comparing crime and related data could produce other measures of integrity problems.

In this book, the discussion of secondary analysis has a special purpose. As we conclude our examination of modes of observation in criminal justice research, you should have developed a full appreciation for the range of possibilities available in finding the answers to questions about crime and criminal justice policy. No single method of getting information unlocks all puzzles, yet there is no limit to the ways you can find out about things. And, more powerfully, you can zero in on an issue from several independent directions, gaining an even greater mastery of it.

✪ *Main Points*

- Data and records produced by formal organizations may be the most common source of data in criminal justice research.
- Many public organizations produce statistics and data for the public record, and these data are often useful for criminal justice researchers.
- All organizations keep nonpublic records for internal operational purposes, and these records are valuable sources of data for criminal justice research.
- Public organizations can sometimes be enlisted to collect new data—through observation or interviews—for use by researchers.
- The units of analysis represented by agency data may not always be obvious, because agencies typically use different, and often unclear, units of count to record information about people and cases.
- Although agency records have many potential research uses, because they are produced for purposes other than research they may be unsuitable for a specific study.
- Researchers must be especially attentive to possible reliability and validity problems when they use data from agency records.
- "Follow the paper trail" and "Expect the expected" are two general maxims for researchers to keep in mind when using agency records in their research.
- Content analysis is a research method appropriate for studying human communications. Because communication takes many forms, content analysis can study many other aspects of behavior.

- Units of communication, such as words, paragraphs, and books, are the usual units of analysis in content analysis.
- Coding is the process of transforming raw data—either manifest or latent content—into a standardized, quantitative form.
- Secondary analysis refers to the analysis of data collected earlier by another researcher for some purpose other than the topic of the current study.
- Archives of criminal justice and other social data are maintained by the ICPSR and the NACJD for use by other researchers.
- The advantages and disadvantages of using secondary data are similar to those for agency records—data previously collected by some researcher may not match our own needs.

✪ *Key Terms*

Latent content	Secondary analysis
Manifest content	

✪ *Review Questions and Exercises*

1. Each year, the BJS publishes the *Sourcebook of Criminal Justice Statistics,* a compendium of data from many different sources. Consult the online edition of the *Sourcebook* (see below), select a table of interest to you, and describe how the data presented in that table were originally collected.

2. In New York City, police officers assigned to a specialized gang squad pay special attention to graffiti, or tagging. In doing so, they conduct a type of content analysis to study actions, threats, and other messages presented in this form of communication. Describe how you would plan a formal content analysis of graffiti. Be sure to distinguish manifest and latent content, units of analysis, and coding rules for your study.

✪ *Internet Exercises*

To ensure that you always have access to live, correct Web links for the Web sites referenced in the following exercises, we provide the necessary links on the companion Web site for *Research Methods for Criminal Justice and Criminology* at http://cj.wadsworth. com/maxfield_babbie/research_methods4e. Once at the companion Web site, select this specific chapter, click Chapter Resources, then click Web Links.

1. The *Sourcebook for Criminal Justice Statistics* is available online and provides summary statistics in many areas of interest to criminal justice researchers. Visit this site, find a table or section that interests you, and bring your information to class to discuss. Be prepared to discuss the source of the data, the units of analysis, the way the constructs were operationalized, and any limitations to the reliability and validity of the data included in the table or section.

2. The Texas Department of Criminal Justice provides access to its State Correctional Department's statistics from its Web page. Search this Web site for information of interest to you; then locate similar information from another state department of corrections Web site and compare your findings. Discuss the limitations of this type of comparative process.

3. Visit the Bureau of Justice Statistics Web site. Select and print a graph from the "Key Facts at a Glance" section. Then search other areas of the BJS site to find data used to prepare the graph you have printed. Download the data into a spreadsheet program. Then conduct secondary analysis on those data—present a different graph, or prepare a graph displaying the data in a different format.

✪ *InfoTrac College Edition*

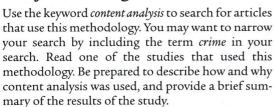

Use the keyword *content analysis* to search for articles that use this methodology. You may want to narrow your search by including the term *crime* in your search. Read one of the studies that used this methodology. Be prepared to describe how and why content analysis was used, and provide a brief summary of the results of the study.

✪ *The NEW Companion Web Site for* **Research Methods for Criminal Justice and Criminology,** *Fourth Edition*

http://cj.wadsworth.com/maxfield_babbie/ research_methods4e

Supplement your review of this chapter by going to the new companion Web site to take one of the Tutorial Quizzes, use the flash cards to master key terms, and check out the many other study aids

you'll find there. You'll also find special features such as quantitative and qualitative data analysis primers to help you with a special project or do some research on your own.

✪ *Additional Readings*

Bureau of Justice Statistics, *Data Quality Guidelines* (Washington, DC: U.S. Department of Justice, Bureau of Justice Statistics, 2002). In 2001, the U.S. Office of Management and Budget directed that all federal agencies develop guidelines to maximize the quality of information they collect and disseminate. This publication describes how the BJS complied with that directive. It provides an excellent overview of validity and reliability issues in series of data often used by criminal justice researchers.

Bureau of Justice Statistics, *Sourcebook of Criminal Justice Statistics* (Washington, DC: U.S. Department of Justice, Bureau of Justice Statistics, annual). As its name implies, this annual compendium of crime and criminal justice data is a comprehensive source of information collected by government agencies and other organizations. Organized into six sections, each year's *Sourcebook* presents hundreds of tables, including extensive notes documenting original sources. You can find the *Sourcebook* on the Internet at http://www.albany.edu/sourcebook.

Geerken, Michael R., "Rap Sheets in Criminological Research: Considerations and Caveats," *Journal of Quantitative Criminology,* Vol. 10 (1994), pp. 3–21. You won't find a more thorough or interesting discussion of how police arrest records are produced and what that means for researchers. Anyone who uses arrest data should read this very carefully.

General Accounting Office, *Content Analysis: A Methodology for Structuring and Analyzing Written Material,* Transfer Paper 10.3.1. (Washington, DC: U.S. General Accounting Office, 1996). As an agency conducting evaluation studies for the U.S. Congress, the GAO uses a variety of research methods. One of a series of "transfer papers" that describe GAO methods, this book presents an excellent overview of content analysis applications and methods.

Jacob, Herbert, *Using Published Data: Errors and Remedies* (Thousand Oaks, CA: Sage, 1984). We have often referred to this small book. It is an extremely valuable source of insight into the promise and pitfalls of using agency records. All social scientists should read this book carefully.

Webb, Eugene T., Campbell, Donald T., Schwartz, Richard D., Sechrest, Lee, and Grove, Janet Belew, *Nonreactive Measures in the Social Sciences* (Boston: Houghton Mifflin, 1981). A compendium of unobtrusive measures, this book includes physical traces, a variety of archival sources, and observation, and provides a good discussion of the ethics involved in and the limitations of such measures.

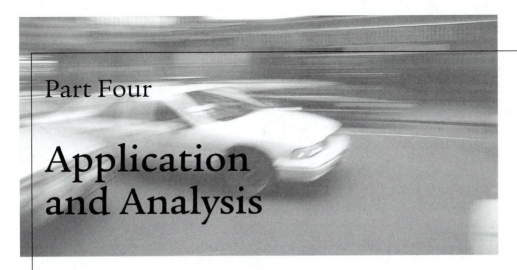

Part Four

Application and Analysis

This final section of the book draws on concepts and ideas from earlier chapters to bring you closer to the actual process of criminal justice research. Having examined the role of theory, cause and effect, measurement, experiments, and different ways of collecting data, we are now ready to see how these pieces come together.

Criminal justice research can be conducted in many ways to answer many different types of questions. We have touched on various research purposes throughout the text, but the first chapter in this section examines a specific research purpose more closely. Because crime is an important and seemingly intractable social problem, applied research is attracting growing interest from researchers and public officials alike.

Chapter 12 describes evaluation research and policy analysis. As we will see, carefully specifying concepts and being attentive to measures are as important for applied research as they are for other research purposes.

Chapter 13 takes up the question of analysis. After we have designed a research project, specified measures, and collected data, our attention will turn to a search for patterns and relationships for description, explanation, or evaluation, depending on the research purpose. In Chapter 13, we take a preliminary look at descriptive and inferential statistics. Our goal is to establish a familiarity with the principles of basic statistical analysis.

Chapter 12

Evaluation Research
and Policy Analysis

In this chapter, our attention centers on applied criminal justice research. Evaluation studies are conducted to learn whether (and why) programs have succeeded or failed. Policy analysis helps officials plan future action and anticipate the possible effects of new programs.

Introduction

Evaluation research is an increasingly important activity for researchers and public officials alike.

Evaluation research—sometimes called "program evaluation"—refers to a research purpose rather than a specific research method. Its special purpose is to evaluate the impact of policies such as mandatory arrest for domestic violence, innovations in probation, and new sentencing laws. Another type of evaluation study, **policy analysis,** helps public officials examine and choose from alternative actions. Virtually all types of designs, measures, and data collection techniques can be used in evaluation research and policy analysis.

Evaluation research in criminal justice is probably as old as criminal justice research generally. Whenever people have instituted a new program for a specific purpose, they have paid attention to its actual consequences, even if they have not always done so in a conscious, deliberate, or sophisticated fashion. Over time, the field of evaluation research has become an increasingly popular and active research specialty, which is reflected in the proliferation of associated textbooks, courses, and projects. As a consequence, you are likely to read increasing numbers of evaluation reports and, as a researcher, to be asked to conduct evaluations.

In part, the growth of evaluation research no doubt reflects increasing desire on the part of criminal justice researchers to actually make a difference in the world. At the same time, we cannot discount the influence of two additional factors: (1) increased federal requirements for program evaluations to accompany the implementation of new programs and (2) the availability of research funds to meet that requirement.

Many people know that the 1994 Crime Bill authorized billions of federal dollars to support community policing, drug courts, and other criminal justice initiatives. Fewer people realize that the Crime Bill also required that most of these new initiatives be evaluated. From the time of Crime Act's passage in 1994 through the 1998–99 fiscal year, the National Institute of Justice alone spent more than $210 million on research and evaluation projects to test the effects of the new legislation (National Institute of Justice, 2001).

By the same token, increased interest in program evaluation and policy analysis has followed heightened concern for the accountability of public officials and public policy. Criminal justice agencies are expected to justify the effectiveness and cost of their actions. If traditional approaches to probation supervision, for example, do not deter future lawbreaking, new approaches should be developed and their effectiveness assessed. Or, if using temporary detention facilities fabricated from recycled semi trailers is less costly than constructing new jails,

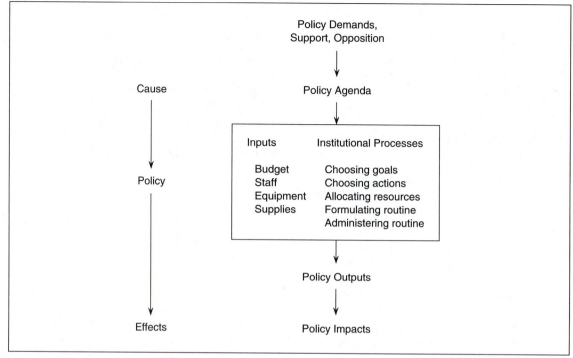

Figure 12.1   The Policy Process
Source: Adapted from Lineberry (1977:42–43).

public officials should consider whether the lower-cost alternative will meet their needs for pretrial detention and short-term incarceration.

Topics Appropriate for Evaluation Research and Policy Analysis

Policy analysis and evaluation are used to develop justice policy and determine its impact.

Most fundamentally, evaluation research is appropriate whenever some policy intervention occurs or is planned. A policy intervention is an action taken for the purpose of producing some intended result. In its simplest sense, evaluation research is a process of determining whether the intended result was produced. Policy analysis focuses more on deciding what intervention, if any, should be pursued. Given alternative

courses of action, which is likely to be least costly, most effective, or least difficult to implement? Our focus, of course, is on the analysis and evaluation of criminal justice policy and criminal justice agencies. However, it will be useful to first consider a simple general model of the policy-making process in order to understand various topics appropriate to evaluation and policy analysis.

The Policy Process

Figure 12.1 presents our model, adapted from Robert Lineberry's (1977:42–43) classic summary of a policy system. A similar type of "input–output" model is described in a National Institute of Justice publication on evaluation guidelines (McDonald and Smith, 1989). Although we will examine each step in turn, recognize that the policy process, like the research process generally (see Chapter 4), is fluid and does not always start at the beginning and conclude at the end.

The policy process begins with some demand that normally appears as support for a new course of action or opposition to existing policy. Such demands can emerge from within a public organization or from outside sources. For example, newspaper stories alleging racial discrimination in drug sentencing can generate demand for revised sentencing policies, or a prosecutor may independently decide to review all sentence recommendations made by deputies who prosecute drug cases. Before any action can be taken, demands must find a place on the policy agenda. A prosecutor might ignore accusations of discrimination published in an alternative newspaper held in low esteem, or she or he may decide not to take actions on suggestions for changes that emerge from within the district attorney's office.

The next step shown in Figure 12.1 actually encompasses several steps. Policy makers consider ultimate goals they wish to accomplish and different means of achieving those goals. Does our prosecutor seek absolute equality in sentences recommended for all white and African American drug defendants, or should there be ranges of permissible variation based on criminal history, severity of charges, and so on? Resources must be allocated from available inputs, including personnel, equipment, supplies, and even time. Who will review sentence recommendations? How much time will that take, and will additional staff be required? Because the word *policy* implies some standard course of action about how to respond to some recurring problem or issue, routine practices and decision rules must be formulated. Will sentence recommendations for each case be reviewed as they are prepared, or is it sufficient to review all cases on a weekly basis?

Policy outputs refer to what is actually produced, in much the same manner that a manufacturer of office supplies produces paper clips and staples. In our hypothetical example, the prosecutor's policy produces the routine review of sentence recommendations in drug cases. Or, to consider a different example, a selective traffic enforcement program intended to reduce auto accidents on a particular roadway may produce a visible police presence, together with traffic citations for speeding.

In the final stage, we consider the impact of policy outputs. Does the prosecutor's review process actually eliminate disparities in sentences? Are auto accidents reduced in the targeted enforcement area?

The distinction between policy outputs and their impacts is important for understanding applications of evaluation to different stages of the policy process. Unfortunately, this difference is often confusing to both public officials and researchers. *Impacts* are fundamentally related to policy goals; they refer to the basic question of what a policy action is trying to achieve. *Outputs* embody the means to achieve desired policy goals. A prosecutor seeks to achieve equality in sentence recommendations (impact), so a review process is produced as a means to achieve that goal (output). Or a police executive allocates officers, patrol cars, and overtime pay to produce traffic citations (outputs) in the expectation that citations will achieve the goal of reducing auto accidents (impact).

Now consider the left side of Figure 12.1. Our policy model can be expressed as a simple cause-and-effect process such as we considered in earlier chapters. Some cause has produced the variation in sentences for African American and white defendants, or some cause has produced a concentration of auto accidents. Policies are formulated to produce some effect or impact. In this sense, a policy can be viewed as a hypothesis in which an independent variable is expected to produce change in some dependent variable. Sentence review procedures are expected to produce a reduction in sentence disparities; targeted enforcement is expected to produce a reduction in auto accidents. Goal-directed public policies may therefore be viewed as if-then statements: *If* some policy action is taken, *then* we expect some result to be produced.

Linking the Process to Evaluation

By comparing this simple model with a general definition of program evaluation given in one of the most widely used texts on the subject (Rossi, Freeman, and Lipsey, 1999), the topics appropriate to applied research will become clearer. Peter Rossi and associates (1999:4) define program evaluation as

> *the use of social science research procedures to systematically assess the effectiveness of social intervention programs.* More specifically, evaluation researchers (evaluators) use social research methods to study, appraise, and help improve social programs in all their aspects, including the diagnosis of the social problems they address, their conceptualization and design, their implementation and administration, their outcomes, and their efficiency. (emphasis in original)

We have been discussing systematic social science research procedures throughout this book. Now let's substitute *criminal justice* for *social programs* and see how this definition and Figure 12.1 help us understand program evaluation applications.

Policy Analysis   Activities listed under "Institutional Processes" in Figure 12.1 refer to conceptualization and design. For example, faced with a court order to maintain prison populations within established capacity, corrections officials might begin by conceiving and designing different ways to achieve this demand. Policy analysis is an example of a social science research procedure that can help corrections officials evaluate alternative actions, choose among them, and formulate routine practices for implementing policy to comply with a court order.

One approach might be to increase rated capacity through new construction or conversion of existing facilities. Another might be to devise a program to immediately reduce the existing population. Still another might be to cut back on the admission of newly sentenced offenders. A more general goal that would certainly be considered is the need to protect public safety. Each goal implies different types of actions, together with different types and levels of resources, that would be considered within constraints implied by the need to protect public safety. If officials from other organizations—prosecutors, judges, or state legislators—were involved in conceptualization and design, then additional goals, constraints, and policies might be considered.

Increasing capacity by building more prisons would be the most costly approach in financial terms, but it might also be viewed as the most certain way to protect public safety. Early release of current inmates would be cheaper and faster than building new facilities, but this goal implies other decisions, such as how persons would be selected and whether they would be released to parole or to halfway houses. And each of these alternatives requires some organizational capacity to choose inmates for release, place them in halfway houses, or supervise compliance with parole. Refusing new admissions would be least costly. Political support must be considered for each possible approach. Each alternative—spending money on new construction, accepting responsibility for early release, or tacitly passing the problem on to jails that must house inmates refused admission to state facilities—requires different types of political influence or courage.

Many other topics in criminal justice research are appropriate for policy analysis. Police departments use such techniques to help determine the boundaries of patrol beats. In most large cities, analysts examine the concentration of calls for service in terms of space and time and consider how street layout and obstacles might facilitate or impede patrol car mobility.

A growing number of law enforcement agencies are using computerized crime maps to detect emerging patterns in crime and develop appropriate responses. Producing computer-generated maps that display reported crimes within days after they have occurred is one of the most important policy planning tools for the New York City Police Department (Silverman, 1999). Other departments have taken advantage of funding and technical assistance made available by the 1994 Crime Bill to enhance mapping and other crime analysis capabilities.

Court administrators often make changes in the way cases are scheduled for individual judges after estimating what effects such changes will have. Estimates are usually based on analysis of past case volume and predicted future volume. Many states now conduct "prison impact" studies to estimate shifts in prison populations that will result from legislative changes in sentence length. Later in this chapter, we will describe an example of a prison population model.

Program Evaluation Policy analysis takes places in the policy-making stage. In contrast, program evaluation studies are conducted in later stages and seek answers to two types of questions: (1) Are policies being implemented as planned? and (2) Are policies achieving their intended goals? Evaluation, therefore, seeks to link the intended actions and goals of criminal justice policy to empirical evidence that policies are being carried out as planned and are having the desired effects. These two types of questions correspond to two related types of program evaluations: process evaluation and impact assessment. Returning to our example of policies to reduce prison population, we will consider first impact assessment and then process evaluation.

Let's assume that corrections department policy analysts select an early-release program to reduce the population of one large institution. Inmates who have less than 120 days remaining on their sentence and who were committed for nonviolent offenses will be considered for early release. Further assume that of those inmates selected for early release, some will be assigned to parole officers, and some will serve their remaining sentence in halfway houses—working at jobs during the week but spending evenings and weekends in a community-based facility.

Table 12.1 Hypothetical Results of Early-Prison-Release Impact Assessment

	Percent New Arrests After 6 Months	Number of Persons
Normal release	26%	142
Early release to halfway houses	17	25
Early parole	33	46
Subtotal early release	27	71
Total	26	213

Note: Preprogram population = 1578; actual population after implementation = 1402; court-imposed population cap = 1350.

The program has two general goals: (1) to reduce prison population to the court-imposed ceiling and (2) to protect public safety. Whereas the first goal is fairly straightforward, the second is uncomfortably vague. What do we mean by "protecting public safety"? For now, let's say we will conclude that the program is successful in this regard if, after 6 months, persons in the two early-release conditions have aggregate rates of arrest for new offenses equal to or less than a comparison group of inmates released after completing their sentences.

Our **impact assessment** would examine data on the prison population before and after the new program was implemented, together with arrest records for the two types of early releases and a comparison group. We might obtain something like the hypothetical results shown in Table 12.1.

Did the program meet its two goals? Your initial reaction might be that it did not, but Table 12.1 presents some interesting findings. The prison population certainly was reduced, but it did not reach the court-imposed cap of 1350. Those released to halfway houses had lower arrest rates than others, but persons placed on early parole had higher arrest rates. Averaging arrest rates for all three groups shows that the total figure is about the same as that for persons released early. Notice also that almost twice as many people were released to early parole as were placed in halfway houses.

The impact assessment results in Table 12.1 would have been easier to interpret if we had conducted a **process evaluation.** A process evaluation focuses on program outputs, as represented in Figure 12.1, seeking answers to the question of whether as the program was implemented as intended. If we had conducted a process evaluation of this early-release program, we might have discovered that something was amiss in the selection process. Two pieces of evidence in Table 12.1 suggest that one of the selection biases we considered in Chapter 7, "creaming," might be at work in this program. Recall that creaming is the natural tendency of public officials to choose experimental subjects least likely to fail. In this case, selectivity is indicated by the failure of the early-release program to meet its target number, the relatively small number of persons placed in halfway houses, and the lower re-arrest rates for these persons. A process evaluation would have monitored selection procedures and probably revealed evidence of excessive caution on the part of corrections officials in releasing offenders to halfway houses.

Ideally, impact assessments and process evaluations are conducted together. Our example illustrates the important general point that process evaluations make impact assessments more interpretable. In other cases, process evaluations may be conducted when an impact assessment is not possible. To better understand how process evaluations and impact assessments complement each other, let's now look more closely at how evaluations are conducted.

Getting Started

Learning policy goals is a key first step in doing evaluation research.

Several steps are involved in planning any type of research project. This is especially true in applied studies, for which even more planning may be required. In evaluating a prison early-release program, we need to think about design, measurement, sampling, data collection procedures, analysis, and so on. We also have to address such practical problems as obtaining access to people, information, and data needed in an evaluation.

In one sense, however, evaluation research differs slightly in the way research questions are developed and specified. Recall that we equated program evaluation with hypothesis testing; policies are equivalent to if-then statements postulating that some intervention will have some desired impact. Preliminary versions of research questions, therefore, will already have been formulated for many types of evaluations. Policy analysis usually considers a limited range of alternative choices; process evaluations focus on whether programs are carried out according to plans; and impact assessments evaluate whether specified goals are attained.

This is not to say that evaluation research is a straightforward business of using social science methods to answer specific questions that are clearly stated by criminal justice officials. It is often difficult to express policy goals in the form of if-then statements that are empirically testable. Another problem is the presence of conflicting goals. Many issues in criminal justice are complex, involving different organizations and people. And different organizations and people may have different goals that make it difficult to define specific evaluation questions. Perhaps most common and problematic are vague goals. Language describing criminal justice programs may optimistically state goals of "enhancing public safety by reducing recidivism" without clearly specifying what is meant by that objective.

In most cases, researchers have to help criminal justice officials formulate testable goals, something that is not always possible. Other obstacles may interfere with researchers' access to important information. Because of these and similar problems, evaluation researchers must first address the question of whether to evaluate at all.

Evaluability Assessment

An evaluability assessment is described by Rossi and associates (1999:157) as sort of a "pre-evaluation," in which a researcher determines whether conditions necessary for conducting an evaluation are present. One obvious condition is support for the study from organizations delivering program components that will be evaluated. The word *evaluation* may be threatening to public officials, who fear that their own job performance is being rated. Thomas Cook and Donald Campbell (1979) referred to this as "evaluation apprehension." Even if officials do not feel personally threatened by an impact assessment or other applied study, evaluation research can disrupt routine agency operations. Ensuring agency cooperation and support is therefore an important part of evaluability assessment. Even if no overt opposition exists, officials may be ambivalent about evaluation. This might be the case, for example, if an evaluation is required as a condition of launching some new program.

This and other steps in evaluability assessment may be accomplished by "scouting" a program and interviewing key personnel (Rossi, Freeman, and Lipsey, 1999:135). The focus in scouting and interviewing should be on obtaining preliminary answers to questions that eventually will have to be answered in more detail as part of an evaluation. What are general program goals and more specific objectives? How are these goals translated into program components? What kinds of records and data are readily available? Who will be the primary consumers of evaluation results? Do other persons or organizations have some direct or indirect stake in the program? Figure 12.2 presents a partial menu of questions that can guide information gathering for the evaluability assessment and later stages.

The answers to these and similar questions should be used to prepare a program description. Although "official" program descriptions may be available, evaluation researchers should

1. Goals
   a. What is the program intended to accomplish?
   b. How do staff determine how well they have attained their goals?
   c. What formal goals and objectives have been identified?
   d. Which goals or objectives are most important?
   e. What measures of performance are currently used?
   f. Are adequate measures available, or must they be developed as part of the evaluation?

2. Clients
   a. Who is served by the program?
   b. How do they come to participate?
   c. Do they differ in systematic ways from nonparticipants?

3. Organization and Operation
   a. Where are the services provided?
   b. Are there important differences among sites?
   c. Who provides the services?
   d. What individuals or groups oppose the program or have been critical of it in the past?

4. History
   a. How long has the program been operating?
   b. How did the program come about?
   c. Has the program grown or diminished in size and influence?
   d. Have any significant changes occurred in the program recently?

Figure 12.2   Evaluation Questions
Source: Adapted from Stecher and Davis (1987:58–59).

always prepare their own description, one that reflects their own understanding of program goals, elements, and operations. Official documents may present incomplete descriptions or ones intended for use by program staff, not evaluators. Even more importantly, official program documents often do not contain usable statements about program goals. As we will see, formulating goal statements that are empirically testable is one of the most important components of evaluation research.

Douglas McDonald and Christine Smith (1989:1) describe slightly different types of questions to be addressed by criminal justice officials and evaluators in deciding whether to evaluate state-level drug control programs:

How central is the project to the state's strategy?

How costly is it relative to others?

Are the project's objectives such that progress toward meeting them is difficult to estimate accurately with existing monitoring procedures?

Such questions are related to setting both program and evaluation priorities. On the one hand, if a project is not central to drug control strategies, or if existing information can help determine project effectiveness, then an evaluation should probably not be conducted. On the other hand, costly projects that are key elements in antidrug efforts should be evaluated so that resources can be devoted to new programs if existing approaches are found to be ineffective.

Although Rossi and associates (1999) describe it as a distinct type of research, an evaluability assessment does not need to be a major project in and of itself. Often, a few questions posed to a few people, together with a careful reading of program documents, will yield sufficient information to decide whether to proceed further. The questions presented in Figure 12.2 are a good guide for developing a scouting report. If the scouting report indicates that a particular program will not be readily evaluable, it is far better to make that determination before beginning a full-blown study.

Problem Formulation

We mentioned that evaluation research questions may be defined for you. This is true in a general sense, but formulating applied research problems that can be empirically evaluated is an important and often difficult step. Evaluation research is a matter of finding out whether something is or is not there, whether something did or did not happen. To conduct evaluation research, we must be able to operationalize, observe, and recognize the presence or absence of what is under study.

This process normally begins by identifying and specifying program goals. The difficulty of this task, according to Rossi and associates (1999:167), revolves around the fact that formal statements of goals are often abstract statements about ideal outcomes. Here are some examples of goal statements paraphrased from actual program descriptions:

> Equip individuals with life skills to succeed (a state-level shock incarceration program; MacKenzie, Layton, Shaw, and Gowdy, 1993).

> Provide a safe school environment conducive to learning (a school resource officer program; Johnson, 1999).

> Encourage participants to accept the philosophy and principles of drug-free living (an urban drug court; Finn and Newlyn, 1993).

> Provide a mechanism that engages local citizens and community resources in the problem-solving process (a probation–police community corrections program; Wooten and Hoelter, 1998).

Each statement expresses a general program objective that must be clarified before we can formulate research questions to be tested empirically. We can get some idea of what the first example means, but this goal statement raises several questions. The objective is for individuals to succeed, but succeed at what? What is meant by "life skills"—literacy, job training, time management, self-discipline? We might also ask whether the program focuses on outputs (equipping people with skills) or on impacts (promoting success among people who are equipped with the skills). On the one hand, an evaluation of program outputs might assess individual learning of skills, without considering whether the skills enhance chances for success. On the other hand, an evaluation of program impacts might obtain measures of success such as stable employment or not being arrested within some specified time period.

In all fairness, these goal statements are taken somewhat out of context; source documents expand on program goals in more detail.

They are, however, typical of stated goals, or initial responses we might get to the question, What are the goals of this program? Researchers, however, require more specific statements of program objectives.

Wesley Skogan (1985) cautions that official goal statements frequently "oversell" what a program might realistically be expected to accomplish. It's natural for public officials to be positive or optimistic in stating goals, and overselling may be evident in goal statements. Another reason officials and researchers embrace overly optimistic goals is that they fail to develop a micromodel of the program production process (Weiss, 1995). That is, they do not adequately consider just how some specified intervention will work. Referring back to Figure 12.1, we can see that developing a micromodel can be an important tool for laying out program goals and understanding how institutional processes are structured to achieve those goals. Skogan (1985:38; emphasis in original) describes a micromodel as

> part of what is meant by a "theory-driven" evaluation. Researchers and program personnel should together consider just how each element of a program should affect its targets. If there is not a good reason why "X" *should* cause "Y" the evaluation is probably not going to find that it did! Micromodeling is another good reason for monitoring the actual implementation of programs.

A micromodel can also reveal another problem that sometimes emerges in applied studies: inconsistent goals.

For example, Michael Maxfield and Terry Baumer (1992) evaluated a pretrial home detention program in which persons awaiting trial for certain types of offenses were released from jail and placed on home detention with electronic monitoring. Five different criminal justice organizations played roles in implementation or had stakes in the program. The county sheriff's department (1) faced pressure to reduce its jail population. Under encouragement from the county prosecutor (2), the pretrial release program was established. Criminal court judges (3) had the ultimate authority to release defendants to home detention, following recommendations by bail commissioners in a county criminal justice services agency (4). Finally, a community corrections department (5) was responsible for actually monitoring persons released to home detention.

Maxfield and Baumer (1992) interviewed persons in each of these organizations and discovered that different agencies had different goals. The sheriff's department was eager to release as many people as possible to free up jail space for convicted offenders and pretrial defendants who faced more serious charges. Community corrections staff, charged with the task of monitoring pretrial clients, were more cautious and sought only persons who presented a lower risk of absconding or committing more offenses while on home detention. The county prosecutor viewed home detention as a way to exercise more control over some individuals who would otherwise be released under less restrictive conditions. Some judges refused to release people on home detention, while others followed prosecutors' recommendations. Finally, bail commissioners viewed pretrial home detention as a form of jail resource management, adding to the menu of existing pretrial dispositions (jail, bail, or release on recognizance).

The different organizations involved in the pretrial release program comprised multiple **stakeholders**—persons and organizations with a direct interest in the program. Each stakeholder had different goals for and different views on how the program should actually operate—who should be considered for pre-trial home detention, how they should be monitored, and what actions should be taken against those who violated various program rules. After laying out these goals and considering different measures of program performance, Maxfield and Baumer (1992:331) developed a micromodel of home detention indicating that electronic monitoring is suitable for only a small fraction of defendants awaiting trial.

Clearly specifying program goals, then, is a fundamental first step in conducting evaluation studies. If officials are not certain about what a program is expected to achieve, it is not possible to determine whether goals are reached. Or, if multiple stakeholders embrace different goals, evaluators must specify different ways to assess those goals. Maxfield (2001) describes a number of different approaches to specifying clear goals, a crucial first step in the evaluation process.

Measurement

After we identify program goals, our attention turns to measurement, considering first how to measure a program's success in meeting goals. Rossi and associates (1999:83–4) state this in terms that should now be familiar:

> For an evaluation question to be answerable, it must be possible to identify in advance some evidence or "observables" that can realistically be obtained and will be credible as the basis for an answer. This generally means developing questions (1) that involve measurable performance dimensions, (2) that are sufficiently unambiguous so that explicit, noncontroversial definitions can be given for each of their terms, and (3) for which the relevant standards or criteria are specified or obvious.

Obtaining evaluable statements of program goals is conceptually similar to the measurement process, in which program objectives represent conceptual definitions of what a program is trying to accomplish. Chapter 5 began with the following sentence: "This chapter describes the progression from having a vague idea about what we want to study to being able to recognize it and measure it in the real world." As evaluation researchers, we must similarly recognize the need to state clear conceptual definitions and then describe specific operational definitions.

Specifying Outcomes   If a criminal justice program is intended to accomplish something, we must be able to measure that something. If

we want to reduce fear of crime, we need to be able to measure fear of crime. If we want to increase consistency in sentences for drug offenses, we need to be able to measure that. Notice, however, that, although outcome measures are derived from goals, they are not the same as goals. Program goals represent *desired outcomes,* whereas outcome measures are *empirical indicators* of whether those desired outcomes are achieved. Furthermore, if a program pursues multiple goals, then researchers may have to either devise multiple outcome measures or select a subset of possible measures to correspond with a subset of goals.

Keeping in mind our program-as-hypothesis simile, outcome measures correspond to dependent variables—the Y in a simple $X \rightarrow Y$ causal hypothesis. Because we have already considered what's involved in developing measures for dependent variables, we can describe how to formulate outcome measures. Pinning down program goals and objectives results in a conceptual definition. We then specify an operational definition by describing empirical indicators of program outcomes.

In our earlier example, Maxfield and Baumer (1992) translated the disparate interests of organizations involved in pretrial home detention into three more specific objectives: (1) Ensure appearance at trial, (2) protect public safety, and (3) relieve jail crowding. These objectives led to corresponding outcome measures: (1) failure-to-appear rates for persons released to pretrial home detention, (2) arrests while on home detention, and (3) estimates of the number of jail beds made available, computed by multiplying the number of persons on pretrial home detention by the number of days each person served on the program. Table 12.2 summarizes the goals, objectives, and measures defined by Maxfield and Baumer.

Let's consider another example. Staff from the Department of the Youth Authority in California conducted an evaluation of a boot camp and intensive parole program known as LEAD—an acronym for qualities the program sought to instill in participants: leadership, esteem, abil-

Table 12.2   Pretrial Home Detention with Electronic Monitoring: Goals, Objectives, and Measures

Actor/Organization	Goals
Sheriff	Release jail inmates
Prosecutor	Increase supervision of pretrial defendants
Judges	Protect public safety
Ball commission	Provide better jail resource management
Community corrections	Monitor defendant compliance
	Return violators to jail

Objectives	Measures
Ensure court appearance	Failure-to-appear courts
Protect public safety	Arrests while on program
Relieve jail crowding	N defendants $\times$ days served

Source: Adapted from Maxfield and Baumer (1992).

ity, and discipline. The three major goals of LEAD were to (1) reduce recidivism, (2) ease crowded conditions in juvenile facilities, and (3) provide a cost-effective treatment option (Department of the Youth Authority, 1997:18).

Evaluators assessed the effectiveness of the LEAD program by comparing LEAD participants with other young offenders who were not in LEAD. Data were collected on lengths of stay in each institution, estimated program costs, and rates of recidivism. Measures of recidivism were obtained from official records of arrests and parole violations for 12-, 18-, and 24-month periods after release. Length of incarceration was used to measure the reduction of institutional crowding, as well as cost savings. It was assumed that LEAD participants would have shorter average lengths of incarceration than youths not participating but that these short-term cost savings would be reduced if LEAD participants were later reincarcerated more rapidly or at higher rates. Recidivism data routinely collected on all subjects were used to examine whether this was the case.

Measuring Program Contexts   Measuring the dependent variables directly involved in an impact assessment is only a beginning. As Ray Pawson and Nick Tilley (1997:69) point out, it is usually necessary to measure the context within which the program is conducted. These variables may appear to be external to the experiment itself, yet they still affect it.

Consider, for example, an evaluation of a job-skills training program coupled with early prison release to a halfway house. The primary outcome measure might be participants' success at gaining employment after completing the program. We will, of course, observe and calculate the subjects' employment rates. We should also be attentive to what has happened to the employment/unemployment rates of the community and state where the program is located. A general slump in the job market should be taken into account in assessing what might otherwise seem to be a low employment rate for subjects. Or, if all the experimental subjects get jobs following the program, that might result more from a general increase in available jobs than from the value of the program itself.

There is no magic formula or set of guidelines for selecting measures of program context, any more than there is for choosing control variables in some other type of research. Just as we read what other researchers have found with respect to some topic we are interested in—say, explanatory research—we should also learn about the production process for some criminal justice program before conducting an evaluation.

Theory also plays an important role. If we study a program to provide job training so that participants can better compete for employment, we need to understand how labor markets operate in general. This is part of a theory-driven evaluation: Understanding how a program should work in theory will better enable researchers to specify measures of program contexts that should be considered (Weiss, 1995).

Measuring Program Delivery   In addition to making measurements relevant to the outcomes of a program, it is necessary to measure the program intervention—the experimental stimulus or independent variable. In some cases, this measurement will be handled by assigning subjects to experimental and control groups, if that's the research design. Assigning a person to the experimental group is the same as scoring that person "yes" on the intervention, and assignment to the control group represents a score of "no." In practice, however, it's seldom that simple.

Let's continue with the job-training example. Some inmates will participate in the program through early release; others will not. But imagine for a moment what job-training programs are actually like. Some subjects will participate fully; others might miss sessions or fool around when they are present. So we may need measures of the extent or quality of participation in the program. And if the program is effective, we should find that those who participated fully have higher employment rates than those who participated less.

An evaluation of a drug court operating in Washington, DC, provides an example of uncommonly thorough attention to program delivery (Carver, Boyer, and Hickey, 1996). First, program staff kept attendance records for training activities and classes that participants were required to attend. In addition, evaluators recorded how attentive participants were and how actively they participated in discussions. Assuming that degree of participation in program activities would affect success rates, evaluators expected lower recidivism among drug users who were more attentive and active.

Other factors may further confound the administration of the experimental stimulus. Suppose we are evaluating a new form of counseling designed to cure drug addiction. Several counselors administer it to subjects composing an experimental group. We can compare the recovery rate of the experimental group with that of a control group (a group that received some other type of counseling or none at all). It might be useful to include the names of the counselors who treat specific subjects in the experimental

group, because some may be more effective than others. If that turns out to be the case, we must find out why the treatment works better for some counselors than for others. What we learn will further elaborate our understanding of the therapy itself.

Michael Dennis (1990) describes an excellent example of the importance of measuring interventions in this type of study. Intravenous drug users were randomly assigned to receive enhanced treatment (the experimental stimulus) or standard treatment from counselors. Recognizing that some counselors might be more skilled than others, Dennis also randomly assigned counselors to provide either enhanced or standard treatments. There was still some potential for variation in counseling within the enhanced and standard treatment groups, so Dennis tape-recorded sample sessions between patients and counselors. Research staff who were blind to the intended level of counseling then rated each recorded session according to whether they felt it represented enhanced or standard counseling.

Obtaining measures of the experimental intervention is very important for many types of evaluation designs. Variation in the levels of treatment delivered by a program can be a major threat to the validity of even randomized evaluation studies. Put another way, uncontrolled variation in treatment is equivalent to unreliable measurement of the independent variable.

Specifying Other Variables   It is usually necessary to measure the population of subjects involved in the program being evaluated. In particular, it is important to define those for whom the program is appropriate. In evaluation studies, such persons are referred to as the program's "target population." If we are evaluating a program that combines more intensive probation supervision with periodic urine testing for drug use, it's probably appropriate for convicted persons who are chronic users of illegal drugs, but how should we define and measure chronic drug use more specifically? The job-skills training program mentioned previously is probably appropriate for inmates who have poor employment histories, but a more specific definition of employment history is needed.

This process of definition and measurement has two aspects. First, the program target population must be specified. This is usually done in a manner similar to the process of defining program goals. Drawing on questions like those in Figure 12.2, evaluators consult program officials to identify the intended targets or beneficiaries of a particular program. Because the hypothetical urine testing program is combined with probation, its target population will include persons who might receive suspended sentences with probation. However, offenders convicted of crimes that carry nonsuspendible sentences will not be in the target population. Prosecutors and other participants may specify additional limits to the target population—employment or no previous record of probation violations, for example.

Most evaluation studies that use individual people as units of analysis also measure such background variables as age, gender, educational attainment, employment history, and prior criminal record. Such measures are made to determine whether experimental programs work best for males, those over age 25, high school graduates, persons with fewer prior arrests, and so forth.

Second, in providing for the measurement of these different kinds of variables, we need to choose whether to create new measures or use ones already collected in the course of normal program operation. If our study addresses something that's not routinely measured, the choice is easy. More commonly, at least some of the measures we are interested in will be represented in agency records in some form or other. We then have to decide whether agency measures are adequate for our evaluation purposes.

Because we are talking about measurement here, our decision to use our own measures or those produced by agencies should, of course, be based on an assessment of measurement re-

liability and validity. If we are evaluating the program that combined intensive probation with urinalysis, we will have more confidence in the reliability and validity of basic demographic information recorded by court personnel than in court records of drug use. In this case, we might want to obtain self-report measures of drug use and crime commission from subjects themselves, rather than relying on official records.

By now, it should be abundantly clear that measurement must be taken very seriously in evaluation research. Evaluation researchers must carefully determine all the variables to be measured and obtain appropriate measures for each. However, such decisions are typically not purely scientific ones. Evaluation researchers often must work out their measurement strategy with the people responsible for the program being evaluated.

Designs for Program Evaluation

Designs used in basic research are readily adapted for use in evaluation research.

Chapter 7 presented a good introduction to a variety of experimental and other designs that researchers use in studying criminal justice. Recall that randomly assigning research subjects to experimental or control groups controls for many threats to internal validity. Here, our attention turns specifically to the use of different designs in program evaluation.

Randomized Evaluation Designs

To illustrate the advantages of random assignment, consider this dialogue from Lawrence Sherman's book *Policing Domestic Violence: Experiments and Dilemmas* (1992:67):

When the Minneapolis domestic violence experiment was in its final planning stage, some police officers asked: "Why does it have to be a randomized experiment? Why can't you just follow up the people we arrest anyway, and compare their future violence risks to the people we don't arrest?"

Since this question reveals the heart of the logic of controlled experiments, I said, "I'm glad you asked. What kind of people do you arrest now?"

"Assholes," they replied. "People who commit aggravated POPO."

"What is aggravated POPO?" I asked.

"Pissing off a police officer," they answered. "Contempt of cop. But we also arrest people who look like they're going to be violent, or who have caused more serious injuries."

"What kind of people do you not arrest for misdemeanor domestic assault?" I continued.

"People who act calm and polite, who lost their temper but managed to get control of themselves," came the answer.

"And which kinds of people do you think would have higher risks of repeat violence in the future?" I returned.

"The ones we arrest," they said, the light dawning.

"But does that mean arrest caused them to become more violent?" I pressed.

"Of course not—we arrested them because they were more trouble in the first place," they agreed.

"So just following up the ones you arrest anyway wouldn't tell us anything about the effects of arrest, would it?" was my final question.

"Guess not," they agreed. And they went on to perform the experiment.

Sherman's dialogue portrays the obvious problems of selection bias in routine police procedures for handling domestic violence. In fact, one of the most important benefits of randomization is to avoid the selectivity that is such a fundamental part of criminal justice decision making. Police selectively arrest people, prosecutors selectively file charges, judges and juries selectively convict defendants, and offenders are selectively punished. In a more general sense,

randomization is the great equalizer: Through probability theory, we can assume that groups created by random assignment will be statistically equivalent.

At the same time, randomized designs are not suitable for evaluating all experimental criminal justice programs. Certain requirements of randomized studies mean that this design cannot be used in many situations. A review of those requirements illustrates many of the limits of randomized designs for applied studies.

Program and Agency Acceptance   Random assignment of people to receive some especially desirable or punitive treatment may not be possible for legal, ethical, and practical reasons. We discussed ethics and legal issues in Chapter 3. Sometimes, practical obstacles may also be traced to a misunderstanding of the meaning of random assignment. It is crucial that public officials understand why randomization is desirable and that they fully endorse the procedure. Joan Petersilia (1989:444) describes how RAND researchers obtained cooperation for an evaluation of intensive probation by appealing to the self-interest of program staff. Staff are better served by learning what works and what doesn't, a determination that can best be made through a randomized experiment. Staff responsible for delivering an experimental program must understand, endorse, and agree to follow procedures for random assignment.

At the same time, justice agencies have expanding needs for evaluations of smaller-scale programs. John Eck (2002) explains how designs that are less elaborate are more likely to be accepted by public agencies.

Minimization of Exceptions to Random Assignment   In any real-world delivery of alternative programs or treatments to victims, offenders, or criminal justice agency staff, exceptions to random assignment are all but inevitable. In a series of experiments on police responses to domestic violence, officers responded to incidents in one of three ways, according to a random assignment procedure

(Sherman, 1992). The experimental treatment was arrest; control treatments included simply separating parties to the dispute or attempting to advise and mediate. Although patrol officers and police administrators accepted the random procedure, exceptions were made as warranted in individual cases, subject to an officer's discretionary judgment.

As the number of exceptions to random assignment increases, however, the statistical equivalence of experimental and control groups is threatened. When police (or others) make exceptions to random assignment, they are introducing bias into the selection of experimental and control groups. Randomized experiments are best suited for programs in which such exceptions can be minimized.

Adequate Caseflow for Sample Size In Chapter 8, we examined the relationship between sample size and accuracy in estimating population characteristics. As sample size increases (up to a point), estimates of population means and standard errors become more precise. By the same token, the number of subjects in groups created through random assignment is related to the researcher's ability to detect significant differences in outcome measures between groups. If each group has only a small number of subjects, statistical tests can detect only very large program effects or differences in outcome measures between the two groups. This is a problem with statistical conclusion validity and sample size, as we discussed in Chapters 7 and 8.

Case flow represents the process through which subjects are accumulated in experimental and control groups. In Sherman's domestic violence evaluations, cases flowed into experimental and control groups as domestic violence incidents were reported to police. Evaluations of other types of programs will generate cases through other processes—for example, offenders sentenced by a court or inmates released from a correctional facility.

If relatively few cases flow through some process and thereby become eligible for random as-

signment, it will take a longer time to obtain sufficient numbers of cases. The longer it takes to accumulate cases, the longer it will take to conduct an experiment and the longer experimental conditions must be maintained. Imagine filling the gas tank of your car with a small cup: It would take a long time, it would test your patience, and you would probably tarnish the paint with spilled gasoline as the ordeal dragged on. In a similar fashion, an inadequate flow of cases into experimental groups risks contaminating the experiment through other problems.

Getting information about case flow in the planning stages of an evaluation is a good way to diagnose possible problems with numbers of subjects. For example, Sherman (1992:293–95) conducted what he calls a "pipeline" study in Milwaukee to determine whether there were enough suitable domestic violence cases for random assignment to three treatment conditions.

Maintaining Treatment Integrity Treatment integrity refers to whether an experimental intervention is delivered as intended. Sometimes called "treatment consistency," treatment integrity is therefore roughly equivalent to measurement reliability. Experimental designs in applied studies often suffer from problems related to treatment inconsistencies. If, for example, serving time in jail is the experimental treatment in a program designed to test different approaches to sentencing drunk drivers, treatment integrity will be threatened if some defendants are sentenced to a weekend in jail while others serve 30 days or longer.

Criminal justice programs can vary considerably in the amount of treatment applied to different subjects in experimental groups. For example, Petersilia (1989) describes how the concept of intensive probation supervision invites problems with treatment integrity. Intensive supervision, the experimental treatment, is defined as increased contact between probation officers and clients. Two types of problems can emerge. First, subjects in the experimental group might not receive enough increased contact with probation officers to constitute intensive supervision. Second, there may be some treatment spillover such that control-group subjects begin to have more contact with probation officers. In either case, subjects in experimental and control groups receive similar levels of treatment, which can reduce the differences between the two groups on outcome measures.

Midstream changes in experimental programs can also threaten treatment integrity. Rossi and associates (1999:297) point out that the possibility of midstream changes means that randomized designs are usually not appropriate for evaluating programs in early stages of development, when such changes are more likely. For example, assume we are evaluating an intensive supervision probation program with randomized experimental and control groups. Midway through the experiment, program staff decide to require weekly urinalysis for everyone in the experimental group (those assigned to intensive supervision). If we detect differences in outcome measures between the experimental and control groups (say, arrests within a year after release), we will not know how much of the difference is due to intensive supervision and how much might be due to the midstream change of adding urine tests.

Summing Up the Limits of Randomized Designs   Randomized experiments therefore require that certain conditions be met. Staff responsible for program delivery must accept random assignment and further agree to minimize exceptions to randomization. Case flow must be adequate to produce enough subjects in each group so that statistical tests will be able to detect significant differences in outcome measures. Finally, experimental interventions must be consistently applied to treatment groups and withheld from control groups.

These conditions, and the problems that may result if they are not met, can be summarized as two overriding concerns in field experiments: (1) equivalence between experimental and control groups before an intervention, and (2) the ability to detect differences in outcome measures after an intervention is introduced. If there are too many exceptions to random assignment, experimental and control groups may not be equivalent. If there are too few cases, or inconsistencies in administering a treatment, or treatment spillovers to control subjects, outcome measures may be affected in such a way that researchers cannot detect the effects of an intervention.

Although these conditions are related to features of experimental design, more often, they are practical issues in experiments in natural settings. David Weisburd and associates (Weisburd, Petrosino, and Mason, 1993) tie many of these issues together by noting something of a paradox. In efforts to gain more precise estimates of treatment effects, researchers commonly increase the size of experimental treatment and control groups. But having larger groups makes experiments more difficult to manage. This, in turn, introduces treatment inconsistencies and other errors that negate the sought-after advantage of a larger sample size.

Let's now look at an example that illustrates both the strengths of random experiments and constraints on their use in criminal justice program evaluations.

Home Detention: Two Randomized Studies

Terry Baumer and Robert Mendelsohn conducted two random experiments to evaluate programs that combine home detention with electronic monitoring (ELMO). In earlier chapters, we examined how different features of these studies illustrated measurement principles; here, our focus is on the mechanics of random assignment and program delivery.

In their first study, Baumer and Mendelsohn evaluated a program that targeted adult offenders convicted of nonviolent misdemeanor and minor felony offenses (Baumer and Mendelsohn, 1990; also summarized in Baumer, Maxfield, and Mendelsohn, 1993). The goal of the program was to provide supervision of offend-

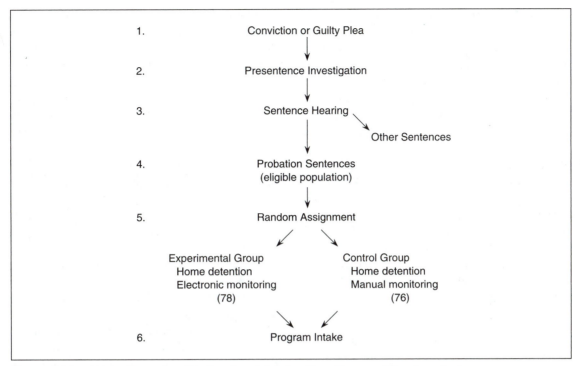

Figure 12.3   Home Detention for Convicted Adults: Case Flow and Random Assignment

ers that was more enhanced than traditional probation but less restrictive and less costly than incarceration. Several measures of outcomes and program delivery were examined, as we have described in earlier chapters.

Baumer and Mendelsohn selected a randomized posttest-only design, in which the target population was offenders sentenced to probation. Subjects were randomly assigned to an experimental group in which the treatment was electronically monitored home detention or to a control group sentenced to home detention without electronic monitoring. Figure 12.3 summarizes case flow into the evaluation experiment. After a guilty plea or trial conviction, probation office staff reviewed offenders' backgrounds and criminal records for the purpose of recommending an appropriate sentence. The next step was a hearing, at which sentences are imposed by a criminal court judge.

Persons sentenced to probation were eligible for inclusion in the experiment. Their case files

were forwarded to staff in the community corrections agency responsible for administering the home detention programs. On receiving an eligible case file, community corrections staff telephoned the evaluation researchers, who, having prepared a random list of case numbers, assigned subjects to either the treatment or control group. Subject to two constraints, this process produced 78 treatment subjects and 76 control subjects.

Thinking back on our consideration of ethics in Chapter 3, you should be able to think of one constraint: informed consent. Researchers and program staff explained the evaluation project to subjects and obtained their consent to participate in the experiment. Those who declined to participate in the evaluation study could nevertheless be assigned to home detention as a condition of their probation. The second constraint was made necessary by the technology of electronic monitoring: Subjects could not be kept in the treatment group if they did not have a telephone that could be connected to the electronic monitoring equipment.

Notice that random assignment was made after sentencing. Baumer and Mendelsohn began their evaluation by randomizing subjects between stages 2 and 3 in Figure 12.3. This produced problems because judges occasionally overruled presentence investigation recommendations to probation, thus overriding random assignment. After detecting this problem, Baumer and Mendelsohn (1990:27–29) moved randomization "downstream," so that judicial decisions could not contaminate the selection process.

Baumer and Mendelsohn (1990:26) obtained agreement from community corrections staff, prosecutors, and judges to use random assignment by getting all parties to accept an assumption of "no difference":

> That is, in the absence of convincing evidence to the contrary, they were willing to assume that there was no difference between the . . . methods of monitoring. This allowed the prosecutor to negotiate and judges to assign home detention as a condition of probation only, while permitting the community corrections agency to make the monitoring decision.

Convinced of the importance of random assignment, the community corrections agency "delegated" to researchers the responsibility for making the monitoring decision, a "decision" that was randomized.

In this example, the experimental condition—electronic monitoring—was readily distinguished from the control condition, home detention without electronic monitoring. There was no possibility of treatment spillover; control subjects could not unintentionally receive some level of electronic monitoring because they had neither the bracelet nor the home-base unit that embodied the treatment. Electronic monitoring could therefore be readily delivered to subjects in the experimental group and withheld from control subjects. This treatment was not necessarily consistent, however.

The second ELMO evaluation conducted by Baumer and Mendelsohn reveals how program delivery problems can undermine the strengths of random assignment (Baumer, Maxfield, and Mendelsohn, 1993). In their study of juvenile burglars, they used similar procedures for randomization, but eligible subjects were placed in one of four groups, as illustrated in this table:

Electronic Monitoring?

Police Visits?	No	Yes
No	C	E1
Yes	E2	E3

Juvenile burglars could be randomly assigned to three possible treatments: electronic monitoring only (E1), police visits to their home after school only (E2), or electronic monitoring and police visits (E3). Subjects in the control group (c) were sentenced to home detention only. As in the adult study, outcome measures included arrests after release.

Although there were no problems with random assignment, inconsistencies in the delivery of each of the two experimental treatments produced uninterpretable results (Maxfield and Baumer, 1991:5):

> Observations of day-to-day program operations revealed that, compared with the adult program, the juvenile court and cooperating agencies paid less attention to delivering program elements and using information from . . . the electronic monitoring equipment. Staff were less well-trained in operating the electronic monitoring equipment, and police visits were inconsistent.

The box titled "Home Detention" in Chapter 1 elaborates on differences in the operation of these two programs and a third ELMO program for pretrial defendants. However, the lesson from these studies bears repeating here: *Randomization does not control for variation in treatment integrity and program delivery.*

Randomized experiments can be powerful tools in criminal justice program evaluations.

At the same time, it is often impossible to maintain the desired level of control over experimental conditions. This is especially true for complex interventions that may change while an evaluation is under way. Experimental conditions are also difficult to maintain when different organizations work together in delivering some service—a community-based drug treatment provider coupled with intensive probation, for example.

Largely because of such problems, evaluation researchers are increasingly turning to other types of designs that are less "fragile"—less subject to problems if rigorous experimental conditions cannot be maintained.

Quasi-Experimental Designs

Quasi-experiments are distinguished from "true" experiments by the lack of random assignment of subjects to an experimental and a control group. Random assignment of subjects is often impossible in criminal justice evaluations. Rather than forgo evaluation altogether in such instances, it is usually possible to create and execute research designs that will permit evaluation of the program in question.

Quasi-experiments may also be "nested" into experimental designs as backups should one or more of the requisites for a true experiment break down. For example, Michael Dennis (1990) describes how a time-series design was nested into a series of random experiments to evaluate enhanced drug abuse counseling. In the event that case flow is inadequate or random assignment to enhanced or standard counseling regimes breaks down, the nested time-series design will salvage a quasi-experiment.

We considered different classes of quasi-experimental designs—nonequivalent groups, cohorts, and time series—in Chapter 7, together with examples of each type. Each of these designs has been used extensively in criminal justice evaluation research.

Ex Post Evaluations Often, a researcher or public official may decide to conduct an evaluation sometime after an experimental program has gone into effect. These so-called ex post evaluations (Rossi, Freeman, and Lipsey, 1999: 312) are not usually amenable to random assignment after the fact. For example, if a new job-skills training program is introduced in a state correctional facility, an ex post evaluation might compare rates of employment among released inmates with similar outcome measures for a matched comparison institution. Or an interrupted time-series design might examine records of alcohol-related accidents before and after a new law that allows administrative suspension of driver's licenses to take effect.

Full-Coverage Programs Interventions such as new national or statewide laws are examples of full-coverage programs in which it is not possible to identify subjects who are not exposed to the intervention, let alone randomly assign persons to receive or not receive the treatment. Quasi-experimental designs may be the strongest possible approach for evaluating such programs. Statewide sentencing guidelines and mandatory minimum sentences are common examples of full-coverage interventions.

Larger Treatment Units Similarly, some experimental interventions may be designed to affect all persons in some larger unit—a neighborhood crime prevention program, for example. It is not possible to randomly assign some neighborhoods to receive the intervention while withholding it from others. Nor is it possible to control which individuals in a neighborhood are exposed to the intervention.

Different types of quasi-experimental designs can be used in such cases. For example, in a Kansas City program to reduce gun violence, police targeted extra patrols at gun crime "hot spots" (Sherman, Shaw and Rogan, 1995). Some beats were assigned to receive the extra patrols, while comparison beats—selected for their similar frequency of gun crimes—did not get the special patrols. Several outcome measures were compared for the two types of areas. After 29 weeks, gun seizures in the target area increased by more than 65 percent and gun crimes dropped by 49 percent. There were no significant changes in either gun crimes or gun seizures in the comparison beat. Drive-by shootings dropped from 7 to 1 in the target area and increased from 6 to 12 in the comparison area. Homicides declined in the target area but not in the comparison area. Citizen surveys showed less fear of crime and more positive feelings about the neighborhood in the target area than in the comparison area.

Nonequivalent-Groups Designs   As we saw in Chapter 7, quasi-experimental designs lack the built-in controls for selection bias and other threats to internal validity. Nonequivalent-groups designs, by definition, cannot be assumed to include treatment and comparison subjects who are statistically equivalent. For this reason, quasi-experimental program evaluations must be carefully designed and analyzed to rule out possible validity problems.

For evaluation designs that use nonequivalent groups, attention should be devoted to constructing experimental and comparison groups that are as similar as possible on important variables that might account for differences in outcome measures. Rossi and associates (1999) caution that procedures for constructing such groups should be grounded in a theoretical understanding of what individual and group characteristics might confound evaluation results. In a study of recidivism by participants in shock incarceration programs, for example, we certainly want to ensure that equal numbers of men and women are included in groups assigned to shock incarceration and groups that received some other sentence. Alternatively, we can restrict our analysis of program effects to only men or only women.

Time-Series Designs   Interrupted time-series designs require attention to different issues because researchers cannot normally control how reliably the experimental treatment is actually implemented. Foremost among these issues are instrumentation, history, and construct validity. In many interrupted time-series designs, conclusions about whether an intervention produced change in some outcome measure rely on simple indicators that represent complex causal processes.

In their evaluation of a Washington, DC, gun control law Colin Loftin and associates (Loftin, McDowall, Wiersema, and Cottey, 1991) examined changes in public health records of death by homicide and suicide. These indicators represented complex processes, including motivation, situational factors, and the presence of other persons who might have prevented a murder or suicide, in addition to the primary concept of interest to the authors—weapon availability. The authors could not control for differences in the circumstances surrounding homicides and suicides. With regard to the gun control law's impact, they concluded that declines in gun-related deaths were not produced by outside factors.

Understanding the causal process that produces measures used in time-series analysis is crucial for interpreting results. Such understanding can come in two related ways. First, we should have a sound conceptual grasp of the underlying causal forces at work in the process we are interested in. Second, we should understand how the indicators used in any time-series analysis are produced.

Patricia Mayhew and associates (Mayhew, Clarke, and Elliott, 1989) concluded that laws requiring motorcycle riders to wear helmets produced a reduction in motorcycle theft. This might seem puzzling until we consider the causal constructs involved in stealing motorcycles. Assuming that most motorcycle thefts are crimes of opportunity, Mayhew and associates argue that few impulsive thieves stroll about carrying helmets. Even thieves are sufficiently rational to recognize that a helmetless motorcycle rider will be unacceptably conspicuous—an insight that deters them from stealing motorcycles. Mayhew and colleagues considered displacement as an alternative explanation for the decline in motorcycle theft, but they found no evidence that declines in motorcycle theft were accompanied by increases in either stolen cars or bicycles. By systematically thinking through the causal process of motorcycle theft, Mayhew and associates were able to conclude that helmet laws were unintentionally effective in reducing theft.

Situational Crime Prevention We conclude our examination of quasi-experimental evaluations by briefly describing certain crime prevention studies that have readily used such designs. In earlier chapters, we outlined the general rationale of situational crime prevention. Carefully considering the interaction between offender motivations and the situations that facilitate different types of crime can reveal approaches to reducing crime opportunities. The motorcycle theft study by Mayhew and colleagues is an example of situational crime prevention, albeit unintentional. Ronald Clarke's (1997a) evaluation of caller ID as a way to reduce obscene phone calls, described in Chapter 7, is another example. The periodical *Crime Prevention Studies* includes several examples of quasi-experimental evaluations based on the theoretical foundations of situational crime prevention.

One of these is a nonequivalent-groups quasi-experiment conducted by David Farrington and associates (1993) to evaluate different approaches to preventing shoplifting. The experiment was carried out in nine electronics stores operated in England by the same retail chain. Stores were placed in one of four groups, created by matching the stores on three characteristics: physical size, sales volume, and type of location. Three experimental interventions to prevent shoplifting were tested: (1) physical redesign of store layout to reduce opportunities for shoplifting, (2) electronic tagging of items so that they would trigger sensors at the exit to each shop, and (3) uniformed guards posted at store entrances. In addition, one store in three of the four groups served as a comparison site, where no new measures to prevent shoplifting were introduced.

The outcome measure was based on a system whereby labels were placed on certain small items thought to be frequently stolen: audiotapes, videotapes, stereo headphones, and photographic film. Each item was fixed with a sticky

Table 12.3 Situational Crime Prevention of Shoplifting

	Percentage of Items Stolen		
	Pretest	**Posttest 1**	**Posttest 2**
Group A			
Store 1 (R)	36.5	15.2	27.1
Store 2 (T)	30.8	7.3	4.4
Group B			
Store 3 (T)	17.3	1.4	5.5
Store 4 (G)	10.7	5.8	8.8
Store 5 (C)	15.3	10.4	NA
Group C			
Store 6 (C)	15.4	21.5	15.0
Store 7 (G)	6.9	8.1	18.6
Group D			
Store 8 (R)	24.4	5.0	NA
Store 9 (C)	13.6	29.6	22.0

Note: Experimental treatments: R = store redesign; T = electronic tagging; G = security guard; C = comparison.

Source: Adapted from Farrington and associates (1993:108).

label that sales clerks were to remove whenever an item was sold. The total number of labeled items before a store opened for the day was known. Comparing this total with the number of labels accumulated by clerks and the number of items remaining in each store at day's end yielded a count of missing items. Pretest measures were obtained for each store over a 3-day period. Two posttest measures were made at most sites, 1 week and 4 weeks after introducing prevention measures. Table 12.3 summarizes the grouping of stores with experimental treatments and the results of the evaluation. The figures in this table represent the number of missing tags as a percentage of all items that left the store (sold or stolen).

Notice first the different mixes of stores and experimental treatments. The four groupings of stores reflect within-group similarities and between-group differences in matching criteria. The experimental and control conditions across stores in different groups were mixed to compare prevention effectiveness with store characteristics.

Although we have omitted tests of statistical significance from Table 12.3, some interesting patterns are evident in the results. Electronic tagging (stores 2 and 3) reduced shoplifting in both the 1- and 4-week posttests. Store redesign was effective only in the first posttest (store 1); a second posttest showed an increase in shoplifting, which suggests that thieves learned to adapt to the new layout (only one posttest was conducted in the other redesign site, store 8). Uniformed guards (stores 4 and 7) had no consistent impact on shoplifting. Shoplifting in the three comparison sites (stores 5, 6, and 9) either increased or declined less than it did in matched experimental sites.

Several features of this evaluation warrant comment. First, randomization was not possible because the experimental treatment was delivered to a small number of large units—electronics stores. Second, Farrington and associates used matching criteria that could reasonably be expected to affect shoplifting rates. A related point is that all sites were franchise stores owned by the same large chain, which minimized differences in inventory mixes, management procedures, and the like. Third, the three experimental conditions were mixed and tested in different groups of matched stores. This produced a stronger test of the relative effectiveness of different prevention measures.

Finally, consider for a moment the degree of cooperation required between researchers and evaluation clients. On the one hand, Farrington and colleagues required some effort from store staff in collecting and counting tagged items, not to mention implementing different crime prevention measures. On the other hand, you should also see the potential benefits to retail stores from this quasi-experiment to determine what works in preventing shoplifting.

Other Types of Evaluation Studies

Earlier in this chapter, we noted how process evaluations are distinct from impact assessments. Whereas the latter seek answers to questions about program effects, process evaluations monitor program implementation, asking whether programs are being delivered as intended.

Process evaluations can be invaluable aids in interpreting results from an impact assessment. We described how Baumer and Mendelsohn were better able to understand outcome measures in their evaluation of ELMO for juvenile burglars because they had monitored program delivery. Similarly, Petersilia (1989) notes the importance of process evaluation in monitoring levels of intensive supervision that were actually delivered to probationers. Without a process evaluation, information about program implementation cannot be linked to outcome measures.

Process evaluations can also be useful for criminal justice officials whose responsibility centers more on the performance of particular tasks than on the overall success of some program. For example, police patrol officers are collectively responsible for public safety in their beat, but their routine actions focus more on performing specific tasks such as responding to a call for service or, in community policing, diagnosing the concerns of neighborhood residents. Police supervisors are attentive to traffic tickets written, arrests made, and complaints against individual officers. Probation and parole officers are, of course, interested in the ultimate performance of their clients, but they are also task-oriented in their use of records to keep track of client contacts, attendance at substance abuse sessions, or job performance. Process evaluations center on measures of task performance—on the assumption that tasks are linked to program outcomes. So process evaluations can be valuable in their own right, as well as important for diagnosing measures of program effects.

Policy Analysis and Scientific Realism

Policy analysis, coupled with scientific realism, helps public officials use research to select and assess alternative courses of action.

Program evaluation differs from policy analysis with respect to the time dimension and where each activity takes place in the policy process.

Policy analysis is used to help design alternative courses of action and choose among them. Because of this, policy analysis is a more future-oriented activity that frequently produces *predictions,* whereas most evaluation studies produce *explanations.*

In reality, the distinction between these two types of applied research is not quite so clear. Similar types of research methods are used to address policy analysis questions (What would happen?) as are brought to bear on program evaluation questions (What did happen?). Consider, for example, a definition of policy analysis from a prominent text: "Attempting to bring modern science and technology to bear on society's problems, policy analysis searches for feasible courses of action, generating information and marshalling evidence of the benefits and other consequences that would follow their adoption and implementation" (Quade, 1989:4). Except for the form of the verb— "would follow"—this is not too different from the way we defined program evaluation.

Results from program evaluations are frequently considered in choosing among future courses of action. Policy analysis depends just as much on clearly specifying goals and objectives as does program evaluation. As a result, the achievement of goals and objectives worked out through policy analysis can be tested through program evaluation. Measurement is also a fundamental concern in both types of applied studies. Let's consider an example of policy analysis to illustrate its similarities to and differences from program evaluation.

Modeling Prison Populations

Growth in state and federal prison populations in the 1980s and 1990s caught many public officials only partly by surprise. For years, researchers like Alfred Blumstein (1988; Blumstein, Cohen, and Miller, 1980) have used mathematical models to forecast future prison populations.

More importantly, such models permit corrections officials and others to frame and answer *what if* questions about future prison pop-ulations. For example, what will be the estimated impact on the number of juveniles in custody if sanctions for juvenile offenders are increased? Or what will happen if a larger proportion of arrested persons have prior felony convictions and therefore must be sentenced to prison under state law? Or will growth in the juvenile population of a state increase pressure on prison crowding over the next 10 years? Researchers and public officials alike have become especially concerned about the impact of changes in juvenile justice policy.

Although the mathematics of modeling juvenile and adult correctional populations can seem intimidating, the principles are relatively straightforward. Our consideration of these principles will draw heavily on prison population models developed in three states: the Pennsylvania model described by Blumstein and associates (1980); a model used by researchers in the New York State Division of Criminal Justice Services, Office of Policy Analysis, Research, and Statistical Services (Greenstein, van Alstyne, and Frederick, 1986); and a series of reports issued by the Texas Criminal Justice Policy Council (Criminal Justice Policy Council, 1996, 2003).

In all cases, population projections are based on data that represent the demographic structure of a state's population, arrest rates broken down by demographic groups, conviction and incarceration rates broken down by groupings of offenses, and functions that represent specific sentences for different offenses. Models are first developed, or "initialized," using current population data and past information about criminal justice processing—arrest, conviction, and incarceration rates.

Figure 12.4 summarizes components of the model used in New York State; it shows the flow of persons from arrest through incarceration. The stages labeled "Arrest Rates," "Probability of Conviction," and "Probability of Prison Sentence" are based on past cases. The latter two are computed from past data that represent the percentage of arrested defendants who are convicted and the percentage of convicted offenders who are sentenced to prison.

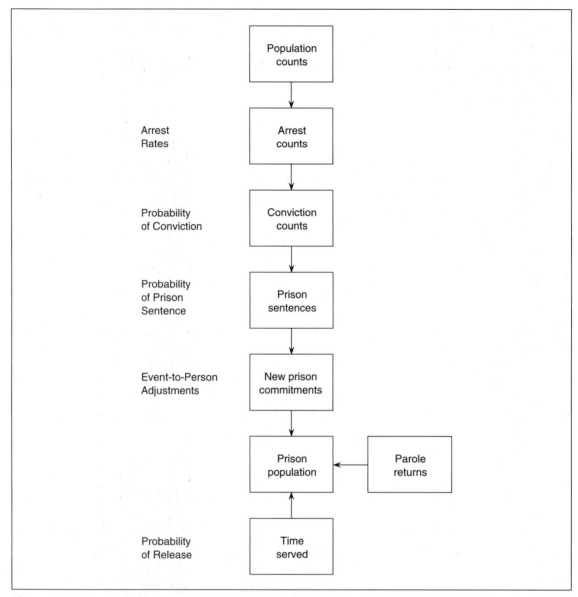

Figure 12.4   Process that Generates a Prison Population
Source: Adapted from Greenstein, van Alstyne, and Frederick (1986:7).

Two other general features of the figure item labeled "New prison commitments" are important. First, commitments are adjusted to include past information on sentence length, a factor that obviously affects prison population. Second, a further adjustment is required because of an especially vexing characteristic of criminal justice enforcement and prosecution.

As we saw in the Chapter 11 box "How Many Parole Violators Were There Last Month?" it's sometimes hard to figure out what to count. People are arrested and prosecuted, but individuals may be charged with and convicted of more than one offense and more than one count for each offense, or more than one offender might be arrested in a single arrest event.

Consider, for example, an armed robbery in which two offenders rob three victims; one victim is struck in the face with a handgun by offender 1, and another is shot and seriously injured by offender 2. Both offenders are arrested the next day when they attempt to buy cocaine from an undercover police officer. This single arrest event could produce two defendants, each of whom faces three counts of robbery and one or more counts of weapon use while committing a felony. Defendant 1 is charged with aggravated assault, and defendant 2 with attempted murder; both also face drug charges; and each has a prior felony conviction that precludes legal handgun ownership. The stage labeled "Event-to-Person Adjustments" in Figure 12.4 reflects the complicated relationships among arrest events, defendants, offenses, counts, and charges that must be taken into account in forecasting prison populations, which are, of course, based on numbers of people. In this case, the number of sentences is adjusted to predict the number of people who will be admitted and the approximate number of years they will serve for each sentence.

The next component of prison population models is an estimate of demographic change. As Blumstein and associates (1980:8) pointed out, changes in demographic composition are based on three social processes: births, deaths, and migration. A state's population change depends on fertility, mortality, and people moving into and out of the state. Fortunately, these social processes are readily modeled, and demographic projections are relatively reliable. Because arrest rates vary by age, gender, and race, prison population forecasts almost always disaggregate demographic projections into groups based on these three characteristics. Data from the National Planning Association were used to predict New York's population, while Texas analysts used population estimates from the state comptroller's office.

One final category of information is needed. Prison population is a function of intake, length of stay, and exits. We have considered the complex process of estimating intake and sen-

tence length; the latter represents an estimate of exits. Because both New York and Texas used some form of parole system, state models incorporate past data on the proportion of inmates paroled to estimate exits.

To summarize, here are the pieces needed to project correctional populations: (1) predictions of future state population, broken down by age, gender, and race; (2) past data on arrest rates for each demographic group, broken down by type of crime; (3) past data on conviction rates for persons arrested in each crime group; (4) past data on incarceration rates and imposed sentence length for persons convicted in each crime group; and (5) past data on parole release rates. Having entered all of these data into a computer and specified the relationships among all components, let's look at some actual projections.

Figure 12.5 presents the model used by Texas to forecast juvenile justice populations (Criminal Justice Policy Council, 1998, 2003). Because we described such models as being most useful as tools for assessing *what if* questions, Figure 12.5 shows projections made at different times over a 2-year period.

We see that the overall trend was for the number of incarcerated youths in Texas to increase, but variations in the three projections reflect changes in circumstances when the estimates were made. For example, the first projection, made in 1996, assumed a 2 percent growth rate in the Texas population ages 10–16. However, two types of legislative changes forced a revision in these estimates. First, increased penalties for a variety of offenses meant that the number of new commitments to juvenile facilities was expected to increase by 15 percent. Second, because sentence length was also increased, the increased numbers of juveniles sentenced to incarceration were sentenced for longer terms.

Thus, three factors combined to produce a projected 75 percent increase in incarcerated juveniles from 1997 through 2002: (1) a very small increase in the size of the juvenile population, (2) a modest increase in the number of offenses that called for incarceration, and (3) a modest

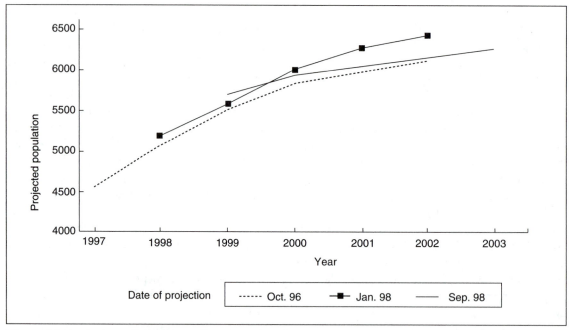

Figure 12.5   Projected Texas Juvenile Justice Population
Source: Adapted from Criminal Justice Policy Council (1998, 2003).

increase in the length of sentences for different offenses. The scientific projection of populations in correctional custody thus involved more than merely figuring out how many juveniles there would be in Texas. How the law affected juvenile offenders had a greater impact. Policy analysis in the form of population projections enabled Texas legislators to consider that expected impact in advance.

Prison population models are clearly useful tools for policy makers. Of course, the accuracy of forecasts diminishes the farther into the future they attempt to project, because intentional or unintentional policy changes may alter the flow of persons through courts to prison. In practice, the conditional probability estimates that form the core of projection models are regularly updated to reflect changes in arrest, conviction, and incarceration rates.

Other Applications of Policy Analysis

In recent years, growing numbers of justice agencies, especially police and sheriff's departments, have taken advantage of rapid advances in computing and telecommunications. Crime analysis used to be restricted primarily to studying pin maps. Computerized mapping systems now permit police to monitor changes in crime patterns on a daily or hourly basis and to develop responses accordingly. Furthermore, simultaneous advances in computing power and declines in the cost of that power make it possible for even small agencies to use mapping tools (Harries, 1999). The ongoing technological advances in mapping have fueled the application of statistical models to geographic clusters of crime problems. Thomas Rich (1999) describes this as analytic mapping, whereby statistical tools supplement the "eyeballing" approach to locating concentrations of crime.

Recent developments include animated maps that combine data about location and time of incidents (Ratcliffe, 2002). Imagine (required, because this printed text has neither color nor animation) a city map on which, over the course of a 24-hour day, hot spots emerge in different areas at different times of day. Let's place you in this hypothetical picture.

Problem-Solving Questions	Evaluation Questions
Scanning	
What is the problem?	How should the problem be measured?
Analysis	
How big is the problem?	How big is the problem?
Who is involved? How?	Who is involved? How?
Where is the problem? Why?	Where is the problem? Why?
Response	
What should be done?	How will accountability be determined?
Who should do it? How?	How will problem changes be measured?
	How will alternative causes be assessed?
Assessment	
Did the response occur as planned?	Did the response occur as planned? (process evaluation)
Did the problem decline?	Did the problem decline? (impact assessment)
What should be done next?	If the problem declined, can alternative causes be ruled out?

Figure 12.6   Problem Solving and Evaluation
Source: Adapted from Eck (2003:6).

You wake up to find that your car, which you parked in your apartment lot the night before, has been broken into. Your break-in becomes part of a 7:00 A.M. hot spot in apartment parking lots, reflecting a pattern of such thefts in recent weeks. You arrive at work a couple of hours later to discover an overnight commercial burglary, adding to a 9:00 A.M. downtown hot spot, as workers discover overnight break-ins when they open up for the day. In this worst of all possible days, you return home to discover that the mailbox of your building has been trashed, thus producing a 6:00 P.M. burglary hot spot in a residential neighborhood.

Though it's unlikely that all such misfortunes will affect one person in one day, this scenario reflects the time/space regularities of different offenses. New computing and mapping tools expand the smaller-scale policy analysis capabilities of police departments. Another way to combine space/time analysis of hot spots might involve tracing monthly changes over a few years to show how new buildings or parking lots produce new hot spots or cause reported crime to shift to different locations within a metropolitan area (Wartell and Mielke, 2003).

Recall that we considered some of the differences between incident-based police data and

traditional summary reports in Chapter 6. One of the most important advantages of incident-based data is the potential for use in the kind of policy analysis we have described. Most crime-mapping and similar tools are developed and used by individual departments, reflecting the fact that crime analysis is based on locally generated data. With incident-based reporting, crime analysis can be conducted on larger units. For example, Donald Faggiani and Colleen McLaughlin (1999) describe how National Incident Based Reporting System (NIBRS) data can show state or regional patterns in drug arrests and offenses. Using NIBRS data for Virginia, the authors demonstrate differences in types of arrests and drugs for different areas of the state.

Problem solving is a policy analysis tool that has long been associated with policing. Problem solving involves four analytic steps; scanning, analysis, response, and assessment (SARA) (Eck and Spelman, 1987). Consider how problem-solving approaches to policing merge the application of problem analysis and assessment of the effects of interventions. Figure 12.6 is adapted from John Eck's (2003) guidebook for police analysts and line officers. It shows how the four principal steps of problem solving relate to key evaluation questions. In this figure, the column labeled "Problem-Solving Questions" signifies policy analysis activities.

Notice first that problem solving begins with a diagnosis of the problem (scanning and analysis), then shifts to devising appropriate responses, and eventually evaluates them (assessment). Notice also how some questions are identical across the problem-solving and evaluation dimensions. This indicates that both applied research activities depend on problem diagnosis and measurement. The two activities differ primarily in that policy analysis focuses on planning responses whereas evaluation focuses on assessing impact. But good policy analysis also includes assessment, and evaluation is best conducted on carefully planned policies. The two activities are usually complementary in this way.

Partly because it has proved helpful in law enforcement applications, problem solving is being adopted by other criminal justice agencies. For example, Veronica Coleman and associates (Coleman, Holton, Olson, Robinson, and Stewart, 1999) describe how local and federal prosecutors in several U.S. cities have formed planning teams to identify crime problems and develop appropriate interventions. Teams include U.S. attorneys, researchers, and other criminal justice professionals who pursue a form of policy analysis labeled Strategic Approaches to Community Safety Initiatives (SACSI). SACSI involves five steps, four of which should look familiar (Coleman et al., 1999:18):

1. Form an interagency working group.
2. Gather information and data about a local crime problem.
3. Design a strategic intervention to tackle the problem.
4. Implement the intervention.
5. Assess and modify the strategy as the data reveal effects.

We have only scratched the surface of policy analysis applications in criminal justice. This is an area of applied research that is growing daily.

Other examples draw on methods of systems analysis, operations research, and economics for such purposes as cost–benefit studies, police patrol allocation, and decisions about hiring probation officers. Cost–benefit analysis, in particular, is used to assess the relative value and expense of alternative policies. Although the mathematical tools that form the base of policy analysis can be sophisticated, the underlying logic is relatively simple.

For example, police departments traditionally used pin maps to represent the spatial and temporal concentrations of reported crime. This example of "low-tech" policy analysis is conceptually identical to computer models of hot spots used in many departments to plan police deployment.

Scientific Realism and Applied Research

Traditional research and evaluation are based on the model of cause and effect we considered in Chapters 4 and 7. An independent variable (cause) produces some change in a dependent variable (effect). Experimental and quasi-experimental designs seek to isolate this causal process from the possible effects of intervening variables. Designs thus try to control for the possible effects of intervening variables.

Situational crime prevention and problem solving represent a bridge between traditional research approaches and applied research that is the foundation of scientific realism. Ray Pawson and Nick Tilley (1997) propose that, instead of trying to explain cause in a traditional sense, evaluators should search for mechanisms acting in context to explain outcomes. As we have seen, experiments do this by producing pretest statistical equivalence between groups of subjects who receive an intervention and groups of subjects who do not. Quasi-experiments using nonequivalent groups seek to control intervening variables by, for example, holding possible intervening variables constant. So, for example, if we believe that employment status might be an intervening variable in the relationship between arrest and subsequent domestic violence, we will try to structure an evaluation to hold employment status constant between treatment and control groups.

Scientific realism treats employment status as the *context* in which an arrest *mechanism* operates on the *outcome* of repeat domestic violence. Rather than try to control for employment status, a scientific realist will study the mechanism in context and conclude, for example, that arrest is effective in reducing subsequent violence in situations in which an offender is employed but is not effective when the offender is unemployed. This finding will be no different from what Sherman (1992) concludes in his assessment of a series of randomized experiments.

What is different is that the scientific realist approach is rooted in the principle that similar interventions can naturally be expected to have different outcomes in different contexts. Most notably, this approach is more compatible with the realities of evaluation than is the experimental approach. Pawson and Tilley (1997:81) put it this way: "Ultimately, realist evaluation would be *mechanism-* and *context-driven* rather than program-led" (emphasis in original). This means that interventions should be designed not so much as comprehensive programs that apply equally in all situations. Instead, interventions should be developed for specific contexts, and evaluations of those interventions must consider context as a key factor in whether the intervention achieves the desired outcome.

Situational crime prevention (Clarke, 1997b) is an example of the scientific realist approach that bridges policy analysis and evaluation because it focuses on what mechanisms operate for highly specific types of crime in specific situations. So, for example, rather than develop and evaluate large-scale programs intended to reduce auto theft generally, situational crime prevention seeks specific interventions that will be effective in reducing particular types of auto theft. Ronald Clarke and Patricia Harris (1992) distinguish several types of auto theft by their purposes: joyriding, temporary transportation,

resale or stripping, or insurance fraud. Theft of certain models for joyriding may be reduced by modest increases in security, while theft of expensive cars for resale or export requires different approaches. And many types of auto theft can be reduced by placing attendants at the exits of parking garages, but car break-ins may not be affected by that intervention.

As we mentioned in Chapter 7, the realist approach resembles a case-study approach. Both are *variable-oriented* strategies for research—they depend on measures of many variables to understand and assess a small number of cases. Detailed data and information are gathered about specific interventions, often in very small areas. Whereas an experimental evaluation uses probability theory to control for intervening variables, the case-study approach depends on detailed knowledge to understand the context in which mechanisms operate.

In his discussion of applied research tools for problem solving, Eck (2002, 2003) makes the case even more strongly. Public officials, he argues, are more interested in solving local problems than in identifying robust cause-and-effect relationships. As Figure 12.6 shows, both problem solving and evaluation are concerned with answering the question "Did the problem decline?" But eliminating alternative explanations for a decline, which is the central concern of internal validity and the rationale for stronger evaluation designs, is important only if officials wish to use the same intervention elsewhere.

In what Eck terms "small-claim, small-area problem solving," analysts develop appropriate interventions for problems in context. This is the essence of the problem-solving process. Like Eck, we emphasize *process*—systematically studying a problem, developing appropriate interventions, and seeing if those interventions have the intended effect. This is quite different from what Eck terms "large-claim interventions"—such as Drug Abuse Resistance Education (D.A.R.E.) or corrections boot camps—that are developed to apply in a wide variety of

PUTTING IT ALL TOGETHER

APPLIED RESEARCH IN THE NYPD

In many respects, applied research was the foundation when the New York City Police Department decided to make basic changes in how it operated. NYPD managers began to more deliberately use information about crime to direct the actions of patrol officers and staff in special units. Former Commissioner William Bratton (1999:15) sums it up this way: "Four . . . principles now guide the department's patrol and investigative work: timely, accurate intelligence; rapid deployment; effective tactics; and relentless follow-up and assessment." If we compare these principles with the process of problem solving discussed in this chapter, we can see that both policy analysis and pro-

gram evaluation are evident, though not in the kind of formal way we have considered. Let's look more closely at the tools of applied research used by the NYPD.

First, *timely intelligence* refers to measures of crime and police activity compiled for department managers on a weekly basis. Such measures are included in a Compstat report for each of the city's 76 precincts. The weekly reports are printed on two sides of one sheet of paper that is headed with a photograph of the precinct commander to symbolize her or his accountability for the week's activity. Reports summarizing data for the previous week are distributed each Monday to precinct commanders and department managers. Then, usually twice a week, the department's top commanders convene Compstat meetings in a high-tech command room at police headquarters. In addition to the data sheets previously distributed,

settings. Because small-claim, small-scale interventions are tailored to highly specific settings, they cannot easily be transferred intact to different settings. However, the *process* of diagnosing local problems, selecting appropriate interventions, and then assessing the effects of those interventions can be generally applied. Anthony Braga (2002) offers more examples of this reasoning. Gloria Laycock presents an even stronger case for scientific realism in applied criminal justice research generally (2002) and in making specific plans for crime prevention (Tilley and Laycock, 2002).

We might rightly be skeptical about the generalizability of small-scale evaluations, whether case studies or something else. But the scientific realists respond that generalizability is not really the point. Instead, they urge combining results from a large number of smaller-scale evaluations as an alternative to trying to generalize from a small number of large-scale evaluations. For example, in a series of studies, Terry Baumer and associates (Baumer, Maxfield, and Mendel-

sohn, 1993) found that home detention with electronic monitoring achieved desired outcomes in some situations, but not in others. Aggregating across the three populations studied, the same intervention delivered in the same city produced different results for convicted adults, convicted juveniles, and pretrial adults. Similarly, Paul Ekblom and Ken Pease (1995:625) describe how an intervention to reduce repeat victimization among domestic violence victims appeared to have no effect when postintervention counts of domestic violence incidents were examined. Breaking the simple measure of domestic violence incidents down into subsets of repeat victimizations and new victimizations showed that counts of repeat victims were substantially lower, but this was offset by an increase in first-time victimizations. This makes sense if we think through the theory of action implied by this program.

Whenever possible, randomized or quasi-experimental evaluations should be conducted. But it is important to recognize the formidable

commanders consult computer-generated maps of crime activity that are projected on a huge screen.

Commanders from two to four precincts are scheduled for Compstat participation. In essence, they are held accountable for crime and police activity in their precincts and are expected to report on *rapid deployment* and *tactics*. Department commanders query precinct commanders about what they have done to address crime problems in their precinct. At one Compstat meeting, the department's chief grilled a Brooklyn commander about auto thefts in his precinct. Not satisfied with his response, or with the responses of other precinct commanders in Brooklyn, the chief demanded that commanders come up with a plan to deal with increases in auto thefts. The implication was that precinct commanders would report on progress in addressing the auto theft problem at a future Compstat meeting, illustrating *follow-up* and *assessment*.

This is the surface of Compstat—a formal meeting at the very highest levels of the department at which precinct commanders are held accountable. But the real analysis and evaluation work is less visible, less spectacular, and more routine. Expecting to be grilled at department Compstat meetings several times per year, precinct commanders conduct their own crime analysis to develop their own tactics. Precinct staff consult Compstat data prepared by department analysts, but they are even more dependent on their own data reflecting crime problems in their precinct.

In this way, the expectation (threat?) of having to account for crime and explain actions to department brass has made policy analysis a tool essential to the survival of precinct commanders. Policy analysis and evaluation are ongoing. Each week, precinct staff review data, plan new tactics, and assess the effects of actions previously taken.

requirements for deploying these designs. The scientific realist approach to evaluation is flexible and may be appropriate in many situations. A scientific realist evaluation or case study can be especially useful in smaller-scale evaluations in which interest centers on solving some particular problem in a specific context more than on finding generalizable scientific truths. In any case, a variety of approaches can satisfy the definition of program evaluation we discussed early this chapter, by systematically applying social science research procedures to an individual program or agency.

Our general advice in this regard is simple: Do the best you can. This requires two things: (1) understanding the strengths and limits of social science research procedures, and (2) carefully diagnosing what is needed and what is possible in a particular application. Only by understanding possible methods and program constraints can we properly judge whether any kind of evaluation study is worth undertaking with an experimental, quasi-experimental, or nonexperimental design, or whether an evaluation should not be undertaken at all.

The Political Context of Applied Research

Public policy involves making choices, and that involves politics.

Applied researchers bridge the gap between the body of research knowledge about crime and the practical needs of criminal justice professionals—a process that has potential political, ideological, and ethical problems. In the final section of this chapter, we turn our attention to the context of applied research, describing some of the special problems that can emerge in such studies.

Some similarities are evident between this material and our discussion of ethics in Chapter 3. Although ethics and politics are often closely intertwined, the ethics of criminal justice research focuses on the methods used, whereas political issues are more concerned with the substance and use of research findings. Ethical and political aspects of applied research also differ in that there are no formal codes of accepted political conduct comparable to the codes of ethical conduct we examined earlier. Although some ethical norms have political aspects—for example, not harming subjects relates to protection of civil liberties—no one has developed a set of political norms that can be agreed on by all criminal justice researchers.

Evaluation and Stakeholders

Most applied studies involve multiple stakeholders—people who have some direct or indirect interest in the program or evaluation results (Rossi, Freeman, and Lipsey, 1999:204–5). Some stakeholders may be enthusiastic supporters of an experimental program, others may oppose it, and still others may be neutral. Different stakeholder interests in programs can produce conflicting perspectives on evaluations of those programs.

For example, in their study of pretrial home detention, Maxfield and Baumer (1992) found support for the program in the prosecutor's office and sheriff's department. Each was pleased by the prospect of freeing up jail space. However, decision makers in the community corrections agency, responsible for delivering home detention, were less supportive, expressing concern over the increased workload and fear that too many persons released to pretrial home detention would be bad risks. And some community corrections staff were more worried about the evaluation than the program, feeling that their job performance was under scrutiny. The National Institute of Justice funded the evaluation, hoping that results would document a successful program that could be adopted in other jurisdictions. Community corrections decision makers had a different perspective on the evaluation—they wanted to know what did and did not work.

Emil Posavec and Raymond Carey (1997: 36–40) describe such problems as dysfunctional attitudes toward program evaluation. Program supporters may have unrealistic expectations that evaluation results will document dramatic success. Conversely, they may worry that negative results will lead to program termination. Agency staff may feel that day-to-day experience in delivering a program imparts a qualitative understanding of its success that cannot be documented by a controlled experiment. Staff and other stakeholders may object that an evaluation consumes scarce resources better spent on actually delivering a program.

We have two bits of advice in dealing with such problems. First, identify program stakeholders, their perspectives on the program, and their likely perspectives on the evaluation. In addition to agency decision makers and staff, stakeholders include program beneficiaries and competitors. For example, store owners in a downtown shopping district might benefit from an experimental program to deploy additional police on foot patrol, while people who live in a nearby residential area might argue that additional police should be assigned to their neighborhood.

Second, educate stakeholders about why an evaluation should be conducted. This is best done by explaining that applied research is conducted to determine what works and what does not. The National Institute of Justice and the Bureau of Justice Assistance have issued brief documents that describe how evaluation can benefit criminal justice agencies by rationalizing their actions (Kirchner, Przybylski, and Cardella, 1994; Maxfield, 2001). Such publications, together with examples of completed evaluations, can be valuable tools for winning the support of stakeholders. It may be possible to point to other benefits of evaluation as well. For example, Petersilia (1989:455) describes the generally high levels of support found in the 11 sites conducting experiments on intensive supervision programs: "The project seems to buy local practitioners visibility with the media and local funders, staff enthusiasm (at least initially), and because an outside agency is interested in studying them, added acceptance with their peers."

For an excellent description of the political and logistical problems involved in a complex evaluation that affects multiple stakeholders, see the appendix to Sherman's (1992) book on domestic violence experiments. He presents a detailed report on the process of planning one experiment in Milwaukee, from initial negotiations through project completion.

More generally, recognize that applied research is very much a cooperative venture. Accordingly, researchers and program staff are mutual stakeholders in designing and executing evaluations. Evaluators' interest in a strong design that will meet scientific standards must be balanced against the main concern of program sponsors—obtaining information that is useful for developing public policy.

Among other things, the existence of mutual stakeholders' perspectives implies that applied researchers have obligations to program sponsors, their collaborative partners in evaluation studies.

The flip side of being cautious about getting caught in stakeholder conflict is the benefit of applied research in influencing public policy. Evaluation studies can provide support for continuing or expanding successful criminal justice programs, or evidence that ineffective programs should be modified or terminated. And policy analysis results can sometimes be used to influence actions by public officials. For an example, see the box titled "When Politics Accommodates Facts," in which Tony Fabelo describes how policy analysis dissuaded Texas legislators from costly lawmaking.

Politics and Objectivity

Politics and ideology can color research in ways even more subtle than those described by Fabelo. You may, for example, consider yourself an open-minded and unbiased person who aspires to be an objective criminal justice researcher. However, you may have strong views about different sentencing policies, believing that proba-

tion and restitution are to be preferred over long prison sentences. Because there is no conclusive evidence to favor one approach over the other, your beliefs would be perfectly reasonable.

Now, assume that one of the requirements for the course you are taking is to write a proposal for an evaluation project on corrections policy. In all likelihood, you will prepare a proposal to study a probation program rather than, say, a program on the use of portable jails to provide increased detention capacity. That is natural, and certainly legitimate, but your own policy preferences will affect the topic you chose.

Or let's say that you deplore racism and racial discrimination in any form. Nonetheless, you know from other courses you have taken that African Americans are disproportionately arrested and imprisoned and even stopped for traffic violations more than white motorists. You also know that there is some evidence of higher crime commission rates among African Americans than whites. You will probably reject an explanation that suggests genetic or other biological factors as the causes, believing that one race is not genetically superior to another. But how might you feel about a research project that looks for relationships between genetics and crime? Because genetic differences between races do exist, does this mean that such research is racist? Probably not, as we have described it here, but you should know that in the past decade the U.S. National Institutes of Health canceled conferences to discuss research on the link between genetics and crime because of the racial implications of such research.

Ronald Clarke (1997b:28) describes political objections to applied studies of situational crime prevention: "Conservative politicians regard it as an irrelevant response to the breakdown in morality that has fueled the postwar rise in crime. Those on the left criticize it for neglecting issues of social justice and for being too accepting of the definitions of crime of those in power." By the same token, electronic monitoring is distrusted for being simultaneously too lenient by allowing offenders to do time at

WHEN POLITICS ACCOMMODATES FACTS

by Tony Fabelo
Executive Director, Texas Criminal Justice
Policy Council

The 1994 federal anticrime bill, and related politics emanating from this initiative, put pressure on
the states to adopt certain sentencing policies as
a condition for receiving federal funds. Among
these policies is the adoption of a "three strikes
and you're out" provision establishing a no-parole
sentence for repeat violent offenders. Facts have
prevented a criminal justice operational gridlock
in Texas by delineating to policy makers the operational and fiscal impact of broadly drafted policies in this area. Facts established through policy
analysis by the Criminal Justice Policy Council
(CJPC) have clearly stated that a broad application of the "three strikes and you're out" policy
will have a tremendous fiscal impact.

Therefore, state policy makers have carefully
drafted policies in this area. For example, during
the last legislative session, the adoption of life with
no parole for repeat sex offenders was considered.
State policy makers, after considering facts presented by the CJPC, adopted a policy that narrowly
defined the group of offenders for whom the law is
to apply. They also adopted a 35-year minimum
sentence that must be served before parole eligibility, rather than a life sentence with no parole. The
careful drafting of this policy limited its fiscal impact while still accomplishing the goal of severely
punishing the selected group of sex offenders.

Unlike Texas, politics did not accommodate
facts in California, where lawmakers adopted a

fiscally unsustainable "three strikes and you're
out" policy.

For my part, I need to maintain personal integrity and the integrity of the CJPC in defining the
facts for policy makers. I have to be judged not
only by "objectivity," which is an elusive concept,
but by my judgment in synthesizing complex information for policy makers. To do this, I follow
and ask my staff to follow these rules:

1. Consider as many perspectives as possible in
   synthesizing the meaning of information, including the perspectives of those stakeholders
   who will be affected.
2. State the limits of the facts and identify
   areas where drawing conclusions is clearly
   not possible.
3. Consult with your peers to verify methodological assumptions and meet accepted criteria to
   pass the scrutiny of the scientific community.
4. Provide potential alternative assumptions behind the facts.
5. Set clear expectations for reviewing reports
   and releasing information so that facts are not
   perceived as giving advantage to any particular
   interest group.
6. Judge the bottom-line meaning of the information for policy action based on a frame of
   reference broader than that of any particular
   party or constituency.
7. Finally, if the above are followed, never succumb to political pressure to change your
   judgment. Integrity cannot be compromised
   even once. In the modern crowded market-
   place of information, your audience will judge
   you first for your motives and then for your
   technical expertise.

Source: Adapted from Fabelo (1996:2, 4).

home and too close to a technological nightmare by enabling the government to spy on individuals. Evaluations of situational crime prevention or ELMO programs may be criticized
for tacitly supporting either soft-on-crime or
heavy-handed police state ideologies.

In this sense, it is difficult to claim that criminal justice research, either applied or basic, is

value-free. Our own beliefs and preferences affect the topics we choose to investigate. Political
preferences and ideology may also influence
criminal justice research agendas by making
funds available for some projects but not others. For example, in 1997, the National Institute
of Justice awarded money for projects to study
these topics: "Evaluation of La Bodega de la Fa-

milia: A Family Drug Crisis Center" and "Evaluation of Wisconsin's Residential Substance Abuse Treatment Program for Female State Prisoners." No funds were awarded, however, for such projects as "The Scope of Institutionalized Racism in the War on Drugs" or "Systematic Bias in Sentences for Crack Possession." It is, of course, possible for researchers—consciously or unconsciously—to become instruments for achieving political or policy objectives in applied research.

For instance, the U.S. General Accounting Office (GAO) conducts evaluations of executive branch agencies in order to help Congress exercise its oversight function. Wallace Earl Walker (1985) has argued that GAO staff selectively plan evaluations, choosing agencies that they believe will show evidence of mismanagement. Or evaluators try to steer congressional staff to "request" evaluations that the GAO is eager to conduct.

It may sometimes seem difficult to maintain an acceptable level of objectivity about or distance from evaluation results in criminal justice research. This task can be further complicated if you have strong views one way or another about a particular program or policy. Researchers who evaluate, say, an experimental program to prevent offenders from repeating probably sincerely hope that the program will work. However, substantially less consensus exists about other criminal justice problems and policies. For example, how do you feel about a project to test the effects of restrictive handgun laws or mandatory jail sentences for abortion protesters? We conclude this chapter with one final example that we expect will make you think about some of the political issues involved in applied research.

In 1990, the elected prosecutor of Marion County, Indiana—in which Indianapolis is located—was sharply criticized in a series of newspaper stories that claimed to present evidence of racial disparity in drug sentences handed down in the county. Convicted minority offenders, it was asserted, received longer prison terms than white offenders. The prosecutor immediately responded, criticizing the data collected and methods used by the investigative reporter. He also contacted Maxfield and asked him to conduct an independent analysis of drug cases accepted for prosecution.

In the first place, the prosecutor claimed, he had had previous feuds with the author of the newspaper stories. Second, he categorically denied any discriminatory policies in making sentence requests in drug cases. Third, he said he knew that the data and methods reported in the newspaper stories were deficient even though the reporter would not reveal details about his sources and information. Finally, if any pattern of racial disparity existed, it was certainly inadvertent, and the prosecutor wanted to know about it so that the problem could be fixed. Maxfield accepted the project and was paid to produce a report.

How do you feel about this example? Did Maxfield sell out? How would you feel if Maxfield turned up clear evidence of disparity in sentences? Or no evidence of disparity? What about political party affiliation—would it make a difference if the prosecutor and Maxfield identified with the same party? With different parties?

✪ Main Points

- Evaluation research and policy analysis are examples of applied research in criminal justice.
- Different types of evaluation activities correspond to different stages in the policy process—policy planning, process evaluation, and impact evaluation.
- An evaluability assessment may be undertaken as a scouting operation or a preevaluation to determine whether it is possible to evaluate a particular program.
- A careful formulation of the problem, including relevant measurements and criteria of success or failure, is essential in evaluation research.
- Organizations may not have clear statements or ideas about program goals. In such cases, researchers must work with agency staff to formulate mutually acceptable statements of goals before proceeding.
- Evaluation research may use experimental, quasi-experimental, or nonexperimental designs. As in studies with other research purposes,

designs that offer the greatest control over experimental conditions are usually preferred.

- The use of randomized field experiments requires careful attention to random assignment, case flow, and treatment integrity.
- Randomized designs cannot be used for evaluations that begin after a new program has been implemented or for full-coverage programs in which it is not possible to withhold an experimental treatment from a control group.
- Process evaluations can be undertaken independently or in connection with an impact assessment. Process evaluations are all but essential for interpreting results from an impact assessment.
- Policy analysis is a more future-oriented applied research technique. However, policy analysis draws on the same social science research methods used in program evaluation. Many variations on policy analysis are used in applied criminal justice research.
- The scientific realist approach to applied research focuses on mechanisms in context, rather than generalizable causal processes.
- Criminal justice agencies are increasingly using policy analysis tools for tactical and strategic planning.
- Problem solving, evaluation, and scientific realism have many common elements.
- Evaluation research entails special logistical, ethical, and political problems because it is embedded in the day-to-day events of public policy and real life.

✪ *Key Terms*

Evaluation research	Problem solving
Impact assessment	Process evaluation
Policy analysis	Stakeholders

✪ *Review Questions and Exercises*

1. In presentations to justice practitioners, Maxfield describes evaluation as answering two questions: "Did you get what you expected?" and "Compared to what?" Discuss how particular sections of this chapter relate to those two questions.
2. When programs do not achieve their expected results, it's due to one of two things: The program was not a good idea to begin with, or it was a good idea but was not implemented properly. Discuss why it is necessary to conduct both a

process and an impact evaluation to learn why a program failed.
3. What are the principal advantages and disadvantages of randomized designs for field experiments? Are such designs used in policy analysis? Explain your answer.

✪ *Internet Exercises*

To ensure that you always have access to live, correct Web links for the Web sites referenced in the following exercises, we provide the necessary links on the companion Web site for *Research Methods for Criminal Justice and Criminology* at http://cj.wadsworth.com/maxfield_babbie/research_methods4e. Once at the companion Web site, select this specific chapter, click on "Chapter Resources," then click on "Web Links."

1. The American Evaluation Association provides links to many sites relevant to program evaluation and policy analysis. Visit the association's Web site for articles and/or links that are interesting to you, summarize the information available at the site, and describe its relevance to criminal justice research, program evaluation, and policy analysis.
2. In Chapter 3, we discussed ethics in criminal justice research. The nature of evaluation research presents many unique challenges to the practitioner. Visit the AEA Program Evaluation Standards Web site, and discuss the ethical issues that seem to be unique to evaluation.
3. The COPS Office was first established to promote community policing by hiring and training police. More recently, this organization has sponsored a series of guides on how to do problem-oriented policing, patterned after seminal work by Herman Goldstein. Visit the POP Center Web site, and select two guides to examining different types of problems. Describe how policy analysis and program evaluation are incorporated into the guides.

✪ *InfoTrac College Edition*

Use the keywords *evaluation* and *prison* to find an article that describes an evaluation that looked at some type of program offered to offenders while incarcerated. Briefly describe the program, the evaluation design, and the findings discussed in the article. Based on what you have learned from this class so far, how would you rate the rigor of this evaluation? Comment on the study from the point of view of internal, external, conclusion, and construct validity. If the article does not provide enough information to adequately comment on one of the above topics, make note of this as well.

✪ *The NEW Companion Web Site for* **Research Methods for Criminal Justice and Criminology,** *Fourth Edition*

http://cj.wadsworth.com/maxfield_babbie/ research_methods4e

Supplement your review of this chapter by going to the new companion Web site to take one of the Tutorial Quizzes, use the flash cards to master key terms, and check out the many other study aids you'll find there. You'll also find special features such as quantitative and qualitative data analysis primers to help you with a special project or do some research on your own.

✪ *Additional Readings*

Connell, James P., Kubisch, Anne C., Schorr, Lisbeth B., and Weiss, Carol H. (eds.), *New Approaches to Evaluating Community Initiatives: Concepts, Methods, and Contexts* (Washington, DC: Aspen Institute, 1995). Although this collection of essays is not specific to criminal justice, it offers much useful advice. Many of the chapters are best suited to readers who have a background in evaluation, but the chapter by Carol Weiss, "Nothing As Practical as Good Theory," is an excellent guide to the importance of thinking through the rationale underlying a program.

Eck, John E., *Assessing Responses to Problems: An Introductory Guide for Police Problem-Solvers* (Washington, DC: U.S. Department of Justice, Office of Community Oriented Policing Services, 2003) (http://www.popcenter.org). This highly recommended guide was written to accompany a series of problem-solving guides that aid police in addressing a wide range of problems. Eck summarizies key elements of user-oriented evaluation.

Fabelo, Tony, "The Critical Role of Policy Research in Developing Effective Correctional Policies," *Corrections Management Quarterly,* Vol. 1, no. 1 (1997), pp. 25–31. The principal criminal justice policy adviser for the state of Texas describes the use of applied research in corrections policy.

Pawson, Ray, and Tilley, Nick, *Realistic Evaluation* (Thousand Oaks, CA: Sage, 1997). The authors describe scientific realism and apply it to the evaluation of crime prevention and other criminal justice policy. This book also presents an interesting critique on the inappropriate use of experimental and quasi-experimental designs in criminal justice evaluation.

Rossi, Peter H., Freeman, Howard E., and Lipsey, Mark W., *Evaluation: A Systematic Approach,* 6th ed. (Thousand Oaks, CA: Sage, 1999). Of the many available "handbooks" on evaluation methods, this is the most widely read. Although the book is uneven in its coverage of recent developments, the authors provide a good general foundation in evaluation methods.

Tilley, Nick (ed.), *Analysis for Crime Prevention* (*Crime Prevention Studies,* Vol. 13, Monsey, NY: Criminal Justice Press, 2002); *Evaluation for Crime Prevention* (*Crime Prevention Studies,* Vol. 14, Monsey, NY: Criminal Justice Press, 2002). These companion volumes present innovative thinking about how policy analysis and program evaluation can be used by public officials in preventing crime. Some of the articles will be controversial. All are interesting and mostly fun to read.

Chapter 13

Interpreting Data

We'll examine a few simple statistics frequently used in criminal justice research. We'll also cover the fundamental logic of multivariate analysis. You'll come away from this chapter able to perform a number of simple, though powerful, analyses to describe data and reach research conclusions.

Introduction

Empirical research usually uses some type of statistical analysis.

Many people are intimidated by empirical research because they feel uncomfortable with mathematics and statistics. And, indeed, many research reports are filled with otherwise unspecified computations. The role of statistics in criminal justice research is very important, but it is equally important for that role to be seen in its proper perspective.

Empirical research is, first and foremost, a logical rather than a mathematical operation. Mathematics is not much more than a convenient and efficient language for accomplishing the logical operations inherent in good data analysis. Statistics is the applied branch of mathematics especially appropriate to a variety of research analyses.

We'll be looking at two types of statistics: descriptive and inferential. **Descriptive statistics** are used to summarize and otherwise describe data in manageable forms. **Inferential statistics** help researchers form conclusions from their observations; typically, that involves forming conclusions about a population from the study of a sample drawn from it.

Before considering any numbers, we want to assure you that the level of statistics used in this chapter has been proven safe for humans. Our introduction to this important phase of criminal justice research is just that—an introduction. Our intent is to familiarize future producers and consumers of empirical criminal justice research with fundamental concepts of quantitative analysis. Many published criminal justice studies use sophisticated statistical techniques that are best learned in specialized courses. But the underlying logic and fundamental techniques of statistics are not at all complicated.

We assume that you are taking a course in research methods for criminology and criminal justice because you are interested in the subjects of crime and criminal justice policy. We suggest that you approach this chapter by thinking about statistics as tools for describing and explaining crime and criminal justice policy. Learning how to use these tools will help you better understand this fascinating subject. And learning how to summarize and interpret data about a subject you find inherently interesting is the least painful and most rewarding way to becoming acquainted with statistics.

Univariate Description

The simplest statistics describe some type of average and dispersion for a single variable.

Descriptive statistics represent a method for presenting quantitative descriptions in a manageable form. Sometimes, we want to describe single variables; this procedure is known as univariate analysis. Other times, we want to describe the associations that connect one variable with another. Bivariate analysis refers to descriptions of two variables, and multivariate analysis examines relationships among three or more variables.

Univariate analysis examines the distribution of cases on only one variable at a time. We'll begin with the logic and formats for the analysis of univariate data.

Distributions

The most basic way to present univariate data is to report all individual cases—that is, to list the attribute for each case under study in terms of the variable in question. Suppose we are interested in the ages of criminal court judges; our data might come from a directory of judges prepared by a state bar association. The most direct manner of reporting the ages of judges is simply list them: 63, 57, 49, 62, 80, 72, 55, and so forth. Such a report will provide readers with complete details of the data, but it is too cumbersome for most purposes. We could arrange our data in a somewhat more manageable form without losing any of the detail by reporting that 5 judges are 38 years old, 7 are 39, 18 are 40, and so forth. Such a format avoids duplicating data on this variable.

For an even more manageable format—with a certain loss of detail—we might report judges' ages as marginals, which are **frequency distributions** of grouped data: 24 judges under 45 years of age, 51 between 45 and 50 years of age, and so forth. Our readers will have less data to examine and interpret, but they will not be able to reproduce fully the original ages of all the judges. Thus, for example, readers will have no way of knowing how many judges are 41 years old.

The preceding example presented marginals in the form of raw numbers. An alternative form is the use of percentages. Thus, for example, we might report that *x* percent of the judges are younger than 45, *y* percent are between 45 and 50, and so forth. The following table shows an example:

Ages of Criminal Court Judges (hypothetical)

Age	Percentage
Under 35	9%
36–45	21
46–55	45
56–65	19
65 and older	6
Total	100% = 433
No data	18

In computing percentages, it is necessary to determine the base from which to compute—the number that represents 100 percent. In the most straightforward situation, the base is the total number of cases under study. A problem arises, however, whenever some cases have missing data. Let's consider, for example, a survey in which respondents are asked to report their ages. If some respondents fail to answer that question, we have two alternatives. First, we might still base our percentages on the total number of respondents, reporting those who fail to give their ages as a percentage of the total. Second, we might use the number of persons who give an answer as the base from which to compute the percentages; this approach is illustrated in the accompanying table. We will still report the number who do not answer, but they will not figure in the percentages.

The choice of a base depends entirely on the purposes of the analysis. If we wish to compare the age distribution of a survey sample with comparable data on the population from which the sample was drawn, we will probably want to omit the "no answers" from the computation. Our best estimate of the age distribution of all respondents is the distribution for those who answered the question. Because "no answer" is not a meaningful age category, its presence among the base categories will only confuse the comparison of sample and population figures.

Measures of Central Tendency

Beyond simply reporting marginals, researchers often present data in the form of summary **averages,** or measures of central tendency. Options in this regard include the **mode** (the most frequent attribute, either grouped or ungrouped), the arithmetic **mean** (the sum of values for all observations, divided by the number of observations), and the **median** (the middle attribute in the ranked distribution of observed attributes). Here's how the three averages are calculated from a set of data.

Suppose we are conducting an experiment that involves teenagers as subjects. They range in age from 13 to 19, as indicated in this frequency distribution:

Age	Number
13	3
14	4
15	6
16	8
17	4
18	3
19	3

Now that we know the actual ages of the 31 subjects, how old are these subjects in general, or on average? Let's look at three different ways we might answer that question.

The easiest average to calculate is the mode, the most frequent value. The distribution of our 31 subjects shows there are more 16-year-olds (eight of them) than any other age, so the modal age is 16, as indicated in Figure 13.1.

Figure 13.1 also demonstrates the calculation of the mean. There are three steps: (1) Multiply each age by the number of subjects who are that age, (2) total the results of all those multiplications, and (3) divide that total by the number of subjects. As indicated in Figure 13.1, the mean age in this illustration is 15.87.

The median represents the "middle" value; half are above it and half below. If we had the precise age of each subject (for instance, 17 years and 124 days), we could arrange all 31 subjects in order by age, and the median for the whole group would be the age of the middle subject.

We do not, however, know precise ages; our data constitute "grouped data" in this regard. Three people who are not precisely the same age have been grouped in the category "13 years old," for example.

Figure 13.1 illustrates the logic of calculating a median for grouped data. Because there are 31 subjects altogether, the "middle" subject is number 16 when they are arranged by age—15 are younger and 17 are older. The bottom portion of Figure 13.1 shows that the middle person is one of the eight 16-year-olds. In the enlarged view of that group, we see that number 16 is the third from the left.

Measures of Dispersion

In the research literature, we find both means and medians presented. Whenever means are presented, we must be aware that they are susceptible to extreme values: A few very large or very small numbers can change the mean dramatically. Because of this, it is usually important to examine measures of **dispersion** about the mean.

The simplest measure of dispersion is the range: the distance separating the highest from the lowest value. Thus, besides reporting that our subjects have a mean age of 15.87, we might also indicate that their ages range from 13 to 19. A somewhat more sophisticated measure of dispersion is the **standard deviation,** which can be described as the average amount of variation about the mean. If the mean is the average value of all observations in a group, then the standard deviation represents the average amount each individual observation varies from the mean. Table 13.1 presents some hypothetical data on the ages of persons in juvenile and adult court that will help illustrate the concepts of deviation and average deviation. Let's first consider the top of Table 13.1.

The first column shows the age for each of 10 juvenile court defendants. The mean age for these 10 juveniles is 14. The second column shows how much each individual's age deviates from the mean. Thus, the first juvenile is 2 years younger than the mean, the second is 1 year older, and the third is the same age as the mean.

You might first think that the average deviation is calculated in the same way as the mean—add up all individual deviations for each case and divide by the number of cases. We did that in Table 13.1, but notice that the total deviation is zero; therefore, the average deviation is zero. In fact, the sum of deviations from the mean will *always* be zero. This is because some

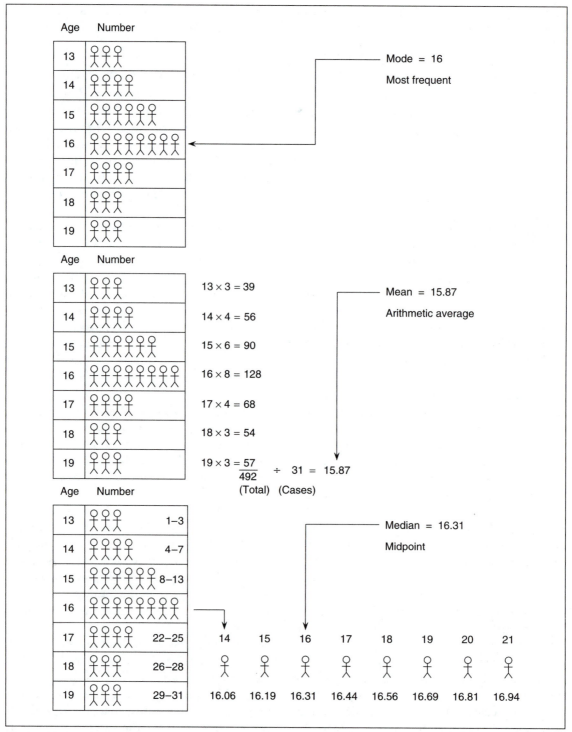

Figure 13.1   Three "Averages"

Table 13.1 Standard Deviation for Two Hypothetical Distributions

		Juvenile Court	
	Age	Deviation from Mean	Squared Deviation from Mean
	12	−2	4
	15	1	1
	14	0	0
	13	−1	1
	15	1	1
	14	0	0
	16	2	4
	16	2	4
	12	−2	4
	13	−1	1
Sum	140	0	20
Average	14	(0)	(2)
Standard deviation			1.41
		Adult Court	
	Age	Deviation from Mean	Squared Deviation from Mean
	18	−10	100
	37	9	81
	23	−5	25
	22	−6	36
	25	−3	9
	43	15	225
	19	−9	81
	50	22	484
	21	−7	49
	22	−6	36
Sum	280	0	1,126
Average	28	(0)	(112.6)
Standard deviation			10.61

individual deviations will be negative and some will be positive—and the positive and negative values will always cancel each other out.

For this reason (and other reasons too complex to describe here), the standard deviation measure of dispersion is based on the squared deviations from the mean. Squaring any number always produces a positive value, so when we add all the squared deviations together, we will not get zero for the total. Summing these squared deviations in the top of Table 13.1 produces a total of 20, and dividing by the number of observations produces an "average" deviation of 2. This quantity—the sum of squared deviations from the mean divided by the number of cases—is called the "variance." Taking the square root of the variance produces the standard deviation, which is 1.41 for juveniles in Table 13.1.

How should we interpret a standard deviation of 1.41, or any other such value, for that matter? By itself, any particular value for the standard deviation has no intuitive meaning. This measure of dispersion is most useful in a comparative sense. Comparing the relative values for the standard deviation and the mean indicates how much variation there is in a group of cases, relative to the average. Similarly, comparing standard deviations for different groups of cases indicates relative amounts of dispersion within each group.

In our example of juvenile court cases, the standard deviation of 1.41 is rather low relative to the mean of 14. Now compare the data for juvenile court to the bottom half of Table 13.1, which presents ages for a hypothetical group of adult court defendants. The mean is higher, of course, because adults are older than juveniles. More important for illustrating the standard deviation, there is greater variation in the distribution of adult court defendants, as illustrated by the standard deviation and the columns that show raw deviations and squared deviations from the mean of 28. The standard deviation for adult cases (10.61) is much higher relative to the mean of 28 than are the relative values of the standard deviation and mean for juvenile cases. In this hypothetical example, the substantive reason for this is obvious: There is much greater age variation in adult court than in juvenile court because the *range* for ages of adults is potentially greater (18 to whatever) than the range for ages in juveniles (1 to 17). As a result, the standard deviation for adult defendants indicates greater variation than the same measure for juvenile defendants.

In addition to providing a summary measure of dispersion, the standard deviation plays a role in the calculation of other descriptive statistics, some of which we will touch on later in this chapter. The standard deviation is also a central component of many inferential statistics used to make generalizations from a sample of observations to the population from which the sample was drawn.

Comparing Measures of Dispersion and Central Tendency

Other measures of dispersion can help us interpret measures of central tendency. One useful indicator that expresses both dispersion and grouping of cases is the percentile, which indicates what percentage of cases fall at or below some value. For example, scores on achievement tests such as the SAT are usually reported in both percentiles and raw scores. Thus, a raw score of 630 might fall in the 80th percentile, indicating that 80 percent of persons who take the SAT achieve scores of 630 or less; alternatively, the 80th percentile means that 20 percent of scores were higher than 630. Percentiles may also be grouped into quartiles, which give the cases that fall in the first (lowest), second, third, and fourth (highest) quarters of a distribution.

Table 13.2 presents a distribution of prior arrests for some hypothetical population of, say, probationers to illustrate different measures of central tendency and dispersion. Notice that, although the number of prior arrests ranges from 0 to 55, cases cluster in the lower end of this distribution. Half the cases have 4 or fewer prior arrests, as indicated by three descriptive statistics in Table 13.2: median, 50th percentile, and 2nd quartile. Only one-fourth of the cases have 8 or more prior arrests.

Notice also the different values for our three measures of central tendency. The mode for prior arrests is 2, and the mean or average number is 5.76. Whenever the mean is much higher than the mode, it indicates that the mean is distorted by a small number of persons with many prior arrests. The standard deviation of 6.64 further indicates that our small population has quite a bit of variability. Figure 13.2 presents a graphic representation of the dispersion of cases and the different values for the three measures of central tendency.

Distributions such as those shown in Table 13.2 and Figure 13.2 are known as "skewed distributions." Although most cases

Table 13.2 Hypothetical Data on Distribution of Prior Arrests

Number of Prior Arrests	Number of Cases	Percentage of Cases	Percentile/ Quartile
0	1	0.56	
1	16	8.89	
2	31	17.22	25th/1st
3	23	12.78	
4	20	11.11	50th/2nd
5	16	8.89	
6	19	10.56	
7	18	10.00	75th/3rd
8	11	6.11	
9	14	7.78	
10	5	2.78	
30	3	1.67	
40	2	1.11	
55	1	0.56	
Total	180	100%	

Mode	2
Median	4
Mean	5.76
Range	0–55
Standard deviation	6.64

cluster near the low end, a few are spread out over very high values for prior arrests. Many variables of interest to criminal justice researchers are skewed in similar ways, especially when examined for some general population. Most people have no prior arrests, but a small number of persons have many. Similarly, most people suffer no victimization from serious crime in any given year, but a small number of persons are repeatedly victimized.

In an appropriately titled article, "Deviating from the Mean," Michael Maltz (1994) cautions that criminologists, failing to recognize high levels of variation, sometimes report means for populations that exhibit a great deal of skewness. When reading reports of criminal justice research, researchers are advised to look closely at measures of both dispersion and central tendency. When the numerical value of the standard deviation is high and that for the mean is low, the mean is not a good measure of central tendency.

The preceding calculations are not appropriate for all variables. To understand this, we must examine two types of variables: continuous and discrete. Age and number of prior arrests are continuous ratio variables; they increase steadily in tiny fractions instead of jumping from category to category as does a discrete variable such as gender or marital status. If discrete variables are being analyzed—a nominal or ordinal variable, for example—then some of the techniques discussed previously are not applicable.

Strictly speaking, medians and means should be calculated for only interval and ratio data, respectively. If the variable in question is gender, for instance, raw numbers or percentage marginals are appropriate and useful measures. Calculating the mode is a legitimate, though not very revealing, tool of analysis, but reports of

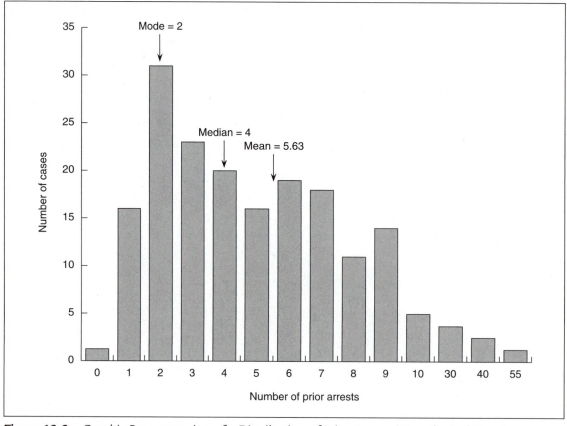

Figure 13.2   Graphic Representation of a Distribution of Prior Arrests (Hypothetical Data)

mean, median, or dispersion summaries would be inappropriate.

Computing Rates

Rates are fundamental descriptive statistics in criminal justice research. In most cases, rates are used to standardize some measure for comparative purposes. For example, the following table shows UCR figures on total murders for 2001 in four states.

	Total Murders, 2001	2001 Population
California	2166	33,359,000
Florida	823	15,222,000
Louisiana	422	3,368,000
Pennsylvania	573	10,397,000

Source: Federal Bureau of Investigation (2002).

Obviously, California had far more murders than the other three states, but these figures are difficult to interpret because of large differences in the states' total populations. Computing rates enables us to standardize by population size and make more meaningful comparisons, as the next table shows.

Murder Rates per 100,000 Population, 2001

California	6.5
Florida	5.4
Louisiana	12.5
Pennsylvania	5.5

We can see that Louisiana, even with the fewest murders in 2001 (among the states reported here), had the highest murder rate. Notice also that the murder rate is expressed as the number of murders per 100,000 population. This is a common convention in reporting rates of crime and other rare events. To get the rate of murder *per person,* move the decimal point five places to the left in each of the figures in the second table. You can clearly see which version is easier to interpret.

The arithmetic of calculating rates could not be much easier. What is not so simple, and in any event requires careful consideration, is deciding on the two basic components of rates: numerator and denominator. The numerator represents the central concept we are interested in measuring, so selecting the numerator involves all the considerations of measurement we have discussed elsewhere. Murder rates, arrest rates, conviction rates, and incarceration rates are common examples in which the numerator is a relatively straightforward count.

Choosing the right denominator can present problems. In most cases, we should compute rates to standardize according to some population eligible to be included in the numerator. Sometimes, the choice is fairly obvious, as in our use of each state's total population to compute murder rates. To compute rates of rape or sexual assault, we should probably use the population of adult women in the denominator, although we should also consider how to handle rapes with male victims. Because households are at risk of residential burglary, burglary rates should be computed using some count of households. Similarly, commercial burglaries should be based on some count of commercial establishments, and auto theft on some indicator of registered autos.

More difficult problems can arise in computing rates to express some characteristic of a mobile population. For example, residents of Miami are at risk of criminal victimization in that city, but so are tourists and other visitors to Miami. Because many nonresidents visit or pass through the city in any given year, a measure of Miami's crime rate based only on the city's resident population (such as the U.S. Census) will tend to overestimate the number of crimes standardized by the population at risk; many people at risk will not be counted in the denominator. Or what about estimating the crime rate on a subway system? The population at risk here is users, who, in New York City, amount to millions of persons per day.

Rates are very useful descriptive statistics that may be easily computed. It is important, however, to be careful in selecting numerators and denominators. Recognize that this caution applies as much to questions of making measurements as it does to questions of computing descriptive statistics. The box titled "Murder on the Job," presented later in this chapter, gives an example of confusion about the meaning of rates.

Detail Versus Manageability

In presenting univariate—and other—data, we are constrained by two often conflicting goals. On the one hand, we should attempt to provide readers with the fullest degree of detail possible regarding those data. On the other hand, the data should be presented in a manageable form. Because these two goals often run counter to each other, researchers must seek the best compromise between them. One useful solution is to report a given set of data in more than one form. In the case of age, for example, we might report the marginals on ungrouped ages plus the mean age and standard deviation.

Our introductory discussion of univariate analysis shows how this seemingly simple matter can be rather complex. The lessons of this section will be important as we move now to a consideration of analysis involving more than a single variable.

Describing Two or More Variables

Descriptive statistics applied to two or more variables are tools to understand relationships among those variables.

Univariate analyses describe the units of analysis of a study and, if they are a sample drawn from some larger population, allow us to make descriptive inferences about the larger population. Bivariate and multivariate analyses are aimed primarily at explanation.

Often, it's appropriate to describe subsets of cases, subjects, or respondents. Table 13.3, for

Table 13.3   Hypothetical Illustration of Subgroup Comparisons: Length of Prison Sentence by Felony Criminal History

Felony Criminal History	Median Sentence Length
No arrests or convictions	6 months
Prior arrests only	11 months
Prior convictions	23 months

Table 13.4   Gun Ownership Among Male and Female Respondents, 2000

	Male	Female
Own a Gun?		
Yes	42%	25%
No	58	75
100% =	(817)	(1040)

Source: 2000 General Social Survey (available at http://sda.berkeley.edu:7502/archive.htm).

example, presents hypothetical data on sentence length for offenders grouped by prior felony record. In some situations, the researcher presents subgroup comparisons purely for descriptive purposes. More often, the purpose of subgroup descriptions is comparative. In this case, comparing sentences for subgroups of convicted offenders implies some causal connection between prior felony record and sentence length. Similarly, if we compare sentence lengths for men and women, it implies that something about gender has a causal effect on sentence length.

Bivariate Analysis

In contrast to univariate analysis, subgroup comparisons constitute a kind of **bivariate analysis** in that two variables are involved. In such situations, we are usually interested in relationships among the variables. Thus, univariate analysis and subgroup comparisons focus on describing the *people* (or other units of analysis) under study, whereas bivariate analysis focuses more on the *variables* themselves.

Notice, then, that Table 13.4 can be regarded as a subgroup comparison: It independently describes gun ownership among male and female respondents in the 2000 General Social Survey. It shows—comparatively and descriptively—that fewer females than males report owning a gun.

The same table viewed as an explanatory bivariate analysis tells a somewhat different story. It suggests that the variable "gender" has an ef-

fect on the variable "gun ownership." The behavior is seen as a dependent variable that is partially determined by the independent variable, gender. Explanatory bivariate analyses, then, involve the "variable language" we introduced in Chapter 1. In a subtle shift of focus, we are no longer talking about male and female as different subgroups but about gender as a variable—a variable that has an influence on other variables.

Adding the logic of causal relationships among variables has an important implication for the construction and reading of percentage tables. One of the chief bugaboos for novice data analysts is deciding on the appropriate "direction of percentaging" for any given table. In Table 13.4, for example, we divided the group of subjects into two subgroups—male and female—and then described the behavior of each subgroup. That is the correct way to construct this table.

Notice, however, that it would have been possible, though inappropriate, to construct the table differently. We could have first divided the subjects into different categories of gun ownership and then described each of those subgroups by the percentage of male and female subjects in each. This method would make no sense in terms of explanation, however; owning a gun does not *make* someone male or female.

Table 13.4 suggests that gender affects gun ownership. Had we used the other method of construction, the table would have suggested that gun ownership affects whether someone is male or female—which makes no sense.

Another, related problem complicates the lives of novice data analysts: How do you *read* a percentage table? There is a temptation to read Table 13.4 as "Among females, only 25 percent owned a gun, and 75 percent did not; therefore, being female makes you less likely to own a gun." That is not the correct way to read the table, however. The conclusion that gender—as a variable—has an effect on gun ownership must hinge on a comparison between males and females. Specifically, we compare the 25 percent of females with the 42 percent of males and note that women are less likely than men to own a gun. The appropriate comparison of subgroups, then, is essential in reading an explanatory bivariate table.

Percentaging a Table In constructing and presenting Table 13.4, we have used a convention called "percentage down." This means that we can add the percentages down each column to total 100 percent. We read this form of table across a row. For the row labeled "Yes," what percentage of the males own a gun? What percentage of the females?

The percentage-down convention is just that—a conventional practice; some researchers prefer to percentage across. They would organize Table 13.4 with "Male" and "Female" on the left side of the table, identifying the two rows, and "Yes" and "No" at the top, identifying the columns. The actual numbers in the table would be moved around accordingly, and each *row* of percentages would total 100 percent. In that case, we would make our comparisons between males and females by reading down, within table columns, still asking what percentage of males and females owned guns. The logic and the conclusion would be the same in either case; only the form would be different.

In reading a table that someone else has constructed, therefore, it's necessary to find out in which direction it has been percentaged. Usually, that will be apparent from the label-

ing of the table or the logic of the variables being analyzed. Sometimes, however, tables are not clearly labeled. In such cases, the reader should add the percentages in each column and each row. If each of the columns totals 100 percent, the table has been percentaged down. If the rows total 100 percent each, the table has been percentaged across. Follow these rules of thumb:

1. If the table is percentaged down, read across.
2. If the table is percentaged across, read down.

By the way, we constructed Table 13.4 from General Social Survey (GSS) data available on the Internet, as you may have guessed from the Internet address shown at the bottom of the table. GSS data from 1976 onward can be accessed directly through the online data analysis capability of the University of California at Berkeley. You can use a simple interactive program at the Berkeley site to construct your own percentage tables for any GSS variables. This will give you invaluable practice in constructing bivariate percentage tables.

Here's another example: Suppose we are interested in investigating newspaper editorial policies regarding the legalization of marijuana. We undertake a content analysis of editorials on this subject that have appeared during a given year in a sample of daily newspapers across the nation. Each editorial has been classified as favorable, neutral, or unfavorable with regard to the legalization of marijuana. Perhaps we wish to examine the relationship between editorial policies and the types of communities in which the newspapers are published, thinking that rural newspapers might be more conservative than urban ones. Thus, each newspaper (and so, each editorial) is classified in terms of the population of the community in which it is published.

Table 13.5 presents some hypothetical data describing the editorial policies of rural and urban newspapers. Note that the unit of analysis in this example is the individual editorial. Table 13.5 tells us that there were 127 editorials

Table 13.5   Hypothetical Data Regarding Newspaper Editorials on the Legalization of Marijuana

Editorial Policy Toward Legalizing Marijuana	Community Size	
	Under 100,000	Over 100,000
Favorable	11%	32%
Neutral	29	40
Unfavorable	60	28
100% =	(127)	(438)

about marijuana in our sample of newspapers published in communities with populations under 100,000. (*Note:* This choice of 100,000 is for simplicity of illustration and does not mean that rural refers to a community of less than 100,000 in any absolute sense.) Of these, 11 percent (14 editorials) were favorable toward the legalization of marijuana, 29 percent were neutral, and 60 percent were unfavorable. Of the 438 editorials that appeared in our sample of newspapers published in communities with more than 100,000 residents, 32 percent (140 editorials) were favorable toward legalizing marijuana, 40 percent were neutral, and 28 percent were unfavorable.

When we compare the editorial policies of rural and urban newspapers in our imaginary study, we find—as expected—that rural newspapers are less favorable toward the legalization of marijuana than are urban newspapers. That is determined by noting that a larger percentage (32 percent) of the urban editorials than the rural ones (11 percent) were favorable. We might note, as well, that more rural than urban editorials were unfavorable (60 percent versus 28 percent). Note, too, that this table assumes that the size of a community might affect its newspaper's editorial policies on this issue, rather than that editorial policy might affect the size of communities.

Constructing and Reading Tables   Before introducing multivariate analysis, let's review the steps involved in the construction of explanatory bivariate tables:

1. Divide the cases into groups according to attributes of the independent variable.
2. Describe each of these subgroups in terms of attributes of the dependent variable.
3. Read the table by comparing the independent variable subgroups with one another in terms of a given attribute of the dependent variable.

In the example of editorial policies regarding the legalization of marijuana, the size of a community is the independent variable, and a newspaper's editorial policy is the dependent variable. The table is constructed as follows:

1. Divide the editorials into subgroups according to the sizes of the communities in which the newspapers are published.
2. Describe each subgroup of editorials in terms of the percentages favorable, neutral, or unfavorable toward the legalization of marijuana.
3. Compare the two subgroups in terms of the percentages favorable toward the legalization of marijuana.

Bivariate analyses typically have an explanatory purpose. This hypothetical example has hinted at the nature of causation as it is used by social scientists. We hope that the rather simplified approach to causation in these examples will have commonsense acceptability at this point.

Bivariate Table Formats   Tables such as those we've been examining are commonly called **contingency tables:** Values of the dependent variable are *contingent* on values of the independent variable. Although contingency tables are commonly used in criminal justice research, their format has never been standardized. As a result, a variety of formats will be found in the research literature. As long as a table is easy to read and interpret, there is probably no reason to strive for standardization; however, these guidelines should be followed in the presentation of most tabular data.

1. Provide a heading or a title that succinctly describes what is contained in the table.

2. Present the original content of the variables clearly—in the table itself if at all possible, or in the text with a paraphrase in the table. This information is especially critical when a variable is derived from responses to an attitudinal question because the meaning of the responses will depend largely on the wording of the question.
3. Clearly indicate the attributes of each variable. Complex categories need to be abbreviated, but the meaning should be clear in the table, and, of course, the full description should be reported in the text.
4. When percentages are reported in the table, identify the base on which they are computed. It is redundant to present all the raw numbers for each category, because these could be reconstructed from the percentages and the bases. Moreover, the presentation of both numbers and percentages often makes a table more difficult to read.
5. If any cases are omitted from the table because of missing data ("no answer," for example), indicate their numbers in the table.

By following these guidelines and thinking carefully about the kinds of causal and descriptive relationships they want to examine, researchers address many policy and research questions in criminal justice. We want to emphasize, however, the importance of thinking through the logic of contingency tables. Descriptive statistics—contingency tables, measures of central tendency, or rates—are sometimes misrepresented or misinterpreted. See the box titled "Murder on the Job" for an example of this.

Multivariate Analysis

A great deal of criminal justice research uses multivariate techniques to examine relationships among several variables. Like much statistical analysis, the logic of **multivariate analysis** is straightforward, but the actual use of many multivariate statistical techniques can be complex. A full understanding requires a solid background in statistics and is beyond the scope of this book. In this section, we briefly discuss the construction of multivariate tables—those constructed from three or more variables—and the comparison of multiple subgroups.

Multivariate tables can be constructed by following essentially the same steps outlined previously for bivariate tables. Instead of one independent variable and one dependent variable, however, we will have more than one independent variable. And instead of explaining the dependent variable on the basis of a single independent variable, we'll seek an explanation through the use of more than one independent variable. Let's consider an example from research on victimization.

Multivariate Tables: Lifestyle and Street Crime If we consult any source of published statistics on victimization (see Chapter 11), we will find several tables that document a relationship between age and personal crime victimization—younger people are more often victims of assault and robbery, for example. An influential book by Michael Hindelang and associates (Hindelang, Gottfredson, and Garofalo, 1978) suggested a "lifestyle" explanation for this relationship. The lifestyle of many younger people—visiting bars and clubs for evening entertainment, for example—exposes them to street crime and potential predators more than does the less active lifestyle of older people. This is certainly a sensible hypothesis, and Hindelang and associates found general support for the lifestyle explanation in their analysis of data from early versions of the National Crime Victimization Survey. But the U.S. crime survey data did not include direct measures of lifestyle concepts.

Questionnaire items in the British Crime Survey (BCS) provided better measures of individual behaviors. Using these data, Ronald Clarke and associates (Clarke, Ekblom, Hough, and Mayhew, 1985) examined the link between exposure to risk and victimization, while holding age and gender constant. Specifically, Clarke and colleagues hypothesized that older persons are less often victims of street crime because

MURDER
ON THE JOB

"High Murder Rate for Women on the Job," read the headline for a brief story in *The New York Times*, reporting on a study released by the U.S. Department of Labor. The subhead was equally alarming, and misleading, to casual readers: "40 percent of women killed at work are murdered, but figure for men is only 15 percent." Think about this statement, in light of our discussion of how to percentage a table. You should be able to imagine something like the following:

Cause of Death at Work

	Women	Men
Murder	40%	15%
Other	60	85
Total	100%	100%

This table indicates that, of those women who die while on the job at work, 40 percent are murdered, and is consistent with the opening paragraphs of the story. Notice that so far nothing has been said about how many women and men are murdered, or how many women and men die on the job from all causes. Later on, the story provides more details:

Vehicle accidents caused the most job-related deaths, 18 percent or 1,121 of the 6,083 work related deaths in 1992. . . . Homicides, including shootings and stabbings, were a close second with 17 percent, or 1,004 deaths, said the study by the department's Bureau of Labor Statistics.

This information enables us to supplement the table by adding row totals: 6083 people died on the job in 1992, 1004 of them were murdered, and 5079 (6083 − 1004) died from other causes.

One more piece of information is needed to construct a contingency table: the total number of men and women killed on the job. The story does not tell us that directly, but it provides enough information to approximate the answer: "Although men are 55 percent of the workforce, they comprise 93 percent of all job-related deaths." Men must therefore be 93 percent of the 6083 total workplace deaths, or approximately 5657; this leaves approximately 426 deaths of women on the job. "Approximate" is an important qualifier here, because computing numbers of cases from percentages creates some inconsistencies due to rounding off percentages reported in the newspaper story. Let's now construct a contingency table to look at the numbers of workplace deaths. The next table shows computed numbers in parentheses. Notice that with the exception of "Total" all numbers have been esti-

they spend less time on the streets. The 1982 BCS asked respondents whether they had left their homes in the previous week (that is, the week before they were interviewed) for any evening leisure or social activities. Those who responded yes were asked which nights they had gone out and what they had done.

Hypothesizing that some types of evening activities are more risky than others, Clarke and associates restricted their analysis to leisure pursuits away from respondents' homes, such as visiting a pub, nightclub, or theater. Their dependent variable—street crime victimization— was also carefully defined to include only crimes against persons (actual and attempted assault,

robbery, rape, and theft) that occurred away from victims' homes or workplaces or the homes of friends. Furthermore, because the leisure behavior questions asked about evening activities, only street crime victimizations that took place between 6:00 P.M. and midnight were included.

Clarke and associates therefore proposed a very specific hypothesis that involves three carefully defined concepts and variables: Older persons are less often victims of street crime because they less often engage in behavior that exposes them to risk of street crime. Parts A–C of Table 13.6 present cross-tabulations for the three possible bivariate relationships among

mated from the newspaper story's percentages for men and women.

Cause of Death at Work

	Women (est.)	Men (est.)	Total	Total (est.)
Murder	(170)	(849)	1004	(1019)
Other	(256)	(4808)	5079	(5064)
Total	(426)	(5657)	6083	

The results are interesting. Although a greater percentage of women than men are murdered, a much larger number of men than women are murdered.

Now, recall the story's headline, "High Murder Rate." This implies that the *number* of women murdered on the job, divided by the total number of women at risk of murder on the job, is higher than the same computed rate for men. We need more information than the story provides to verify this claim, but there is a clue. Women are about 45 percent of the workforce, so there are about 1.2 men in the workforce for every woman (55 percent ÷ 45 percent). But about five times as many men as women are murdered on the job (849 ÷ 170).

This should tip you off that the headline is misleading. If the ratio of male-to-female murders is 5 to 1, but the ratio of male-to-female workers is 1.2 to 1, how could the murder rate for women be higher? You could compute actual rates of murder on the job by finding a suitable denominator; in this case, the number of men and women in the workforce would be appropriate. Consulting the Census Bureau publication *Statistical Abstract of the United States* would provide this information and enable you to compute rates, as in our final table:

	Women	Men
Civilian workforce (1,000s)	53,284	63,593
Murdered at work	170	849
On-the-job murder rate per 100,000 workers	0.319	1.335

So *The New York Times* got it wrong; there is a higher murder rate for men on the job. Women are less often killed on the job by any cause, including murder. But women who die on the job (in much smaller numbers than men) are more likely to die from murder than are men who die on the job. A murder rate expresses the number of people murdered divided by the population at risk.

Rates are often computed with inappropriate denominators. But it is less common to find the term *rate* used so inaccurately.

Source: "High Murder Rate for Women on the Job" (1993); U.S. Bureau of the Census (1992).

these variables: evening street crime victimization by age and by evening leisure pursuits, and evening leisure pursuits by age.

The relationships illustrated in these tables are consistent with the lifestyle hypothesis of personal crime victimization. First, victimization was more common for younger people (ages 16–30) and for those who pursued leisure activities outside their home three or more evenings in the previous week (parts A and B of Table 13.6). Second, as shown in part C, the attributes of young age and frequent exposure to risk were positively related: About 41 percent of the youngest group had gone out three or more nights, compared with 20 percent of those ages 31–60 and only 10 percent of those over age 60.

However, because we are interested in the effects of two independent variables—lifestyle and age—on victimization, we must construct a table that includes all three variables.

Several of the tables we have presented in this chapter are somewhat inefficient. When the dependent variable—street crime victimization—is dichotomous (two attributes), knowing one attribute permits us to easily reconstruct the other. Thus, if we know from Table 13.6A that 1 percent of respondents ages 31–60 were victims of street crime, then we know automatically that 99 percent were not victims. So

Table 13.6A   Evening Street Crime Victimization by Age

Street Crime Victim	16–30	31–60	61+
Yes	4.8%	1.0%	0.3%
No	95.2	99.0	99.7
100% =	(2738)	(4460)	(1952)

Table 13.6B   Evening Street Crime Victimization by Evenings Out During Previous Week

Street Crime Victim	None	1 or 2	3+
Yes	1.2%	1.6%	3.8%
No	98.9	98.4	96.2
100% =	(3252)	(3695)	(2203)

Table 13.6C   Evening Out During Previous Week by Age

Evenings Out	16–30	31–60	61+
None	20.6%	35.2%	57.2%
1 or 2	38.6	44.9	32.5
3+	40.9	19.8	10.2
100% =	(2738)	(4460)	(1952)

Table 13.6D   Evening Street Crime Victimization by Age and Evenings Out

Evenings Out	Percentage of Victims		
	16–30	31–60	61+
None	3.9	1.0	0.2
	(563)	(1572)	(1117)
1 or 2	3.8	0.9	0.2
	(1056)	(2004)	(635)
3+	6.2	1.4	1.1
	(1119)	(884)	(200)
Total N =	(2738)	(4460)	(1952)

Note: Percentages and numbers of cases computed from published tabulations.

Source: Adapted from Clarke, Ekblom, Hough, and Mayhew (1985: Tables 1, 2, and 3).

reporting the percentages for both values of a dichotomy is unnecessary. On the basis of this recognition, Table 13.6D presents the relationship between victimization and two independent variables in a more efficient format.

In Table 13.6D, the percentages of respondents who reported a street crime victimization are shown in the cells at the intersections of the two independent variables. The numbers presented in parentheses below each percentage are the numbers of cases on which the percentages are based. Thus, for example, we know that 563 people ages 16–30 did not go out for evening leisure in the week before their interview and that 3.9 percent of them were victims of street crime in the previous year. We can calculate from this that 22 of those 563 people were victims and the other 541 people were not victims.

Let's now interpret the results presented in this table:

- Within each age group, persons who pursue outside evening leisure activities three or more times per week are more often victimized. There is not much difference between those who go out once or twice per week and those who stayed home.
- Within each category for evening leisure activities, street crime victimization declines as age increases.
- Exposure to risk through evenings out is less strongly related to street crime victimization than is age.
- Age and exposure to risk have independent effects on street crime victimization. Within a given attribute of one independent variable, different attributes of the second are still related to victimization.
- Similarly, the two independent variables have a cumulative effect on victimization. Younger people who go out three or more times per week are most often victimized.

Returning to the lifestyle hypothesis, what can we conclude from Table 13.6D? First, this measure of exposure to risk is, in fact, related to street crime victimization. People who go out more frequently are more often exposed to risk and more often victims of street crime. As Clarke and associates point out, however, differences in exposure to risk do not account for lower rates of victimization among older persons: Within categories of exposure to risk, victimization still declines with age. So lifestyle is related to victimization, but this measure of behavior—exposure to risk of street crime—does not account for all age-related differences in victimization. Furthermore, what we might call lifestyle "intensity" plays a role here. Going out once or twice a week does not have as much impact on victimization as going out more often. The most intensely active night people ages 30 or younger are most often victims of street crime.

Multivariate contingency tables are powerful tools for examining relationships between a dependent variable and multiple independent variables measured at the nominal or categorical level. Contingency tables can, however, become cumbersome and difficult to interpret if independent variables have several categories or if more than two independent variables are included. In practice, criminal justice researchers often employ more sophisticated techniques for multivariate analysis of discrete or nominal variables. Although the logic of such analysis is not especially difficult, most people learn these techniques in advanced courses in statistics.

Multiple-Subgroup Comparisons: Social Disorganization and Boston Neighborhoods
Just as subgroup comparisons can constitute a type of bivariate analysis, comparing values on some dependent variable across multiple subgroups is a type of multivariate analysis. In a sense, Table 13.6D compared victimization for multiple subgroups defined by age and evening leisure activities.

Multiple-subgroup comparisons are most frequently used to compare values for dependent variables measured at the interval or ratio level. For example, we might wish to compare crime rates among urban areas that have been

Table 13.7 Assault Rates, Poverty, and Mobility in 60 Boston Neighborhoods

	Mobility		
Poverty	Low	High	Total
Low	12.2 (22)	19.5 (21)	15.8 (43)
High	43.8 (4)	25.0 (13)	29.4 (17)
Total	17.1 (26)	21.6 (34)	19.6 (60)

Note: Row and column total assault rates computed from published tabulations.
Source: Adapted from Warner and Pierce (1993: Table 2).

classified according to different attributes. Table 13.7 is adapted from research by Barbara Warner and Glenn Pierce (1993) that examined the relationship between measures of social disorganization and crime problems.

Drawing on earlier studies by Clifford Shaw and Henry McKay (1969) and by William Julius Wilson (1987), Warner and Pierce compared calls for police service from 60 Boston neighborhoods to two measures of social disorganization—poverty and population mobility—each computed from census data for Boston neighborhoods. Their poverty measure expresses the percentage of neighborhood residents with incomes below the poverty line in 1980; their population mobility measure expresses the percentage of residents who lived in the same dwelling for less than 5 years. Classifying each neighborhood as high or low on each of these two measures produces the two subgroups shown in Table 13.7. Each cell indicates the mean rate of police calls to report assaults for neighborhoods in each subgroup.

As the table shows, assaults were more common in high-poverty neighborhoods, regardless of residential mobility. No surprises here; this finding is consistent with virtually all research on social disorganization, from Shaw and McKay onward. However, the relationship between mobility and assaults varied, depending on neighborhood poverty levels. In low-poverty

Table 13.8   Hypothetical Raw Data on Education and Support for Gun Control Laws

Support for Gun Control	Educational Level				
	None	Grade School	High School	College	Graduate Degree
Low	23	34	156	67	16
Medium	11	21	123	102	23
High	6	12	95	164	77

areas (the first row of Table 13.7), the mean assault rate was greater for high-mobility neighborhoods, but the opposite was true for high-poverty neighborhoods (the second row). Warner and Pierce refer to Wilson's influential book, *The Truly Disadvantaged: The Inner City, the Underclass, and Public Policy* (1987), to interpret this finding: Assaults were most common in poor, stable neighborhoods—those where poverty was persistent and mobility limited. As Warner and Pierce (1993:507) state, these are "neighborhoods where people remain because they have no choice. This type of stability appears to have an impact on crime in a very different way. Rather than building cohesiveness, it may build resentment, frustration, and isolation."

Notice also how it is necessary to compare the *combined* categories of poverty and mobility to reveal this finding. If we examined the mean number of assaults for each variable separately, shown in the row and column totals for Table 13.7, we would conclude that assaults are more common in high-poverty and high-mobility neighborhoods. Comparing multiple subgroups defined by the intersection of poverty and mobility is a form of multivariate analysis that enabled Warner and Pierce to sort out the subtle relationships between these two independent variables and neighborhood assault rates. Later in this chapter, we will return to this study to illustrate the use of a more powerful multivariate technique. But multiple-subgroup comparisons can provide useful information about the relationship between more

than one independent variable and dependent variables measured at the interval or ratio level.

Measures of Association

As we've suggested, descriptive statistics is a method for presenting quantitative descriptions in a manageable form. Sometimes, we want to describe single variables; other times, we want to describe the associations that connect one variable with another.

Bivariate contingency tables are one way to examine the association between two variables. But contingency tables can be quite complex, presenting several different response categories for row and column variables. Nevertheless, a contingency table represents the association between two variables as a data matrix. Table 13.8 presents such a matrix, showing hypothetical data for the joint frequency distribution of education and support for gun control laws. It provides all the information needed to determine the nature and extent of the relationship between education and support for gun control. Notice, for example, that 23 people (1) have no education and (2) scored low on support for gun control; 77 people (1) have graduate degrees and (2) scored high on support for gun control.

However, this matrix presents more information than we can easily comprehend. Studying the table carefully shows that as education increases from "none" to "graduate degree" there is a general tendency for gun control support to increase. A variety of descriptive statistics can summarize this data matrix. Selecting the appropriate measure depends initially on the nature of the two variables.

We'll turn now to some of the options available for summarizing the association between two variables. Each measure of association we'll discuss is based on the same model—**proportionate reduction of error (PRE).**

To see how this model works, suppose we ask you to guess respondents' attributes on a given variable—for example, whether they answered yes or no to a given questionnaire item. To assist you, let's first assume you know the overall distribution of responses in the total sample—say, 60 percent yes and 40 percent no. You will make the fewest errors in this process if you always guess the modal (most frequent) response: yes.

Second, let's assume you also know the empirical relationship between the first variable and some other variable—say, gender. Now, each time we ask you to guess whether a respondent said yes or no, we'll tell you whether the respondent is a man or a woman. If the two variables are related, you should make fewer errors the second time. It is possible, therefore, to compute the PRE by knowing the relationship between the two variables: the stronger the relationship, the greater the reduction of error.

This basic PRE model is modified slightly to take account of different levels of measurement—nominal, ordinal, or interval. The following sections will consider each level of measurement and present one measure of association appropriate to each. However, the three measures discussed are only a partial representation of the many appropriate measures.

Nominal Variables If the two variables consist of nominal data (for example, gender, marital status, or race), lambda (λ) is one appropriate measure. Lambda is based on your ability to guess values on one of the variables: the PRE achieved through knowledge of values on the other variable. A simple example will illustrate the logic and method of lambda.

Table 13.9 Hypothetical Data Relating Gender to Fear of Crime

Fear	Men	Women	Total
Safe	900	200	1100
Unsafe	100	800	900
Total	1000	1000	2000

Table 13.9 presents hypothetical data relating gender to a common measure of fear of crime, based on the question "How safe do you feel, or would you feel, walking alone on your neighborhood streets at night?" Overall, we note that 1100 people answered "safe" on the fear question, and 900 answered "unsafe." If you try to predict how people will respond to the fear-of-crime question, knowing only the overall distribution on that variable, you will always predict "safe" because that will result in fewer errors than always predicting "unsafe." Nevertheless, this strategy will result in 900 errors out of 2000 predictions.

But suppose you have access to the data in Table 13.9 and are told each person's gender before making your predictions about fear of crime. Your strategy will change: For every man, you will predict "safe," and for every woman, you will predict "unsafe." In this instance, you will make 300 errors—the 100 men who responded "unsafe" and the 200 women who responded "safe"—600 fewer errors than you would make without knowing the person's gender.

Lambda, then, represents the reduction in errors as a proportion of the errors that would have been made on the basis of the overall distribution. In this hypothetical example, lambda equals .67—that is, 600 fewer errors divided by the 900 total errors based on fear of crime alone. In this fashion, lambda measures the statistical association between gender and fear of crime.

If gender and fear were statistically independent, we would find the same distribution of fear of crime for men and women. In this case, knowing gender will not affect the number of errors made in predicting fear, and the resulting lambda will be zero. If, however, all men responded "safe" and all women responded "unsafe," then by knowing gender you can avoid all errors in predicting fear of crime. You will make 900 fewer errors (out of 900), so lambda will equal 1.0—a perfect statistical association.

Lambda is only one of several measures of association appropriate to the analysis of two nominal variables. Any statistics textbook will describe other appropriate measures.

Ordinal Variables If the variables being related are ordinal (for example, occupational status or education), gamma (γ) is one appropriate measure of association. Like lambda, gamma is based on the ability to guess values on one variable by knowing values on another. Instead of exact values, however, gamma is based on the ordinal arrangement of values. For any given pair of cases, you guess that their ordinal ranking on one variable will correspond (positively or negatively) to their ordinal ranking on the other. For example, if you suspect that political conservatism is negatively related to support for gun control, and if person A is more conservative than person B, then you guess that A is less supportive of gun control than B. Gamma is the proportion of paired comparisons that fits this pattern.

Table 13.10 presents hypothetical data relating political ideology to support for gun control. The general nature of the relationship between these two variables is that, as conservatism increases, support for gun control decreases. There is a negative association between conservatism and support for gun control.

Gamma is computed from two quantities: (1) the number of pairs that have the same ranking on the two variables, and (2) the number of pairs that have the opposite ranking on the two variables. The pairs that have the same ranking are computed as follows: The frequency of each cell in the table is multiplied by the sum of all cells appearing below and to the right of it—with all these products being summed. In Table 13.10, the number of pairs with the same

Table 13.10 Hypothetical Data Relating Political Ideology and Support for Gun Control

Support for Gun Control	Liberal	Moderate	Conservative
Low	200	400	700
Medium	500	900	400
High	800	300	100

ranking is 200(900 + 300 + 400 + 100) + 500 (300 + 100) + 400(400 + 100) + 900(100), or 340,000 + 200,000 + 200,000 + 90,000 = 830,000.

The pairs that have the opposite rankings on the two variables are computed as follows: The frequency of each cell in the table is multiplied by the sum of all cells appearing below and to the left of it—with all these products being summed. In Table 13.10, the number of pairs with opposite rankings is 700(500 + 800 + 900 + 300) + 400(800 + 300) + 400(500 + 800) + 900(800), or 1,750,000 + 440,000 + 520,000 + 720,000 = 3,430,000. Gamma is computed from the numbers of same-ranked pairs and opposite-ranked pairs as follows:

$$\text{Gamma} = \frac{\text{same} - \text{opposite}}{\text{same} + \text{opposite}}$$

In our example, gamma equals (830,000 − 3,430,000) divided by (830,000 + 3,430,000), or −.61. The negative sign in this answer indicates the negative association suggested by the initial inspection of the table. Conservatism and support for gun control, in this hypothetical example, are negatively associated. The numerical figure for gamma indicates that 61 percent more of the pairs examined had opposite rankings than the same ranking.

Note that whereas values of lambda vary from 0 to 1, values of gamma vary from −1 to +1 and represent both the direction and the magnitude of the association. Because nominal variables have no ordinal structure, it makes no sense to speak of the direction of the relationship. A negative lambda indicates that we made more errors in predicting values on one variable while knowing values on the second than we made in ignorance of the second, and that's not logically possible.

Interval or Ratio Variables If interval or ratio variables (for example, age, income, or number of arrests) are being analyzed, one appropriate measure of association is Pearson's product-moment correlation (r). The derivation and computation of this measure of association are beyond the scope of this book, so we will make only a few general comments here.

Like both gamma and lambda, r is based on guessing the value of one variable by knowing the other. For a continuous interval or ratio variable, however, it is unlikely that we can predict the precise value of the variable. At the same time, predicting only the ordinal arrangement of values on the two variables does not take advantage of the greater amount of information conveyed by an interval or ratio variable. In a sense, r reflects how closely we can guess the value of one variable through our knowledge of the value of the other.

To understand the logic of r, let's consider how we might hypothetically guess values that particular cases have on a given variable. With nominal variables, we have seen that the best guess is the modal value. But for interval or ratio data, we can minimize our errors by always guessing the mean value of the variable. Although this practice produces few, if any, perfect guesses, it will minimize the extent of our errors.

In the computation of lambda, we noted the number of errors produced by always guessing the modal value. In the case of r, errors are measured in terms of the sum of the squared differences between the actual value and the mean. This sum, called the "total variation," is calculated in much the same way as the standard deviation, discussed earlier in this chapter.

To understand that concept, we must expand the scope of our examination. Let's look at the logic of regression analysis, and we'll return to correlation within that context.

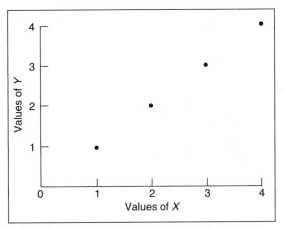

Figure 13.3 Simple Scattergram of Values of X and Y

Regression Analysis The general formula for describing the association between two variables is $Y = f(X)$. This formula is read, "Y is a function of X," which means that values of Y can be explained in terms of variations in the values of X. Stated more strongly, we might say that X causes Y, so the value of X determines the value of Y. **Regression analysis** is a method of determining the specific function relating Y to X. There are several forms of regression analysis, depending on the complexity of the relationships being studied. Let's begin with the simplest.

The regression model can be seen most clearly in the case of a perfect *linear* association between two variables. Figure 13.3 is a scattergram presenting in graphic form the values of X and Y produced by a hypothetical study. It shows that for the four cases in our study the values of X and Y are identical in each instance. The case with a value of 1 on X also has a value of 1 on Y, and so forth. The relationship between the two variables in this instance is described by the equation $Y = X$; this is the regression equation. Because all four points lie on a straight line, we can superimpose that line over the points; this is the regression line.

The linear regression model has important descriptive uses. The regression line offers a graphic picture of the association between X

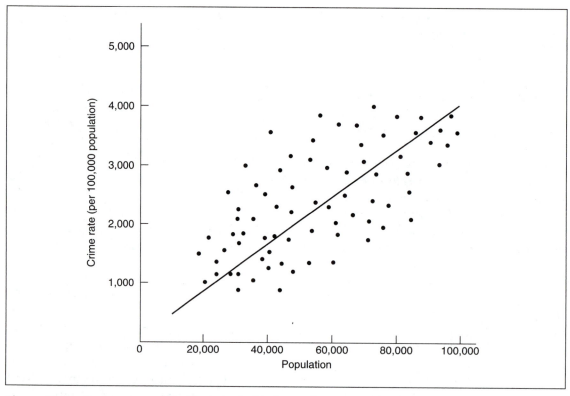

Figure 13.4   Scattergram of the Hypothetical Values of Two Variables with Regression Line Added

and Y, and the regression equation is an efficient form for summarizing that association. The regression model has inferential value as well. To the extent that the regression equation correctly describes the general association between the two variables, it may be used to predict other sets of values. If, for example, we know that a new case has a value of 3.5 on X, then we can predict the value of 3.5 on Y as well.

In practice, of course, studies are seldom limited to four cases, and the associations between variables are seldom as clear as the one presented in Figure 13.3.

Figure 13.4 is a somewhat more realistic example that represents a hypothetical relationship between population and crime rate in small to medium-size cities. Each dot in the scattergram is a city, and each dot's placement reflects that city's population and its crime rate. As in our previous example, the values of Y

(crime rates) generally correspond to those of X (populations), and as values of X increase, so do values of Y. However, the association is not nearly as clear as it was in Figure 13.3.

It is not possible in Figure 13.4 to superimpose a straight line that will pass through all the points in the scattergram. But we can draw an approximate line showing the best possible linear representation of the several points.

If you've ever studied geometry, you know that any straight line on a graph can be represented by an equation of the form $Y = a + bX$, where X and Y are values of the two variables. In this equation, a equals the value of Y when X is zero, and b represents the slope of the line. If we know the values of a and b, we can estimate Y for every value of X.

Regression analysis is a technique for establishing the regression equation representing the geometric line that comes closest to the distribution of points. This equation is valuable both descriptively and inferentially. First, the regression equation provides a mathematical description of the relationship between the variables. Second, it allows us to infer values of Y when we have values of X. Referring to Figure 13.4, we can estimate crime rates of cities if we know their populations.

To improve our guessing, we construct a regression line, stated in the form of a regression equation that permits the estimation of values on one variable from values on the other. The general format for this equation is $Y' = a + b(X)$, where a and b are computed values, X is a given value on one variable, and Y' is the estimated value on the other. The values of a and b are computed to minimize the differences between the actual values of Y and the corresponding estimates (Y') based on the known value of X. The sum of squared differences between actual and estimated values of Y is called the "unexplained variation" because it represents errors that exist even when estimates are based on known values of X.

The "explained variation" is the difference between the total variation and the unexplained variation. Dividing the explained variation by the total variation produces a measure of the proportionate reduction of error corresponding to the similar quantity in the computation of lambda. In the present case, this quantity is the correlation squared: r^2. Thus, if $r = .7$, then $r^2 = .49$, which means that about half the variation has been explained.

In practice, we compute r rather than r^2 because the product-moment correlation can take either a positive or a negative sign, depending on the direction of the relationship between the two variables. Computing r^2 and taking a square root will always produce a positive quantity, which means we will lose information about the direction of the relationship between X and Y. Consult any standard statistics textbook for the method of computing r. In practice, this and other measures of association are easily calculated with a variety of computer programs, including popular spreadsheet and database applications.

Multiple Regression Analysis Often, criminal justice researchers find that a given dependent variable is affected by several independent variables simultaneously. Multiple regression analysis provides a means for analyzing such situations. That was the case when Warner and Pierce (1993) set about studying social disorganization and calls for police services in Boston neighborhoods. Their expectations may be stated in the form of a multiple regression equation:

$$AR = b_0 + b_1X_1 + b_2X_2 + b_3X_3 + e$$

where

AR = assault rate
X_1 = poverty
X_2 = residential mobility
X_3 = racial heterogeneity
b = regression weight
e = residual

Notice that, in place of the single X variable in a linear regression, there are three X's, as well as three b's instead of just one. Also, the equation ends with a residual factor (e), which represents error—the variance in Y that is not accounted for by the X variables analyzed.

Warner and Pierce then calculated the values of the several b's to show the relative contributions of the several independent variables in neighborhood assault rates. They also calculated the multiple-correlation coefficient as an indicator of the extent to which the three independent variables predict the dependent variable. This follows the same logic as the simple bivariate correlation discussed earlier, and it is traditionally reported as a capital R. In this case, $R = .77$, which means that about 59 percent ($.77^2$) of the variance in neighborhood assault rates is explained by the three variables acting in concert.

Cautions in Regression Analysis The use of regression analysis for statistical inferences is based on the same assumptions made for

PUTTING IT ALL TOGETHER

ANALYZING NYPD CRIME DATA

Rutgers University researchers examined an enormous amount of data in their efforts to assess the impact the NYPD had on crime. Most of these data were nonpublic measures (see Chapter 11) based on different units of analysis. Much of the analysis included rather complex statistical models (see Sousa, 2003); here, we present relatively simple tabulations to illustrate some principles of descriptive statistics on data that have been slightly disguised.

The accompanying tables show five measures routinely listed on Compstat reports. Data are presented for a report issued in June 1999 covering 13 Brooklyn precincts. Data are real measures presented in an actual Compstat report, but the identity of the individual 13 is not presented.

Descriptive Statistics Only

These data are for a nonrandom selection of Brooklyn, New York, precincts, so we cannot use them as examples of statistical inference. The

Brooklyn Precinct Activity Measures

Precinct	Gun Arrests	Drug Arrests	Summons	Felony Assault	Domestic Incident Reports
1	10	25	3,452	66	652
2	12	32	1,339	143	1,251
3	5	46	489	127	1,128
4	5	61	767	85	433
5	4	63	990	117	1,071
6	0	103	1,077	95	554
7	1	143	1,369	89	991
8	20	335	2,437	260	1,947
9	11	374	905	70	572
10	39	389	2,323	246	2,350
11	47	465	3,361	403	3,504
12	8	497	2,325	114	1,230
13	5	626	1,674	212	1,124
N = 13					
Range	0–47	25–626	489–3,452	66–403	554–3,504
Median	8	143	1369	117	1124
Mean	12.8	243.0	1731.4	155.9	1292.8
Standard deviation	13.9	202.6	929.8	94.5	825.2

Note: Units are anonymous police precincts in Brooklyn, New York.
Data shown are totals for the period 1 January 1999 through 20 June 1999.

Units: Gun arrests: people arrested for illegal gun possession.
Drug arrests: people arrested for drug law violations.
Summons: people issued summons for "quality of life" violations.
Felony assault: serious assault incidents reported to police.
Domestic incident reports: incidents of domestic violence reported to police.

Correlation Matrix, Brooklyn Precinct Activity Measures

	Gun Arrests	Drug Arrests	Summons	Felony Assault	Domestic Incidence Reports
Gun Arrest	1.0				
Drug Arrest	0.44	1.0			
Summons	0.64	0.38	1.0		
Felony Assault	0.85	0.56	0.54	1.0	
Domestic Incidence Reports	0.92	0.48	0.64	0.95	1.0

Note: Entries are Pearson product moment correlations between row and column variables.

table labeled "Brooklyn Precinct Activity Measures" shows counts of different indicators from the June 1999 Compstat report. All data are totals for the period January 1, 1999, through June 20, 1999. Notice, in the key to this table, that some indicators are based on people as units, while others are based on incidents. The column labeled "Summonses" shows people charged with certain minor criminal offenses, popularly referred to as quality-of-life crimes.

As the descriptive statistics for this table show, quite a lot of variation exists among these 13 Brooklyn precincts. This is more true for certain measures—notably, gun arrests—than for others, such as domestic violence incident reports. For which measures is the mean a good measure of central tendency? For which measures is the mean less appropriate?

Bivariate Description

The second table presents a matrix of correlation coefficients (r). It's customary to use a matrix like this to show correlations among a number of variables. Notice that the coefficient along the diagonal is always 1.0; each variable is perfectly correlated with itself.

Many of the correlations in this table are rather high. The value of 0.95 for the correlation between felony assault and domestic violence incident reports means that these two measures are strongly related. Summons arrests and arrests for drug offenses are weakly related to each other.

The coefficients in this table can be transformed to reflect the general proportionate reduction in error model we considered earlier. By squaring each coefficient, you can find the proportion of variation in one variable "explained" by the other. Determining if one *really* explains the other requires making some assumptions about cause, an issue we discussed in other chapters.

Another useful exercise is to plot the covariation among a pair of measures and then to draw a straight line that passes closest to all plotted points. You will find this task easier for pairs of variables that are highly correlated. Why? If appropriate statistical software is available to you, computing regression models will help you answer that question. Finally, compare your graph of measures from Brooklyn precincts with Figure 13.4.

These simple exercises with actual NYPD crime data will give you some hands-on experience with powerful statistical techniques. You will also gain insight into the relationships between measures of police activity and different measures of crime. For example, three indicators shown in the Brooklyn table are more direct measures of police activity, whereas the other indicators measure crime problems reported to police. Discussing which are which, and then conducting appropriate analysis on those variables, will help you learn about the relationship between police and crime, and how social scientists study such relationships.

correlational analysis: simple random sampling, the absence of nonsampling errors, and continuous interval data. Because data in criminal justice research seldom completely satisfy these assumptions, caution is always advised in assessing the results of regression analyses.

Also, regression lines can be useful for interpolation (estimating cases that lie between those observed), but they are less trustworthy when used for extrapolation (estimating cases that lie beyond the range of observations). This limitation on extrapolations is important in two ways. First, it's not uncommon to find regression equations that seem to make illogical predictions. An equation that links population and crimes, for example, might seem to suggest that small towns with, say, a population of 1000 should produce −123 crimes a year. This failure in predictive ability does not disqualify the equation, but it does dramatize that its applicability is limited to a particular range of population sizes. Second, researchers sometimes overstep this limitation, drawing inferences that lie outside their range of observation.

Inferential Statistics

When we generalize from samples to larger populations, we use inferential statistics to test the significance of an observed relationship.

Many criminal justice research projects examine data collected from a sample drawn from a larger population. A sample of people may be interviewed in a survey; a sample of court records may be coded and analyzed; a sample of newspapers may be examined through content analysis. Researchers seldom, if ever, study samples merely to describe the samples per se; in most instances, their ultimate purpose is to make assertions about the larger population from which the sample has been selected. Frequently, then, we will want to interpret our univariate and multivariate sample findings as the basis for inferences about some population.

This section examines the statistical measures used for making such inferences and their logical bases. We'll begin with univariate data and then move to bivariate.

Univariate Inferences

The opening sections of this chapter dealt with methods of presenting univariate data. Each summary measure was intended to describe the sample studied. Now we will use those measures to make broader assertions about the population. This section will focus on two univariate measures: percentages and means.

If 50 percent of a sample of people say they received traffic tickets during the past year, then 50 percent is also our best estimate of the proportion of people who received traffic tickets in the total population from which the sample was drawn. Our estimate assumes a simple random sample, of course. It is rather unlikely, however, that precisely 50 percent of the population got tickets during the year. If a rigorous sampling design for random selection has been followed, we will be able to estimate the expected range of error when the sample finding is applied to the population.

The section in Chapter 8 on sampling theory covered the procedures for making such estimates, so they will only be reviewed here. The quantity

$$s = \sqrt{\frac{p \times q}{n}}$$

where p is a percentage, q equals $1 - p$, and n is the sample size, is called the "standard error." As noted in Chapter 8, this quantity is very important in the estimation of sampling error. We may be 68 percent confident that the population figure falls within plus or minus 1 standard error of the sample figure, 95 percent confident that it falls within plus or minus 2 standard errors, and 99.9 percent confident that it falls within plus or minus 3 standard errors.

Any statement of sampling error, then, must contain two essential components: the confidence level (for example, 95 percent) and the confidence interval (for example, 2.5 percent).

If 50 percent of a sample of 1600 people say they have received traffic tickets during the year, we might say we are 95 percent confident that the population figure is between 47.5 and 52.5 percent.

Recognize in this example that we have moved beyond simply describing the sample into the realm of making estimates (inferences) about the larger population. In doing that, we must be wary of three assumptions.

First, the sample must be drawn from the population about which inferences are being made. A sample taken from a telephone directory, for example, cannot legitimately be the basis for statistical inferences about the population of a city.

Second, the inferential statistics assume simple random sampling, which is virtually never the case in actual sample surveys. The statistics assume sampling with replacement, which is almost never done, but that is probably not a serious problem. Although systematic sampling is used more frequently than random sampling, that, too, probably presents no serious problem if done correctly. Stratified sampling, because it improves representativeness, clearly presents no problem. Cluster sampling does present a problem, however, because the estimates of sampling error may be too small. Clearly, street-corner sampling does not warrant the use of inferential statistics. This standard error sampling technique also assumes a 100 percent completion rate. This problem increases in seriousness as the completion rate decreases.

Third, inferential statistics apply to sampling error only; they do not take account of **nonsampling errors.** Thus, although we might correctly state that between 47.5 and 52.5 percent of the population (95 percent confidence) will report getting a traffic ticket during the previous year, we can not so confidently guess the percentage that had actually received them. Because nonsampling errors are probably larger than sampling errors in a respectable sample design, we need to be especially cautious in generalizing from our sample findings to the population.

Tests of Statistical Significance

There is no scientific answer to the question of whether a given association between two variables is significant, strong, important, interesting, or worth reporting. Perhaps the ultimate test of significance rests with our ability to persuade readers (present and future) of the association's significance. At the same time, a body of inferential statistics—known as parametric tests of significance—can assist in this regard. As the name suggests, parametric statistics make certain assumptions about the parameters that describe the population from which the sample is selected.

Although tests of statistical significance are widely reported in criminal justice literature, the logic underlying them is subtle and often misunderstood. Tests of significance are based on the same sampling logic that has been discussed elsewhere in this book. To understand that logic, let's return to the concept of sampling error with regard to univariate data.

Recall that a sample statistic normally provides the best single estimate of the corresponding population parameter, but the statistic and the parameter are seldom identical. Thus, we report the probability that the parameter falls within a certain range (confidence interval). The degree of uncertainty within that range is due to normal sampling error. The corollary of such a statement is, of course, that it is improbable that the parameter will fall outside the specified range only as a result of sampling error. Thus, if we estimate that a parameter (99.9 percent confidence) lies between 45 and 55 percent, we say by implication that it is extremely improbable that the parameter is actually, say, 70 percent if our only error of estimation is due to normal sampling. That is the basic logic behind tests of significance.

The Logic of Statistical Significance

The logic of statistical significance can be illustrated in a series of diagrams representing the selection of samples from a population. The elements in the logic we will illustrate are

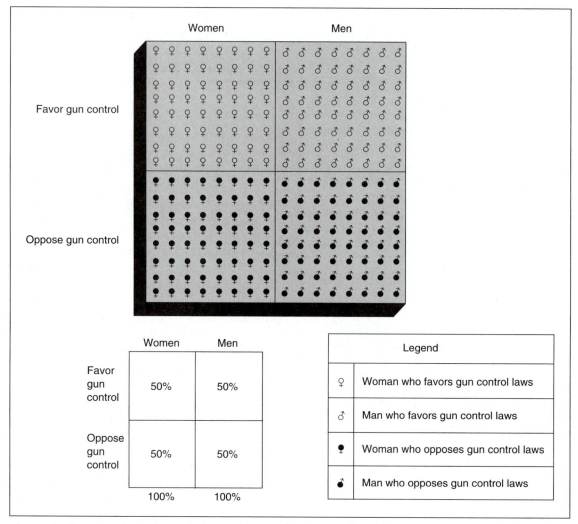

Figure 13.5   Hypothetical Population of Men and Women Who Either Favor or Oppose Gun Control Laws

(1) assumptions regarding the *independence* of two variables in the population study, (2) assumptions regarding the *representativeness* of samples selected through conventional probability sampling procedures, and (3) the observed *joint distribution* of sample elements in terms of the two variables.

Figure 13.5 represents a hypothetical population of 256 people, half women and half men. The diagram indicates how each person feels about laws restricting gun ownership. In the diagram, those who favor gun control laws have open circles; those who oppose it have their circles shaded in.

The question we'll be investigating is whether there is any relationship between gender and opinions about gun control laws. More specifically, we'll investigate whether women are more likely to favor gun control than men. Take a moment to look at Figure 13.5 and see what the answer to that question might be.

The figure indicates that there is no relationship between gender and attitudes about gun control. Exactly half of each group favors gun

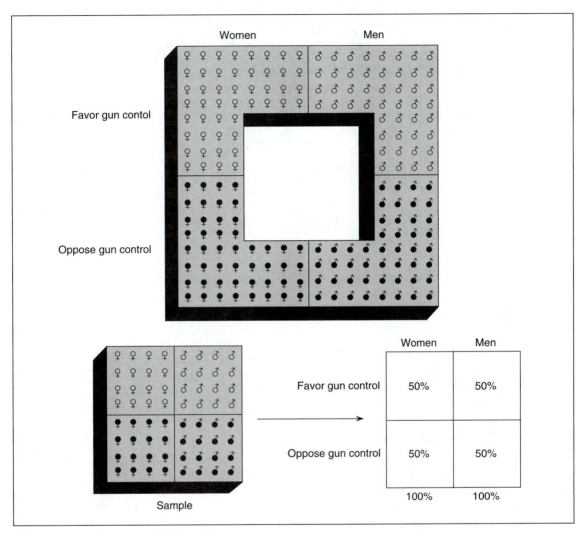

Figure 13.6 Representative Sample

control, and half opposes it. Recall the earlier discussion of proportionate reduction of error. In this instance, knowing a person's gender will not reduce the "errors" we make in guessing his or her attitude toward gun control laws. The chart at the bottom of Figure 13.5 provides a tabular view of what can be observed in the graphic diagram.

Figure 13.6 represents the selection of a one-fourth sample from the hypothetical population. In terms of the graphic illustration, a "square" selection from the center of the popu-lation provides a representative sample. Notice that our sample contains 16 of each type of per-son: Half are men and half are women; half of each gender group favors gun control, and the other half opposes it.

The sample selected in Figure 13.6 allows us to draw accurate conclusions about the rela-tionship between gender and attitudes toward gun control in the larger population. Following the sampling logic presented in Chapter 8, we note that there is no relationship between gen-der and gun control attitudes in the sample.

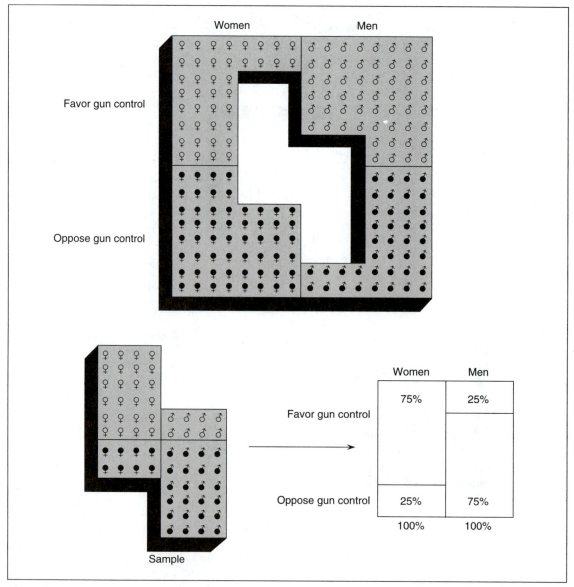

Figure 13.7   Unrepresentative Sample

Thus, we conclude that there is similarly no relationship in the larger population—because we've presumably selected a sample according to the conventional rules of sampling.

Of course, real-life samples are seldom such perfect reflections of the populations from which they are drawn. It would not be unusual for us to have selected, say, one of two extra men who oppose gun control and a couple of extra women who favor it—even if there was no relationship between the two variables in the population. Such minor variations are part and parcel of probability sampling, as we saw in Chapter 8.

Figure 13.7, however, represents a sample that falls far short of the mark in reflecting the

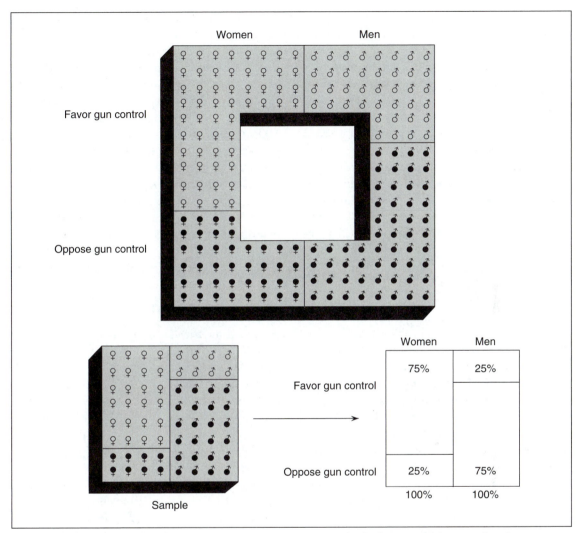

Figure 13.8 Representative Sample from a Population in Which the Variables Are Related

larger population. Notice that far too many supportive women and too many opposing men are selected. As the table shows, three-fourths of the women in the sample support gun control, but only one-fourth of the men do so. If we selected this sample from a population in which the two variables were unrelated, we would be sorely misled by the analysis of our sample.

As you'll recall, it's unlikely that a properly drawn probability sample will ever be as inaccurate as the one shown in Figure 13.7. In fact, if we actually select a sample that gives us those re-

sults, we should look for a different explanation. Figure 13.8 illustrates that other explanation.

Notice that the sample selected in Figure 13.8 also shows a strong relationship between gender and opinion about gun control. The reason is quite different this time. We've selected a perfectly representative sample, but we see that there is actually a strong relationship between the two variables in the population at large. In this figure, women are more likely to support gun control than men: That's the case in the population, and the sample reflects it.

In practice, of course, we never know what's so for the total population; that's why we select samples. So, if we select a sample and find the strong relationship presented in Figures 13.7 and 13.8, we need to decide whether that finding accurately reflects the population or is simply a product of sampling error.

The fundamental logic of tests of statistical significance, then, is this: Faced with *any* discrepancy between the assumed independence of variables in a population and the observed distribution of sample elements, we may explain that discrepancy in either of two ways: (1) We attribute it to an unrepresentative sample, or (2) we reject the assumption of independence. The logic and statistics associated with probability sampling methods offer guidance about the varying probabilities of different degrees of unrepresentativeness (expressed as sampling error). Most simply put, there is a high probability of a small degree of unrepresentativeness and a low probability of a large degree of unrepresentativeness.

The **statistical significance** of a relationship observed in a set of sample data, then, is always expressed in terms of probabilities. Significant at the .05 level ($p \le .05$) simply means that the probability of a relationship as strong as the observed one being attributable to sampling error alone is no more than 5 in 100. Put somewhat differently, if two variables are independent of each other in the population, and if 100 probability samples were selected from that population, then no more than 5 of those samples should provide a relationship as strong as the one that has been observed.

There is, then, a corollary to confidence intervals in tests of significance, which represent the probability of the measured associations being due only to sampling error. This is called the **level of significance.** Like confidence intervals, levels of significance are derived from a logical model in which several samples are drawn from a given population. In the present case, we assume that no association exists between the variables in the population, and then we ask what proportion of the samples drawn from

that population would produce associations at least as great as those measured in the empirical data. Three levels of significance are frequently used in research reports: .05, .01, and .001. These mean, respectively, that the chances of obtaining the measured association as a result of sampling error are no more than 5 in 100, 1 in 100, and 1 in 1000.

Researchers who use tests of significance normally follow one of two patterns. Some specify in advance the level of significance they will regard as sufficient. If any measured association is statistically significant at that level, they will regard it as representing a genuine association between the two variables. In other words, they are willing to discount the possibility of its resulting from sampling error only.

Other researchers prefer to report the specific level of significance for each association, disregarding the conventions of .05, .01, and .001. Rather than reporting that a given association is significant at, say, the .05 level, they might report significance at the .023 level, indicating that the chances of its having resulted from sampling error as no more than 23 in 1000.

Visualizing Statistical Significance

In a Bureau of Justice Statistics publication describing the National Crime Victimization Survey (NCVS) for a nontechnical audience, Michael Maltz and Marianne Zawitz (1998) introduce a very useful technique for using graphical displays to show statistical significance.

Recall that the NCVS is a national sample designed to estimate nationwide rates of victimization. We also saw in earlier chapters that the NCVS is based on large samples in order to estimate crimes that are relatively rare—most notably, rape and robbery. Maltz and Zawitz use visual displays of estimates and their confidence intervals to demonstrate the relative precision of victimization rates disclosed by the survey.

Figure 13.9, reproduced from Maltz and Zawitz, presents an example of this approach. The figure shows annual rates of change in all violent victimizations from 1973 through 1996. Notice

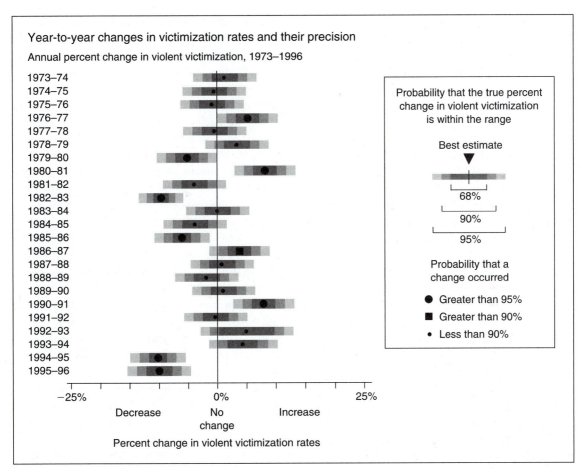

Figure 13.9 Point Estimates and Confidence Intervals
Source: Maltz and Zawitz (1998:4).

the vertical line in Figure 13.9, representing no change in violent victimization rates for each year. Estimates of annual rates of change are shown in horizontal bars arrayed along the vertical line. The horizontal bars for each year present parameter estimates for annual change, signified by a dot or square, bracketed by the confidence intervals for each parameter estimate at three confidence levels: 68 percent (1 standard error), 90 percent (1.6 standard errors), and 95 percent (2 standard errors).

Consider first the topmost bar, showing estimates for change from 1973 to 1974. The small dot signifying the point estimate (an increase of 1.24 percent) is just to the right of the no-

change vertical line. But notice also that the confidence intervals of 1, 1.6, and 2 standard errors cross over the no-change line; the estimate of a 1.24 percent increase is less than 2 standard errors above zero. This means that, using the .05 (2 standard errors) criterion, the estimated increase is not statistically significant. To further emphasize this point, notice the key in Figure 13.9, which shows different probabilities that a change occurred each year; the small dot representing the point estimate for 1973–74 change indicates the probability that a change actually occurred is less than 90 percent.

Now consider the most recent estimate shown in this figure—change from 1995 to

1996. The point estimate of −9.9 percent is well below the no-change line, and the confidence intervals are well to the left of this line. Bracketing the point estimate by 2 standard errors produces an interval estimate of between −15.7 percent (point estimate *minus* 2 standard errors) and −4.05 percent (point estimate *plus* 2 standard errors). This means we can be 95 percent certain that the violent victimization rate declined from 1995 to 1996 by somewhere between −4.05 and −15.7 percent. Because the point estimate of −9.9 percent is more than 2 standard errors from zero, we can confidently say there was a statistically significant decline in violent victimization.

Displaying point and interval estimates in this way accurately represents the concepts of statistical inference and statistical significance. Sample-based estimates of victimization, or any other variable, are just that—estimates of population values, bounded by estimates of standard error. Statistical significance, in this example, means that our estimates of change are above or below zero, according to some specified criterion for significance.

Annual publications documenting changes in victimization rates from the NCVS now routinely present visual displays like that in Figure 13.9. See Callie Rennison (2002:4) for an example that shows declines in violent victimization continuing through the year 2001.

Studying Figure 13.9 will enhance your understanding of statistical inference. We suggest that you consider the point and interval estimates for each year's change. Pay particular attention to the confidence intervals and their position relative to the no-change line. Then classify the statistical significance (at the .05 level) for change each year into one of three categories: (1) no change, (2) significant increase, and (3) significant decrease. You'll find our tabulation in the exercises at the end of this chapter.

Chi Square

Chi square (χ^2) is a different type of significance test that is widely used in criminal justice research. It is based on the **null hypothesis:** the as-

sumption that there is no relationship between two variables in a population. Given the observed distribution of values on two variables in a contingency table, we compute the joint distribution that would be *expected* if there were no relationship between the two variables. The result of this operation is a set of expected frequencies for all the cells in the contingency table. We then compare this expected distribution with the *empirical* distribution—cases actually found in the data—and determine the probability that the difference between expected and empirical distributions could have resulted from sampling error alone. Stated simply, chi square compares what you get (empirical) with what you expect given a null hypothesis of no relationship. An example will illustrate this procedure.

Let's assume we are interested in the possible relationship between gender and whether people avoid areas near their home because of crime, which we will refer to as "avoidance behavior." To test this relationship, we select a sample of 100 people at random. Our sample is made up of 40 men and 60 women; 70 percent of our sample report avoidance behavior, and the remaining 30 percent do not.

If there is no relationship between gender and avoidance behavior, then 70 percent of the men in the sample should report avoiding areas near their home, and 30 percent should report no avoidance behavior. Moreover, women should describe avoidance behavior in the same proportion. Table 13.11 (part I) shows that, based on this model, 28 men and 42 women say they avoid areas at night, with 12 men and 18 women reporting no avoidance.

Part II of Table 13.11 presents the observed avoidance behavior for the hypothetical sample of 100 people. Note that 20 of the men say they avoid areas at night, and the remaining 20 say they do not. Among the women in the sample, 50 avoid areas and 10 do not. Comparing the expected and observed frequencies (parts I and II), we note that somewhat fewer men report avoidance behavior than expected, whereas somewhat more women than expected avoid areas near their home at night.

Table 13.11 Hypothetical Illustration of Chi Square

I. Expected Cell Frequencies

	Men	Women	Total
Avoid areas*	28	42	70
Do not avoid areas	12	18	30
Total	40	60	100

II. Observed Cell Frequencies

	Men	Women	Total
Avoid areas	20	50	70
Do not avoid areas	20	10	30
Total	40	60	100

III. (Observed − Expected)^2 ÷ Expected

	Men	Women	
Avoid areas	2.29	1.52	Chi sq. = 12.70
Do not avoid areas	5.33	3.56	$p < .001$

*"Is there any area around here—that is, within a city block—that you avoid at night because of crime?"

Chi square is computed as follows: For each cell in the tables, we (1) subtract the expected frequency for that cell from the observed frequency, (2) square this quantity, and (3) divide the squared difference by the expected frequency. This procedure is carried out for each cell in the tables, and the results are added. Part III of Table 13.11 presents the cell-by-cell computations. The final sum is the value of chi square—12.70 in this example.

This value is the overall discrepancy between the observed distribution in the sample and the distribution we would expect if the two variables were unrelated. Of course, the mere discovery of a discrepancy does not *prove* that the two variables are related, because normal sampling error might produce discrepancies even when there is no relationship in the total population. The magnitude of the value of chi square, however, permits us to estimate the probability of that having happened.

To determine the statistical significance of the observed relationship, we must use a standard set of chi-square values. That will require the computation of the degrees of freedom. For chi square, the degrees of freedom are computed as follows: The number of rows in the table of observed frequencies, minus one, is multiplied by the number of columns, minus one. This may be written as $(r - 1)(c - 1)$. In the present example, we have two rows and two columns (discounting the totals), so there is 1 degree of freedom.

Turning to a table of chi-square values (see the inside back cover), we find that, for 1 degree of freedom and random sampling from a population in which there is no relationship between two variables, 10 percent of the time we should expect a chi square of at least 2.7. Thus, if we select 100 samples from such a population, we should expect about 10 of those samples to produce chi squares equal to or greater than 2.7. Moreover, we should expect chi-square values of at least 6.6 in only 1 percent of the samples and chi-square values of 10.8 in only 0.1 percent of the samples. The higher the chi-square value, the less probable it is that the value can be attributed to sampling error alone.

In our example, the computed value of chi square is 12.70. If there is no relationship between gender and avoidance behavior, and a large number of samples were selected and studied, we can expect a chi square of this magnitude in fewer than 0.1 percent of those samples.

Table 13.12   Hypothetical Illustration of Chi-Square Sensitivity to Sample Size

I. Expected Cell Frequencies

	Men	Women	Total
Avoid areas*	5.6	8.4	14
Do not avoid areas	2.4	3.6	6
Total	8	12	20

II. Observed Cell Frequencies

	Men	Women	Total
Avoid areas	4	10	14
Do not avoid areas	4	2	6
Total	8	12	20

III. (Observed − Expected)^2 ÷ Expected

	Men	Women	
Avoid areas	0.46	0.30	Chi sq. = 2.54
Do not avoid areas	1.07	0.71	$10 < p < 20$

*"Is there any area around here—that is, within a city block—that you avoid at night because of crime?"

Thus, the probability of obtaining a chi square of this magnitude is less than 0.001 if random sampling has been used and there is no relationship in the population. We report this finding by saying that the relationship is statistically significant at the .001 level. Because it is so improbable that the observed relationship could have resulted from sampling error alone, we are likely to reject the null hypothesis and assume that a relationship does, in fact, exist between the two variables.

Many measures of association can be tested for statistical significance in a similar manner. Standard tables of values permit us to determine whether a given association is statistically significant and at what level.

Cautions in Interpreting Statistical Significance

Tests of significance provide an objective yardstick against which to estimate the significance of associations between variables. They assist us in ruling out associations that may not represent genuine relationships in the population under study. However, the researcher who uses or reads reports of significance tests should be aware of certain cautions in their interpretation.

First, we have been discussing tests of *statistical* significance; there are no objective tests of *substantive* significance. Thus, we may be legitimately convinced that a given association is not due to sampling error but still assert, without fear of contradiction, that two variables are only slightly related to each other. Recall that sampling error is an inverse function of sample size: the larger the sample, the smaller the expected error. Thus, a correlation of, say, .1 might well be significant (at a given level) if discovered in a large sample, whereas the same correlation between the same two variables would not be significant if found in a smaller sample. Of course, that makes perfect sense if one understands the basic logic of tests of significance: In the larger sample, there is less chance that the correlation is simply the product of sampling error.

Consider, for example, Table 13.12, in which 20 cases are distributed in the same proportions across row and column categories as in Table 13.11. In each table, 83 percent of women report avoidance behavior (10 out of 12 in Table 13.12, and 50 out of 60 in Table 13.11).

But with one-fifth the number of cases in Table 13.12, the computed value of chi square is only one-fifth that obtained in Table 13.11. Consulting the distribution of chi-square values (inside back cover), we see that the probability of obtaining a chi square of 2.54 with 1 degree of freedom lies between .1 and .2. Thus, if there is no relationship between these two variables, we can expect to obtain a chi square of this size in 10–20 percent of samples drawn. Most researchers would not reject the null hypothesis of no relationship in this case.

We mentioned the point illustrated by this example in Chapter 12 because sample size is especially important for applied studies that use experimental designs. With small sample sizes, even moderately large differences might result from sampling error. Because randomized experiments are costly and time consuming, they are often conducted with relatively small numbers of subjects in experimental and control groups. With small numbers of subjects, only large differences in outcome variables will be statistically significant.

The distinction between statistical and substantive significance is perhaps best illustrated by those cases in which there is absolute certainty that observed differences cannot be a result of sampling error. That is the case when we observe an entire population. Suppose we are able to learn the age and gender of every murder victim in the United States for 1996. For argument's sake, let's assume that the average age of male murder victims is 25, as compared with, say, 26 for female victims. Because we have the ages of all murder victims, there is no question of sampling error. We know with certainty that the female victims are older than their male counterparts. At the same time, we can say that the difference is of no substantive significance. We conclude, in fact, that they are essentially the same age.

Second, lest you be misled by this hypothetical example, statistical significance should not be calculated on relationships observed in data collected from whole populations. Remember, tests of statistical significance measure the likelihood of relationships between variables being only a product of sampling error, which, of course, assumes that data come from a sample. If there's no sampling, there's no sampling error.

Third, tests of significance are based on the same sampling assumptions we used to compute confidence intervals. To the extent that these assumptions are not met by the actual sampling design, the tests of significance are not strictly legitimate.

In practice, tests of statistical significance are frequently used inappropriately. If you were to review any given issue of an academic journal in criminal justice, we'd be willing to bet you would find one or more of these technically improper uses:

- Tests of significance computed for data representing entire populations
- Tests based on samples that do not meet the required assumptions of probability sampling
- Tests applied to measures of association that have been computed in violation of the assumptions made by those measures (for example, Pearson product-moment correlations computed from ordinal data)
- Interpretation of statistical significance as a measure of association (a "relationship" of $p \leq .001$ is "stronger" than one of $p \leq .05$)

We do not mean to a suggest a "purist" approach by these comments. We encourage you to use any statistical technique—any measure of association or any test of significance—on any set of data if it will help you understand your data. In doing so, however, you should recognize what measures of association and statistical significance can and cannot tell you, as well as the assumptions required for various measures. Any individual statistic or measure tells only part of the story, and you should try to learn as much of the story as you can.

Visualizing Discernible Differences

In this spirit, Michael Maltz proposes a compromise in the use of statistical significance tests on populations and on samples that

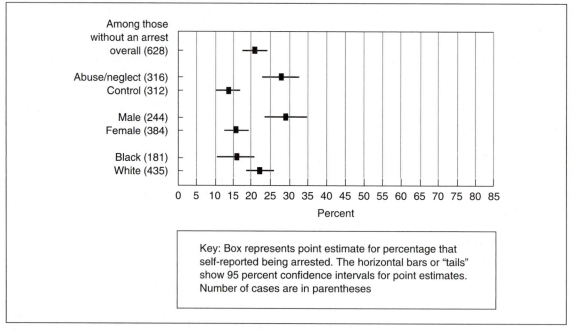

Figure 13.10   Displaying Data: Percentage that Self-Report Arrests
Source: Adapted from Maxfield, Weiler, and Widom (2000:100, Figure 1).

violate the assumptions of probability sampling. Acting on a suggestion by criminologist Alfred Blumstein, Maltz (1994:440) advises researchers to use the phrase "statistically discernible difference" rather than "statistically significant difference" when using significance tests on inappropriate samples or populations. A **statistically discernible difference** is one that would be considered statistically significant if found in a random sample. Being careful with our language in this way alerts readers that, although significance tests are not technically appropriate, they can be used as a gauge to show the magnitude of deviation from the null hypothesis.

Researchers can also use the Maltz and Zawitz technique for presenting bounded point estimates to assess relationships between two or more variables. For example, Maxfield and associates (Maxfield, Weiler, and Widom, 2000) compared self-reports of arrests to actual records of arrests for Cathy Spatz Widom's

(1992) sample of child abuse/neglect victims and matched controls. Their research question centered on the relationship between two measures of offending—official records of arrests and self-reported arrests. Self-report measures, gathered through interviews with almost 1200 subjects, were compared with arrest records obtained from local, state, and federal law enforcement agencies.

Recall from earlier chapters that Widom's subjects were selected purposively: Abuse/neglect victims were identified through court records, and controls were individually matched to victims. Because this sample can in no way be considered random, tests of statistical significance are not technically appropriate.

Figure 13.10 presents point and interval estimates of self-reported arrests for different subgroups of subjects who did not have an official arrest record. The first point estimate shows that, of the 628 subjects with no official arrest record, 21 percent told interviewers that they *had* been arrested. This estimate is bracketed by 95 percent confidence intervals, showing the point estimate plus or minus 2 standard errors.

Now consider the separate estimates for abuse/neglect victims and their controls. A larger percentage of abuse/neglect victims (28 percent) self-reported arrests compared with control subjects (14 percent). Furthermore, when these point estimates are bounded by 2 standard errors, the "tails" of the two estimates do not overlap. This means that the estimates of self-reported arrests for abuse/neglect victims are more than 2 standard errors higher than those for control subjects. The last pair of subgroupings compares self-reported arrests by black and white subjects, regardless of whether they were abuse/neglect victims or controls. In this case, the tails of bounded estimates for the two groups overlap, indicating that self-reported arrests for black and white subjects are less than 2 standard errors apart.

Because the analysis shown in Figure 13.10 is not based on a random sample, it violates the assumptions of statistical significance tests. However, it's still possible to assess the relative size of differences in self-reported arrests by comparing bounded point estimates. Following the suggestion of Blumstein and Maltz, we can make the following observation: There is a statistically discernible difference in self-reported arrests between abuse/neglect victims and control subjects, but not between black and white subjects.

✪ *Main Points*

- Descriptive statistics are used to summarize data under study.
- A frequency distribution shows the number of cases that have each of the attributes of a given variable.
- Measures of central tendency reduce data to an easily manageable form, but they do not convey the detail of the original data.
- Measures of dispersion give a summary indication of the distribution of cases around an average value.

- Rates are descriptive statistics that standardize some measure for comparative purposes.
- Bivariate analysis and subgroup comparisons examine some type of relationship between two variables.
- The rules of thumb in interpreting bivariate percentage tables are (1) "Percentage down" and "read across" in making the subgroup comparisons, or (2) "Percentage across" and "read down" in making subgroup comparisons.
- Multivariate analysis is a method of analyzing the simultaneous relationships among several variables and may be used to more fully understand the relationship between two variables.
- Many measures of association are based on a proportionate reduction of error (PRE) model, which measures improvement in predictions about one variable, given information about a second variable.
- Lambda (λ) and gamma (γ) are PRE-based measures of association for nominal and ordinal variables, respectively.
- Pearson's product-moment correlation (r) is a measure of association used in the analysis of two interval or ratio variables.
- Regression equations are computed on the basis of a regression line—the geometric line that represents, with the least amount of discrepancy, the actual location of points in a scattergram. The equation for a regression line predicts the values of a dependent variable on the basis of values of one or more independent variables.
- Inferential statistics are used to estimate the generalizability of findings arrived at in the analysis of a sample to the larger population from which the sample has been selected.
- Inferences about some characteristic of a population—such as the percentage that favors gun control laws—must contain an indication of a confidence interval (the range within which the value is expected to be—for example, between 45 and 55 percent favor gun control) and an indication of the confidence level (the likelihood that the value does fall within that range—for example, 95 percent confidence).
- Tests of statistical significance estimate the likelihood that an association as large as the observed one could result from normal sampling error if no such association exists between the variables in the larger population.
- Statistical significance must not be confused with substantive significance, which means that

an observed association is strong, important, or meaningful.

- Tests of statistical significance, strictly speaking, make assumptions about data and methods that are almost never satisfied completely by real social research. Claiming a "statistically discernible relationship" is more appropriate when assumptions are not satisfied.

✪ Key Terms

Average	Multivariate analysis
Bivariate analysis	Nonsampling errors
Contingency table	Null hypothesis
Descriptive statistics	Proportionate
Dispersion	reduction of error
Frequency	Regression analysis
distributions	Standard deviation
Inferential statistics	Statistical significance
Level of significance	Statistically discernible
Mean	difference
Median	Univariate analysis
Mode	

✪ Review Questions and Exercises

1. Using the data in the accompanying table, construct and interpret tables showing:
   a. The bivariate relationship between age and attitude toward capital punishment
   b. The bivariate relationship between political orientation and attitude toward capital punishment
   c. The multivariate relationship linking age, political orientation, and attitude toward capital punishment

Age	Political Orientation	Attitude Toward Capital Punishment	Frequency
Young	Conservative	Favor	90
Young	Conservative	Oppose	10
Young	Liberal	Favor	60
Young	Liberal	Oppose	40
Old	Conservative	Favor	60
Old	Conservative	Oppose	10
Old	Liberal	Favor	15
Old	Liberal	Oppose	15

2. Distinguish between measures of association and tests of statistical significance.

3. Here are our answers to the question about statistical significance relating to Figure 13.9: Fifteen years show no significant change in violent victimization; significant increases are shown for 3 years; violent victimization decline significantly in 5 years. The increase from 1976 to 1977 and the decrease from 1979 to 1980 are close; notice the edge of the 95 percent confidence interval borders the no-change line. We recommend that you read the Maltz and Zawitz publication. It's listed in the bibliography and can be downloaded from the Bureau of Justice Statistics Web site at http://www.ojp.usdoj.gov/bjs/abstract/dvctue.htm.

✪ Internet Exercises

To ensure that you always have access to live, correct Web links for the Web sites referenced in the following exercises, we provide the necessary links on the companion Web site for *Research Methods for Criminal Justice and Criminology* at http://cj.wadsworth.com/maxfield_babbie/research_methods4e. Once at the companion Web site, select this specific chapter, click on "Chapter Resources," then click on "Web Links."

1. The Texas Department of Criminal Justice (TDCJ) provides detailed information on offenders who have been executed in that state since the reinstatement of the death penalty. Go to the TDCJ Web site and use some of the descriptive statistical techniques you have learned in this chapter to summarize what you find—for example, the average age of the executed offenders, their ethnic distribution, and the percentage female. What other questions might you be able to answer if you took the time to record the additional information included on the offender information form that is provided for most of the offenders?

2. Go to the General Social Survey Web site.
   a. Prepare bivariate contingency tables for analyzing the relationship between gun ownership and these variables: political party affiliation, education, and rural/urban/suburban residence.
   b. Prepare a three-way contingency table for analyzing gun ownership, gender, and each of the variables from the first part of this exercise.

3. Visit the online data analysis site maintained by the National Archive of Criminal Justice Data. Read the introductory material for on-line data analysis. Then select a study from the lists provided, and produce two contingency tables using four variables of interest to you. Present percentages computed in the correct direction. Also include descriptive statistics for each variable.

✪ InfoTrac College Edition

Search InfoTrac College Edition to find a research article on a topic you are interested in learning more about. What is the primary research question that guides the study? How does the author use statistics to answer this research question? Does the author use descriptive statistics? How? Does the author use inferential statistics? How? Do you think that the author's use of statistics helped her or him to "make a case" for the conclusions drawn?

✪ The NEW Companion Web Site for Research Methods for Criminal Justice and Criminology, *Fourth Edition*

http://cj.wadsworth.com/maxfield_babbie/research_methods4e

Supplement your review of this chapter by going to the new companion Web site to take one of the Tutorial Quizzes, use the flash cards to master key terms, and check out the many other study aids you'll find there. You'll also find special features such as quantitative and qualitative data analysis primers to help you with a special project or do some research on your own.

✪ Additional Readings

Babbie, Earl, Halley, Fred, and Zaino, Jeanne, *Adventures in Social Research* (Newbury Park, CA: Pine Forge Press, 2000). This book introduces you to data analysis through SPSS, a widely used computer program for statistical analysis. Several of the basic techniques described in this chapter are illustrated and discussed further.

Finkelstein, Michael O., and Levin, Bruce, *Statistics for Lawyers* (New York: Springer-Verlag, 1990). Law school trains people to be analytic, but few lawyers know much about statistics. This book provides a straightforward explanation of many basic statistical concepts. Examples are drawn from actual cases to illustrate how to calculate and interpret statistics. In addition, readers gain insight into how to reason with statistics.

Mohr, Lawrence B., *Understanding Significance Testing* (Thousand Oaks, CA: Sage, 1990). An excellent and comprehensive examination of the topic, this book covers both the technical details and the substantive meaning of significance tests.

Morgan, Susan E., Reichart, Tom, and Harrison, Tyler R., *From Numbers to Words: Reporting Statistical Results in the Social Sciences* (Boston: Allyn & Bacon, 2002). This book provides basic but uncommonly useful information on how to use and present basic statistical techniques. Each section includes general guidelines and examples from research studies. This book is helpful as an introduction for beginning researchers and a reference for more experienced analysts.

Weisburd, David, and Britt, Chester, *Statistics in Criminal Justice*, 2nd ed. (Belmont, CA: Wadsworth, 2002). This text presents an excellent basic introduction to statistics using examples from criminal justice.

Glossary

Aggregate Groups of units—people, prisons, court-rooms, or stolen autos, for example. Although criminal justice professionals are usually most concerned with individual units, social science searches for patterns that are reflected in aggregations of units. For example, a probation officer focuses on probation clients as individuals, whereas a social scientist focuses on groups of probation clients, or aggregates. See Chapter 1.

Anonymity The identity of a research subject is not known, and it is therefore impossible to link data about a subject to an individual's name. Anonymity is one tool for addressing the ethical issue of privacy. Compare to *confidentiality*. See Chapter 3.

Attributes Characteristics of persons or things. See *variables* and Chapter 1.

Average An ambiguous term that generally suggests typical or normal. The mean, median, and mode are specific mathematical averages. See Chapter 13.

Binomial variable A variable that has only two attributes is binomial. Gender is an example; it has the attributes male and female.

Bivariate analysis The analysis of two variables simultaneously for the purpose of determining the empirical relationship between them. The construction of a simple percentage table and the computation of a simple correlation coefficient are examples of bivariate analyses. See Chapter 13.

Case-oriented research A research strategy in which many cases are examined to understand a comparatively small number of variables. Examples include experiments (Chapter 7) and surveys (Chapter 9).

Case study A research strategy in which the researcher's attention centers on an in-depth examination of one or a few cases on many dimensions. Case studies can be exploratory, descriptive, or explanatory. Case studies can also be used in evaluation research. See Chapters 7 and 12.

Classical experiment A research design well suited to inferring cause, the classical experiment involves three major pairs of components: (1) independent and dependent variables, (2) pretesting and posttesting, and (3) experimental and control groups, with subjects randomly assigned to one group or the other. See Chapter 7.

Closed-ended questions Survey questions in which the respondent is asked to select an answer from a list provided by the researcher. Closed-ended questions are especially popular in surveys because they provide a greater uniformity of responses and are more easily analyzed than closed-ended questions. See Chapter 9.

Cluster sample A multistage sample in which natural groups (clusters) are sampled initially, with the members of each selected group being subsampled afterward. For example, you might select a sample of municipal police departments from a directory, get lists of the police officers at all the selected departments, then draw samples of officers from each. See Chapter 8.

Cohort study A study in which some specific group is studied over time, although data may be collected from different members in each set of observations. See Chapter 4.

Computer-assisted interviewing Survey research by computer, in which questionnaires are presented on computer screens instead of paper. In computer-assisted personal interviewing, an interviewer reads items from the computer screen and keys in responses. In computer-assisted self-interviewing, respondents read (silently) items on the screen of a laptop computer and key in their answers. Another variation is audio-assisted self-interviewing, whereby respondents hear questions through headphones, then key in their answers. Both types of self-interviewing are especially useful for sensitive questions like self-reports. See Chapter 9.

Concept The words or symbols in language that we use to represent mental images. "Crime," for example, is a concept that represents our men-tal images of violence and other acts that are prohibited and punished by government. We use conceptual definitions to specify the meaning of concepts. Compare to *conception*. See Chapter 5.

Conception The mental images we have that represent our thoughts about things we routinely encounter. We use the word *speeding* (a concept) to represent our mental image (conception) of traveling above the posted speed limit. See Chapter 5.

Conceptual definition Defining concepts by using other concepts. Concepts are abstract—the words and symbols that are used to represent mental images of things and ideas. This means that a conceptual definition uses words and symbols to define concepts. In practice, conceptual definitions represent explicit statements of what a researcher means by a concept. A conceptual definition of "prior record" might be "recorded evidence of one or more convictions for a criminal offense." See also *operational definition* and Chapter 5.

Conceptualization The mental process whereby fuzzy and imprecise notions (concepts) are made more specific and precise. So you want to study fear of crime? What do you mean by fear of crime? Are there different kinds of fear? What are they? See Chapters 5 and 6.

Confidence interval The range of values within which a population parameter is estimated to lie. A survey, for instance, may show that 40 percent of a sample favor a ban on handguns. Although the best estimate of the support that exists among all people is also 40 percent, we do not expect it to be exactly that. We might, therefore, compute a confidence interval (for example, from 35 to 45 percent) within which the actual percentage of the population probably lies. Note that it is necessary to specify a confidence level in connection with every confidence interval. See Chapters 8 and 13.

Confidence level The estimated probability that a population parameter lies within a given confidence interval. Thus, we might be 95 percent confident that between 35 and 45 percent of all residents of California favor an absolute ban on handguns. See Chapters 8 and 13.

Confidentiality Researchers know the identity of a research subject but promise not to reveal any information that can be attributed to an individual subject. Anonymity is similar, but sometimes researchers need to know subjects' names in order to link information from different sources. Assuring confidentiality is one way of meeting our ethical obligation to not harm subjects. See Chapter 3.

Construct validity (1) The degree to which a measure relates to other variables as expected within a system of theoretical relationships. See Chapter 5. (2) How well an observed cause-and-effect relationship represents the underlying causal process a researcher is interested in. See Chapters 4 and 7. Also see *validity threats*.

Content validity The degree to which a measure covers the range of meanings included within the concept. See Chapter 5.

Contingency table A format for presenting the relationship among variables in the form of percentage distributions. See Chapter 13.

Control group In experimentation, a group of subjects to whom no experimental stimulus is administered and who should resemble the experimental group in all other respects. The comparison of the control group and the experimental group at the end of the experiment indicates the effect of the experimental stimulus. See Chapter 7.

Criterion-related validity The degree to which a measure relates to some external criterion. For example, the validity of self-report surveys of drug use can be shown by comparing survey responses to laboratory tests for drug use. See Chapter 5.

Cross-sectional study A study based on observations that represent a single point in time. Compare to *longitudinal study*. See Chapter 4.

Deduction The logical model in which specific expectations of hypotheses are developed on the basis of general principles. Starting from the general principle that all deans are meanies, you might anticipate that this one won't let you change courses. That anticipation would be the result of deduction. See also *induction* and Chapters 1 and 4.

Dependent variable The variable assumed to depend on or be caused by another variable (called the independent variable). If you find that sentence length is partly a function of the number of prior arrests, then sentence length is being treated as a dependent variable. See Chapters 1 and 7.

Descriptive statistics Statistical computations that describe either the characteristics of a sample or the relationship among variables in a sample. Descriptive statistics summarize a set of sample observations, whereas inferential statistics move beyond the description of specific observations to make inferences about the larger population from which the sample observations were drawn. See Chapter 13.

Dimension A specifiable aspect or facet of a concept. See Chapter 5.

Dispersion The distribution of values around some central value, such as an average. The range is a simple measure of dispersion. Thus, we may report that the mean age of a group is 37.9 and the range is from 12 to 89. See Chapter 13.

Disproportionate stratified sampling Deliberately drawing a sample that over- or underrepresents some characteristic of a population. We may do this to ensure that we obtain a sufficient number of uncommon cases in our sample. For example, believing violent crime to be more common in large cities, we might oversample urban residents to obtain a specific number of crime victims. See Chapter 8.

Ecological fallacy Erroneously drawing conclusions about individuals based solely on the observation of groups. See Chapter 4.

Empirical From experience. Social science is said to be empirical when knowledge is based on what we experience. See Chapter 1.

Environmental survey Structured observations undertaken in the field and recorded on specially designed forms. Note that interview surveys record a respondent's answers to questions, while environmental surveys record what an observer sees in the field. For example, a community organization may conduct periodic environmental surveys to monitor neighborhood parks—whether facilities are in good condition, how much litter is present, and what kinds of people use the park. See Chapter 10.

Equal probability of selection method (**EPSEM**) A sample design in which each member of a population has the same chance of being selected into the sample. See Chapter 8.

Evaluation research An example of applied research, evaluation involves assessing the effects of some program or policy action, usually in connection with the goals of that action. Determining whether a sex-offender treatment program attained its goal of reducing recidivism by participants would be an example. Compare to *policy analysis*. See Chapter 12.

Experimental group In experimentation, a group of subjects who are exposed to an experimental stimulus. Subjects in the experimental group are normally compared to subjects in a control group to test the effects of the experimental stimulus. See Chapter 7.

External validity Whether a relationship observed in a specific population, at a specific time, in a specific place would also be observed in other populations, at other times, in other places. External validity is concerned with generalizability from a relationship observed in one setting to the same relationship in other settings. Replication enhances external validity. See Chapters 4 and 7.

Face validity The quality of an indicator that makes it seem a reasonable measure of some variable. That sentence length prescribed by law is some indication of crime seriousness seems to make sense without a lot of explanation; it has face validity. See Chapter 5.

Fact As generally used in social science research, a fact is some phenomenon that has been observed. Compare to *law* and *theory*. See Chapter 2.

Focus group Small groups (of 12 to 15) engaged in a guided discussion of some topic. Participants selected are from a homogeneous population. Although focus groups cannot be used to make statistical estimates about a population, members are nevertheless selected to represent a target population. Focus groups are most useful in two situations: (1) when precise generalization to a larger population is not necessary, and (2) when focus group participants and the larger population they are intended to represent are relatively homogeneous. See Chapter 9.

Frequency distribution A description of the number of times the various attributes of a variable are observed in a sample. The report that 53 percent of a sample were men and 47 percent were women is a simple example of a frequency distribution. Another example is the report that 15 of the cities studied had populations of less than 10,000, 23 had populations between 10,000 and 25,000, and so forth. See Chapter 13.

Generalizability That quality of a research finding that justifies the inference that it represents something more than the specific observations on which it was based. Sometimes, this involves the generalization of findings from a sample to a population. Other times, it is a matter of concepts: If you are able to discover why people commit burglaries, can you generalize that discovery to other crimes as well? See Chapter 7.

Grounded theory A type of inductive theory that is based on (grounded in) field observation. The researcher makes observations in natural settings, then formulates a tentative theory that explains those observations. See Chapter 2.

Hypothesis An expectation about the nature of things derived from a theory. It is a statement of something that ought to be observed in the real world if the theory is correct. See *deduction* and Chapters 2 and 7.

Hypothesis testing The determination of whether the expectations that a hypothesis represents are indeed found in the real world. See Chapters 2 and 7.

Idiographic A mode of causal reasoning that seeks detailed understanding of all factors that contribute to a particular phenomenon. Police detectives trying to solve a particular case use the idiographic mode of explanation. Compare to *nomothetic*. See Chapters 1 and 4.

Impact assessment A type of applied research that seeks to answer the question: Did a public program have the intended effect on the problem it was meant to address? If, for example, a new burglary prevention program has the goal of reducing burglary in a particular neighborhood, an impact assessment would try to determine whether burglary was, in fact, reduced as a result of the new program. Compare to *process evaluation*. See Chapter 12.

Incident-based measure Refers to crime measures that express characteristics of individual crime incidents. The FBI Supplementary Homicide Reports are well-known examples, reporting details on each homicide incident. Compare to *summary-based measure*. See Chapter 6.

Independent variable An independent variable is presumed to cause or determine a dependent variable. If we discover that police cynicism is partly a function of years of experience, then experience is the independent variable and cynicism is the dependent variable. Note that any given variable might be treated as independent in one part of an analysis and dependent in another part of the analysis. Cynicism might become an independent variable in the explanation of job satisfaction. See Chapters 1 and 7.

Induction The logical model in which general principles are developed from specific observations. Having noted that teenagers and crime victims are less supportive of police than older people and nonvictims are, you might conclude that people with more direct police contact are less supportive of police and explain why. That would be an example of induction. See also deduction and Chapters 1 and 4.

Inferential statistics The body of statistical computations relevant to making inferences from findings based on sample observations to some larger population. See also *descriptive statistics* and Chapter 13.

Internal validity Whether observed associations between two (or more) variables are, in fact, causal associations or are due to the effects of some other variable. The internal validity of causal statements may be threatened by an inability to control experimental conditions. See also *validity threats* and Chapters 4 and 7.

Intersubjective agreement That quality of science (and other inquiries) whereby two different researchers studying the same problem arrive at the same conclusion. Ultimately, this is the practical criterion for what is called objectivity. We agree that something is "objectively true" if independent observers with different subjective orientations conclude that it is "true." See Chapter 2.

Interval measure A level of measurement that describes a variable whose attributes are rank ordered and have equal distances between adjacent attributes. The Fahrenheit temperature scale is an example of this because the distance between 17 and 18 is the same as that between 89 and 90. See also *nominal measure, ordinal measure,* and *ratio measure* and Chapter 5.

Latent content As used in connection with content analysis, this term describes the underlying meaning of communications as distinguished from their manifest content. See Chapter 11.

Law As used in scientific theory, a law is a universal generalization about groupings of facts. See Chapter 2.

Level of significance In the context of tests of statistical significance, the degree of likelihood that an observed, empirical relationship could be attributable to sampling error. A relationship is significant at the .05 level if the likelihood of its being only a function of sampling error is no greater than 5 out of 100. See Chapter 13.

Longitudinal study A study design that involves the collection of data at different points in time, as contrasted to a cross-sectional study. See also *trend study, cohort study,* and *panel study* and Chapter 4.

Manifest content In connection with content analysis, the concrete terms contained in a communication, as distinguished from latent content. See Chapter 11.

Mean An average, computed by summing the values of several observations and dividing by the number of observations. If you now have a grade-point average of 4.0 based on 10 courses, and you get an F in this course, then your new grade-point (mean) average will be 3.6. See Chapter 13.

Median Another average, representing the value of the "middle" case in a rank-ordered set of observations. If the ages of five people are 16, 17, 20, 54, and 88, then the median is 20. (The mean is 39.) See Chapter 13.

Mode Still another average, representing the most frequently observed value or attribute. If a sample contains 1000 residents of California, 275 from New Jersey, and 33 from Minnesota, then California is the modal category for residence. See Chapter 13.

Multivariate analysis The analysis of the simultaneous relationships among several variables. Examining simultaneously the effects of age, gender, and city of residence on robbery victimization is an example of multivariate analysis. See Chapter 13.

Nominal measure A level of measurement that describes a variable whose different attributes are only different, as distinguished from ordinal, interval, and ratio measures. Gender is an example of a nominal measure. See Chapter 5.

Nomothetic A mode of causal reasoning that tries to explain a number of similar phenomena or situations. Police crime analysts trying to explain patterns of auto thefts, or burglaries, or some other offense use nomothetic reasoning. Compare to *idiographic*. See Chapters 1 and 4.

Nonprobability sample A sample selected in some fashion other than those suggested by probability theory. Examples are purposive, quota, and snowball samples. See Chapter 8.

Nonsampling error Imperfections of data quality that are a result of factors other than sampling error. Examples are misunderstandings of questions by respondents, erroneous recordings by interviewers and coders, and data entry errors. See Chapter 13.

Null hypothesis In connection with hypothesis testing and tests of statistical significance, the hypothesis that suggests there is no relationship between the variables under study. You may conclude that the two variables are related after having statistically rejected the null hypothesis. See Chapter 13.

Objectivity Doesn't exist. See also *intersubjective agreement* and Chapter 2.

Open-ended questions Questions for which the respondent is asked to provide his or her own answers. Chapter 9.

Operational definition Specifying what operations should be performed to measure a concept. The operational definition of "prior record" might be "Consult the county (or state or FBI) criminal history records information system. Count the number of times a person has been convicted of committing a crime." See Chapter 5.

Operationalization One step beyond conceptualization. Operationalization is the process of developing operational definitions by describing how actual measurements will be made. See Chapters 4 and 5.

Ordinal measure A level of measurement that describes a variable whose attributes may be rank ordered along some dimension. An example is socioeconomic status as composed of the attributes high, medium, and low. See also *nominal measure, interval measure,* and *ratio measure* and Chapter 5.

Panel study A type of longitudinal study in which data are collected from the same subjects (the panel) at several points in time. See Chapter 4.

Paradigm A fundamental perspective or model that organizes our view of the world. Thomas Kuhn (1970) coined this term in the philosophy of science. Paradigms affect how we select and define problems for research, together with the methods we use in conducting research. Compare to *theory.* See Chapter 2.

Policy analysis Using social science research to determine which of two or more alternative policy actions will be selected. For example, examining patterns of auto theft to decide what preventive and enforcement strategies should be pursued is policy analysis. Compare to *evaluation research.* See Chapter 12.

Population All people, things, or other elements we wish to represent. Researchers often study only a subset or sample of a population, then generalize from the people, things, or other elements actually observed to the larger population of all people, things, or elements. See Chapter 8.

Population parameter The summary description of a particular variable in the population. For example if the mean age of all professors at your college is 43.7, then 43.7 is the population parameter for professors' mean age. Compare to *sample statistic* and *sampling distribution.* See Chapter 8.

Probabilistic A type of causal reasoning that certain factors make outcomes more or less likely to happen. Having an arrest as a juvenile makes it more likely that someone will be arrested as an adult. See Chapter 4.

Probability sample The general term for a sample selected in accord with probability theory, typically involving some random selection mechanism. Specific types of probability samples include area probability sample, equal probability of selection method (EPSEM), simple random sample, and systematic sample. See Chapter 8.

Problem solving An example of applied research that combines elements of evaluation and policy analysis. The most widely known approach to problem solving in policing is the SARA model, which stands for scanning, analysis, response, and assessment. See Chapter 12.

Process evaluation A type of applied research that seeks to answer the question: Was a public program implemented as intended? For example, a burglary prevention program might seek to reduce burglaries by having crime prevention officers meet with all residents of some target neighborhood. A process evaluation would determine whether meetings with neighborhood residents were taking place as planned. Compare to *impact assessment.* See Chapter 12.

Proportionate reduction of error (PRE) A logical model for assessing the strength of a relationship by asking how much knowing values on one variable might reduce our errors in guessing values on the other. For example, if we know how much education people have, we can improve our ability to guess how much they earn, thus indicating that there is a relationship between the two variables.

Prospective approach A type of longitudinal study that follows subjects forward in time. "How many people who were sexually abused as children are convicted of a sexual offense as an adult?" is an example of a prospective question. Compare to *retrospective.* See Chapter 4.

Purposive sample A type of nonprobability sample in which you select the units to be observed on the basis of your own judgment about which ones will be best suited to your research purpose. For example, if you were interested in studying community crime prevention groups affiliated with public schools and groups affiliated with religious organizations, you would probably want to select a purposive sample of school- and church-affiliated groups. Most television networks use purposive samples of voting precincts to project winning candidates on election night; precincts that always vote for winners are sampled. See Chapter 8.

Quasi-experiment A research design that includes most, but not all, elements of an experimental design. *Quasi-* means "sort of," and a quasi-experiment is sort of an experiment. Two general classes of quasi-experiments are nonequivalent groups and time-series designs. Compare to *classical experiment* and see Chapter 7.

Questionnaire A document that contains questions and other types of items designed to solicit information appropriate to analysis. Questionnaires are used primarily in survey research and also in field research. See Chapter 9.

Quota sample A type of nonprobability sample in which units are selected into the sample on the basis of prespecified characteristics, so that the total sample will have the same distribution of characteristics as are assumed to exist in the population being studied. See Chapter 8.

Randomization A technique for randomly assigning experimental subjects to experimental groups and control groups. See Chapter 7.

Range A measure of dispersion, the distance that separates the highest and lowest values of a variable in some set of observations. In your class, for example, the range of ages might be from 17 to 37. See Chapter 13.

Ratio measure A level of measurement that describes a variable whose attributes have all the qualities of nominal, ordinal, and interval measures and in addition are based on a "true zero" point. Length of prison sentence is an example of a ratio measure. See Chapter 5.

Reductionism A fault of some researchers: a strict limitation (reduction) of the kinds of concepts to be considered relevant to the phenomenon under study. See Chapter 4.

Regression analysis A method of data analysis in which the relationships among variables are represented in the form of an equation called a regression equation. See Chapter 13.

Reification The process of regarding as real things that are not real. This is usually a problem in measurement. See Chapter 5.

Reliability That quality-of-measurement standard whereby the same data would have been collected each time in repeated observations of the same phenomenon. We would expect that the question "Did you see a police officer in your neighborhood today?" would have higher reliability than the question "About how many times in the past 6 months have you seen a police officer in your neighborhood?" This is not to be confused with validity. See Chapter 5.

Replication Repeating a research study to test the findings of an earlier study, often under slightly different conditions or for a different group of subjects. Replication results either support earlier findings or cause us to question the accuracy of an earlier study. See Chapter 1.

Representativeness That quality of a sample having the same distribution of characteristics as the population from which it was selected. Representativeness is enhanced by probability sampling and provides for generalizability and the use of inferential statistics. See Chapter 8.

Retrospective research A type of longitudinal study that looks backward, asking subjects to recall events that happened earlier in their lives or tracing official records of someone's previous actions. "How many current sex offenders were sexually abused as children?" is a retrospective question. Compare to *prospective*. See Chapter 4.

Sample element That unit about which information is collected and that provides the basis of analysis. Typically, in survey research, elements are people. Other kinds of units can be the elements for criminal justice research—correctional facilities, gangs, police beats, or court cases, for example. See Chapter 8.

Sample statistic The summary description of a particular variable in a sample. For example, if the mean age of a sample of 100 professors on your campus is 41.1, then 41.1 is the sample statistic for professors' age. We usually use sample statistics to estimate population parameters. Compare to *sampling distribution*. See Chapter 8.

Sampling distribution The range or array of sample statistics we would obtain if we drew a very large number of samples from a single population. With random sampling, we expect that the sampling distribution for a particular statistic (mean age, for example) will cluster around the population parameter for mean age. Furthermore, sampling distributions for larger sample sizes will cluster more tightly around the population parameter. See Chapter 8.

Sampling frame That list or quasi-list of units composing a population from which a sample is selected. If the sample is to be representative of the population, it is essential that the sampling frame include all (or nearly all) members of the population. See Chapter 8.

Sampling units Like sampling elements, these are things that may be selected in the process of sampling; often, sampling units are people. In some types of sampling, however, we often begin by selecting large groupings of the eventual elements we will analyze. *Sampling units* is a generic term for things that are selected in some stage of sampling but are not necessarily the objects of our ultimate interest. See Chapter 8.

Scientific realism An approach to evaluation that studies what's called "local causality." Interest focuses more on how interventions and measures of effect are related in a specific situation. This is different from a more traditional social science interest in finding causal relationships that apply generally to a variety of situations. As explained by Ray Pawson and Nick Tilley (1997), scientific realism is especially useful for evaluating justice programs because it centers on analyzing interventions in local contexts. See Chapters 4 and 12.

Secondary analysis A form of research in which the data collected and processed by one researcher are re-analyzed—often for a different purpose—by another. This is especially appropriate in the case of survey data. Data archives are repositories or libraries for the storage and distribution of data for secondary analysis. See Chapter 11.

Self-report survey Self-report surveys ask people to tell about crimes they have committed. This method is best for measuring drug use and other so-called victimless crimes. Confidentiality is especially important in self-report surveys. See Chapters 6 and 9.

Simple random sample A type of probability sample in which the units composing a population are assigned numbers, a set of random numbers is then generated, and the units that have those numbers are included in the sample. Although probability theory and the calculations it provides assume this basic sampling method, it is seldom used for practical reasons. An alternative is the systematic sample (with a random start). See Chapter 8.

Snowball sampling A method for drawing a non-probability sample. Snowball samples are often used in field research. Each person interviewed is asked to suggest additional people for interviewing. See Chapters 8 and 10.

Stakeholders Individuals with some interest, or stake, in a specific program. Any particular program may have multiple stakeholders with different interests and goals. See Chapter 12.

Standard deviation A measure of dispersion about the mean. Conceptually, the standard deviation represents an "average" deviation of all values relative to the mean. See Chapter 13.

Standard error A measure of sampling error, the standard error gives us a statistical estimate of how much a member of a sample might differ from the population we are studying, solely by chance. Larger samples usually result in smaller standard errors. See Chapters 8 and 13.

Statistical conclusion validity Whether we can find covariation among two variables. This is the first of three requirements for causal inference (see Chapter 4 for the other two). If two variables do not vary together (covariation), there cannot be a causal relationship between them. See Chapters 4 and 7 for more on statistical conclusion validity. Chapter 13 describes the role of sample size in finding statistical significance, which is conceptually related to statistical conclusion validity.

Statistical significance A general term for the unlikeliness that relationships observed in a sample could be attributed to sampling error alone. See also *test of statistical significance* and Chapter 13.

Statistically discernible difference Tests of statistical significance should not normally be used unless our data meet certain assumptions about sampling and variation. Citing a finding as a "statistically discernible difference" allows us to use the tools of statistical inference while alerting readers that the use of these tools is not technically appropriate. See Chapter 13.

Stratification The grouping of the units composing a population into homogeneous groups (or strata) before sampling. This procedure, which may be used in conjunction with simple random, systematic, or cluster sampling, improves the representativeness of a sample, at least in terms of the stratification variables. See Chapter 8.

Summary-based measure Crime measures that report only total crimes for a jurisdiction or other small area are summary-based measures of crime. The FBI Uniform Crime Reports is one well-known summary measure. Compare to *incident-based measure*. See Chapter 6.

Surveillance measure Data routinely collected to monitor some phenomenon—accidents, injuries, communicable disease incidents, drug emergencies—are surveillance measures. U.S. agencies use surveillance measures to obtain estimates of drug use and, more recently, injuries produced by violent crime. See Chapter 6.

Systematic sample A type of probability sample in which every kth unit in a list is selected for inclusion in the sample—for example, every 25th student in the college directory of students. We compute k (also called the sampling interval) by dividing the size of the population by the desired sample size. Within certain constraints, systematic sampling is a functional equivalent of simple random sampling and is usually easier to do. Typically, the first unit is selected at random. See Chapter 8.

Test of statistical significance A class of statistical computations that indicate the likelihood that the relationship observed between variables in a sample can be attributed to sampling error only. See also *inferential statistics* and Chapter 13.

Theory A theory is a systematic explanation for the observed facts and laws that relate to a particular aspect of life. For example, routine activities theory (see Cohen and Felson, 1979) explains crime as the result of three key elements coming together: a suitable victim, a motivated offender, and the absence of capable guardians. See Chapter 2.

Trend study A type of longitudinal study in which a given characteristic of some population is monitored over time. An example is the series of annual Uniform Crime Report totals for some jurisdiction. See Chapter 4.

Typology Classifying observations in terms of their attributes. Sometimes referred to as "taxonomies," typologies are typically created with nominal variables. For example, a typology of thieves might group them according to the types of cars they steal and the types of locations they search to find targets. See Chapter 5.

Units of analysis The what or whom being studied. Units of analysis may be individual people, groupings of people (a juvenile gang), formal organizations (a probation department), or social artifacts (crime reports). See Chapter 4.

Univariate analysis The analysis of a single variable for purposes of description. Frequency distributions, averages, and measures of dispersion are examples of univariate analysis, as distinguished from bivariate and multivariate analyses. See Chapter 13.

Validity (1) Whether statements about cause and effect are true (valid) or false (invalid). See Chapters 4 and 7; also see *validity threats*. (2) A descriptive term used for a measure that accurately reflects what it is intended to measure. For example, police records of auto theft are more valid measures than police records of shoplifting. It is important to realize that the ultimate validity of a measure can never be proved. Yet we may agree as to its relative validity on the basis of face validity, criterion-related validity, content validity, and construct validity. This must not be confused with reliability. See Chapter 5.

Validity threats Possible sources of invalidity, or making false statements about cause and effect. Four categories of validity threats are linked to fundamental requirements for demonstrating cause: statistical conclusion validity, internal validity, construct validity, and external validity (see separate entries in this Glossary). In general, statistical conclusion validity and internal validity are concerned with bias; construct validity and external validity are concerned with generalization. See Chapters 4 and 7.

Variable-oriented research A research strategy whereby a large number of variables are studied for one or a small number of cases or subjects. Time-series designs and case studies are examples. See Chapter 7.

Variables Logical groupings of attributes. The variable gender is made up of the attributes male and female. See Chapter 1.

Victim survey A sample survey that asks people about their experiences as victims of crime. Victim surveys are one way to measure crime, and they are especially valuable for getting information about crimes not reported to police. The National Crime Victimization Survey is an example. See Chapters 6 and 9.

Bibliography

Academy of Criminal Justice Sciences. 2000. "Code of Ethics." Greenbelt, MD: Academy of Criminal Justice Sciences. http://www.acjs.org/new_page_13.htm. Accessed 19 January 2003.

American Association of University Professors. 2001. *Protecting Human Beings: Institutional Review Boards and Social Science Research.* AAUP Redbook. Washington, DC: American Association of Univer-sity Professors. http://www. aaup.org/statements/Redbook/repirb.htm. Accessed 24 January 2003.

American Psychological Association. 2002. *Ethical Principles of Psychologists and Code of Conduct.* Washington, DC: American Psychological Association. http://www.apa. org/ethics. Accessed 19 January 2003.

American Sociological Association. 1997. "Code of Ethics." Washington, DC: American Sociological Association. http://www.asanet.org/ecoderev.htm. Accessed 19 January 2003.

Babbie, Earl, Fred Halley, and Jeanne Zaino. 2000. *Adventures in Social Research.* Newbury Park, CA: Pine Forge Press.

Babbie, Earl. 1990. *Survey Research Methods.* Belmont, CA: Wadsworth.

———. 1994. *The Sociological Spirit.* Belmont, CA: Wadsworth.

———. 2001. *The Practice of Social Research,* 9th ed. Belmont, CA: Wadsworth.

Bachman, Ronet, and Linda E. Saltzman. 1995. *Violence Against Women: Estimates from the Redesigned Survey.* Washington, DC: U.S. Department of Justice, Office of Justice Programs, Bureau of Justice Statistics.

Bachman, Ronet, and Bruce M. Taylor. 1994. "The Measurement of Family Violence and Rape by the Redesigned National Crime Victimization Survey." *Justice Quarterly* 11:499–512.

Baldus, David C., Charles Pulaski, and George Woodworth. 1983. "Comparative Review of Death Sentences: An Empirical Study of the Georgia Experience." *Journal of Criminal Law and Criminology* 74:661–753.

Ball, John C., Lawrence Rosen, John A. Flueck, and David N. Nurco. 1982. "Lifetime Criminality of Heroin Addicts in the United States." *Journal of Drug Issues* 3:225–39.

Baron, Stephen W., and Timothy F. Hartnagel. 1998. "Street Youth and Criminal Violence." *Journal of Research in Crime and Delinquency* 35(2):166–92.

Baumer, Eric, Janet L. Lauritsen, Richard Rosenfeld, and Richard Wright. 1998. "The Influence of Crack Cocaine on Robbery, Burglary, and Homicide Rates: A Cross-City Longitudinal Analysis." *Journal of Research in Crime and Delinquency* 35:316–40.

Baumer, Terry L., and Robert I. Mendelsohn. 1990. *The Electronic Monitoring on Non-Violent Convicted Felons: An Experiment in Home Detention.* Final Report to the National Institute of Justice. Indianapolis: Indiana University, School of Public and Environmental Affairs.

Baumer, Terry L., and Dennis Rosenbaum. 1982. *Combatting Retail Theft: Programs and Strategies.* Boston: Butterworth.

Baumer, Terry L., Michael G. Maxfield, and Robert I. Mendelsohn. 1993. "A Comparative Analysis of Three Electronically Monitored Home Detention Programs." *Justice Quarterly* 10:121–42.

Bennis, Jason, Wesley G. Skogan, and Lynn Steiner. 2003. "The 2002 Beat Meeting Observation Study." Community Policing Working Paper No. 26. Evanston, IL: Northwestern University, Center for Policy Research. http://www.northwestern.edu/ipr/publications/policing.html. Accessed 27 April 2003.

Best, Joel. 2001. *Damned Lies and Statistics: Untangling Numbers from the Media, Politicians, and Activists.* Berkeley: University of California Press.

Beveridge, William I. B. 1950. *The Art of Scientific Investigation.* New York: Vintage Books.

Bichler, Gisela, and Ronald V. Clarke. 1996. "Eliminating Pay Phone Toll Fraud at the Port Authority Bus Terminal in Manhattan." In *Preventing Mass Transit Crime,* ed. Ronald V. Clarke, 93–115. *Crime Prevention Studies,* Vol. 6. Monsey, NY: Criminal Justice Press.

Black, Donald. 1970. "The Production of Crime Rates." *American Sociological Review* 35:733–48.

Block, Carolyn Rebecca. 1995. "STAC Hot Spot Areas: A Statistical Tool for Law Enforcement Agencies." In *Crime Analysis Through Computer Mapping,* ed. Carolyn Rebecca Block, Margaret Dabdoub, and Suzanne Fregly, 15–32. Washington, DC: Police Executive Research Forum.

Block, Richard L. 1995. "Spatial Analysis in the Evaluation of the CAPS Community Policing Program in Chicago." In *Crime Analysis Through Computer Mapping,* ed. Carolyn Rebecca Block, Margaret Dabdoub, and Suzanne Fregly, 251–58. Washington, DC: Police Executive Research Forum.

Block, Richard L., and Carolyn Rebecca Block. 1980. "Decisions and Data: The Transformation of Robbery Incidents into Official Robbery Statistics." *Journal of Criminal Law and Criminology* 71:622–36.

Blumstein, Alfred. 1988. "Prison Populations: A System Out of Control?" In *Crime and Justice: An Annual Review of Research,* ed. Michael Tonry and Norval Morris, 231–66. Chicago: University of Chicago Press.

Blumstein, Alfred, Jacqueline Cohen, and Harold D. Miller. 1980. "Demographically Disaggregated Projections of Prison Populations." *Journal of Criminal Justice* 8:1–26.

Blumstein, Alfred, Jacqueline Cohen, and Richard Rosenfeld. 1991. "Trend and Deviation in Crime Rates: A Comparison of UCR and NCS Data for Burglary and Robbery." *Criminology* 29:237–63.

Blumstein, Alfred, Jacqueline Cohen, Jeffrey A. Roth, and Christy A. Visher, eds. 1986. *Criminal Careers and "Career Criminals."* Washington, DC: National Academy Press.

Blumstein, Alfred, and Richard Rosenfeld. 1998. "Explaining Recent Trends in U.S. Homicide Rates." *Journal of Criminal Law and Criminology* 88 (Summer):1175–216.

Boba, Rachel. 2003. *Problem Analysis in Policing.* Washington, DC: Police Foundation.

Boland, Barbara. 1986. "What Is Community Prosecution?" *National Institute of Justice Journal* 231 (August):35–40.

Bonta, James. 1996. "Risk–Needs Assessment and Treatment." In *Choosing Correctional Options That Work,* ed. Alan T. Harland, 18–32. Thousand Oaks, CA: Sage.

Bonta, James, and Laurence L. Motiuk. 1990. "Classification to Halfway Houses: A Quasi-Experimental Evaluation." *Criminology* 28:497–506.

Braga, Anthony A. 2002. *Problem-Oriented Policing and Crime Prevention.* Monsey, NY: Criminal Justice Press.

Braga, Anthony A., David M. Kennedy, Elin J. Waring, and Anne Morrison Piehl. 2001. "Problem-Oriented Policing and Youth Violence: An Evaluation of Boston's Operation Ceasefire." *Journal of Research in Crime and Delinquency* 38 (August):195–225.

Brantingham, Patricia L., and Paul J. Brantingham. 1991. "Notes on the Geometry of Crime." In *Environmental Criminology,* 2nd ed., ed. Paul J. Brantingham and Patricia L. Brantingham, 27–54. Prospect Heights, IL: Waveland.

Brantingham, Paul J., and Patricia L. Brantingham, eds. 1991a. *Environmental Criminology,* 2nd ed. Prospect Heights, IL: Waveland.

———. 1991b. "Introduction: The Dimensions of Crime." In *Environmental Criminology,* 2nd ed., ed. Paul J. Brantingham and Patricia L. Brantingham, 7–26. Prospect Heights, IL: Waveland.

Brantingham, Paul J., and C. Ray Jeffery. 1991. "Afterword: Crime, Space, and Criminological Theory." In *Environmental Criminology,* 2nd ed., ed. Paul J. Brantingham and Patricia L. Brantingham, 227–37. Prospect Heights, IL: Waveland.

Bratton, William, with Peter Knobler. 1998. *Turnaround: How America's Top Cop Reversed the Crime Epidemic.* New York: Random House.

———. 1999. "Great Expectations: How Higher Expectations for Police Departments Can Lead to a Decrease in Crime." In *Measuring What Matters.* Proceedings from the Policing Research Institute Meetings, ed. Robert Langworthy, 11–26. Washington, DC: U.S. Department of Justice, Office of Justice Programs, National Institute of Justice.

Brownstein, Henry H. 1996. *The Rise and Fall of a Violent Crime Wave: Crack Cocaine and the Social Construction of a Crime Problem.* Guilderland, NY: Harrow & Heston.

Bureau of Justice Assistance. 1993. *A Police Guide to Surveying Citizens and Their Environment.* NCJ-143711. Washington, DC: U.S. Department of Justice, Office of Justice Programs, Bureau of Justice Assistance.

Bureau of Justice Statistics. 1993. *Performance Measures for the Criminal Justice System.* Discussion Papers from the BJS–Princeton Project. Washington, DC: U.S. Department of Justice, Office of Justice Programs, Bureau of Justice Statistics.

———. 1994. *Criminal Victimization in the United States, 1992.* Washington, DC: U.S. Department of Justice, Office of Justice Programs, Bureau of Justice Statistics.

———. 1996. *Criminal Victimization in the United States, 1993.* Washington, DC: U.S. Department of Justice, Office of Justice Programs, Bureau of Justice Statistics.

———. 1997. *Criminal Victimization in the United States, 1994.* Washington, DC: U.S. Department of Justice, Office of Justice Programs, Bureau of Justice Statistics.

———. 2002. *Correctional Populations in the United States, 1998.* BJS Internet Report. Washington, DC: U.S. Department of Justice, Office of Justice Programs, Bureau of Justice Statistics.

Burgess, Ernest W. 1925. "The Growth of the City." In *The City: Chicago,* ed. Robert E. Park, Ernest W. Burgess, and Roderic D. Mckenzie. Chicago: University of Chicago Press.

Campbell, Donald T. 1979. "Assessing the Impact of Planned Social Change." *Evaluation and Program Planning* 2:67–90.

———. 1994. "Introduction." In *Case Study Research: Design and Methods,* 2nd ed., ed. Robert K. Yin, ix–xi. Thousand Oaks, CA: Sage.

Campbell, Donald T., and Julian Stanley. 1966. *Experimental and Quasi-Experimental Designs for Research.* Chicago: Rand McNally.

Carver, Jay, Kathryn R. Boyer, and Ronald Hickey. 1996. "Management Information Systems and Drug Courts: The District of Columbia Approach." Paper presented at the Annual Training Conference of the National Association of Drug Court Professionals. Washington, DC: District of Columbia Pretrial Services Agency.

Casady, Tom. 1999. "Privacy Issues in the Presentation of Geocoded Data." *Crime Mapping News* 1 (Summer). Washington, DC: Police Foundation.

Caspi, Avshalom, Terrie E. Moffitt, Phil A. Silva, Magda Stouthamer-Loeber, Robert F. Krueger, and Pamela S. Schmutte. 1994. "Are Some People Crime Prone? Replications of the Personality–Crime Relationship Across Countries, Genders, Races, and Methods." *Criminology* 32:163–95.

Chaiken, Jan M., and Marcia R. Chaiken. 1982. *Varieties of Criminal Behavior.* Santa Monica, CA: Rand.

———. 1990. "Drugs and Predatory Crime." In *Crime and Justice: A Review of Research: Vol. 13. Drugs and Crime,* ed. Michael Tonry and James Q. Wilson. Chicago: University of Chicago Press.

Chermak, Steven. 1998. "Predicting Crime Story Salience: The Effects of Crime, Victim, and Defendant Characteristics." *Journal of Criminal Justice* 26:61–70.

Chermak, Steven M., and Alexander Weiss. 1997. "The Effects of the Media on Federal Criminal Justice Policy." *Criminal Justice Policy Review* 8:323–41.

Chicago Community Policing Evaluation Consortium. 1999. *Community Policing in Chicago, Years Five and Six.* Chicago: Illinois Criminal Justice Information Authority.

————. 2003. *Community Policing in Chicago, Years Eight and Nine.* Chicago: Illinois Criminal Justice Information Authority.

Clarke, Ronald V. 1995. "Situational Crime Prevention." In *Building a Safer Society: Strategic Approaches to Crime Prevention,* ed. Michael Tonry and David Farrington, 91–150. *Crime and Justice: An Annual Review of Research.* Chicago: University of Chicago Press.

————. 1996. "The Distribution of Deviance and Exceeding the Speed Limit." *British Journal of Criminology* 36.

————. 1997a. "Deterring Obscene Phone Callers: The New Jersey Experience." In *Situational Crime Prevention: Successful Case Studies,* 2nd ed., ed., Ronald V. Clarke, 90–97. New York: Harrow & Heston.

————. 1997b. "Introduction." In *Situational Crime Prevention: Successful Case Studies,* 2nd ed., ed., Ronald V. Clarke, 2–43. New York: Harrow & Heston.

Clarke, Ronald, Paul Ekblom, Mike Hough, and Pat Mayhew. 1985. "Elderly Victims of Crime and Exposure to Risk." *The Howard Journal* 24(1):1–9.

Clarke, Ronald V., and Patricia M. Harris. 1992. "Auto Theft and Its Prevention." In *Crime and Justice: An Annual Review of Research,* 1–54. Chicago: University of Chicago Press.

Clarke, Ronald V., and Patricia Mayhew. 1980. *Designing Out Crime.* London: Her Majesty's Stationery Office.

Coleman, Veronica, Walter C. Holton, Jr., Kristine Olson, Stephen C. Robinson, and Judith Stewart. 1999. "Using Knowledge and Teamwork to Reduce Crime." *National Institute of Justice Journal* (October):16–23.

Committee on Science, Engineering, and Public Policy. 1995. *On Being a Scientist: Responsible Conduct in Research.* Washington, DC: National Academy Press.

Connell, James P., Anne C. Kubisch, Lisbeth B. Schorr, and Carol H. Weiss, eds. 1995. *New Approaches to Evaluating Community Initiatives: Concepts, Methods, and Contexts.* Washington, DC: Aspen Institute.

Cook, Thomas D., and Donald T. Campbell. 1979. *Quasi-Experimentation: Design and Analysis Issues for Field Settings.* Boston: Houghton Mifflin.

Corman, Hope, and H. Naci Mocan. 2000. "A Time-Series Analysis of Crime, Deterrence, and Drug Abuse in New York City." *American Economic Review* 90(3):584–604.

Cornish, D. B., and Ronald V. Clarke, eds. 1986. *The Reasoning Criminal: Rational Choice Perspectives on Offending.* New York: Springer-Verlag.

Cornwell, J. Phillip, Michael J. Doherty, Eric L. Mitter, and Scarlet L. Drayer. 1989. *Roadside Observation Survey of Safety Belt Use in Indiana.* Bloomington: Indiana University, Transportation Research Center.

Criminal Justice Policy Council. 1996. *Projection of Correctional Populations in Texas Fiscal Years 1997–2002.* Austin, TX: Criminal Justice Policy Council.

————. 1998. *Projection of Adult and Juvenile Correctional Population and Capacity, FY 1999 to FY 2003.* Austin, TX: Criminal Justice Policy Council.

————. 2003. *Adult and Juvenile Correctional Population Projections, FY 2003 to FY 2008.* Austin, TX: Criminal Justice Policy Council.

Cullen, Francis T., and Paul Gendreau. 2000. "Assessing Correctional Rehabilitation: Policy, Practice, and Prospects." In *Policies, Processes, and Decisions of the Criminal Justice System,* ed. Julie Horney, 109–75. *Criminal Justice 2000,* Vol. 3. Washington, DC: U.S. Department of Justice, Office of Justice Programs, National Institute of Justice.

D'Alessio, Stewart J., Lisa Stolzenberg, and W. Clinton Terry. 1999. "'Eyes on the Street': The Impact of Tennessee's Emergency Cellular Telephone Program on Alcohol Related Crashes." *Crime and Delinquency* 45(4):453–66.

Daly, Martin, and Margo Wilson. 1988. *Homicide.* Hawthorne, NY: Aldine de Gruyter.

Davis, Sean. 1996. "Environs of Rapid Transit Stations: A Focus for Street Crime or Just Another Risky Place?" In *Preventing Mass Transit Crime,* ed. Ronald V. Clarke, 237–57. *Crime Prevention Studies,* Vol. 6. Monsey, NY: Criminal Justice Press.

Decker, Scott H., Susan Pennell, and Ami Caldwell. 1997. *Illegal Firearms: Access and Use by Arrestees.* Research in Brief. Washington, DC: U.S. Department of Justice, Office of Justice Programs, National Institute of Justice.

Decker, Scott H., and Barrik Van Winkle. 1996. *Life in the Gang: Family, Friends, and Violence.* New York: Cambridge University Press.

Dennis, Michael L. 1990. "Assessing the Validity of Randomized Field Experiments: An Example from Drug Abuse Treatment Research." *Evaluation Review* 14:347–73.

Department of the Youth Authority. 1997. *LEAD: A Boot Camp and Intensive Parole Program: The Final Impact Evaluation.* Sacramento: State of California, Department of the Youth Authority.

Devine, Joel A., and James D. Wright. 1993. *The Greatest of Evils: Urban Poverty and the American Underclass.* Hawthorne, NY: Aldine de Gruyter.

Dillman, Don A. 1978. *Mail and Telephone Surveys: The Total Design Method.* New York: Wiley.

————. 1999. *Mail and Internet Surveys: The Tailored Design Method,* 2nd ed. New York: Wiley.

Donnerstein, Edward, Daniel Linz, and Stephen Penrod. 1987. *The Question of Pornography: Research Findings and Policy Implications.* New York: Free Press.

Eck, John E. 2002. "Learning from Experience in Problem-Oriented Policing and Situational Prevention: The Positive Functions of Weak Evaluations and the Negative Functions of Strong Ones." In *Crime Prevention Studies,* Vol. 14, ed. Nick Tilley, 93–117. Monsey, NY: Criminal Justice Press.

————. 2003. *Assessing Responses to Problems: An Introductory Guide for Police Problem-Solvers.* Washington, DC: U.S. Department of Justice, Office of Community Oriented Policing Services.

Eck, John E., and Nancy G. LaVigne. 1994. *Using Research: A Primer for Law Enforcement Managers,* 2nd ed. Washington, DC: Police Executive Research Forum.

Eck, John E., and William Spelman. 1987. *Problem-Solving: Problem-Oriented Policing in Newport News.* Washington, DC: Police Executive Research Forum.

Eisenberg, Michael. 1999. *Three Year Recidivism Tracking of Offenders Participating in Substance Abuse Treatment Programs.* Austin, TX: Criminal Justice Policy Council.

Eisenstein, James, and Herbert Jacob. 1977. *Felony Justice: An Organizational Analysis of Criminal Courts.* Boston: Little, Brown.

Ekblom, Paul, and Ken Pease. 1995. "Evaluating Crime Prevention." In *Building a Safer Society: Strategic Approaches to Crime Prevention,* ed. Michael Tonry and David Farrington, 585–662. *Crime and Justice: An Annual Review of Research.* Chicago: University of Chicago Press.

Elliott, Delbert S., and David Huizinga. 1984. "The Relationship Between Delinquent Behavior and ADM Problems." Unpublished paper, prepared for the Alcohol, Drug Abuse, and Mental Health Administration/Office of Juvenile Justice and Delinquency Prevention State-of-the-Art Conference on Juvenile Offenders with Serious Drug, Alcohol, and Mental Health Problems.

Elliott, Delbert S., David Huizinga, and Suzanne S. Ageton. 1985. *Explaining Delinquency and Drug Use.* Thousand Oaks, CA: Sage.

Elliott, Delbert S., David Huizinga, and Scott Menard. 1989. *Multiple Problem Youth: Delinquency, Substance Use, and Mental Health Problems.* New York: Springer-Verlag.

Ericson, Richard V., Patricia M. Baranek, and Janet B. L. Chan. 1991. *Representing Order: Crime, Law, and Justice in the News Media.* Toronto: University of Toronto Press.

Esbensen, Finn-Aage, and Delbert S. Elliott. 1994. "Continuity and Discontinuity in Illicit Drug Use: Patterns and Antecedents." *Journal of Drug Issues* 24(1):75–97.

Fabelo, Tony. 1995. "What Is Recidivism? How Do You Measure It? What Can It Tell Policy Makers?" *Bulletin from the Executive Director* No. 19. Austin, TX: Criminal Justice Policy Council.

———. 1996. "When Politics Accommodate Facts to Make Better Criminal Justice Policies." *Bulletin from the Executive Director* No. 21. Austin, TX: Criminal Justice Policy Council.

———. 1997. "The Critical Role of Policy Research in Developing Effective Correctional Policies." *Corrections Management Quarterly* 1(1):25–31.

Fagan, Jeffrey, Franklin E. Zimring, and June Kim. 1998. "Declining Homicide in New York City: A Tale of Two Trends." *Journal of Criminal Law and Criminology* 88 (Summer):1277–323.

Faggiani, Donald, and Colleen McLaughlin. 1999. "Using National Incident-Based Reporting System Data for Strategic Crime Analysis." *Journal of Quantitative Criminology* 15 (June).

Farrell, Graham, Alan Edmunds, Louise Hibbs, and Gloria Laycock. 2000. *RV Snapshot: UK Policing and Repeat Victimisation.* Crime Reduction Research Series, Paper 5. London: Home Office, Policing and Reducing Crime Unit, Research, Development, and Statistics Directorate.

Farrell, Ronald A., and Victoria Lynn Swigert. 1978. "Prior Offense Record as a Self-fulfilling Prophecy." *Law and Society* 12:437–53.

Farrington, David P., Sean Bowen, Abigail Buckle, Tony Burns-Howell, John Burrows, and Martin Speed. 1993. "An Experiment in the Prevention of Shoplifting." In *Crime Prevention Studies,* Vol. 1., ed. Ronald V. Clarke, 93–119. Monsey, NY: Criminal Justice Press.

Farrington, David P., Rolf Loeber, Magda Stouthamer-Loeber, Welmoet B. Van Kammen, and Laura Schmidt. 1996. "Self-Reported Delinquency and a Combined Delinquency Seriousness Scale Based on Boys, Mothers, and Teachers: Concurrent and Predictive Validity for African-Americans and Caucasians." *Criminology* 34:493–517.

Farrington, David P., Lloyd E. Ohlin, and James Q. Wilson. 1986. *Understanding and Controlling Crime: Toward a New Research Strategy.* New York: Springer-Verlag.

Federal Bureau of Investigation. 1999. *Crime in the United States 1998.* Washington, DC: U.S. Department of Justice, Federal Bureau of Investigation.

———. 2000. *National Incident-Based Reporting System: Vol. 1. Data Collection Guidelines.* Washington, DC: U.S. Department of Justice, Federal Bureau of Investigation.

———. 2002. *Crime in the United States 2001.* Washington, DC: U.S. Department of Justice, Federal Bureau of Investigation. http://www.fbi.gov/ucr/01cius.htm. Accessed 13 May 2003.

Felson, Marcus. 1998. *Crime and Everyday Life,* 2nd ed. Thousand Oaks, CA: Pine Forge Press.

———. 2002. *Crime and Everyday Life,* 3rd ed. Thousand Oaks, CA: Sage.

Felson, Marcus, Mathieu E. Belanger, Gisela M. Bichler, Chris D. Bruzinski, Glenna S. Campbell, Cheryl L. Fried, Kathleen C. Grofik, Irene S. Mazur, Amy B. O'Regan, Patricia J. Sweeney, Andrew L. Ulman, and LaQuanda M. Williams. 1996. "Redesigning Hell: Preventing Crime and Disorder at the Port Authority Bus Terminal." In *Preventing Mass Transit Crime,* ed. Ronald V. Clarke, 5–92. *Crime Prevention Studies,* Vol. 6. Monsey, NY: Criminal Justice Press.

Felson, Marcus, and Ronald V. Clarke. 1998. *Opportunity Makes the Thief: Practical Theory for Crime Prevention.* Police Research Series, Paper 98. London: Home Office, Policing and Reducing Crime Unit, Research, Development, and Statistics Directorate.

Fendrich, Michael, Timothy P. Johnson, Seymour Sudman, Joseph S. Wislar, and Vina Spiehler. 1999. "Validity of Drug Use Reporting in a High-Risk Community Sample: A Comparison of Cocaine and Heroin Survey Reports with Hair Tests." *American Journal of Epidemiology* 149 (May):955–62.

Finkelhor, David, and Richard Ormond. 2001. *Child Abuse Reported to the Police.* Juvenile Justice Bulletin. Washington, DC: U.S. Department of Justice, Office of Justice Programs, Office of Juvenile Justice and Delinquency Prevention.

Finkelstein, Michael O., and Bruce Levin. 1990. *Statistics for Lawyers.* New York: Springer-Verlag.

Finn, Peter, and Andrea K. Newlyn. 1993. *Miami's Drug Court: A Different Approach.* Program Focus. Washington, DC:

U.S. Department of Justice, Office of Justice Programs, National Institute of Justice.

Fishman, Mark. 1980. *Manufacturing the News*. Austin: University of Texas Press.

Forster, Emma, and Alison McCleery. 1999. "Computer Assisted Personal Interviewing: A Method of Capturing Sensitive Information." *IASSIST Quarterly* 23 (Summer):26–38. http://iassistdata.org/publications/iq/index.html. Accessed 14 May 2003.

Fox, James Alan. 2000. "Demographics and U.S. Homicide." In *The Crime Drop in America,* ed. Alfred Blumstein and Joel Wallman, 288–317. New York: Cambridge University Press.

Gant, Frances, and Peter Grabosky. 2001. *The Stolen Vehicle Parts Market.* Trends and Issues, Canberra: Australian Institute of Criminology.

Geerken, Michael R. 1994. "Rap Sheets in Criminological Research: Considerations and Caveats." *Journal of Quantitative Criminology* 10:3–21.

General Accounting Office. 1991. *Using Structured Interviewing Techniques.* Transfer Paper 10.1.5. Washington, DC: U.S. General Accounting Office.

———. 1992. *Using Statistical Sampling.* Transfer Paper 10.1.6. Washington, DC: U.S. General Accounting Office.

———. 1996. *Content Analysis: A Methodology for Structuring and Analyzing Written Material.* Transfer Paper 10.3.1. Washington, DC: U.S. General Accounting Office.

———. 2000. *Racial Profiling: Limited Data Available on Motorist Stops.* Report to the Honorable James E. Clyburn, Chairman Congressional Black Caucus. GAO/GGD-00-41. Washington, DC: U.S. General Accounting Office.

Gerbner, G., and L. Gross. 1980. "The Violent Face of Television and Its Lessons." In *Children and the Faces of Television,* ed. E. Palmer and A. Doerr, 149–62. New York: Academic Press.

Gfroerer, Joseph. 1993. "An Overview of the National Household Survey on Drug Abuse and Related Methodological Research." In *Proceedings of the Survey Research Section of the American Statistical Association, August 1992.* Boston: American Statistical Association.

———. 1996. *Preliminary Estimates from the 1995 National Household Survey on Drug Abuse.* Advance Report 18. Rockville, MD: U.S. Department of Health and Human Services, Substance Abuse and Mental Health Services Administration. http://www.health.org/pubs/95hhs/ar18txt.htm. Accessed 18 December 1996.

Gfroerer, Joseph, Joe Eyerman, and James Chromy, eds. 2002. *Redesigning an Ongoing National Household Survey: Methodological Issues.* Publication No. SMA 03–3768. Rockville, MD: Office of Applied Studies, Substance Abuse and Mental Health Services Administration. http://www.samhsa.gov/oas/methods.htm. Accessed 18 March 2003.

Gladwell, Malcolm. 2000. *The Tipping Point: How Little Things Can Make a Big Difference.* Boston: Little, Brown.

Glaser, Barney G., and Anselm Strauss. 1967. *The Discovery of Grounded Theory.* Chicago: University of Chicago Press.

Glassbrenner, Donna. 2002. *Safety Belt and Helmet Use in 2002: Overall Results.* Technical Report. DOT HS 809 500. Washington, DC: U.S. Department of Transportation, National Highway Traffic Safety Administration, National Center for Statistics and Analysis.

———. 2003. *Safety Belt Use in 2002: Use Rates in the States and Territories.* Research Note. DOT HS 809 587. Washington, DC: U.S. Department of Transportation, National Highway Traffic Safety Administration, National Center for Statistics and Analysis.

Glueck, Sheldon, and Eleanor T. Glueck. 1950. *Unraveling Juvenile Delinquency.* Cambridge, MA: Harvard University Press.

Goldkamp, John S., and Doris Weiland. 1993. *Assessing the Impact of Dade County's Felony Drug Court.* Research in Brief. Washington, DC: U.S. Department of Justice, Office of Justice Programs, National Institute of Justice.

Gordon, Margaret T., Janet Reis, and Thomas Tyler. 1979. *Crime in the Newspapers: Some Unintended Consequences.* Evanston, IL: Northwestern University, Center for Urban Affairs and Policy Research.

Gottfredson, Michael R., and Travis Hirschi. 1987. "The Methodological Adequacy of Longitudinal Research on Crime." *Criminology* 25:581–614.

———. 1990. *A General Theory of Crime.* Stanford, CA: Stanford University Press.

Gottfredson, Stephen D., and Don M. Gottfredson. 1994. "Behavioral Prediction and the Problem of Incapacitation." *Criminology* 32:441–74.

Grayson, Betty, and Morris I. Stein. 1981. "Attracting Assault: Victims' Nonverbal Cues." *Journal of Communication* 31:68–75.

Greenstein, Steven C., David J. van Alstyne, and Bruce C. Frederick. 1986. *A Model for Forecasting Long-Term Trends in the New York State Prison Population.* Albany: New York State Division of Criminal Justice Services, Office of Policy Analysis, Research, and Statistical Services.

Greenwood, Peter. 1975. *The Criminal Investigation Process.* Santa Monica, CA: RAND.

Gurr, Ted Robert. 1976. *Rogues, Rebels, and Reformers.* Thousand Oaks, CA: Sage.

———. 1989. "Historical Trends in Violent Crime: Europe and the United States." In *Violence in America: The History of Crime,* ed. Ted Robert Gurr. Thousand Oaks, CA: Sage.

Hale, Chris. 1996. "Fear of Crime: A Review of the Literature." *International Review of Victimology* 4:74–150.

Hall, Richard A. Spurgeon, Carolyn Brown Dennis, and Tere L. Chipman. 1999. *The Ethical Foundations of Criminal Justice.* Boca Raton, FL: CRC Press.

Haney, Craig, Curtis Banks, and Philip Zimbardo. 1973. "Interpersonal Dynamics in a Simulated Prison." *International Journal of Criminology and Penology* 1:69–97.

Hanmer, Jalna, Sue Griffiths, and David Jerwood. 1999. *Arresting Evidence: Domestic Violence and Repeat Victimisation.* Police Research Series, Paper 104. London: Home Office, Policing and Reducing Crime Unit, Research, Development, and Statistics Directorate.

Harland, Alan T. 1996. "Correctional Options That Work: Structuring the Inquiry." In *Choosing Correctional Options*

That Work, ed. Alan T. Harland, 1–17. Thousand Oaks, CA: Sage.

Harries, Keith. 1999. *Mapping Crime: Principle and Practice.* Washington, DC: U.S. Department of Justice, Office of Justice Programs, National Institute of Justice.

Harries, Keith D., Stephen J. Stadler, and R. T. Zdorkowski. 1984. "Seasonality and Assault: Explorations in Inter-Neighborhood Variation, Dallas 1980." *Annals of the Association of American Geographers* 74:590–604.

Harris, David A. 1997. "'Driving While Black' and All Other Traffic Offenses: The Supreme Court and Pretextual Traffic Stops." *Journal of Criminal Law and Criminology* 87(2):544–82.

Heeren, Timothy, Robert A. Smith, Suzette Morelock, and Ralph W. Hingson. 1985. "Surrogate Measures of Alcohol Involvement in Fatal Crashes: Are Conventional Indicators Adequate?" *Journal of Safety Research* 16:127–34.

Hempel, Carl G. 1952. "Fundamentals of Concept Formation in Empirical Science." In *International Encyclopedia of Unified Science: Foundations of the Unity of Science,* Vol. 2. Chicago: University of Chicago Press.

Hesseling, Rene B. P. 1994. "Displacement: A Review of the Empirical Literature." In *Crime Prevention Studies,* Vol. 3., ed. Ronald V. Clarke, 197–230. Monsey, NY: Criminal Justice Press.

Heumann, Milton, and Colin Lofton. 1979. "Mandatory Sentencing and the Abolition of Plea Bargaining: The Michigan Felony Firearm Statute." *Law and Society Review* 13:393–430.

Hindelang, Michael J., Michael R. Gottfredson, and James Garofalo. 1978. *Victims of Personal Crime: An Empirical Foundation for a Theory of Personal Victimization.* Cambridge, MA: Ballinger.

Homan, Roger. 1991. *The Ethics of Social Research.* New York: Longman.

Homel, Ross, and Jeff Clark. 1994. "The Prediction and Prevention of Violence in Pubs and Clubs." In *Crime Prevention Studies,* Vol 3., ed. Ronald V. Clarke, 1–46. Monsey, NY: Criminal Justice Press.

Homel, Ross, Steve Tomsen, and Jennifer Thommeny. 1992. "Public Drinking and Violence: Not Just an Alcohol Problem." *Journal of Drug Issues* 22:679–97.

Hood-Williams, John, and Tracey Bush. 1995. "Domestic Violence on a London Housing Estate." *Research Bulletin* 37:11–18.

Hoover, Kenneth R. 1992. *The Elements of Social Scientific Thinking,* 5th ed. New York: St. Martin's Press.

Horney, Julie, and Ineke Haen Marshall. 1992. "An Experimental Comparison of Two Self-Report Methods for Measuring Lambda." *Journal of Research in Crime and Delinquency* 29(1):102–21.

Hough, Michael, and Pat Mayhew. 1985. *Taking Account of Crime.* Home Office Research Study 85. London: Her Majesty's Stationery Office.

Huizinga, David, and Delbert S. Elliott. 1986. "Reassessing the Reliability and Validity of Self-Report Delinquency Measures." *Journal of Quantitative Criminology* 2(4):293–327.

Humphreys, Laud. 1975. *The Tearoom Trade.* Enlarged edition with perspectives on ethical issues. Chicago: Aldine.

Hunter, Rosemary S., and Nancy Kilstrom. 1979. "Breaking the Cycle in Abusive Families." *American Journal of Psychiatry* 136:1318–22.

Idaho State Police. 2002. *Crime in Idaho 2001.* Meridian: Idaho State Police, Bureau of Criminal Identification, Uniform Crime Reporting Unit. http://www.isp.state. id.us/identification/ucr/crime_idaho.html. Accessed 6 May 2003.

Inciardi, James A. 1986. *The War on Drugs: Heroin, Cocaine, Crime, and Public Policy.* Palo Alto: CA: Mayfield.

———. 1993. "Some Considerations on the Methods, Dangers, and Ethics of Crackhouse Research." Appendix A in *Women and Crack Cocaine,* ed. James A. Inciardi, Dorothy Lockwood, and Anne E. Pettieger, 147–57. New York: Macmillan.

Jacob, Herbert. 1984. *Using Published Data: Errors and Remedies.* Thousand Oaks, CA: Sage.

Jacobs, Bruce A. 1996. "Crack Dealers' Apprehension Avoidance Techniques: A Case of Restrictive Deterrence." *Justice Quarterly* 13:359–81.

Jacobs, Bruce A., and Jody Miller. 1998. "Crack Dealing, Gender, and Arrest Avoidance." *Social Problems* 45(4):550–69.

Jeffery, C. Ray. 1977. *Crime Prevention Through Environmental Design,* 2nd ed. Thousand Oaks, CA: Sage.

Johansen, Helle Krogh, and Peter C. Gotzsche. 1999. "Problems in the Design and Reporting of Trials of Antifungal Agents Encountered During Meta-Analysis." *Journal of the American Medical Association* 282 (November):1752–59.

Johnson, Bruce D., Paul Goldstein, Edward Preble, James Schmeidler, Douglas S. Lipton, Barry Spunt, and Thomas Miller. 1985. *Taking Care of Business: The Economics of Crime by Heroin Abusers.* Lexington, MA: Lexington Books.

Johnson, Bruce, Andrew Golub, and Eloise Dunlap. 2000. "The Rise and Decline of Hard Drugs, Drug Markets, and Violence in Inner-City New York." In *The Crime Drop in America,* ed. Alfred Blumstein and Joel Wallman, 164–206. New York: Cambridge University Press.

Johnson, Ida M. 1999. "School Violence: The Effectiveness of a School Resource Officer Program in a Southern City." *Journal of Criminal Justice* 27:173–92.

Johnston, Lloyd D., Patrick M. O'Malley, and Jerald G. Bachman. 2003. *Monitoring the Future National Results on Adolescent Drug Use: Overview of Key Findings, 2002.* NIH Publication No. 03–5374. Rockville, MD: National Institute on Drug Abuse.

Jolin, Annette, William Feyerhorn, Robert Fountain, and Sharon Friedman. 1998. *Beyond Arrest: The Portland, Oregon Domestic Violence Experiment.* Final Report to the National Institute of Justice. Washington, DC: U.S. Department of Justice, Office of Justice Programs, National Institute of Justice.

Justice Research and Statistics Association. 1996. *Domestic and Sexual Violence Data Collection.* Report to Congress Under the Violence Against Women Act. Washington, DC: U.S. Department of Justice, Office of Justice

Programs, National Institute of Justice and Bureau of Justice Assistance.

——. 2003. "FBI's Status of NIBRS in the States." IBR Resource Center. Washington, DC: Justice Research and Statistics Association. http://www.jrsa.org/ibrrc/status_nibrs/nibrs_states.html. Accessed 6 May 2003.

Kalichman, Seth C. 2000. *Mandated Reporting of Suspected Child Abuse: Ethics, Law, and Policy,* 2nd ed. Washington, DC: American Psychological Association.

Kaplan, Abraham. 1964. *The Conduct of Inquiry.* San Francisco: Chandler.

Karmen, Andrew. 2000. *New York Murder Mystery: The True Story Behind the Crime Crash of the 1990s.* New York: New York University Press.

Kelling, George L., and William J. Bratton. 1998. "Declining Crime Rates: Insiders' Views of the New York City Story." *Journal of Criminal Law and Criminology* 88(4):1217–31.

Kelling, George L., and Catherine M. Coles. 1996. *Fixing Broken Windows: Restoring Order and Reducing Crime in Our Communities.* New York: Free Press.

Kelling, George L., Tony Pate, Duane Dieckman, and Charles E. Brown. 1974. *The Kansas City Preventive Patrol Experiment: A Technical Report.* Washington, DC: Police Foundation.

Kelling, George L., and William H. Sousa, Jr. 2001. *Do Police Matter? An Analysis of the Impact of New Yow City's Police Reforms.* Civic Report. New York: Manhattan Institute Center for Civic Innovation.

Kennedy, David M. 1998. "Pulling Levers: Getting Deterrence Right." *National Institute of Justice Journal* 236 (July):2–8.

Kennedy, David M., Anne M. Piehl, and Anthony A. Braga. 1996. "Youth Gun Violence in Boston: Gun Markets, Serious Youth Offenders, and a Use Reduction Strategy." *Law and Contemporary Problems* 59 (Winter):147–96.

Kershaw, Chris, Tracey Budd, Graham Kinshott, Joanna Mattinson, Pat Mayhew, and Andy Myhill. 2000. *The 2000 British Crime Survey: England and Wales.* Home Office Statistical Bulletin. London: Research and Statistics Directorate, Home Office.

Kessler, David A. 1999. "The Effects of Community Policing on Complaints Against Officers." *Journal of Quantitative Criminology* 15(3):333–72.

Killias, Martin. 1993. "Gun Ownership, Suicide and Homicide: An International Perspective." *Canadian Medical Association Journal* 148:289–306.

Kim, Julia Yun Soo, Michael Fendrich, and Joseph S. Wislar. 2000. "The Validity of Juvenile Arrestees' Drug Use Reporting: A Gender Comparison." *Journal of Research in Crime and Delinquency* 37 (November):419–32.

Kim, So Young, and Wesley G. Skogan. 2003. "Statistical Analysis of Time Series Data on Problem Solving." Community Policing Working Paper no. 27. Evanston, IL: Northwestern University, Center for Policy Research. http://www.northwestern.edu/ipr/publications/policing. html. Accessed 27 April 2003.

Kindermann, Charles, James Lynch, and David Cantor. 1997. *Effects of the Redesign on Victimization Estimates.* Bureau of Justice Statistics National Crime Victimization Survey

Report. Washington, DC: U.S. Department of Justice, Office of Justice Programs, National Institute of Justice.

Kirchner, Robert A., Roger Przybylski, and Ruth A. Cardella. 1994. *Assessing the Effectiveness of Criminal Justice Programs.* Assessment and Evaluation Handbook Series no. 1. Washington, DC: U.S. Department of Justice, Office of Justice Programs, Bureau of Justice Assistance.

Kish, Leslie. 1965. *Survey Sampling.* New York: Wiley.

Kitsuse, John I., and Aaron V. Cicourel. 1963. "A Note on the Use of Official Statistics." *Social Problems* 11:131–38.

Krohn, Marvin. 1991. "Control and Deterrence Theories." In *Criminology,* ed. Joseph F. Sheley. Belmont, CA: Wadsworth.

Krueger, Richard A., and Mary Anne Casey. 2000. *Focus Groups: A Practical Guide for Applied Research,* 3rd ed. Thousand Oaks, CA: Sage.

Kuhn, Thomas. 1996. *The Structure of Scientific Revolutions,* 3rd ed. Chicago: University of Chicago Press.

Lamberth, John. 1996. "Report of John Lamberth, Ph.D." Summary of Court Testimony. American Civil Liberties Union. ACLU in the Courts. http://www.aclu.org/court/lamberth.html. Accessed 28 August 2001.

Lane, Roger. 1997. *Murder in America: A History.* Columbus: Ohio State University Press.

Langan, Patrick A., Lawrence A. Greenfeld, Steven K. Smith, Matthew R. Durose, and David J. Levin. 2001. *Contacts Between Police and the Public: Findings from the 1999 National Survey.* Washington, DC: U.S. Department of Justice, Office of Justice Programs, Bureau of Justice Statistics.

Lange, James E., Kenneth O. Blackman, and Mark B. Johnson. 2001. *Speed Violation Survey of the New Jersey Turnpike: Final Report.* Calverton, MD: Public Services Research Institute. http://www.northjersey.com (pdf version). Accessed 26 March 2002.

Langworthy, Robert, ed. 1999. *Measuring What Matters.* Proceedings from the Policing Research Institute Meetings. Washington, DC: U.S. Department of Justice, Office of Justice Programs, National Institute of Justice.

Larson, Richard C. 1975. "What Happened to Patrol Operations in Kansas City? A Review of the Kansas City Preventive Patrol Experiment." *Journal of Criminal Justice* 3:267–97.

Latané, Bibb, and John M. Darley. 1970. *The Unresponsive Bystander: Why Doesn't He Help?* Englewood Cliffs, NJ: Prentice-Hall.

Lattimore, Pamela K., and Joanna R. Baker. 1992. "The Impact of Recidivism and Capacity on Prison Populations." *Journal of Quantitative Criminology* 8:189–215.

Lauritsen, Janet L., Robert J. Sampson, and John H. Laub. 1991. "The Link Between Offending and Victimization Among Adolescents." *Criminology* 29:265–92.

Laycock, Gloria. 2002. "Methodological Issues in Working with Policy Advisers and Practitioners." In *Analysis for Crime Prevention,* ed. Nick Tilley, 205–37. *Crime Prevention Studies,* Vol. 13. Monsey, NY: Criminal Justice Press.

Leiber, Michael J., and Jayne M. Stairs. 1999. "Race, Contexts, and the Use of Intake Diversion." *Journal of Research in Crime and Delinquency* 36(1):56–86.

Lempert, Richard O. 1984. "From the Editor." *Law and Society Review* 18:505-13.

Levine, Robert. 1997. *A Geography of Time: The Temporal Misadventures of a Social Psychologist.* New York: Basic Books.

Lineberry, Robert L. 1977. *American Public Policy.* New York: Harper & Row.

Loeber, Rolf, Magda Stouthamer-Loeber, Welmoet van Kammen, and David P. Farrington. 1991. "Initiation, Escalation and Desistance in Juvenile Offending and Their Correlates." *Journal of Criminal Law and Criminology* 82(1): 36-82.

Loftin, Colin. 1986. "The Validity of Robbery-Murder Classifications in Baltimore." *Violence and Victim* 1:191-204.

Loftin, Colin, David McDowall, Brian Wiersema, and Talbert J. Cottey. 1991. "Effects of Restrictive Licensing of Handguns on Homicide and Suicide in the District of Columbia." *New England Journal of Medicine* 325:1615-20.

Lopez, Patricia. 1992. "'He Said . . . She Said . . .': An Overview of Date Rape from Commission Through Prosecution Through Verdict." *Criminal Justice Journal* 13:275-302.

Luntz, Barbara, and Cathy Spatz Widom. 1994. "Antisocial Personality Disorder in Abused and Neglected Children Grown Up." *American Journal of Psychiatry* 151:670-74.

Lynch, James P. 1990. "The Current and Future National Crime Survey." In *Measuring Crime: Large-Scale, Long-Range Efforts,* ed. Doris L. MacKenzie, Phyllis J. Baunach, and Roy R. Roberg, 97-118. Albany: State University of New York Press.

McCaig, Linda, and Janet Greenblatt. 1996. *Preliminary Estimates from the Drug Abuse Warning Network.* Advance Report No. 17. Rockville, MD: U.S. Department of Health and Human Services, Substance Abuse and Mental Health Services Administration, Office of Applied Studies. http://www.health.org/pubs/96dawn/ar17.htm. Accessed 18 December 1996.

McCall, George J. 1978. *Observing the Law: Field Methods in the Study of Crime and the Criminal Justice System.* New York: Free Press.

McCleary, Richard. 1992. *Dangerous Men: The Sociology of Parole,* 2nd ed. New York: Harrow & Heston.

McCleary, Richard, Barbara C. Nienstedt, and James M. Erven. 1982. "Uniform Crime Reports as Organizational Outcomes: Three Time Series Experiments." *Social Problems* 29:361-72.

McDonald, Douglas C., and Christine Smith. 1989. *Evaluating Drug Control and System Improvement Projects.* Washington, DC: U.S. Department of Justice, Office of Justice Programs, National Institute of Justice.

McDowall, David, Colin Loftin, and Brian Wiersema. 2000. "The Impact of Youth Curfew Laws on Juvenile Crime Rates." *Crime and Delinquency* 46(1):76-91.

Macintyre, Stuart, and Ross Homel. 1997. "Danger on the Dance Floor: A Study of the Interior Design, Crowding and Aggression in Nightclubs." In *Policing for Prevention: Reducing Crime, Public Intoxication, and Injury.* In *Crime Prevention Studies,* Vol. 7, ed. Ross Homel, 91-114. Monsey, NY: Criminal Justice Press.

MacKenzie, Doris Layton, Phyllis J. Baunach, and Roy R. Roberg, eds. 1990. *Measuring Crime: Large-Scale, Long-Range Efforts.* Albany: State University of New York Press.

MacKenzie, Doris Layton, Katherine Browning, Stacy B. Skroban, and Douglas A. Smith. 1999. "The Impact of Probation on the Criminal Activities of Offenders." *Journal of Research in Crime and Delinquency* 36(4):423-53.

MacKenzie, Doris Layton, James W. Shaw, and Voncile B. Gowdy. 1993. *An Evaluation of Shock Incarceration in Louisiana.* Research in Brief. Washington, DC: U.S. Department of Justice, Office of Justice Programs, National Institute of Justice.

McVicker, Steve, and Roma Khanna. 2003. "DNA Find Sparks Call for Review: New Look at Policies in DA's Office Urged." In *Houston Chronicle,* 15 March, A1.

Maher, Lisa. 1997. *Sexed Work: Gender, Race, and Resistance in a Brooklyn Drug Market.* Oxford, UK: Clarendon Press.

Maltz, Michael D. 1994. "Deviating from the Mean: The Declining Significance of Significance." *Journal of Research in Crime and Delinquency* 31:434-63.

———. 1998. "Which Homicides Decreased? Why?" *Journal of Criminal Law and Criminology* 88 (Summer):1489-96.

———. 1999. *Bridging Gaps: Estimating Crime Rates from Police Data.* Washington, DC: U.S. Department of Justice, Office of Justice Programs, Bureau of Justice Statistics.

Maltz, Michael, Andrew C. Gordon, David McDowall, and Richard McCleary. 1980. "An Artifact in Pretest-Posttest Designs: How It Can Mistakenly Make Delinquency Programs Look Effective." *Evaluation Review* 4:225-40.

Maltz, Michael D., and Marianne W. Zawitz. 1998. *Displaying Violent Crime Trends Using Estimates from the National Crime Victimization Survey.* Bureau of Justice Statistics Technical Report. Washington, DC: U.S. Department of Justice, Office of Justice Programs, Bureau of Justice Statistics.

Maple, Jack, with Chris Mitchell. 1999. *Crime Fighter: Putting the Bad Guys Out of Business.* New York: Doubleday.

Marshall, Catherine, and Gretchen B. Rossman. 1995. *Designing Qualitative Research.* Thousand Oaks, CA: Sage.

Marx, Karl. [1880] 1956. *Revue Socialist* (5 July). Reprinted in *Karl Marx: Selected Writings in Sociology and Social Philosophy,* ed. T. N. Bottomore and Maximilien Rubel. New York: McGraw-Hill.

Mastrofski, Stephen D., Roger B. Parks, Jr., Albert J. Reiss, Robert E. Worden, Christina DeJong, Jeffrey B. Snipes, and William Terrill. 1998. *Systematic Observation of Public Police: Applying Field Research Methods to Policy Issues.* Research Report. Washington, DC: U.S. Department of Justice, Office of Justice Programs, National Institute of Justice.

Mastrofski, Stephen D., and R. Richard Ritti. 1999. "Patterns of Community Policing: A View from Newspapers in the United States." COPS Working Paper No. 2. Washington, DC: U.S. Department of Justice, Office of Community Oriented Policing Services.

Maxfield, Michael G. 1987a. *Explaining Fear of Crime: Evidence from the 1984 British Crime Survey.* Research and Planning Unit Paper 43. London: Home Office.

———. 1987b. "Incivilities and Fear of Crime in England and Wales and the United States: A Comparative Analysis." Unpublished paper, prepared for presentation at the Annual Meeting of the American Society of Criminology.

———. 1989. "Circumstances in Supplementary Homicide Reports: Variety and Validity." *Criminology* 26(4):123–55.

———. 1999. "The National Incident-Based Reporting System: Research and Policy Applications." *Journal of Quantitative Criminology* 15 (June):119–49.

———. 2001. *Guide to Frugal Evaluation for Criminal Justice.* Final Report to the National Institute of Justice. Washington, DC: U.S. Department of Justice, Office of Justice Programs, National Institute of Justice.

Maxfield, Michael G., and W. Carsten Andresen. 2002. *Evaluation of New Jersey State Police In-Car Mobile Video Recording System.* Final Report to the Office of the Attorney General. Newark, NJ: Rutgers University, School of Criminal Justice.

Maxfield, Michael G., and Terry L. Baumer. 1991. "Electronic Monitoring in Marion County Indiana." *Overcrowded Times* 2:5, 17.

———. 1992. "Home Detention with Electronic Monitoring: A Nonexperimental Salvage Evaluation." *Evaluation Review* 16:315–32.

Maxfield, Michael G., Barbara Luntz Weiler, and Cathy Spatz Widom. 2000. "Comparing Self-Reports and Official Records of Arrests." *Journal of Quantitative Criminology* 16 (March):87–110.

Maxfield, Michael G., and Cathy Spatz Widom. 1996. "The Cycle of Violence: Revisited Six Years Later." *Archives of Pediatrics and Adolescent Medicine* 150:390–95.

Maxwell, Christopher D., Joel H. Garner, and Jeffrey A. Fagan. 2001. *The Effects of Arrest on Intimate Partner Violence: New Evidence from the Spouse Assault Replication Program.* Research in Brief. Washington, DC: U.S. Department of Justice, Office of Justice Programs, National Institute of Justice.

Maxwell, Joseph A. 1996. *Qualitative Research Design: An Interactive Approach.* Thousand Oaks, CA: Sage.

Maxwell, Sheila Royo. 1999. "Examining the Congruence Between Predictors of Release-on-Recognizance and Failure to Appear." *Journal of Criminal Justice* 27(2):127–41.

Mayhew, Patricia, Ronald V. Clarke, and David Elliott. 1989. "Motorcycle Theft, Helmet Legislation, and Displacement." *Howard Journal* 28:1–8.

Mednick, Sarnoff, William Gabrielli, and Barry Hutchings. 1984. "Genetic Influences in Criminal Convictions: Evidence from an Adoption Cohort." *Science* 224:891–94.

MEGG Associates. 1996. *A NIBRS Overview.* Richmond, VA: MEGG Associates. http://www.crisnet.com/m-nibrs3.html#nib_hist. Accessed 23 December 1996.

Mesch, Gustavo S., and Gideon Fishman. 1999. "Entering the System: Ethnic Differences in Closing Criminal Files in Israel." *Journal of Research in Crime and Delinquency* 36(2):75–93.

Mieczkowski, Thomas. 1990. "Crack Distribution in Detroit." *Contemporary Drug Problems* 17:9–30.

Mieczkowski, Thomas M. 1990. "The Accuracy of Self-Reported Drug Use: An Evaluation and Analysis of New Data." In *Drugs, Crime, and the Criminal Justice System,* ed. Ralph Weisheit, 275–302. Cincinnati, OH: Anderson.

———. 1996. "The Prevalence of Drug Use in the United States." In *Crime and Justice: An Annual Review of Research,* ed. Michael Tonry, 349–414. Chicago: University of Chicago Press.

Milgram, Lester. 1965. "Some Conditions of Obedience to Authority." *Human Relations* 18:57–76.

Mirrlees-Black, Catriona. 1995. "Estimating the Extent of Domestic Violence: Findings from the 1992 BCS." *Research Bulletin* (37):1–9.

———. 1999. *Domestic Violence: Findings from a New British Crime Survey Self-Completion Questionnaire.* Home Office Research Study. London: Home Office, Research, Development, and Statistics Directorate.

Mirrlees-Black, Catriona, Pat Mayhew, and Andrew Percy. 1996. *The 1996 British Crime Survey: England and Wales.* Home Office Statistical Bulletin. London: Home Office, Research, Development, and Statistics Directorate.

Mitford, Jessica. 1973. *Kind and Usual Punishment: The Prison Business.* New York: Random House.

Mohr, Lawrence B. 1990. *Understanding Significance Testing.* Thousand Oaks, CA: Sage.

Monahan, John, Paul S. Appelbaum, Edward P. Mulvey, Pamela Clark Robbins, and Charles W. Lidz. 1993. "Ethical and Legal Duties in Conducting Research on Violence: Lessons from the MacArthur Risk Assessment Study." *Violence and Victims* 8(4):387–96.

Morgan, Susan E., Tom Reichart, and Tyler R. Harrison. 2002. *From Numbers to Words: Reporting Statistical Results in the Social Sciences.* Boston: Allyn & Bacon.

Mott, Joy, and Catriona Mirrlees-Black. 1995. *Self-Reported Drug Misuse in England and Wales: Findings from the 1992 British Crime Survey.* Research and Planning Unit Paper 89. London: Home Office.

Murray, Charles A., and L. A. Cox. 1979. *Beyond Probation: Juvenile Corrections and the Chronic Delinquent.* Thousand Oaks, CA: Sage.

National Institute of Justice. 1996. *1995 Drug Use Forecasting: Annual Report on Adult and Juvenile Arrestees.* Washington, DC: U.S. Department of Justice, Office of Justice Programs, National Institute of Justice.

———. 1999a. *1998 Annual Report on Drug Use Among Adult and Juvenile Arrestees.* Washington, DC: U.S. Department of Justice, Office of Justice Programs, National Institute of Justice.

———. 1999b. *NIJ Awards in Fiscal Year 1998.* Washington, DC: U.S. Department of Justice, Office of Justice Programs, National Institute of Justice.

———. 2001. *Annual Report to Congress.* Washington, DC: U.S. Department of Justice, Office of Justice Programs, National Institute of Justice.

———. 2002. *Drug Use and Related Matters Among Adult Arrestees, 2001.* Washington, DC: U.S. Department of Justice, Office of Justice Programs, National Institute of Justice. http://www.adam-nij.net/report.asp. Accessed 13 May 2003.

———. 2003a. *2000 Arrestee Drug Abuse Monitoring: Annual Report.* Research Report. Washington, DC: U.S. Department of Justice, Office of Justice Programs, National Institute of Justice. http://www.adam-nij.net/report.asp. Accessed 13 May 2003.

———. 2003b. *Solicitation for Evaluations of Bureau of Justice Assistance Discretionary Funds Projects.* Washington, DC: U.S. Department of Justice, Office of Justice Programs, National Institute of Justice.

National Research Council. 1996. *The Evaluation of Forensic DNA Evidence.* Washington, DC: National Academy Press.

———. 2001. *Informing America's Policy on Illegal Drugs: What We Don't Know Keeps Hurting Us,* ed. Charles F. Manski, John V. Pepper, and Carol V. Petrie. Committee on Data and Research for Policy on Illegal Drugs. Washington, DC: National Academy Press.

National Youth Gang Center. 1999. *1997 National Youth Gang Survey: Summary.* Washington, DC: U.S. Department of Justice, Office of Justice Programs, Office of Juvenile Justice and Delinquency Prevention.

Newman, Oscar. 1972. *Defensible Space.* New York: Macmillan.

———. 1996. *Creating Defensible Space.* Washington, DC: U.S. Department of Housing and Urban Development, Office of Policy Development and Research.

New York Times. 1993. "High Murder Rate for Women on the Job." (3 October).

Nolan, James J., and Yoshio Akiyama. 1999. "An Analysis of Factors That Affect Law Enforcement Participation in Hate Crime Reporting." *Journal of Contemporary Criminal Justice* 15(1):111–27.

Nolan, James J., Yoshio Akiyama, and Samuel Berhanu. 2002. "The Hate Crime Statistics Act of 1990: Developing a Method for Measuring the Occurence of Hate Violence." *American Behavioral Scientist* 46(1):136–53.

NOP Market Research Limited. 1985. *1984 British Crime Survey Technical Report.* London: NOP Market Research Limited.

O'Brien, Robert M. 1985. *Crime and Victimization Data.* Thousand Oaks, CA: Sage.

Office of National Drug Control Policy. 1996. *Pulse Check: National Trends in Drug Abuse Spring 1996.* Washington, DC: Executive Office of the President, Office of Drug Control Policy.

———. 2003. *Pulse Check: Trends in Drug Abuse November 2002.* Washington, DC: Executive Office of the President, Office of Drug Control Policy. http://www.whitehousedrug policy.gov/publications. Accessed 1 April 2003.

Office of the Mayor. 2003. "My Neighborhood Statistics." New York: New York City, Office of the Mayor, Office of Operations. http://www.nyc.gov/html/ops/html/my_stats.html. Accessed 14 April 2003.

Painter, Kate. 1991. *An Evaluation of Public Lighting as a Crime Prevention Strategy with a Special Focus on Women and Elderly People.* Manchester, England: University of Manchester, Faculty of Economic and Social Studies.

———. 1996. "The Influence of Street Lighting Improvements on Crime, Fear and Pedestrian Street Use After Dark." *Landscape and Urban Planning* 35:193–201.

Painter, Kate, and David P. Farrington. 1998. "Marital Violence in Great Britain and Its Relationship to Marital and Non-Marital Rape." *International Review of Victimology* 5(3/4):257–76.

Park, Robert E., and Ernest W. Burgess. 1921. *Introduction to the Science of Sociology.* Chicago: University of Chicago Press.

Pate, Anthony M., Mary Ann Wycoff, Wesley G. Skogan, and Lawrence W. Sherman. 1986. *Reducing Fear of Crime in Houston and Newark: A Summary Report.* Washington, DC: Police Foundation.

Patton, Michael Quinn. 1990. *Qualitative Evaluation Research Methods,* 2nd ed. Thousand Oaks, CA: Sage.

———. 2001. *Qualitative Research and Evaluation Methods,* 3rd ed. Thousand Oaks, CA: Sage.

Pawson, Ray, and Nick Tilley. 1997. *Realistic Evaluation.* Thousand Oaks, CA: Sage.

Pease, Ken, and Gloria Laycock. 1996. *Revictimization: Reducing the Heat on Hot Victims.* Washington, DC: U.S. Department of Justice, Office of Justice Programs, National Institute of Justice.

Perkins, Craig, and Darrell K. Gilliard. 1992. *National Corrections Reporting Practices, 1988.* Washington, DC: U.S. Department of Justice, Office of Justice Programs, Bureau of Justice Statistics.

Petersilia, Joan. 1989. "Implementing Randomized Experiments: Lessons from BJA's Intensive Supervision Project." *Evaluation Review* 13:435–58.

Petersilia, Joan, and Susan Turner. 1991. "An Evaluation of Intensive Supervision in California." *Journal of Criminal Law and Criminology* 82:610–58.

Pettiway, Leon E. 1995. "Copping Crack: The Travel Behavior of Crack Users." *Justice Quarterly* 12(3):499–524.

Poklemba, John J. 1988. *Measurement Issues in Jail and Prison Overcrowding.* Albany, NY: New York Division Of Criminal Justice Services, Criminal Justice Information Systems Improvement Program.

Pollard, Paul. 1995. "Pornography and Sexual Aggression." *Current Psychology* 14:200–221.

Pollock, Joycelyn M. 1997. *Ethics in Crime and Justice: Dilemmas and Decisions,* 3rd ed. Belmont, CA: Wadsworth.

Posavec, Emil J., and Raymond G. Carey. 1997. *Program Evaluation: Methods and Case Studies,* 5th ed. Englewood Cliffs, NJ: Prentice-Hall.

President's Commission on Law Enforcement and Administration of Justice. 1967. *The Challenge of Crime in a Free Society.* Washington, DC: Government Printing Office.

Quade, E. S. 1989. *Policy Analysis for Public Decisions,* 3rd ed., rev. Grace M. Carter. New York: North-Holland.

Ragin, Charles C. 2000. *Fuzzy-Set Social Science.* Chicago: University of Chicago Press.

Ragin, Charles C., and Howard S. Becker. 1992. *What Is a Case? Exploring the Foundations of Social Inquiry.* Cambridge: Cambridge University Press.

Ramsay, Malcolm, and Sarah Partridge. 1999. *Drug Misuse Declared in 1998: Results from the British Crime Survey.* Home Office Research Study 197. London: Her Majesty's Stationery Office.

Ramsay, Malcolm, and Andrew Percy. 1996. *Drug Misuse Declared: Results of the 1994 British Crime Survey.* Home Office Research Study 151. London: Her Majesty's Stationery Office.

Rasinski, Kenneth A. 1989. "The Effect of Question Wording on Public Support for Government Spending." *Public Opinion Quarterly* 53:388–94.

Ratcliffe, Jerry H. 2002. "Aoristic Signatures and the Spatio-Temporal Analysis of High-Volume Crime Patterns." *Journal of Quantitative Criminology* 18 (March):23–43.

Reaves, Brian A. 1993. *Using NIBRS Data to Analyze Violent Crime.* Bureau of Justice Statistics Technical Report. Washington, DC: U.S. Department of Justice, Office of Justice Programs, Bureau of Justice Statistics.

Reiss, Albert J., Jr. 1971. *The Police and the Public.* New Haven, CT: Yale University Press.

Rennison, Callie. 2002. *Criminal Victimization 2001: Changes 2000–01 with Trends 1993–2001.* Washington, DC: U.S. Department of Justice, Office of Justice Programs, Bureau of Justice Statistics.

Rennison, Callie Marie. 2001. *Intimate Partner Violence and Age of Victim, 1993–99.* BJS Special Report. Washington, DC: U.S. Department of Justice, Office of Justice Programs, Bureau of Justice Statistics.

Reuter, Peter, Robert MacCoun, and Patrick Murphy. 1990. *Money from Crime: A Study of the Economics of Drug Dealing in Washington, DC.* Santa Monica, CA: RAND.

Reynolds, Paul D. 1979. *Ethical Dilemmas and Social Research.* San Francisco: Jossey-Bass.

Rich, Thomas F. 1999. "Mapping the Path to Problem Solving." *National Institute of Justice Journal* (October):2–9.

Risler, Edwin A., Tim Sweatman, and Larry Nackerud. 1998. "Evaluating the Georgia Legislative Waiver's Effectiveness in Deterring Juvenile Crime." *Research on Social Work Practice* 8:657–67.

Roberts, James C. 2002. *Serving Up Trouble in the Barroom Environment.* Unpublished Ph.D. dissertation, Rutgers University School of Criminal Justice, Newark, NJ.

Robins, Lee N. 1978. "Sturdy Childhood Predictors of Adult Antisocial Behavior: Replications from Longitudinal Studies." *Psychological Medicine* 8:611–22.

Roethlisberger, Fritz J., and William J. Dickson. 1939. *Management and the Worker.* Cambridge, MA: Harvard University Press.

Rosenbaum, Dennis P., Susan F. Bennett, Betsy D. Lindsay, Deanna L. Wilkinson, Brenda Davis, Chet Taranowski, and Paul Lavrakas. 1992. *The Community Responses to Drug Abuse National Demonstration Program: Executive Summary.* Chicago: Center for Research in Law and Justice.

Rosenbaum, Dennis P., Sandy Yeh, and Deanna L. Wilkinson. 1994. "Impact of Community Policing on Police Personnel: A Quasi-Experimental Test." *Crime and Delinquency* 40(3):331–53.

Rosenfeld, Richard. 2000. "Patterns in Adult Homicide: 1980–1995." In *The Crime Drop in America,* ed. Alfred Blumstein and Joel Wallman, 130–63. New York: Cambridge University Press.

Rosenfeld, Richard, Timothy M. Bray, and Arlen Egley. 1999. "Facilitating Violence: A Comparison of Gang-Motivated, Gang-Affiliated, and Nongang Youth Homicides." *Journal of Quantitative Criminology* 15(4):495–516.

Rosenfeld, Richard, and Scott H. Decker. 1993. "Discrepant Values, Correlated Measures: Cross-Sectional and Longitudinal Comparisons of Self-Reports and Urine Tests of Cocaine Use Among Arrestees." *Journal of Criminal Justice* 21:223–31.

Rossi, Peter H., Howard E. Freeman, and Mark W. Lipsey. 1999. *Evaluation: A Systematic Approach,* 6th ed. Thousand Oaks, CA: Sage.

Sampson, Robert J., and John H. Laub. 1993. *Crime in the Making: Pathways and Turning Points Through Life.* Cambridge, MA: Harvard University Press.

Sampson, Robert J., and Stephen W. Raudenbush. 1999. "Systematic Social Observation of Public Spaces: A New Look at Disorder in Urban Neighborhoods." *American Journal of Sociology* 105 (November):603–51.

Schmalleger, Frank. 1991. *Criminal Justice Ethics: Annotated Bibliography and Guide to Sources.* New York: Greenwood Press.

Schmitt, Erica Leah, Patrick A. Langan, and Matthew R. Durose. 2002. *Characteristics of Drivers Stopped by Police, 1999.* Washington, DC: U.S. Department of Justice, Office of Justice Programs, Bureau of Justice Statistics.

Schneider, Anne L. 1990. *Deterrence and Juvenile Crime.* New York: Springer-Verlag.

Seidman, David, and Michael Couzens. 1974. "Getting the Crime Rate Down: Political Pressure and Crime Reporting." *Law and Society Review* 8:457–93.

Shannon, David M., Todd E. Johnson, Shelby Searcy, and Alan Lott. 2002. "Using Electronic Surveys: Advice from Professionals." *Practical Assessment, Research and Evaluation* 8(1). http://ericae.net/pare/getvn.asp?v=8&n=1. Accessed 13 May 2003.

Shaw, Clifford R., and Henry D. McKay. 1969. *Juvenile Delinquency and Urban Areas.* Chicago: University of Chicago Press.

Shea, Christopher. 2000. "Don't Talk to Humans: The Crackdown on Social Science Research." *Lingua Franca* 10 (September).

Shearing, Clifford D., and Phillip C. Stenning. 1992. "From the Panopticon to Disney World: The Development of Discipline." In *Situational Crime Prevention: Successful Case Studies,* ed. Ronald V. Clarke, 249–55. New York: Harrow & Heston.

Sherman, Lawrence W. 1992. *Policing Domestic Violence: Experiments and Dilemmas.* New York: Free Press.

———. 1995. "Hot Spots of Crime and Criminal Careers Places." In *Crime and Place,* ed. John E. Eck and David Weisburd, 15–32. *Crime Prevention Studies,* Vol. 4. Monsey, NJ: Criminal Justice Press.

Sherman, Lawrence W., and Richard A. Berk. 1984. *The Minneapolis Domestic Violence Experiment.* Washington, DC: Police Foundation.

Sherman, Lawrence W., and Ellen G. Cohn. 1989. "The Impact of Research on Legal Policy: The Minnesota Domestic Violence Experiment." *Law and Society Review* 23: 117–44.

Sherman, Lawrence W., Patrick R. Gartin, and Michael E. Buerger. 1989. "Hot Spots of Predatory Crime: Routine Activity and the Criminology of Place." *Criminology* 27: 27–55.

Sherman, Lawrence W., James W. Shaw, and Dennis P. Rogan. 1995. *The Kansas City Gun Experiment.* Research in Brief. Washington, DC: U.S. Department of Justice, Office of Justice Programs, National Institute of Justice.

Sieber, Joan E. 2001. *Summary of Human Subjects Protection Issues Related to Large Sample Surveys.* Washington, DC: U.S. Department of Justice, Office of Justice Programs, Bureau of Justice Statistics.

Silberman, Charles. 1978. *Criminal Violence, Criminal Justice.* New York: Random House.

Silverman, Eli B. 1999. *NYPD Battles Crime: Innovative Strategies in Policing.* Boston: Northeastern University Press.

Sinauer, Nancy, Michael J. Bowling, Kathryn E. Moracco, Carol W. Runyan, and John D. Butts. 1999. "Comparisons Among Female Homicides Occurring in Rural, Intermediate, and Urban Counties in North Carolina." *Homicide Studies* 3: 107–28.

Singleton, Royce A., Jr., Bruce C. Straits, and Margaret Miller Straits. 1993. *Approaches to Social Research,* 2nd ed. New York: Oxford University Press.

Skogan, Wesley G. 1974. "The Validity of Official Crime Statistics: An Empirical Investigation." *Social Science Quarterly* 55: 25–38.

———. 1985. *Evaluating Neighborhood Crime Prevention Programs.* The Hague, Netherlands: Ministry of Justice, Research and Documentation Centre.

———. 1988. "Community Organizations and Crime." In *Crime and Justice: An Annual Review of Research,* ed. Michael Tonry and Norville Morris, 39–78. Chicago: University of Chicago Press.

———. 1990. *Disorder and Decline: Crime and the Spiral of Decay in American Neighborhoods.* New York: Free Press.

Skogan, Wesley G., and Michael G. Maxfield. 1981. *Coping with Crime: Individual and Neighborhood Reactions.* Thousand Oaks, CA: Sage.

Smith, Steven K., and Carolyn C. DeFrances. 2003. *Assessing Measurement Techniques for Identifying Race, Ethnicity, and Gender: Observation-Based Data Collection in Airports and at Immigration Checkpoints.* Washington, DC: U.S. Department of Justice, Office of Justice Programs, Bureau of Justice Statistics.

Smith, Steven K., Greg W. Steadman, Todd D. Minton, and Meg Townsend. 1999. *Criminal Victimization and Perceptions of Community Safety in 12 Cities, 1998.* Washington, DC: U.S. Department of Justice, Office of Justice Programs, Bureau of Justice Statistics, and Office of Community Oriented Police Services.

Snyder, Howard N. 2000. *Sexual Assault of Young Children As Reported to Law Enforcement: Victim, Incident, and Offender Characteristics.* NIBRS Statistical Report. Washington, DC: U.S. Department of Justice, Office of Justice Programs, Bureau of Justice Statistics.

Sousa, William H. 2003. *Crime Reduction in New York City: The Impact of the NYPD.* Unpublished Ph.D. dissertation, Rutgers University School of Criminal Justice, Newark, NJ.

Spelman, William. 2000. "The Limited Importance of Prison Expansion." In *The Crime Drop in America,* ed. Alfred Blumstein and Joel Wallman, 97–129. New York: Cambridge University Press.

Spergel, Irving A. 1990. "Youth Gangs: Continuity and Change." In *Crime and Justice: An Annual Review of Research,* ed. Norval Morris and Michael Tonry, 171–275. Chicago: University of Chicago Press.

Spohn, Cassia. 1990. "The Sentencing Decisions of Black and White Judges: Expected and Unexpected Similarities." *Law and Society Review* 24: 1197–216.

Spohn, Cassia, and Julie Horney. 1991. "The Law's the Law, but Fair Is Fair: Rape Shield Laws and Officials' Assessment of Sexual History Evidence." *Criminology* 29: 137–61.

Stecher, Brian M., and W. Alan Davis. 1987. *How to Focus an Evaluation.* Thousand Oaks, CA: Sage.

Stewart, D. W., and P. N. Shamdasani. 1990. *Focus Groups: Theory and Practice.* Thousand Oaks, CA: Sage.

Straus, Murray A. 1999. "The Controversy over Domestic Violence by Women: A Methodological, Theoretical, and Sociology of Science Analysis." In *Violence in Intimate Relationships,* ed. Ximena Arriaga and Stuart Oskamp, 17–44. Thousand Oaks, CA: Sage.

Strom, Kevin J. 2001. *Hate Crimes Reported in NIBRS, 1997–99.* BJS Special Report. Washington, DC: U.S. Department of Justice, Office of Justice Programs, Bureau of Justice Statistics.

Substance Abuse and Mental Health Services Administration. 2002a. *Results from the 2001 National Household Survey on Drug Abuse: Vol. 1. Summary of National Findings.* Rockville, MD: Office of Applied Studies, Substance Abuse and Mental Health Services Administration. http://www.samhsa.gov/oas/NHSDA/2k1nhsda/vol1. Accessed 25 January 2003.

———. 2002b. *Emergency Department Trends from the Drug Abuse Warning Network, Preliminary Estimates January–June 2002.* DAWN Series D-22, DHHS Publication No. 03-3779. Rockville, MD: Substance Abuse and Mental Health Services Administration, Office of Applied Studies. http://www.samhsa.gov/oas/trends. Accessed 27 April 2003.

Surette, Ray. 1992. *Media, Crime, and Justice: Images and Reality.* Pacific Grove, CA: Brooks/Cole.

Takeuchi, David. 1974. *Grass in Hawaii: A Structural Constraints Approach.* Unpublished master's thesis, Department of Sociology, University of Hawaii.

Taxman, Faye S., and Lori Elis. 1999. "Expediting Court Dispositions: Quick Results, Uncertain Outcomes." *Journal of Research in Crime and Delinquency* 36(1): 30–55.

Taylor, Ralph B. 1999. *Crime, Grime, Fear, and Decline: A Longitudinal Look.* Research in Brief. Washington, DC: U.S. Department of Justice, Office of Justice Programs, National Institute of Justice.

Taylor, Ralph B., Sally A. Shumaker, and Stephen D. Gottfredson. 1985. "Neighborhood-Level Links Between Physical Features and Local Sentiments." *Journal of Architectural Planning and Research* 2:261–75.

"Telemarketing Sales Rule." 2003. *Federal Register* 68(19): 4669.

Tilley, Nick. 2000. "The Evaluation Jungle." In *Secure Foundations: Key Issues in Crime Prevention, Crime Reduction and Public Saftey,* ed. Scott Ballintyne, Ken Pease, and Vic McLaren, 115–30. London: Institute for Public Policy Research.

———, ed. 2002a. *Analysis for Crime Prevention. Crime Prevention Studies,* Vol. 13. Monsey, NY: Criminal Justice Press.

———, ed. 2002b. *Evaluation for Crime Prevention. Crime Prevention Studies,* Vol. 14. Monsey, NY: Criminal Justice Press.

Tilley, Nick, and Gloria Laycock. 2002. *Working Out What to Do: Evidence-Based Crime Reduction.* Crime Reduction Research Series, Paper 11. London: Home Office, Policing and Reducing Crime Unit, Research, Development, and Statistics Directorate.

Tjaden, Patricia, and Nancy Thoennes. 2000. *Full Report of the Prevalence, Incidence, and Consequences of Violence Against Women.* Findings from the National Violence Against Women Survey. Research Report. Washington, DC: U.S. Department of Justice, Office of Justice Programs, National Institute of Justice.

Toch, Hans, and J. Douglas Grant. 1991. *Police as Problem Solvers.* New York: Plenum.

Tonry, Michael. 1999. "Why Are U.S. Incarceration Rates So High?" *Crime and Delinquency* 45(4):419–37.

Turner, Jonathan. 1974. *The Structure of Sociology Theory.* Homewood, IL: Dorsey Press.

U.S. Bureau of the Census. 1992. *Statistical Analysis of the United States.* Washington, DC: Government Printing Office.

———. 1994. *Technical Background on the Redesigned National Crime Victimization Survey.* Washington, DC: U.S. Department of Justice, Office of Justice Programs, Bureau of Justice Statistics.

———. 2002. *Statistical Abstract of the United States.* Washington, DC: Government Printing Office.

U.S. Department of Justice. 1995. *The Nation's Two Crime Measures.* NCJ-122795. Washington, DC: U.S. Department of Justice.

Van Kirk, Marvin. 1977. *Response Time Analysis.* Washington, DC: U.S. Department of Justice, National Institute of Law Enforcement and Administration of Justice.

Walker, Jeffrey T. 1994. "Fax Machines and Social Surveys: Teaching an Old Dog New Tricks." *Journal of Quantitative Criminology* 10 (June):181–88.

Walker, Samuel. 1994. *Sense and Nonsense About Crime and Drugs: A Policy Guide,* 3rd ed. Belmont, CA: Wadsworth.

Walker, Wallace Earl. 1985. "The Conduct of Program Evaluation Reviews in the General Accounting Office." *Evaluation and Program Planning* 8:271–80.

Ward, V. M., J. T. Bertrand, and L. E. Brown. 1991. "The Comparability of Survey and Focus Group Results." *Evaluation Review* 15:266–83.

Warner, Barbara D., and Glenn L. Pierce. 1993. "Reexamining Social Disorganization Theory Using Calls to Police as a Measure of Crime." *Criminology* 31:493–517.

Wartell, Julie, and Philip Mielke. 2003. "Cross-Jurisdictional Analysis of Vehicle Theft: Issues and Results." Paper presented at the 11th International Symposium on Environmental Criminology and Crime Analysis, Cincinnati, OH.

Weis, Joseph G. 1986. "Issues in the Measurement of Criminal Careers." In *Criminal Careers and "Career Criminals,"* Vol. 2, ed. Alfred Blumstein, Jacqueline Cohen, Jeffrey A. Roth, and Christy A. Visher, 1–51. Washington, DC: National Academy Press.

Weisburd, David. 1997. *Reorienting Crime Prevention Research and Policy: From the Causes of Criminality to the Context of Crime.* Paper presented at the 1996 Conference on Criminal Justice Research and Evaluation. Research Report. Washington, DC: U.S. Department of Justice, Office of Justice Programs, National Institute of Justice.

Weisburd, David, and Chester Britt. 2002. *Statistics in Criminal Justice,* 2nd ed. Belmont, CA: Wadsworth.

Weisburd, David, and Lorraine Green. 1995. "Policing Drug Hot Spots: The Jersey City Drug Market Analysis Experiment." *Justice Quarterly* 12:711–35.

Weisburd, David, Cynthia M. Lum, and Anthony Petrosino. 2001. "Does Research Design Affect Study Outcomes in Criminal Justice?" *The Annals* 578 (November):50–70.

Weisburd, David, Anthony Petrosino, and Gail Mason. 1993. "Design Sensitivity in Criminal Justice Experiments." In *Crime and Justice: An Annual Review of Research,* ed. Michael Tonry, 337–79. Chicago: University of Chicago Press.

Weisel, Deborah. 1999. *Conducting Community Surveys: A Practical Guide for Law Enforcement Agencies.* Washington, DC: U.S. Department of Justice, Office of Justice Programs, Bureau of Justice Statistics, and Office of Community Oriented Police Services.

Weiss, Carol H. 1995. "Nothing As Practical as Good Theory: Exploring Theory-Based Evaluation for Comprehensive Community Initiatives for Children and Families." In *New Approaches to Evaluating Community Initiatives: Concepts, Methods, and Contexts,* ed. James P. Connell, Anne C. Kubisch, Lisbeth B. Schorr, and Carol H. Weiss, 65–92. Washington, DC: Aspen Institute.

West, Donald J., and David P. Farrington. 1977. *The Delinquent Way of Life.* London: Heinemann.

Widom, Cathy Spatz. 1989a. "The Cycle of Violence." *Science* 244 (14 April):160–66.

———. 1989b. "Child Abuse, Neglect, and Adult Behavior: Research Design and Findings on Criminality, Violence, and Child Abuse." *American Journal of Orthopsychiatry* 59: 355–67.

———. 1989c. "Does Violence Beget Violence? A Critical Examination of the Literature." *Psychological Bulletin* 106: 3–28.

———. 1992. *The Cycle of Violence.* Research in Brief. Washington, DC: U.S. Department of Justice, Office of Justice Programs, National Institute of Justice.

Widom, Cathy Spatz, Barbara Luntz Weiler, and Linda B. Cotler. 1999. "Childhood Victimization and Drug Abuse: A Comparison of Prospective and Retrospective Findings." *Journal of Consulting and Clinical Psychology* 67(6): 867–80.

Wikström, Per-Olof H. 1995. "Preventing City-Center Crimes." In *Building a Safer Society: Strategic Approaches to Crime Prevention,* ed. Michael Tonry and David Farrington, 429–68. *Crime and Justice: An Annual Review of Research.* Chicago: University of Chicago Press.

Williams, Kent M. 1991. "Using Battered Woman Syndrome Evidence with a Self-Defense Strategy in Minnesota." *Law and Inequality* 10:107–36.

Williams, Terry. 1989. *The Cocaine Kids.* Reading, MA: Addison-Wesley.

Williams, Terry, Eloise Dunlap, Bruce D. Johnson, and Ansley Hamid. 1992. "Personal Safety in Dangerous Places." *Journal of Contemporary Ethnography* 21(3):343–74.

Wilson, James Q., and Richard J. Herrnstein. 1985. *Crime and Human Nature.* New York: Simon & Schuster.

Wilson, James Q., and George Kelling. 1982. "Broken Windows: The Police and Neighborhood Safety." *Atlantic Monthly* (March):29–38.

Wilson, O. W., and Roy Clinton McLaren. 1963. *Police Administration.* 3rd ed. New York: McGraw-Hill.

Wilson, William Julius. 1987. *The Truly Disadvantaged.* Chicago: University of Chicago Press.

———. 1996. *When Work Disappears: The World of the New Urban Poor.* New York: Knopf.

Wilt, Susan A., and Celia S. Gabrel. 1998. "A Weapon-Related Injury Surveillance System in New York City." *American Journal of Preventive Medicine* 15 (October):75–82.

Winner, Lawrence, Lonn Lanza-Kaduce, Donna M. Bishhop, and Charles E. Frazier. 1997. "The Transfer of Juveniles to Criminal Court: Reexamining Recidivism over the Long Term." *Crime and Delinquency* 43:548–63.

Wolfgang, Marvin E., Robert M. Figlio, and Thorsten Sellin. 1972. *Delinquency in a Birth Cohort.* Chicago: University of Chicago Press.

Wolfgang, Marvin E., Robert M. Figlio, Paul E. Tracy, and Simon I. Singer. 1985. *The National Survey of Crime Severity.* NCJ-96017. Washington, DC: U.S. Department of Justice, Office of Justice Programs, Bureau of Justice Statistics.

Woodward, Lianne J., and David M. Fergusson. 2000. "Childhood and Adolescent Predictors of Physical Assault: A Prospective Longitudinal Study." *Criminology* 38 (February):233–61.

Wooten, Harold B., and Herbert J. Hoelter. 1998. "Operation Spotlight: The Community Probation–Community Police Team Process." *Federal Probation* 62(2):30–35.

Wright, Doug, Peggy Barker, Joseph Gfroerer, and Lanny Piper. 2002. "Summary of NHSDA Design Changes in 1999." In *Redesigning an Ongoing National Household Survey: Methodological Issues,* ed. Joseph Gfroerer, Joe Eyerman, and James Chromy, 9–22. Publication No. SMA 03-3768. Rockville, MD: Office of Applied Studies, Substance Abuse and Mental Health Services Administration. http://www.samhsa.gov/oas/methods.htm. Accessed 18 March 2003.

Wright, Richard, and Trevor Bennett. 1990. "Exploring the Offender's Perspective: Observing and Interviewing Criminals." In *Measurement Issues in Criminology,* ed. Kimberly L. Kempf, 138–51. New York: Springer-Verlag.

Wright, Richard T., and Scott H. Decker. 1994. *Burglars on the Job: Streetlife and Residential Break-Ins.* Boston: Northeastern University Press.

———. 1997. *Armed Robbers in Action: Stickups and Street Culture.* Boston: Northeastern University Press.

Wycoff, Mary Ann, Wesley G. Skogan, Anthony M. Pate, and Lawrence W. Sherman. 1985a. *Citizen Contact Patrol: Technical Report.* Washington, DC: Police Foundation.

Wycoff, Mary Ann, Wesley G. Skogan, Anthony M. Pate, and Lawrence W. Sherman. 1985b. *Police Community Stations: Technical Report.* Washington, DC: Police Foundation.

Yin, Robert K. 1994. *Case Study Research: Design and Methods,* 2nd ed. Thousand Oaks, CA: Sage.

Zimring, Franklin E. 1998. *American Youth Violence.* New York: Oxford University Press.

Name Index

Subject Index

Distribution of Chi Square

Probability

df	.99	.98	.95	.90	.80	.70	.50
1	.0³157	.0³628	.00393	.0158	.0642	.148	.455
2	.0201	.0404	.103	.211	.446	.713	1.386
3	.115	.185	.352	.584	1.005	1.424	2.366
4	.297	.429	.711	1.064	1.649	2.195	3.357
5	.554	.752	1.145	1.610	2.343	3.000	4.351
6	.872	1.134	1.635	2.204	3.070	3.828	5.348
7	1.239	1.564	2.167	2.833	3.822	4.671	6.346
8	1.646	2.032	2.733	3.490	4.594	5.528	7.344
9	2.088	2.532	3.325	4.168	5.380	6.393	8.343
10	2.558	3.059	3.940	4.865	6.179	7.267	9.342
11	3.053	3.609	4.575	5.578	6.989	8.148	10.341
12	3.571	4.178	5.226	6.304	7.807	9.034	11.340
13	4.107	4.765	5.892	7.042	8.634	9.926	12.340
14	4.660	5.368	6.571	7.790	9.467	10.821	13.339
15	5.229	5.985	7.261	8.547	10.307	11.721	14.339
16	5.812	6.614	7.962	9.312	11.152	12.624	15.338
17	6.408	7.255	8.672	10.085	12.002	13.531	16.338
18	7.015	7.906	9.390	10.865	12.857	14.440	17.338
19	7.633	8.567	10.117	11.651	13.716	15.352	18.338
20	8.260	9.237	10.851	12.443	14.578	16.266	19.337
21	8.897	9.915	11.591	13.240	15.445	17.182	20.337
22	9.542	10.600	12.338	14.041	16.314	18.101	21.337
23	10.196	11.293	13.091	14.848	17.187	19.021	22.337
24	10.856	11.992	13.848	15.659	18.062	19.943	23.337
25	11.524	12.697	14.611	16.473	18.940	20.867	24.337
26	12.198	13.409	15.379	17.292	19.820	21.792	25.336
27	12.879	14.125	16.151	18.114	20.703	22.719	26.336
28	13.565	14.847	16.928	18.939	21.588	23.647	27.336
29	14.256	15.574	17.708	19.768	22.475	24.577	28.336
30	14.953	16.306	18.493	20.599	23.364	25.508	29.336

For larger values of df, the expression $\sqrt{2\chi^2} - \sqrt{2df-1}$ may be used as a normal deviate with unit variance, remembering that the probability of χ^2 corresponds with that of a single tail of the normal curve.